Third Supplement to Torrey

THIRD SUPPLEMENT TO TORREY'S

New England Marriages
Prior to 1700

Melinde Lutz Sanborn

GENEALOGICAL PUBLISHING CO., Inc.

For Ruth and Lowell

INTRODUCTION

Torrey's manuscript, *New England Marriages Before 1700*, was unquestionably the most complete index of its kind. Over more than forty years, Torrey combed the collection of books and periodicals in the library of the New England Historic Genealogical Society, extracting almost every available reference to marriages of early New England settlers. Only a few of his references came from the Society's considerable manuscript collections, and an even smaller number of citations came from items outside its holdings. Still, it was an extraordinary undertaking, and estimates that it covers almost 99% of the married couples in New England before 1700 are not far off. Among his entries were discoveries not yet in print, showing that he was in close communication with the leading researchers of the day, who, like their present counterparts, are generally open and generous with the results of their investigations.

Following Torrey's death in 1962, his manuscript was used extensively in the reading room at NEHGS. After his arrival in the 1970s, librarian David Dearborn began periodically updating the bound photocopy kept there. In 1985 NEHGS and Genealogical Publishing Company collaborated with Elizabeth P. Bentley and Gary Boyd Roberts to produce a single, typed volume that omitted the references but included a new index. It immediately became a bestseller. More than a decade later, NEHGS produced a version of "Torrey" on CD, complete with references, which brought access to the genealogical literature through 1962 to countless thousands of private users. A section on the NEHGS website devoted to updates and corrections may one day materialize.

Despite its great popularity and very frequent use, most people do not appear to understand what it is that Torrey did. Some insist on using Torrey as a reference, when his work is in actuality an *index* to references. Clarence Torrey did not perform the research that determined his entries; his work was a faithful index of what others discovered and published. Thus, his index contains many entries that are incorrect or contradictory; it remains for the user of the index to evaluate the references cited.

The present work is the *Third Supplement to Torrey's New England Marriages Prior to 1700*, and it is primarily an index to the major genealogical periodicals published since Torrey's death (the first and second supplements were published by Genealogical Publishing Company in 1991 and 1995, respectively). Covering the period from 1962 through the spring of 2003, the *Third Supplement* incorporates *all* of the information from the first and second supplements, plus an additional 80% of new material. In all, approximately 6,000 entries, referring to as many as 20,000 people, are included. An impressive number of new entries were spontaneously offered by some of the leading genealogical researchers in this area from their own unpublished work. Such entries are an advance look at what may be appearing in print or online in the years to come.

A fair number of important discoveries have been posted on the World Wide Web and have not appeared in the traditional print media. This is a problem for several reasons, but most significantly, it does not allow for peer review of the quality that comes to bear on journal articles. Since there is some exceptional work being published on the web, and only on the web, some few entries appear here for the first time, citing a current web page. Such pages come and go, so the user is forewarned.

Another improvement introduced in this supplement is the inclusion of marriages for previously ignored groups. While it is true that little has been written in New England genealogical literature about families of African or Native American origin, there were more than sixty such marriages performed and recorded by the civil authorities, or implied by the recording of children's births, prior to 1700. These are no longer omitted. Records are also included for the several hundred cases of children born too soon to couples who eventually married but did not pay to record the marriage date. In instances where the couples did not marry but did have a child, a notation appears.

The *Third Supplement* contains references to additional, or supplementary, information, published in the form of corrections, new discoveries, significant new biographical detail, or deletions to Torrey's original work. Since these new discoveries and corrections tend to make their way into the periodical literature more frequently than elsewhere, this is effectively an index to the major genealogical journals published since Torrey's death (as seen in the reference list). Several long-term projects undertaken by family associations are emerging in print, some with strong contributions to the early New England literature. Lastly, a few corrections, particularly in the form of deletions, are offered. Earlier editions of this supplement included corrections of major typographical errors in the original printed Torrey. With the appearance of the Torrey CD, many of these errors have been corrected and are not repeated here.

There are many more discoveries of these types out there. I continue to keep a file of them and appreciate the many people who have brought such entries to my attention.

Arrangement

The presentation of entries here follows a simple format. Torrey originally used a fairly complex set of notations, such as "[ ]" to show a maiden name not found in a marriage record. After polling a number of readers at the New England Historic Genealogical Society who were frequent users of Torrey's work, and finding that they were happily oblivious of the meaning of most of his special notations, the notation system was dropped here.

Entries are arranged alphabetically by groom. An every-name index follows the main text.

The groom is presented first in the entries: last name in capitals, first name and a superscript indicating his generation from the immigrant if this information is provided in the source, followed by the years of his birth (or baptism, indicated by "bp") and death in parentheses. If these dates are approximate, they are preceded by a "c" as an abbreviation for "circa." The next element is the indicator of which marriage this is for the groom. If it is an only marriage, an "&" is used. If it is one of multiple marriages for the groom, a 1/wf, 2/wf, etc., appears. If the couple did not marry but had children, the symbol ~ is used.

The bride's name appears next: first name first, a superscript if her generation is indicated in the reference work, then her surname in capitals. If her maiden name is unknown, and it is her first marriage, her given name is followed by a blank: " _____." If she is a widow or divorced, her maiden name appears in parentheses, in the usual manner, the parentheses remaining empty if her maiden name is unknown. Other married names are presented in order, with all but the last in parentheses. If her subsequent or previous marriages or divorces are mentioned in the article being referenced, they are listed after her dates of birth and death. In many cases, her father's name is also given after her dates.

The marriage place and date, if given, are the next elements, followed by the place(s) of primary residence. If no marriage date is known, but an early occurrence such as a child's birth, joint deed, or court appearance is mentioned, that year with "by," "bef" for before, or "aft" for after is shown. Sometimes, when a range of dates for an event is given in the literature, these dates are entered with "bet" for between or a hyphen between two numbers.

Lastly, the reference for the entire item is entered in abbreviated form with volume and page number, if applicable.

A few additional abbreviations are used, e.g., "+" indicates that a person lived beyond the listed date; "m" is married; "int." means intention. State, or more properly, colony, designations are given only when it may be unclear whether the town in New England or England is meant.

Use

With either the printed version of the original *New England Marriages Prior to 1700* (Genealogical Publishing Co., 1985) or the CD version (New England Historic Genealogical Society, 1995), this Torrey supplement can be used in a variety of ways to develop clues for eighteenth- and nineteenth-century research, as well as to identify or eliminate seventeenth-century ancestors. Search features on the CD make it possible to do limited Boolean searches when very little information is known. For instance, a woman whose birth date is known, but whose later career and possible marriage is a mystery, can be targeted by typing in just her first name, say "Rebecca," and the town in which she was born, say "Braintree." The hits generated by that search can then be sorted by a likely date of marriage range—women usually married about age 20 in this time period. If, for instance, she was single when her father wrote his will, this added time refinement can be used to sort the candidates. If her name is distinctive, it's possible that it was also her mother's name, so marriages from a generation earlier can also be considered. Once some possible marriages are found, this supplement can be consulted to learn if more has been written about either the potential bride or groom's families.

Although many of the entries here are drawn from articles concerned with the identification of a woman's maiden name, often from English records, a good percentage come from multi-generational studies, often running five or six generations, well into the eighteenth century. Thus, this indexes not only the seventeenth-century couple but also later generations of many families.

The appearance of certain given names can provide clues to possible ancestry. For instance, many unusual women's names tend to run in families. Names such as "Olive," "Jael," "Jerusha," "Violet," "Rooksby," and "Desire" are strongly identified with particular surnames and can be indicative of the maiden name of a mother or grandmother when seen in later generations. Surnames used as first names for boys, such as "Otis," "Wyatt," or "Cutting," can also lead to a mother's maiden name.

The geographical distribution of certain surnames can often provide clues for later work. Especially in the cases of very common surnames, such as Smith or Brown, the identification of the locality can do much to limit a search by way of process of elimination. Use of the locality listing at the end of each of these entries, combined with a knowledge of likely migration patterns, may determine the area of a later search.

Patterns in the New Discoveries

Significant new discoveries pertaining to seventeenth-century New England are appearing at an accelerated rate, thanks to special projects being undertaken by a number of dedicated researchers. A significant proportion of the entries in this supplement derive from three areas of study: abstracts of English probate records, English marriages of colonial immigrants, and the study of immigrant clusters.

The first area is best represented by the efforts of Mr. Leslie Mahler, whose prolific appearances in print stem largely from his abstracts of the London Commissary Court records. The second was neglected in Torrey's time, not so much from lack of trying, but because convenient indexes were not readily available. The International Genealogical Index online has done much to make long-distance research easier, and a fair number of recent discoveries owe their success to its use as an index. The appearance of Peter Wilson Coldham's two volumes of seventeenth-century emigration records— *The Complete Book of Emigrants 1607–1660* (Genealogical Publishing Company, 1987) and *The Complete Book of Emigrants 1661–1699* (Genealogical

Publishing Company, 1990)—has been material in filling the information void for this type of research. In recent years, the great popularity of old classics in reprint form, such as Henry F. Waters' two-volume set, *Genealogical Gleanings in England,* and Michael Ghirelli's *A List of Emigrants from England To America 1682–1692*, has made this early information much more accessible. The *NEHGS Register* online has revolutionized a previously tedious necessity—the checking of related literature for clues and details already in print. While its index, which is a revised and improved version of the index in print, contains every citation to individual names in the *Register*, the present index weeds out the casual aside and gives the user a direct line to significant contributions, whether in the *Register* or elsewhere.

Several of the unpublished items submitted from the work of leading researchers are the results of techniques neglected since the era of the great town histories, when entire settlements—rather than simply individual families—were studied. Most notable among these efforts is *The Great Migration Study Project*, sponsored by the New England Historic Genealogical Society and led by Robert Charles Anderson, F.A.S.G. By looking at communities in their entirety, missing links have been discovered, or at least deduced, with a reasonable degree of certainty. *GMSP* has re-examined families long taken for granted, and the results have been both sensational and sobering.

Douglas Richardson can be credited with many impressive discoveries in England and the colonies. Many of these discoveries have been published in the leading journals, and others appeared in John B. Threlfall's *Great Migration* volumes (see References). His kind letters have contained many new finds for this index effort, some of which have been published since earlier editions of this supplement.

It was my privilege to work for many years with Dean Crawford Smith, C.G., whose idea of publishing a series of books in the general style of Walter Goodwin Davis blossomed into many new discoveries in England and early New England.

The study of immigrant clusters in their English home parishes has brought many breakthroughs and is expected to continue to do so. An excellent example of this cluster phenomenon, highlighting several Lynn, Massachusetts, families, appeared in *The American Genealogist* in April 1990 (65:65-9). The continuing efforts of the General Society of Mayflower Descendants to publish the first five generations of *Mayflower* descendants from the original passengers, as well as the appearance of several single surname genealogies by large family associations, have brought decades of effort into the public eye.

A relatively small number of discoveries presented here were made through the re-examination of original records that had been misused or misread. Some long-lost records have been recovered in recent years, most notably the first Newport court book for very early Rhode Island cases, now transcribed by Jane Fletcher Fiske, F.A.S.G., and the original Towcester, Northamptonshire, parish register for the 1500s and 1600s.

The major journals indexed here, *The American Genealogist, The New England Historical and Genealogical Register, The National Genealogical Society Quarterly, The New York Genealogical and Biographical Record,* and *The Genealogist,* are covered through issues that appeared by January 2003.

REFERENCES

Abel Lunt — Walter Goodwin Davis, *The Ancestry of Abel Lunt, 1769–1806 of Newbury, Massachusetts* (Portland, Maine: The Anthoensen Press, 1963)

AEBK, AEBK 1 — Dean Crawford Smith, *The Ancestry of Eva Belle Kempton, Part I* (Boston: New England Historic Genealogical Society, 1995)

AEBK 3 — Dean Crawford Smith, *The Ancestry of Eva Belle Kempton, Part III*, manuscript in preparation

AEBK 4 — Dean Crawford Smith, *The Ancestry of Eva Belle Kempton, Part IV* (Boston: New England Historic Genealogical Society, 2000)

AEJA — Dean Crawford Smith, *The Ancestry of Emily Jane Angell* (Boston: New England Historic Genealogical Society, 1992)

AmacE — The unpublished research of Andrew B.W. MacEwen, P.O. Box 97, Stockton Springs, ME 04981

ASBO — Dean Crawford Smith, *The Ancestry of Samuel Blanchard Ordway* (Boston: New England Historic Genealogical Society, 1990)

Aspinwall — *A Volume Relating to the Early History of Boston Containing The Aspinwall Notarial Records from 1644 to 1651* (Boston, 1903)

BB — The unpublished research of Barbara Baxter, 330 Fairway, Southern Pines, NC 28387-2714

Boston VR — *A Report of the Record Commissioners Containing Boston Births, Baptisms, Marriages, and Deaths, 1630–1699* (Boston, 1883)

BTR — *Records of the Town of Braintree, 1640–1793*, Samuel A. Bates, ed. (Randolph, 1886)

CG — Elaine Chadbourne Bacon, comp., *The Chadbourne Family in America: A Genealogy* (North Waterboro, Maine: The Chadbourne Family Association, 1994)

Charlestown VR — Roger D. Joslyn, *Vital Records of Charlestown, Massachusetts, to the Year 1850*, Vol. 1 (Boston: New England Historic Genealogical Society, 1984)

Colver Gen — Valerie Dyer Giorgi, *Colver-Culver Family Genealogy* (Santa Maria, Calif.: The Author, 1984)

DCD   The unpublished research of David Curtis Dearborn, Reference Librarian, New England Historic Genealogical Society, 101 Newbury Street, Boston, MA 02116

DCS   The unpublished research of the late Dean Crawford Smith, Smith-Sanborn manuscript collection, New England Historic Genealogical Society, 101 Newbury Street, Boston, MA 02116

DR   The unpublished research of Douglas Richardson, 216 West Buffalo Street, #3, Chandler, AZ 85224

EIHC   *Essex Institute Historical Collections* (Salem, Mass.: Essex Institute, 1859–)

EQC   *Records and Files of the Quarterly Courts of Essex County, Massachusetts.* 9 vols. (Salem, Mass.: Essex Institute, 1911–1975)

Essex Probate   Original probate records at the Registry of Probate for Essex County, Salem, MA

Fiske   *Thomas Cooke of Rhode Island: A Genealogy of Thomas Cooke alias Butcher of Netherbury, Dorsetshire, England, who came to Taunton, Massachusetts, in 1637 and settled in Portsmouth, Rhode Island in 1643.* 2 vols. (Boxford, Mass.: The Author, 1987)

GBS   The unpublished research of Gregory Bell Smith, 6106 N. 31st Place, Phoenix, AZ 85016

Gen.Adv.   *The Genealogical Advertiser, A Quarterly Magazine of Family History*, Lucy Hall Greenlaw, ed. 4 vols. 1898–1901 (Reprint 4 vols. in 1. Baltimore: Genealogical Publishing Co., 1974)

Genealogy of Edward Small   Lora Altine Woodbury Underhill, *Descendants of Edward Small of New England.* 2 vols. (Boston: Houghton Mifflin Co., 1934)

GFS   The unpublished research of George Freeman Sanborn Jr., Librarian, New England Historic Genealogical Society, 101 Newbury Street, Boston, MA 02116

GM   Robert Charles Anderson, George Freeman Sanborn Jr., and Melinde Lutz Sanborn, *The Great Migration* (Boston: New England Historic Genealogical Society, 1999–)

GMB   Robert Charles Anderson, *The Great Migration Begins.* 3 vols. (Boston: New England Historic Genealogical Society, 1995)

GMSP   The unpublished research stemming from the Great Migration Study Project, New England Historic Genealogical Society, 101 Newbury Street, Boston, MA 02116

Hale, House   Donald Lines Jacobus and Edgar Francis Waterman, *Hale, House and Related Families, Mainly of the Connecticut River Valley* (Hartford: Connecticut Historical Society, 1952)

Harris — The unpublished research of Gale Ion Harris, 1312 Basswood Circle, East Lansing, MI 48823

Hempstead Diary — "Diary of Joshua Hempstead, 1711–1758," in *Collections of the New London County Historical Society*, Vol. 1 (New London, Conn., 1901)

HQ — *Heritage Quest: The International Genealogy Forum*, P.O. Box 540670, North Salt Lake, UT 84054

Higgins — The unpublished research of Smith Higgins, Jr., 6041 Guion Road, Indianapolis, IN 46254

Hist. of N.B. — David N. Camp, *The History of New Britain* (1889)

ITC — The unpublished research of Isabel Tuell Coburn, HC 62, Box 146, New Harbor, ME 04554

JEA — The unpublished research of Jerome E. Anderson, P.O. Box 1089, 95 School Street, Warren, MA 01083

JHM — The unpublished research of John Hollister McCallum, 1385 Northview Drive, Marion, IA 52302

JHO — The unpublished research of Julie Helen Otto, New England Historic Genealogical Society, 101 Newbury Street, Boston, MA 02116

JP — The unpublished research of John Plummer, 148 Grant Street, Apt. 34, Waterbury, CT 06702

LB — Melinde Lutz Sanborn, *Lost Babes* (Derry, N.H.: The Author, 1992)

LCF — Benjamin Franklin Wilbour, *Little Comptom Families*, 2nd edition (Little Compton. R.I.: Little Compton Historical Society, 1974)

LCVR — Benjamin Franklin Wilbour, *Little Compton Families, from Records Compiled by Benjamin Franklin Wilbour* (Little Compton, R.I.: Little Compton Historical Society, 1967)

LMM — The unpublished research of Leslie Mahler, 169 Kenbrook Circle, San Jose, CA 95111

LND — Sybil Noyes, Charles Thornton Libby, and Walter Goodwin Davis, *The Genealogical Dictionary of Maine and New Hampshire.* 5 parts. 1928–1939 (Reprint 5 parts in 1. Baltimore: Genealogical Publishing Co., 1972)

LN Tyler — The unpublished research of LN Tyler

Loyal Dissenter — Roland L. Warren, *Loyal Dissenter, The Life and Times of Robert Pike* (Lanham, Md.: University Press of America, 1992)

Manwaring — Charles William Manwaring, *Early Connecticut Probate Records, Hartford District 1700–1729, vol. II.* (originally published 1904, reprint Baltimore, Md.: Genealogical Publishing Co., 1995).

MD   *The Mayflower Descendant*, 376 Boylston Street, Suite B, Boston, MA 02116

MF5G   *Mayflower Families Through Five Generations Vol. 6: Stephen Hopkins* (General Society of Mayflower Descendants, 1992)

MK   The unpublished research of Marshall Kirk

ML   The unpublished research of Mrs. Marilyn Labbe, 380 Pond Hill Road, Moosup, CT 06354

MLS   The unpublished research of Melinde Lutz Sanborn, P.O. Box 706, Derry, NH 03038

NGSQ   *The National Genealogical Society Quarterly*, 4527 Seventeenth Street North, Arlington, VA 22207-2399

NHGR   *The New Hampshire Genealogical Record*, P.O. Box 2316, Concord, NH 03302-2316

NYGBR   *The New York Genealogical and Biographical Record*, 122 East 58th Street, New York, NY 10022

PCR   *Records of the Colony of New Plymouth in New England*, Nathaniel B. Shurtleff and David Pulsifer, eds. 12 vols. (Boston: Commonwealth of Massachusetts, 1855–1861)

PCRG   Plymouth Colony Research Group, unpublished research offered by the late Ruth Wilder Sherman

Pillsbury Ancestry
     Mary Lovering Holman, *Ancestry of Charles Stinson Pillsbury and John Sargent Pillsbury* (Concord, N.H., 1938)

Plymouth Court   *Plymouth Court Records 1686–1859*, David Thomas King, ed. CD edition. (Boston: The Pilgrim Society & The New England Historic Genealogical Society, 2002)

PRC   *The Public Records of the Colony of Connecticut Prior to the Union with New Haven Colony, May, 1665 . . .* , J. Hammond Trumbull, ed. (Hartford, 1850).

Pynchon Court Book
     Colonial Justice in Western Massachusetts, Joseph H. Smith, ed. (Cambridge: Harvard University Press, 1961)

REG   *The New England Historical and Genealogical Register* (Boston: New England Historic Genealogical Society, 1845–)

RCA   The unpublished research of Robert Charles Anderson, 2 Fenway, Derry, NH 03038

RI Court Records   *Records of the Court of Trials of the Colony of Providence Plantations, 1662–1670.* Vol. II (Providence, 1922)

RI Friends records Per PCRG
From the Rhode Island Friends records, available on microfilm at the Rhode Island Historical Society, Providence, RI, pointed out by the Plymouth Colony Research Group

Robin Bush The unpublished research of Robin Bush, former Somerset Archivist, Somersetshire, England

Savage James Savage, *A Genealogical Dictionary of the First Settlers of New England, Showing Three Generations of Those Who Came Before May, 1692, on the Basis of Farmer's Register.* 4 vols. (Baltimore: Genealogical Publishing Co., reprint, 1969)

Saxbe The unpublished research of William Bart Saxbe, Jr., F.A.S.C., 864 Hancock Road, Williamstown, MA 01267

Sewall's Diary M. Halsey Thomas, ed., *The Diary of Samuel Sewall* (New York: Farrar, Straus and Giroux, 1973)

SD *Suffolk Deeds*, vols. 1–14 (Boston: Suffolk Registry of Deeds [1880–1906])

SJC Supreme Judicial Court, Massachusetts, files at Massachusetts Archives, Columbia Point, MA

Smith Frederick Kinsman Smith, *The Family of Richard Smith of Smithtown, L.I.* (Smithtown, N.Y.: The Author, 1967)

SPC The unpublished research of Susan P. Canney, 285 Morgan Street, South Hadley, MA 01075

Sprague Waldo C. Sprague, Thayer Family Genealogies, 1949, Sprague Collection, manuscript holdings of the New England Historic Genealogical Society, 101 Newbury Street, Boston, MA 02116

Stanley Israel P. Warren, *The Stanley Families of America, Descended from John, Timothy and Thomas Stanley of Hartford, Conn., 1636* (Portland, Maine: B. Thurston & Co., 1887)

Stevens-Miller Ancestry
Mary Lovering Holman, *Ancestry of Colonel John Harrington Stevens and his wife Frances Helen Miller.* 2 vols. (Wayzata, Minn.: Helen Pendleton Winston Pillsbury, 1948, 1952)

Story of the Bloods
Roger Deane Harris, *The Story of the Bloods; Including an Account of the Early Generations of the Family in America in Genealogy Lines from Robert Blood of Concord and Richard Blood of Groton* (Boston: The Author, 1960)

Suffolk Deed Original deeds at the Registry of Deeds for Suffolk County at Boston, MA

Swansea Book A Original Swansea, Massachusetts town records

TAG *The American Genealogist*, P.O. Box 398, Demorest, GA 30535-0398

TEG *The Essex Genealogist*, The Essex Society of Genealogists, P.O. Box 313, Lynnfield, MA 01940-0313

TG *The Genealogist*, 25 Rodeo Drive 22, Sausalito, CA 94965-1783

VR per PCRG From vital records of the indicated towns pointed out by the Plymouth Colony Research Group

Watertown VR "Records of Births, Deaths and Marriages—First Book and Supplement," Section three in *Watertown Records Comprising the First and Second Books of Town Proceedings . . .* , Vol. 1 (Watertown, 1894)

Wilson Ken Stevens, *Descendants of Henry Wilson of Dedham, Massachusetts*, forthcoming

Winthrop Papers *Winthrop Papers 1638–1644*, Vol. 4 (Boston: The Massachusetts Historical Society, 1944)

WMJ Medical Journals of John Winthrop, Jr., manuscript original, Massachusetts Historical Society, 1154 Boylston Street, Boston, MA 02215

26 GMC John Brooks Threlfall, *Twenty-six Great Migration Colonists to New England and Their Origins* (Madison, Wis.: The Author, 1993)

50 GMC John Brooks Threlfall, *Fifty Great Migration Colonists to New England and Their Origins* (Madison, Wis.: The Author, 1990)

THIRD SUPPLEMENT
TO TORREY'S
New England Marriages
Prior to 1700

_____ (Indian) ~ Ruth EVERETT; Scituate [Plymouth Court Mar 1686/7]

_____, _____ & Elizabeth² CARTER [GM 2:29]

_____, _____ & Elizabeth² TRUANT; m by 1678 Marshfield [GMB 3:1840]

_____, _____ & Elizabeth² WOODWORTH; m by 26 Nov 1685 [GMB 3:2066]

_____, _____ & Hannah WELD, d/c Mr. Joseph Weld; m bet 1642-1654 [Boston VR 6:18]

_____, _____ & Jane² TRUANT; m by 1678 Marshfield [GMB 3:1840]

_____, _____ & Mary SWAIN, d/o William; m aft 1635 New Haven Colony [RCA]

_____, _____ & Sarah SMITH (c1645-53-bef 1687/8); m bef 1687/8 Watertown [AEBK 1:436]

_____, _____ (negro of Mr. Jocelen's) ~ May 1647 [WP 5:152]

_____, Angola (-1674/5) (negro) & Elizabeth _____ (-1692+) (negro); m Boston 20 April 1654 [Boston VR 1:48]

_____, Jo (negro) ~ Sarah CURTICE; Scituate [Plymouth Court Sept 1698]

_____, Mingo (negro) & _____ _____; m bef 19 May 1641 [Boston VR 1:11]

_____, Mingo (negro) & Mott _____ (negro); m Charlestown 10 Dec 1686 [Charlestown VR 1:25]

_____, Narramore & Ruth NEWELL; by 13 June 1698 [SJC #3762]

_____, Nimrod (negro) ~ Hannah² BONNEY; in court 27 Oct 1685 [GM 1:342]

_____, Roco (-1695+) & Sue _____ (-1695+); 1 Dec 1687 Springfield/Stratford? (John Pynchon's freed slaves) [REG 148:42; Harris]

_____, Sam (Indian) & _____ _____ [Plymouth Court Mar 1687/8]

_____, Toby (negro) & Jane _____ (negro); m Boston 15 Aug 1695 [Boston VR 1:vii]

ABBOTT, Daniel (c1610-1647) & Mary _____ (-1643); by 1630 Providence [GMB 1:2]

ABBOTT, Daniel² (1654[/5]-) & Hannah BROOKS, dau of John; m by 1694 New Haven [GM 1:4]

ABBOTT, George & Mary² WEED; m c1657 [GMB 3:1957]

ABBOTT, George & Sarah[2] FARNHAM; m2 Henry INGALLS; m Andover 26 Apr 1658 [GM 2:494]

ABBOTT, Joseph[2] (1652-   ) & Anna SANFORD, perhaps dau of Thomas; m by 1700 East Haven [GM 1:4]

ABBOTT, Nehemiah & Mary[2] HOWE (c1639-   ); m Ipswich 14 Dec 1659 [GM 3:434]

ABBOTT, Peter[2] (c1632-hanged 1667) & Elizabeth EVARTS, dau of John; m bef 1667 Branford [GM 1:3]

ABBOTT, Robert[1] (c1605-1658) & 1/wf _____ _____; m c1630 Watertown/Wethersfield/ Branford [GM 1:3]

ABBOTT, Robert[1] (c1605-1658) & 2/wf Mary _____; m2 John ROBBINS; m by 1649 Watertown/Wethersfield/Branford [GM 1:3]

ABBOTT, Thomas (c1643-1712/3) & Elizabeth GREEN; Kittery [TAG 70:87]

ABDY, Matthew[1] (c1620-1682+) & 1/wf Tabitha REYNOLDS (-1661), dau of Robert; m by 1648 Boston [GM 1:6]

ABDY, Matthew[1] (c1620-1682+) & 2/wf Alice COX (-1682+); m Boston 24 May 1662 [GM 1:6]

ABDY, Matthew[2] (c1658-   ) & 1/wf Deborah (STIMSON) WILSON; m1 Robert WILSON; m Cambridge 10 Apr 1688 [GM 1:7]

ABELL, James & Sarah BOWEN; m 1686 Rehoboth [VR per PCRG]

ABELL, Robert[1] (c1605-1663) & Joanna _____, m2 William HYDE; m bef 1639 Stapenhill, Derbyshire/Weymouth/Rehoboth [GMSP]

ADAMS, Abraham (c1639-1714) & Mary PETTINGILL (1652-1705); m Newbury 16 Nov 1670 [Abel Lunt, p.53]

ADAMS, Edward & Elizabeth[2] BUCKLAND (1640[/1]-   ); m2 James MILES; m Windsor 25 May 1660 [GM 1:452]

ADAMS, Edward[2] & Lydia[2] PENNIMAN (bp 1634[/5]-1675/6); m c1652 Medfield [TAG 71:16; GMB 3:1429]

ADAMS, George[1] (-1696) & Frances TAYLOR (-1696+); m bef 1645 Watertown [TAG 55:207]

ADAMS, James & Frances[2] VASSALL; m Scituate 16 July 1646 [GMB 3:1872]

ADAMS, Jeremy (c1611-1683) & 1/wf Rebecca (BASEDEN) GREENHILL (-bef 1682); m1 Samuel Greenhill; m bef 1637 Cambridge/Hartford [GMSP]

ADAMS, Jeremy (c1611-1683) & 2/wf Rebecca (FLETCHER) WARNER (c1638-1715); m1 Andrew Warner; m c1683 Hartford [GMSP]

ADAMS, John & Abigail[2] PINNEY (1654-   ); m Windsor 6 Dec 1677 [GMB 3:1480]

ADAMS, John & Hannah WEBB; m c1683 Braintree [TAG 71:21]

ADAMS, John (-1633) & Ellen NEWTON (c1598-1681); m2 Kenelm WINSLOW; m c1625 Plymouth [GMSP]

ADAMS, Jonathan & Elizabeth[2] HOLMAN (1644-   ); m by 1665 [GM 3:390]

ADAMS, Jonathan[2] (c1643-1707) & Rebecca ANDREWS (c1655-1731); m c1671 Falmouth [TG 3:62]

ADAMS, Moses (1645-1724) & Lydia[3] WHITNEY (1657-1719); m Sherborn 15 Apr 1684 [AEBK 1:539]

ADAMS, Richard[1] (c1606-1674) & 1/wf Mary (_____) CHEAME (-1642+); m by 1635 Malden [GM 1:10]

ADAMS, Richard[1] (c1606-1674) & 2/wf Elizabeth _____ (-1656); m aft 1642 Malden [GM 1:10]

ADAMS, Richard[1] (c1606-1674) & 3/wf Elizabeth _____; m by 1662 Malden [GM 1:10]

ADAMS, Richard[1] (c1606-1679+) & Susan _____; m by 1635 Salem [GM 1:12]

ADAMS, Samuel & Mehitable[2] NORTON (c1645-); m Ipswich 20 Dec 1664 [GMB 2:1338]

ADAMS, Walter & Hannah[2] MOULTON (bp 1641-); m Charlestown 15 Dec 1657 [GMB 2:1308]

ADDINGTON, Isaac & Ann[2] LEVERETT (bp 1619[/20]-); m by 1644 Boston [GMB 2:1177]

ADDIS, William[1] & Millicent WOOD; m bef 1623 Harescomb, Gloucestershire/New London [TAG 58:215; 57:181]

ADGETT, John & Sarah[2] HAYWARD (1653-); Wethersfield [GM 3:284]

AGER, William (c1610-1654) & Alice _____ , m2 Henry TOTTINGHAM; m by 1636 Salem [GMSP]

AINES, Alexander & Katherine _____; m bef 3 Feb 1656/7 [TAG 71:145]

ALBEE, John (-1675) & Jane HOLBROOK; m2 Alexander BALCOM; m 18 Oct 1671 Medfield/Mendon [TAG 48:122]

ALBERTSON, Derrick[1] & Willmet _____; Oyster Bay [NYGBR 109:205]

ALBERTSON, Derrick[2] & Dinah COLES; m bef 10 Nov 1692 Oyster Bay [NYGBR 109:206]

ALBRO, John[1] (c1620-1712) & Dorothy (_____) POTTER (-1696/7); m1 Nathaniel POTTER; m c1645 Portsmouth [GM 1:18]

ALBRO, John[2] & Mary STOKES; m Portsmouth 27 Apr 1693 [GM 1:19]

ALBRO, John[2] ~ Margaret HALL; in court May 1679 [GM 1:19]

ALBRO, Samuel[2] (c1645-1739) & Isabel LAWTON; m c1670 Narragansett [GM 1:19]

ALCOCK, George (c1605-1640) & 1/wf Anne? HOOKER (-1630/1); m by 1626 Roxbury [GMSP]

ALCOCK, George (c1605-1640) & 2/wf Elizabeth _____, m2 Dr. Henry DEENGAINE; m bef 1637 Roxbury [GMSP]

ALCOCK, John & Sarah[2] PALGRAVE (c1621-1665); m by 1649 Roxbury [GMB 3:1375]

ALCOCK, Philip (c1648-1715) & 2/wf Sarah (GREEN) BUTLER (1642-); m1 Nathaniel BUTLER; m 4 Apr 1699 New Haven/Wethersfield [TAG 46:10]

ALCOCK, Samuel (1665-1708) & Elizabeth[3] CHADBOURNE (1667-1743); m c1690s Kittery [CG, 31]

ALCOCK, Thomas (bef 1614-1657) & Margery _____, m2 John BENHAM, m3 Richard PRITCHARD; m bef 1635 Boston [GMSP]

ALDEN, David & Mary² SOUTHWORTH; m by 1674 [GMB 3:1711]

ALDEN, John¹ (c1599-1687) & Priscilla² MULLINS (c1603-1651+); m Plymouth by 1623 [GMB 2:1316]

ALDEN, Jonathan² & Abigail² HALLETT (c1642-); m Duxbury 10 Dec 1672 [GM 3:198]

ALDEN, Joseph & Mary² SIMONSON (c1641-); m c1660 [GMB 3:1683]

ALDERMAN, John¹ (c1584-1657) & Jane _____ perhaps CLAPP; m by 1636 Dorchester/Salem [GM 1:21]

ALDIS, John & Sarah² ELIOT (bp 1628/9-); m Dedham 27 Sept 1650 [GM 2:416]

ALDRIDGE, Jacob (-1695) & Huldah³ THAYER (1657-1694+); m Medfield 25 June 1675 [AEBK 3]

ALDRIDGE, Jacob (1676-1753) & 1/wf Margery³ HAYWARD (c1676-1717+); m Mendon 15 Sept 1699 [AEBK 3]

ALDUS, John² (bp 1627/8-1700) & Sarah ELIOTT; m Dedham 27 Sept 1650 [REG 150:489]

ALDUS, Nathan (bp 1592-) & Mary _____; m by 1623 England/Dedham [REG 150:489]

ALFORD, Elisha² & _____ _____; m by Apr 1676 [GM 1:26]

ALFORD, John & Charity DIKE [GMB 1:546]

ALFORD, Nathaniel² (bp 1636/7-) & _____ _____; m by 1676 Salem [GM 1:25]

ALFORD, William¹ (c1605-1676/7) & 1/wf Mary DRAPER; m St John, Hackney, Middlesex 10 June 1630 [GM 1:24]

ALFORD, William¹ (c1605-1676/7) & 2/wf Ann _____; m by 1658 Boston [GM 1:25]

ALGER, Allen (c1610-c1675) & Agnes _____ (c1620-1668+); m bef 1640 Richmond Island/Scarborough [GMSP]

ALLEN, _____ & Elizabeth GREENWAY (c1612-); probably William Allen of Manchester as 2nd wife [GMB 2:816]

ALLEN, _____ & Elizabeth² GREENWAY (bp 1608[/9]-); m by 5 Feb 1650[/1] [TAG 74:195]

ALLEN, Benjamin (1647-1678) & Hannah BULLARD (1645-1678+); m Medfield 6 Mar 1668/9 [AEBK 1:210]

ALLEN, Caleb & Elizabeth SISSON; m 28 Apr 1670 [TAG 67:30]

ALLEN, George¹ (c1592-1648) & 1/wf _____ _____; m c1617 Weymouth/Sandwich [GM 1:28]

ALLEN, George¹ (c1592-1648) & 2/wf Katherine _____; m2 John COLLINS; m by 1627 Weymouth/Sandwich [GM 1:28]

ALLEN, George² (c1619-) & 1/wf Hannah _____; m by 1648 Sandwich [GM 1:28]

ALLEN, George² (c1619-) & 2/wf Sarah _____; m 1682+ [GM 1:29]

ALLEN, Gideon[2] & Sarah PRUDDEN, dau of Peter; m by 1671 Boston [GM 1:29]

ALLEN, Henry[2] & 1/wf Sarah HILL; m by 1663 Milford [GM 1:29]

ALLEN, Henry[2] & 2/wf Rebecca (_____) ROSE; m1 Robert ROSE; m 1685 Wethersfield [GM 1:29]

ALLEN, James did not marry Hannah Dummer [GMB 1:591]

ALLEN, James[3] (c1678-1723/4) & Mary BOURNE (1678-1722); m c1700 Chilmark [REG 118:204]

ALLEN, Jedediah & Elizabeth[2] HOWLAND (c1647-); m c1669 [GMB 2:1019]

ALLEN, John & Bethia[2] PENNIMAN (c1643-1698+); m bef 22 Dec 1673 [TAG 71:17; GMB 3:1429]

ALLEN, John & Elizabeth BACON; m 1650 [RI Friends records per PCRG]

ALLEN, John[1] (c1605-by 1662) & Anne _____; m2 Michael PIERCE; m by 1635 Plymouth [GM 1:38]

ALLEN, John[2] & Mary[2] HANNUM (1650-); m Northampton Dec 1669 [GM 3:212]

ALLEN, John[2] (c1610-) & Christian _____; m Barnstable [GM 1:28]

ALLEN, John[4] & Rebecca _____; m2 Joseph[2] LANDERS [REG 124:45]

ALLEN, Joshua & Mary ?CROWELL (-1727); m2 William MORE; m bef 1682 [REG 125:232-4]

ALLEN, Mathew[2] (c1629-) & Sarah KIRBY; m Sandwich 6 June 1657 [GM 1:29]

ALLEN, Nehemiah & Sarah[2] WOODFORD (bp 1649-); m Northampton 21 Sept 1664 [GMB 3:2059]

ALLEN, Ralph (-c1659) & Esther[2] SWIFT (bp 1629-); m c1646 Sandwich [TAG 77:172]

ALLEN, Ralph[2] & Susanna _____; m c1642 [GM 1:28; REG 155:212]

ALLEN, Richard (1673-1730/1) & Hannah BUTLER (c1673-); m c1695 Sandwich [REG 127:24]

ALLEN, Samuel & Hannah[2] WOODFORD; m Northampton 29 Nov 1659 [GMB 3:2059]

ALLEN, Samuel[3] (1665/6-1717) & 1/wf Mary BALDWIN (c1665-1689/90+); m Northampton 14 July 1687 [REG 156:103, 110]

ALLEN, Samuel[3] (1665/6-1717) & 2/wf Mercy WRIGHT (-1727/8); m Northampton 16 Dec 1692 [REG 156:103, 111]

ALLEN, Thomas (1668/9-1719) & Anna BARNES (1668/9-1758); m Swansea 24 Sept 1694 [AEJA]

ALLEN, William (c1627-) & Priscilla BROWNE, dau of Peter; m Sandwich 21 Mar 1649 [GM 1:29]

ALLEN, William (c1637-1684) & Rebecca HAZARD (bp 1639-); m by 11 Feb 1669/70 Boston [REG 156:217]

ALLEN, William[1] (bef 1648-1738) & Elizabeth TWITCHELL (c1651-1717); m Medfield 15 Feb 1668/9 [AEBK 3]

ALLEN, William¹ (c1602-1678/9) & 1/wf Alice _____ (-1631/2); m bef 1630 Salem/Manchester [GMSP]

ALLEN, William¹ (c1602-1678/9) & 2/wf Elizabeth _____ (perhaps Greenway) (- 1685+); by 1634 Salem/Manchester [GMB 1:34]

ALLERTON, Isaac (c1586-1658/9) & 1/wf Mary NORRIS (-1620/1); m Leiden, Holland 4 Nov 1611 Marblehead/New Amsterdam/New Haven [GMSP]

ALLERTON, Isaac (c1586-1658/9) & 2/wf Fear BREWSTER (-c1634); m bet 1623-1627 Plymouth/New Haven [GMSP]

ALLERTON, Isaac (c1586-1658/9) & 3/wf Joanna SWINNERTON; m bet 1634-44 Plymouth/New Haven [GMB 1:37, MD 42:124, REG 124:133, TAG 60:159]

ALLERTON, Isaac (c1630-) & Elizabeth SWINNERTON; by 1652 Plymouth [GMB 1:37]

ALLEY, Hugh¹ (c1608-1673[/4]) & Mary _____ (-1674+); m by 1641 Lynn [GM 1:41]

ALLEY, Hugh² (1653-) & Rebecca HOOD; m Lynn 9 Dec 1681 [GM 1:41]

ALLEY, John² (1646-) & Joanna FURNELL; m Lynn Aug 1670 [GM 1:41]

ALLING, Abraham¹ (c1645-1711+) & Mary _____; m c1669/70 Marblehead [NYGBR 129:80]

ALLING, Thomas² (c1670-1716+) & Elizabeth³ WEEKS; m bef 1698 Oyster Bay/Marblehead/Hempstead [NYGBR 129:183]

ALLYN, John & Ann/Hannah² SMITH (c1635-), dau of Henry; m Springfield 19 Nov 1651 [GMB 3:1691]

ALLYN, Matthew (bp 17 Apr 1605-1670/1) & Margret WYOT (-12 Sept 1675); m Braunton, Devonshire 2 Feb 1626/7 Cambridge/Hartford/Windsor [GMSP]

ALLYN, Thomas & Abigail² WARHAM (bp 1638-); m Windsor 21 Oct 1658 [GMB 3:1927]

ALMY, Christopher² (c1632-) & Elizabeth CORNELL, dau of Thomas; m 9 July 1661 Portsmouth [GM 1:44]

ALMY, Job² & Mary UNTHANK, dau of Christopher; m by 1664 Warwick [GM 1:45]

ALMY, John² & Mary COLE (c1634-), dau of James; m2 John POCOCKE; m by 1668 Plymouth [GMB 1:423; GM 1:44]

ALMY, William¹ (c1601-1676/7-7) & Audrey BARLOW, dau of Stafford; m by lic 17 July 1626 South Kilworth, Leicestershire/Lutterworth, Leicestershire/Lynn/Portsmouth [GM 1:44]

ALSOP, Joseph¹ (c1621-1698) & Elizabeth PRESTON, dau of William; m by 1647 New Haven [GM 1:50]

ALSOP, Joseph² & Abigail THOMPSON, dau of John; m2 John MILES; m New Haven 25 Nov 1672 [GM 1:50]

ALSOP, Richard & Hannah² UNDERHILL (1666-); m by 1687 [GMB 3:1862]

ALVORD, Benedict & Joan NEWTON (bp 1616/7-), sister of Anthony; m 1640 Watertown [TAG 65:14-16]

AMBROSE, Henry (1649-) & Susannah (_____) WORCESTER; m1 Timothy
WORCESTER; m Oct 1672 Salisbury [NHGR 9:55]

AMBROSE, Henry (bp 13 June 1613- bef 1658) & Susannah _____ (-1692+); m2 John
SEVERANCE; m c1640 Kersey, Suffolk/Hampton/Boston [NHGR 9:49]

AMBROSE, Samuel (bp 25 July 1641-) & Hope LAMBERTON (c1636-bef 1704); m2
_____ HERBERT, m3 William CHENEY; m bef 1665 div. New Haven
[NHGR 9:55]

AMES, John & Elizabeth[2] HAYWARD (c1628-); m 20 Oct 1645 [GM 3:291]

AMES, John[2] & Sarah WILLIS, dau of John; m c1671 Bridgewater [AEBK 3]

AMES, William[1] (bp 1605-1653[/4]) & Hannah _____ (-1702/3); m2 John NILES; m by
1641 Braintree [AEBK 3]

ANDREW, Hester ~ pled married [Plymouth Court Mar 1698/9]

ANDREW, Samuel (bp 1619/20-1701) & Elizabeth WHITE (bp 1630/1-); m Cambridge
22 Sept 1652 [REG 150:194]

ANDREW, William[3] & Seeth[3] GRAFTON (1665-1745+); m2 1704 Zechariah[3] HICKS; m
by 1685 [TAG 71:27]

ANDREWS, Henry & Mary[2] WADSWORTH; m c1659 [GMB 3:1891]

ANDREWS, James[2] (1625/6-) & 2/wf Margaret (PHIPS) HALSEY; m Boston by int 6
Aug 1696 [GM 1:57]

ANDREWS, James[2] (1625/6-1704) & 1/wf Dorcas[2] MITTON (c1627-1695/6); m c1645-6
St. James, Garlickhithe, London/Saco/Portland [TG 3:59; GM 1:57]

ANDREWS, John & Judith[2] BELCHER (1658-); m c1684 Ipswich [GM 1:235]

ANDREWS, John (c1620-1708) & Jane JORDAN (c1622-1705+); m c1645 Ipswich [50
GMC]

ANDREWS, John[2] & 1/wf _____ LILLY; m by 1669 [GM 1:66]

ANDREWS, John[2] (c1628-) & Sarah HOLYOKE (bp 1623-), dau of Edward;
Tanworth, Warwickshire/Lynn [GM 1:54]

ANDREWS, Joseph[2] (c1597-1679/80) & Elizabeth _____; m by 1632 Hingham [GM
1:61]

ANDREWS, Nathan & Deborah[2] ABBOTT; m New Haven Oct 1661 [GM 1:3]

ANDREWS, Robert[1] (c1593-1643/4) & Elizabeth _____ (probably a widow); m c1618
Ipswich [GM 1:53]

ANDREWS, Samuel[1] (c1598-bef 1633) & Jane _____ (-1676); m2 Arthur
MACKWORTH; m by 1625 Saco [GM 1:57]

ANDREWS, Samuel[2] & Elizabeth[2] SPENCER, dau of Thomas; m c1668 [GMB 3:1720;
GM 1:66]

ANDREWS, Thomas & Mary[2] BELCHER; m Ipswich 9 Feb 1681/2 [GM 1:235]

ANDREWS, Thomas[1] (c1572-1643) & _____ _____; m c1597 Hingham [GM 1:61]

ANDREWS, Thomas[1] (c1611-1673) & Ann _____ (-1684[/5]); m c1636 Dorchester
[GM 1:60]

ANDREWS, Thomas[2] (1638-) & Hannah KIRBY, dau of John; m c1670 [GM 1:66]

ANDREWS, Thomas[2] (bp 1639-) & Phebe[2] GOARD (bp 1645/6-); m Dorchester 31 Dec 1667 [GM 1:60, 3:80]

ANDREWS, William & Anne (TAPP) GIBBARD New Haven [TAG 72:79]

ANDREWS, William (-1638) & _____ _____, a widow (-1640+); by 1638 Lynn [GMB 1:46]

ANDREWS, William[1] (c1607-1659) & Abigail _____ (-1682/3), perhaps GRAVES; m2 Nathaniel BARDING; m by 1632 Cambridge/Hartford [GM 1:65]

ANGELL, James (c1650s-1710/11) & Abigail DEXTER (1655-1711+); m 30 or 3 Sept 1678 Providence, RI [AEJA]

ANGELL, John (c1646-1720) & Ruth FIELD (c1649-1727+); m 7 Jan 1669/70 Providence, RI [AEJA]

ANGELL, Thomas (-1685-94) & Alice ASHTON (bp 1617/8-1694); m by 1642 Providence, RI [AEJA]

ANNABLE, Anthony (c1595-1674) & 1/wf Jane MOUMFORD (-1643); m All Saints, Cambridge, Cambridgeshire 26 Apr 1619 Plymouth/ Scituate/Barnstable [GMSP]

ANNABLE, Anthony (c1595-1674) & 2/wf Ann ELCOCK or CLARK (-1678+); m Barnstable 3 Mar 1644 or 1 Mar 1645 Plymouth/Scituate/ Barnstable [GMSP]

ANNIS, Abraham[2] (1668-bef 1751) & Hannah ?BADGER (1673-by 1724); m c1692 Newbury [ASBO, p.127]

ANNIS, Anthony & Jane RUNDLETT, delete - error for John ANTHONY [LND, p.66]

ANNIS, Cormac & Sarah CHASE; m Newbury 15 May 1666 [TAG 70:239]

ANNIS, Isaac[2] (c1673-by 1712) & Rebecca[4] BAILEY (1675-1748); m2 Shimuel GRIFFIN; m by 1700 Newbury [ASBO, p.124]

ANTHONY, John & Susanna[2] ALBRO; m Portsmouth 3 Jan 1693/4 [GM 1:19]

ANTROBUS, Walter (-1614) & Jane ARNOLD (c1567-1635+); m St Albans, Hertfordshire 8 Feb 1586/7 [GM 1:68]

ANTROBUS, William[2] (bp 1587-) & Alice DENTON; m St Albans, Hertfordshire 6 July 1607 Ipswich [GM 1:68]

ANTRUM, Obadiah[2] (bp 1640-) & Martha BAKER; m2 Thomas ANDREWS; m c1664 Salem [GM 1:71]

ANTRUM, Thomas[1] (bp 1601-1662[/3]) & Jane BATTER; m St Edmunds, Salisbury, Wiltshire 24 May 1630 Salem [GM 1:70]

APPLEGATE, Bartholomew[2] & Hannah/Anneken[2] PATRICK (c1631-), dau of Daniel; m Oct 1650 Gravesend [GM 1:73; GMB 3:1405]

APPLEGATE, John[2] (c1630-1712) & Avis GOULDING, dau of William; m by 1662 Gravesend [GM 1:73]

APPLEGATE, Thomas[1] (c1598-1656-7) & Elizabeth _____; m c1623 Weymouth/Newport/Gravesend [GM 1:72]

APPLEGATE, Thomas[2] & Johanna GIBBONS, dau of Richard; perhaps second marriage for Thomas [GM 1:73]

ARCHER, Henry[1] (1604/5-1673+) & Elizabeth[2] STOW (bp 1617-1669); m Roxbury 4 Dec 1639 Ipswich [AEBK 3]

ARCHER, John[1] (-1675) & Alse _____; m2 John BRICK; m by 1657 Portsmouth/Fall River/Jamestown [REG 157:110]

ARCHER, John[2] (c1659-by 1724/5) & Mehitable SHEARS; m Bristol 5 Jan 1692 [REG 157:111]

ARCHER, Samuel (c1608-1667) & Susanna _____ (-1674); m2 Richard HUTCHINSON; m bef 1657 Salem [GMSP]

ARMITAGE, Godfrey & Mary[2] COGSWELL (bp 1618-); m by 1651 Boston [GM 2:138]

ARMITAGE, Thomas[1] (c1601-by 1667) & 1/wf _____ _____; m c1626 Plymouth/Sandwich [GM 1:79]

ARMITAGE, Thomas[1] (c1601-by 1667) & 2/wf Martha _____ (-by 1659); m by 1650 Plymouth/Sandwich/Stamford/Hempstead/Oyster Bay [GM 1:79]

ARMITAGE, Thomas1 (c1601-by 1667) & 3/wf Anne LILLESTONE; m2 probably Samuel BARRETT; m by 1659 Plymouth/Sandwich/Stamford/Hempstead/ Oyster Bay [GM 1:79]

ARMS, William & Joanna[2] HAWKES (1653[/4]-); m Hatfield 21 Nov 1677 [GM 3:260]

ARNOLD, Benedict[2] (1615-) & Damaris WESTCOTT; m 17 Dec 1640 [GM 1:88]

ARNOLD, Daniel[2] & Elizabeth OSBORN, dau of James; m by 1676 [GM 1:83]

ARNOLD, Isaac[1] (c1640-1706) & 1/wf _____ _____; Southold [NYGBR 125:91]

ARNOLD, Isaac[1] (c1640-1706) & 2/wf Sarah (CORNELL) WASHBURN (bp 4 July 1657-); m1 John Washburn; m lic. 30 Oct 1691 Southold [NYGBR 125:92]

ARNOLD, John[1] (c1603-1664) & Susanna _____ (-1666/7+); m c1628 Hartford [GM 1:83]

ARNOLD, Joseph[2] & Elizabeth WAKEMAN, dau of Samuel; m bet 21 Aug 1659-11 Feb 1659/60 [GM 1:83; GME 3:1901]

ARNOLD, Richard (1642-1710) & Mary ANGELL (1640s-aft 1685); m aft 24 Oct 1666 Providence, RI [AEJA]

ARNOLD, Samuel[2] & Sarah[2] HOLMES; m c1671 Marshfield [REG 145:376]

ARNOLD, Stephen[2] (1622-) & Sarah SMITH, dau of Edward; m Providence 24 Nov 1646 Ilchester, Somersetshire [GM 1:89]

ARNOLD, William[1] (1587-1675-7) & Christian PEAK (1583-), dau of Thomas; m by 1611 Hingham/Providence [GM 1:88]

ASHCRAFT, John & Hannah OSBORN; m Stonington 12 Dec 1670 [TAG 74:129]

ASHLEY, Jonathan & Sarah[2] WADSWORTH (bp 1649[/50]-); m 10 Nov 1669 Hartford [GMB 3:1895]

ASHLEY, Joseph (1652-1698) & Mary PARSONS (1661-1711); m2 Joseph WILLISTON; m Springfield 16 Oct 1685 [REG 148:220]

ASHTON, James & Lucretia FOXWELL (c1646-); c1666 Piscataqua [GMB 1:695]

ASLEBEE, John (c1614-1671) & Rebecca AYER (-bef 1702); m2 George KEYSER, 8 Oct 1648 Newbury [TAG 40:231]

ASPINWALL, Peter & Remember[2] PALFREY (bp 16 Oct 1638-   ); m Boston 12 Feb 1661[/2] [GMB 3:1371]

ASPINWALL, William[1] (c1605-1662+) & Elizabeth GOODYEAR (-1650+), dau of Thomas; m bef 1630 Leiden/Charlestown/Boston/Portsmouth/New Haven/Manchester, Eng. [REG 154:379; GMB 1:56]

ASTWOOD, James & Sarah PRUDDEN; m Kings Walden, Hertfordshire 30 Apr 1633 [TAG 16:27]

ASTWOOD, John[1] (c1609-1654) & 1/wf Dinis STALLWORTH (-1634); m Missenden, Hertfordshire 13 Feb 1633/4 Roxbury/Milford [GM 1:93]

ASTWOOD, John[1] (c1609-1654) & 2/wf Martha _____, perhaps CARTER; m by 1635 Roxbury/Milford [GM 1:93]

ASTWOOD, John[1] (c1609-1654) & 3/wf Sarah (_____) BALDWIN (-1669); m1 Sylvester BALDWIN; m by 2 Aug 1640 Milford [GM 1:93]

ATKINSON, Hugh & Ellen _____ (c1623-1663/4) [AEBK 4:399]

ATKINSON, Theodore[1] (c1614-1701) & 1/wf Abigail CHAMBERS (-1663+), dau of Thomas; m by 1642 [GM 1:101]

ATKINSON, Theodore[1] (c1614-1701) & 2/wf Mary (WHEELWRIGHT) LYDE, dau of John; m1 Edward LYDE; m aft 21 Oct 1667 [GM 1:101]

ATKINSON, Theodore[2] (1644-   ) & Elizabeth MITCHELSON, dau of Edward; m2 Henry DEERING; m c1668 [GM 1:102]

ATWATER, Joshua (grandson of Rev. Adam Blackman of Stratford)(-1691/2) & Mary (MAVERICK) SMITH (1661-1688); m bef Apr 1688 [Sewall's Diary, 165 & 288]

ATWOOD, John[1] (-1675/6) & Sarah MASTERSON (1619+-1701); m aft 1637 Plymouth [MD 44:138]

ATWOOD, Nathaniel[2] (1651/2-1724) & Mary LUCAS? (c1659+-1736); m by 1684 Plymouth/Plympton/Carver [MD 44:139, TAG 41:202]

ATWOOD, Oliver[2] (1671-   ) & Anna BETTS; m Charlestown 30 Mar 1699 [GM 1:106]

ATWOOD, Philip[1] (c1620-1700[/1]) & 1/wf Rachel[2] BACHELOR (-1674), dau of William; m by 1653 [GM 1:105, 124]

ATWOOD, Philip[1] (c1620-1700[/1]) & 2/wf Elizabeth GROVER (-1676); m Malden 7 Apr 1675 [GM 1:105]

ATWOOD, Philip[1] (c1620-1700[/1]) & 3/wf Elizabeth _____ (-1688); m aft 1676 Malden [GM 1:105]

ATWOOD, Philip[2] (1658-1722) & Sarah TENNEY; m Salem 23 July 1684 [GM 1:106]

AUGER, Matthew & Martha (_____) CARVER, m1 Robert CARVER; Boston [RCA]

AULGAR, John & Hannah[2] BAKER (1644-   ); m by 1679 Boston [GM 1:131]

AUSTIN, John (1671-1759+) & Sarah[3] HALL (1679/80-1760); m Taunton 23 Nov 1699 [AEBK 4:333]

AUSTIN, Jonas[1] (bp 1598-1683) & 1/wf Constance (_____) ROBINSON (-1667); m1 William ROBINSON; m Tenterden, Kent 22 Jan 1626/7 Taunton [GM 1:108]

AUSTIN, Jonas[1] (bp 1598-1683) & 2/wf Frances (_____) HILL (-1676); m1 John HILL; m Taunton 14 Dec 1667 [GM 1:108]

AUSTIN, Jonas[2] (bp 1629/30-) & Esther _____; m c1661 [GM 1:108]

AUSTIN, Matthew (c1624-1684+) & _____[2] CANNEY; m bef 1658 [NHGR 20:6]

AUSTIN, Richard & Abigail[2] BACHELOR (bp 1637-); m Charlestown 11 Nov 1659 [GM 1:125]

AVERY, Christopher & 1/wf Margery STEPHENS; m Abbots Kerswell, Devonshire 28 Aug 1616 Wolborough & Newton Abbott, Devonshire [BB; JAN]

AVERY, Jonathan & Sybil SPARHAWK (c1655-1708) [REG 156:318]

AVERY, Joseph[1] (c1600-drowned 1635) & _____ _____ (-drowned 1635); m by 1623 Romsey, Hampshire/Newbury [GM 1:110]

AVERY, Thomas & Hannah[2] MINOR (1655-); m 22 Oct 1672 [GMB 2:1265]

AVERY, Thomas[1] (c1622-1658+) & Susanna _____ (-1657/8+); m by 1654 Salem [GM 1:114]

AVERY, William & Mary (WOODMANSEE) TAPPIN (c1629-1707); m1 John TAPPIN; m bef 8 Nov 1679 Boston [REG 147:45]

AWKLEY, Miles[1] (c1610-c1638) & Mary _____; m by 1635 Boston [GM 1:115]

AXTELL, Henry[2] (bp 1641-killed 1676) & Hannah MERRIAM (1645-1683); m Marlborough 14 June 1665 [AEBK 3]

AXTELL, Thomas[1] (bp 1618/9-164[5/]6) & Mary _____; m2 John MAYNARD; m c1639 Sudbury [AEBK 3]

AXTELL, Thomas[3] (1672-1750) & Sarah[3] BARKER (1679-1747); m Concord 2 Nov 1697 [AEBK 3]

AYER, Joseph (1658/9-1698+) & Sarah[2] CORLISS (1663/4-1698+); m 24 Nov 1686 Haverhill [ASBO, p.212]

AYER, Zachariah[3] (1657-1696+) & Elizabeth[2] CHASE (1657-1696+); did not m2 Daniel FAVOR; m 27 June 1673 Andover [ASBO, p.175]

AYERS, Robert[2] & Elizabeth PALMER; Haverhill [NHGR 10:71]

AYERS, Simon & Elizabeth (ALLERTON) STARR; New Haven 22 July 1679 [TAG 67:30]

AYERS, William[1] (c1620s-1662+) & _____ _____; m by 1653 England/Hartford [TAG 75:205]

AYRES, John[1] & Susanna SYMONDS (c1615-1682-/3?] Ipswich [TAG 74:116]

AYRES, Samuel & Abigail[2] FELLOWS; m Ipswich 16 Apr 1677 [GM 1:511]

AYRES, Thomas[2] (c1656-1726/7+) & Sarah[3] REYNOLDS; m2 Pardon TILLINGHAST; m bet 15 Oct 1692 & 28 Nov 1696 [TAG 75:302]

AYRES, William (-1662+) & _____ _____ (-1662+); c1653 Hartford [Harris]

AYRES, William[1] (c1620s-1671+) & Judith _____ (-1668+); m c1653 [TAG 75:303]

BACHELOR, David (1643-) & Hannah PLUMMER; m Reading 30 Dec 1679 [GM 1:120]

BACHELOR, John[1] (c1610-1676) & Rebecca _____ (-1661/2); m c1635 Reading [GM 1:120]

BACHELOR, John[2] & 1/wf Sarah LUNT, dau of Henry; m Reading 7 Jan 1662 [GM 1:120]

BACHELOR, John[2] & 2/wf Hannah (BOYNTON) WARNER (-1693), dau of John; m1 Nathaniel WARNER; m Reading 10 May 1687 [GM 1:120]

BACHELOR, John[2] & 3/wf Hannah _____; m Reading 12 June 1694 [GM 1:120]

BACHELOR, Joseph[2] (1644-) & Agnes (WADLAND) GILLINGHAM; m1 William GILLINGHAM; m Charlestown 22 Dec 1670 [GM 1:125]

BACHELOR, William[1] (c1596-1669[/70]) & 1/wf Jane _____ (-1637); m c1633 [GM 1:124]

BACHELOR, William[1] (c1596-1669[/70]) & 2/wf Rachel BATE (-1676); m by 1637 [GM 1:124]

BACHILER, Rev. Stephen[1] (c1561-1656) & 1/wf _____ _____ (a relative to Rev. John Bate) (-c1610-24); m bef 1590 Ipswich/Yarmouth/Newbury/Hampton/ Portsmouth [NHGR 8:14-17, GMB 1:62]

BACHILER, Rev. Stephen[1] (c1561-1656) & 2/wf Christian WEARE (-bef 1627); m Abbots Ann, Hampshire 2 Mar 1623/4 Ipswich/Yarmouth/Newbury/Hampton/ Portsmouth [NHGR 8:14-17, GMB 1:62]

BACHILER, Rev. Stephen[1] (c1561-1656) & 3/wf Helena MASON (c1583-by 1647); m Abbots Ann, Hampshire 26 Mar 1627 Ipswich/Yarmouth/ Newbury/ Hampton/Portsmouth [NHGR 8:14-17, GMB 1:62]

BACHILER, Rev. Stephen[1] (c1561-1656) & 4/wf Mary (_____) BEEDLE; m1 Robert BEEDLE; m bef 14 Feb 1648/9 Ipswich/Yarmouth/Newbury/Hampton/ Portsmouth [NHGR 8:14-17, GMB 1:62]

BACON, George[1] (c1592-1642) & 1/wf _____ _____; m c1623 England/Hingham [GM 1:128]

BACON, George[1] (c1592-1642) & 2/wf Margaret _____ (-1682/3); m2 Edward GOLD; m bet 1635-40 Hingham [GM 1:128]

BACON, Peter[2] (bp 1654-) & 1/wf Sarah JENKINS; m Hingham 25 May 1670 [GM 1:128]

BACON, Peter[2] (bp 1654-) & 2/wf Martha (HOWLAND) DAMON (-1732); m1 John DAMON; m Hingham 19 Feb 1679/80 [GM 1:129]

BACON, Samuel & Martha[2] FOXWELL (163[7/]8-); m Barnstable 9 May 1659 [GM 2:567]

BACON, Samuel[2] (c1623-) & Mary JACOB, dau of John; m Hingham 17 Dec 1675 [GM 1:128]

BACON, William[1] & Rebecca[1] POTTER (bp 1610-) [TAG 73:26]

BADGER, John & Elizabeth[2] HAYDEN (c1643-); m Charlestown 16 June 1663 [GM 3:280]

BADLAM, William[1] (c1650s-bef 1718) & 1/wf Joane _____ (c1660-c1687-90); m bef 1684, Boston/Weymouth [REG 141:3]

BADLAM, William[1] (c1650s-bef 1718) & 2/wf Mary FRENCH (1662-bef 1718); m c1690 Weymouth/Boston [REG 141:3]

BAGLEY, Orlando[2] (1658-c1728/9) & 1/wf Sarah[2] SARGENT (1651/2-1701); m 22 Dec 1681 Amesbury [ASBO, p.124; GMB 3:1632]

BAILEY, Guido & 2/wf Ruth (RATCHELL?) (GURNEY) BUNDY; m1 John GURNEY; m2 John BUNDY [TAG 33:138]

BAILEY, James & Mary[2] CARR (1651/2-); m Newbury 17 Sept 1672 [GM 2:20]

BAILEY, John & Ann BOURNE; m2 Thomas TRANTOR; m 9 May 1677 Marshfield [TAG 40:33-4]

BAILEY, John & Eleanor[2] EMERY (bp 1624-); m by 1641 Salisbury [GM 2:449]

BAKER, Alexander[1] (c1607-1684/5-5) & Elizabeth _____ (c1612-1684/5+); m by 1632 Boston [GM 1:131]

BAKER, Cornelius & Hannah[2] WOODBURY (bp 1636-); m Salem 26 Apr 1658 [GMB 3:2055]

BAKER, Jeffrey & Joan[2] ROCKWELL (bp 1625-); m2 Richard INGRAM; m Windsor 15 Nov 1642 [GMB 3:1596]

BAKER, John & Alice[2] PIERCE (bp 1650-); m c1672 Yarmouth [GMB 3:1468]

BAKER, John & Katharine[2] PERKINS (1648-); m Ipswich 13 May 1667 [GMB 3:1436]

BAKER, John (-1641) & Charity _____; m by 1631 Charlestown/Newbury/York/Boston [GMSP]

BAKER, Joseph (1660/1-1590+) & Hannah BANKS (1666-); m Woburn 4 Oct 1686 Chelmsford [AEBK 4:63]

BAKER, Joshua[2] (1642-) & Hannah (____) MINTER; m1 Tristram MINTER; m New London 13 Sept 1674 [GM 1:131]

BAKER, Josiah (1654[/5]-) & Mary _____; m by 1680 Boston [GM 1:132]

BAKER, Nathaniel & Mary[2] PIERCE (c1645-); m c1670 [GMB 3:1468]

BAKER, Nathaniel[1] (c1614-1682) & 1/wf _____ LANE, dau of William; m by 1639 Hingham [GM 1:138]

BAKER, Nathaniel[1] (c1614-1682) & 2/wf Sarah _____; m aft 28 Feb 1650[/1] Hingham [GM 1:138]

BAKER, Nicholas[1] (c1610-1678) & 1/wf _____ _____ (-1661); m by 1638 Scituate [GM 1:143]

BAKER, Nicholas[1] (c1610-1678) & 2/wf Grace (____) DIPPLE; m 29 Apr 1662 Scituate [GM 1:143]

BAKER, Nicholas[2] & Experience COLLIER, dau of Thomas; m c1687 [GM 1:144]

BAKER, Samuel & Ellen[2] WINSLOW; m Marshfield 20 Dec 1656 [GMB 3:2035]

BAKER, Samuel (c1665-) & Sarah SNOW (1680-); m 27 Feb 1699 Marshfield [REG 124:119]

BAKER, Samuel[2] (bp 1638-) & 1/wf Fear[2] ROBINSON (bp 1644/5-), dau of Isaac; m by 1664 Hingham [GM 1:143; GMB 3:1593]

BAKER, Samuel[2] (bp 1638-) & 2/wf Abigail (LATHROP) HUNTINGTON [GM 1:143]

BAKER, Thomas & Mary HAUGH [REG 156:389]

BAKER, Thomas & Sarah[2] CARR (1654-); m by 1678 Boston [GM 2:21]

BAKER, William & _____ _____, m bef 1636 Watertown [RCA]

BAKER, William & a Pequot woman of Plymouth 1632 [RCA]

BAKER, William (c1613-1658) & Joan _____ (-1669); m by 1633 Charlestown/Billerica [GMB 1:82]

BAKER, William (c1655-1743) & 1/wf Sarah FITTS (1661-bef 1722); m 30 Dec 1689 Ipswich [ASBO, p.89]

BAKER, William[2] (1647-) & Eleanor _____; m by 1669 Boston [GM 1:132]

BALCH, Benjamin & 3/wf Grace (_____) MALLOTT; m1 Hosea MALLOTT [JHM]

BALCH, John & 1/wf Sarah GARDNER (c1627-); by c1650 Cape Ann [GMB 2:734]

BALCH, John & Mary CONANT (c1632-); m2 William DODGE; by 1652 Salem [GMB 1:454]

BALCH, John[1] (c1605-1648) & 1/wf Margery _____ (-1636+); m by 1636 or earlier Cape Ann/Salem/Beverly [GMSP]

BALCH, John[1] (c1605-1648) & 2/wf Annia _____ (-by 1657); m after 1636 Cape Ann/Salem/Beverly [GMSP]

BALCOM, Alexander (-1711) & 1/wf _____ _____; Portsmouth [TAG 71:145]

BALCOM, Alexander[1] & Jane (HOLBROOK) ALBEE; m1 John ALBEE; m c1676 Providence [TAG 48:122]

BALDWIN, Henry & Phebe[2] RICHARDSON (bp 1632-); m Woburn 1 Nov 1649 [GMB 3:1582]

BALDWIN, James (c1667-1748+) & 1/wf Elizabeth _____; m bef 1703 Milford [REG 156:111]

BALDWIN, John & Hannah[2] BIRCHARD (bp 1633-); m Guilford 12 Apr 1653 [GM 1:296]

BALDWIN, Joseph[1] (-1684) & 1/wf Hannah WHITLOCK? [REG 156:104-108]

BALDWIN, Joseph[1] (-1684) & 2/wf Isabel (NORTHAM) CATLIN [REG 156:108-111]

BALDWIN, Joseph[1] (-1684) & 3/wf Elizabeth _____ (HITCHCOCK) WARRINER [REG 156:104-111]

BALDWIN, Joseph[2] (bp 1644-1681) & 1/wf Elizabeth _____; m about 1662 [REG 156:104-11]

BALDWIN, Joseph[2] (bp 1644-1681) & 2/wf Sarah COLEY, dau. of Samuel (-1689); m bet 1675/6-77/8 Hadley [REG 156:104-111]

BALDWIN, Joseph[3] (1663-1714) & Elizabeth GROVER (1669-1744/5); m Malden 16 June 1691 [REG 156:110]

BALLANTINE, William & Hannah[2] HOLLARD (1635-   ); m2 William LONG; m Boston 23 July 1652 [GM 3:379]

BALLARD, John (c1634-   ) & Rebecca _____; m by 1669 [GM 1:148]

BALLARD, Nathaniel[2] (c1636-   ) & Rebecca HUTSON; m Lynn 16 Dec 1662 [GM 1:148]

BALLARD, William[1] (c1603-1638/9-9) & Elizabeth _____; m2 William KNIGHT; m3 Allen BREAD; m c1633 [GM 1:148; TEG 13:230]

BALLINE, Samuel & Experience SABIN; m 1672 Rehoboth [VR per PCRG]

BANBRIDGE, Guy[1] (c1595-1645) & Justice _____ (-1672/3); m c1620 Cambridge [GM 1:153]

BANFIELD, John & Mary[2] PICKERING (c1643-   ); m c1673 [GMB 3:1460]

BANGS, Edward (c1591-1677) & 1/wf Lydia[2] HICKS (bp 6 Sept 1612- c1635); m by 1633 Plymouth/Eastham [GMB 1:89, 2:927]

BANGS, Edward (c1591-1677) & 2/wf Rebecca _____ (-1655); m by 1635 Plymouth/Eastham [GMSP]

BANGS, John & Hannah[2] SMALLEY (1641-   ); m Eastham 23 Jan 1660[/1] [GMB 3:1689]

BANGS, Jonathan (1640-1728) & 1/wf Mary MAYO (-1711); m 16 July 1664 Eastham [TAG 60:159 & MD 4:29]

BANKS, John[1] (c1631-1683) & Hannah[2] JENKINS (c1645-1716); m say 1665 Chelmsford [AEBK 4:61]

BANKS, Lydia is not connected to Roger Mowry, she was d/o John and Mary (Fisher) Banks of Maidstone, Kent [RCA]

BARBER, John[2] (bp 1642-   ) & Bathsheba COGGINS; m Springfield 2 Sept 1663 [GM 1:155]

BARBER, Josiah[2] (1653/4-   ) & 2/wf Abigail LOOMIS; m Windsor 22 Nov 1677 [GM 1:156]

BARBER, Samuel[2] (bp 1648-   ) & 1/wf Mary COGGINS; m Windsor 1 Dec 1670 [GM 1:156]

BARBER, Samuel[2] (bp 1648-   ) & 2/wf RUTH DRAKE; m Windsor 25 Jan 1676[/7] [GM 1:156]

BARBER, Thomas & Mary[2] PHELPS (1644-   ); m Windsor 17 Dec 1663 [GMB 3:1446]

BARBER, Thomas (c1645-1690+) & Anne[2] CHASE (1647-1690+); m 27 Apr 1671 Newbury/Suffield [ASBO, p.172]

BARBER, Thomas[1] (bp 1612-1662) & Jane _____ (-1662); m Windsor 7 Oct 1640 Stamford, Lincolnshire/Windsor [GM 1:155; TAG 71:112]

BARBER, Thomas[2] (1644-   ) & Mary PHELPS; m Windsor 17 Dec 1663 [GM 1:155]

BARKER, Francis[1] (-by 1655) & _____ _____; m by 1645 [AEBK 3]

BARKER, Isaac & Judith[2] PRENCE (c1645-); m2 William TUBBS; m Plymouth 28 Dec 1665 [GMB 3:1523]

BARKER, James & Sarah[2] JEFFREYS (c1650-); m c1675 [GMB 2:1084]

BARKER, John[2] (c1645-by 1718) & 1/wf Juda SIMONDS (c1646-1704); m Concord 9 Dec 1668 [AEBK 3]

BARKER, John[3] (1669-1734/5) & Dorothy SHEPARD (1669-1746); m c1688 Concord [AEBK 3]

BARKER, Robert[1] (c1616-by 1691/2) & Lucy (not Williams) (-1681/2+); by 1642 Plymouth/Marshfield/Duxbury [GMB 1:94]

BARKER, William[3] (1674-1703) & Dorothy HAYWARD (1673[/4?]-1755); m Concord 12 Mar 1695/6 [AEBK 3]

BARLOW, Edward/Edmund & Mary[2] PEMBERTON (bp 1636-); m c1656 [GMB 3:1420]

BARNAART, Casper & Elizabeth FLETCHER (bp 1604-); m2 Michiel VOOREHOTEN; bef 1636 [GMB 1:681]

BARNABY, James ~ Elizabeth HUGHES; Plymouth [Plymouth Court Sept 1691]

BARNARD, Bartholomew & Sarah[2] BIRCHARD (bp 1624-); m Hartford 25 Oct 1647 [GM 1:296]

BARNARD, Benjamin (c1650-) & Sarah WENTWORTH, dau of William; m by 1687 [GM 1:164]

BARNARD, James & Abigail[2] PHILLIPS (c1643-); m Watertown 8 Oct 1666 [GMB 3:1449]

BARNARD, John & Mary PEGREM; m by 1634 [LMM; GM 1:158-61]

BARNARD, John (1657-1727-32) & 1/wf Sarah[2] CUTTING (1661-1684+); m Watertown 5 Mar 1682/3 [AEBK 1:265; GM 2:274]

BARNARD, John (1657-1727-32) & 2/wf Elizabeth STONE (-1694); m 17 Nov 1692 [AEBK 1:265]

BARNARD, John (1657-1727-32) & 3/wf Mary MORSE; m 23 July 1694 [AEBK 1:265]

BARNARD, John[1] (c1598-1664) & Mary STACE (-c1665); m by 1634 [GM 1:160]

BARNARD, John[1] (c1607-1646) & Phebe WHITING (-1685), dau of Anthony; m c1632 Dedham, Essex/Watertown [GM 1:163]

BARNARD, John[2] (c1632-) & Sarah FLEMING, dau of John; m 15 Nov 1654 [GM 1:163]

BARNARD, Joseph & Lydia[2] HAYWARD (1660-); m c1691 Wethersfield [GM 3:284]

BARNARD, Nathaniel (c1634-by 1659) & Mary LUGG (1642-1659+); m Boston 11 Feb 1658/9 [AEBK 4:494]

BARNARD, Stephen & Rebecca[2] HOWE (c1652-); m Andover 1 May 1671 [GM 3:434]

BARNARD, Thomas & Abigail[2] BULL (c1653-); m Salem 28 Apr 1696 [GM 1:475]

BARNES, John (-by 1679/80) & Elizabeth[2] HEATON (1643-by 1710); m by 1 Mar 1669/70 Boston [AEBK 4:392; GM 3:305]

BARNES, John[1] (c1608-1667/8-71) & 1/wf Mary PLUMMER (-1651); m Plymouth 12 Sept 1633 [GMSP]

BARNES, John[1] (c1608-1667/8-71) & 2/wf Joan _____ (-1682/3+); m bef 1 Mar 1652/3 Plymouth [GMSP]

BARNES, Jonathan & Elizabeth[2] HEDGES (1647-); m Plymouth 4 Jan 1665[/6] [GMB 2:906]

BARNES, Thomas (1670/1-1706) & Sarah STONE (-1699); m Providence 25 Mar 1697 [AEJA]

BARNES, Thomas (c1602-1672) & Anna _____ (c1610s-1672+); m by 1643 Hingham [AEJA]

BARNES, William (c1610-) & Rachel _____; m bef 1640 Salisbury [50 GMC]

BARNETT alias BARBANT, John & Mary[2] BISHOP (c1634-); m2 John DURLAN/DARLING; m Salem 14 June 1661 [GM 1:310]

BARNEY, Jacob (c1601-1673) & 1/wf Anna _____; by 1632 Salem [GMB 1:106]

BARNEY, Jacob (c1601-1673) & 2/wf Elizabeth _____ (-1676/7+); by 1673 Salem [GMB 1:106]

BARNUM, Thomas & Sarah (THOMPSON) HURD (-1717/8); m1 John HURD [TAG 50:3]

BARRETT, James (c1644-1672-9) & Dorcas[2] GREEN (1654-1682); m Malden 1 Jan 1671/2 [AEBK 4:306]

BARRETT, James[2] & Abiel PHILLIPS, dau of George; m Watertown 8 Oct 1666 [GM 1:164]

BARRETT, John (-1715) & Deborah[2] HOWE (1666/7-1743); m c1690 Marlborough [AEBK 3]

BARRETT, Jonathan (1654-1743) & 1/wf Abigail (EAMES) WESTON (-1706); m Woburn 26 June 1696 [AEBK 4:439]

BARRETT, Jonathan (1654-1743) & 2/wf Sarah LEARNED (1653-1694/5); m c1679 [AEBK 4:439]

BARRETT, Samuel & Hannah[2] BETTS (bp 1639/40-) [GM 1:279]

BARRETT, Samuel & Sarah[2] BUTTRICK (1662-); m Chelmsford 21 Feb 1683[/4]? [GM 1:524]

BARRETT, William & Mary[2] BARNARD (1639-); m Cambridge 16 June 1662 [GM 1:164]

BARRETT, William & Sarah (POOLE) CHAMPNEY possibly [GMB 2:1494-96]

BARRON, Ellis (c1633-1711-12) & 1/wf Hannah[2] HAWKINS (1636-1673); m Watertown 14 Dec 1653 [AEBK 1:128; GMB 2:889]

BARRON, Ellis (c1633-1711-12) & 2/wf Lydia (PRESCOTT) FAIRBANKS (-1712+); m1 Jonas FAIRBANKS; m say 1674 Watertown/Groton [AEBK 1:129]

BARRON, Ellis[1] (c1610-1676) & 1/wf Grace _____ (c1610-bef 1653); by 1630 Watertown [AEBK 1:119]

BARRON, Ellis[1] (c1610-1676) & 2/wf Anne (HAMMOND) HAWKINS (bp 1616-1685); m1 by 1637 Timothy HAWKINS; m Watertown 14 Dec 1653 [AEBK 1:119]

BARRON, John (c1638-1692/3) & Elizabeth HUNT (-1704); m Concord 1 Apr 1664 [AEBK 1:130]

BARRON, Moses (1643/4-by 1719/20) & Mary[3] LEARNED (1647-1728+); m by 1669 Chelmsford [AEBK 1:130, 4:438]

BARSHAM, William (c1610-1684) & Anabel SMITH alias BLAND (c1615-by 1683); m by 1635 Watertown [GMSP]

BARSTOW, George[1] (c1614-1652/3) & Susanna MARRIOTT (-1654), dau of Thomas; m by 1649 Cambridge [GM 1:169]

BARSTOW, George[2] (bp 1653-) & Mercy CLARK, dau of James; m c1684 Boston [GM 1:169]

BARSTOW, Joseph[2] (1639-) & Susanna LINCOLN; m Hingham 16 May 1666 [GM 1:177]

BARSTOW, Michael[1] (bp 17 Nov 1600-1674) & 1/wf Grace HALSTEAD (bp 1597-by 1635); m Halifax, Yorkshire 15 Feb 1624/5 Charlestown/Watertown [REG 146:230; GM 1:173]

BARSTOW, Michael[1] (bp 17 Nov 1600-1674) & 2/wf Mercy _____ (-by 1642); m possibly in England by 5 Dec 1635 Charlestown/Watertown [REG 146:234; GM 1:173]

BARSTOW, Michael[1] (bp 17 Nov 1600-1674) & 3/wf Grace (WALKER) CARVER (- 1672); m1 Richard CARVER; m c1641 Charlestown/Watertown [REG 146:234; GM 1:174]

BARSTOW, William[1] (c1612-1668/9) & Ann HUBBARD; m2 John PRINCE; m Dedham 8 July 1638 [GM 1:177]

BARSTOW, William[2] (bp 1652-) & Martha _____ (-1711); m by 1676 Scituate [GM 1:178]

BARTHOLOMEW, Henry (bp 1654-1694-8) & Katherine HUTCHINSON (1652/3- 1730+); m2 Richard JANVERIN; m 1675-1692 Salem [REG 145:264)

BARTHOLOMEW, Henry[1] & Elizabeth[2] SCUDDER (c1622-1682); m 1640s Salem [TAG 72:294]

BARTHOLOMEW, William[1] (c1603-1680/1) & Ann _____ (-1682/3); m by 1653 Charlestown [GM 1:183]

BARTLETT, Benjamin & Susanna[2] JENNY (c1634-); m by 1654 [GMB 2:1093]

BARTLETT, Henry[1] (c1656-1718+) & Mary[2] BUSH (1662-1704+); m Marlborough 6 Dec 1682 [AEBK 3]

BARTLETT, John & Bethia DEVEREUX; by Mar 1680 [GMB 1:533]

BARTLETT, Joseph & Hannah[2] POPE (c1639-1710[/1?]); m c1663 [GMB 3:1498]

BARTLETT, Joseph (-1703) & Lydia GRISWOLD (-1752); m Plymouth 6 June 1692 [REG 155:249]

BARTLETT, Robert (c1604-1676) & Mary[2] WARREN (-by 1683); m c1629 Plymouth [GMB 3:1936]

BARTLETT, Robert (c1612-1675/6) & Ann _____ (-1676); m c1637
   Cambridge/Hartford/Northampton [GMSP]

BARTLETT, Thomas (c1594-1654) & Hannah _____ (-1674+); m by 1636/7
   Watertown [GMSP]

BARTLETT, William & Sarah[2] PURCHASE (c1669-); did NOT marry Gamaliel
   PHIPPEN; m Marblehead 27 Dec 1688 [GMB 3:1532]

BARTON, Elisha & Mary CROCKETT; by 28 Oct 1684 [GMB 1:497]

BARTRAM, William (c1616-21-1690) & Sarah (or Hannah)(likely JOHNSON) BURT
   (bp 12 Nov 1624 or 23 Mar 1627/8-bet 1688-1694); m1 Hugh BURT; m c 1654
   Ware, Great Amwell, Hertfordshire/Roxbury/Lynn/Swansea [TEG 4:178-185;
   AEJA; GMB 2:1108; REG 146:275, 149:230; Gen. Adv. 4:58]

BASCOMB, Thomas[1](c1605-1682) & Avis _____ (-1676); m c1630 Northampton [GM
   1:187]

BASCOMB, Thomas[2] (1641/2-) & Mary NEWELL, dau of Thomas; m Northampton 20
   Mar 166[6/]7 [GM 1:188]

BASS, Samuel (c1600-1694) & Ann SAVELL (c1600-1693); m Saffron Walden, Essex 25
   Apr 1625 Roxbury/Braintree [GMSP]

BASSETT, John[2] (1653-) & ?Mary _____; m c1687 [GM 1:193]

BASSETT, Nathaniel[2] (c1628-1709/10) & Dorcas JOYCE (not Mary) (c1640-1707); m
   c1661 Yarmouth/Chatham [TAG 43:3]

BASSETT, Thomas[1] (c1598-1669/70) & 1/wf _____ _____; m by 1651 [GM 1:190]

BASSETT, Thomas[1] (c1598-1669/70) & 2/wf Joanna (____) BEARDSLEY; m1 Thomas
   BEARDSLEY; m aft July 1656 [GM 1:190]

BASSETT, Thomas[2] & Sarah perhaps BALDWIN, dau of Josiah; m c1690 [GM 1:190]

BASSETT, William & Mary[2] RAINSFORD (1632-); m2 James PERCIVAL; m c1652
   Sandwich [GMB 3:1546]

BASSETT, William (c1600-1667) & 1/wf Elizabeth _____ (-1634+); m by 1623
   Plymouth/Duxbury/Bridgewater [GMSP]

BASSETT, William (c1600-1667) & 2/wf Mary (TILDON) LAPHAM; m1 Thomas
   LAPHAM; m bet 1651-1664 Plymouth/Duxbury/Bridgewater [GMSP]

BASSETT, William[1] (bp 1624-1703) & Sarah _____; m c1647 Lynn [GM 1:192]

BASSETT, William[2] & Sarah HOOD. m Lynn 25 Oct 1675 [GM 1:193]

BATCHELDER, John & Sarah[2] GOODALE (c1638-); m Wenham 4 May 1666 [GM
   3:106]

BATE, Benjamin[2] (bp 1632-) & Jane WEEKS [GM 1:197]

BATE, Clement[1] (bp 1594/5-1671) & Ann _____ (-1669); m by 1621 Hingham [GM
   1:197]

BATE, Edward[1] (bp 1606-1586) & Susanna PUTNAM (bp 1609/10-); m 26 Jan 1631/2
   Drayton Beauchamp, Buckinghamshire/Weymouth [TAG 65:94]

BATE, James (bp 1582-1655-5/6) & Alice GLOVER (-1657); m Saltwood, Kent 16 Sept
   1603 [GM 1:199]

BATE, James[2] (bp 1624-) & Hannah WITHINGTON; m c1648 Dorchester [GM 1:200]

BATE, Joseph[2] (bp 1628-) & Esther HILLIARD; m Hingham Jan 1657/8 Biddenden, Kent [GM 1:197]

BATE, Samuel (bp 1638/9-) & Lydia LAPHAM, dau of Thomas; m Hingham 20 Feb 1666/7 [GM 1:197]

BATES, Edward (c1616-1644-5) & Lydia _____, may have m2 William FLETCHER; m by 1641 Boston [GMSP]

BATES, James & Ruth[2] LYFORD (c1619-); m Hingham 19 Apr 1643 [GMB 2:1215; GM 197]

BATES, John (c1640s-1718/9) & Elizabeth (BECKWITH) GERRARD, m1 Robert GERRARD, div.; m mid-1670s Lyme/Haddam, CT [AEJA]

BATH, William & Eleanor (_____) ELLENWOOD (c1636-); m1 Ralph ELLENWOOD; m bef June 1677 Beverly [EQC 4:216; 6:288]

BATT, Nicholas[1] (c1608-1677) & Lucy _____ (-1678[/9]); m c1633 Newbury [GM 1:203]

BATTELLE, Thomas[1] (c1620s-1705/6) & Mary[2] FISHER (bp 1622/3-1691); m Dedham 5 Sept 1648 [AEBK 4:235]

BATTEN, Hugh[1] & Ursula[2] GREENWAY (bp 1603-1682); m aft 5 Feb 1650[/1] Dorchester [TAG 74:195; GMB 816]

BATTER, Edmund[1] (c1609-1685) & 1/wf Sarah VERIN (bp 1609-1669), dau of Philip; m c1630 Sarum/Salem [GM 1:210]

BATTER, Edmund[1] (c1609-1685) & 2/wf Mary GOOKIN (-1702-2/3), dau of Daniel; m Salem 8 June 1670 [GM 1:210]

BATTER, Edmund[2] (1673/4-) & 1/wf Martha PICKMAN; m Salem 26 Oct 1699 [GM 1:210]

BAULSTON, William (c1605-1677/8+) & Elizabeth _____; m by 1630 Boston/Portsmouth, RI [GMSP]

BAXTER, Gregory (c1607-1659) & Margaret ?PADDY (-1661/2); m bef 1632 Roxbury/Braintree/Boston [GMSP]

BAXTER, John (1639-1719) & Hannah WHITE (c1638-1717/8+); m Braintree 24 Nov 1659 [AEBK 1:502]

BAXTER, Simon & Sarah[2] BELL (1640-); m All Hallows Barking, London [GM 1:241]

BAYLEY, _____ & Sarah WILLIAMS (c1675-bef 1705); m c1690 New London/Groton [AEJA]

BAYLEY, Thomas[2] & Hannah RAWLINGS (c1644-1721); m bef 1687 Weymouth [AEBK 1:404]

BAYLY, John[1] (c1586-1651) & Ann BAYLY (-1659); m Bromhan, Wiltshire July 1611 Salisbury/Newbury [TAG 77:243]

BAYLY, John[2] (bp 1613-1690/1) & Eleanor[2] EMERY, dau. of John; m c1640 Newbury [TAG 77:245]

BEACKINTON, _____ & Ann PEDRICK?; m bef 1693, Marblehead [LB]

BEAL, John & Mary (GILMAN) JACOB; m1 Nicholas Jacob; m Hingham 10 Mar 1658/9 [GMB 2:959]

BEAL, Thomas & Sarah[1] _____; perhaps [GM 1:213]

BEAL, Thomas[1] (bp 1599-1661) & Sarah _____ (-1677+); Biddenden, Kent/Cambridge [GM 1:216]

BEALE, Arthur & Agnes[2] HILTON (c1647-); m by 1667 [GMB 2:954]

BEAMON, Gamaliel[1] (c1623-1678/9) & Sarah _____; m c1649 Dorchester [GM 1:218]

BEAMON, John[1] (c1612-by 1647) & _____ _____; m2 John TUCKER; m c1640 Salem [GM 1:220]

BEAMON, Noah[2] (1661-) & Patience TRESCOTT; m Dorchester 1 Jan 1684/5 [GM 1:218]

BEAMON, Samuel[2] (1656/7-) & Hester BUCKINGHAM, dau of Thomas; m c1690 Saybrook/New London [GM 1:221]

BEAMON, Thomas[2] (c1649-) & Elizabeth WILLIAMS; m Marlborough 26 July 1678 [GM 1:218]

BEAMON, William[2] (c1608-1698/9) & Lydia DANFORTH (bp 1625-1686), dau of Nicholas; m Saybrook 9 Dec 1643 [GM 1:221; 2:283]

BEAMSLEY, William (c1607-1658) & 1/wf Anne _____ (-1643+); m bef 1630 Boston [50 GMC & GMSP]

BEARDSLEY, Daniel[2] (c1645-1730) & Ruth GOODWIN, dau of Thomas; m by 1682 Stratford [GM 1:226]

BEARDSLEY, John[1] (c1633-) & Hannah _____; m c 1656 [GM 1:225]

BEARDSLEY, Joseph[2] (c1634-) & _____ _____; m c1666 Stratford [GM 1:226]

BEARDSLEY, Samuel[2] & Abigail CLARK, dau of John; m c1664 New Haven [GM 1:226]

BEARDSLEY, William[1] (c1605-1660-) & Mary HARVEY (bp 1605-1674+); m Ilkeston, Derbyshire 26 Jan 1631/2 Concord/Stratford [GM 1:225]

BEASLEY, Robert & Sarah BROWN (c1652-); by 26 Nov 1672 Charlestown [GMB 1:252]

BECK, Alexander (c1613-1668) & 1/wf Mary _____ (-1639); by 1639 Boston [GMSP]

BECK, Alexander (c1613-1668) & 2/wf Elizabeth HINDS; m by 1640 Boston [GMSP]

BECK, Caleb[2] & Hannah BOLLES (1649-), dau of Joseph; m c1670 Portsmouth [GM 1:229]

BECK, Henry[1] (c1617-1693/4+) & Anna _____; m c1640 Dover/Portsmouth [GM 1:229]

BECK, Henry[2] (c1654-) & Elizabeth _____; m c1686 [GM 1:230]

BECK, Thomas[2] & Mary _____, perhaps FROST; m c1683 [GM 1:230]

BECKWITH, Matthew (c1645-1727) & 3/wf Sarah (_____) STARKEY (-1728/9+); m1 John STARKEY; m by 1714 New London/Lyme [AEJA]

BECKWITH, John (c1665-1757) & Prudence MANWARING (c1667-8-1740); c1687 New London [AEJA]

BECKWITH, Joseph (1679-1741) & Mary LEE (1676-1759-61); m2 Daniel STERLING, m3 John RIGGS; m 18 May 1699 Lyme, CT [AEJA]

BECKWITH, Joseph (c1653-1707+) & Susanna TALLMAN (-1711+); m c1675 Lyme [AEJA]

BECKWITH, Matthew (c1612-1681) & Mary _____ (c1625-1682+); m c1643 probably New London, CT [AEJA]

BECKWITH, Matthew (c1645-1727) & 1/wf Elizabeth _____; m c1666 New London/Lyme, CT [AEJA]

BECKWITH, Matthew (c1645-1727) & 2/wf Elizabeth (GRISWOLD) (ROGERS) PRATT (-by 1700); m1 John ROGERS; div.; m2 Peter PRATT; m c1688 Lyme [AEJA]

BECKWITH, Nathaniel (c1656-1725-6) & Martha _____; by 1679 Lyme [AEJA]

BEECHER, Thomas (c1600-1636/7) & Christian (_____) COOPER; m1 Thomas COOPER; m by 1630 Charlestown [GMSP]

BEERS, Eliezer (-1691) & Susannah (HARRINGTON) CUTTING; m3 1703 Peter CLOYSE [AEBK 1:263]

BEERS, Richard & Elizabeth FIRMIN (bp 1615-); m by 1639 Watertown [GMB 1:677]

BEGGARLY, Richard & Alice _____, m2 John GREENE; m bef 1630 Providence [GMSP]

BELCHER, Andrew & Elizabeth[2] DANFORTH (bp 1619-); m Cambridge 1 Oct 1639 [GM 2:283]

BELCHER, Edward (c1600-by 1672/3) & 1/wf _____ _____; m by 1630 Boston [GMSP]

BELCHER, Edward (c1600-by 1672/3) & 2/wf Christian (TALMAGE) WORMOOD; m1 William WORMWOOD; between 1646-1655/6 Boston [GMB 1:150]

BELCHER, Jeremy[1] (c1614-1674+) & 1/wf _____ _____; m c1639 [GM 1:234]

BELCHER, Jeremy[1] (c1614-1674+) & 2/wf Mary LOCKWOOD (-1700), dau of Edmund probably; m contract 30 Sept 1652 [GM 1:234]

BELCHER, Jeremy[2] (c1641-1722/3) & 1/wf Sarah (WEEDEN) SENTER, dau of Edward; m1 John SENTER; m by 1668 Boston [GM 1:235]

BELCHER, Josias & Ranis[2] RAINSFORD (1638-); m Boston 3 Mar 1655 [GMB 3:1546]

BELCHER, Richard[2] (1665-) & Mary SIMPSON; m Ipswich 20 May 1689 [GM 1:235]

BELCHER, Samuel[2] (c1639-1713/4) & 1/wf Mary COBBETT; m c1668 [GM 1:234]

BELCHER, Samuel[2] (c1639-1713/4) & 2/wf Mercy (WIGGLESWORTH) BRACKENBURY, dau of Michael; m1 Samuel BRACKENBURY [GM 1:234]

BELDEN, Richard[1] (c1598-) & Margaret ACKRENDEN; Heptonstall, Yorkshire/Wethersfield [TAG 76:20-28, 128]

BELKNAP, Abraham (bp 10 Mar 1589/90-1643) & Mary STALLON (bp 24 Dec 1595-); m 28 Oct 1617 Latton, Essex/Lynn [50 GMC]

BELL, James[1] (c1633-1676) & Hester LUGG (bp 1632/3-1713/4+; m2 Richard MARSHALL; m bet 1655-58 Taunton [AEBK 4:87]

BELL, James[2] (1663-1713+) & Hannah PRAY (1665/6-); m bef 1698 Taunton [AEBK 4:93]

BELL, Thomas[1] (c1606-1672) & Susanna BRYDON (bp 1604-1672/3), dau of John; m Bury St. Edmunds St. James, Suffolk 15 Aug 1631 [GM 1:241]

BELL, Thomas[1] (c1610-1655) & Anne ?ESSEX; m2 1656 William[2] MULLINS; m by 1638 Boston [TAG 74:285]

BELL, Thomas[2] (1642-by 1695) & Anna _____ (-1696+); m by 1689 Boston/Stonington [TAG 74:285]

BELL, Thomas[2] (c1633-) & Jane _____ [GM 1:241]

BELLINGHAM, Richard[1] (c1592-1672) & 1/wf Elizabeth BACKHOUSE, dau of Samuel [GM 1:247]

BELLINGHAM, Richard[1] (c1592-1672) & 2/wf Penelope PELHAM (-1702); m 9 Nov 1641 Boston [GM 1:247]

BELLINGHAM, Samuel[2] & 1/wf Lucy _____; m c1650 Boston [GM 1:247]

BELLINGHAM, Samuel[2] & 2/wf Elizabeth (SMITH) SAVAGE; m St James Dukes Place, London 18 Apr 1695 [GM 1:247]

BELLOWS, Eleazer[2] (1671-) & Esther BARRETT; m Marlborough 11 Oct 1692 [GM 1:252]

BELLOWS, John[1] (c1624-1683) & Mary WOOD (-1707), dau of John; m Concord 9 May 1655 [GM 1:251]

BELLOWS, John[2] (1666-) & Hannah NEWTON, dau of Moses; m by 1695 Marlborough [GM 1:251]

BENDALL, Edward (bp 1607-1657+) & 2/wf Mary _____ (-1644); Roxbury/Boston [GMB 1:153]

BENDALL, Edward (bp 1607-1657+) & 3/wf Jane (___) GOWER (-1661+); by 1648 London [GMB 1:154]

BENEDICT, Thomas & Mary MESSENGER (c1646-c1699); m Jan 1665 Norwalk [REG 152:363]

BENHAM, John (c1605-by 1661/2) & 1/wf _____ _____ (-1660); by 1630 Dorchester/New Haven [GMB 1:158]

BENJAMIN, Daniel (1660-1719) & Elizabeth[3] BROWNE (1664-1719+); m Watertown 25 Mar 1687 [AEBK 1:190]

BENJAMIN, Joseph & Jemima[2] LOMBARD (c1637-), dau of Thomas; m Boston 10 June 1661 [GMB 2:1197]

BENNETT, Arthur & Mary[2] GODDARD (c1645-); m2 Joseph FIELD; m3 Hans WOLFORD; m by 1664 [GM 3:87]

BENNETT, Elisha[2] & Dorothy _____; m c1690 Boston [GM 1:259]

BENNETT, Henry & Elizabeth[2] (GOODALE) SMITH (c1636-); m1 John SMITH; m Salem Mar 1674/5 [GM 3:105]

BENNETT, Henry & Lydia[2] PERKINS (bp 1632-); m c1651 Ipswich [GMB 3:1432]

BENNETT, James (1645-1736) & 1/wf Mary JOY (c1647-by 1684); m c1667/8 Fairfield [REG 154:334]

BENNETT, John & Mary[2] COBBETT (1640-); m2 Richard MEADES; m c1660 Salisbury [GM 2:117]

BENNETT, John & Sarah HARRIS (1677-1705); m 25 Oct 1699 Boston [REG 152:335]

BENNETT, John (-1717/8) & Deborah GREEN (bp 1648-); by 1671 Salem/Middleborough [GMB 2:825]

BENNETT, John (c1612-1663) & Margaret _____ (-1673/4+); by 1638 Marblehead [GMB 1:167]

BENNETT, John[2] (c1645-) & Aphra (_____) ADAMS; m1 _____ ADAMS; m by 1677 Boston [GM 1:258]

BENNETT, Samuel[1] (c1610-1682/3+) & Sarah _____ (-1682/3), a niece of Boniface BURTON; m by 3 Dec 1656 Boston [GM 1:258]

BENNETT, Samuel[2] & Sarah HARGRAVE, dau of William; m c1665 [GM 1:258]

BENNETT, William[1] (c1620-1682) & Jane _____ (c1622-1693); m bef 1643 East Budleigh, Devonshire/Manchester [ASBO, p.139]

BENSON, Isaac[3] & Mary[3] BUMPUS (bp 1671-); m 17 Mar 1698/9 Scituate [TAG 43:69]

BENSON, John[1] (c1608-1678) & Mary WILLIAMS (c1610-1681); m 14 Oct 1633 Caversham, Eng/Hull [REG 142:269]

BENSON, John[2] (c1635-1711) & Elizabeth MARSH (1646-1704); m c1664, Hull [REG 142:270]

BENTON, Andrew & Martha[2] SPENCER (1657[/8]-); m by 1677 [GMB 3:1721]

BERNARD, Musachiell[1] (bp 1607-1666+) & Mary _____ (c1607-); m c1632 [GM 1:262]

BERRY, Benjamin & Elizabeth[2] WITHERS (c1663-); m2 Dodavah CURTIS; m by 14 Mar 1690/1 [GMB 3:2046]

BERRY, Edward & Elizabeth[2] (HARDY) HASKELL; m by 1669 [GM 3:220]

BESBEECH, Thomas[1] (bp 1589/90-1673/4) & Anna BASEDEN (-1634); m Biddenden, co Kent 14 Jan 1618/9 [GM 1:265]

BESSEY, Anthony[1] (c1609-1656/7-7) & Jane _____ (-1693); m2 George BARLOW; m c1639 [GM 1:268]

BESSEY, Nehemiah (c1643-) & Mary RANSON, dau of Robert; m c1680 Sandwich [GM 1:268]

BESWICK, George (-1672) & _____ _____; Wethersfield/Glastonbury [REG 145:324; Connecticut Colonial Probate 3:126; Harris]

BETSCOMBE, Richard[1] (bp 1601-1647+) & Mary STRONG (-1646), dau of Philip; m St Mary the Virgin, The Devizes, Wiltshire 24 Aug 1630 Hingham [GM 1:271]

BETTS, John[1] (c1594-1662/3) & Elizabeth BRIDGE (c1599-1663/4); Cambridge [GM 1:275]

BETTS, John[2] & Susanna _____ [GM 1:280]

BETTS, Richard & Sarah HUSTIS (c1663-); Newtown [NYGBR 129:205]

BETTS, Richard[1] & Joanna[1] CHAMBERLAIN (bp 1630-1711+) TAG 72:297]

BETTS, Samuel[2] (bp 1642/3-) & Ruth _____ [GM 1:280]

BETTS, William[1] (c1614-1673[/4?]-5[/6]) & Alice _____; m 27 or 28 Feb 1638/9 [GM 1:279]

BETTYS, _____ & Miriam[2] TYLER (c1655-8-), dau. of John; m aft 1697 Portsmouth, RI [TAG 52:221]

BIAM, Abraham & Experience ALVORD; m 1672 Scituate [VR per PCRG]

BICKFORD, John & Susannah[2] FURBER (1664-); m by 1685 Dover [GM 2:611]

BICKFORD, John & Temperance[2] HULL (bp 1625/6-); m c1650 Northleigh, Devonshire [GM 3:455]

BICKFORD, Thomas & Bridget[2] FURBER; m c1688 [GM 2:611]

BICKNELL, John[1] (c1624-) & 1/wf Mary _____; m c1654 Weymouth [GM 1:282]

BICKNELL, John[1] (c1624-) & 2/wf Mary PORTER; m Weymouth 2 Dec 1658 [GM 1:282]

BICKNELL, Zachary[1] (1590-by 1636/7) & Agnes _____ (c1608-1643); m2 Richard ROCKET; m by 1624 Weymouth [GM 1:282]

BIDFORD, Samuel & Sarah JOANS; m Harwich 18 Nov 1697 [TAG 60:158]

BIDWELL, Samuel & 1/wf Elizabeth[3] STOW; m Roxbury 14 Nov 1672 [AEBK 3]

BIGELOW, James (c1660-) & Patience[3] BROWNE (1668/9 by 1690/1); m Watertown 25 Mar 1687 [AEBK 1:191]

BIGELOW, John (c1617-1703) & 1/wf Mary[2] WARREN (bp 1624-1691); m Watertown 30 Oct 1642 [AEBK 1:473; GMB 3:1934]

BIGELOW, John (c1617-1703); & 2/wf Sarah BEMIS (1642/3-); m Watertown 2 Oct 1694 [AEBK 1:473]

BIGG, Smallhope (bp 1585-) & Ellen _____ [GM 1:286]

BIGGE, John (c1561-1605) & Rachel MARTIN (bp 17 June 1565-1647); m Tenterden, Kent 14 Sept 1583 Dorchester [50 GMC; GM 1:286]

BIGGS, William (c1666-) & 1/wf Mary[2] WILLIAMS (c1658-1712+); m c1687/8 Middletown [TAG 69:181-3]

BILL, James[1] & 1/wf Anne ?TUTTLE (-bef 1627); m bef 11 Sep 1613 Ringstead, Nottinghamshire [TAG 60:200]

BILL, James[1] & 2/wf Dorothy _____ (-1640+); m bef Mar 1626/7 Boston [TAG 60:200]

BILLINGS, John[1] (c1616-by 1646) & Elizabeth _____; m2 Rice THOMAS; m c1641 [GM 1:291]

BILLINGS, John[2] (c1641-) & Ann ANDREWS; m by 1671 Piscataqua [GM 1:291]

BIRCHARD, John[2] (bp 1627/8-) & 1/wf Christian ANDREWS; m Hartford/Saybrook 22 July 1653 [GM 1:296]

BIRCHARD, John[2] (bp 1627/8-) & 2/wf Jane (LEE) HYDE, dau of Thomas; m c1680 [GM 1:296]

BIRCHARD, Thomas[1] (bp 1595-by 1684) & 1/wf Mary ROBINSON (1596-1655); m 23 Oct 1620 Fairstead, Essex/Roxbury [TAG 51:18; GM 1:295]

BIRCHARD, Thomas[1] (bp 1595-by 1684) & 2/wf Katherine (_____) ANDREWS; m by 1659 Roxbury [TAG 51:18; GM 1:296]

BIRCHARD, Thomas[1] (bp 1595-by 1684) & 3/wf Deborah _____ (-1680); Roxbury [TAG 51:18]

BIRD, James & Lydia[2] STEELE; m Farmington 31 Mar 1657 [GMB 3:1759]

BIRD, Joseph & Mary[2] CLARK (c1638-); m by 1660 Farmington [GM 2:84]

BIRD, Simon (c1615-1666) & Mary _____ (-1679); m c1643 Billerica [GM 1:300]

BIRDSALL, Henry[1] (c1585-by 1651) & Agnes KEMPE; m St Stephen, Norwich, Norfolk 9 Apr 1610 Boston/Salem [GM 1:301]

BIRDSALL, Nathan[2] (bp 1620-) & _____ _____; Salem/Easthampton [GM 1:302]

BIRGE, Daniel & Deborah[2] HOLCOMBE (1650/1-); m Hartford 5 Nov 1668 [GMB 2:966]

BISBY, John & Joanna[2] BROOKS (bp 1659-); m Marshfield 13 Sept [GM 1:414]

BISHOP, _____ & Mary[2] WILLIAMS; m by 1650 [GMB 3:2005]

BISHOP, Edward (not Edward[1]) & Bridget (PLAYFER)(WASSILBE) OLIVER (-1692); m2 Thomas OLIVER; m bef 1680 Salem [TAG 57:129-38, 64:207]

BISHOP, Job & Elizabeth[2] PHILLIPS (c1628-); m by 1651 [GMB 3:1449]

BISHOP, John[2] & Mary _____ [GM 1:309]

BISHOP, Nathaniel[1] (c1607-1687) & Alice _____ (-1674+); m by 1634 Boston [GM 1:304]

BISHOP, Nathaniel[2] & _____ _____; m c1665 [GM 1:309]

BISHOP, Richard[1] (c1603-1674) & 1/wf _____ _____; m c1628 Salem [GM 1:309]

BISHOP, Richard[1] (c1603-1674) & 2/wf Dulsabel (_____) KING (c1604-1658); m1 Richard KING; m by June 1635 Salem [GM 1:309]

BISHOP, Richard[1] (c1603-1674) & 3/wf Mary (_____) GAULT, (-1659); m1 William GAULT; m Salem 22 July 1660 contract of 12 July 1660 Salem [GM 1:309]

BISHOP, Thomas[2] & Lydia NORMAN, dau of John; m c1661 Salem [GM 1:309]

BISHOP, Townsend[1] (c1612-1645+) & _____ _____; m by 1637 Salem [GM 1:311]

BISSELL, John & Israel[2] MASON (c1638-); m Windsor 17 June 1658 [GMB 2:1228]

BISSELL, Nathaniel & Mindwell[2] MOORE (1643-); m Windsor 25 Sept 1662 [GMB 2:1277]

BISSELL, Samuel & Abigail[2] HOLCOMBE (bp 1638/9-); m Windsor 11 June 1658 [GMB 2:966]

BISSELL, Thomas & Abigail[2] MOORE (1639[/40]-); m Windsor 11 Oct 1655 [GMB 2:1277]

BITFIELD, Samuel[1] (bp 1601/2-1660) & perhaps 2/wf Elizabeth _____ (-1669); Wrington, Somersetshire/Boston [TAG 67:240]

BIXBY, Joseph (bp 28 Oct 1621-) & Sarah (RIDDLESDALE) HEARD (bp 16 Nov 1623-); m contract 15 Dec 1647 [26 GMC]

BLACK, Daniel & Faith[2] BRIDGES (c1645-); m bet 1660-1664 [GM 1:391]

BLACK, John[1] (c1591-1674/5) & _____ _____ (not Susanna)(-1646+); m by 1636 Salem/Beverly [GFS; GMB 1:176]

BLACK, John[2] & 1/wf Freeborn (WOLFE) SALLOWS; m Beverly [GFS]

BLACK, John[2] & 2/wf Mary[3] (PHIPPEN) WALLIS (bp 1643/4-1691+); m1 John WALLIS; m aft Sept 1690 Beverly [GFS]

BLACK, John[3] & 1/wf Deborah _____; m Beverly [GFS]

BLACK, John[3] & 2/wf Mary MORGAN; m int Beverly 18 Aug 1700 [GFS]

BLACKLEACH, Benjamin[3] (c1660s-1703+) & Mary (HOLMAN) (BILL) BUCKNELL (1667-1703+); m1 Thomas BILL, m2 Samuel BUCKNELL; m Boston 18 Sept 1693 [REG 148:34-5]

BLACKLEACH, Benoni/Benjamin (1643-say 1711) & ? 2/wf Hannah _____ (-1729+); m2 John Clove; c1680 Wethersfield/Delaware/Maryland [REG 148:31; Harris]

BLACKLEACH, Benoni[2] (1643-1667+) & Dorcas BOWMAN (-1683), dau of Nathaniel; m2 Hugh MARCH; m bef 1663 Salem/Wethersfield/Newbury [REG 148:30; GM 1:316]

BLACKLEACH, John[1] (1600+-1683) & Elizabeth BACON (bp 6 Aug 1609-1683), dau of Robert; m London bef Aug 1630 Wethersfield [REG 148:5+; GM 1:316]

BLACKLEACH, John[2] (bp 10 Jan 1631/2-1703) & 1/wf Elizabeth perhaps SHEAFE; m bef 1660 Hartford [REG 148:21-2; GM 1:316]

BLACKLEACH, John[2] (bp 10 Jan 1631/2-1703) & 2/wf Elizabeth HARBERT (c1638-1708); m Hartford [REG 148:22; GM 1:316]

BLACKLEACH, John[3] (1660/1-1698) & Susannah (FENN) HOOKER (1669-1697); m1 William HOOKER; m bet 1689-1693 Boston/Farmington [REG 148:33]

BLACKLEACH, Nathaniel[3] (1666-bef 1726) & Mary (MILBURY) FREETHY (-1735); m1 James FREETHY; m bef June 1695 Cambridge, Yorkshire [REG 148:36]

BLACKLEACH, Richard[1] (c1654-1731) & 1/wf Abigail HUDSON (1654-1712/3); m Stratford 8 Dec 1680 [REG 148:40]

BLACKLEACH, Solomon[2] (bp 1648-1678) & Sindeniah _____ (-1678+); m bef 1678 Boston/Wethersfield/London/Plymouth [REG 148:19; Harris; GM 1:317]

BLACKMAN, Deliverance[2] & Hannah (OSBORN) ASHCRAFT; m1 1670 John ASHCRAFT [TAG 74:128]

BLAISDELL, Henry[2] & 1/wf Mary HADDON (c1637-), dau of Garrett; m by 17 Oct 1657 Salisbury [GMB 2:833; GM 1:321]

BLAISDELL, Henry[2] & 2/wf Elizabeth _____ [GM 1:321]

BLAISDELL, John[3] (1668-1733) & Elizabeth[2] (CHALLIS) HOYT (bef 1671-1744+); m 6 Jan 1692/3 Amesbury [ASBO, p.151]

BLAISDELL, Ralph[1] (c1607-by 1651) & Elizabeth _____ (-1667); m c1632 Salisbury [GM 1:321]

BLAKE, James & Elizabeth^2 CLAPP (c1634-); m by 1652 Dorchester [GM 2:78]

BLAKE, Jasper (c1623-1673) & Deborah^2 EVERETT (bp 1628-1678); m by 1649 Hampton [AEBK 4:213; REG 154:287]

BLANCHARD, John (-1692/3-3/4) & 1/wf Elizabeth^2 HILLS (bp 1627-1658/9-62); m c1656 Dunstable [AEBK 4:416]

BLANCHARD, John (-1692/3-3/4) & 2/wf Hannah (BRACKETT) KINSLEY; m1 Samuel KINSLEY; m c1662 [AEBK 4:416]

BLANCHARD, William & Hannah^2 EVERILL; m2 George MANNING; m c1648 [GM 2:474]

BLAND, John (alias SMITH) (-1667) & 1/wf Isabel DRAKE (-1639); m bef 1613 Eng [TAG 61:22]

BLANEY, John^2 (1661-1726) & Elizabeth^2 PURCHASE (not WILLIAMS) (c1645-1726+); m Marblehead 20 Dec 1683 [GMB 3:1532; TG 3:54]

BLINMAN, Richard (-1687) & Mary ?PARKE, m bef 1642 Gloucester/New London [TG 4:182]

BLINN, James^2 (c1673-1731) & Margaret DENNISON (1677-1736); m 6 Dec 1698 Boston [REG 143:310]

BLINN, Peter^2 & Hannah ?CRAMPTON; m bef 7 Mar 1696/7 Guilford [REG 143:308]

BLISH, Abraham (1654-1734/5) & 1/wf Martha SHAW (1655-1706); m say 1679 Boston [TG 10:100; REG 155:288]

BLISS, Jonathan^2 & Miriam HARMON; m c1648 Braintree/Rehoboth [REG 149:216]

BLISS, Thomas (-1650/1) & 1/wf Margaret HULINS (c1595-1684); m 18 Oct 1621 St. Nicholas, Gloucester, Gloucestershire/Hartford [TAG 52:193; 60:202]

BLODGETT, Daniel^2 (bp 1631-) & 1/wf Mary BUTTERFIELD; m Chelmsford 15 Sept 1653 [GM 1:325]

BLODGETT, Daniel^2 (bp 1631-) & 2/wf Sarah UNDERWOOD; m Chelmsford 10 Mar 1669[/70]

BLODGETT, Samuel^2 (bp 1633-) & Ruth EGGLETON; m Woburn 13 Dec 1655 [GM 1:325]

BLODGETT, Thomas^1 (c1605-1641-2) & Susanna _____ (-1660/1); m2 James THOMSON; m by 1627 Cambridge [GM 1:325]

BLOIS, Edmund^1 (c1588-1679-80/1) & 1/wf Mary _____ (-1672); m c1623 Watertown [GM 1:328]

BLOIS, Edmund^1 (c1588-1679-80/1) & 2/wf Ruth PARSONS, dau of Hugh; m Cambridge 27 Sept 1675 [GM 1:328]

BLOIS, Richard^2 (c1623-) & Micaell JENNISON, dau of Robert; m Watertown 10 Feb 1657[/8] [GM 1:328]

BLOOD, Joseph (-by 1692) & Mercy BUTTERWORTH [Story of the Bloods, p. 165]

BLOOD, Robert & Hannah (JENKINS) PARKER (-1716); m Concord 8 Jan 1690/1 [REG 153:91]

BLOOMFIELD, William[1] (c1605-1666/7+) & 1/wf Sarah _____; m c1633 Newtown [GM 1:332]

BLOOMFIELD, William[1] (c1605-1666/7+) & 2/wf Isabel (PEARCE) SACKETT (-1682+); m1 Simon SACKETT; m by 1639 [GM 1:332]

BLOSSOM, Peter & Sarah[2] BOTFISH; m Barnstable 21 June 1663 [GM 1:358]

BLOSSOM, Thomas & Sarah[2] EWER (bp 1629-); m2 Nicholas DAVIS; m Barnstable 18 June 1645 [GM 2:481]

BLOSSOM, Thomas[1] (c1580-1633) & Anne [H]ELSDON; m2 Henry ROWLEY; m St Clement, Cambridge, Cambridgeshire 10 Nov 1605 Plymouth [GMB 1:182, TAG 63:74]

BLOTT, Robert[1] (alias John Black)(c1580s-1665) & only wife Susanna SELBEE (-1659/60); m Harrold, Bedfordshire 31 Aug 1609 Boston [TAG 67:67; GM 1:335]

BLOWER, John[1] (-1675) & Tabitha _____; m bef 1654/5 Barnstable/ Boston [TAG 52:74]

BLOWER, John[2] (bp 1627/8-) & Tabitha _____; m c1654 [GM 1:339]

BLOWER, Pyam[2] (c1638-) & Elizabeth BELCHER; m Cambridge 31 Mar 1668 [GM 1:339]

BLOWER, Thomas[1] (bp 1587-by 1639) & Alice FROST (bp 1594-), dau of Edward; m2 William TILLY; m Stanstead, Suffolk 19 Nov 1612 Boston [TAG 71:113; GM 1:338]

BLUNDEN, _____ & Sarah[2] MULLINS (c1598-); m c1622 [GMB 2:1316]

BOAD, Henry (-1657) & Anne (DALTON) REWSE; m West Wratting, Cambridgeshire, 19 July 1621 Wells, Maine [REG 154:264]

BOND, William & Hepzibah[2] HASTINGS (1663/4-); m Watertown 2 June 1680 [GM 3:239]

BONFIELD, George & Rebecca[2] BRADSTREET; m by Oct 1665 [GM 1:387]

BONHAM, George & Sarah[2] MORTON (c1620-); m Plymouth 20 Dec 1644 [GMB 2:1297]

BONNEY, James (c1672-1723/4) & 1/wf Abigail BISHOP; m Duxbury 12 June 1695 [GM 1:342]

BONNEY, John[2] (c1664-1745) & Elizabeth BISHOP, dau of James; m by 1690 [GM 1:342]

BONNEY, Thomas[1] (c1614-1688/9-93) & Mary _____ (-1688/9+); m by 1655 Charlestown/Duxbury [GM 1:341]

BONNEY, Thomas[2] & 1/wf Dorcas[2] SAMSON (c1652-), dau of Henry; m by 1684 [GMB 3:1623; GM 1:341]

BONNEY, Thomas[2] & 2/wf Sarah STUDLEY; m Duxbury 18 July 1695 [GM 1:341]

BONNEY, William[2] & Ann _____; m by 1693 Plymouth [GM 1:342]

BONNEY, William[2] & Mehitable KING; m Plymouth 11 July 1700 [GM 1:342]

BONYTHON, John[2] & Agnes _____; m c1650 [GM 1:345]

BONYTHON, Richard[1] (bp 1580-bef 1654) & Lucretia LEIGH, dau of William; m c1607
    [GM 1:345]

BOOSY, James[1] (c1604-1649) & Alice _____ (-1683); m2 James WAKELEY; m by
    1629 Wethersfield [GM 1:349]

BOOSY, Joseph & Esther perhaps WARD; m2 Jehu BURR; m by 1655 Westherfield
    [GMB 3:1920; GM 1:349]

BOOTH, Benjamin[2] (1667-bef 1746) & 1/wf Mary[3] SUTTON (1665/6-1709+); m c1690
    Scituate/Middleborough [TAG 74:181]

BOOTH, George & Elizabeth WILKINS; m bef 30 Dec 1692 Salem [REG 144:54]

BOOTH, John[1] & (perhaps) Elizabeth[2] GRANGER (c1638-); m Feb 1659
    Scituate/Marshfield [MD 42:55; TAG 74:181]

BOOTH, Joseph ~ Mary SUTTON; Scituate [Plymouth Court Oct 1686]

BORDEN, John[1] (bp 1606/7-c1635) & Joanna _____ (-1691); m2 John GAY; m by 1627
    Dedham [REG 130:39; GM 1:350]

BORDEN, John[2] (1635-) & Hannah HOUGH; m New London 11 Feb 1661[/2?] [GM
    1:351]

BORDMAN, Andrew & Ruth[2] BULL (c1643-); m Cambridge 15 Oct 1669 [GM 1:474]

BOREMAN, Daniel[2] & Hannah HUTCHINSON, dau of Richard; m Ipswich 12 Apr 1662
    [GM 1:354]

BOREMAN, Thomas[1] (bp 1601-1673) & Margaret OFFING (-1676); m St. Helen's
    Bishopgate, London 17 Aug 1630 Ipswich [GM 1:354]

BOREMAN, Thomas[2] (c1644-1719) & Elizabeth PERKINS; m Ipswich 1 Jan 1667/8
    [GM 1:354]

BOSTON, Walter & Ann DEVEREUX; m2 Robert NICHOLS; by June 1668 [GMB
    1:533]

BOSWORTH, Benjamin[2] (c1615-) & 1/wf _____ _____; m c1645 Hingham [GM
    1:356]

BOSWORTH, Benjamin[2] (c1615-) & 2/wf Beatrice (HAMPSON) JOSSELYN; m
    Lancaster 16 Nov 1671 [GM 1:356]

BOSWORTH, Edward[1] (c1586-1634) & Mary _____ (-1648); m c1611 Boston [GM
    1:356]

BOSWORTH, Jonathan & Hannah[2] HOWLAND (c1637-); m Swansea 6 July 1661
    [GMB 2:1023]

BOSWORTH, Jonathan (c1613-1687/8) & Elizabeth _____ (c1614-1705); by 1636
    Cambridge/Hingham/Rehoboth [GMB 1:189; GM 1:356]

BOSWORTH, Nathaniel[2] & Bridget BELLAMY, dau of Jeremiah; m c1644 Hingham
    [GM 1:356]

BOTFISH, Joseph[2] (1651-) & Elizabeth BESSEY, dau of Anthony; m by 1674 Sandwich
    [GM 1:358, 1:269]

BOTFISH, Robert[1] (c1614-165[ ]) & Bridget _____; m2 Samuel HINCKLEY; m c1639
    Sandwich/Barnstable [GM 1:358]

BOTSFORD, Samuel[3] (1670-1745) & Hannah (not widow SMITH) (-1732); m bef 1700 Milford [TAG 59:196]

BOTTS, Isaac & Elizabeth[2] FREETHY; m2 Moses SPENCER; m by 1673 [GM 2:585]

BOUENTON, Thomas, see BUFFINGTON

BOULTER, Nathaniel[1] & Grace SWAINE (bp 1627/8-); m c1647 [TAG 74:248]

BOURNE, Henry[1] (c1613-1670+) & Sarah _____ (-1684); m by 1638 Hingham/Scituate [GM 1:359]

BOURNE, Jared[1] (c1614-1673/4) & 1/wf Mary _____ (-1644); m by 1643 Boston [GM 1:362]

BOURNE, Jared[1] (c1614-1673/4) & 2/wf _____ _____; m by 1651 Boston [GM 1:362]

BOURNE, Jared[2] (1651/2-) & Elizabeth BRAYTON, dau of Francis; m by 1690 Portsmouth [GM 1:362]

BOURNE, Job & Ruhama[2] HALLETT (c1644-); m Sandwich 14 Dec 1664 [GM 3:198]

BOURNE, John & Alice[2] BESBEECH; m Marshfield 18 July 1645 [GM 1:265]

BOURNE, Shearjashub (c1643-1718/19) & Bathsheba SKIFFE (1648-1714); m c1673 Sandwich [REG 118:203]

BOURNE, Timothy[3] (1666-1744) & Temperance SWIFT (c1668-1746); m c1688 Sandwich [REG 118:205]

BOWDEN, Richard & Martha[2] BLAISDELL; m2 Thomas? SEALEY; m3 John Clough; m by 1661 Boston [GM 1:322]

BOWDISH, Nathaniel[3] & Mary _____ [TAG 71:73]

BOWDITCH, William (-1681) & Sarah BEARE (-1699+); m 15 Sep 1663 Thornecombe, Devonshire/Salem [NGSQ 69:278]

BOWEN, Griffith[1] & Margaret FLEMING (only wife); m 1627 Wales/Boston/Swanzey [NGSQ 67:163]

BOWEN, Obadiah[2] (c1627-28-1710) & Mary _____; m c1650 [TAG 76:277]

BOWEN, Richard (c1631-1718) & 1/wf Esther SUTTON (-1688); m Rehoboth 4 Mar 1656 [TAG 76:274-77]

BOWEN, Richard (c1631-1718) & 2/wf Martha (ALLEN) SABEN; m1 William SABEN; m Rehoboth 20 Jan 1689/90 [TAG 76:277]

BOWEN, Richard[1] (c1594-1674/5) & 1/wf _____ _____ (not Ann) (a welsh woman); Wales/Rehoboth [TAG 76:263-77]

BOWEN, Richard[1] (c1594-1674/5) & 2/wf Elizabeth (_____) MARSH (-1675); m1 George MARSH; Weymouth/Rehoboth [TAG 76:263-76]

BOWEN, Thomas (c1634-1663+) & Elizabeth NICHOLS; m2 Samuel FULLER; m by 1659 [TAG 76:278; MD 39:86]

BOWERMAN, Thomas[2] (1648-) & Mary[2] HARPER (1655-); m 7 June 1678 Sandwich [TAG 48:217]

BOWKER, John (c1647-1721) & Mary[2] HOWE (1659-1723); m Marlborough 8 Jan 1678[/9] [AEBK 3]

BOWLES, John & Elizabeth[2] HEATH (bp 1629/30-); m Roxbury 2 Apr 1649 [GM 3:302]

BOWNE, Andrew (bp 1638-) & Elizabeth _____; m by 1667 New York [GM 1:364]

BOWNE, James[2] (bp 1636-) & Mary STOUTE; m Gravesend 26 Dec 1665 [GM 1:364]

BOWNE, John[2] & Lydia HOLMES, dau of Obadiah; m c1664 Gravesend [GM 1:364]

BOWNE, William[1] (c1609-by 1677[/8]) & Anne _____; m c1634 [GM 1:364]

BOYCE, Antipas & Hannah[2] HILL (1638/9-); m Boston 24 Jan 1659[/60?] [GM 3:324]

BOYDEN, Jonathan[2] (1651/2-) & Mary CLARK; m Medfield 26 Sept 1673 [GM 1:368]

BOYDEN, Thomas[1] (c1613-1678+) & 1/wf Frances _____ (-1657/8); m by 1639 Scituate/Watertown/Boston [GM 1:367]

BOYDEN, Thomas[1] (c1613-1678+) & 2/wf Hannah (PHILLIPS) MORSE (-1676); m1 Joseph MORSE; m Boston 3 Nov 1658 [GM 1:367]

BOYDEN, Thomas[2] (1639-) & Martha HOLDEN (1645[/6]-), dau of Richard; m by 1667 Watertown [GM 1:367, 3:366]

BOYES, Samuel & Lydia[2] BEAMON (1644/5-); m2 Alexander PYGAN; m Saybrook 3 Feb 1667/8 [GM 1:221]

BOYLSTON, Thomas[1] (c1615-1652+) & Sarah _____ (-1704); m2 John CHENERY; m c1640 Watertown [GM 1:371]

BOYLSTON, Thomas[2] (1644/5-) & Mary GARDNER; m Charlestown 13 Dec 1665 [GM 1:371]

BOYNTON, Caleb (c1649-1708) & Hannah HARRIMAN (1655-1725); m Rowley 26 May 1674 [REG 150:44]

BOYNTON, Joshua & Sarah[2] BROWN (1657-); m Newbury 7 Apr 1678 probably [GM 1:434]

BRACKENBURY, Richard (c1600-1684) & Ellen _____ (-1667+); m by 1628 Salem/Beverly [GMB 1:198]

BRACKENBURY, Samuel (1645/6-1678) & Mercy WIGGLESWORTH (1655/6-1728); m by 3 Feb 1672/3 [REG 156:319]

BRACKENBURY, William (c1602-1668) & 1/wf Anne _____ (-by 1645); by 1632 Charlestown [GMB 1:202]

BRACKENBURY, William (c1602-1668) & 2/wf Alice _____ (1600-1670); by 1645 Charlestown/Malden [GMB 1:202; REG 156:319]

BRACKETT, John & Hannah[2] FRENCH; m Braintree 6 Sept 1661 [GM 2:592]

BRACKETT, John[2] (1641-1666) & Sarah STEDMAN (1643-1729/30); m2 1667/8 Samuel ALCOCK; m3 1682 Thomas GRAVES; m4 1697+ John PHILLIPS; m Cambridge 23 Aug 1662 [REG 155:285]

BRACKETT, Peter[1] (1608-1688) & 1/wf Martha RAY; m Cavendish, Suffolk 4 Oct 1632 [TAG 52:73, REG 155:283]

BRACKETT, Peter[1] (1608-1688) & 2/wf Priscilla _____; m by 1642 [TAG 52:73, REG 155:284]

BRACKETT, Peter[1] (1608-1688) & 3/wf Mary (_____) WILLIAMS (-1679); m1
    Nathaniel WILLIAMS; m by Dec. 1666 Boston [TAG 52:73, REG 155:284]

BRACKETT, Richard (bp 1610-1691) & Alice[2] BLOWER (bp 1615-1690); m 16 Jan
    1633/4 St. Katherine by the Tower, London/ Boston [TAG 52:65; 56:99; REG
    127:17, 50 GMC, GMB 1:205; GM 1:338]

BRACY, John[2] (c1640-1708/9) & Anne (PEARCE) CARMICHAEL, dau of John; m1
    John CARMICHAEL; m aft 1677 [GM 1:374]

BRACY, Thomas[1] (bp 1601-by 1649) & 1/wf Hannah HART; m London 30 Jan 1626/7
    [GM 1:373]

BRACY, Thomas[1] (bp 1601-by 1649) & 2/wf Phebe BISBY, dau of William; m2 Samuel
    MARTIN; m St Lawrence Jewry, London 4 Aug 1631 [GM 1:373]

BRACY, Thomas[2] & Mary OSBORN, dau of James; m c1672 [GM 1:373]

BRADBURY, Thomas[1] (bp 28 Feb 1610/11-1694/5) & Mary[2] PERKINS (bp 3 Sept 1615-
    1700); m c1636 Wicken Bonhunt, Essex/Hillmorton, Warwickshire/Salisbury
    [50 GMC; GMB 3:1432; GM 1:379]

BRADBURY, William (1649-) & Rebecca (WHEELWRIGHT) MAVERICK, dau of
    John; m1 Samuel MAVERICK; m Salisbury 12 Mar 1671/2 [GM 1:380]

BRADBURY, Wymond[2] (1637-) & Sarah PIKE; m2 John STOCKMAN; m Salisbury 7
    May 1661 [GM 1:379]

BRADFORD, Joseph[3] & 1/wf Anne[2] FITCH, dau. Rev. James[1] [REG 155:246]

BRADFORD, Joseph[3] & 2/wf Mary (SHERWOOD) FITCH, dau. of Mathew; m1 Daniel[2]
    FITCH [REG 155:246]

BRADFORD, William[2] & 1/wf Alice RICHARDS (bp 1629-1671); m c1650 [GMB
    3:1577; REG 155:245]

BRADFORD, William[2] & 2/wf Sarah (_____) GRISWOLD, wid. Francis[2], m c1673
    [REG 155:245-50]

BRADFORD, William[2] & 3/wf Mary (WOOD) HOLMES, by 1677 [REG 155:245]

BRADHURST, Ralph & Hannah[2] GORE (1645-); m Roxbury 13 June 1677 [GM 3:119]

BRADISH, James[2] (c1634-1664-5) & Katherine _____ (-1689+); m2 1665 Peter
    SYMONS; m c1657 Newtown, L.I. [TAG 75:49]

BRADISH, John[2] (1645-) & Susanna _____; m by 1674 Boston [GM 1:384]

BRADISH, Joseph[2] (1638-) & Mary FROST, dau of Edmund; m Sudbury 10 Apr 1664
    [GM 1:383]

BRADISH, Robert[1] (c1607-1657-9) & 1/wf Mary _____ (-1638); m c1630 Cambridge
    [GM 1:383]

BRADISH, Robert[1] (c1607-1657-9) & 2/wf Vashti (_____) MORRILL (-by 1672/3); m1
    _____ MORRILL; m c1639 Cambridge [GM 1:383; TAG 75:47]

BRADSHAW, Humphrey & Martha (DAVIES) RUSSELL (-1695); m1 William
    RUSSELL; m3 Thomas HALL [TAG 44:83]

BRADSTREET, Dudley (1648-1706) & Anne WOOD (not WHITE) PRICE; m1 Theodore
    PRICE; m Salem 12 Nov 1673 [REG 139:139]

BRADSTREET, Humphrey[1] (c1594-1655) & Bridget _____ (c1604-1665); m c1625 Ipswich [GM 1:386]

BRADSTREET, John[2] (c1630-) & Hannah PEACH, dau of John; m2 William WATERS; m by 1660 [GM 1:386]

BRADSTREET, Moses[2] (c1643-) & Elizabeth HARRIS; m Ipswich 11 Mar 1661/2 [GM 1:387]

BRADSTREET, Simon[1] & Anne[1] (DOWNING) GARDNER; m 6 June 1676 [TAG 74:174]

BRAINERD, Daniel & Hannah[2] SPENCER (unproven) [GMB 3:1720]

BRANKER, John (c1601-1662) & Abigail SEARLE (1612-1684); m2 Rev. John WARHAM; m Honiton, Devonshire 13 Jan 1629/30 Dorchester/Windsor [Assoc. for the Promotion of Scholarship in Genealogy, Occasional Publication #1, pp. 59-69; GMB 1:217; REG 149:305]

BREED, Allen[1] (c1599-1690/1) & 1/wf Elizabeth WHEELER; m Pullowhill, Bedfordshire 16 Nov 1622 Lynn [TEG 11:198]

BREED, Allen[1] (c1599-1690/1) & 2/wf Elizabeth (_____) (BALLARD) KNIGHT (c1609-1661+); m1 William BALLARD, m2 William KNIGHT; m Lynn 28 Mar 1656 [TEG 11:198]

BRENTON, William & Hannah DAVIS; by 1680 [GMB 1:222]

BRENTON, William (c1610-1674) & 1/wf Dorothy _____; by 1634 Boston [GMB 1:222]

BRENTON, William (c1610-1674) & 2/wf Martha BURTON (-1672+); by 1644 Portsmouth [GMB 1:222]

BREWER, Daniel & Hannah[2] MORRILL (1636-); m Roxbury 5 Nov 1652 [GMB 2:1291]

BREWSTER, Nathaniel & 2/wf Sarah[2] LUDLOW (c1643-); m after Feb 1660 Dublin, Ire/Boston/Setauket [NGSQ 51:234; GMB 2:1212]

BREWSTER, William (c1557-66-1644) & Mary STUBBE? (-1627); m bef 1593 Eng/Plymouth [REG 128:288, GMB 1:228]

BRIDGE, John[1] (c1593-1665) & 1/wf _____ _____ (-1654+); m by 1618 Cambridge [GM 1:395]

BRIDGE, John[1] (c1593-1665) & 2/wf Elizabeth (_____) (BANCROFT) SAUNDERS (-1686[/7?); m1 Roger BANCROFT; m2 Martin SAUNDERS; m4 Edward TAYLOR; m contract 29 Nov 1658 [GM 1:395]

BRIDGE, Matthew[2] (c1618-) & Anne[2] DANFORTH (bp 1622-), dau of Nicholas; m by 1645 Cambridge [GM 1:396, 2:283]

BRIDGE, Thomas[2] & Dorcas _____; m by 1648 Cambridge [GM 1:396]

BRIDGES, Edmund[1] (c1612-1684/5) & 1/wf Elizabeth _____ (-1664); m c1636 Ipswich [GM 1:390]

BRIDGES, Edmund[1] (c1612-1684/5) & 2/wf Mary (LANGTON) LITTLEHALE; m1 Richard LITTLEHALE; m Ipswich 6 Apr 1665 [GM 1:390]

BRIDGES, Edmund[2] (c1636-) & Sarah TOWNE, dau of William; m Topsfield 11 Jan 1659/60 [GM 1:391]

BRIDGES, Hackaliah[2] (-1671) ~ Mary QUILTER; in court Sept 1657 [GM 1:391]

BRIDGES, Hackaliah[2] (-1671) ~ Sarah FRENCH; in court Sept 1656 [GM 1:391]

BRIDGES, John[2] & 1/wf Sarah[2] HOWE (c1646-); m Ipswich 5 Dec 1666 [GM 1:391, 3:434]

BRIDGES, John[2] & 2/wf Mary (TYLER) POST; m1 Richard POST; m Andover 1 Mar 1677/8 [GM 1:391]

BRIDGES, Josiah (c1654-) & 1/wf Elizabeth NORTON (c1654-); m Ipswich 13 Nov 1676 [GM 1 392; GMB 2:1338]

BRIDGES, Josiah (c1654-) & 2/wf Ruth GREENSLIP; m Ipswich 19 Sept 1677 [GM 1:392]

BRIDGES, Obadiah[2] & 1/wf Mary SMITH; m Ipswich 25 Oct 1671 [GM 1:392]

BRIDGES, Obadiah[2] & 2/wf Elizabeth ____; m by 1677 [GM 1:392]

BRIDGES, William (c1615-by 1648/9) & Persis PIERCE; by 1643 Charlestown [GMB 1:231]

BRIDGHAM, Henry[1] & Elizabeth[1] HARDING (bp 1622/3-); m by 1645 Boreham, Essex/Boston [GM 3:217]

BRIGDEN, Thomas[1] (c1604-1668) & Thomasine ____ (-1669); m c1629 Boston/Charlestown [GM 1:399]

BRIGDEN, Thomas[2] (c1629-) & Mildred[2] CARTHRICK, dau of Michael; m by 1655 [GM 1:399, 2:32]

BRIGGS, George & Sarah KNIGHT (1656-); m Boston [Boston VR 1:55]

BRIGGS, Hugh[2] (-1692+) & Martha[2] EVERSON (-1736/7); m 1 Mar 1682/3 Taunton/Plympton [REG 125:82]

BRIGGS, John[1] (bp 1595-) & Agnes THAYER (bp 1607-); m 11 Nov 1633 Thornbury, Gloucestershire/Taunton, MA [TAG 59:179]

BRIGGS, John[3] (1672-1750) & 1/wf Hannah HOLLOWAY (-bef 1727); m bef 1699 Norton/Taunton [REG 125:84]

BRIGGS, Jonathan (1635-) & Experience ____; by 1664 Weymouth [GMB 1:236]

BRIGGS, Peter (1680-) & 1/wf Elizabeth ____ (-1704+); c1700 Boston [Harris]

BRIGGS, Richard & Rebecca[2] HOSKINS (c1642-); m Taunton 15 Aug 1662 [GM 3:417]

BRIGGS, Samuel (-1705/6) & Mary[3] HALL (1672-1723-5); m2 Benjamin CASWELL; m Taunton 27 July 1692 [AEBK 4:332]

BRIGGS, Samuel[2] (-1675+) & Elizabeth ELLIS (c1645-1675+); m c1664 Sandwich [REG 119:172]

BRIGGS, William[2] (c1649-1728) & 1/wf Sarah MACOMBER (c1643-1680); m 6 Nov 1666 Dorchester/Marshfield [REG 125:82]

BRIGGS, William[2] (c1649-1728) & 2/wf ?Abigail MASON; m 2 July 1680 Dedham [REG 125:82]

BRIGHAM, John[2] (1644/5-) & 1/wf Sarah DAVIS; m by 1673 Marlborough [GM 1:403]

BRIGHAM, John[2] (1644/5-   ) & 2/wf Deborah (HAYNES) BROWN; m aft 1698 [GM 1:403]

BRIGHAM, Samuel[2] (c1655-1713) & Elizabeth[2] HOWE (1665-1739); m Marlborough [no day or month] 1683 [AEBK 3; GM 1:403]

BRIGHAM, Thomas[1] (c1603-1653) & Mercy _____ (-1693); m2 Edmund RICE; m3 William HUNT; m c1641 Cambridge/ Holme-on-Spalding-Moor, Lancashire [GM 1:402]

BRIGHAM, Thomas[2] (c1641-1717) & 1/wf Mary RICE; m Marlborough 27 Dec 1665 [GM 1:402]

BRIGHAM, Thomas[2] (c1641-1717) & 2/wf Susannah (SHATTUCK)(MORSE) FAY (-1716); m1 Joseph MORSE; m2 John FAY; m Marlborough 30 July 1695 [GM 1:402]

BRIGHT, Henry[1] & Anne[2] GOLDSTONE (bp 1615-   ); m by 1635 Boston [GM 3:100]

BRIGHT, Nathaniel & Mary[3] COOLIDGE (1660-1717); m Watertown 21 July 1681 [AEBK 3]

BRIGHT, Rev. Francis & _____ _____; by 2 Feb 1628/9 (probably earlier) Salem, Charlestown; returned [GMB 1:238]

BRIMBLECOM, John (-1656+) & Barbara (   ) DAVIS; m1 George DAVIS, m3 Thomas CHADWELL; m 14 Jan 1655 Lynn/Boston [DCD]

BRIMBLECOM, John[1] (bp 1622-1678) & Tabitha _____ (only wife); m c1640 Modbury, Devonshire/Marblehead [DCD]

BRISCO, Joseph & Abigail[2] COMPTON; m2 Abraham BUSBY; m Boston 30 Jan 1651/2 [GM 2:171]

BROCK, Henry & Elizabeth ALDOUS (bp 1593/4-   ); m c1619 Dedham [REG 144:130]

BROCK, Peter (-1707) & Sarah _____ (c1677-1717); m2 Henry BEERE/BEERS; m c1696 Newport/W.I. [TAG 65:195]

BROCKWAY, Wolston & Hannah (BRIGGS) HARRIS; m by Sept 1664 [REG 152:344]

BRONSON, Isaac[2] (c1645-bef 1718/9) & Mary[2] ROOT (c1650-1719/20+); m c1669 Farmington [TAG 71:207]

BRONSON, John (1602-1680) & Frances HILLS (-1680+); m 19 Nov 1626 Halstead, Essex/Farmington, CT [TAG 38:199]

BRONSON, John (c1673-1748) & 1/wf Mary HICKOX (-1713); m Waterbury 9 Nov 1697 [TAG 71:210]

BRONSON, Richard (-1687) & 2/wf _____ _____ (-c1665); m c1646/7 Farmington [TAG 38:206]

BRONSON, Richard (-1687) & 3/wf Elizabeth (_____) (CARPENTER) ORVIS, m1 David CARPENTER; m2 George ORVIS; m c1666 Farmington, CT [TAG 38:206]

BROOKES, William & Susanna[2] (HANFORD) WHISTON (c1615-   ); m by 1665 Scituate [GM 3:206]

BROOKIN, John & Elizabeth[2] HOLLARD (1638-   ); m2 Edward GROVE; m by 1659 Boston [GM 3:379]

BROOKINGS, William & Mary[2] WALFORD (c1635-); m2 William WALKER; m c1659 [GMB 3:1904]

BROOKS, _____ & Mary[2] GRIGGS (c1627-); m by 1655 Boston [GM 3:157]

BROOKS, Gilbert[1] (c1621-1695) & 1/wf Elizabeth _____ (-1687); m by 1646 [GM 1:410]

BROOKS, Gilbert[1] (c1621-1695) & 2/wf Sarah (REDWAY) CARPENTER, dau of James; m1 Samuel CARPENTER; m Rehoboth 18 Jan 1687[8] [GM 1:410]

BROOKS, Nathaniel[2] (bp 1646-) & Elizabeth CURTIS; m Scituate 24 Dec 1678 [GM 1:414]

BROOKS, Richard & Mary (BLANCHARD) COOPER (c1645-60-bef 1729); m1 Josiah COOPER [REG 140:315]

BROOKS, Robert & Elizabeth[2] WINSLOW; m2 George CURWIN; m c1656 [GMB 3:2025]

BROOKS, Thomas[2] (bp 1657-) & Hannah BISBY; m Scituate 6 June 1687 [GM 1:414]

BROOKS, Timothy & Mehitable[2] MOWRY; m2 Eldad KINGSLEY [GMB 2:1314]

BROOKS, William[1] (c1615-1680+) & 1/wf _____ _____ (-by 1665); m by 1644 Scituate/Marshfield [GM 1:413]

BROOKS, William[1] (c1615-1680-) & 2/wf Susannah (HANFORD)WHISTON, dau of Jeffrey; m1 John WHISTON; m by 1665 Scituate/Marshfield [GM 1:414] or Susanna (DOWNE) WHITSTON [not HANFORD; TAG 30:154]

BROUGH, Edmund & Mary CHANDLER; m by 1653 Marshfield/ Boston [TAG 67:31]

BROUGHTON, John & Hannah[2] BASCOMB; m2 William JANES; m Windsor 15 Nov 1650 [GM 1:188]

BROWN, Abraham (1649-1733) & Elizabeth[2] SHEPARD (c1655-1733+); m 15 June 1675 Salisbury [ASBO, p.373]

BROWN, Benjamin[2] & _____ _____; Charlestown [GM 1:443]

BROWN, Boaz (1641/2-1724) & 1/wf Mary WINSHIP (1641-bef 1695); m Concord 8 Nov 1664 [REG 140:317]

BROWN, Boaz (1641/2-1724, not Jr.) & 2/wf Mary (FULLER) RICHARDS (-1715); m1 John RICHARDS; m 30 Sept 1695 Stow/Dedham [REG 140:317]

BROWN, Francis[2] (bp 1632/3-) & Mary MORSE; m Newbury 31 Dec 1679 [REG 152:350; GM 1:437]

BROWN, Francis[2] (bp 1632/3-1691) & 1/wf Mary JOHNSON (-1679); m Newbury 21 Nov 1653 [REG 152:350; GM 1:437]

BROWN, George[1] (c1613-1642 & _____ _____; m by 1642 Newbury [GM 1:419]

BROWN, Henry & Wait[2] WATERMAN [GMB 3:1942]

BROWN, Hugh (c1605-) & Elizabeth _____; by 1631 Salem [GMB 1:247]

BROWN, Isaac[2] (c1638-1674); m Rebecca BAILEY (-1731); m2 John DOGGETT; m Newbury 22 Aug 1661 [GM 1:437; REG 152:351]

BROWN, James (c1604-1676) & Judith/Elizabeth _____ (-by 1647); by 1638 Charlestown [GMB 1:252]

BROWN, James (c1615-1651) & Grace _____ (-1651); by 1645 Boston [GMB 1:249]

BROWN, James² & Lydia² HOWLAND (c1633-), dau of Henry; m c1655 [GMB 2:1023; GM 1:426]

BROWN, John & Ann² MASON (1650-); m Swansea 8 Nov 1672 [GMB 2:1228]

BROWN, John¹ (c1591-1662) & Dorothy _____ (-1673/4); m c1616 Rehoboth [GM 1:426]

BROWN, John² & 1/wf _____ _____; m by 1650 Rehoboth [GM 1:426]

BROWN, John² & Lydia² BUCKLAND (-1660), dau of William; m2 William LORD; m3 Thomas DUNK; m4 Abraham POST; m c1661 Rehoboth [GM 1:426, 455]

BROWN, Joseph² & Mehitable BRENTON (1652-1676), dau of William; m by 3 Oct 1675 Charlestown [GMB 1:222, 443]

BROWN, Joshua² (1642-) & Sarah SAWYER; m Newbury 15 Jan 1668[/9?] [GM 1:434]

BROWN, Josiah & Mary² FELLOWS; m Reading 23 Feb 1666/7 [GM 2:510]

BROWN, Nathaniel¹ (c1622-1658) & Eleanor WATTS (-1703); m2 Jasper CLEMENTS; m3 Nathaniel WILLETT; m Hartford 23 Dec 1647 [GM 1:430]

BROWN, Nathaniel² (1654-) & Martha HUGHES; m Middletown 2 July 1677 [GM 1:430]

BROWN, Nicholas² (c1645-1705) & Mary LINFORTH (-1717+); m Haverhill 27 Jan 1669/70 [REG 152:351; GM 1:437]

BROWN, Richard (c1576-1660) & 2/wf Elizabeth _____ (-1676/7); m2 Richard JACKSON; m c1657 Watertown [GMB 1:265]

BROWN, Richard¹ (c1613-1661) & 1/wf Edith _____ (-1647); m by 1638 Newbury [GM 1:434]

BROWN, Richard¹ (c1613-1661) & 2/wf Elizabeth (GREENLEAF) BADGER, dau of Edmund; m1 Giles BADGER; m Newbury 1[torn] Feb 164[/7/8] [GM 1:434]

BROWN, Richard² (1650/1-) & Mary JAQUES; m Newbury 7 May 1674 [GM 1:434]

BROWN, Thomas (1667-1739) & Rachel POULTER (1670/1-1710+); m c1690 Lexington [REG 141:221]

BROWN, Thomas¹ (c1606-1686/7) & Mary HEALY (-1654); m Christian Malford, Wiltshire 20 Aug 1632 [GM 1:437]

BROWN, William & Persis BRIDGES (c1645-); by 1664 Boston [GMB 1:232]

BROWN, William¹ (c1609-1687/8) & 1/wf Mary _____ (c1609-by 1638); m by 1635 Salem [GM 1:443]

BROWN, William¹ (c1609-1687/8) & 2/wf Sarah SMITH, dau of Samuel; m by 1639 Salem [GM 1:443]

BROWN, William¹ (c1669-1740+) & Mary _____ (c1674-1732+); m by 1694 Leicester [AEBK 4:98]

BROWN, William² (1639-) & 1/wf Hannah CORWIN; m Salem 29 Dec 1664 [GM 1:443]

BROWN, William² (1639-) & 2/wf Rebecca BAYLEY; m Salem 26 Apr 1694 [GM 1:443]

BROWNE, Abraham¹ (bɔ 1588-1645-48) & 1/wf Joan SHELTON (c1599-1628); m South Weald, Essex 21 Sept 1619 [AEBK 1:180; GMB 3:2087]

BROWNE, Abraham¹ (bɔ 1588-1645-48) & 2/wf Lydia ____ (c1609-1686); m2 1659 Andrew HODGES; m say 1629 [AEBK 1:180; GMB 1:245, 3:2087]

BROWNE, Abraham² (1539/40-1657) & Mary DIX (-1678); m2 1668 Samuel RICE; m Watertown 5 Feb 1662/3 [AEBK 1:187]

BROWNE, Abraham³ (1571-1729) & Mary HYDE (-1723); m c1691 Watertown [AEBK 1:191]

BROWNE, Edmund¹ (bp 1600-1655) & Elizabeth OKLYE (c1630-1669-72); m Boston 14 Feb 1653/4 [AEBK 1:174; GM 1:416]

BROWNE, James & Elizabeth² CARR; m2 Samuel GARDINER; m c1672 [GM 2:25]

BROWNE, John¹ (bp 1598-1636) & Dorothy ____; perhaps m2 William POTTER; m bef 1634 Watertown [AEBK 1:174]

BROWNE, Jonathan² (1635-1690/1) & Mary SHATTUCK (1645-1732); m Watertown 11 Feb 1661/2 [AEBK 1:187]

BROWNE, Robert & Sarah HARKER (bp 1646-); by 2 Mar 1674/5 Boston [GMB 2:863; Suffolk Deed 12:282]

BROWNE, Thomas (c1626-1693) & Mary² NEWHALL (bp 1637-1693+); m c1658/9 [AEBK 4:508]

BROWNE, William & Elizabeth² RUGGLES (bp 1633-); m Boston 24 Apr 1655 [GMB 3;1606]

BROWNE, William & Mary² BESBEECH (bp 1619/20-); m Sudbury 15 Nov 1641 [GM 1:265]

BROWNING, Nathaniel & Sarah² FREEBORN (bp 1631-); m by 1652 [GM 2:575]

BRUCE, Roger² (c1670-1733) & Elizabeth FORBUSH (1669-by 1746); m c1690 Sudbury/Marlborough [REG 136:301]

BRUCE, Thomas¹ (-c1714-21) & Magdalen ____ (-c1706-9); m bef 1665 Sudbury/Marlborough [REG 136:296]

BRUCE, William & Elizabeth (CUMMINGS) GOULD; m Charlestown 15 Mar 1693 [REG 153:68-69]

BRUFF, Stephen & Damaris THREENEEDLES; m bef 1699 Boston [TAG 67:31]

BRUNDISH, John¹ (c1604-1639) & Rachel ____; m2 Anthony WILSON; m c1629 Wethersfield [GM 1:447]

BRUNDISH, John² (c1636-) & Hannah ____; Fairfield [GM 1:447]

BRUNING, Joseph & Marah² COBBETT (1652-); m2 John ROGERS; m by 1691 Boston [GM 2:118]

BRYANT, Stephen & Abigail² SHAW (c1624-); m c1643 [GMB 3:1661]

BUCK, Emmanuel[1] (1621-1705-7) & 2/wf Mary[2] ARNOLD (-bef 1664); m 17 Apr 1658 Wethersfield [TAG 44:169; GM 1:83]

BUCK, Roger[2] (c1617-) & Susan _____; m by 1642 Cambridge [GM 1:449]

BUCK, Samuel & Rachel[2] LEVENS (bp 1646-); m Cambridge 16 Mar 1669/70 [GMB 2:1175]

BUCK, William[1] (c1585-1657/8) & _____ _____ (-by 1635); m c1617 Cambridge [GM 1:449]

BUCKINGHAM, Daniel (-1725) & Sarah LEE (1674/5-1750/1+); m2 Nathaniel LYNDE; m Lyme 24 May 1693 [AEJA]

BUCKINGHAM, Thomas & Esther[2] HOSMER (c1647-); m Saybrook 20 Sept 1666 [GMB 2:1004]

BUCKLAND, Benjamin[2] (bp 1640-) & Rachel WHEATLEY; m by 1663 Rehoboth [GM 1:455]

BUCKLAND, Joseph[2] & Deborah ALLEN; m Rehoboth 5 Nov 1659 [GM 1:455]

BUCKLAND, Nicholas[2] (1646[/7]-) & 1/wf Martha WAKEFIELD; m Windsor 14 Apr or 21 Oct 1668 [GM 1:452]

BUCKLAND, Nicholas[2] (1646[/7]-) & 2/wf Elizabeth DRAKE; m Windsor 3 Mar 1685/6 [GM 1:452]

BUCKLAND, Nicholas[2] (1646[/7]-) & 3/wf Hannah (SMITH) (TRUMBULL) STRONG, dau of Hugh; m1 Joseph TRUMBULL; m2 John STRONG; m Windsor 16 June 1698 [GM 1:452]

BUCKLAND, Thomas[1] (c1613-1662) & Temperance DENSLOW (-1681), dau of Nicholas; m by 10 Mar 1638 Windsor [GM 1:452; GMB 1:528]

BUCKLAND, Thomas[2] (1650[/1]-) & Hannah COOK, dau of Nathaniel; m Windsor 21 Oct 1675 [GM 1:453]

BUCKLAND, Timothy[2] (1638[/9]-) & Abigail VORE, dau of Richard; m Windsor 27 Mar 1662 [GM 1:452]

BUCKLAND, William[1] (c1609-1683) & Mary[2] BOSWORTH (-1687), dau of Edward; m c1634 Hingham/Rehoboth/Boston [GM 1:356, 455]

BUCKLAND, William[2] (c1644-1691) & Elizabeth[2] WILLIAMS (c1648-bef 1712); m by Dec 1666 Hingham/Hartford [TAG 69:174; GM 1:455-6]

BUCKNAM, Joses & 1/wf _____[2] KNOWER (c1648-); m by 1666 Malden [GMB 2:1147]

BUCKNAM, William & _____[2] WILKINSON; m c1638 [GMB 3:1996]

BUCKNELL, Samuel & Sarah[2] BISHOP (1634[/5]-); m Boston 18 Sept 1654 [GM 1:304]

BUFFINGTON, Benjamin[2] (1675-bef 1739) & Hannah SOUTHWICK (1677-1735+); m bef 1699 Salem/Swansea [TAG 62:182]

BUFFINGTON, Thomas (1644-bef 28 Aug 1729) & Sarah SOUTHWICK (1644-1733+); Salem/Swansea [TAG 62:184]

BUGBEE, Edward[3] (1668-1702/3) & Abigail[4] HOLBROOK (1674-1729); m bef Oct 1694 Roxbury [TAG 67:8-10]

BUGBY, Edward[1] (c1594-1668/9) & Rebecca ____; m by 1630 Roxbury [GM 1:458]

BUGBY, Joseph[2] (1640-) & Experience PITCHER, dau of Andrew; m by 1664 Roxbury/Dorchester [GM 1:458]

BULKELEY, Gershom[2] (c1636-1713) & Sarah CHAUNCY; m Concord 6 Oct 1659 [GM 1:463]

BULKELEY, John[2] (bp 1619/20-) & 1/wf Ann TRY; m Odell, Bedfordshire 19 Mar 1650[/1?] [GM 1:463]

BULKELEY, John[2] (bp 1619/20-) & 2/wf Elizabeth (____) OKES; m by lic Harrow-on-the-Hill, Middlesex 6 Sept 1667 [GM 1:463]

BULKELEY, John[2] (bp 1619/20-) & 3/wf Avis ____ [GM 1:463]

BULKELEY, Peter[1] (1582/3-1658/9) & 1/wf Jane ALLEN (bp 1587/8-1626), dau of Thomas; m. Goldington, Bedfordshire 12 Apr 1613 Odel, Bedfordshire [GM 1:462]

BULKELEY, Peter[1] (1582/3-1658/9) & 2/wf Grace CHETWOOD (c1602-1669), dau of Richard; m Apr 1635 Concord [GM 1:462]

BULKELEY, Peter[2] (1643-) & Margaret ____; m by 1670 Concord [GM 1:463]

BULKELEY, Thomas[2] (bp 1617-) & Sarah[2] JONES (c1619/20-); m2 1659 Anthony WILSON; m c1640 Concord [GM 1:462; TAG 71:54]

BULL, David[2] (bp 1650[/1]-) & Hannah CHAPMAN; m Saybrook 27 Dec 1677 [GM 1:475]

BULL, Henry[1] & 2/wf Esther (SWIFT) ALLEN (bp 1629-1676); m1 Ralph ALLEN; m Sandwich 14 Feb 1664 [TAG 77:172, 283]

BULL, Henry[1] & 3/wf Ann (CLAYTON) EASTON; m1 Nicholas EASTON; m 28 Mar 1677 [TAG 77:283]

BULL, Henry[1] (c1610-1693/4) & 1/wf Elizabeth ____ (-1665) (perhaps GOFFE [GM 3:99]); m by 1638 Newport [GM 1:468; TAG 77:282]

BULL, Isaac & Sarah PARKER (bp 1632-); m Boston 22 June 1652 [TAG 76:188]

BULL, Jonathan[2] (bp 1649-) & Sarah WHITING; m Hartford 19 Mar 1684/5 [GM 1:475]

BULL, Joseph[2] (c1641-) & 1/wf Sarah MANNING; m by 1672 Hartford [GM 1:474]

BULL, Joseph[2] (c1641-) & 2/wf Hannah HUMPHREY; m by 1697 Hartford [GM 1:474]

BULL, Robert[1] & Phebe GOSSE, Saybrook "about" 15 Dec 1649 [TAG 69:140]

BULL, Thomas[1] (c1610-1684) & Susanna ____ (-1680); m c1639 Hartford [GM 1:473]

BULL, Thomas[2] (c1647-) & 1/wf Esther COWLES; m Farmington 29 Apr 1669 [GM 1:474]

BULL, Thomas[2] (c1647-) & 2/wf Mary (CHEEVER) LEWIS, dau of Ezekiel; m1 William LEWIS; m Farmington 13 Jan 1692/3 [GM 1:475]

BULLARD, Benjamin & Martha[2] PIDGE (1642/3-); m Dedham 5 Apr 1659 [GMB 3:1466]

BULLARD, George (say 1607-1688/9) & 1/wf Margaret _____ (-1639); m 1630s
Watertown [AEBK 1:206]

BULLARD, George (say 1607-1688/9) & 2/wf Beatrice HALL; m aft Feb 1640 [AEBK
1:206]

BULLARD, George (say 1607-1688/9) & 3/wf Mary (RICHARDS) MAPLEHEAD; m
Watertown Apr 1655 [AEBK 1:206]

BULLARD, George (say 1607-1688/9) & 4/wf Jane (LISHAM) ELLIS; m Charlestown 2
May 1672 [AEBK 1:206]

BULLARD, John[1] (c1602-1678) & 1/wf Magdalen MARTIN (c1608-1661); m say 1633
Barnham, Suffolk/Medfield [AEBK 1:207; REG 146:280]

BULLARD, John[1] (c1602-1678) & 2/wf Ellen (_____) DICKERMAN (-by 1678); m1
Thomas DICKERMAN; m bet 1661-63/4 Medfield [AEBK 1:207]

BULLARD, Joseph[2] (1643-by 1722) & Sarah _____ (c1644-1722); m by 1665
Weston/Dedham [AEBK 1:212]

BULLARD, Joseph[3] (1665-1711+) & Margaret[3] CHENEY (1670-1711+); m Medfield 25
June 1691 [AEBK 1:213]

BULLARD, Robert (c1600-1639) & Anne MARTYN (c1604-bef 1660); m c1625
Barnham, Suffolk/Watertown [REG 146:280; AEBK 1:205]

BULLARD, William[1] (c1594-1686) & 1/wf Mary _____ (-bef 1653) [AEBK 1:205]

BULLARD, William[1] (c1594-1686) & 2/wf Mary (_____)(_____) GRISWOLD (-1655);
m2 Francis GRISWOLD; m Cambridge 4 Jan 1653 [AEBK 1:205]

BULLARD, William[1] (c1594-1686) & 3/wf Mary _____ (-1679+); m aft 1655 [AEBK
1:205]

BULLOCK, Edward[1] (c1603-1649-56/7) & _____ (_____) JOHNSON; Dorchester [GM
1:476]

BULLOCK, Henry[1] (c1595-1663) & 1/wf Susan _____ (-1644); m c1627 Salem [GM
1:479]

BULLOCK, Henry[1] (c1595-1663) & 2/wf Elizabeth _____; m bet 2 Nov 1644 and 21 Dec
1663 [GM 1:479]

BULLOCK, Henry[2] (c1627-) & Alice FLINT, dau of William; m by 1654 Salem [GM
1:479]

BULLOCK, John (1664-1739) & Elizabeth BARNES (1674/5-1761); m 29 Jan 1695
Swansea [AEJA]

BUMPAS, Edward (1636-) & Sarah _____; by 1671 Scituate [GMB 1:275]

BUMPAS, John (1636-1715/6)& Sarah _____ (-1710+); m bef 1670 Scituate/
Middleboro/Rochester [TAG 43:69]

BUMSTEAD Jeremiah & 1/wf Hannah[2] ODLIN (1643-); m bef 1664 Boston [GMB
2:1349]

BUNCE, Thomas & Susannah[2] BULL (c1645-) [GM 1:474]

BUNDY, James[2] (1664-) & Mary _____; m by 1690 Braintree/Pt. Judith, R.I. [TAG
67:30; GM 1:481]

BUNDY, John[2] (c1617-1681) & 1/wf Martha CHANDLER (-1674), dau of Roger; m by 1649 Plymouth/Boston/Taunton/Duxbury [GMB 1:331; GM 1:481]

BUNDY, John[2] (c1617-1681) & 2/wf Ruth (____) GURNEY; m1 John GURNEY; m3 Guido BAILEY; m Taunton 5 Jan 1676 [GM 1:481]

BUNKER, Benjamin[2] (bp 1635-) & Mary CHICKERING, dau of Francis; m2 William SYMMES; m3 Samuel TORREY [GM 1:486]

BUNKER, George[1] (c1599-1663/4-4) & 1/wf Judith MAJOR (-1646); m Odell, Bedfordshire 8 Sept 1624 [GM 1:486]

BUNKER, George[1] (c1599-1663/4-4) & 2/wf Margaret (WELLS) HOWE (bp 1590-1660); m1 Edward HOWE; m aft 8 Apr 1647 Watertown [GM 1:486; TAG 70:177]

BUNKER, John[2] (bp 1630-) & Hannah MELLOWS; m Malden Sept 1655 [GM 1:486]

BUNKER, Jonathan[2] (bp 1638-) & Mary HOWARD; m Charlestown 30 Jan 1662/3 [GM 1:486]

BURDEN, George[1] (c1611-1652-57) & Ann SOULBY; m St. Nicholas, Newcastle upon Tyne, Northumberland 4 Feb 1634/5 Boston/Barbados [REG 155:91+; GM 1:489]

BURDETT, George[1] (c1602-1671) & Susan _____, perhaps m St Stephen Coleman St., London 8 Nov 1627, then Susanna COOCKE; m by 1634 Dover/Dublin [GM 1:493]

BURDETT, George[1] (c1602-1671) ~ Mary, wife of George PUDDINGTON [GM 1:493]

BURDETT, George[1] (c1602-1671) ~ Ruth, wife of John GOOCH; c1640 [GM 1:493]

BURGE, John (c1615-1678) & 1/wf Rachel _____ (-1661) [AEBK 4:278]

BURGE, John (c1615-1678) & 2/wf Mary (STEARNS) LEARNED; m Chelmsford 9 June 1662 [AEBK 4:278, 433]

BURGE, John (c1615-1678) & 3/wf Grizzell[2] (FLETCHER)(JEWELL)(GREGGS) (KIBBY) GURNEY (c1619-1669); m Chelmsford 3 July 1667 [AEBK 4:278]

BURGE, John (c1615-1678) & 4/wf Jane (____) GORNELL (-1678); m Chelmsford 6 Sept 1677 [AEBK 4:278]

BURGESS, Joseph & Patience FREEMAN [TAG 40:104]

BURGESS, Roger & Sarah[2] (GRIGGS) KING; m by 1659 Boston [GM 3:158]

BURGETT, James[1] (c1621-1670/1) & Lydia MEAD (-1670/1+), dau of Gabriel; m Boston 19 Oct 1652 [GM 1:497]

BURKBY, Thomas[1] & Martha[2] (CHENEY) SADLER (bp 1626-); m by 1655 [TAG 76:247]

BURKE, Richard (1671-) & Abigail SAWTELL (1671/2-1716); m bef 1691 Sudbury [REG 126:6]

BURMAN, Thomas & Hannah _____; m bef 1663 Barnstable [MD 18:63]

BURNAP, Isaac & Hannah[2] ANTRUM (bp 1638-); m Salem 8 Nov 1658 [GM 1:70]

BURNAP, Robert & Ann _____ [REG 155:355]

BURNAP, Thomas[2] (-1690/1) & Mary PEARSON (-1690/1); m Lynn 3 Dec 1663
[REG 155:353]

BURNHAM, John[2] (c1652-1721) & Mary[3] CATLIN (1666-1721+); m by 26 Dec 1686
[TAG 74:36]

BURNHAM, Moses & Ann[2] BELCHER; m by 1699 Ipswich [GM 1:235]

BURNHAM, Richard[2] (1656-1744) & Sarah[2] HUMPHRIES (1658-); m 11 June 1680
[TAG 74:36]

BURNHAM, Samuel (1658-1728) & 1/wf Mary[2] FITCH (c1657-1700-1727); m 8 Oct
1684 [TAG 68:96; 74:37]

BURNHAM, Thomas (-1694) & Marie LAWRENCE (bp 10 Apr 1625-1715); St Albans
Abbey, Hertfordshire/Ipswich [TG 10:22]

BURNHAM, Thomas[1] (c1620-1688) & Ann[2] WRIGHT (c1622-1705+); m bef 1646 [TAG
74:35; GMB 3:2073]

BURNHAM, Thomas[2] (c1649-1726) & Naomi[3] HULL (1656/7-1726+); m Killingworth 4
Jan 1676 [TAG 74:35]

BURNHAM, William[2] (c1645-1720-33) & 1/wf Elizabeth[3] LOOMIS (1655-1717); m
Windsor 28 June 1681 [TAG 74:35]

BURR, Jehu & Hester[2] WARD [GMB 3:1920]

BURR, Jehu (c1605-by 1654) & _____ _____; by 1631 Roxbury/Springfield/Fairfield
[GMB 1:279]

BURR, John & Mary[2] WARD [GMB 3:1920]

BURR, Nathaniel & Sarah[2] WARD; m c1662 [GMB 3:1920]

BURRAGE, John & Joanna[2] STOWERS (c1624-); m by 1657 Charlestown [GMB
3:1781]

BURRELL, John[1] (c1609-1654-56/7) & Sarah _____ (-1657+); m c1634 Roxbury [GM
1:500]

BURROUGHS, George (-hanged 1692) & 1/wf Hannah FISHER (1652/3-1681); m
c1672-4 [AEBK 4:257; TAG 76:18]

BURROUGHS, George (-hanged 1692) & 2/wf Sarah (RUCK) HAWTHORNE; m
c1682 [AEBK 4:257]

BURROUGHS, George (?1650-hanged 1692) & 3/wf Mary _____ (-1712+); m2 Michael
HOMER, m3 Christopher HALL; m c1690 Salem [TAG 56:43; AEBK 4:257]

BURROUGHS, Jeremiah & _____ HEWES; m2 John MENDALL [TAG 40:33]

BURROUGHS, John & Hannah COLVER (1652-1733); m New London 14 Dec 1670
[Colver Gen, 23]

BURSLEY, John[1] & Joanna[2] HULL (c1620-); m2 Dolor[1] DAVIS; m Sandwich c28 Nov
1639 [GM 3:455]

BURSLEY, Thomas & Joanna _____; m bef 1660 [PCR 3:201]

BURT, Edward[2] (bp 1626-) & Elizabeth[2] BUNKER (bp 1628-); m by 1657
Charlestown [GM 1:486, 502]

BURT, Hugh[1] (bp 1590-1661) & 1/wf Ursula _____ (-1628); m by 1614 Dorking, Surrey [GM 1:502]

BURT, Hugh[1] (bp 1590-1661) & 2/wf Ann (HOLLAND) BASSETT (-1664[/5?]-73); m1 Roger BASSETT; m by 1635 Dorking, Surrey/Lynn [GM 1:502]

BURT, Hugh[2] (bp 1621-) & Sarah JOHNSON, dau of John; m by 1647 Roxbury/Lynn [GM 1:502]

BURT, James[1] (-1679-80) & Anna _____ (-1665); not widow of Humphrey GALLOP Taunton [TAG 75:109]

BURT, James[2] (c1659-1743) & Mary THAYER (-1743+); m Taunton 2 Sept 1685 [TAG 75:113]

BURT, Richard[2] (-1685+) & Charity[2] (HALL) GALLOP (c1635-1711); m about 1656 Taunton [AEBK 4:326]

BURTON, Boniface[1] (c1579-1669) & Frances _____ (-1669[/70]-79); m by Feb 1666/7 Lynn/Reading [GM 1:505]

BURTON, Stephen & Abigail BRENTON; by 1677 [GMB 1:223]

BURWELL, Samuel (bp 1667-1712) & Deborah MERWIN (1670-1706); m c1698 Milford [REG 149:308]

BUSH, Samuel (c1652-1733) & 1/wf Mary[3] GOODENOW (1659-1687); m 1 May 1677 [AEBK 3]

BUSH, Samuel (c1652-1733) & 2/wf Abigail LEE; m 11 May 1688 [AEBK 3]

BUSHNELL, Edmund[1] (bp 1606-1636) & Martha HALLOR; m2 William BEAMSLEY; m Horsham, Sussex 2 Aug 1627 Boston [GM 1:508]

BUSHNELL, Francis[1] (1608/9-1681) & Mary GROMBRIDGE (bp 1605/6-), dau of Thomas; m Horsham, Sussex 27 June 1631 [GM 1:511]

BUSHNELL, John[1] (bp 1615-1667) & Jane _____; m by 1651 Horsham, Sussex/Boston [GM 1:513]

BUSHNELL, John[2] & Sarah SCRANTON; m Guilford May 1665 [GM 1:511]

BUSHNELL, John[2] (c1644-) & Sarah (LOVERING) PLACE; m by 1687 Boston [GM 1:514]

BUSHNELL, Samuel[2] & Ruth SANFORD; m 17 Apr 1684 Saybrook [GM 1:511]

BUSHROD, Peter & Elizabeth[2] HANNUM (1645-); m by 1680 [GM 3:212]

BUSICOTE, Peter[1] & Mary MAY; m 20 Nov 1631 Hartland, Devonshire/Warwick, RI [TAG 58:230]

BUSS, John & Elizabeth[2] BRADBURY (1651-); m Salisbury 12 May 1673 [GM 1:380]

BUSS, John & Elizabeth[2] HILL (bp 1651-); m by 1680 Boston [GM 3:325]

BUSWELL, Samuel & Sarah[2] KEYES (1633-); m Salisbury 8 July 1656 [GMB 2:1129]

BUTLER, Daniel[2] (c1642-bef 1717) & Elizabeth HOUSE (-1689-1717); m 8 April 1665 Sandwich [REG 127:22]

BUTLER, James (-killed 1736) & Lydia[3] SNOW (1676-1723); m c1698 Lancaster [AEBK 3]

BUTLER, Nathaniel (1641-1697/8) & Sarah GREEN (1642-), dau. of Bartholomew; m2
   Philip ALCOCK; m bef 1668 Wethersfield [TAG 46:10, GMB 1:287]

BUTLER, Peter & Mary[2] ALFORD (bp 1631-); m2 Hezekiah USHER; m3 Samuel
   NOWELL; m by 1654 Boston [GM 1:25]

BUTLER, Samuel (1640-) & Elizabeth _____ (-1681); m bef 1665 Haddam, CT [TAG
   60:29]

BUTLER, Thomas & Sarah[2] STONE; m by 1657 [GMB 3:171]

BUTLER, William & Sarah[2] CROSS; m by 1677 Ipswich [GM 2:244]

BUTMAN, Jeremiah & Mehitable (GILES) COLLINS [TAG 72:300]

BUTTERWORTH, Benjamin (1672-by 1711) & Huldah[3] HAYWARD (c1672-1714+); m
   Swansea 6 Jan 1692 [AEBK 3]

BUTTERWORTH, John[2] (c1624-1708) & Sarah _____ (-1666/7+); m c1650 Bristol
   [TAG 77:303]

BUTTERWORTH, John[3] (1651-1731) & Hannah WHEATON (1654-1724); m Rehoboth 4
   Sept 1674 [TAG 77:303]

BUTTOLPH, George[3] (1667-1696) & Elizabeth probably BUCK, (1670-1752); m2 Robert
   LATIMER; m bef 1690 Wethersfield [TAG 58:138]

BUTTOLPH, John (1639[/40]-1692/3) & 2/wf Abigail (FITCH) MASON (1650-); m1
   John[2] MASON; m Wethersfield 27 June 1682 Norwich [TAG 40:54; GM 1:520]

BUTTOLPH, John[2] (1639[/40]-) & 1/wf Hannah GARDNER, dau of George; m Salem
   16 Oct 1663 [GM 1:520]

BUTTOLPH, John[2] (1639[/40]-1692/3) & 3/wf Susanna (CLARK)(KELLY) SANFORD;
   m1 James KELLY; m2 Nathaniel SANFORD; m bef 1687 Wethersfield [GM
   1:520; TAG 58:136]

BUTTOLPH, Thomas[1] (c1603-1667) & Ann HARDING (-1680); m by 1635 Boreham,
   Essex/Boston [GM 1:519]

BUTTOLPH, Thomas[2] (1637-) & Mary BAXTER; m Boston 5 Sept 1660 [GM 1:520]

BUTTON, John & 3/wf Mary (_____) SIMMONS, m1 John SIMMONS; m bef 1670
   Boston [RCA]

BUTTRICK, John[2] (1653-) & Mary BLOOD, dau of Robert; m Stow 8 Apr 1679 [GM
   1:523]

BUTTRICK, Samuel[2] (1654[/5]-) & Elizabeth BLOOD, dau of Robert; m Concord 21
   June 1677 [GM 1:523]

BUTTRICK, William[1] (c1616-1698) & 1/wf Mary HASTINGS, dau of John; m by 1648
   Concord [GM 1:523]

BUTTRICK, William[1] (c1616-1698) & 2/wf Sarah _____ (-1664); m by 1653 Concord
   [GM 1:523]

BUTTRICK, William[1] (c1616-1698) & 3/wf Jane (_____) GOODENOW; probably m1
   Thomas[2] GOODENOW; m Concord 21 Feb 1667[/8] [GM 1:523]

BUTTRY, Nicholas[1] (c1602-by 1636) & Martha _____; m2 Miles IVES; m c1634
   Cambridge [GM 1:526]

CABLE, John (c1615-1682) & 1/wf Sarah _____; by 1640 Springfield/Fairfield [GMB 1:30]

CADE, James & Margaret _____; m by 19 Mar 164[2/]3 Boston [GM 2:2]

CADY, Nicholas & Judith[2] KNOPF (bp 1629-); m by 1650 Watertown [GMB 2:1145]

CAIN, Arthur & Sarah[2] GOULD (c1648-); m Hingham 29 Nov 1675 [GM 3:122]

CAKEBREAD, Thomas[1] (c1595-1642/3) & Sarah _____; m2 Philemon WHALE; by 1620 Sudbury [GMB 1:303]

CALDWELL, John & Sarah DILLINGHAM; c1654 [GMB 1:549]

CALL, John & Hannah[2] KETTLE (bp 1639-); m Charlestown 21 Jan 1656 [GMB 2:1125]

CALL, Thomas & Lydia[2] SHEPARDSON (bp 1637-1723); m2 Thomas SKINNER; m Malden 22 July 1657 [GMB 3:1665]

CALLENDER, Ellis (-1728) & 1/wf Mary _____ ; m bef 1674 Boston [REG 144:196]

CALLOW, Oliver (-1674/5) & Judith (_____) CLOCK (-by 1684); m Boston 29 Feb 1655/6 [Boston VR 53]

CALLUM, Caleb[2] (c1660s-by 1692/3) & Elizabeth DYNN (-1716); m2 Richard COMER/COMAN; m c1680 Salem [DCD; TAG 70:104]

CALLUM, John[2] (1661-by 1743) & 2/wf Elizabeth[2] BEANS (-1716+) (she did not m2 Richard COMER/COMAN); m Salem 30 Nov 1685 [DCD; TAG 70:5]

CAMMOCK, _____ & Martha[2] SMITH (1641-); m by 1681 [GMB 3:1692]

CAMMOCK, Thomas (bp 1592/3-by 1643) & Margaret _____; m2 Henry JOSSELYN; by 1640 Piscataqua [GMB 1:306]

CAMP, Nicholas & Mehitable[2] (GUNN) FENN (bp 1641-); m1 Benjamin FENN; m by 1690 Milford [GM 3:168]

CAMPBELL, John & Sarah (ROGERS) HACKLETON; m Southampton 9 Mar 1686/7 [NYGBR 127:74]

CANE, Christopher[1] (c1513-1653) & Margery _____ (-1687); m by 1640 Cambridge [GM 2:5]

CANE, Jonathan[2] (1640-) & Deborah WELCH, dau of Thomas; m Cambridge 14 May 1674 [GM 2:5]

CANE, Nathaniel[2] (1642-) & 1/wf Elizabeth _____; m by 1678 Boston [GM 2:5]

CANE, Nathaniel[2] (1642-) & 2/wf Sarah GREEN; m Kittery 2 Nov 1688 [GM 2:5]

CANFIELD, Nathaniel & Sarah WILLOUGHBY; m bef 12 May 1662 Eng/Norwalk [REG 118:296]

CANFIELD, Samuel (bp 1645-1690) & Elizabeth MERWIN (not WILLOUGHBY) (bef 1650-1697+); m c 1672 or bef 1697 Norwich/Norwalk [REG 118:296; 149:307]

CANNEY, Joseph (c1643-by 1690) & 1/wf Mary _____; m c1665 Dover [NHGR 20:7]

CANNEY, Joseph (c1643-by 1690) & 2/wf Mary CLEMENTS; m 25 Dec 1670 [NHGR 20:7]

CANNEY, Joseph (c1643-by 1690) & 3/wf Mary DAMM; m c1673 Dover [NHGR 20:7]

CANNEY, Thomas (c1639-1677) & Sarah TAYLOR; m2 John WINGATE; m Dover 3 Oct 1666 [NHGR 20:7]

CANNEY, Thomas[1] (c1600-1681+) & Jane _____; m bef 1652 Dover [NHGR 20:6]

CAPEN, Bernard (c1562-1638) & Joan PURCHASE (c1578-1653); m Dorchester, Dorsetshire 31 May 1596 Dorchester, MA [GMSP]

CAPEN, John[1] (1612/3-1692) & 1/wf Radigon[1] CLAPP (bp 1609-1645); m Dorchester 20 Oct 1637 [AEBK 4:129]

CAPEN, John[1] (1612/3-1692) & 2/wf Mary BASS; m Dorchester 20 Sept 1647 [AEBK 4:129]

CARDER, James[2] (1655-) & Mary WHIPPLE, dau of John; m Warwick 6 Jan 1686/7 [GM 2:9]

CARDER, John[2] & 1/wf Mary HOLDEN, dau of Randall; m Warwick 1 Dec 1671 [GM 2:9]

CARDER, John[2] & 2/wf Hannah _____; bef 13 Sept 1700 [GM 2:9]

CARDER, Joseph[2] (c1658-1693/4) & Bethiah _____; m by 1693 Warwick [GM 2:9]

CARDER, Richard[1] (c1615-1675+) & 1/wf _____ _____; m c1641 Roxbury/Boston/Warwick [GM 2:9]

CARDER, Richard[1] (c1615-1675+) & 2/wf Mary _____ (-1691/2); m c1646 Roxbury/Boston/Warwick [GM 2:9]

CARGILL, David (c1661-1734) & Janet SMITH (c1664-1745); m c1680 Derry, No. Ireland/Londonderry, NH [REG 117:244]

CARMAN, Caleb (1639/40-) & Elizabeth _____; by 1666 Hempstead [GMB 1:312]

CARMAN, John[1] (-c1654) & Florence _____, m2 John HICKS; m bef 1633 Roxbury/Hempstead [GMSP]

CARPENTER, Abiah (1643-) & ?Mary[2] REDWAY [TAG 70:204]

CARPENTER, David & Elizabeth _____; m2 George ORVIS; m3 Richard BRONSON [TAG 38:206]

CARPENTER, John[3] (bp 1626-) & Hannah ?SMITH [TAG 70:203]

CARPENTER, Joseph (bp 1634-) & Margaret[2] SUTTON; m Rehoboth 25 Nov 1655 [TAG 70:204]

CARPENTER, Samuel (c1636-) & Sarah[2] REDWAY; m Rehoboth 25 May 1660 [TAG 70:204]

CARPENTER, William & Elizabeth[2] ARNOLD (1611-); m c1635 [GM 1:88]

CARPENTER, William (bp 1631-) & 1/wf Priscilla BENNETT; m Rehoboth 5 Oct 1651 [TAG 70:204]

CARPENTER, William (bp 1631-) & 2/wf Miriam SALE; m Rehoboth 10 Feb 1663[/4] [TAG 70:204]

CARPENTER, William[1] (c1576-c1638) & ?Alice CARPENTER (-1637/8); m bef 1605 Shalbourne, Wiltshire [TAG 70:205]

CARPENTER, William[2] (c1605-1658/9?) & Abigail BRIANT (bp 1604-1686/7); m Shalbourne, Wiltshire/Rehoboth [TAG 70:203]

CARR, Caleb & Phillipa GREENE (1658-by 1706), dau of John; m2 Charles DICKINSON; m by 1678 Jamestown [TAG 42:189; GM 2:25]

CARR, Caleb[1] (c1625-1695) & 1/wf Mercy _____ (-1675); m c1654 Newport [GM 2:14]

CARR, Caleb[1] (c1625-1695) & 2/wf Sarah (CLARKE) PINNER, dau of Jeremiah; m1 John PINNER; m 21 Dec 1675 Newport [GM 2:14]

CARR, Caleb[2] (1657-) & Deborah _____; m by 1680 Jamestown [GM 2:14]

CARR, Edward[2] & Hannah STANTON, dau of John; m Jamestown 6 Oct 168[6] [GM 2:15]

CARR, Esek[2] & Susanna _____; m c1685 Little Compton [GM 2:26]

CARR, George[1] (c1613-1682) & Elizabeth _____ (-1691); m by 1642 Salisbury [GM 2:20]

CARR, George[2] (1644-) & Anne COTTEN; m Salisbury 8 Nov 1677 [GM 2:20]

CARR, John[2] & Wait EASTON, dau of Peter; m c1686 not Newport [GM 2:15]

CARR, Nicholas[2] (1654-) & Rebecca NICHOLSON; m by 1679 Jamestown [GM 2:14]

CARR, Richard[2] (1659-) & 1/wf Dorothy BOYCE; m Killingworth 10 Feb 1684[/5?] [GM 2:21]

CARR, Robert[1] (c1614-1681) & _____ _____ (-1681+); m c1650 Portsmouth/Newport [GM 2:25]

CARR, Robert[2] & Elizabeth LAWTON; m c1683 [GM 2:26]

CARR, Samuel[2] (1658-) & _____ _____; m by 1689 Newport [GM 2:15]

CARR, William[2] (164[7/?]8-) & Elizabeth PIKE; m Salisbury 20 Aug 1672 [GM 2:20]

CARRELL, Nathaniel (c1637-8-) & 2/wf Hannah _____; by 1691 [TAG 70:207]

CARRELL, Nathaniel (c1637-8-) & Mary[2] PEASE (c1636-bef 1683), dau. of Robert[1]; m c1660 Salem [TAG 70:207; 71:145]

CARRINGTON, Edward (c1615-1684) & Elizabeth _____ (c1618-1658); by 1638 Charlestown [GMB 1:316]

CARTER, John[2] (1650-) & Martha BROWN, dau of William; m by 1681 Salisbury [GM 2:29]

CARTER, Thomas & Elizabeth[2] (GOBLE) WHITE (c1633-); m1 John WHITE; m Sudbury 7 June 1682 [GM 3:83]

CARTER, Thomas[1] (c1610-1676) & Mary _____; m c1641 Salisbury [GM 2:28]

CARTHRICK, Michael[1] (c1610-1646/7) & Sarah _____ (-1659+); m c1635 Ipswich [GM 2:32]

CARTWRIGHT, Edward (-1671) & Elizabeth MORRISON (bp 1623/4-1673); m bef 1664 Boston [REG 146:277]

CARVER, John (c1585-1621) & Catherine (WHITE) LEGGATT (-1621); by 1609 Leiden/Plymouth [GMB 1:321]

CARVER, Richard (c1577-1638-41) & 1/wf Margaret SKURRIE (-1618); m Filby, Norfolk 24 Nov 1614 [REG 146:234]

CARVER, Richard (c1577-1638-41) & 2/wf Elizabeth _____ (-1622); m after 16 Nov 1618 Filby, Norfolk [REG 146:234]

CARVER, Richard (c1577-1638-41) & 3/wf Grace WALKER, m2 Michael BARSTOW; m St Stephen, Norwich 7 July 1623 [REG 146:234]

CARY, John & Abigail² PENNIMAN (1651-1729); m c1670 Bristol/Bridgewater [TAG 71:18; GMB 3:1429]

CASE, Henry & Martha² CURWIN; m2 Thomas HUTCHINSON; m Southold Nov 1658 [GM 2:266]

CASE, Henry (1659-1740) & Tabitha VAIL (-1735); Southold, LI [TAG 38:183]

CASE, John & Sarah² SPENCER; m c1656 [GMB 3:1724]

CASS, Joseph² & Mary HOBBS; Hampton [NYGBR 131:299]

CASWELL, John² (1656-1713-13/4) & Elizabeth³ HALL (1670-1739); m2 1716 Benjamin NEWLAND; m Taunton 26 Nov 1689 [AEBK 4:331-2]

CASWELL, Thomas² (1650\1-1725-6) & 2/wf Mary RAMSDEN; m 2 Dec 1691 Taunton [MD 39:69]

CAVERLEY, George & _____ _____; m bef 8 May 1698 Newport [TAG 69:119, 185]

CAZNEAU, Paix (-1720) & Margaret GERMAINE (1671-1769); m bef 1696 Boston/Roxbury/Wrentham [REG 142:127]

CHADBOURNE, Humphrey² (bp 23 Apr 1615-1667) & Lucy² TREWORGYE (c1632-1704-8), dau of James, m2 Thomas WILLS; m3 Elias STILEMAN; m c1652 Kittery [GM 2:33; CG, 9]

CHADBOURNE, Humphrey³ (c1653-1694) & Sarah BOLLES (1657-probably after 1707); m2 Benjamin NASON; m bef 1678 Kittery [CG, 23]

CHADBOURNE, James³ (c1655-1686) & Elizabeth³ HEARD (-1702+); m2 Samuel SMALL; m c1680 Kittery [CG, 27 & Genealogy of Edward Small, 1:466-7]

CHADBOURNE, William¹ (bp 30 Mar 1582-1652) & Elizabeth SPARRY (c1589-1623+); m St Editha, Tamworth, Staffordshire 8 Oct 1609 Kittery [CG & NHGR 10:110; GM 2:33]

CHADBOURNE, William² (bp 15 Oct 1620-1667+) & Mary _____ (c1620s-1644+); m bef 1644 Boston and possibly Cecil Co., Maryland [CG, 17; GM 2:33]

CHADWELL, Thomas & 2/wf Barbara (_____) (DAVIS) BRIMBLECOM; m1 George DAVIS; m2 John BRIMBLECOM; m aft 1656 Lynn/Boston [DCD]

CHADWICK, Charles (c1596-1682) & Elizabeth _____ (-1684/5); m2 1683 Thomas FOX; before 1630 Watertown [GMB 1:323-24]

CHALKER, Abraham² (1655-1730/1) & 2/wf Sarah² INGHAM (1658-1687); m Saybrook 23 Sep 1686 [TAG 68:137]

CHALLIS, John² (c1677-1742) & Sarah² FRAME (c1680-1751+); m 26 Jan 1698/9 Salisbury [ASBO, p.153]

CHALLIS, Thomas² (1673-c1752) & 1/wf Mary³ COLBY (c1669-bef 1727); m bef 3 Sep 1696 Amesbury [TAG 49:172; ASBO, p.154]

CHALLIS, William[2] (1663-by 1726) & Margaret[3] FOWLER (1673-1726+); m 2 Jan 1698/9 Salisbury [ASBO, p.152]

CHAMBERLAIN, Francis & perhaps Agnes HAIDEN; m 1613/4 Ugley, Essex [TAG 51:151]

CHAMBERLAIN, Richard & Sarah[2] BUGBY (c1630-); m by 1665 [GM 1:458]

CHAMBERLAIN, Thomas & Mary (?POPE)(POULTER)(AYLETT) PARKER (c1596-1692/3); m1 John[1] POULTER; m2 John AYLETT; m3 John PARKER [REG 141:217; see 153:89]

CHAMBERLAIN, William & Eunice[2] EWELL; m Scituate 9 Sept 1678 [GM 2:479]

CHAMPNEY, Christopher & Margaret _____; delete - mistake for Christopher CAINE [RCA]

CHAMPNEY, Daniel[2] (1644[/5]-) & 1/wf Dorcas BRIDGE; m Cambridge 3 Jan 1665[/6] [GM 2:45]

CHAMPNEY, Daniel[2] (1644[/5]-) & 2/wf Hepzibah (CORLETT) MINOT; m Cambridge 9 June 1684 [GM 2:45]

CHAMPNEY, John[1] (c1610-by 1643) & Joan _____; m2 Golden MOORE; m by 1635 Cambridge [GM 2:38]

CHAMPNEY, Joseph[2] (bp 1632-) & Sarah POOLE, dau of John; m c1656 Billerica [GM 2:45]

CHAMPNEY, Richard[1] (c1604-1669) & Jane _____; m c1629 Cambridge [GM 2:44]

CHAMPNEY, Samuel[2] (1635-) & 1/wf Sarah HUBBARD; m Billerica 13 Oct 1657 [GM 2:45]

CHAMPNEY, Samuel[2] (1635-) & 2/wf Ruth (MITCHELSON) GREEN, dau of Edward [GM 2:45]

CHANDLER, Benjamin & Elizabeth BUCK; m by 1672 Scituate [GMB 1:328]

CHANDLER, Edmund (c1587-1662) & 1/wf _____ _____; by 1612 Plymouth, Devonshire [GMB 1:326-30]

CHANDLER, Edmund (c1587-1662) & 2/wf _____ _____; by 1632 Plymouth/Duxbury [GMB 1:326-30]

CHANDLER, John[2] & Elizabeth DOUGLAS (1641-); m Roxbury 16 Feb 1658[/9?] [TAG 74:280]

CHANDLER, Joseph & Mercy _____; by 1673 Duxbury [GMB 1:328]

CHANDLER, William[1] (1595-1641/2) & 1/wf Alice THOROUGHGOOD; Roxbury [TAG 73:51]

CHANDLER, William[1] (1595-1641/2) & 2/wf Agnes BAYFORD; Roxbury [TAG 73:51]

CHANEY, Joseph (-1704) & 1/wf Hannah[2] THURSTON (1650-1690); m Medfield 12 Mar 1667/8 [AEBK 3]

CHANTRELL, John[1] (c1640-1694) & Mary MELLOWS (c1642-1729); m by 1670 Boston [AEBK 1:217]

CHANTRELL, Joseph (1673-1710) & Amie GARDNER (c1675-1710+); m Boston 13 Dec 1697 Newport [AEBK 1:222]

CHAPLIN, Clement[1] (bp 1593-1656) & Sarah HINDES (-1661[/2?]); m Rushbrooke, Suffolk 5 May 1618 [GM 2:50]

CHAPMAN, Edward & Elizabeth SHERWIN; m bef 31 Mar 1696 [REG 144:54]

CHAPMAN, Edward[1] & Mary SYMONDS (c1612-1658) Ipswich [TAG 74:116]

CHAPMAN, Isaac[2] (1647-) & Rebecca LEONARD; m Barnstable 2 Sept 1678 [GM 2:53]

CHAPMAN, John & Elizabeth[2] BEAMON (1650-); m Saybrook 26 Mar 1677 [GM 1:221]

CHAPMAN, John (c1613-by 1657) & Martha (____) LAWRENCE; m1 Thomas LAWRENCE; m3 Francis BROWNE; Watertown/Wethersfield/New Haven/Fairfield/Stamford [GMB 1:332-35]

CHAPMAN, Jonathan & Hannah[2] SPENCER (unproven) [GMB 3:1720]

CHAPMAN, Ralph[1] (bp 1657-) & 1/wf Mary ____; m by 1679 Scituate [GM 2:53]

CHAPMAN, Ralph[1] (bp 1657-) & 2/wf Abigail ____; m by 1693 Scituate [GM 2:53]

CHAPMAN, Ralph[1] (c1615-1671-71/2) & Lydia WILLS, dau of Isaac; m Marshfield 23 Nov 1642 [GM 2:53]

CHAPPELL, Caleb[2] (1671-1733) & Ruth ROYCE (1669-1768); m Norwich 4 June 1694 [REG 150:71]

CHAPPELL, George[1] (c1615-by 1682) & 1/wf Christian ____; m by 1644 New London [GM 2:56; REG 150:54]

CHAPPELL, George[1] (c1615-by 1682) & 2/wf Margaret ____ (-1714+); m by 1653 [GM 2:57; REG 150:54]

CHAPPELL, George[2] (1653/4-1712) & 1/wf Alice WAY; m New London 3 Oct 1676 [REG 150:61; GM 2:57]

CHAPPELL, John[2] & Elizabeth (CARPENTER) JONES (1644-1694+); m1 Richard JONES; m3 ____ HILL: m bet 1671 and 1674 Lyme [REG 150:57; GM 2:57; TAG 41:42]

CHAPPELL, Nathaniel[2] (1668-1712) & Hopestill ROSE-MORGAN (1669-1753); m2 Thomas BOLLES; m by 1694 New London [REG 150:67; GM 2:57]

CHASE, Aquila[2] (1652-1720) & Esther BOND (1655-1722/3+); m c1673 Newbury [ASBO, p.174]

CHASE, Benjamin (bp 1652-) & Philip[2] SHERMAN (1652-); by c1674 Yarmouth [GMB 1:337-38, 3:1672]

CHASE, Daniel[2] (1661-1706/7) & Martha[3] KIMBALL (1664-1713+); m 25 Aug 1683 Newbury [ASBO, p.175]

CHASE, John[2] (1655-1739/40) & 1/wf Elizabeth[2] BINGLEY (1660-bef 1687); m 23 May 1677 Newbury [ASBO, p.175]

CHASE, John[2] (1655-1739/40) & 2/wf Lydia[2] CHALLIS (1665-1736+); m 21 Dec 1687 Salisbury [ASBO, p.175]

CHASE, Thomas[2] (1654-1732-4) & 1/wf Rebecca[2] FOLLANSBEE (c1658-1711); m 22 Nov 1677 Newbury [ASBO, p.174]

CHASE, William & Hannah² SHERMAN (1647-); m c1678 [GMB 3:1672]

CHASE, William (c1605-1659) & Mary _____ (-1659); Roxbury/Yarmouth [GMB 1:336-39]

CHATER, John & Alice² EMERY; m by 1644 Newbury [GM 2:449]

CHECKLEY, John & Anna² EYRE (c1630-); m Boston 5 Mar 165[1/]2 [GM 2:487]

CHEESEBOROUGH, Elisha & Rebecca² PALMER (c1646-); m2 John BALDWIN; m Stonington 20 Apr 1665 [GMB 3:1383]

CHEESEBOROUGH, Nathaniel & Hannah DENISON; by 1660 Stonington [GMB 1:342]

CHENEY, Daniel² (c1625-) & Sarah BAILEY; m Newbury 8 Oct 1665 [TAG 76:247; GM 2:62]

CHENEY, John¹ (c1600-1666) & 1/wf Amy _____; m by 1625 Mistley, Essex [TAG 76:246]

CHENEY, John¹ (c1600-1666) & 2/wf Martha SMITHE (-1666+); m Lawford, Essex 3 Mar 1630/1 Newbury [TAG 76:246; GM 2:61]

CHENEY, John² (bp 1628-) & Mary² PLUMMER (c1640-); m2 David BENNETT; m Newbury 20 Apr or 29 May 1660 [TAG 76:247; GMB 3:1485; GM 2:62]

CHENEY, Joseph (1647-1704) & 2/wf Mehitable (PLIMPTON) HINSDILL (-1704+); m1 Ephraim HINSDALE; m3 1717 Jonathan ADAMS; m Medfield 21 July 1691 [AEBK 1:234]

CHENEY, Joseph² (1647-1704) & 1/wf Hannah THURSTON (1650-1690); m Medfield 12 Mar 1667/8 [AEBK] see Chaney

CHENEY, Peter, Jr. & Mary ( ) HOLMES; m1 Samuel¹ HOLMES [ASBO, p.341]

CHENEY, Peter² (c1638-) & Hannah² NOYES; m Newbury 14 May 1663 [TG 76:247; GM 2:62]

CHENEY, Thomas² (c1630-1693-5) & Jane ATKINSON (-1724); m Roxbury 11 Jan 1655/6 [AEBK 1:231]

CHENEY, William (c1604-1667) & Margaret _____ (c1603-1686); m England bef 1623 Boston [AEBK 1:225]

CHENEY, William (c1635-hanged 1681) & Deborah WISWALL; m2 Ebenezer WILLIAMS; m bef 1661 Roxbury/Dorchester/Medfield [AEBK 1:232]

CHESHOLM, Thomas¹ (c1604-1671) & Isabel _____; m c1658 Cambridge [GM 2:66]

CHESLEY, Philip & Sarah² RAWLINS (c1658-); m c1678 [GMB 3:1553]

CHESTER, John & Sarah WELLES; by 1654 Wethersfield [GMB 1:347]

CHESTER, John (-1628) & Dorothy HOOKER (c1589-by 1662), dau of Thomas; m Birkstall, Leicestershire 1 June 1609 [GM 2:67]

CHESTER, Leonard (c1610-1648) & Mary _____; m2 Richard RUSSELL; by 1634 Wethersfield [GMB 1:345-49; GM 2:67]

CHICK, Thomas (bp 17 Dec 1641-1683+) & Elizabeth³ SPENCER (c1640-1687+); m2 Nicholas TURBET; m by 1674 Berwick [CG, 22]

CHILD, Ephraim[1] (c1593-1663) & Elizabeth (BOND) PALMER; m1 Samuel PALMER; m 1624/5 Nayland, Suffolk/Watertown [TAG 62:29]

CHILD, John & Hannah[2] FRENCH (1676[/7?]-); m Watertown 5 Oct 1693 [GM 2:592]

CHILD, John (-1676) & Mary[3] WARREN (1651-1734); m2 Nathaniel FISKE; m Watertown 29 May 1668 [AEBK 1:478]

CHILD, Richard & Mary[2] TRUANT; m Marshfield 24 Jan 1664[/5] [GMB 3:1840]

CHILD, Richard & Mehitable[2] DIMMOCK (bp 1642-); m Watertown 17 Apr 1662 [GM 2:349]

CHILD, Shubael (1665-) & Abigail SANDERSON (-1693); m 27 Oct 1687 Watertown [REG 127:182]

CHILDS, Joseph & Elizabeth TROUANT; m bef 11 Apr 1696 Marshfield [TAG 40:33]

CHILDS, Joseph ~ Marshfield [Plymouth Court Sept 1691]

CHIPMAN, John & Hope[2] HOWLAND (1629-); m c1646 [GMB 2:1022]

CHITTENDEN, Henry[2] (c1629-) & _____ _____; m c1656 Scituate [GM 2:72]

CHITTENDEN, Isaac[2] (c1625-) & Martha VINALL; m Scituate Apr 1646 [GM 2:72]

CHITTENDEN, Israel & Deborah[2] BAKER (bp 1652-); m Scituate 25 Apr 1678 [GM 1:144]

CHITTENDEN, Thomas (c1584-1668) & Rebecca BAMFORT (c1595-); Wouldham, Kent 8 Aug 1621 Scituate [GM 2:72]

CHRISTOPHERS, Christopher & 2/wf Elizabeth (BREWSTER) BRADLEY (1637-); m by June 1677 New London [TAG 68:182]

CHUBB, Thomas (c1609-1688) & Avis _____; by 1637 Beverly [GMB 1:356]

CHUBB, William & _____ _____; by 1684 Beverly [GMB 1:357]

CHUBBOCK, John[2] (1648-) & Martha BEALE; m Hingham 2 Dec 1668 [GM 2:75]

CHUBBOCK, Nathaniel[2] (bp 1635-) & Mary (_____) GARNET; m1 John GARNET; m Hingham 18 June 1669 [GM 2:75]

CHUBBOCK, Thomas[1] (c1606-1676) & Alice[2] HOBART (bp 1606[/7]-1674/5), dau of Edmund; m Hardingham, Norfolk 28 Feb 1631[/2?] [GM 2:75; GMB 2:959]

CHURCH, Benjamin & Alice[2] SOUTHWORTH; m 26 Dec 1667 [GMB 3:1711]

CHURCH, Caleb & Joanna[2] SPRAGUE (bp 1645-); m Hingham 16 Dec 1667 [GMB 3:1737]

CHURCH, Caleb (c1646-bef 1722) & 3/wf Rebecca (_____) SCOTTOW; m1 John SCOTTOW; m 6 Nov 1691 Watertown [TAG 60:135]

CHURCH, David (1657-) & Mary _____; by 1687 Watertown [GMB 1:359]

CHURCH, Garrett (c1611-1685+) & Sarah _____; by 1637 Watertown [GMB 1:358-60]

CHURCH, Nathaniel & Sarah[2] BARSTOW (bp 1645-); m 1666 [GM 1:178]

CHURCH, Richard & Elizabeth[2] WARREN; m c1635/6 [GMB 3:1936]

CHURCHILL, John & Hannah[2] PONTUS (c1624-); m2 Giles RICKARD; m Plymouth 18 Dec 1644 [GMB 3:1492; TAG 71:115]

CHURCHILL, John (-1723) & 1/wf Rebecca DELANO (-1709); m 28 Dec 1686 Plymouth [TAG 60:139; MD 13:204]

CHURCHILL, Josiah & Elizabeth FOOTE (bp 1617/8-); m by 1639 Wethersfield [GM 2:542]

CLAPP, Edward[1] (c1609-1664/5) & 1/wf Prudence[1] CLAPP (c1606-bef 1655), dau of Nicholas; m c1634 Dorchester [AEBK 4:128; GM 2:78]

CLAPP, Edward[1] (c1609-1664/5) & 2/wf Susanna COCKERILL (-1688), dau of William; m c1646 Dorchester [GM 2:78, 122]

CLAPP, Ezra[2] (1640-) & 1/wf Abigail _____; m by 1667 Milton [GM 2:78]

CLAPP, Ezra[2] (1640-) & 2/wf Experience HOUGHTON; m Dorchester 22 May 1684 [GM 2:78]

CLAPP, Increase (c1647-1716) & Elizabeth (BURSLEY) GOODSPEED (bp 1649-1706/7); m Barnstable Oct 1675 [AEBK 4:138]

CLAPP, John[1] (c1616-1655) & Joan _____ (c1624-1703/4); m c1644 Medfield [AEBK 4:131]

CLAPP, Joshua[3] (c1667-1728) & 1/wf Mary BOYDEN (-by 1718); m Dedham 22 Dec 1696/7 [AEBK 4:144]

CLAPP, Nehemiah[2] (bp 1646-) & Sarah LEAVITT; m Hingham 17 Apr 1678 Dorchester [GM 2:78; AEBK 3]

CLAPP, Nicholas[1] (1612-1679) & 1/wf Sarah CLAPP (bp 1611-by 1667); m say 1636 Dorchester [AEBK 4:130]

CLAPP, Nicholas[1] (1612-1679) & 2/wf Abigail _____; m by 1667 Dorchester [AEBK 4:130]

CLAPP, Nicholas[1] (1612-1679) & 3/wf Anna (_____) ANNIBALL [AEBK 4:130]

CLAPP, Samuel[2] (c1641-1722-33) & Hannah GILL (bp 1645-1722); m Scituate 14 June 1666 [AEBK 4:137]

CLAPP, Thomas[1] (c1608-1684) & 1/wf Jane _____ (c1617-1656/7); m c1637 Scituate [AEBK 4:132]

CLAPP, Thomas[1] (c1608-1684) & 2/wf Abigail (WRIGHT) SHARP (c1623-1702-8); m c1655-7 Rehoboth [AEBK 4:132]

CLAPP, Thomas[2] (1638/9-1688) & Mary FISHER (1643/4-1704+); m Dedham 10 Nov 1662 [AEBK 4:140]

CLAPP, Thomas[3] (1663-1703/4) & Mary _____ (c1666-1722+); m2 Benjamin CHENNERY; m c1686 Dedham [AEBK 4:144]

CLARGETT, William & Mary NEGGRES; m Boston 25 May 1687 [Boston VR 1:vii]

CLARK, Andrew (c1644-) & Mehitable SCOTTO; by 1672 Boston [GMB 1:378]

CLARK, Christopher & Rebecca[2] EYRE (c1626-); m by 1647 Boston/Watertown [TAG 65:21; GM 2:487]

CLARK, Isaac (c1666-1768) & Sarah[4] STOW (1673[/4]-1761); m c1691 [AEBK 3]

CLARK, James & Elinor/Elizabeth[2] WRIGHT; m c1644 [GMB 3:2073]

CLARK, John & Rebecca[2] COOPER (1657-); m 12 July 1677 [GM 2:211]

CLARK, John (-1726/7) & Sarah² SMITH (1660-c1731); m bef 1683 Beverly [TAG 43:23]

CLARK, John (c1640-   ) & Sarah _____; by 1668 Boston [GMB 1:377]

CLARK, John² (c1642-   ) & Mary BURNHAM, dau of Thomas; m Ipswich 9 Oct 1672 [GM 2:8]

CLARK, Jonathan² (c1649-   ) & Lydia TITCOMB; m Newbury 15 May 1683 [GM 2:88]

CLARK, Joseph¹ (c1611-1641) & _____ _____ (-1639); m c1636 Windsor [GM 2:84]

CLARK, Josiah² & Sarah (_____) SAMPSON; m1 Richard SAMPSON; m by 1677 [GM 2:88]

CLARK, Josiah² ~ Sarah WARR; c1671 [GM 2:88]

CLARK, Latham & Ann NEWBERRY; m 1698 Portsmouth/ Newport [TAG 67:21]

CLARK, Nathaniel² & Elizabeth SOMERBY, dau of Henry; m Newbury 23 Nov 1663 [GM 2:88]

CLARK, Nicholas (c1613-1680) & _____ _____; by 1640 Hartford [GMB 1:373-75]

CLARK, Samuel (bp 1659-1705) & Hannah (PAINE)(ELIOT) FAYERWEATHER; m Boston 23 June 1698 [REG 146:380]

CLARK, Samuel² (c1645-   ) & Anne LEADER, dau of Richard; m c1668 [GM 2:88]

CLARK, Susannah ~ Plymouth [Plymouth Court Sept 1688]

CLARK, Thomas & Abigail² COGSWELL; m c1666 Ipswich [GM 2:139]

CLARK, Thomas (c1599-1696/7) & 1/wf Susanna² RING; by July 1631 Plymouth [GMB 1:375-80, 3:1587]

CLARK, Thomas (c1599-1696/7) & 2/wf Alice (HALLETT) NICHOLS (-by 1671); after 20 Jan 1664/5 Plymouth [GMB 1:375-80]

CLARK, Thomas¹ (c1613-1689/90) & Sarah _____; m c1638 Ipswich [GM 2:88]

CLARK, Thomas² & Rebecca _____; m c1667 [GM 2:88]

CLARK, Thurston¹ (c1590-1661) & Faith _____ (-by 1663); m c1617 [GM 2:100]

CLARK, Timothy (1657-1737) & Sarah RICHARDSON (1657-1726); m c1678 Boston/Bristol [Sewall's Diary, 3:373-374]

CLARK, William & Hannah GRISWOLD (1658-1687/8); m Plymouth 7 Mar 1677/8 [REG 155:249]

CLARK, William & Martha² NASH (c1630-   ); m c1650 Duxbury [GMB 2:1323]

CLARK, William (-1682) & Margaret (_____) THOMPSON; m1 John THOMPSON; m c1639-1640 Watertown [RCA]

CLARKE, George¹ (c1615-1690) & Sarah _____ Milford [TAG 74:73]

CLARKE, John & Rebecca² BEAMON (1659-   ); m Saybrook 17 Dec 1684 [GM 1:222]

CLARKE, William & Martha² FARR; m Boston 18 Sept 1661 [GMB 3:2079]

CLARKE, William (c1608-1682/3) & Mary SHERMAN (-1693); m c1640 Lynn [TAG 39:101]

CLEAVES, William & Martha EDWARDS (not dau. of Giles Corey); by 1683 Wenham/Beverly [155:226]

CLEEVE, George[1] & 2/w² Alice SHORTOLL/STANSTALL?; m 22 Sept 1614 St Peter's Cornhill, London [REG 140:181]

CLEEVE, George[1] & 3/wf Frances OLNEY (-bef 1618); m c1615 London [REG 140:181]

CLEEVE, George[1] & 4/wf Joan PRICE; m 7 Sept 1618 Shrewsbury/Portland [REG 140:181]

CLEEVE, George[1] (c1586-1666+) & 1/wf Alice (____) ABROOK (c1581-by 1618); m London 17 Oct 1612 Portland [GMB 1:385; REG 140:180]

CLEMENCE, Richard[2] (c1659-1723) & Sarah SMITH (-1725); m by 1688 Providence [REG 155:138-42]

CLEMENCE, Thomas[1] (by 1625-by 1688) & Elizabeth ____ (c1630-by 1725); m by 1650s Providence [REG 155:133]

CLEMENT, Augustine[1] (c1603-1674) & Elizabeth perhaps BULLOCK; m Wokingham, Berkshire 3 July 1628 Dorchester [GM 2:104]

CLEMENT, James & Martha[2] DEANE; m2 Ralph POWELL; m Marshfield 28 Dec 1674 [GM 2:336]

CLEMENT, Robert & Elizabeth[2] FAWNE (bp 1633-1665/6+); m Haverhill 8 Dec 1652 St Olave Old Jewry, London [GM 2:506; TAG 77:31]

CLEMENT, Samuel[2] (1635-) & 1/wf Hannah INGS, dau of Maudit; m Boston 2 July 1657 [GM 2:104]

CLEMENT, Samuel[2] (1635-) & 2/wf Deborah ____; m by 1669 Boston [GM 2:104]

CLIFTON, Savery (c1665-1753+) & Dorothy BURGES (1670-1725-7); m by 1690 Rochester [NGSQ 59:158]

CLINTON, Lawrence & Rachel[2] HAFFIELD (c1629-); m by 1666 div 1681/2 [GM 3:186]

CLOUGH, John[1] (c1614-1691) & 1/wf Jane ____ (-1679/80); m c1642 Salisbury [GM 2:113]

CLOUGH, John[1] (c1614-1691) & 2/wf Martha (BLAISDELL)(BOWDEN) CILLEY, dau of Ralph; m1 Richard BOWDEN; m2 Thomas? CILLEY; m Dover 15 Jan 1686[/7?] [GM 2:113]

CLOUGH, John[2] (1648/9-) & Mercy PAGE; m Salisbury 13 Nov 1674 [GM 2:113]

CLOUGH, Samuel[2] (1656/7-) & Elizabeth BROWN; m Salisbury 3 Aug 1679 [GM 2:113]

CLOUGH, Thomas[2] (1651-) & 1/wf Hannah GUILE; m 10 Mar 1679/80 [GM 2:113]

CLOUGH, Thomas[2] (1651-) & 2/wf Ruth CONNOR; m Salisbury 1688 or 89 [GM 2:113]

COBB, Edward & Mary[2] HOSKINS (c1640-); m2 Samuel PHILLIPS; m3 Richard GODFREY; m Plymouth 28 Nov 1660 [GM 3:417]

COBB, Henry (c1607-1679) & 1/wf Patience[2] HURST (c1612-1648); m by 1632 Barnstable [GMB 1:394, 2:1047]

COBB, Henry[1] & Sarah[2] HINCKLEY (bp 1629-); m Barnstable 12 Dec 1649 [GM 3:334]

COBB, John & Susannah BRIGGS; m bef 1696 Providence [NGSQ 73:25]

COBBETT, Joshua[2] (164[7/]8-) & Elizabeth _____; m by 1686 Boston [GM 2:118]

COBBETT, Josiah[1] (c1614-1691/2+) & Mary[2] HAFFIELD (c1618-), dau of Richard; m by 1640 Boston [GM 2:117, 3:185]

COBBETT, Josiah[2] (1642-) & Deborah _____; m c1672 Boston [GM 2:117]

COCHRAN, Peter (c1626-1722) & Christian WALLACE; m c1650s Londonderry, Ireland [AEJA]

COCHRAN, William (c1660s-1738) & 1/wf Agnes COCHRAN; m by 1689 Londonderry, NH [AEJA]

COCKE, Joseph & Susanna[2] UPSALL (1639/40-); m Boston 10 Nov 1659 [GMB 1:429, 3:1868]

COCKERILL, William[1] (c1601-by 1661) & Elizabeth _____ (-by 1664); m c1626 [GM 2:122]

COCKERUM, William[1] (c1609-1657[/8]-60) & Christian IBROOKE (c1611-1657[/8]+); m c1633 [GM 2:124]

CODDINGTON, Nathaniel & Susanna HUTCHINSON (bp 1649-1716+); m Newport 19 Apr 1677 [REG 145:263]

CODDINGTON, Thomas & 1/wf Priscilla[2] JEFFREYS (c1652-); m c1682 [GMB 2:1084]

CODDINGTON, William (c1601-1678) & 1/wf Mary _____; by 1626 Boston [GMB 1:397]

CODDINGTON, William (c1601-1678) & 2/wf Mary MOSELEY; 2 Sep 1631 Terling, Essex [GMB 1:397]

CODDINGTON, William (c1601-1678) & 3/wf Ann BRINLEY (c1628-1708); by 1650 Newport [GMB 1:397]

COE, Benjamin[2] (bp 1628-) & Abigail CARMAN, dau of John; m c1660 Roxbury [GM 2:130]

COE, John & Hannah (BARRETT) JENNER; m1 _____ JENNER; m by 1666 [LMM; TAG forthcoming]

COE, John[2] (bp 1625-) & _____ _____; m c1657 [GM 2:130]

COE, Robert[1] (bp 1596-1687-90) & 1/wf Mary _____ (-1628); m by 1625 Thorpe-Morieux, Suffolk [GM 2:130]

COE, Robert[1] (bp 1596-1687-90) & 2/wf Hannah DEARSLAY; m Assington, co. Suffolk 29 Apr 1630 [GM 2:130]

COE, Robert[1] (bp 1596-1687-90) & 3/wf Jane (_____)(SMITH) ROUSE; m1 Bartholomew SMITH; m2 Edward ROUSE; m aft 15 Feb 1674 [GM 2:130]

COE, Robert[2] (bp 1626-) & Hannah MITCHELL, dau of Matthew; m by 1651 Stratford [GM 2:130]

COFFIN, Peter[3] & Apphia DOLE (1668-); m c1688 [TAG 74:57]

COGGAN, Henry[1] (bp 1607-1649) & Abigail BISHOP (-1653); m2 John PHINNEY; m Bridport, Dorsetshire 14 Mar 1636/7 [GM 2:134]

COGGAN, John (1590/1-1658) & 1/wf Mary JORDAIN (bp 1595-); 26 Jan 1619/20 St Mary Arches, Exeter, Devon [GMB 1:403]

COGGAN, John (1590/1-1658) & 2/wf Anne _____; by 1634 Boston [GMB 1:403]

COGGAN, John (1590/1-1658) & 3/wf Mary _____; by 1652 Boston [GMB 1:403]

COGGAN, John (1590/1-1658) & 4/wf Martha (RAINSBOROUGH) (COYTMORE) WINTHROP (-1660); 10 Mar 1651/2 Boston [GMB 1:403]

COGGAN, John (bp 1642/3-) & Mary LONG; m Charlestown 22 Dec 1664 [GM 2:135]

COGGESHALL, John & Mary (HEDGES) STURGES; m Yarmouth 1 Oct 1679 [GMB 2:906]

COGGESHALL, John (bp 1601-1647) & Mary _____ (-1684); by 1624 Halstead, Essex; Newport [GMB 1:406]

COGSWELL, Adam³ (1666/7-1749) & Abigail WISE (1666-); m c1687 Ipswich [TAG 56:82; 60:159]

COGSWELL, John¹ (bp 1592-1669) & Elizabeth THOMPSON, dau of William; m Westbury Leigh, Wiltshire 10 Sept 1615 Ipswich [GM 2:138]

COGSWELL, John² (bp 1622-) & _____ _____; m c1647 [GM 2:139]

COGSWELL, William² (bp 1619/20-1700) & Susanna² HAWKES (c1633-), dau of Adam; m c1654 Charlestown/Ipswich [GM 2:138, 3:255]

COKER, Benjamin (1650-) & Martha PERLEY; m Newbury 31 May 1678 [GM 2:143]

COKER, Joseph (1640-) & 1/wf Sarah² HATHORNE (1634/5-), dau of William; m1 and div Edward HELWISE; m Newbury 13 Apr 1665 [GM 2:143; GMB 2:885]

COKER, Joseph (1640-) & 2/wf Mary (JONES) WOODBRIDGE, dau of Ann; m1 Thomas WOODBRIDGE; m bet 8 Feb 1687/8 and 16 Dec 1697 [GM 2:143]

COKER, Robert² (c1606-1680) & Catherine _____ (-1678); m Newbury 19 Nov 1680 [GM 2:143]

COLBORN, Nathaniel & Mary² BROOKS (bp 1649-); m Dedham 19 Nov 1669 [GM 1:410]

COLBRON, William (c1593-1662) & Margery _____ (-1663/4+); by 1621 Boston [GMB 1:412]

COLBURN, Daniel² & Sarah BLOOD; m Chelmsford 18 June 1685 [GM 2:148]

COLBURN, Edward¹ (c1618-1700[/1]) & Hannah _____; m c1645 Chelmsford [GM 2:147]

COLBURN, Ezra² (1658[/9?]-) & Hannah VARNUM; m Chelmsford 22 Nov 1681 [GM 2:148]

COLBURN, John² & Susannah READ; m Chelmsford 10 or 18 Mar 1671[/2] [GM 2:148]

COLBURN, Joseph² (1661-) & 1/wf Hannah _____; m by 1684 Chelmsford [GM 2:148]

COLBURN, Robert¹ (c1507-1685) & Alice _____; Ipswich [GM 2:151]

COLBURN, Robert² (c1547-) & Mary BISHOP, dau of Edward; m c1670 Chelmsford [GM 2:148]

COLBURN, Samuel & Marcy PARTRIDGE; m Dedham 12 Mar 1682/3 [AEBK 4:264]

COLBURN, Thomas[2] & 1/wf Hannah ROUF; m Chelmsford 6 Aug 1672 [GM 2:148]

COLBURN, Thomas[2] & 2/wf Mary RICHARDSON; m Chelmsford 17 Nov 1681 [GM 2:148]

COLBY, Anthony (bp 8 Sept 1605-1660/1) & Susannah (____) WATERMAN (c1608-1689); m1 ____ WATERMAN, m3 William WHITRIDGE; m bef 1633 Horbling, Lincolnshire/Cambridge/Salisbury/Boston [50 GMC; GMB 1:415]

COLBY, James & ____ ____; m bef 1679 Rehoboth [PCR 6:8, 13]

COLBY, Samuel & Elizabeth[2] SARGENT (1648-); m by 1668 [GMB 3:1632]

COLCORD, Edward[1] (c1615-1681/2) & Anne WARD (c1622-1688/9); m c1640 Hampton [REG 141:120]

COLDHAM, Thomas (c1602-1675) & 1/wf ____ ____ (-by 1646); by 1625 [GMB 1:418]

COLDHAM, Thomas (c1602-1675) & 2/wf Joanna ____ (-1687); by 1646 Lynn [GMB 1:418, REG 125:24]

COLE, Abraham[2] (1636-) & Mary WEDGWOOD, dau of John; m Hampton 15 Mar 1666[/7] [GM 2:156]

COLE, Daniel[2] & Mercy FULLER [TAG 75:129]

COLE, Daniel[2] (c1667-1736) & Mercy FREEMAN (c1673-1735) [TAG 75:128]

COLE, Hugh & Mary[2] FOXWELL (1635-); m Plymouth 8 Jan 1654[/5] [GM 2:567]

COLE, Isaac[1] (c1607-1674) & 1/wf Joan JONES; m St. Peter, Sandwich, Kent 25 July 1631 [GM 2:155]

COLE, Isaac[1] (c1607-1674) & 2/wf Jane (____) (EGGLETON) BRITTON (-1687); m 2 James BRITTON; m Woburn 1 Feb 1659[/60?] [GM 2:155]

COLE, Jacob[2] (1641-) & Sarah TRAIN, dau of John; m Charlestown 12 Oct 1669 [GM 2:156]

COLE, James & Ann ?WALLINGTON (-1679/80); m 6 Dec 1625 St Dunstan's Stepney/Hartford [TAG 40:74]

COLE, James (-1652) & 2/wf Damaris SEABROOK (-1625); m St Botolph without Aldgate, London 9 Nov 1623 Hartford [DR]

COLE, James (-1652) & 3/wf Anne (____) EDWARDS (not Wallington)(d/o of Mrs. Julian Munter by a prior marriage -1680); m1 Richard EDWARDS; m St Dunstan, Stepney 6 Dec 1625 Hartford [DR]

COLE, James (-1652) (kinsman of Henry Cole of Hartford) & 1/wf Frances ____ (not Munter) (-1623); m England bef 1617 near St. Mary Whitechapel/Hartford [DR]

COLE, James (c1600-1678) & Mary TIBBES; 1 May 1625 Barnstaple, Devonshire, Plymouth [GMB 1:422]

COLE, James (c1625-) & Ruth ____; m2 Henry MUDD; by 28 Aug 1655 [GMB 1:429]

COLE, James[2] & 1/wf Mary TILSON (-1678+); m Plymouth 23 Dec 1652 [TAG 67:244]

COLE, James[2] & 2/wf Esther ____; m by Sept 1698 Plymouth [TAG 67:244]

COLE, James[3] (1655-) & Mary[2] CADMAN?; m bef 1696 Swanzey [TAG 64:140]

COLE, John & Rachel[2] HART (c1642-); m by 1664 [GMB 2:872]

COLE, John & Ruth[2] SNOW (c1644-); m Eastham 10 Dec 1666 [GMB 3:1704]

COLE, John & Susanna[2] HUTCHINSON (bp 1633-); m Boston 30 Dec 1651 [GM 3:481]

COLE, John (c1623-) & Ursula _____; not Susanna Upshur; by 1655 [GMB 1:429]

COLE, John ~ Susanna _____; Plymouth [Plymouth Court June 1688]

COLE, Nathaniel & Martha JACKSON; m Warwick 30 Aug 1667 Hempstead [NYGBR 131:9]

COLE, Nathaniel & Sarah[2] BONNEY; m by 1680 Duxbury [GM 1:341]

COLE, Rice (c1590-1646) & Arrald DUNNINGTON (-1661); by c1616 Charlestown [LMM; GMB 1:421, 429]

COLE, Robert (c1616-) & Philip _____; m2 William MORRIS; by 1649 Charlestown [GMB 1:429]

COLE, Samuel (c1597-1666) & 1/wf Ann _____ (-by 1647); by 1622 [GMB 1:433]

COLE, Samuel (c1597-1666) & 2/wf Margaret (_____) GREENE; by 30 Sept 1647 [GMB 1:433]

COLE, Samuel (c1597-1666) & 3/wf Ann (MANSFIELD) KEAYNE; m1 Robert KEAYNE; m Boston 16 Oct 1660 [GMB 1:433; REG 155:24-29]

COLE, William[1] (-1640-4) & Elizabeth DOUGHTY (bp 1606/7-1652+); m 1620+ All Saints, Bristol, Gloucestershire/Boston [TAG 77:16]

COLEFAX, Jonathan (1658/9-1711) & Sarah[3] EDWARDS (1671-1725); m2 Robert WEBSTER; m Wethersfield 28 May 1696 [REG 145:337; TAG 71:240]

COLEMAN, Edward & Margaret[2] LOMBARD (bp 1623-); m Nauset 27 Oct 1648 [GMB 2:1197]

COLEMAN, John[2] & Joanna FOLGER; m by 1667 Nantucket [GM 2:161]

COLEMAN, Joseph[2] (1642-) & Ann BUNKER, dau of George; m c1675 Nantucket [GM 2:161]

COLEMAN, Thomas & Frances[1] (ALBRIGHT) WELLES (c1600-1678); m1 Thomas Welles; m bef 6 Mar 1638 England/Wethersfield, CT/Hadley, MA [REG 146:32]

COLEMAN, Thomas & Margaret MUSHIT; m 10 Dec 1679 Marshfield [TAG 60:159]

COLEMAN, Thomas[1] (c1602-1682) & 1/wf Susan RAWLINES (-1650); m Wootton Rivers, Wiltshire 24 Nov 1623 [GM 2:160]

COLEMAN, Thomas[1] (c1602-1682) & 2/wf Mary (_____) JOHNSON (-1662/3); m1 Edmund JOHNSON; m 16 July 1651 Hampton [GM 2:160]

COLEMAN, Thomas[1] (c1602-1682) & 3/wf Margery (FOWLER) (OSGOOD) ROWELL, dau of Philip; m1 Christopher OSGOOD; m2 Thomas ROWELL; m4 Thomas OSBORNE [GM 2:160]

COLEMAN, Tobias[2] & Lydia JACKSON; m Rowley 16 Apr 1668 [GM 2:160]

COLEPOT, _____ & Sarah PIERCE (-1702-); m2 William HARRIS; by Aug 1662 Boston [REG 11:174; SD 16:119-20; Harris]

COLES, Daniel (c1637-) & Mahershallalhashbaz GORTON; by 1662 [GMB 1:438]

COLES, John (c1630-) & Ann _____; by 1683 Oyster Bay [GMB 1:438]

COLES, Robert (c1605-1655) & 1/wf Mary _____ (c1637); by 1630 [GMB 1:437]

COLES, Robert (c1605-1655) & 2/wf Mary HAWKSHURST; m2 Mathias HARVEY; by c1637 Pawtuxet/Warwick [GMB 1:437]

COLLER, James (c1671-1749) & 1/wf Elizabeth _____; by 1695/6 Oxford [AEBK 1:255]

COLLER, John & Hannah² CUTLER (1638-); m c1659 Watertown [GM 2:270]

COLLER, John (1661-1718+) & Elizabeth ROSS (c1672-1718); m aft 1692 Cambridge/Natick [AEBK 1:254]

COLLER, John¹ (c1633-1702+) & 1/wf Hannah _____ (c1638-); m by 1658 Cambridge [AEBK 1:249]

COLLER, John¹ (c1633-1702+) & 2/wf Mary² CUTLER (1643-); m bef 1684 Cambridge [AEBK 1:249]

COLLER, Nathaniel (c1667-by 1714) & Mary BARRETT; m Chelmsford 10 Oct 1693 [AEBK 1:255]

COLLICOTT, Richard (c1604-1686) & 1/wf Joanna THORNE; Barnstaple, Devon 25 Sep 1627 [GMB 1:443]

COLLICOTT, Richard (c1604-1686) & 2/wf Thomasine _____ (c1618-1692); by 1641 Boston [GMB 1:443]

COLLICUT, Preserved (bp 1648/9-) & Deborah DOWSE; by 1671 Dorchester/Boston [GMB 1:443]

COLLIER, Moses² & 1/wf Elizabeth JONES; m Hingham 29 Mar or 25 Nov 1655 [GM 2:164]

COLLIER, Moses² & 2/wf Elizabeth BULLARD; m Hingham 17 Dec 1657 [GM 2:164]

COLLIER, Thomas¹ (c1597-1647) & Susan _____ (-1667); m c1622 Hingham [GM 2:163]

COLLIER, Thomas² & Jane CURTIS; m Hingham 30 Dec 1647 [GM 2:163]

COLLIER, William (c1585-1670+) & Jane CLARK (perhaps a widow) (-1653+); m St Olave Southwark, Surrey 16 May 1611, Duxbury [GMB 1:448, TAG 42:119-121, 215-216; 51:58, 92-93]

COLLINS, Benjamin² & 1/wf Priscilla KIRTLAND; m Lynn 25 Sept 1673 [GM 2:168]

COLLINS, Benjamin² & 2/wf Elizabeth (_____) PUTNAM; m Lynn 5 Sept 1677 [GM 2:168]

COLLINS, Francis & Elizabeth² COCKERILL [GM 2:122]

COLLINS, Henry¹ (c1606-1686/7) & Ann _____ (-1691); m c1630 Lynn [GM 2:167]

COLLINS, Henry² (1630-) & Mary TOLMAN, dau of Thomas; m by 1651 Lynn [GM 2:167]

COLLINS, John² & Mehitable GILES (bp 1637-); m2 Jeremiah BUTMAN; m Salem 9 Mar 1658/9 [TAG 72:300]

COLLINS, John[2] (1631/2-) & Abigail JOHNSON, dau of Richard; m c1656 Lynn [GM 2:167]

COLLINS, Joseph[2] (c1643-) & 1/wf Sarah SILSBEE; m c1669 Lynn [GM 2:168]

COLLINS, Joseph[2] (c1643-) & 2/wf Mariah SMITH; m Lynn 15 Oct 1684 [GM 2:168]

COLLINS, Robert & Esther (_____) ROLF [GM 2:563]

COLLINS, William & Anne[2] HUTCHINSON (bp 1626-); m by 1641 [GM 3:481]

COLSTON, Nathaniel (-1684) & 2/wf Margaret _____ (-1684+); aft. 8 June 1678 Newport/Boston/Jamaica [Harris]

COLT, Abraham (1666-1734+) & Hannah[3] LOOMIS (1661/2-); m Windsor 1 Jan 1690 [REG 145:330]

COLT, Benjamin (1669-1739) & 1/wf _____ _____ (-1701+); c1700 Windsor/Hartford [REG 145:331; Harris]

COLT, John (c1630s -1703) & 2/wf Hester[2] EDWARDS (1641-c1679/80); m 1665 Windsor [REG 145:318]

COLT, John[1] & Mary SKINNER; m by 1661 [TAG 74:98]

COLTMAN, John[1] (bp 1613-1688-) & Mary _____ perhaps Taylor; m2 Theophilus3 SHERMAN; m "about" 24 Sept 1667 Wethersfield [TAG 77:256]

COLTON, Isaac & Mary[2] COOPER (1651-); m2 Edward STEBBINS; m Springfield 30 June 1670 [GM 2:210]

COLTON, John (1659-1726/7) & Abigail PARSONS (1666-1689); m Springfield 19 Feb 1684/5 [REG 148:221]

COLWELL, Robert & Margaret WHITE; div Providence [TAG 73:100]

COMER/COMAN, Richard & Martha GILBERT; m 23 Oct 1663 Salem [DCD]

COMER/COMAN, Richard[2] (-1716) & 1/wf Martha REWE; m 25 Oct 1683 Salem [DCD]

COMER/COMAN, Richard[2] (-1716) & 2/wf Elizabeth (DYNN) CALLUM; m1 Caleb CALLUM; m 4 Feb 1692/3 Salem/Providence [DCD]

COMINS, Richard (-c1675) & Susannah BOYNTON; Saco [REG 153:54]

COMINS, Richard (c1602-1679) & Jane PETER; Sheviock, Cornwall 1632 Portsmouth [REG 153:53]

COMPTON, John[1] (c1607-1651/2-64) & Susannah _____ (-by 1664); m c 1632 Roxbury [GM 2:171]

COMSTOCK, John (-by 1680) & Abigail[2] CHAPPELL (1644-1713/4+); m2 Moses HUNTLEY; m by Apr 1662 Lyme [REG 150:56; GM 2:57]

CONANT, Christopher (bp 1588-1630+) & 1/wf Sicily CROXON; St Ann Blackfriars, London 13 Aug 1617 [GMB 1:450-51]

CONANT, Christopher (bp 1588-1630+) & 2/wf Anne (_____) WILTON; Shobrooke, Devon 14 Sep 1619 [GMB 1:450-51]

CONANT, Exercise (bp 1637-) & Sarah _____; by 1668/9 Beverly [GMB 1:455]

CONANT, Joshua & 1/wf Christian[2] MORE (bp 1652-); m Salem 31 Aug 1676 [GMB 2:1286]

CONANT, Joshua & Seeth GARDNER (bp 1636-); m2 John/Joseph Grafton; by 1657 Salem [GMB 1:454, 2:734]

CONANT, Lot (c1624-) & Elizabeth WALTON (bp 1629-); m2 Andrew MANSFIELD [GMB 1:454]

CONANT, Roger & Elizabeth[2] WESTON; m bef 22 Jan 1661[/2] [GMB 3:1968]

CONANT, Roger[1] (bp 1592-1679) & Sarah HORTON (-by 1677/8); St Ann Blackfriars, London 11 Nov 1618 Salem/Manchester [GMB 1:454, REG 148:107-29]

CONANT, Roger[2] & Elizabeth _____; by 1661/2 Salem [GMB 1:454]

CONCKLYNE, Joseph[3] (c1670-1716) & Mary EDWARDS (1674-1752); m by 1697 Southold, L.I. [TAG 71:240]

CONGDON, Benjamin & Elizabeth[2] ALBRO; m c1670 [GM 1:19]

CONKLIN, Ananias & Mary LAUNDER; m St Peters, Nottingham, Nottinghamshire 23 Feb 1630/1 [TAG 71:195]

CONKLIN, Jeremiah & Mary[2] GARDINER (1638-); m c1658 Saybrook [GM 3:10]

CONKLIN, Joseph[3] (c1670-1716) & Mary EDWARDS (1674-1752); m by 1697 Southold, L.I. [REG 145:338]

CONVERSE, Allen (bp 1616-1679) & Elizabeth _____ (-1691); m by 1641 [REG 153:96]

CONVERSE, Edward (bp 1588/9-1663) & 2/wf Sarah _____; m by 14 Oct 1632 Charlestown [REG 153:93]

CONVERSE, Edward (bp 1588/9-1663) & 3/wf Joan (WARREN) SPRAGUE (-1680/1); m1 Ralph SPRAGUE; m Woburn 9 Sept 1662 [REG 153:93 GMB 1:462]

CONVERSE, Edward[1] (bp 1588/9-1663) & 1/wf Sarah PARKER (c1596-1625); m Great Burstead, Essex 29 June 1614 Woburn [REG 153:92, 146:130; GMB 1:462]

CONVERSE, James (bp 1620-1715) & Anne LONG (bp 1623-1691); m Woburn 24 Oct 1643 [REG 153:94]

CONVERSE, Josiah (bp 1618-1690/1) & Esther[2] CHAMPNEY (bp 1630-1713); m2 Jonathan DANFORTH; m Woburn 26 Mar 1651 Stisted, Essex [GM 2:244; REG 153:94]

COOK, George[2] (c1647-1711+) & Ann _____ (-1689+); m bef 1683 Long Island [Fiske 1:40]

COOK, John (-1718) & Naomi[3] THAYER (1662/3-1694+); m Mendon 16 Apr 1684 [AEBK 3]

COOK, John[3] (1656-1737) & Ruth SHAW (1660-1737+); m c1680 Portsmouth, RI/Tiverton [Fiske 1:63]

COOK, John[3] (c1652-1727) & Mary HAVENS? (c1656-1754); m bef 1675 Tiverton [Fiske 1:47]

COOK, Robert & Submit WEEKES; m Boston 26 Oct 1693 [REG 155:391]

COOK, Samuel (c1659/60-c1752) & Lydia[3] WHITE (1662-1701+); m Medfield 27 Apr 1681 [AEBK 1:511]

COOKE, Aaron (bp 1613/4-1690) & 1/wf _____ _____ (-by 1650); by 1638 Dorchester [GMB 1:465]

COOKE, Aaron (bp 1613/4-1690) & 2/wf Joan DENSLOW (-1676); by 1650 Westfield [GMB 1:465, 528]

COOKE, Aaron (bp 1613/4-1690) & 3/wf Elizabeth NASH; New Haven 2 Dec 1676 [GMB 1:465]

COOKE, Aaron (bp 1613/4-1690) & 4/wf Rebecca (Foote) SMITH (-1701); m1 Philip SMITH; Hadley 2 Oct 1638 [GMB 1:465]

COOKE, Elisha[2] & Elizabeth LEVERETT, dau of John; m c1670 Boston [GM 2:188]

COOKE, Ellis & Martha[2] COOPER (bp 1629-); m c1650 [GM 2:204]

COOKE, Francis (c1583-1663) & Hester MAHIEU; Leiden 20 July 1603 [GMB 1:469]

COOKE, George[1] (c1610-by 1652) & Anne _____; m by 1640 Cambridge [GM 2:175]

COOKE, Henry & Judith[2] BIRDSALL (bp 1611-); m Salem June 1639 [GM 1:302]

COOKE, Jacob & 2/wf Elizabeth (Lettice) SHURTLEFF; Plymouth 18 Nov 1669 [GMB 1:470]

COOKE, Jacob[2] & 1/wf Damaris[2] HOPKINS (c1628-); m aft 10 June 1646 Plymouth [GMB 1:470 2:988; TAG 73:171]

COOKE, John & 2/wf Hannah HARRIS; m c1690 Providence/Middletown [TAG 52:6]

COOKE, John & Sarah[2] WARREN; m Plymouth 28 Mar 1634 [GMB 3:1936]

COOKE, John[2] (-1704/5) & Phebe WEEDEN (-1734+); m2 William PECKHAM; m c1676 Warwick div 1684 [TAG 52:5; 60:159]

COOKE, Joseph[1] (c1608-1679+) & Elizabeth[2] HAYNES (bp 1624-), dau of John; m by 1643 Hingham/Cambridge [GM 2:181; GMB 2:896]

COOKE, Joseph[2] (1643-) & Martha STEDMAN; m Cambridge 4 Dec 1665 [GM 2:181]

COOKE, Josias (c1610-1673) & Elizabeth (_____) DEANE; m1 Stephen DEANE; Plymouth 16 Sep 1635 [GMB 1:474]

COOKE, Richard[1] (c1610-1673) & Elizabeth _____ (c1616-1690); m c1636 Boston [GM 2:187]

COOKE, Thomas[1] (bp 1600-1677) & 1/wf Mary _____ (-by 1673) Taunton [Fiske 1:13]

COOKE, Thomas[1] (bp 1600-1677) & 2/wf Mary ?SHEARMAN (1645-) not SLOCUM, m2 Jeremiah BROWN c1679; Kingstown [Fiske 1:13]

COOKE, Walter (-1695/6) & Catherine BRENTON? (-1695/6); m bef 1674 Mendon [REG 128:154]

COOKERY, Henry & Mary[2] BEAMON (bp 1657-); m Charlestown 22 or 23 Jan 1688/9 [GM 1:218]

COOLIDGE, John[1] (bp 1604-1691) & Mary[1] RAVENS (bp 1602-1691); m c1630 Watertown [AEBK 3; GM 2:195; TAG 62:164]

COOLIDGE, John[2] (c1630-1690/1) & 1/wf Hannah LIVERMORE (c1633-1678), dau of John; m Watertown 14 Nov 1655 [AEBK 3; GM 2:195]

COOLIDGE, John[2] (c1630-1690/1) & 2/wf Mary (WELLINGTON) MADDOCK (1640/1-1690/1), dau of Roger; m1 Henry MADDOCK; m Watertown 16 Sept 1679 [AEBK 3; GM 2:195]

COOLIDGE, Jonathan[2] (1646/7-1723/4) & Martha RICE; m Watertown 3 Dec 1679 [AEBK 3; GM 2:196]

COOLIDGE, Joseph[3] (1666-1737) & Rebecca FROST (1669-1750); m c1659 Watertown [AEBK 3]

COOLIDGE, Nathaniel[2] (c1636-1711) & Mary BRIGHT (1639-1681+), dau of Henry; m Watertown 15 Oct 1657 [AEBK 3; GM 2:196]

COOLIDGE, Obadiah[3] (1663-1707) & Elizabeth ROSE (1665-by 1732); m Sudbury 28 Feb 1686/7 [AEBK 3]

COOLIDGE, Simon[2] (c1632-) & 1/wf Hannah[2] BARRON (c1637-1680), dau of Ellis; m Watertown 17 Nov 1658 [GM 2:196; AEBK 3; AEBK 1:129]

COOLIDGE, Simon[2] (c1632-1693) & 2/wf Priscilla ROGERS (c1647-1717); m Watertown 19 Jan 1681/2 [AEBK 3; GM 2:196; AEBK 1:129]

COOLIDGE, Stephen[2] (1639-) & Rebecca _____ (-1702); Watertown [GM 2:196]

COOMBS, Francis[2] & 2/wf Mary (BARKER) PRATT; m c1678 [TAG 71:248; GMB 1:478]

COOMBS, Francis[2] (c1635-1682) & 1/wf Deborah MORTON; m c1672 [TAG 71:248; GMB 1:478]

COOMBS, Humphrey & Bathsuah[2] RAYMENT (bp 1637-); m Salem 29 July 1659 [GMB 3:1564]

COOMBS, John (1664-1709/10) & Elizabeth (BALLENTINE) (GREENLAND) YELLINGS (1659-); m1 David GREENLAND; m2 Roger YELLINGS; m c1687/8 Boston [TAG 46:130]

COOMBS, John[1] (c1610-by 1646) & Sarah[2] PRIEST (c1614-); m c1632 Plymouth [GMB 1:478, 3:1526; TAG 71:247]

COOMBS, John[2] & Elizabeth (ROYALL?) BARLOW; m Boston 24 Feb 1661/2 [TAG 71:248]

COOPER, Anthony[1] (c1584-1635/6) & 1/wf Margaret CLARKE (-1617); m Hingham, Norfolk 25 July 1609 [GM 2:198]

COOPER, Anthony[1] (c1594-1635/6) & 2/wf Frances _____ (-by 1672); m c1626 Hingham [GM 2:198]

COOPER, John[1] (c1594-1662+) & Wibroe (GRIGGS) PEIRSON; m1 William PEIRSON; m Olney, Buckinghamshire 18 Oct 1618 Lynn/Southampton [GM 2:203; TAG 64:196]

COOPER, John[1] (c1609-1681-83[/4?]) & Priscilla (CARPENTER) WRIGHT (c1598-1689); m1 William WRIGHT; m Plymouth 27 Nov 1634 [GM 2:201]

COOPER, John[2] (bp 1624/5-) & Sarah[1] MEW (bp 1630-); m c1650 Southampton, L.I. [TAG 66:48, TAG 76:15; GM 2:204]

COOPER, Josiah (-1678) & 2/wf Mary BLANCHARD (c1645-50-bef 1729); m2 Richard BROOKS; m bef 1676 Boston [REG 140:315]

COOPER, Josiah[2] & 1/wf Waitawhile MAKEPEACE, dau of Thomas; m Boston 13 Sept 1661 [GM 2:199]

COOPER, Josiah[2] & 2/wf Mary GARDNER, dau of Richard (or step dau); m by 1678 [GM 2:199]

COOPER, Samuel (1646/7-1727) & Mary HARRIMAN (c1660-1732); m Rowley 25 June 1691 [REG 150:44]

COOPER, Thomas[1] (bp 1626/7-) & Mary RAYNOR, dau of Thurston; m c1665 [GM 2:204]

COOPER, Thomas[1] (c1617-1675) & Sarah SLYE (bp 1615-); m2 William CLARKE; m c1642 Springfield [GM 2:210]

COOPER, Thomas[2] (1646-) & Desire LAMBERTON, dau of George; m Springfield Aug 1669 [GM 2:210]

COOPER, Timothy[1] (c1610s-bef 1659) & Elizabeth _____; bef 1641 Lynn [TEG 11:212]

COOPER, Timothy[2] (1644-) & Elizabeth MUNSON, dau of Thomas; m Springfield 19 Oct 1664 [GM 2:210]

COPP, Aaron[3] (c1675-bef 1730) & Mary[3] HEATH (1672-1730+); m 30 Dec 1698 Haverhill [ASBO, p.316]

CORBETT, Robert (-1695) & 2/wf Abiel[3] TWITCHELL (1663-1744); m2 John BUGBEE; m 1690 Woodstock [AEBK 3]

CORBETT, William & Eleanor/Ellen BARTRUM (1660-); m Bristol 19 Sept 1683 [REG 149:231]

CORLISS, George[1] (c1617-1686) & Joanna[2] DAVIS (c1624-1690s); m2 James[1] ORDWAY; m 26 Oct 1645 Haverhill [ASBO, p.207; GM 2:315]

CORLISS, John[2] (1647/8-1697/8) & 1/wf Mary[2] WILFORD (1667-); m2 William[2] WHITTAKER; m 17 Dec 1684 Haverhill [ASBO, p.213]

CORNELIS, Arent & Patience[2] PATRICK; m by 24 June 1662 Flushing [GMB 3:1405]

CORNELL, Samuel[2] & Grissell (STRANGE) FISH (c1650-); m1 Thomas[2] FISH; m c1686 Dartmouth [TAG 54:25]

CORNELL, Thomas & Elizabeth[2] FISHCOCK; m2 John MORRICE; m New Amsterdam 2 Nov 1642 [GM 2:527]

CORNELL, Thomas[2] (1627-1673) & 1/wf Elizabeth _____ (not FISCOCK); m bef 1657 Portsmouth [TAG 58:78]

CORNISH, Richard[1] (c1609-drowned 1644) & Katharine _____ (-executed c1644); by 1634 York [GM 2:213]

CORNWALL, William (bp 1609-1577/8) & 1/wf Joan RANKE; m Fairfield, Essex 27 Sept 1632 [GMB 1:483, TAG 51:115]

CORNWALL, William (bp 1609-1577/8) & 2/wf Mary _____; by 1640 Middletown [GMB 1:483]

CORWIN, George & Elizabeth (HERBERT) WHITE (bp 1611-1668); m c1634 Salem [REG 150:193]

CORWIN, John (1636-) & Margaret WINTHROP; m Salem May 1665 [REG 150:195]

CORY, William (bp 1634-1681/2) & Mary EARLE (c1640-1718); m2 Joseph TIMBERLAKE; m c1657 Portsmouth, RI [REG 147:163; 145:124]

COTTA, John[2] (bp 1645-) & Mary MOORE, dau of Jeremiah; m by 1667 Boston [GM 2:216]

COTTA, Robert[1] (c1611-1664) & Joan _____ (-1664+); m by 1636 Salem [GM 2:216]

COTTON, John (-1679+) & Marie[3] STOW (1643[/4]-1706+); m by 1666 Concord [AEBK 3]

COTTON, John (1585-1652) & 1/wf Elizabeth HORROCKS (-1630+); by 1612 [GMB 1:486]

COTTON, John (1585-1652) & 2/wf Sarah (_____) STORY; m3 Richard MATHER; by 3 Oct 1632 Boston [GMB 1:486]

COTTON, William & Abigail[2] PICKERING (c1653-); perhaps [GMB 3:1460]

COTTRELL, Nicholas (not Jabez) (-c1711) & Anna PEABODY (-bef 1711); m bef 22 Mar 1686/7 Stonington/Newport [REG 117:97]

COTTRELL, Nicholas[2] (c1630s-1711/2) & Em[2] PEABODY (c1644-); m say 1664 [AEBK 1:370]

COUNTS, Edward & Sarah[2] ADAMS (1637-); m Malden 25 Feb 1662 [GM 1:10]

COURSER, John[2] (bp 1642-) & Margaret _____; m c1668 Boston [GM 2:220]

COURSER, William[1] (c1608-1673) & Joan _____; m c1637 Boston [GM 2:220]

COVELL, Philip & Elizabeth[2] ATWOOD (1669-); m Malden 16 Nov 1688 [GM 1:106]

COVELL, Richard & Sarah[2] BUSHNELL (1655[/6?]-); m by 5 Oct 1678 Salem [GM 1:513]

COWDALL, John & 2/wf Joan _____; m by 1668 [RI Court Records 2:51]

COWDREY, Nathaniel & Mary[2] BACHELER; m Reading 22 Nov 1660 [GM 1:120]

COWEN, Israel ~ Hannah _____; Scituate [Plymouth Court Sept 1691]

COX, Moses[1] & Prudence (MARSTON) SWAINE; m Hampton 16 June 1658 [TAG 74:248]

COY, Richard & Martha[2] HAFFIELD (c1627-); m by 1652 [GM 3:186]

CRACKBONE, Benjamin[2] (c1631-) & Elizabeth DUTTON; m Cambridge 6 Nov 1657 [GM 2:226]

CRACKBONE, Gilbert[1] (c1596-1671/2) & 1/wf Judith SQUIRE (-1626); m Great Coggeshall, Essex 13 Aug 1621 [GM 2:225]

CRACKBONE, Gilbert[1] (c1596-1671/2) & 2/wf Mary EASTWOOD (-1655); m Great Coggeshall, Essex 18 June 1627 [GM 2:225]

CRACKBONE, Gilbert[1] (c1596-1671/2) & 3/wf Elizabeth (_____) COOLEY; m1 John COOLEY; m Cambridge 17 June 1656 [GM 2:225]

CRACKSTONE, John & _____ _____; by 1600 Plymouth [GMB 1:488]

CRAFTS, Griffin & 1/wf Alice _____; by 1628 [GMB 1:490-91]

CRAFTS, Griffin & 2/wf Ursula (ADAMS) (STREETER)(HOSIER) ROBINSON; m1
    Samuel STREETER, m2 Samuel HOSIER, m3 William ROBINSON;
    Dorchester 13 July 1673 [GMB 1:490-91]

CRAFTS, Griffin & 3/wf Dorcas (FRENCH) PEAKE; m1 Christopher PEAKE [GMB
    1:490-91]

CRAFTS, Moses & Rebecca[2] GARDNER (1647-); m Roxbury 24 June 1667 [GM
    3:14]g

CRAFTS, Samuel & Elizabeth[2] SEAVER (bp 1643-); m Roxbury 16 Oct 1661 [GMB
    3:1645]

CRAM, Benjamin[2] & Argentine CROMWELL, dau of Giles; m Hampton 28 Nov 1662
    [GM 2:229]

CRAM, John[1] (bp 1596/7-1681/2) & Esther WHITE (-1677); m Bilsby, Lincolnshire 8?
    June 1624 Hampton [GM 2:228]

CRAM, Thomas (1646-) did not die 1751, this was his son [LN Tyler]

CRAM, Thomas[2] (c1644-) & Elizabeth WEARE; m Hampton 20 Dec 1681 [GM 2:229]

CRAMPTON, John & Sarah ROCKWELL (c1654-); m Norwalk 8 Oct 1676 [TAG
    77:109]

CRANSTON, William & Mercy ARCHER (-1732); m2 Samuel GIBBS; Jamestown
    [REG 157:114]

CRAWFORD, _____[1] (c1609-1634) & Winifred _____; m2 John WOLCOTT; m3
    Thomas ALLYN; m by 1634 Watertown (perhaps m St Vedast Foster Lane,
    London 2 Feb 1629/30 John Craford & Winifred Longman) [GM 2:231]

CREBER, Thomas & _____[2] MOSES (c1644-); m by 25 May 1665 [GMB 2:1301]

CRISP, Benjamin (c1610-1683) & 1/wf Bridget _____; by 1636 Watertown [GMB 1:494]

CRISP, Benjamin (c1610-1683) & 2/wf Joanna (Goffe?) LONGLEY; m1 William
    LONGLEY Sr.; after 29 Nov 1680 [GMB 1:494]

CRISPE, Eleazar (1641/2-1726+) & Elizabeth _____; m bef 1700 Groton [TAG 62:27]

CRITTENDEN, Abraham Jr. (-1694) & Susanna GREGSON (c1637-1712); m 13 May
    1661 New Haven [REG 128:73]

CROCKER, Francis & Mary GAUNT (-1693?); lic. 2 Mar 1646/7 Barnstable/Scituate
    [TAG 60:159]

CROCKER, John & Mary[2] BOTFISH; m Barnstable Nov 1659 [GM 1:358]

CROCKER, Thomas (c1633-1715/6) & Rachel[2] CHAPPELL (1649-); m by 1668 New
    London [REG 150:57; GM 2:57]

CROCKETT, Elihu & 1/wf Mary WINNOCK [GMB 1:497]

CROCKETT, Elihu & 2/wf _____ _____ [GMB 1:497]

CROCKETT, Ephraim & Ann _____; by 1667 Kittery [GMB 1:497]

CROCKETT, Hugh & Margaret _____; by 1697 York [GMB 1:497]

CROCKETT, Joseph & Hannah CLEMENTS [GMB 1:497]

CROCKETT, Joshua & Sarah TRICKEY [GMB 1:497]

CROCKETT, Thomas (c1615-by 1678/9) & Ann _____; m2 Digory JEFFRIES; by 1644 Kittery [GMB 1:497]

CROMWELL, John & Seaborn[2] BACHELOR (bp 1634/5-); m2 Robert PARIS; m by 1657 Charlestown [GM 1:125]

CROOKE, Joseph (c1670-2-) & _____ _____; Southold [TAG 70:169]

CROOKE, Samuel (-1672+) & Sarah[2] RISLEY (1640-1716); m2 John PAYNE; m by 1666 East Hartford [TAG 70:162-70, 71:145]

CROOKE, Samuel[2] & _____ _____; Southold [TAG 70:169]

CROSBY, Anthony & Prudence[2] WADE; m2 Seaborn COTTON; m3 John HAMMOND; m Rowley 28 Dec 1659 [GMB 3:1886]

CROSBY, Joseph & Sarah[2] FRENCH (1671-); m Billerica 6 May 1691 [GM 2:592]

CROSBY, Joseph[2] (1638[/9]-) & 1/wf Sarah BRACKETT, dau of Richard; m Braintree 1 June 1675 [GM 2:235]

CROSBY, Joseph[2] (1638[/9]-) & 2/wf Eleanor (VEASEY) PAINE, dau of William; m1 Stephen PAINE; m Braintree 5 Oct 1693 [GM 2:235]

CROSBY, Simon[1] (c1609-1639) & Ann BRIGHAM (-1675); m2 William THOMPSON; m Holme-on-Spalding-Moor, Yorkshire/Cambridge [GM 2:235]

CROSBY, Simon[2] (1637-) & Rachel BRACKETT, dau of Richard; m Braintree 15 July 1659 [GM 2:235]

CROSBY, Thomas & Deborah[2] FIFIELD (1660/1-); m Hampton 29 Oct 1685 [GM 2:525]

CROSBY, Thomas[2] (bp 1634/5-) & Sarah _____; m by 1663 Eastham [GM 2:235]

CROSS, John[1] (c1584-1650-51) & Ann _____ (c1596-1669); m c1634 Watertown [GM 2:239]

CROSS, Robert[1] (c1612-1695+) & 1/wf Anna[2] JORDAN (c1615-1677); m 20 Aug 1635 Ipswich [GM 2:243; ASBO, p. 223]

CROSS, Robert[1] (c1613-bef 1702) & 2/wf Mary _____ (c1653-1695+); m bet 1677-1680 Ipswich [GM 2:243; ASBO, p.223]

CROSS, Robert[2] (c1642-) & Martha TREADWELL; m Ipswich 19 Feb 1664/5 [GM 2:243]

CROSS, Stephen[2] (c1647-) & Elizabeth CHENEY (1647/8-), dau of John; m c1672 Newbury/Ipswich/Roxbury [TAG 76:247; GM 2:62, 244]

CROSS, Thomas[3] (1667-by 1698) & Esther _____ (c1670-1702+); m c1690 Ipswich [ASBO, p.237]

CROSSMAN, Robert & Hannah[2] BROOKS (bp 1659-); m Taunton 21 July 1679 [GM 1:411]

CROSSMAN, Samuel & 1/wf Elizabeth[2] BELL (1668-by 1696); m Taunton 19 Dec 1689 [AEBK 4:93]

CROSSMAN, Samuel & 2/wf Mary SAWYER; m Taunton 22 Dec 1696 [AEBK 4:94]

CROW, John[1] (c1590-1651/2+) & Elishua _____; m c1615 Yarmouth [GM 2:247]

CROW, John[2] & Mehitable _____; m c1656 Yarmouth [GM 2:247]

CROW, William & Hannah[2] WINSLOW (1644-   ); m2 John STURTEVANT; m Plymouth 5 Apr 1664 [GMB 3:2033]

CROW, Yelverton[2] & Elizabeth _____; m c1642 Charlestown [GM 2:247]

CROWELL, Christopher[1] (c1629-1688) & 1/wf Deliverance[2] BENNETT (bp 1643-1680); m 8 Oct 1657 Salem [ASBO, p.249]

CROWELL, Christopher[1] (c1629-1688) & 2/wf Margaret _____ (-1695+); m bef 1688 Boston [ASBO, p.249]

CUDWORTH, Israel[2] (bp 1641-) & _____ _____; m c1678 Scituate [GM 2:254]

CUDWORTH, James[1] (bp 1612-1681) & Mary PARKER; m Northam, Devonshire 1 Feb 1633/4 Scituate [GM 2:254]

CUDWORTH, James[2] (bp 1635-) & Mary[2] HOWLAND (c1643-), dau of Henry; m c1665 Scituate [GM 2:254; GMB 2:1018]

CUDWORTH, Jonathan[2] & Sarah JACKSON; m Scituate 31 May 1667 [GM 2:254]

CULLIMORE, Isaac[1] (c1613-1674-76) & 1/wf Margaret _____ (-1651); m by 1643 Boston [GM 2:260]

CULLIMORE, Isaac[1] (c1613-1674-76) & 2/wf Margery PAGE; m Boston 22 Jan 1651[/2] [GM 2:260]

CUMINS, David (-1693) & Elizabeth _____; m by 1671 Boston [REG 153:56]

CUMMING, Philip (-1707) & Elizabeth _____ (-1707+); m by 1691 Portsmouth, RI [REG 153:57]

CUMMINGS, Isaac[1] (1600-1677) & Ann _____; m bef 1629 Mistley, Essex/Topsfield [REG 145:240]

CUMMINGS, Isaac[2] (bp 1632/3-1721) & Mary ANDREWS (c1640-by 1712); m Topsfield 27 Nov 1659 [REG 145 240]

CUMMINGS, John & Sarah[2] HOWLETT (c1639-); m by 1658 [GMB 2:1027]

CUMMINGS, Richard & Elizabeth[2] BONYTHON (bp 1612-); m c1647 [GM 1:345]

CUMMINS, Timothy (-c1708) & 1/wf Grace PRIDEUX; m Marblehead 13 Oct 1687 [REG 153:58]

CURRIER, Samuel & Mary HARDY (c1645-); by 1665 Bradford [GMB 2:860]

CURTIS, Ephraim[2] & Elizabeth KILBORNE; m Rowley 6 Sept 1693 [GM 2:263]

CURTIS, Henry & Mary TAINTOR; m bef 1642 Watertown/Sudbury [TAG 65:22-3]

CURTIS, Israel & Rebecca[2] BEARDSLEY; m2 James BEEBE; m by 1666 Stratford [GM 1:226]

CURTIS, John & Dorcas[2] PEAKE (1639-); m aft 1675 [GMB 3:1414]

CURTIS, John & Miriam[2] BROOKS (bp 1652-); m Scituate 4 Apr 1678 [GM 1:414]

CURTIS, John[2] (1673-) & probably 1/wf Charity MAY; m bef 1696 Plymouth & Plympton [TAG 67:2-7]

CURTIS, John[2] (c1649-) & Mary LOOKE, dau of Thomas; m Topsfield 4 Dec 1672 [GM 2:262]

CURTIS, Philip³ & Obedience² HOLLAND (bp 1642-); m2 1677/8 Benjamin³ GAMBLIN; m Roxbury 20 Oct 1658 [TAG 68:181; GM 3:376]

CURTIS, Samuel & Sarah² (SALMON) EDWARDS [TAG 76:296]

CURTIS, William (bp 1592-1672) & 1/wf Mary RAWLYNS; m St Margaret Moses, London 3 Dec 1615 [GMB 1:500]

CURTIS, William (bp 1592-1672) & 2/wf Sarah ELIOT (bp 1599/1600-); m Nazeing, Essex 6 Aug 1618 Roxbury [GMB 1:500]

CURTIS, William² (1662-) & 2/wf Lydia HILL; m bef 4 Feb 1698/9 Salem [TAG 59:75]

CURTIS, Zaccheus¹ (c1619-by 1682) & Jane/Johannah _____ (c1624-); m by 1659 Rowley [GM 2:262]

CURTIS, Zaccheus² (c1646-) & Mary BLAKE; m Topsfield 4 Dec 1673 [GM 2:262]

CURWEN, Theophilus² & Mary _____; m by 1678 Southold [GM 2:266]

CURWIN, John² & Mary GLOVER; m Southold 4 Feb 1658/9 [GM 2:266]

CURWIN, Matthias¹ (c1602-1658) & Margaret SHATSWELL, dau of Judith; m by 1627 Sibbertoft, Northamptonshire/Southold [GM 2:266]

CUSHING, Mathew & Sarah² JACOB (c1636-); m Hingham 25 Feb 1652/3 [GMB 2:1070]

CUSHMAN, Robert (1664-1757) & 1/wf Persis LEWIS? (c1671-1774); c1697 Plymouth [TAG 67:31]

CUSHMAN, Robert (bp 1577/8-1625) & 1/wf Sara REDER (-1616); St Alphage, Canterbury, Kent 31 July 1606 [GMB 1:503]

CUSHMAN, Robert (bp 1577/8-1625) & 2/wf Mary SHINGELTON; Leiden 5 June 1617 [GMB 1:503]

CUSHMAN, Thomas & Ruth² HOWLAND (c1646-); m Plymouth 17 Nov 1664 [GMB 2:1023]

CUSHMAN, Thomas (bp 1607/8-) & Mary ALLERTON; by 1636 Plymouth [GMB 1:503]

CUTLER, James¹ (c1606-1694) & 1/wf Ann _____ (-1644); m c1635 Watertown [GM 2:269]

CUTLER, James¹ (c1606-1694) & 2/wf Mary (_____) KING; m1 Thomas KING; m Watertown 9 Mar 164[4/]5 [GM 2:269]

CUTLER, James¹ (c1606-1694) & 3/wf Phebe² PAGE (c1627-by 1684); m c1661 Watertown [GM 2:270; GMB 3:1366]

CUTLER, James² (1635-) & Lydia (MOORE) WRIGHT; m1 Samuel WRIGHT; m Sudbury 15 June 1665 [GM 2:270]

CUTLER, John & Anna WOODMANSEE (c1626-1683); m c1651 [REG 147:45]

CUTLER, John² & Olive² THOMSON; m Woburn 3 Sept 1650 [GMB 3:1811; TAG 74:104]

CUTLER, John² (1662/3-) & Mary STEARNS; m Cambridge 1 Jan 1693/4 [GM 2:270]

CUTLER, John[2] (c1625-1678) & Mary (BROWNE) LEWIS (bp 1623/4-1693/4); m say 1663 Malden [AEBK 1:185]

CUTLER, Samuel (1661-1773!) & Sarah SAWTELL (1673/4-1731+); m 20 Jan 1691/2 Salem [REG 126:6]

CUTLER, Thomas & Mary GILES (c1635-); m2 1684 Matthew SMITH; m Reading 19 Mar 1659/60 [TAG 72:300]

CUTLER, Thomas[2] & Abigail _____; m c1674 Cambridge [GM 2:270]

CUTTER, Richard & Elizabeth ?WILLIAMS; Cambridge/Roxbury [TAG 74:292]

CUTTING, James[2] (1657/8-1721+) & Hannah COLLER (c1659-1699+), dau of John; m Watertown 16 June 1679 [AEBK 1:245, 266; GM 2:274]

CUTTING, John[2] (c1642-1689) & Susannah HARRINGTON (1649-1704/5+); m Watertown 9 Feb 1671; m2 1690 Eliezer BEERS, m3 1703 Peter CLOYSE [AEBK 1:263; GM 2:274]

CUTTING, Richard (bp 1594-1627) & Susannah[1] STONE (bp 1597-1684); m2 Henry KEMBALL; m3 Thomas LOW; m Great Bromley, Essex 3 Aug 1620 Watertown [AEBK 1:258; TAG 55:26]

CUTTING, Richard (bp 1621/2-1695/6) & Sarah _____ (c1625-1685); m say 1642-5 Watertown [AEBK 1:261; GM 2:274]

CUTTING, Zachariah (c1645-1732) & Sarah _____ (c1650-1709+); m say 1669 Watertown [AEBK 1:264; GM 2:274]

DADY, William (c1605-1682) & 1/wf Dorothy _____ (-1670); by 1633 Charlestown [GMB 1:507]

DADY, William (c1605-1682) & 2/wf Martha (_____) MARCH; m1 John MARCH [not Elizabeth]; Charlestown 29 June 1670 [GMB 1:507]

DAGGETT, John & Mehitable[2] TRUANT; m Marshfield 23 Sept 1691 [GMB 3:1840]

DALTON, Philemon (c1590-1662) & 1/wf Ann COLE (c1600-by 1656); m Dennington, Suffolk 11 Oct 1625 Dedham/Hampton [NHGR 9:109 & 10:81; REG 154:263+; GM 2:279]

DALTON, Philemon[1] (c1590-1662) & 2/wf Dorothy _____; m2 Godfrey DEARBORN; m c1656 Hampton [GM 2:279; REG 154:283]

DALTON, Samuel[2] (c1629-) & Mehitable PALMER, dau of Henry; m by 1654 Hampton [GM 2:279]

DALTON, Timothy (c1577-1661) & Ruth LEETE (bp 8 May 1579-1666); m Gislingham, Suffolk 13 June 1615 [50 GMC, REG 154:263+; TAG 52:113]

DAM, John & Elizabeth[2] FURBER; m Dover 9 Nov 1664 [GM 2:609]

DAMAN, Zachary & Martha[2] WOODWORTH; m Scituate June 1679 [GMB 3:2066]

DAMON, Ebenezer (1665-6-) & _____ _____ (not Bacon); Scituate [NGSQ 71:89-90]

DANFORTH, Jonathan[2] (bp 1628['9?]-) & 1/wf Elizabeth POULTER, dau of John; m Boston 22 Nov 1654 [GM 2:283]

DANFORTH, Jonathan[2] (bp 1628['9?]-) & 2/wf Esther (CHAMPNEY) CONVERSE (c1638-1713), dau of Richard; m1 Josiah CONVERSE; m Billerica 17 Nov 1690 [GM 2:283; REG 153:94]

DANFORTH, Nicholas[1] (bp 1589[/90?]-1638) & Elizabeth BARBER; m Aspall, Suffolk 11 Feb 1617/8 [GM 2:283]

DANFORTH, Samuel[2] (bp 1626-) & Mary[2] WILSON (1633-), dau of John; m2 Joseph ROCK; m 5 Nov 1651 Boston [GM 2:283; GMB 3:2015]

DANFORTH, Thomas[2] (bp 1623-) & Mary WITHINGTON, dau of Henry; m Cambridge 23 Feb 1643[/4?] [GM 2:283]

DANIEL, Davy & Naomi[2] HULL (bp 1639/40-) [GM 3:456]

DANIEL, William & Katherine GREENWAY (c1626-); by 18 Oct 1646 Dorchester [GMB 2:817]

DANIELS, John & Mary[2] CHAPPELL; m New London 19 Jan 1664/5 [GM 2:57; REG 150:55]

DANIELS, Joseph (-1715) & Mary[3] FAIRBANKS (1647-1682); m Medfield 16 Nov 1665 [AEBK 3]

DANIELS, Samuel (-1695) & Mary (BECKWITH) GRANT (1643-1692/3+); m Watertown 10 May 1671 [AEJA]

DANIELS, William[1] & Katherine GREENWAY (c1626-); m by 18 Oct 1646 Dorchester/Milton [TAG 74:195]

DARLING, Cornelius (1675-1763+) & 1/wf Mary FREEBERY (c1676-); m c1694 [AEBK 1:290]

DARLING, Dennis[1] (c1640-1717/8) & Hannah FRANCIS (c1642-1713/14+); m Braintree 3 Jan 1662/3 [AEBK 1:287]

DARLING, Ebenezer (1679-by 1705) & Mary (WHEATON) MANN (1656-1745); m Rehoboth 30 Mar 1698 (curious) [AEBK 1:291]

DARLING, John & Elizabeth DOWNHAM; m Braintree 13 May 1664 [AEBK 1:287]

DARLING, John (1664-1753) & 1/wf Elizabeth THOMPSON (-1687); m by 1686 Mendon/Bellingham [AEBK 1:289]

DARLING, John (1664-1753) & 2/wf Anne ROCKWOOD (-1690); m Boston 2 Jan 1687/8 Mendon [AEBK 1:289]

DARLING, John (1664-1753) & 3/wf Elizabeth MORSE (-1713+); m aft 1690 Mendon/Bellingham [AEBK 1:289-90]

DARLING, Richard & Abigail MESSENGER (c1644-); m c1662; div 7 July 1674 [REG 152:362]

DART, Richard (1667-1740/1) & Elizabeth STRICKLAND (bp 1 Aug 1675-1748/9); m New London 22 June 1699 [AEJA]

DASSETT, John & Hannah[2] FLINT (1643[/4?]-); m Braintree 15 Nov 1662 [GM 2:536]

DAVENPORT, Eleazer & Rebecca ADDINGTON; by 1670 Boston [GMB 1:511]

DAVENPORT, Nathaniel & Elizabeth THACHER; m2 Samuel DAVIS; Boston [GMB 1:511]

DAVENPORT, Rev. John (1597-1670) & 1/wf Elizabeth _____ not (WOLLEY) (1603-1676); m bef 1635 Boston [TAG 52:216]

DAVENPORT, Richard[1] (c1606-1665) & Elizabeth HATHORNE; m by 1635 Salem/Boston [GMB 1:511, 2:886]

DAVENPORT, William[2] (c1665-1742) & 1/wf Elizabeth NICHOLS? (c1670-1697); m c1690s Hartford [TAG 43:86]

DAVIS, _____ & Margaret _____ (c1603-1669); m2 Charles GRICE; m by 1626 Boston/Braintree [GM 2:303]

DAVIS, Barnabas[1] (c1599-1685) & Patience JAMES (bp 1603-1690); m Tewkesbury, Gloucestershire 1 July 1628 [GM 2:288]

DAVIS, Dolor[1] (c1599-1672-73) & 1/wf Margery WILLARD (bp 1602-1658+); m East Farleigh, Kent 29 Mar 1624 Barnstable [GM 2:296]

DAVIS, Dolor[1] (c1599-1672-73) & 2/wf Joanna (HULL) BURSLEY, dau of Joseph; m1 John BURSLEY [GM 2:296]

DAVIS, Elisha (1670-1738/9) & Grace SHAW (c1670-by 1741); m Haverhill 14 June 1694 [TG 10:98-110]

DAVIS, George (-1655) & Barbara _____, m2 John BRIMBLECOM, m3 Thomas CHADWELL; m bef 1647 Boston [DCD]

DAVIS, Hopewell[2] (c1646-) & 1/wf Sarah BOYNTON; m Charlestown 14 Nov 1682 [GM 2:289]

DAVIS, Hopewell[2] (c1646-) & 2/wf Mercy _____ (-1717/8); Charlestown [GM 2:289]

DAVIS, James[1] & Cicely THAYER; m Thornbury, Gloucestershire 11 June 1618 Haverhill [TAG 73:81]

DAVIS, James[1] (c1606-1661) & Joanna _____ (-1678[/9]-9); m by 1631 Boston [GM 2:300]

DAVIS, James[2] (bp 1633-) & Elizabeth RANDALL, dau of William; m c1673 Charlestown [GM 2:288]

DAVIS, John & Sarah[2] CARTER, m Newbury 8 Apr 1681 [GM 2:29]

DAVIS, John[2] (c1626-) & Hannah LINNETT, dau of Robert; m Eastham 15 Mar 1648/9 [GM 2:296]

DAVIS, John[2] (c1631-1687) & Sarah _____ (-1688[/9]); Charlestown [GM 2:288]

DAVIS, Nathaniel[2] (c1644-) & 1/wf Mary CONVERSE; m Woburn 31 Mar 1675 [GM 2:289]

DAVIS, Nathaniel[2] (c1644-) & 2/wf Mary EDMUNDS; m Charlestown 15 July 1692 [GM 2:289]

DAVIS, Nicholas[1] (c1595-1667-69/70) & 1/wf Sarah _____ (c1586-1643); m by 1620 Woburn [GM 2:307]

DAVIS, Nicholas[1] (c1595-1667-69/70) & 2/wf Elizabeth (_____) ISAAC; m1 Joseph ISAAC; m Woburn 12 July 1643 [GM 2:307]

DAVIS, Richard & Sarah[2] BURRELL (1634-); m2 Samuel CHANDLER; m by 19 Feb 1656/7 [GM 1:500]

DAVIS, Samuel[2] & 1/wf Mary MEDDOWES; m Lynn 11 Jan 1665/6 [GM 2:296]

DAVIS, Samuel[2] (bp 1629-) & Mary WATERS; m c1658 Charlestown [GM 2:288]

DAVIS, Simon[2] (c1637-1713) & Mary BLOOD; m Concord 12 Dec 1660 [GM 2:296]

DAVIS, Stephen (-1684+) & 1/wf _____ _____ (-1667+); by 1652 East Hartford/Newark, NJ [WMJ 81, 717; Harris]

DAVIS, Thomas[1] (c1603-1683) & Christian BELLSIRE (-1668); m Chipping Sodbury, Gloucestershire 14 Nov 622 [GM 2:315; DR]

DAVIS, Timothy & Joanna[2] MOSES (c1649-) [GMB 2:1301]

DAVIS, Tobias & Sarah[2] MORRILL (c1625-); m c1646 Roxbury [GMB 2:1291]

DAVIS, William & Margaret[2] PYNCHON (c1624-); m Springfield 31 Oct 1644 [GMB 3:1538]

DAVIS, William[1] (c1597-1643/4) & 1/wf _____ _____; m c1622 [GM 2:317]

DAVIS, William[1] (c1597-1643/4) & 2/wf Mary _____ (-by 1668); m2 John COWDALL; m by 1635 Boston [GM 2:317]

DAVIS, William[2] & Mary[2] PARKER (c1631-), dau of Nicholas; m by 1655 Boston [GM 2:317; GMB 3:1395]

DAVOL, Jonathan (-1698+) & not Hannah ODLIN [TAG 65:148]

DAVOL, Jonathan (-1709) & Mary (not Hannah) _____ (-1709+); Dartmouth [TAG 65:148]

DAVOL, Joseph & Mary SOULE (1679+-); m bef 1700 Dartmouth [TAG 38:165]

DAVOL, Joseph (not Benjamin) (-1715/6) & 2/wf Elizabeth PEABODY (c1650-1716+); m bef 22 Mar 1686 Newport/Westerly [AEBK 1:371; REG 117:97]

DAWES, Ambrose[2] (1642-) & Mary BUMSTEAD; m c1664 Boston [GM 2:322]

DAWES, Jonathan[2] (1661-) & Hannah MORSE, dau of John; m c1687 Boston [GM 2:323]

DAWES, William[1] (c1619-1703/4) & Susanna[2] MILLS (c1623-1694[/5]+); m c1642 Braintree [GM 2:322; GMB 2:1261]

DAY, James & Susanna _____; m by 1684 Ipswich [GM 2:331]

DAY, John[2] & Sarah PENGRY; m Ipswich 20 Apr 1664 [GM 2:331]

DAY, John[2] (c1643-) & 1/wf Mary GAYLORD, dau of Walter; m by 1670 [GM 2:328]

DAY, John[2] (c1643-) & 2/wf Sarah BUTLER; m c1690 [GM 2:328]

DAY, Ralph (-1677) & Susan[2] FAIRBANKS (bp 1627-1659); m Dedham 12 Oct 1647 [AEBK 3]

DAY, Robert[1] (c1604-1648) & 1/wf Mary _____ (c1606-c1634); m by 1634 Cambridge [GM 2:327]

DAY, Robert[1] (c1604-1648) & 2/wf Editha STEBBINS (-1688); m2 John MAYNARD; m c1636 Cambridge [GM 2:327]

DAY, Robert[1] (c1605-1683) & Hannah _____ (-1663[/4]+); m c1638 Ipswich [GM 2:331]

DAY, Thomas[2] & Ann WOODWARD; m Ipswich 20 Oct 1672 [GM 2:331]

DAY, Thomas[2] & Sarah[2] COOPER, dau of Thomas; m Springfield 27 Oct 1659 [GM 2:210, 327]

DAYTON, Caleb (1659-) & Hannah SAYRE?; m c1680-1 Southampton, LI [TAG 38:228]

DEACON, John[1] (c1602-1678+) & 1/wf Alice _____ (-1657); m by 1635 Lynn [GM 2:334-5]

DEACON, John[1] (c1602-1678+) & 2/wf Elizabeth (____) PICKERING (-1661); m1 John PICKERING; m Lynn 25 Dec 1657 [GM 2:335]

DEACON, John[1] (c1602-1678+) & 3/wf Ann _____ (-1690); m c1670 Boston [GM 2:335]

DEANE, _____ & Rachel[1] _____; m2 Joseph BIDDLE; m bef 1635 [GM 2:336]

DEANE, Daniel & Mary[2] GOBLE (bp 1635/6-) [GM 3:83]

DEANE, Stephen (c1605-1633/4) & Elizabeth[2] RING (c1609-); m2 Josias COOKE; by 1630 Plymouth [GMB 1:516, 3:1587]

DEANE, Thomas & Sarah[2] BROWN (1649-); m by 1666 Boston [GM 1:443]

DEANE, Walter (bp 1612-1693+) & Eleanor STRONG (c1613-1693+); m bef 1638 Taunton [TAG 59:227]

DEARING, George[1] (c1613-1645) & Elizabeth _____; m2 Jonas BAILEY [GM 2:337]

DEGALON, _____ (-by 1705?) & Abigail CLARK (1662-1725+); by 1699 Cambridge/Boston [Middlesex Probate #4537; Middlesex Deeds 61:192-93; Sewall's Diary 2:1040; Harris]

DELANO, John & Mary WESTON; by 1679 Duxbury [GMB 1:520]

DELANO, Philip[1] (1603-) & 2/wf Mary (PONTUS) GLASS, m1 James GLASS; m by 17 Jan 1653/4 Plymouth/Duxbury/Bridgewater/ Middleborough [GMB 1:519]

DELANO, Philip[1] (1603-1681) & 1/wf Hester DEWSBERY; m Plymouth 19 Dec 1634 Leyden/Plymouth/Duxbury/ Bridgewater/Middleborough [GMB 1:519]

DELANO, Philip[2] (c1637-) & Elizabeth SAMPSON; by 1670 Plymouth [GMB 1:519]

DELANO, Samuel & Elizabeth STANDISH; by 1679 [GMB 1:520]

DELANO, Thomas & Rebecca ALDEN; by 1667 Plymouth [GMB 1:520]

Delete Roger MOWRY & 1/wf Elizabeth _____ [TAG 44:234]

DENASHA, Thomas & Agnes CROCKER; m 16 Mar 1698/9 Boston [REG 132:38]

DENISON, George & 2/wf Ann BORODELL; after 1643 England/Roxbury/Stonington [GMB 1:523]

DENISON, George (1671-) & Mary (WETHERELL) HARRIS (1668-1711); m 1694 [REG 156:156]

DENISON, John & Phebe LAY [REG 156:156]

DENISON, William (bp 1571-1653/4) & Margaret (CHANDLER) MONK (-1645/6); m1 Henry MONK; m Bishop's Stortford, Hertfordshire 7 Nov 1603 Roxbury [GMB 1:523; TAG 73:51]

DENNING, William (c1616-1653/4) & Ann _____, by 1635 Boston [GMB 1:526]

DENNIS, Robert & Sarah[2] HOWLAND (c1645-1712); m Portsmouth 19 Nov 1672 [GMB 2:1018]

DENNIS, Samuel[2] (c1645-1707-8) & 1/wf Sarah SCULLARD (1645-1683[/4]) Nantucket/Woodbridge [TAG 75:186]

DENNISON, William & Alice[2] PARKER (bp 1633/4-); m Boston 27 Oct 1659 [TAG 76:188]

DENSLOW, Nicholas (c1590-1666/7) & Elizabeth _____ (-1669); by 1618 Windsor [GMB 1:528]

DENTON, Nathaniel[2] (bp 1629-1690) & Sarah _____; m by 1653 Long Island [NYGBR 120:12]

DENTON, Samuel[2] (bp 1631-by 1713/4) & Mary SMITH; m c1664 Hempstead [NYGBR 120:14]

DERRICK/RICH, Michael & Mary[2] BASSETT (1657[/8?]-); m c1676 [GM 1:193]

DESBOROUGH, Henry & Margaret _____; m c1662 [GM 2:343]

DESBOROUGH, Isaac[1] (bp 1615-1658) & Elizabeth _____; m c1644 [GM 2:338]

DESBOROUGH, Peter[2] & Sarah[2] KNAPP (1638/9-), dau of Nicholas; m Stamford 6 Apr 1657 [GM 2:343; GMB 2:1136]

DESBOROUGH, Walter[1] (c1584-c1641) & Phebe PERRY; m Sawbridgeworth, Hertfordshire 13 July 1612 Roxbury [LMM; GM 2:342]

DESBOROW, Samuel (c1615-1690) & Rose (HOBSON) PENNOYER (c1616-1698); m1 Samuel PENNOYER; m aft 1654 Guilford [NGSQ 60:248]

DEVEREUX, Humphrey & Elizabeth _____; by June 1681 [GMB 1:534]

DEVEREUX, John & Susanna HARTSHORN; Marblehead [GMB 1:533]

DEVEREUX, John (-1694) & Ann _____ (c1621-1708); by 1645 Salem/Marblehead [GMB 1:533]

DEVEREUX, Robert & Hannah BLANEY [GMB 1:533]

DEWEY, Jedediah (1647-) & Sarah ORTON; by 28 Mar 1673 Westfield [GMB 1:539]

DEWEY, Thomas & Constant[2] HAWES (1642-); m Dorchester 1 June 1663 [GM 3:252]

DEWEY, Thomas (c1613-1648) & Frances (_____) CLARK; Windsor 22 Mar 1638/9 [GMB 1:539]

DEXTER, John & Mehitable[2] HALLETT (c1663-); m Sandwich 10 Nov 1682 [GM 3:198]

DEXTER, Stephen (1657-1730) & Anna[3] SANDERS (c1673-1729/30+); m 27 Apr 1696 Barnstable [REG 127:252]

DEXTER, Stphen & Abigail[2] WHIPPLE; m2 William HOPKINS; m c1674 [GMB 3:1973]

DEXTER, Thomas & _____ _____; by 1619 Lynn/Barnstable [GMB 1:543]

DEXTER, Thomas & Elizabeth _____; by 11 Aug 1649 Sandwich [GMB 1:543]

DIBBLE, Robert[1] (c1586-1641[/2]) & _____ _____; m c1611 [GM 2:346]

DIBBLE, Samuel[3] & 1/wf Abigail GRAVES (-1667) [REG 155:273-78]

DIBBLE, Thomas[2] (c1613-) & 2/wf Elizabeth (____)(HAWKES) HINSDALE; m1 John HAWKES; m2 Robert HINSDALE; m Windsor 25 June 1683 [GM 2:346]

DIBBLE, Thomas[2] (c1613-) & Miriam ____; m c1637 Windsor [GM 2:346]

DICKERMAN, Thomas (-1657) & Eleanor WHITINGTON; m Little Missenden, Buckinghamshire. 20 Oct 1631 [AEBK 1:207]

DICKINSON, Charles (-1740) & 2/wf Phillipa (GREENE) CARR (1658-by 1706); m1 Caleb CARR; m bef 1693 So. Kingstown, RI [TAG 42:189]

DICKINSON, John & Frances[2] FOOTE (c1629-); m2 Francis BARNARD; m by 1648 Wethersfield [GM 2:542]

DICKINSON, Joseph & Phebe[2] BRACY; m2 John ROSE; m3 Samuel HALE; m c1658 [GM 1:373]

DICKINSON, Nathaniel & Hannah[2] BEARDSLEY; m c1662 [GM 1:226]

DICKINSON, Obadiah & Sarah[2] BEARDSLEY; m Hadley 8 Jan 1668/9 [GM 1:227]

DICKSEY, John & Elizabeth ALLEN; m 1668 Swansea [Swansea Book A, p.93]

DIGGINS, Jeremiah[1] (c1650-1736) & Mary[2] CADWELL (1659/60-1731+); m bef Sept 1676 Hartford [TAG 70:22]

DIKE, Anthony & Margery ____; m2 John POLIN; by 1665 [GMB 1:546]

DIKE, Anthony[1] (c1610-1638) & Tabitha ____; m2 Nathaniel PITTMAN; by 1636 Plymouth/Salem [GMB 1:546]

DILLINGHAM, John (bp 1606-) & Sarah CALY (-1636); by 1639 Ipswich/Boston/Lynn [GMB 1:549; LMM]

DIMMOCK, Shubael[2] (bp 1644-) & Joanna BURSLEY, dau of John; m Barnstable Apr 1653 [GM 2:349]

DIMMOCK, Thomas[1] (c1610-by 1658) & Ann ____; m c1635 Barnstable [GM 2:349]

DIMON, Moses & Abigail ____; m2 Edward HOWARD; m by 1672 [GMB 3:1920]

DINELEY, Fathergone[2] (1638-bef 1675) & Hannah PORTER (1639-); m Roxbury Apr 1663 [REG 148:53; GM 2:354]

DINELY, John[2] (bp 1633-1669) & ____ ____; m c1668 [GM 2:353]

DINELY, William[1] (c1606-1638) & Alice CLOSE (-1645); m2 Richard CRITCHLEY; m Boston, Lincolnshire 9 June 1631 [GM 2:353]

DIRKYE, William & Martha[2] CROSS (1643[/4]-); m Ipswich 20 Dec 1664 [GM 2:243]

DISBROW, Thomas & Mercy[2] (HOLBIDGE) NICHOLS; m1 ____ NICHOLS; m by 1680 [GM 3:349]

DIVEN, John & Hester ____; m by 1647 Lynn [Essex Probate #7719]

DIX, Edward & 1/wf Jane ____; by 1637 Watertown [GMB 1:552]

DIX, Edward & 2/wf Susannah ____ (-1661+); Watertown [GMB 1:552]

DIX, John & Elizabeth[2] BARRETT; m Watertown 7 Jan 1670/1 [GM 1:164]

DIX, John² (c1661-1711) & Rebecca² GOFFE (1651-1711); m bef Feb 1684/5
    Wethersfield [TAG 68:113-118]

DIXEY, William (c1607-1688) & Ann _____; by 1636 Lynn/Salem/Beverly [GMB 1:556]

DOANE, Daniel (c1637-1712) & 1/wf _____ _____; by 1669 [GMB 1:562]

DOANE, Daniel (c1637-1712) & 2/wf Hepsibah (Cole) CRISPE; m1 George CRISPE;
    after 28 July 1682 [GMB 1:562]

DOANE, Ephraim (c1642-) & Mary (Smalley) SNOW; after 1692 Eastham [GMB
    1:562]

DOANE, John (c1590-1685/6) & 1/wf Ann _____; by 4 Dec 1648, by 1625? Eastham
    [GMB 1:562]

DOANE, John (c1590-1685/6) & 2/wf Lydia _____; by 1 Apr 1659 [GMB 1:562]

DOBYSON, _____ & Sarah² MASTERS (c1609-) [GMB 2:1236]

DODD, George & Mary² DAVIS; m2 Matthew AUSTIN; m3 William WRIGHT; m c1646
    [GM 2:308]

DODGE, John (bp 1636-) & 2/wf Elizabeth (_____) WOODBURY; m1 John
    WOODBURY; Salem [GMB 1:565]

DODGE, William (-1685+) & Elizabeth _____; by 1636 Salem [GMB 1:565]

DOGGETT, John & 3/wf Rebecca (BAILEY) BROWN (-1731); m Newbury 22 June
    1697 [REG 152:351]

DOGGETT, John & Persis² SPRAGUE (bp 1643-); m by 1674 Marshfield [GMB
    3:1737]

DOGGETT, John (c1600-1673) & 2/wf Bathsheba (_____) PRATT; m1 Joshua PRATT
    [GMB 1:569]

DOGGETT, John¹ (c1600-1673) & 1/wf Alice¹ BROTHERTON (bp 1602/3-by 1667); m
    Marston Moretain, Bedfordshire 29 Aug 1622 Watertown/Rehoboth [TAG
    72:100; GMB 1:569, 2091]

DOGGETT, John² (bp 1624-) & Anne² SUTTON; m Rehoboth 23 Nov 1651 [TAG
    72:100]

DOGGETT, Joseph (c1647-) & a sister of Putuspaquin; m c1665 [TAG 72:100; GMB
    1:570]

DOGGETT, Thomas (c1632-) & Hannah² MAYHEW (1635-); m c1652 Martha's
    Vineyard [GMB 1:570; 2:1245; TAG 72:100]

DOLE, Abner² (1671/2-) & 1/wf Mary³ JEWETT; 1 or 8 Nov 1694 Newbury/Rowley
    [TAG 74:57]

DOLE, Abner² (1671/2-) & 2/wf Sarah³ BELCHER; m Boston 5 Jan 1698/9 [TAG
    74:57]

DOLE, Henry (1662/3-) & Sarah³ BROCKLEBANK; m Newbury 3 Nov 1686 [TAG
    74:57]

DOLE, John² (1648-) & Mary² GERRISH; m Newbury 23 Oct 1676 [TAG 74:56]

DOLE, Richard¹ (bp 1621-by 1705) & 1/wf Hannah² ROLFE (-1678); m Newbury 3
    May 1647 [TAG 74:55]

DOLE, Richard[1] (bp 1621-by 1705) & 2/wf Hannah (_____) BROCKLEBANK (-1690); m Newbury 4 Mar 1678[/9?] [TAG 74:56]

DOLE, Richard[1] (bp 1621-by 1705) & 3/wf Patience[2] (JEWETT) WALKER; m contract 29 Oct 1690 [TAG 74:56]

DOLE, Richard[2] (1650-) & Sarah[3] GREENLEAF; m Newbury 7 June 1677 [TAG 74:57]

DOLE, William[2] (1660-) & Mary[3] BROCKLEBANK; m Newbury 13 Oct 1684 [TAG 74:57]

DOLLIVER, Samuel & Mary[2] ELWELL; m2 James GARDNER; m Gloucester 15 Aug 1654 [GM 2:429]

DONNELL, Samuel[2] (1645/6-1718) & Alice[3] CHADBOURNE (c1661-1744); m2 Jeremiah Moulton; m Barnstable 5 Nov 1677 [CG, 29]

DORCHESTER, James (-1732) & Sarah PARSONS (1656-1740); m Springfield 1 Mar 1676/7 [REG 148:223]

DORMAN, Ephraim[2] (c1645-) & Mary _____; m c1674 Topsfield [GM 2:359]

DORMAN, John[2] & Mary COOPER, dau of Peter; m Topsfield 21 Nov 1660 [GM 2:359]

DORMAN, Thomas[1] (c1600-1670) & Ellen _____ (-1667/8); m c1663 Topsfield [GM 2:358]

DORMAN, Thomas[2] & Judith WOOD; m Topsfield 6 Nov 1662 [GM 2:359]

DORRYFALL, Barnaby (c1615-1680/1) & Elizabeth _____ (-1679); Braintree [GMB 1:572]

DOTEN, Martha, dau. of Thomas ~ Plymouth [Plymouth Court Sept 1690]

DOTEY, Joseph[2] (1651-c1732) & Deborah[2] ELLIS (c1652-1711); m c1673/4 Rochester [REG 119:173; GMB 1:575]

DOTY, Edward (c1599-1655) & 1/wf _____ _____; bef 1635 [GMB 1:574]

DOTY, Edward[1] (c1599-1655) & 2/wf Faith CLARKE (c1617-1675); m2 John PHILLIPS; Plymouth 6 Jan 1634/5 [GMB 1:574; GM 2:100]

DOTY, Isaac (1647/8-) & Elizabeth ENGLAND; by 1673 [GMB 1:575]

DOTY, John & 1/wf Elizabeth COOKE; by 24 Aug 1668 Plymouth [GMB 1:575]

DOTY, John & 2/wf Sarah ?RICKARD; by c1695 [GMB 1:575]

DOTY, Thomas[2] (1641/2-1678) & 1/wf Mary (_____) CHURCHILL; m2 Henry CHURCHILL; by 1675 Plymouth [GMB 1:575; TAG 71:114]

DOUD, Henry[1] & Elizabeth _____ [TAG 76:298]

DOUD, John[2] (1650-by 1711) & 1/wf Hannah[2] SALMON (c1653-1687); m 14 June 1679 Wethersfield/Guilford [TAG 76:296-8]

DOUG, John[2] (1650-by 1711) & 2/wf Mary BARTLETT; m Guilford Jan 1687/8 [TAG 76:298]

DOUGHTY, Francis (c1607-1669+) & 1/wf Bridget _____ [TAG 77:2-17]

DOUGHTY, Francis (c1607-1669+) & 2/wf Anne (GROVES) (COTTON) EATON [TAG 77:2-17]

DOUGHTY, Francis[1] & _____ _____; by 1632[/3] [TAG 74:57]

DOUGHTY, James & Lydia[2] TURNER; m Scituate 15 Aug 1649 [GMB 3:1845]

DOUGLAS, Robert (bp 1638[/9]-) & Mary[2] HEMPSTEAD; m New London 28 Sept 1665 [TAG 74:280]

DOUGLAS, William (c1610-1682) & Anne[1]MOTLEY (bp 1601-1670+); m c1635 Denford, Northamptonshire/New London [TAG 74:278]

DOUGLAS, William[2] (1645-) & 1/wf Abiah[2] HOUGH; m New London 18 Dec 1667 [TAG 74:280]

DOW, Joseph[3] (1663-1734/5) & 1/wf Mary[2] CHALLIS (1668-1697); m 25 May 1687 Salisbury [ASBO, p.152]

DOW, Stephen[2] & Joanna[2] (CORLISS) HUTCHINS (1650-1734); m1 Joseph[2] HUTCHINS [ASBO, p.210]

DOW, Thomas[2] (1653-1728) & 2/wf Susanna HILL (-1724); m by 1685 [TAG 60:75]

DOWNE, _____ & Eglin[1] HANFORD (bp 1586-1653[/4?]+); m2 Jeffrey HANFORD; m3 Richard[1] SILLIS; m by 1609 Winkleigh, Devonshire/Scituate [GM 3:205]

DOWNES, Thomas & Susannah (ELIOT) HOBART (1641-); by 13 May 1674 Boston [GMB 1:629]

DOWNING, Emanuel[1] (bp 1585-1660+) & 1/wf Anne WARE Ipswich, Suffolk [TAG 74:173]

DOWNING, Emanuel[1] (bp 1585-1660+) & 2/wf Lucy[1] WINTHROP (-1679); m Groton, Suffolk 10 Apr 1622 Westminster, Middlesex [TAG 74:173]

DOWNING, George (c1624-1684) & Frances HOWARD; m 1654 [TAG 74:173]

DOWNING, John[1] (bp 1639/40-1694) & _____ _____ Salem/Boston [TAG 74:174]

DOWNING, Joshua[1] (bp 1627/8-) & _____ Salem/Barbados/Glasgow 1658 [TAG 74:174]

DOWSE, John[2] & Relief[2] HOLLAND (bp 1650-); m2 Timothy FOSTER; m3 Henry LEADBETTER; m Charlestown 31 Oct 1672 [GM 3:376; TAG 68:181]

DRAKE, _____ & Joan _____ (c1595-by 1637); m by 1634 Boston [GM 2:361]

DRAKE, Job & Mary[2] WOLCOTT; m Windsor 25 June 1646 [GMB 3:2051]

DRAKE, John & Hannah[2] MOORE (c1628-); m Windsor 30 Nov 1648 [GMB 2:1277]

DRAKE, Thomas & Jane[2] HOLBROOK (c1637-); m by 1657 [GM 3:353]

DRINKER, Edward[2] (bp 1621-) & 1/wf Elizabeth _____ [GM 2:364]

DRINKER, John[2] (bp 1626-) & Elizabeth _____; m c1653 Charlestown [GM 2:365]

DRINKER, Philip[1] (bp 1595-1647) & 1/wf Mary ABRAHAM (-1627/8); m Hernehill, Kent 29 Oct 1620 [GM 2:364]

DRINKER, Philip[1] (bp 1595-1647) & 2/wf Thomasine SHRUBSOLE (-1634); m Hernehill, Kent 13 Oct 1628 [GM 2:364]

DRINKER, Philip[1] (bp 1595-1647) & 3/wf Elizabeth RICHARDS (-by 1651); m Hernehill, Kent 13 Jan 1634/5 [GM 2:364]

DRIVER, John[2] & _____ _____; m c1673 Lynn [GM 2:367]

DRIVER, Robert[1] (c1592-1680) & Phebe _____ (-1682/3); m c1634 Lynn [GM 2:366]

DRIVER, Robert[2] & Sarah SALMON; m Lynn 6 Jan 1663/4 [GM 2:366]

DUCY, John & Joan[2] VINES; m by 1667 [GMB 3:1879]

DUDLEY, Francis & Sarah[2] WHEELER (1640-1713); m Concord 26 Oct 1665 [AEBK 3]

DUDLEY, Paul & Mary LEVERETT; m2 Penn TOWNSEND; by 1676 Roxbury [GMB 1:585]

DUDLEY, Samuel (bp 1608-) & 1/wf Mary[2] WINTHROP (bp 1611/2-); m by 1632 [GMB 1:584-85, 3:2040]

DUDLEY, Samuel (bp 1608-) & 2/wf Mary BYLEY; by 1644 [GMB 1:584/85]

DUDLEY, Samuel[2] (1608-1683) & 3/wf Elizabeth (?SMITH) GILMAN; dau. of Richard; m1 Edward[2] GILMAN; m c1655 Cambridge/Salisbury/Exeter [AMacE, GMB 1:584-85]

DUDLEY, Thomas (bp 1576-1653) & 1/wf Dorothy YORKE (-1643; Hardingstone, Northamptonshire 25 Apr 1603 [GMB 1:584]

DUDLEY, Thomas (bp 1576-1653) & 2/wf Katherine (DEIGHTON) HAGBORN; m1 Samuel HAGBORNE; m3 John ALLIN Roxbury 4 Apr 1644 [GMB 1:584]

DUMBLETON, John[1] (-1702) & Mercy[2] MARSHFIELD (probably d/o Thomas[1] Marshfield) (-1704); m c1648 Windsor/Springfield [TAG 63:161-63 & Hale House, 521-524 & TAG 67:11-14]

DUMMER, Jeremiah & Ann ATWATER; m aft 3 Sept 1672 [GMB 1:591]

DUMMER, Richard & 1/wf Jane MASON; by 1632 Newbury [GMB 1:590-91]

DUMMER, Richard & 2/wf Frances _____ (-1682); by 1645 Newbury [GMB 1:590-91]

DUMMER, Shubael & Lydia ALCOCK; m say 1656 Newbury [GMB 1:591]

DUNCAN, Nathaniel (bp 1586-by 1668/9) & Elizabeth JOURDAINE; St. Mary Arches, Exeter, Devon 6 Jan 1616 [GMB 1:595]

DUNCAN, Peter & Mary EPES; by 10 Nov 1655 Boston [GMB 1:598]

DUNHAM, Daniel (c1639-) & Hannah _____; say 1670 Plymouth [GMB 1:603]

DUNHAM, John (c1589-1668/9) & 2/wf Abigail BARLOW; m Leiden 22 Oct 1622 [GMB 1:602; TAG 71:131]

DUNHAM, John (c1616-1692) & Mary _____; by 1642 Plymouth [GMB 1:602]

DUNHAM, John[1] (c1589-1668/9) & 1/wf Susanna KENO; m Clophill, Bedfordshire 17 Aug 1612 Plymouth [GMB 1:602; TAG 71:131]

DUNHAM, Nathaniel[3] (c1662-) & 1/wf Mary TILSON (-1714); m 21 Jan 1691/2 Plymouth [TAG 62:7]

DUNHAM, Thomas apparently did not marry anyone [TAG 30:148-9]

DUNKIN, Samuel[1] (c1619-1680/1+) & Mary _____; m c1645 Boston [GM 2:370]

DUNKIN, Samuel[2] & Deliverance _____; m by 1667 Roxbury [GM 2:370]

DUNNE, Richard (negro) & Grace _____ (negro); m by 1654 [Boston VR 1:42]

DURKEE, William[1] (c1634-1712) & Martha[2] CROSS (1643-1726/7); m 20 Dec 1664 Ipswich [ASBO, p.230]

DURRELL, Philip[1] (-1749) & _____ ?PURINGTON (-killed 1726); m bef 1685 Kennebunkport [REG 132:117]

DUTCH, Samuel & Abigail[2] GIDDINGS (c1650-); m Ipswich 12 Feb 1673[/4?] [GM 3:55]

DUTCH, Samuel & Susanna[2] MORE (bp 1650-); m2 Richard HUTTON; m c1675 [GMB 2:1285]

DWELLY, John ~ _____ _____; Scituate [Plymouth Court Oct 1686]

DWELLY, Richard & Elizabeth[2] SIMONSON (c1651-); m c1673 [GMB 3:1683]

DWIGHT, John[1] (c1601-1660[/1]) & 1/wf Hannah _____ (-1656); m by 1626 Dedham [GM 2:375]

DWIGHT, John[1] (c1601-1660[/1]) & 2/wf Elizabeth (_____) (THATCHER) RIPLEY; m1 Thomas THATCHER; m2 William RIPLEY; m Dedham 20 Jan 1657[/8?] [GM 2:375]

DWIGHT, Timothy & Dorcas[2] WATSON (1639-); m2 John ADAMS; m Medfield 8 July 1669 [GMB 3:1949]

DWIGHT, Timothy[2] (c1631-1717/8) & 1/wf Sarah PENNAN; m 11 Nov 1651 [GM 2:376]

DWIGHT, Timothy[2] (c1631-1717/8) & 2/wf Sarah POWELL, dau of Michael; m Dedham 3 May 1653 [GM 2:376]

DWIGHT, Timothy[2] (c1631-1717/8) & 3/wf Anna FLINT; m Dedham 9 Jan 1664/5 [GM 2:376]

DWIGHT, Timothy[2] (c1631-1717/8) & 4/wf Mary (POOLE) EDWARDS, dau of John; m1 Matthew EDWARDS; m Dedham 7 Jan 1686/7 [GM 2:376]

DWIGHT, Timothy[2] (c1631-1717/8) & 5/wf Esther (HUNTING) FISHER, dau of John; m1 Nathaniel FISHER; m Dedham 31 July 1690 [AEBK 4:244; GM 2:376]

DWIGHT, Timothy[2] (c1631-1717/8) & 6/wf Bethia MOSS; m Dedham 1 Feb 1691/2 [GM 2:376]

DYER, Charles[2] & 1/wf Mary _____, not proven dau of John LIPPETT [GM 2:383]

DYER, Charles[2] & 2/wf Martha (BROWNELL) WAIT; m c1690 [GM 2:383]

DYER, George (c1590s-1672) & Abigail _____; by late 1636 or earlier Dorchester [GMB 1:605]

DYER, Henry[2] & Elizabeth SANFORD, dau of John; Boston [GM 2:382]

DYER, Mahershallalhashbaz[2] (c1642-) & Martha PEARCE, dau of Richard [GM 2:383]

DYER, Samuel[2] (bp 1635-) & Anne HUTCHINSON, dau of Edward; m c1663 Boston [GM 2:382]

DYER, William[1] (bp 1609-bef 1677) & 1/wf Mary BARRETT (-hanged 1660); m St. Martin-in-the-Fields, Middlesex 27 Oct 1633 [GM 2:381]

DYER, William[1] (bp 1609-bef 1677) & 2/wf Katherine _____ (-1687+); m c1664 [GM 2:381]

DYER, William[2] & Mary _____; not proven to be dau of Richard WALKER [GM 2:383]

DYKS, Leonard ~ Ruth FISH, in court 10 July 1645 [PCR 1:129]

DYRE, Samuel (bp 1635-bef 1679) & Anne HUTCHINSON (1643-1716/7); m2 Daniel VERNON; m c1660-2 Kingstown, RI [REG 145:262]

EAMES, Anthony[1] (c1592-1670+) & Margery _____; m c1615 Fordington, Dorsetshire/Charlestown/Hingham/Marshfield [GM 2:389]

EAMES, Gershom & Hannah[2] BRIGHAM (1650/1-); m2 William WARD; m by 1671 Marlborough [GM 1:403]

EAMES, Jonathan & Hannah[2] TRUANT; m Marshfield 11 Jan 1682[/3] [GMB 3:1840]

EAMES, Justus[2] (bp 1627-) & Mehitable CHILLINGSWORTH; m Marshfield 2 May 1661 [GM 2:390]

EAMES, Mark[2] & Elizabeth _____: m Hingham 26 May 1648 [GM 2:389]

EARLE, Ralph (1632-1716) & Dorcas[2] SPRAGUE (c1638-); m by 1660 Duxbury/Portsmouth/Dartmouth [GMB 3:1727]

EARLE, William & Mary[2] WALKER; m c1654 [GMB 3:1907]

EASTON, John[2] (bp 1624-) & 1/wf Mehitable GANT (-1673); m 4 Jan 1661 Newport [GM 2:401]

EASTON, John[2] (bp 1624-) & 2/wf Alice _____ (-1689); m aft 1673 [GM 2:401]

EASTON, John[2] (c1639-) & Elizabeth _____; m c1668 Hartford [GM 2:395]

EASTON, Joseph[1] (c1614-1688) & _____ _____; m c1639 Hartford [GM 2:395]

EASTON, Joseph[2] (c1643-) & Hannah[2] ENSIGN (c1645-), dau of James; m by 1668 Hartford [GM 2:396, 457]

EASTON, Nicholas[1] (c1593-1675) & 1/wf Mary _____ (-1629[/30]); m c1622 Romsey, Hampshire [GM 2:400]

EASTON, Nicholas[1] (c1593-1675) & 2/wf Christian (_____) (COOPER) BEECHER (- 1665); m1 Thomas COOPER; m2 Thomas BEECHER; m by 1637 Newport [GM 2:400]

EASTON, Nicholas[1] (c1593-1675) & 3/wf Ann CLAYTON (-1707/8); m2 Henry BULL; m 2 Mar 1671 Newport [GM 2:400]

EASTON, Peter[2] (bp 1622-) & Ann COGGESHALL, dau of John; m 15 Nov 1643 Newport [GM 2:400]

EASTON, Thomas & Jerusha WING; m 12 Dec 1684 Sandwich Quaker Meeting [TAG 67:31]

EASTWICK, Pheasant[1] (by 1642-1699/1700+) & Sarah[2] BARRON (1640-1699/1700); m by 1671 Watertown/Boston/Portsmouth/Cambridge [AEBK 1:130]

EATON, Benjamin[2] & Sarah[2] HOSKINS (1637-); m Plymouth 4 Dec 1660 [GM 3:417]

EATON, Francis[1] (bp 1596-1633) & 1/wf Sarah _____ (-1621); by 1620 Plymouth [TAG 72:304; GMB 1:609]

EATON, Francis[1] (bp 1596-1633) & 2/wf Dorothy _____ (-1622) [TAG 72:304; GMB 1:609]

EATON, Francis[1] (bp 1596-1633) & 3/wf Christian PENN; m2 Francis BILLINGTON; m c1624 Plymouth [TAG 72:304; GMB 1:609]

EATON, John (bp 26 Dec 1590-1668) & 1/wf Anne _____ (-1660/1); m c1618 Hatton, Warwickshire/Haverhill [26 GMC, TAG 68:52]

EATON, John[1] (bp 1590-1668) & 2/wf Phebe (_____) DOW, m1 Thomas[1] DOW; m Haverhill 20 Nov 1661 [TAG 68:52]

EATON, John[1] (c1605-1658) & Abigail (_____) DAMON; m St. James, Dover, Kent 5 Apr 1630 Dedham [GM 2:405]

EATON, John[2] & Alice _____; m c1665 Dedham [GM 2:405]

EATON, Samuel & 1/wf Elizabeth _____; by 1646 Plymouth [GMB 1:609]

EBORNE, Samuel & Susannah[2] TRASK (bp 1638-); m Salem 19 Feb 1663[/4] [GMB 3:1836]

ECLES, John (c1600-1641+) & _____ _____; by 1624 Dorchester [GMB 2:619]

EDDY, _____ & Edith BROWNSON (1655-); m bef 27 Feb 1684/5 Farmington [TAG 38:208]

EDDY, John & 1/wf Amy DOGGETT (-c1645); by 1622 Watertown [GMB 1:612]

EDDY, John & 2/wf Abigail (_____) SMITH; m1 Jeremiah SMITH; after 1692 [GMB 1:616-17]

EDDY, John & 2/wf Joanna (_____) MEADE (c1603-1683); m1 Gabriel MEADE; after 12 May 1666 Watertown [GMB 1:612]

EDDY, John[2] & 1/wf Hepzibah[2] DOGGETT; by 1659 Swansea [TAG 72:100; GMB 1:570, 616]

EDDY, Obadiah (c1645-) & Bennet ELLIS; by 1669 Swansea [GMB 1:617]

EDDY, Samuel (bp 1608-1688) & Elizabeth _____ (c1607-1689); by 1637 Cranbrook, Kent/Swansea [GMB 1:616]

EDENDEN, Edmund (bp 21 Oct 1599-) & 2/wf Elizabeth WHITMAN (bp 31 Aug 1606-); m2 Samuel SKIFT; m Maidstone, Kent 1 Feb 1631/2 Charlestown [26 GMC]

EDGE, Robert & Florence _____ York/Kittery [GM 3:3]

EDGECOMB, Robert & Rachel[2] GIBBONS (1660-); m c1682 [GM 3:47]

EDGERTON, Peter (c1650s-) & 1/wf Clemence _____ (-by 1678); m by 1671 Boston [MK]

EDGERTON, Peter (c1650s-) & 2/wf Mary _____; m by 1678 Boston [MK]

EDMONDS, John[2] & 1/wf Sarah HUDSON (-1682[/3]); m Lynn 16 Dec 1662 [GM 2:410]

EDMONDS, John[2] & 2/wf Mary (_____) GEORGE; m Marblehead 17 Sept 1683 [GM 2:410]

EDMONDS, Joseph[2] (c1643-) & 1/wf Susanna _____; m by 1670 Lynn [GM 2:410]

EDMONDS, Joseph[2] (c1643-) & 2/wf _____ _____; m by 1673 Lynn [GM 2:410]

EDMONDS, Joseph[2] (c1643-) & 3/wf Elizabeth BURGESS; m Lynn 27 Jan 1685[/6] [GM 2:410]

EDMONDS, Samuel[2] & 1/wf Elizabeth MERRIAM; m Lynn 11 Aug 1675 [GM 2:410]

EDMONDS, William[1] (c1610-1681+) & 1/wf Mary _____; m by 1638 Lynn [GM 2:409]

EDMONDS, William[1] (c1610-1681+) & 2/wf Ann (_____) MARTIN (-1686); m Boston 1 Sept 1657 [GM 2:409]

EDMUNDS, Daniel[2] & Mary[2] SPRAGUE (bp 1634-); m by 1664 Charlestown [GMB 3:1730]

EDMUNDS, Walter (c1595-1667) & Dorothy _____ (-1671); m c1619 Gainsborough, Lincolnshire/Concord/Charlestown [DR & 26 GMC]

EDSON, Samuel (bp 5 Sept 1613-1692) & Susanna _____ (not Orcutt) (c1618-1699/1700); Salem [26 GMC]

EDWARDS, John & Elizabeth[2] PALGRAVE (c1625-); m by 8 June 1651 [GMB 3:1375]

EDWARDS, John[1] (c1600-1664) & 1/wf _____ _____; England/ Wethersfield [REG 145:318]

EDWARDS, John[1] (c1600-1664) & 2/wf Dorothy (MOULTON) FINCH; m1 Abraham FINCH; m3 Richard TOWSLEY; m bef 1638 Wethersfield [REG 145:318]

EDWARDS, Joseph[2] (1648-1681) & Sarah[2] SALMON (c1648-1716+); m2 1683 Samuel[2] CURTIS; m Wethersfield 12 Nov 1670 [REG 145:336; TAG 71:238, 296]

EDWARDS, Matthew & Mary[2] POOLE (c1637-); m2 Timothy DWIGHT; m Reading 2 Dec 1657 [GMB 3:1495]

EDWARDS, Robert[1] (c1613-by 1646) & Christian _____; m by 1640 Concord [GM 2:412]

EDWARDS, Thomas[2] (c1623-1683) & _____ (_____) LOVELAND, m1 _____ LOVELAND; m c1649 [REG 145:322]

EDWARDS, William[1] (bp 1618-c1680) & Agnes[1] (HARRIS) SPENCER (bp 1604-1680+); m1 William SPENCER; m 11 Dec 1645 Hartford [TAG 40:72; 63:41]

EELES, John (c1600-1641+) & _____ _____; by 1624 Dorchester [GMB 1:619]

EELES, Samuel[2] & Ann LENTHALL; m Lynn 4 Aug 1663 [TAG 72:3]

EGGLESTON, Bigod (bp 1586/7-1674) & 1/wf _____ _____; by 1612 Settrington, Yorkshire/Windsor [GMB 1:622]

EGGLESTON, Bigod (bp 1586/7-1674) & 2/wf _____ _____; by 1634 Settrington, Yorkshire/Windsor [GMB 1:622]

EGGLESTON, James (c1620-) & Esther[2] KELSEY (c1636-); m2 James ENO; m3 John WILLIAMS; m by 1 Jan 1656/7 Windsor [GMB 1:622, 2:1119]

EGGLESTON, Samuel (c1634-) & Sarah DISBOROUGH; by 6 Mar 1663 Middletown [GMB 1:622]

ELDRED, Nathaniel (-1676+) & Anne HAYNES (bp. 1623-); m by 27 Oct 1646 Barbadoes [DR; GMB 2:896]

ELDREDGE, Thomas & 1/wf Mary STEBBINS (1642/3-by 1684); m bef 1668 Boston [TAG 41:95-6]

ELIOT, Asaph (bp 1651-) & 1/wf Elizabeth DAVENPORT; by 30 July 1678 Boston [GMB 1:511, 629]

ELIOT, Asaph (bp 1651-) & 2/wf Hannah PAINE (1666-1717); m2 Thomas FAYERWEATHER, m3 Samuel CLARK; m by 2 Oct 1682 Boston [GMB 1:629; REG 146:380]

ELIOT, Edmond & Sarah HADDON (c1639/40-); m2 Samuel YOUNGLOVE; by 25 Sept 1660 Salisbury [GMB 2:833]

ELIOT, Jacob (bp 1606-1651) & Margery _____ (-1661); by 1632 Widford, Hertfordshire/ Boston [GMB 1:628]

ELIOT, John & Sarah[2] WILLET (1643-); m by 1662 [GMB 3:2000]

ELIOT, John (bp 1604-1690) & Ann MOUNTFORD (-1686/7); Widford, Hertfordshire 4 Sept 1632 [sic] Roxbury [GMB 1:631]

ELIOT, John[2] (1636-) & Mary WILLET; by 21 Sept 1662 Roxbury [GMB 1:631]

ELIOT, Joseph & 1/wf Sarah BRENTON; by 6 Oct 1676 Guilford [GMB 1:631]

ELIOT, Joseph & 2/wf Mary WILLIS; by 7 Nov 1685 Gilford [GMB 1:631]

ELIOT, Philip[1] (bp 1602-1657) & Elizabeth SYBTHORPE, dau of Robert; m by lic 20 Oct 1624 Little Hallingbury, Essex/Roxbury [GM 2:415]

ELITHORP, Nathaniel & Mary[2] BATT; m Rowley 16 Dec 1657 [GM 1:203]

ELKINS, Eleazer[2] & Deborah BLAKE, dau of Jasper; m Hampton 31 Dec 1673 [GM 2:419]

ELKINS, Gershom[2] (c1641-) & Mary SLEEPER, dau of Thomas; m Hampton 15 May 1667 [GM 2:419]

ELKINS, Henry[1] (c1613-1668) & Mary _____ (-1658/9); m c1638 Hampton [GM 2:419]

ELKINS, Oliver (c1660-c1723) & Jane[2] PURCHASE (c1663-1716); m c1686 Lynn [TG 3:54; GMB 3:1532]

ELLENWOOD, Benjamin (1668-) & Mary _____; m c1688 Beverly [GM 2:423]

ELLENWOOD, John[2] (1659-) & 1/wf Elizabeth ROWLANDSON, dau of Thomas; m Marblehead 8 Jan 1684/5 [GM 2:423]

ELLENWOOD, John[2] (1659-) & 2/wf Sarah MORRELL; m Beverly 30 Mar 1698 [GM 2:423]

ELLENWOOD, Ralph[1] (c1608-1673[/4]) & 1/wf Elizabeth _____; m by 1641 perhaps earlier Salem [GM 2:422]

ELLENWOOD, Ralph[1] (c1608-1673[/4]) & 2/wf Ellen LYN (c1636-); m2 William BATH; m Salem 14 Mar 165[4/]5 [GM 2:422]

ELLENWOOD, Ralph[2] (165[6/]7-) & 1/wf Katherine _____; m by 1682 ; annulled [GM 2:422]

ELLENWOOD, Ralph[2] (165[6/]7-) & 2/wf Martha ROWLANDSON, dau of Thomas; m Marblehead 19 Aug 1691 [GM 2:422]

ELLET, John (c1608-1658+) & Margaret _____ (-1658); by 1633 Watertown/Stamford [GMB 1:633]

ELLICOTT, Thomas & Margaret[2] VINES; m St. Michael Parish, Barbados 18 Oct 1649 [GMB 3:1879]

ELLIS, Edward & Sarah[2] BLOTT (bp 1631-); m Boston 6 Oct 1652 [GM 1:336]

ELLIS, John & Elizabeth[3] FREEMAN (bp 1624-); m by 1644 [GM 2:580]

ELLIS, John (c1615-1697) & Joan (____) CLAPP (c1624-1703/4); m Medfield 16 June 1655 [AEBK 4:131]

ELLIS, John[3] (c1680-1758) & Sarah HOLMES (c1682-1762); m 7 Nov 1700 Plymouth [REG 120:26]

ELLIS, Manoah[2] (c1659-) & Mary[3] ?BURGESS; m c1679 Sandwich [REG 119:267]

ELLIS, Matthias[2] (1657-1748) & Mercy _____ (not NYE) (-1744+); m bef 1679 Sandwich/Yarmouth [REG 119:262, 125:140]

ELLIS, Richard & Elizabeth[2] FRENCH (c1629-); m Dedham 19 Sept 1650 [GM 2:591]

ELLIS, Richard? & Mary LANE (1653-) [REG 156:148]

ELLIS, William[2] (c1665-1716) & Lydia ?BRIGGS (-1734+); m c1696 Middleborough [REG 119:271]

ELLSWORTH, Josiah & Elizabeth[2] HOLCOMBE (c1634-); m Windsor 16 Nov 1654 [GMB 2:966]

ELLSWORTH, Josias[1] (-1689) & Elizabeth HOLCOMB (-1712) [REG 156:335]

ELLSWORTH, Josias[2] & Martha GAYLORD [REG 156:335]

ELMER, Edward (c1613-1676) & Mary _____; m2 Thomas CATLIN; by 1644 Cambridge/Hartford [GMB 1:636]

ELMER, Edward (c1654-) & 1/wf Rebecca FITCH; by 1686 Hartford [GMB 1:637]

ELMER, Edward (c1654-) & 2/wf Hannah _____; by 1696 [GMB 1:637] see below

ELMER, John (c1644-) & Rosamund GINNUARIE; about Oct 1669 Hartford [GMB 1:636]

ELMER, Samuel (bp 1646/7-) & Elizabeth _____; by 1677 Hartford [GMB 1:636]

ELMER/ELMORE, Edward[2] (c1654-1725) & 2/wf Hannah _____ (-1710); bef 14 July 1696 Hartford/Windsor [TAG 68:102; Harris]

ELMES, Jonathan[2] (1663-) & Patience SPUR; m Milton 24 May 1693 [GM 2:426]

ELMES, Rhodolphus[1] (c1620-1711/2) & Catharine WHITCOMB, dau of John; m Scituate 25 Dec 1644 [GM 2:425]

ELMES, Rhodolphus[2] (1668-); m Bethiah DODSON; m Scituate 20 Feb 1695/6 [GM 2:426]

ELMORE, Edward[2] & 1/wf Rebecca[2] FITCH (1663/4-bef 1696); m bef 1686 [TAG 68:98-100] see Elmer

ELMORE, Samuel[2] & Elizabeth GARRETT (c1653/4-1703+); m2 1693 Simeon[2] BOOTH (1641-1692/3); m c1677 Hartford [TAG 71:99]

ELWELL, Isaac[2] (bp 1641/2-) & 1/wf Mehitable MILLET, dau of Thomas; m by 1666 Gloucester [GM 2:429]

ELWELL, Isaac[2] (bp 1641/2-) & 2/wf Mary (PRINCE) ROWE, dau of Thomas; m1 Hugh ROWE; m by 1700 [GM 2:430]

ELWELL, John[1] (bp 1639/40-) & Jane DURIN; m Salem 1 Oct 1667 [GM 2:429]

ELWELL, Joseph[2] (c1648-) & Mary DUTCH, dau of Osmond; m Gloucester 22 June 1669 [GM 2:430]

ELWELL, Josiah[2] (bp 1639-) & Mary COLLINS, dau of John; m Gloucester 15 June 1666 [GM 2:429]

ELWELL, Robert[1] (c1609-1683) & 1/wf Joan _____ (-1675); m c1634 Gloucester [GM 2:429]

ELWELL, Robert[1] (c1609-1683) & 2/wf Alice (_____) LEACH (-1691); m1 Robert LEACH; m Gloucester 29 May 1676 [GM 2:429]

ELWELL, Samuel[2] (c1635-) & Esther DUTCH, dau of Osmond; m Gloucester 7 June 1658 [GM 2:429]

ELWELL, Thomas[1] (bp 1655-) & Sarah[2] BASSETT; m Gloucester 23 Nov 1675 [GM 1:193, 2:430]

ELY, Nathaniel[1] (c1609-1675) & Martha _____ (-1683); m c1634 Springfield [GM 2:438]

ELY, Samuel[2] & Mary[2] DAY, dau of Robert; m2 Thomas STEBBINS; m3 John COLEMAN; m Springfield 28 Oct 1659 [GM 2:328, 438]

EMERSON, John & Mary[2] BATTER (bp 1676/7-); m Salem 14 May 1696 [GM 1:210]

EMERSON, John[1] (c1615-1640+) & Barbara LOTHROP, dau of John; m Duxbury 19 July 1638 [GM 2:439]

EMERSON, Joseph & Elizabeth WOODMANSEE (c1628-1663-5); m perhaps Ipswich c1646 [REG 147:45]

EMERY, Anthony[1] (bp 1601-1680/1-1700) & Frances _____ (-1660+); m by 1631 Romsey, Hampshire/Newbury/Kittery/Portsmouth [GM 2:443]

EMERY, James & Margaret[2] HITCHCOCK (1664-); m c1686 [GM 3:341]

EMERY, James[2] (bp 1631-) & 1/wf Elizabeth _____; m c1657 [GM 2:444]

EMERY, James[2] (bp 1631-) & 2/wf Elizabeth (NEWCOMB) PIDGE; m1 John PIDGE; m Dedham 28 Dec 1695 [GM 2:444]

EMERY, John[1] (bp 1599-1683) & 1/wf Alice GRANTHAM, dau of Walter; m Whiteparish, Wiltshire 26 June 1620 Newbury [GM 2:448; TAG 65:213]

EMERY, John[1] (bp 1599-1683) & 2/wf Mary (SHATSWELL) WEBSTER (-1694); m1 John WEBSTER; m Newbury 29 Oct 1647 [GM 2:448]

EMERY, John[2] (bp 1628/9-) & Mary _____, NOT stepsister; m by 1650 [GM 2:449]

EMERY, Jonathan[2] (1652-) & Mary WOODMAN; m Newbury 29 Nov 1676 [GM 2:449]

EMERY, Zachariah (c1660-) & Elizabeth GOODWIN (c1666-1736); m2 Philip
   HUBBARD; m Berwick 9 Dec 1686 [CG, 45]

EMMONS, Samuel & Mary² SCOTT (1642[/3]-); m Boston 16 Aug 1660 [GMB
   3:1640]

ENDICOTT, John (c1600-1664/5) & 1/wf Anne GOWEN; by 1628 [GMB 1:642]

ENDICOTT, John (c1600-1664/5) & 2/wf Elizabeth (COGAN) GIBSON (-1674+); m1
   _____ GIBSON; by 18 Aug 1630 Boston [GMB 1:642, 2:642]

ENDICOTT, Zerubbabel & 1/wf Mary SMITH?; m c1654 Salem [GMB 1:643]

ENDICOTT, Zerubbabel & 2/wf Elizabeth (WINTHROP) NEWMAN; m1 Antipas
   NEWMAN [GMB 1:643]

ENGLISH, Richard & Jane² BUSHNELL (1662-); m by 27 Jan 1681/2 [GM 1:513]

ENSIGN, David² (c1643-) & 1/wf Mehitable² GUNN, dau of Thomas; m Hartford 22 Oct
   1663; div 1682 [GM 2:456, 3:172]

ENSIGN, David² (c1643-) & 2/wf Sarah (WILCOX) LONG, dau of John; m1 Thomas
   LONG; m aft 1682 [GM 2:456]

ENSIGN, James¹ (bp 1606-1670) & Sarah _____ (-1676); m by 1631 Hartford [GM
   2:456; TAG 75 14]

ENSIGN, John² (-killed 1676) & _____ _____; m by 1665 [TAG 73;250]

ENSIGN, Thomas¹ (c1604-1663-4) & 2/wf Elizabeth WILDER (-1676+); m 17 Jan
   1638[/9] Scituate [TAG 60:99, 73:244]

ENSIGN, Thomas¹ (c1605-1663-4) & 1/wf Anne/Hannah WYBORNE (-bef 1639); m
   Cranbrook, Kent 27 Apr 1629 Scituate [TAG 56:219, 60:99, 73:244; 75:233]

ERRINGTON, William (1592-) & Anne LIDDELL (bp 1598-1653); m 16 Sept 1619 All
   Saints, Newcastle, Shropshire/Cambridge [REG 132:49]

ESTOW, William¹ (c1600-1655) & Mary ( ) MOULTON; m 15 July 1623 Ormsby,
   Norfolk/ Hampton [REG 142:259]

ETHERINGTON, Thomas (-1664) & Mary³ SPENCER (c1634-1664); m c1656
   Newichewannok [CG, 20]

EVANS, Gilbert & Mercy HARKER; m bef 1680s Boston [Suffolk Deed 12:282]

EVANS, William (-by 1671) & Ann ?HAILSTONE (c1637-1672+); m c1657 Taunton
   [AEBK 4:317]

EVELETH, Isaac³ & 1/wf Sarah⁴ PERKINS, dau. of Jacob [AMacE]

EVELETH, Sylvester¹ (bp 1603/4-1688/9) & 1/wf Susan NUBERY (c1607-1659); m 21
   Sep 1630 Exeter, Devonshire [REG 134:299]

EVERARD alias WEBB. John¹ (c1613-drowned 1668) & Mary (_____) FAIRWEATHER
   (-1680); m3 William GOODHUE; m bet 21 June and 7 Aug 1639
   Boston/Chelmsford [GM 2:465]

EVERARD, Jedediah² (1656-by 1699) & Rachel _____; m by 1681 Dedham [REG
   154:289]

EVERARD, Richard[1] (bp 1597-1682) & 1/wf Sarah DALTON (c1595-c1630); m Woolverstone, Suffolk 24 Sept 1623 [AEBK 4:207; REG 154:263-87; GM 2:279]

EVERARD, Richard[1] (bp 1597-1682) & 2/wf Mary _____; m by 1636 Dedham [AEBK 4:207; REG 154:287]

EVERETT, Israel (1651-1678) & Abigail MORSE (1645/6-1737); m by 1675 Dedham [AEBK 4:215]

EVERETT, Jedediah (1656-by 1699) & Rachel _____; m by 1681 Dedham [AEBK 4:216]

EVERETT, John (c1636-1710+) & Elizabeth PEPPER (1645-1710+); m Dedham 13 May 1662 [AEBK 4:213]

EVERETT, Samuel (1640-1717/8) & Mary PEPPER (bp 1651-1718+); m Dedham 28 Oct 1669 [AEBK 4:214]

EVERILL, Abiel[2] & Elizabeth PHILLIPS, dau of William; m2 John ALDEN; m Boston 6 July 1655 [GM 2:474]

EVERILL, James[1] (c1603-1682) & 1/wf Elizabeth _____ (-1674+); m c1628 [GM 2:474]

EVERILL, James[1] (c1603-1682) & 2/wf Mary _____ (-by 1705); m by 4 Mar 1680/1 [GM 2:474]

EVERSON, Richard ~ Elizabeth _____ [Plymouth Court June 1698]

EWELL, Gershom[2] (1650-) & Mary _____; m by 1682 Scituate [GM 2:479]

EWELL, Henry[1] (c1613-1683-88/9) & Sarah ANNIBALL, dau of Anthony; m Marshfield 22 or 23 Nov 1638 [GM 2:478]

EWELL, Ichabod[2] (1659-) & Mehitable GWINNE; m Scituate 1 May 1689 [GM 2:479]

EWELL, John[2] (bp 1639/40-) & Mary GOODALE, dau of Richard; m by 1666 [GM 2:478]

EWER, John & Mary[2] WALLEN; m2 John JENKINS; m c1648 [GMB 3:1916]

EWER, John[2] (bp 1627/8-) & Mary _____; m by 1625 [GM 2:481]

EWER, Robert & Elizabeth CODDINGTON; m 1690 RI [TAG 67:20]

EWER, Thomas (bp 1592/3-1638) & 2/wf Sarah[2] LEARNED (c1607-), dau of William; m2 Thomas LATHROP; m St Mary Magdalene, Bermondsey, Surrey 13 Jan 1623/4 [AEBK 4:431; GMB 2:1165; GM 2:481]

EWER, Thomas[1] (bp 1592/3-1638) & 1/wf Bridget HIPSLEY (-1623); m Strood, Kent/Bermondsey, Surrey 13 Sept 1614 [GM 2:481; AEBK 4:431]

EWER, Thomas[2] (bp 1633/4-) & Hannah _____; m c1667 [GM 2:482]

EYRE, John[2] (1653[/4?]-) & Catharine BRATTLE, dau of Thomas; m 20 May 1680 [GM 2:488]

EYRE, Simon[1] (bp 1588-1658) & 1/wf Dorothy PAINE (c1597-1650), dau of William; m by 1619 Lavenham, Suffolk/Boston [GM 2:486]

EYRE, Simon[1] (bp 1588-1658) & 2/wf Martha (HUBBARD) WHITTINGHAM (-1687), dau of William; m1 John WHITTINGHAM; m by 1652 Boston [GM 2:486]

EYRE, Simon[2] (c1624-) & Lydia STARR (-1653); m by 1652 [GM 2:487]

FABER, Joseph[1] (c1609-1640+) & _____ _____; m by 1639 Boston [GM 2:491]

FAIRBANKS, Eleazur[3] (1655-1745) & Martha LOVETT (1654-1749/50); m c1678 Braintree/Sherborn [AEBK 3]

FAIRBANKS, George[2] (bp 1619-drowned 1682[/3?]) & Mary ADAMS (-1711); m Dedham 26 Oct 1646 [AEBK 3]

FAIRBANKS, George[3] (1650-1737) & 1/wf Rachel ADAMS (c1650/1-1678); m Medfield 1 Dec 1671 [AEBK 3]

FAIRBANKS, George[3] (1650-1737) & 2/wf Susanna _____ (-1750); m c1679 [AEBK 3]

FAIRBANKS, John[2] (c1618-1684) & Sarah FISKE (-1683); m Dedham 16 Mar 1641 [AEBK 3]

FAIRBANKS, Jonas[2] (bp 1625-killed 1675/6) & Lydia PRESCOTT (1641-1712+); m Lancaster 28 May 1658 [AEBK 3]

FAIRBANKS, Jonathan[1] (c1594-1668) & Grace SMITH (1597-1673); m Halifax, West Riding, Yorkshire 20 May 1617 Dedham [AEBK 3]

FAIRBANKS, Jonathan[2] (c1620s-1711/2) & Deborah SHEPARD (-1705); m c1654 Dedham [AEBK 3]

FAIRBANKS, Jonathan[4] (c1660-drowned 1719) & 1/wf Sarah _____ (-1713); m c1685 Sherborn [AEBK 3]

FAIRBANKS, Richard (c1608-1654/5+) & Elizabeth _____; by 1633 Boston [GMB 1:648]

FAIRCHILD, Thomas[2] (1645/6-1686) & Susanna _____ (-1686+); m bef 1672 Stratford/Woodbury [TAG 69:225]

FAIRWEATHER, John & Sarah[2] TURNER (1640/1-); m Boston 15 Nov 1660 [GMB 3:1854]

FAIRWEATHER, Thomas (c1613-1638/9) & Mary _____; m2 John EVERARD ALIAS WEBB; m3 William GOODHUE; by 1634 Boston [GMB 1:651]

FALES, John (1658-1735) & Abigail[2] HAWES (1662-1732); m Wrentham 20 June 1684 [AEBK 3]

FARNHAM, Henry[1] (-1700) & Joan[2] (RUCK) (SWAN) HALSEY (bp 1620/1-1689), dau. of Thomas[1] & Elizabeth; m1 Henry SWAN; div wife of George HALSEY; m bef 3 Dec 1662 Roxbury/Killingworth [TAG 62:35]

FARNHAM, John[2] & Rebecca KENT; m Andover 12 Nov 1667 [GM 2:494]

FARNHAM, Ralph[2] (bp 1633-) & Elizabeth[2] HOLT (1636-); m Andover 26 Oct 1657 [GM 2:494, 3:400]

FARNHAM, Thomas[2] (bp 1631-) & Elizabeth SIBBORNS/SEBORNE, perhaps dau of Mary; m Andover 8 July 1660 [GM 2:494]

FARNSWORTH, Jonathan & Ruth _____ (not Shattuck) (c1678-) [JP]

FARNUM, Ralph[1] (1601-by 1648) & Alice _____, m2 Solomon MARTIN; m bef 1628 St Peter's Church, Cornhill, London/Ipswich/Rochester, co. Kent [50 GMC; GM 2:493; TAG 69:35, 77:282]

FARR, Benjamin[2] & Elizabeth BURRILL; m Lynn 28 July 1680 [GMB 3:2079]

FARR, George & Elizabeth[2] STOWERS (-by 1672), dau of Nicholas; m c1630 [TAG 75:149; GMB 3:1781, 2078]

FARR, Joseph[2] (c1643-1727) & 1/wf Hannah WALDEN; m Lynn 22 Sept 1680 [GMB 3:2079]

FARR, Joseph[2] (c1643-1727) & 2/wf Rebecca KNIGHT; m Lynn 15 Sept 1696 [GMB 3:2079]

FARRINGTON, Edmund[1] (c1588-1670/1) & Elizabeth NEWHALL (c1586-1678); m Sherington, Buckinghamshire. 29 Nov 1613 Lynn [GM 2:496; TAG 65:67; AEBK 4:503]

FARRINGTON, Edward[2] & Dorothy BOWNE, dau of Thomas; m by 1651 [GM 2:496]

FARRINGTON, John[2] (bp 1622-) & Elizabeth KNIGHT, dau of William; m by 1661 Lynn [GM 2:496]

FARRINGTON, Matthew[2] (bp 1620/1-) & _____ _____; m by 1657 Lynn [GM 2:496]

FARRINGTON, Thomas & Helena[2] APPLEGATE, dau of Thomas; m2 Louis HULET; m3 Carle MORGYN; m c1644 [GM 1:73, 2:496]

FARROW, John[1] (c1608-1687) & Frances _____ (-1688/9); m by 1633 Hingham [GM 2:500]

FARROW, John[2] (bp 1639-) & 1/wf Mary HILLIARD, dau of William; m Hingham 14 Aug 1664 [GM 2:500]

FARROW, John[2] (bp 1639-) & 2/wf Frances _____; m Hingham 16 Nov 1691 [GM 2:500]

FARROW, Nathan[2] (1654-) & 1/wf Mary GARNET; m Hingham 5 Dec 1683 [GM 2:500]

FARWELL, Henry[1] (-1670) & Olive WELBY (-1691/2); Concord [TAG 70:100]

FARWELL, Joseph[2] & Hannah[3] LEARNED (1649-); m Chelmsford 25 Dec 1666 [AEBK 4:439]

FASSETT, John (-by 1736) & Mary[3] HILL (1667-1749); m 31 Mar 1697 Billerica [NGSQ 72:11]

FAUNCE, John (c1608-1653) & Patience[2] MORTON (c1615-1691); m2 Thomas WHITNEY; c1633 Plymouth [GMB 1:652, 2:1297]

FAWER, Barnabas[1] (c1614-1654) & 1/wf Dinah _____ (-1642); m by 1639 Boston/Dorchester [GM 2:503]

FAWER, Barnabus[1] (-by 1654/5) & 2/wf Grace NEGUS (poss bp 1603/4-1671); m2 John JOHNSON; m bef 10 Mar 1643/4 Boston/Dorchester [TG 6:196; GM 2:503]

FAWER, Eleazer[2] (1642-) & Mary PRESTON; m2 Samuel JENKINS; m Boston 28 May 1662 [GM 2:504]

FAWNE, John[1] (c1596-1650+) & Elizabeth _____; m by 1633 St. Olave, Old Jewry, London/Ipswich/Haverhill [TAG 77:30; GM 2:506]

FAXON, Richard[2] (bp 1626-1674) & Elizabeth _____; m c1654 [TAG 74:47]

FAXON, Thomas[1] (c1600-1680) & 1/wf Jane FAWDRY (bp 1603-1662+); m Swalcliffe, Oxfordshire 25 June 1625 [TAG 74:45]

FAXON, Thomas[1] (c1600-1680) & 2/wf Sarah (MULLINS)(GANNETT) SAVILL; m Braintree 5 Sept 1670 [TAG 74:45]

FAXON, Thomas[2] (bp 1630-1662) & Deborah[2] THAYER; m Braintree 11 Apr 1653 [TAG 74:47]

FAY, John & Mary[2] BRIGHAM; m c1669 Marlborough [GM 1:403]

FAYERWEATHER, Thomas (1661-by 1693/4) & Hannah (PAINE) ELIOT (1666-1717); m1 Asaph ELIOT; m after 27 Aug 1688 Boston [REG 144:16, 146:380]

FEAKE, Henry & 1/wf Jane WOOLSTONE; St Saviour's, Southwark, Surrey 22 Jan 1615/6 [GMB 1:655]

FEAKE, Henry & 2/wf Joanna (____) WHEELER; by 1657 Long Island [GMB 1:655]

FEAKE, Robert (bp 1642-) & Sarah ____; by 1669 Hellgate [GMB 1:659]

FEAKE, Robert (c1602-1660/1) & Elizabeth (FONES) WINTHROP; m1 Henry WINTHROP; by 27 Jan 1631/2 Watertown [GMB 1:658]

FELLOWS, Ephraim[2] (c1641-) & 1/wf Mary ____ (-1671) [GM 2:510]

FELLOWS, Ephraim[2] (c1641-) & 2/wf Ann (CROSS) MARSHALL, dau of Robert; m1 Thomas MARSHALL; m by 1683 Ipswich [GM 2:510]

FELLOWS, Isaac[2] (c1637-1721) & Joanna[2] BOREMAN, dau of Margaret; m Ipswich 29 Jan 1672[/3] [GM 1:354, 2:510]

FELLOWS, Joseph & Ruth FRAIL; m Ipswich 19 Apr 1675 [GM 1:510]

FELLOWS, William[1] (c1610-1676) & Mary ____ (-1676+); m c1637 Ipswich [GM 2:510]

FELT, George & Philippa[2] ANDREWS; m2 Samuel PLATTS; m3 Thomas NELSON; m Falmouth 25 Nov 1662 [GM 1:58]

FELT, George (c1614-1692+) & Elizabeth ____, daughter of widow Prudence (____) WILKINSON; by 1635 Charlestown/Malden [GMB 1:662, 3:1996]

FELT, Jonathan (c1672-1702) & Elizabeth (WILLIAMS) PURCHASE; m1 Thomas PURCHASE; m 3 Jan 1694/5 Salem [TG 3:56]

FELT, Moses (c1651-) & Lydia MAINS; by 1677 Malden [GMB 1:663]

FELTON, Benjamin[1] (bp 1604-by 1689) & Mary STORY; m St. Nicholas, Great Yarmouth, Norfolk 2 Sept 1628 Salem [GM 2:514]

FELTON, John[2] (bp 1639-) & 1/wf Mary TOMPKINS (-1688); m Salem 29 Nov 1670 [GM 2:515]

FELTON, John[2] (bp 1639-) & 2/wf Hannah ____; m by 1693 Salem [GM 2:515]

FELTON, Nathaniel & Ann[2] HORNE (bp 1656/7-); m c1680 [GMB 2:993]

FELTON, Nathaniel & Mary[2] SKELTON (bp 1627-); m c1646 Salem [GMB 3:1686]

FENN, Benjamin & Mehitable[2] GUNN (bp 1641-); m2 Nicholas CAMP; m Milford 20 Dec 1660 [GM 3:168]

FENNER, Arthur & Mehitable[2] WATERMAN; m c1650 [GMB 3:1942]

FENNER, Arthur[1] & Sarah BROWNE; m bef 1622 Ifield, Sussex/RI [TAG 44:126]

FERN, John & Susannah COATS; m 25 June 1695 Lynn [REG 144:54]

FERRIS, James[2] & _____ _____; m c1670 [GM 2:521]

FERRIS, Jeffrey[1] (c1604-1666) & 1/wf _____ _____ (-1658); m c1629 Stamford [GM 2:520]

FERRIS, Jeffrey[1] (c1604-1666) & 2/wf Susanna (NORMAN) LOCKWOOD (-1660), dau of Richard; m1 Robert LOCKWOOD; m c1659 Greenwich [GM 2:520]

FERRIS, Jeffrey[1] (c1604-1666) & 3/wf Judith (FEAKE) PALMER, dau of James; m1 William PALMER; m c1662 Greenwich [GM 2:520]

FERRIS, John[2] (c1640-) & 2/wf Grace _____ [GM 2:520]

FERRIS, John[2] (c1640-1704+) & 1/wf Mary JACKSON; m c1666 Hempstead [GM 2:520; NYGBR 131:7]

FERRIS, Joseph[2] & Ruth[2] KNAPP (1640/1-), dau of Nicholas; m Stamford 20 Nov 1657 [GMB 2:1136; GM 2:520]

FERRIS, Peter[2] & 1/wf Elizabeth REYNOLDS; m Stamford 15 July 1654 [GM 2:520]

FIELD, Joseph & Mary[2] (GODDARD) BENNETT (c1645-); m1 Arthur BENNETT; m3 Hans WOLFORD; m after 11 Apr 1683 [GM 3:87]

FIFIELD, _____[A] & Mary _____ (c1603-1683) (perhaps a relative of Ruth [Leete] Dalton); Hampton [NHGR 10:32]

FIFIELD, Benjamin[2] (c1648-) & Mary COLCORD; m Hampton 28 Dec 1670 [GM 2:524]

FIFIELD, John[3] (-c1748) & 1/wf Abigail[3] WEARE (1676-1701+); m bef 1698 Hampton [TAG 55:18-19, 59:93]

FIFIELD, William[1] (c1615-1700) & Mary _____ (c1621-); m c1646 Hampton [GM 2:524]

FIFIELD, William[2] (1651/2-) & Hannah CRAM; m Hampton 26 Oct 1693 [GM 2:524]

FILER, Walter (c1613-1683) & Jane _____ (-1690); c1642 Windsor [GMB 1:666]

FILLIBROWN, Thomas & Hannah[2] COLE (bp 1632-); m c1662 Charlestown [GM 2:155]

FINCH, Abraham (c1610-) & Dorothy[2] MOULTON; m2 John EDWARD; m3 Richard TOUSLEY; by 1637 Fairfield [GMB 1:668, 2:1305]

FINCH, Abraham (c1648-) & _____ _____; by 1670 [GMB 1:670]

FINCH, Daniel & 1/wf _____ _____; by c1610 [GMB 1:668]

FINCH, Daniel & 2/wf Elizabeth (_____) THOMPSON; after 25 Dec 1657 Fairfield [GMB 1:668]

FINCH, Daniel & 3/wf Mary (_____) DICKERSON; m1 Thomas DICKERSON; m3 Nicholas PINION; by 4 Apr 1660 [GMB 1:668]

FINCH, Isaac (c1635-) & 2/wf Ann _____; by 1682 Stamford [GMB 1:670]

FINCH, John (c1595-1657) & 1/wf _____ _____; by 1620 [GMB 1:670]

FINCH, John (c1595-1657) & 2/wf Martha _____; m2 John GREEN; by c1635 Stamford [GMB 1:670]

FINCH, John[2] (c1620-) & 1/wf _____ _____; Stamford [GMB 1:670]

FINCH, John[2] (c1620-) & 2/wf Hannah (Marsh) FULLER; m1 Launcelot FULLER; after 8 Nov 1652 Stamford [GMB 1:670]

FINCH, Nathaniel & 1/wf Mary HEMINGWAY; by 1691 [GMB 1:668]

FINCH, Nathaniel & 2/wf Elizabeth HEMINGWAY; by 1694 Fairfield [GMB 1:668]

FINCH, Nathaniel & 3/wf Mary (_____)(FRISBIE)(DARBY) HOADLEY; m1 Jonathan FRISBIE; m2 Robert DARBY [GMB 1:668]

FINCH, Samuel (c1613-1673/4) & 1/wf Katherine _____ (-1640+); by 1638 Roxbury [GMB 1:672-73]

FINCH, Samuel (c1613-1673/4) & 2/wf Judith (ALWARD)(GRAVES) POTTER; m1 John Graves; m2 William Potter; Roxbury 13 Dec 1654 [GMB 1:672-73]

FINCH, Samuel (c1638-) & Sarah[2] HOYT; by 1663 Stamford [GMB 1:670, 2:1031]

FIRMAN, Samuel & Miriam[2] HOYT (c1641-); m Fairfield 25 Mar 1662 [GMB 2:1030]

FIRMIN, Giles[1] (c1590-1634) & _____ _____; not Martha DOGGETT; by 1614 Boston [GMB 1:674]

FIRMIN, Giles[2] (c1614-) & Susan WARD; by 1639 Boston [GMB 1:674]

FIRMIN, John (c1588-by 1642) & 1/wf _____ _____ (-1617/8); by 1615 Nayland, Suffolk [GMB 1:677]

FIRMIN, John (c1588-by 1642) & 2/wf Susan (_____) WARREN; m1 _____ Warren; Nayland, Suffolk 30 June 1618 Watertown [GMB 1:677]

FISH, Nathan & Deborah BARROWS; m 20 Dec 1687 Plymouth [TAG 60:159; MD 13:203]

FISH, Thomas[2] (-c1684) & Grissell STRANGE (c1650-); m2 Samuel[2] CORNELL; m 10 Dec 1668 Portsmouth [TAG 54:25]

FISHCOCK, Edward[1] (c1595-by 1645) & Joan SKOBBELL; m2 Jan HAES; m St Andrews, Plymouth, Devonshire 23 Mar 1619/20 Richmond Island/New Amsterdam [GM 2:527]

FISHER, Anthony[1] (bp 1591-1671) & 1/wf Alice _____ (c1594-1662/3); m c1614 Syleham, Suffolk [AEBK 4:239]

FISHER, Anthony[1] (bp 1591-1671) & 2/wf Isabel (_____)(RIGBY) BRECK; m Dorchester 14 Nov 1663 [AEBK 4:239]

FISHER, Anthony[2] (bp 1623-1669/70) & Joanna FAXON (bp 1628-1694); m Dedham 7 Sept 1647 [AEBK 4:242; TAG 74:47]

FISHER, Cornelius[2] (bp 1629-1700) & 1/wf Leah HEATON (bp 1634-1663/4); m Dedham 22 Feb 1652/3 [AEBK 4:260; GM 3:305]

FISHER, Cornelius[2] (bp 1629-1700) & 2/wf Sarah[2] EVERETT (1644-1675/6); m Dedham 25 July 1665 [AEBK 4:214, 260]

FISHER, Cornelius[3] (1659/60-1743) & 1/wf Anna[3] WHITNEY (1660-1701/2); m by 1690
    [AEBK 1:539, 4:263-4]

FISHER, Daniel (bp 1618-1683) & Abigail MERRIOTT (-1683); m Dedham 17 Nov
    1641 [AEBK 4:242]

FISHER, Edward[1] & Judith[1] SMITH (bp 1606-1680+); m c1639 Alford,
    Lincolnshire/Portsmouth, RI [TAG 67:200]

FISHER, Eleazer (1663-1733) & 1/wf Hannah LEONARD (1671-by 1718); m Wrentham
    21 Mar 1688 [AEBK 4:266]

FISHER, John & Elizabeth[2] BOYLSTON; m Medfield 6 Apr 1658 [GM 1:371]

FISHER, John (1651/2-1727) & 1/wf Judith _____ (-c1673); m c1673 Dedham [AEBK
    4:256]

FISHER, John (1651/2-1727) & 2/wf Hannah ADAMS (1655/6-1746); m Medfield 6 Mar
    1673/4 [AEBK 4:257]

FISHER, John[2] (bp 1633/4-1668) & 1/wf Elizabeth BOYLSTON (1640-1665); m Medfield
    6 Apr 1658 [AEBK 4:236]

FISHER, John[2] (bp 1633/4-1668) & 2/wf Mary[2] TREADWAY (1642-1677); m Sudbury
    12 Sept 1665 [AEBK 1:459, 4:236]

FISHER, Joshua (bp 1587/8-1674) & 2/wf Anne ORSOR (not LUSON) (-1676/7); m
    Syleham, Suffolk 7 Feb 1638/9 [RCA, TAG 66:134; AEBK 4:231]

FISHER, Joshua (1650/1-1708/9) & Esther WISWALL (-1710/1); m Medfield 23 Apr
    1674 [AEBK 4:256]

FISHER, Joshua (bp 1587/8-1674) & 1/wf Elizabeth _____ (c1599-1638); m c1618
    Redenhall, Norfolk [AEBK 4:231]

FISHER, Joshua[2] (bp 1621-1672) & 1/wf Mary[2] ALDIS (bp 1623-1653); m Dedham 15
    Mar 1642/3 [AEBK 4:245; REG 150:489]

FISHER, Joshua[2] (bp 1621-1672) & 2/wf Lydia (_____) OLIVER (-1682/3); m Dedham
    16 Feb 1653/4 [AEBK 4:245]

FISHER, Nathaniel (bp 1626-1676) & Esther HUNTING (bp 1631-1690/1); perhaps m2
    Timothy Dwight; m Dedham 26 Dec 1649 [NGSQ 78:94; AEBK 4:243]

FISHER, Samuel[2] & Meletiah SNOW, dau of Thomas; m Boston 22 Mar 165[8/]9 [GM
    2:530]

FISHER, Thomas[1] (c1604-1638) & Elizabeth ALLEN (-1651[/2?]); m Saxlingham-juxta-
    Mare, Norfolk 21 Sept 1629 [TAG 67:29; GM 2:530]

FISHER, Thomas[2] & Rebecca WOODWARD; m Dedham 11 Dec 1666 [GM 2:530]

FISHER, Vigilance (1654-1713) & 1/wf Rebecca PARTRIDGE (-1694); m Dedham 27
    Nov 1678 [AEBK 4:258]

FISHER, Vigilance (1654-1713) & 2/wf Hannah (HEWINS) LYON (1665-1713+); m
    Dorchester 14 Apr 1696 [AEBK 4:258]

FISKE, John & Lydia FLETCHER (1646/7-1730); m2 Nathaniel[2] HILL [NGSQ 72:8]

FISKE, John (-1715) & Hannah BALDWIN; m 1681 Milford [REG 149:239]

FISKE, Joseph (1648-) & Elizabeth (BARTRAM) HAMMOND; m1 William HAMMOND; m Lynn 22 May 1677 [REG 149:232]

FISKE, Nathaniel (1653-1735) & Mary[3] (WARREN) CHILD (1651-1734); m1 1668 John CHILD; m Watertown 13 Apr 1677 [AEBK 1:478]

FISKE, Thomas & Rebecca[2] PERKINS (1662-); m 3 Nov 1678 [GMB 3:1436]

FISKE, William & Bridget MATCHET; m by 1648 Wenham [REG 149:232]

FITCH, James & Priscilla[2] MASON (1641-); m Norwich 8 Oct 1664 [GMB 2:1228]

FITCH, James[1] (c1605-by 1645[/6]) & Abigail MUNNINGS (c1611-); m Earls Colne, Essex 28 Apr 1635 Boston [GM 2:532]

FITCH, James[2] & Elizabeth[2] MASON (1654-); m Norwich Jan 1676/7 [GMB 2:1228]

FITCH, Jeremiah & Sarah[2] CHUBBOCK; m Boston 25 Sept 1657 [GM 2:75]

FITCH, Joseph[1] (c1630-1719-1727) & only wife Mary[3] STONE (-1687+); m bef Dec 1657 probably Hartford [TAG 68:100; GMB 3:1771]

FITCH, Joseph[2] & Mary STONE; Windsor [TAG 73:272]

FITCH, Joseph[2] (1665/6-1740) & Ann ____; m bef 1697 East Windsor [TAG 68:102-3]

FITHIAN, William (-1678) & Margaret ____; m bef 1646 East Hampton, L.I. [DR]

FitzRANDOLPH, Isaac & Ruth[2] HIGGINS; m2 Stephen TUTTLE; m Woodbridge 23 Apr 1692 [GMB 2:931]

FLACK, Cotton (bp 1577-1656 & 2/wf Jane ____ (-1658+); by 1642 Boston [GMB 1:680]

FLACK, Cotton (bp 1577-1656) & 1/wf Dorothy WRIGHT (-1623); Saffron Walden, Essex 1 July 1611 [GMB 1:680]

FLACK, Samuel (bp 1621-) & 1/wf Mary ____; by 12 Mar 1652/3 [GMB 1:680]

FLACK, Samuel (bp 1621-) & 2/wf Ann WORMWOOD; by 1659 Boston [GMB 1:680]

FLANDERS, Stephen & Abigail[2] CARTER (1652[/3]-); m Salisbury 28 Dec 1670 [GM 2:29]

FLATMAN, Thomas & ____ ____; m bef 7 May 1640 Salem/ Braintree [Savage 2:172]

FLETCHER, Francis[2] (c1630-1704+) & Elizabeth WHEELER (1635[/6?]-1704); m Concord 11 Oct 1656 [AEBK 3; 4:278]

FLETCHER, Moses (c1565-1621) & 1/wf Mary EVANS (-1609+); St Peter's Sandwich, Kent 30 Oct 1589 [GMB 1:681]

FLETCHER, Moses (c1565-1621) & 2/wf Sarah DENBY; Leiden, Holland 21 Dec 1613 Plymouth [GMB 1:681]

FLETCHER, Robert[1] (c1593-1677) & ____ ____ (-1672+); m say 1618 [AEBK 4:274]

FLETCHER, Samuel[2] (c1632-1697) & 1/wf Margaret HAILSTONE (c1639-1674/5-7); m Chelmsford 14 Oct 1659 [AEBK 4:280]

FLETCHER, Samuel[2] (c1632-1697) & 2/wf Hannah FOSTER (c1649-1683); m
    Chelmsford 16 [blank] 1677 [AEBK 4:280]

FLETCHER, Samuel[2] (c1632-1697) & 3/wf Mary (____) COTTEN (c1639-1700+); m
    Chelmsford 3 Sept 1684 [AEBK 4:280]

FLETCHER, Samuel[3] (1664-1704/5) & Mary COTTEN (c1677-1704/5); m Chelmsford 7
    June 1692 [AEBK 4:282]

FLETCHER, Samuel[3] (c1652-) & Hannah[2] WHEELER (-1697); m Chelmsford 5 July
    1673 [AEBK 3]

FLETCHER, William[2] (c1618-1677) & 1/wf Rachel _____ (c1624-by 1645); m say 1644
    Concord/Chelmsford [AEBK 4:276]

FLETCHER, William[2] (c1618-1677) & 2/wf Lydia (____) BATES (c1620-1704); m
    Concord 7 Nov 1645 Chelmsford [AEBK 4:276]

FLINT, Edward & Elizabeth[2] HART (c1639-); m Salem 20 Oct 1659 [GM 3:229]

FLINT, Henry[1] (c1615-1668) & Margery (HOAR) MATTHEWS (-1686/7), dau of
    Charles; m by 1642 Braintree [GM 2:536]

FLINT, Josiah[2] (1645-) & Hester[2] WILLET (1648-), dau of Thomas; m 24 Jan 1671/2
    Dorchester/Swansea [GMB 3:2000; GM 2:536]

FLINT, Thomas & Abigail BRADELL; m by lic 5 Dec 1629 Harby,
    Leicestershire/Matlock, Derbyshire/Concord [LMM]

FLOOD, Joseph[1] (c1590-1646+) & Jane WEST; m Sutton Courtenay, Berkshire 2 Oct
    1621 [GM 2:538]

FLOUNDERS, Thomas (-1670) & Sarah GREENE; m bef 9 May 1670 Newport, RI
    [TAG 59:146]

FOBES, William & Martha _____; Little Compton [LCVR]

FOBES, William (1649/50-1712) & 1/wf ?Elizabeth SOUTHWORTH delete; Little
    Compton [TAG 67:31]

FOGG, Ezekiel (bp 1638-) & Ann _____; by 25 May 1676 Salem [GMB 1:686]

FOGG, John & Grace _____ (-1674/5+); by 1 Aug 1665 Barnstable, England [GMB
    1:686]

FOGG, Ralph (c1600-1673/4) & Susanna _____ (-1673/4); by 1636 Salem [GMB 1:686]

FOLLETT, Abraham[2] (1671-1724) & 1/wf Sarah CALLUM (-1714); m Salem 30 Mar
    1697 [TAG 70:4]

FOLLETT, John[2] (1669-1719) & 1/wf Martha[2] CALLUM (1670-1706) [TAG 70:3-4]

FOLSOM, Nathaniel & Hannah[2] FARROW (bp 1648-); m Hingham 9 June 1674 [GM
    2:500]

FOOTE, Joshua[1] & Elizabeth _____ Providence [TAG 71:149, 72:55]

FOOTE, Nathaniel[1] (-1644) & Elizabeth _____ Wethersfield [TAG 71:149, 72:55]

FOOTE, Nathaniel[1] (1592-1644) & Elizabeth _____ (-1682-3) perhaps DEMING; m2
    Thomas WELLS; m by 1617 Watertown/Wethersfield [GM 2:542]

FOOTE, Nathaniel[2] (bp 1619/20-) & Elizabeth SMITH, dau of Samuel; m2 William
    GULL; m by 1647 [GM 2:542]

FOOTE, Robert[2] (c1627-) & Sarah POTTER, dau of William; m by 1660 [GM 2:542]

FORD, _____ (c1592-1621+) & Martha _____ (-by 1630); m2 Peter Brown; by 1617 Plymouth [GMB 1:687]

FORD, Andrew[2] (c1650/1-1725) & Abiah PIERCE? (c1654-1721-25); m c1679/80 Weymouth [REG 119:103]

FORD, Nathaniel[2] (1658-1733) & Joanna[3] BICKNELL (1663-1739); m c1682 Weymouth [REG 119:110]

FORD, Thomas (c1591-1676) & 1/wf Elizabeth (CHARD) COOKE (-1643); m1 Aaron COOKE; Bridport, Dorset 19 June 1616 Windsor [GMB 1:689]

FORD, Thomas (c1591-1676) & 2/wf Ann (_____) SCOTT (-1675); m1 Thomas SCOTT; Hartford 7 Nov 1644 [GMB 1:689]

FOSDICK, John[2] (c1625-) & 1/wf Ann (SHAPLEIGH) BRANSON, dau of Nicholas; m2 Henry BRANSON; m bef 1685 [GM 2:549]

FOSDICK, John[2] (c1625-) & 2/wf Elizabeth (_____)(LISLEY) BETTS; m1 Robert LISLEY div; m2 John BETTS; m bet 1685-1687 Charlestown [GM 2:549]

FOSDICK, Stephen[1] (c1584-1664) & 1/wf Anna HARRE; m Hadleigh, Suffolk 10 June 1612 [GM 2:547]

FOSDICK, Stephen[1] (c1584-1664) & 2/wf Sarah _____, perhaps WETHERELL; m c1620s [GM 2:548]

FOSDICK, Thomas[2] & Damaris _____; m2 James HADLOCK; m c1648 [GM 2:548]

FOSKETT, John (c1636-1689) & Hannah (HAZARD) LISCOMB (bp 1642-1701/2); m aft 31 Jan 1682/3 Boston/Charlestown [REG 156:218]

FOSKETT, John[1] & 1/wf Elizabeth LEACH; m bef 1670 Charlestown [TAG 43:37]

FOSS, Stephen & Mary JACKSON (bp 6 Aug 1615-); m Paignton, Devon 14 Feb 1632 [REG 144:30]

FOST, John[1] (-1699) & 1/wf Mary[3] CHADBOURNE (1644-bef 1686/7); m bef 1666 Boston/Dover [CG, 31]

FOSTER, Benjamin & Lydia _____; m by 1669 Southampton [GM 2:553]

FOSTER, Christopher[1] (c1603-1684+) & Frances STEVENS; m Ewell, Surrey 24 Dec 1628 [GM 2:553]

FOSTER, Edward[1] (c1610-1643) & Lettice[2] HANFORD (bp 1617-); m2 Edward[1] JENKINS; m Scituate 8 Apr 1635 [GMB 1:691; GM 3:206]

FOSTER, Hopestill[2] (c1621-) & Mary[2] BATE (bp 1619-), dau of James; m by 1640 Dorchester [GM 1:199, 2:555]

FOSTER, John[2] (bp 1634-) & _____ SHAW; m by 1662 [GM 2:553]

FOSTER, Joseph[2] & _____ _____; m c1665 Southampton [GM 2:553]

FOSTER, Nathaniel[2] (bp 1632-) & _____ _____ [GM 2:553]

FOSTER, Richard & Patience BIGGE (bp 5 May 1588-1637/8+); m bet 1609-1630 Cranbrook, Kent/Biddenden, Kent/Dorchester [50 GMC; GM 1:286, 2:554]

FOSTER, Samuel & Margery (_____) PITTS; m bef 30 Dec 1692 Salem [REG 144:545]

FOSTER, Thomas & Sarah[2] PARKER (1640-   ); m2 Peter BRACKETT; m Roxbury 15 Oct 1662 [GMB 3:1399]

FOSTER, Timothy[2] & Relief[2] (HOLLAND) DOWSE, m3 1691/2 Henry LEADBETTER; m 9 Mar 1680/1 Dorchester [TAG 68:181]

FOUNELL, John (c1607-1672/3) & Mary BROWNE (c1611-1696); m2 William HUDSON; m 18 Apr 1633 Hertford, Hertfordshire/Charlestown [TAG 40:29-30]

FOWKES, Henry[1] (c1614-1640+) & Jane _____; m2 William HOSFORD; m by 1640 Dorchester/Windsor [GM 2:560]

FOWLE, Isaac & Rebecca[3] BURROUGHS (bp 1674-   ); m2 1716 Ebenezer TOLMAN; Charlestown 1 Dec 1698 [TAG 76:19]

FOWLER, Joseph[2] (bp 1626-   ) & Martha KIMBALL, dau of Richard; m c1649 [GM 2:563]

FOWLER, Philip & Elizabeth[2] HERRICK (bp 1647-); m Ipswich 23 Jan 1672 [GMB 2:912]

FOWLER, Philip[1] (c1591-1679) & 1/wf Mary _____ (-1659); m by 1615 Ipswich [GM 2:562]

FOWLER, Philip[1] (c1591-1679) & 2/wf Mary (_____) NORTON; m1 George NORTON; m by 1615 Ipswich [GM 2:562]

FOWLER, Samuel (c1660-1737) & Hannah WATHEN (1663-1730); m Salisbury 5 Dec 1684 [REG 154:345]

FOWLER, William[2] & Mary TAPP (c1622-by 1670); m by 1645 New Haven/Milford [TAG 72:79]

FOX, Deborah ~ [Plymouth Court June 1700]

FOX, Eliphalet (-1711) & 1/wf Mary[2] WHEELER (1645-1678/9); m Concord 26 Oct 1665 [AEBK 3]

FOXWELL, John (c1639-) & Deborah[2] JOHNSON (c1653-   ); m2 John HARMON; m by 1673 Boston [GMB 1:695, 2:1097]

FOXWELL, Philip (c1651-) & Eleanor BRACKETT; by 1694 Piscataqua [GMB 1:695]

FOXWELL, Richard (c1604-by 1677) & Susanna[2] BONYTHON (bp 1614/5-); m by 12 Feb 1635/6 Boston [GMB 1:345, 695]

FOXWELL, Richard[1] (c1610-1668) & Anne SHELLEY, dau of Robert; m by 1635 Boston/Roxbury/Scituate [GM 2:567]

FRANKLIN, James & Elizabeth HAMMOND (1673-1760); m2 1722 Jonathan HAYWARD; m3 1735 John CHAFFEE; m Swansey 17 Apr 1695 [REG 149:223]

FRANKLIN, William[1] (c1608-by 1658) & 1/wf Alice[2] ANDREWS, dau of Robert; m by 1638 Boston [GM 1:53, 2:570]

FRANKLIN, William[1] (c1608-by 1658) & 2/wf Phebe _____; m2 Augustine LYNDON; m by 1644 Boston [GM 2:570]

FREAME, Thomas (c1650-1708+) & Mary ROWELL (1649/50-1708+); m 18 Sept 1673 Amesbury/Minsterworth, Gloucestershire [50 GMC, TAG 55:44]

FREEBORN, Gideon[2] & 1/wf Sarah BROWNELL; m 1 June 1658 [GM 2:575]

FREEBORN, Gideon[2] & 2/wf Mary (BOOMER) LAWTON, dau of Matthew; m1 John LAWTON; m Portsmouth 3 June 1678 [GM 2:575]

FREEBORN, William[1] (c1594-1670) & Mary WILSON (c1601-1670); m St Mary, Maldon, Essex 25 July 1625 Portsmouth [GM 2:574]

FREEMAN, Edmond[1] (bp 1596-1682) & 1/wf Bennett HODSOLL (-1630); m Cowfold, Sussex 16 June 1617 Lynn/Sandwich [GM 2:579]

FREEMAN, Edmond[1] (bp 1596-1682) & 2/wf Elizabeth _____ (c1600-1675[/6]); m c1635 Lynn/Sandwich [GM 2:579]

FREEMAN, Edmund[2] (bp 1620-) & 1/wf Rebecca[2] PRENCE (1625-), dau of Thomas; m Plymouth 22 Apr 1646 [GMB 3:1523; GM 2:579]

FREEMAN, Edmund[2] (bp 1620-) & 2/wf Margaret PERRY; m Sandwich 18 July 1651 [GM 2:580]

FREEMAN, Henry & Anna/Hannah[2] STEARNS (bp 1628-); m Watertown 25 Dec 1650 [GMB 3:1749]

FREEMAN, Henry[2] (c1625-) & Mary SHERMAN [TAG 75:174]

FREEMAN, James[3] (c1659-) & Rachel BOND; m Boston 17 Oct 1700 [TAG 75:174, 293]

FREEMAN, John (bp 1626/7-) & Mercy[2] PRENCE (c1631-); m Eastham 13 Feb 1649/50 [GM 2:580; GMB 3:1523]

FREEMAN, Samuel & Mercy[2] SOUTHWORTH; m Eastham 12 May 1658 [GMB 3:1711]

FREEMAN, Samuel (c1600-1644+) & Apphia QUICK (-by 1668); m2 Thomas PRENCE; St Ann Blackfriars, London 14 July 1624 Watertown [GMB 1:699]

FREEMAN, Stephen & Hannah[2] ASTWOOD; m2 Robert PORTER; m3 John? CLARK; m by 1653 Milford [GM 1:94]

FREEMAN, Thomas[3] (1664-) & Alice TEWELL; m Boston Nov 1700 [TAG 75:174, 297]

FREETHY, James[2] & Mary MILBURY, dau of Henry; m c1683 York [GM 2:585]

FREETHY, John & Hannah BRAY, dau of Richard; m c1681 [GM 2:585]

FREETHY, William[1] (c1617-1688+) & Elizabeth _____; NOT BARKER; m c1651 Richmond Island/Portsmouth/York [GM 2:585; ME]

FRENCH, Edward[1] & Ann WORCESTER; m St Andrew, Rugby, Warwickshire 3 Nov 1626 Salisbury [www.worcesterfamily.com/intro.htm]

FRENCH, Jacob[2] (1639[/40?]-) & 1/wf Mary[2] CHAMPNEY (-1681), dau of Richard; m Billerica 20 Sept 1665 [GM 2:545, 92]

FRENCH, Jacob[2] (1639[/40?]-) & 2/wf Mary CONVERSE; m Billerica 30 June 1685 [GM 2:592]

FRENCH, Jacob[2] (1639[/40?]-) & 3/wf Mary _____ (-drowned 1709) [GM 2:592]

FRENCH, John & Deliverance CHUBB; m bet 1656-61 Gloucester [RCA]

FRENCH, John (c1635-) & Phebe KEYES (1639-); by 1657 Ipswich [GMB 1:705, 2:1129]

FRENCH, John[2] (c1635-) & 1/wf Abigail[2] COGGAN (bp 1638-), dau of Henry; m Barnstable 21 June 1659 [GM 2:135, 591]

FRENCH, John[2] (c1635-) & 2/wf Hannah BURRIDGE (-1667); m Billerica 3 July 1662 [GM 2:592]

FRENCH, John[2] (c1635-) & 3/wf Mary ROGERS (-1677); m Billerica 14 Jan 1667/8 [GM 2:592]

FRENCH, John[2] (c1635-) & 4/wf Mary (LITTLEFIELD) KITTEREDGE, dau of Francis; m1 John KITTEREDGE; m Billerica 16 Jan 1677/8 [GM 2:592]

FRENCH, Joseph & Sarah EASTMAN (1655-1748); m2 Solomon[2] SHEPARD [ASBO, p.374]

FRENCH, Samuel (1667-1732) & Abigail HUBBELL (c1672-1741+); m by 1694 Stratfield [REG 154:337+]

FRENCH, Samuel[2] & 2/wf Esther[2] (JACKMAN) MUZZEY; m1 Joseph[2] MUZZEY; m3 John SWEET; m c1682/3 Newbury [AMacE]

FRENCH, Stephen (bp 1600-1678/9) & Mary _____ (-1655); by 1635 Weymouth [GMB 1:702]

FRENCH, Stephen (c1635-) & 2/wf Hannah (Jacob) LORING; by 1679 Weymouth [GMB 1:702]

FRENCH, Thomas (-1679+) & Deborah (WATHEN) JOY; m by 1667 perhaps Guilford [REG 154:329]

FRENCH, Thomas (bp 27 Nov 1608-1680) & Mary MORTON?; m c1631 Assington, Suffolk/Boston/Ipswich [50 GMC; GMB 1:705]

FRENCH, William[1] (c1604-1681) & 1/wf Elizabeth _____ (-1668); m by 1625 Billerica [GM 2:591]

FRENCH, William[1] (c1604-1681) & 2/wf Mary (LOTHROP) STEARNS; m1 John STEARNS; m3 Isaac MIXER; m Billerica 6 May 1669 [GM 2:591]

FRIEND, John & Mary DEXTER; Oct 1639 [GMB 1:543]

FROST, Charles (c1632-) & Mary BOLLES; by 1664 Kittery [GMB 1:707]

FROST, Edmond[1] (c1609-1672) & 1/wf Thomasine CLENCH (bp 1608-), dau of Robert; m Earls Colne, Essex 16 Apr 1634 [GM 2:596]

FROST, Edmond[2] (c1609-1672) & 2/wf Reana (____) (JAMES) (ANDREWS) DANIEL; m1 Edmund JAMES; m2 William ANDREWS; m3 Robert DANIEL; m by 15 Dec 1665 [GM 2:596]

FROST, Ephraim[2] (c1651-) & Hepzibah _____; m by 1678 Cambridge [GM 2:597]

FROST, James[2] (1643-) & 1/wf Rebecca HAMLET, dau of William; m Billerica 7 Dec 1664 [GM 2:596]

FROST, James[2] (1643-) & 2/wf Elizabeth FOSTER; m Billerica 22 Jan 1666/7 [GM 2:597]

FROST, John[2] & Mehitable[2] BUTTOLPH (1651-1678); m 1 June 1668 Boston [TAG 58:132; GM 1:520]

FROST, John[2] & Rebecca ANDREWS; m Cambridge 26 June 1666 [GM 2:596]

FROST, Joseph[2] (1639-) & Hannah MILLER, dau of John; m Charlestown 22 May 1666 [GM 2:596]

FROST, Nicholas (c1595-1663) & _____ _____; by 1632 Kittery [GMB 1:707]

FROST, Samuel[2] (1638-) & Mary COLE; m Cambridge 12 Oct 1663 [GM 2:596]

FROST, Thomas[2] & 1/wf Mary (GIBBS) GOODRIDGE, dau of Mathew; m1 John GOODRIDGE; m Sudbury 12 Nov 1678 [GM 2:597]

FROST, Thomas[2] & 2/wf Hannah JOHNSON; m Sudbury 9 July 1691 [GM 2:597]

FROTHINGHAM, Nathaniel[2] & Mary[2] HETT (bp 1649-); m Charlestown 6 Dec 1667 [GMB 2:917; JP]

FROTHINGHAM, William (c1605-1651) & Anne _____; by 1630 Charlestown [GMB 1:710, 2:710]

FRY, Anthony[1] (by 1645-1695) & Hannah BOWERMAN (1646-1719+); m by 1670 Yarmouth [TAG 77:305]

FRY, John[2] (1671-) & Deliverance HUMMERY (1674-5-); m Bristol 18 June 1695 [TAG 77:307, 311]

FULKE, John & _____ _____; m 1661 Scituate [VR per PCRG]

FULLER, Edward (bp 1575-1620/1) & _____ _____ (-1620/1); by 1605 Plymouth [GMB 1:712]

FULLER, Elizabeth ~, in court 21 Aug 1646 [PCR 1:143]

FULLER, James[2] (c1644-) & Mary RING; m Ipswich 20 Oct 1672 [GM 2:599]

FULLER, John & Elizabeth[2] FARRINGTON (bp 1624-); m c1648 Lynn [GM 2:497]

FULLER, John & Judith[2] GAY; m Dedham 8 Jan 1672[/3?] [GM 3:41]

FULLER, John[1] (bp 1617-1666) & Elizabeth[2] EMERSON (bp 1623-), dau of Thomas; m2 Thomas PERRIN; m c1644 Chelmsford, Essex/Bishops Stortford, Hertfordshire/Ipswich [TAG 77:270; GM 2:599]

FULLER, John[2] (c1646-) & Rachel BRABROOK; m Hampton 19 Mar 1676/7 [GM 2:599]

FULLER, Jonathan & Elizabeth WILMOT; m 14 Dec 1664 [TAG 76:275]

FULLER, Joshua & Hannah[2] (GRIGGS) RAINSFORD (1659-); m1 David RAINSFORD [TAG 56:174; REG 139:307]

FULLER, Matthew (c1605-) & Frances _____; by 1630 Plymouth [GMB 1:712]

FULLER, Robert[1] & Sarah[2] BOWEN (c1624-); m c1643 Rehoboth [TAG 76:274-7]

FULLER, Samuel & 1/wf Alice GLASCOCK (-by 1613) [GMB 1:716]

FULLER, Samuel & 2/wf Agnes CARPENTER (-by 1617); Leiden 23 Apr 1613 [GMB 1:716]

FULLER, Samuel & 3/wf Bridget LEE (-1667+); Leiden 27 May 1617 Plymouth [GMB 1:716]

FULLER, Samuel (c1629-1695) & 2/wf Elizabeth (NICHOLS) BOWEN (c1637-1713); m1 Thomas BOWEN; m c1660s Plympton/Middleborough [MD 39:86, GMB 1:716]

FULLER, William[1] (bp 1609/10-1693) & Frances _____ (-1699) ; m bef 1693 Hampton [TAG 77:269; GM 2:605]

FULLER, William[2] & Susannah (PERKINS) BUSWELL; m Hampton 22 June 1680 [GM 2:600]

FURBER, Jethro[2] & Amy COWELL; m 19 Oct 1678 [GM 2:610]

FURBER, William[1] (c1614-1687-89) & Elizabeth _____; m by 1644 Ipswich/Dover [GM 2:609]

FURBER, William[2] (c1646-) & 1/wf Esther _____ NOT proven STARBUCK; m by 1673 [GM 2:609]

FURBER, William[2] (c1646-) & 2/wf Elizabeth (HEARD) NUTE; m 13 Aug 1694 Dover [GM 2:610]

GAGE, Benjamin & 1/wf Mary[2] KEYES (1645-by 1671); m Andover 16 Feb 1663/4 [GMB 2:1129]

GAGE, John (c1605-1672/3) & 1/wf Amy _____ (-1658); by 1638 Ipswich [GMB 2:721]

GAGE, John (c1605-1672/3) & 2/wf Sarah (_____) KEYES; m1 Robert KEYES; Ipswich 7 Nov 1658 [GMB 2:721]

GAGE, Nathaniel & Mary _____; perhaps widow of Thomas GREEN of Malden; by 15 Apr 1695 Ipswich [GMB 2:721]

GAGER, John (bp 1620-) & Elizabeth GORE; by 1647 Boston [GMB 2:723]

GAGER, Samuel & Rebecca (LAY) RAYMOND; m Apr 1695 Norwich [REG 156:153]

GAGER, William (bp 1592-1630) & _____ _____ (-1630); by 1618 Little Waldingfield, Suffolk/Boston [GMB 2:723]

GAINES, Henry & Jane PARTRIDGE; m 17 May 1634 Olney, Buckinghamshire/ Lynn [TAG 65:68]

GAINES, Samuel & Ann[2] WRIGHT; m Lynn 7 Apr 1665 [GMB 3:2073]

GAINES, Samuel[2] (c1637-by 1700) & 2/wf Hannah[2] BURNHAM (c1646-1716/7); m by 1668 [TAG 74:35]

GALE, Edmund & Sarah DIXEY; by 1666 Salem [GMB 1:556]

GALLEY, John[1] (c1605-1683) & Florence _____ (c1606-1686); m c1634-5 Salem/Beverly [GM 3:2-3]

GALLOP, Humphrey & Anne _____; Dorchester [GMB 2:724]

GALLOP, John (-1656) & Charity[2] HALL (c1635-1711); m2 Richard BURT; m about 1652 [AEBK 4:326]

GALLOP, John (bp 1620/1-) & Hannah LAKE; by 1644 Boston [GMB 2:726]

GALLOP, John[1] (c1593-1649/50) & Christabell BRUSHETT; m St Marys, Bridport, Dorsetshire 19 Jan 1617/8 Boston [GMB 2:726, TAG 68:13]

GALLUP, Samuel & Elizabeth[2] SOUTHWORTH; m Bristol 12 May 1685 [GMB 3:1711]

GAMLIN, Robert (c1585-1642) & _____ _____(-aft 1615 in England); bef 1610 Roxbury/Concord [GMB 2:728]

GAMLIN, Robert (c1610-) & Elizabeth (____) MAYO (-1681/2); m1 John MAYO; by 1634 Roxbury [GMB 2:728]

GARDE, Roger & Martha BRENTON; about 1664 Charlestown [GMB 1:222]

GARDINER, David[2] (1636-) & Mary HERINGMAN; m St. Margaret, Westminster 4 June 1657 [GM 3:10]

GARDINER, Lyon[1] (c1599-by 1664) & Mary DUERCANT (-1665); m by 1624 Saybrook/L.I. [GM 3:10]

GARDNER, Benjamin[2] (1663-) & Margaret _____; m Wethersfield 21 June 1688 [GM 3:15]

GARDNER, Ezekiel & Ruth EDDY (c1645-); by 1 Aug 1671 Boston [GMB 1:613]

GARDNER, George (c1616-) & 1/wf Hannah _____; by 1644 Cape Ann [GMB 2:734]

GARDNER, George (c1616-) & 2/wf Elizabeth (Freestone) TURNER; m1 Robert TURNER; by 1654 [GMB 2:734]

GARDNER, George (c1616-) & 3/wf Elizabeth (Allen) STONE; m1 Rev. Samuel STONE [GMB 2:734]

GARDNER, Joseph[2] (1658/9-) & Mary CORBIN, dau. of Clement; m c1681 [GM 3:14-15]

GARDNER, Joseph[2] (c1630-) & Anne DOWNING (bp 1633-1713); m2 Simon BRADSTREET; m Aug 1656 [GMB 2:734; TAG 74:174]

GARDNER, Peter[1] (c1617-1698) & Rebecca CROOKE (bp 1628-1675); m Roxbury 9 May 1646 [GM 3:14; LMM]

GARDNER, Richard (c1632-) & Sarah SHATTUCK; c1652 Salem [GMB 2:734]

GARDNER, Samuel & 1/wf Mary WHITE (bp 1632-1675); m by 5 Aug 1658 Salem [GMB 2:734; REG 150:195, 455]

GARDNER, Samuel & 2/wf Elizabeth (____) PAINE; m1 _____ PAINE; m 2 Aug 1680 Salem [GMB 2:734]

GARDNER, Thomas (c1592-1674) & 1/wf _____ _____; m by 1614 Salem [GMB 2:733]

GARDNER, Thomas (c1592-1674) & 2/wf Margaret _____; m by 1634 Salem [GMB 2:733]

GARDNER, Thomas (c1592-1674) & 3/wf Damaris (____) SHATTUCK (-1674); after 1641 Salem [GMB 2:733]

GARDNER, Thomas[2] (c1614-) & 1/wf _____ HAPSCOTT; m by 1643 Cape Ann [GMB 2:734]

GARDNER, Thomas[2] (c1614-) & 2/wf Elizabeth[2] HORNE (c1634-); Cape Ann [GMB 2:734, 992]

GARFIELD, Benjamin (c1643-) & 2/wf Elizabeth BRIDGE; m Watertown 17 Jan 1677/8 [REG 156:332; GM 3:21]

GARFIELD, Benjamin (c1643-) & Mehitable[2] HAWKINS (aft 1640-); m by 1674 Watertown [GMB 2:889, REG 156:332; GM 3:21]

GARFIELD, Edward[1] (bp 1583-1672) & 1/wf _____ _____; m by 1611 Hillmorton, Warwickshire/Watertown [REG 156:332; GM 3:20]

GARFIELD, Edward[1] (bp 1583-1672) & 2/wf Rebecca _____ (-1661); m by 1635 Watertown [REG 156:332; GM 3:20]

GARFIELD, Edward[1] (bp 1583-1672) & 3/wf Joanna (_____) BUCKMASTER; m1 Thomas BUCKMASTER; m Watertown 1 Sept 1661 [GM 3:20; REG 156:332]

GARFIELD, Joseph[2] (1637-) & Sarah[2] GALE; m Watertown 3 Apr 1663 [GM 3:20; REG 156:332]

GARFIELD, Samuel (bp 1613-) & 2/wf Mary BENFIELD; m Watertown 28 Sept 1652 [REG 156:332; GM 3:20]

GARFIELD, Samuel[2] (bp 1613-) & 1/wf Susanna _____; m by 1644 Watertown [REG 156:332; GM 3:20]

GARFORD, Jarvis[1] (1590-1657+) & Ann _____; m c1615 Salem [GM 3:24]

GARRETT, Daniel (c1652-1675+) & _____ _____ Windsor [TAG 71:98]

GARRETT, Daniel[1] (1612-1687) & 2/wf ?Margaret _____ (-1668+); by 1665 Hartford [Harris; TAG 71:94]

GARRETT, Daniel[1] (c1612-1687+) & perhaps 1/wf Maria USHER; m St Mary's Bocking, Essex 22 May 1636 Hartford [TAG 71:93]

GARRETT, Joseph[2] (c1657-1728/9+) & 1/wf Mary[2] ELMORE (1658-); not Jeremiah DIGGINS; m c1678 Hartford/Wethersfield [TAG 71:100; GMB 1:637]

GARRETT, Richard (c1595-1630) & _____ _____ (-1643+); by say 1620 Charlestown [GMB 2:738]

GATCHELL, Jeremiah[2] (c1648-) & 1/wf Hannah SAITH; m Charlestown 3 Feb 1672[/3] [GM 3:30]

GATCHELL, Jeremiah[2] (c1648-) & 2/wf Elizabeth BOUDE; m c1682 [GM 3:30]

GATCHELL, John[1] (c1615-1686+) & Wyboro _____ (c1615-1684); m c1639 Marblehead [GM 3:29]

GATCHELL, Jonathan[2] (c1646-) & Mary (TRIPP) WODELL; m1 Gershom WODELL; m Portsmouth 5 Mar 1682[/3] [GM 3:30]

GATCHELL, Joseph[2] (c1652-) & Judith _____; m by 1679 [GM 3:30]

GATCHELL, Samuel[1] (c1617-1686-97) & Dorcas _____ (-1684-5); m c1642 Salsibury [GM 3:34]

GATCHELL, Samuel[2] (1657/8-) & Elizabeth JONES; m 27 Nov 1679 [GM 3:35]

GATCHELL, Samuel[2] (c1639-) & Bethia EVANS; m by 1670 [GM 3:29]

GATCHELL, Thomas[2] (c1654-) & Sarah BRAYTON [GM 3:30]

GATES, Simon & Margaret[2] BARSTOW (bp 1649/50-); m Nov 1670 Scituate [GM 1:169]

GATTENSBY, John (-1670) & Susanna[3] SPENCER (c1636-1684+); m2 Ephraim JOY; m c1657 Berwick [CG, 20]

GATTENSBY, Moses (c1660s-bef 1718) & _____ _____; m bef 1690s Berwick [CG, 50]

GAUNT, Hannaniah[2] & Dorothy BUTLER (1650-); m 10 May 1678 Sandwich [REG 127:22, NGSQ 62:252]

GAWDREN, _____ & Mary COLE (c1628-) [GMB 1:434]

GAY, Eleazer (1647-1726) & Lydia[2] HAWES (1648/9-1717); m c1676 Wrentham/Dedham [AEBK 3; GM 3:40]

GAY, John[1] (c1613-1688/9) & Joanna (_____) BORDEN; m1 John BORDEN; m by 1638 Dedham [GM 3:39; REG 130:39]

GAY, John[2] (1651-) & Rebecca BACON; m Dedham 13 Feb 1678/9 [GM 3:41]

GAY, Jonathan[2] (1653-) & Mary BULLARD; m Dedham 29 Aug 1682 [GM 3:41]

GAY, Nathaniel[2] (1642/3-) & Lydia STARR; m by 1675 [GM 3:40]

GAY, Samuel[2] (1638/9-) & Mary BRIDGE; m Dedham 23 Nov 1661 [GM 3:39]

GAY, Samuel[3] (1662/3-1753) & Mary CURTIS? (1667-1744); m c1687 Roxbury/Swansey [TG 1:77]

GAYLORD, Benjamin[3] (1555-) & Ruth WILLIAMS (c1655-1690/1) [TAG 71:49]

GAYLORD, Samuel & Elizabeth[2] HULL (bp 1625-); m Windsor 4 Dec 1646 [GMB 2:1042]

GAYLORD, Walter & 2/wf Sarah[2] ROCKWELL (c1639-); m Windsor 22 Mar 1658[/9?] [GMB 3:1596]

GAYLORD, Walter & Mary[2] STEBBINS; m Windsor 29 Apr 1648 [GMB 3:1753]

GAYLORD, William (c1590-1673) & _____ _____ (-1657); bef 1615 Crewkerne, Somersetshire/Windsor [GMB 2:742]

GAYLORD, William[1] (1582-) & Jone ASHWOOD; m 11 June 1610 Long Sutton, Somersetshire/Dorchester [TAG 58:220]

GEARY, Nathaniel[2] & Anne[2] DOUGLAS (c1635-); m2 1683 Thomas BISHOP; m Roxbury 14 Oct 1658 [TAG 74:279]

GEE, John[1] (c1635-1702) & Mary _____ (-1703+) Eastchester [NYGBR 113:65]

GEE, Joseph[2] (1676-1716) & 1/wf Sarah ?LANCASTER (-c1700); Eastchester [NYGBR 113:65]

GEER, Daniel[2] & 1/wf Hannah _____ (-by 1728); m bef 1700 Preston [REG 142:46]

GEER, Joseph (1664-1743) & 1/wf Sarah HOWARD (1668-by 1713); m 17 Jan 1692/3 Preston [TAG 49:27; 71:223]

GEERE, Dennis[1] (c1605-1635+) & Elizabeth MONK; m Ovingdean, Sussex 21 Nov 1630 Lynn [GM 3:44]

GEORGE, John & Anne (_____) GOLDSTONE (c1590-1670); m1 Henry[1] GOLDSTONE; m by 1647 Watertown [GM 3:100]

GEORGE, John[1] (bp 1673-1715/6) & Ann[1] SWADDOCK (c1670s-1763); m 5 Nov 1698 St. James Pockthorpe, Norwich/Haverhill [ASBO, p.277]

GEREARDY, John & Renewed[2] SWEET; m c1652 [GMB 3:1790]

GERRARD, Robert (c1640s-1674+) & Elizabeth BECKWITH (c1647-1719+); m c1665 Lyme [AEJA]

GIBBARD, William & Anne[2] TAPP; m2 William ANDREWS; New Haven [TAG 72:79]

GIBBONS, Ambrose (c1592-1656) & Rebecca _____ (-1655); bef 1617 Dover [GMB 2:746]

GIBBONS, Edward (c1606-1654) & Margaret _____; by 1631 Boston [GMB 2:542]

GIBBONS, Giles (c1600-1641) & 1/wf _____ _____ (-by 1629); by 1625 St. Sidwell, Exeter, Devonshire [GMB 2:757]

GIBBONS, James[1] (c1614-1690+) & Judith[2] LEWIS (c1626-by 1687); m by 1648 Saco/Kittery [GM 3:47; GMB 2:1182]

GIBBONS, James[2] (1648[/9?]-) & Dorcas SEELEY; m Saco Dec 166[8] [GM 3:47]

GIBBONS, Jotham (1633-by 1658) & Susanna _____ (-1658+); m by c1655 Boston/Bermuda [GMB 2:753]

GIBBS, Benjamin (c1635-) & Lydia SCOTTOW; by 1676 Windsor [GMB 2:758]

GIBBS, Giles (-1641) & 1/wf _____ _____ (-bef 1629); m c1617 probably near Crewkerne, Somerset/Dorchester/Windsor [DR]

GIBBS, Giles[1] (c1600-1641) & 2/wf Katherine CARWITHE (-1660); St. Sidwell, Exeter, Devonshire 13 Apr 1629 Dorchester [GMB 2:757; TAG 61:33]

GIBBS, Gregory (c1625-) & Joyce (Smith) OSBORN; m1 James OSBORN; after 1676 Windsor [GMB 2:575]

GIBBS, John[2] (1644-1725) & 1/wf Jane[2] BLACKWELL (c1650-1711-16); m c1669 Sandwich [REG 117:183, 123:56]

GIBBS, Matthew & Mary[2] BRADISH; m c1652 [GM 1:383]

GIBBS, Samuel & 2/wf Patience BUTLER (1648-); m 5 Mar 1676 Sandwich [REG 127:22]

GIBSON, Christopher (c1600-1674) & 1/wf Sarah SALE (-by 1636); Chesham, Bucks. 23 Aug 1625 [GMB 2:763]

GIBSON, Christopher (c1600-1674) & 2/wf Marie _____ (-by 1655); by 1636 Dorchester/Boston [GMB 2:763]

GIBSON, Christopher (c1600-1674) & 3/wf Margaret[2] BATE (bp 1621-); by 1655 Dorchester/Boston [GMB 2:763, 3:2007; GM 1:200]

GIBSON, John[1] (c1601-c1688) & 1/wf Rebecca _____ (-1661); m c1634 Cambridge/Roxbury [GM 3:50]

GIBSON, John[1] (c1601-c1688) & 2/wf Joanna (_____) PRENTICE; m1 Henry PRENTICE; m Cambridge 24 July 1662 [GM 3:50]

GIBSON, John[2] (c1641-) & Rebecca ERRINGTON; m Cambridge 9 Dec 1668 [GM 3:51]

GIBSON, Richard & Mary[2] LEWIS (bp 1619-); m late 1638 Saco [GMB 2:1182]

GIBSON, Samuel[2] (1644-) & 1/wf Sarah[2] PEMBERTON (bp 1638-); m Cambridge 30 Oct 1668 [GMB 3:1420; GM 3:51]

GIBSON, Samuel[2] (1644-   ) & 2/wf Elizabeth STEDMAN; m Cambridge 14 June 1679 [GM 3:51]

GIDDINGS, George[1] (bp 24 Sep 1609-1676) & Jane LAWRENCE (bp 18 Dec 1614-1680/1?); m St Peter, St Albans, Hertfordshire 20 Feb 1633/4 Ipswich [TG 10:22; GM 3:54]

GIDDINGS, James[2] (c1640-   ) & Elizabeth ANDREWS; m c1670 [GM 3:54]

GIDDINGS, John[2] (c1638-   ) & Sarah ALCOCK; m c1664 [GM 3:54]

GIDDINGS, Joseph & Elizabeth ROSS; m bef 29 Mar 1698 [REG 144:54]

GIDDINGS, Joseph[2] (c1646-   ) & Susanna RING; m Ipswich 20 July 1671 [GM 3:54]

GIDDINGS, Samuel[2] (c1644-   ) & Hannah MARTIN; m Ipswich 4 Oct 1671 [GM 3:54]

GIDDINGS, Thomas[2] (c1636-   ) & Mary[2] GOODHUE; m Ipswich 23 Feb 1668[/9?] [GM 3:54, 114]

GIFFORD, _____ & Abigail _____; m England bef 1634 [GM 3:56]

GIFFORD, William & Mary[2] MILLS; m Sandwich 16 July 1683 [GMB 3:2082]

GILBERT, _____ (not Thomas) & Lydia _____ (-1654 executed for witchcraft); Windsor [DR]

GILBERT, Giles[2] (c1627-   ) & 1/wf Sarah (_____) PARKER; m aft 1667 [GM 3:59]

GILBERT, Giles[2] (c1627-   ) & 2/wf Mary (WILMARTH) ROCKETT; m1 Joseph ROCKETT; m Taunton 28 Oct 1686 [GM 3:59]

GILBERT, John & Mary (_____) HEATON; m Boston [AEBK 4:391; GM 3:305]

GILBERT, John (bp 1644-1673) & Sarah GREGSON (c1646-1697); m 12 Dec 1667 New Haven [REG 128:73]

GILBERT, John[1] (bp 1580-1656-7) & 1/wf Mary STREET (-1605); m Bridgewater, Somersetshire 17 Jan 1602[/3] [GM 3:58]

GILBERT, John[1] (bp 1580-1656-7) & 2/wf Alice HOPKINS (-1618); m Sept 1606 Bridgewater, Somersetshire [GM 3:58]

GILBERT, John[1] (bp 1580-1656-7) & 3/wf Winifred (_____) COMBE; m1 Joseph COMBE; m c1620 [GM 3:58]

GILBERT, John[2] (bp 1614-   ) & Frances COLLARD; m by 1678 [GM 3:59]

GILBERT, Jonathan & Mary[2] WHITE (bp 1626-); m 29 Jan 1645/6 [GMB 3:1978]

GILBERT, Joseph[2] (c1629-   ) & _____ SLOCUM; m c1663 [GM 3:59]

GILBERT, Thomas & Deborah[2] BEAMON (1652-); m Saybrook 27 Sept 1681 [GM 1:221]

GILBERT, Thomas[1] (bp 1589-1659) & Elizabeth BENNETT (-1659); m Yardley, Worcs. 29 Aug 1610 Braintree/Windsor/Wethersfield [TAG 67:165]

GILBERT, Thomas[2] (c1613-   ) & Jane[2] ROSSITER (c1614-   ); m Taunton 23 Mar 1639/40 [GM 3:59; GMB 3:1601]

GILES, Edward (c1610-1649) & (only wife?) Bridget (_____) VERRY (-by Nov 1680); m1 Thomas? VERRY; by 6 Oct 1635 Salem [GMB 2:765]

GILES, Eleazer (bp 1640-   ) & 1/wf Sarah MORE; m Salem 25 Jan 1664/5 [TAG 72:300]

GILES, Eleazer (bp 1640-) & 2/wf Elizabeth² BISHOP; m Salem 25 Sept 1677 [TAG 72:300]

GILES, John (1645-) & 1/wf _____ _____; Salem [GMB 2:765]

GILES, John² (1645-) & 2/wf Elizabeth² (GALLEY) TRASK (c1643-); m1 Osmund TRASK; m Beverly 5 May 1679 [GMB 2:765]

GILL, John¹ (c1660s-1735) & Mary MacCARWITHY (1663-1737); m Cambridge 31 Dec 1686 Dedham [AEBK 4:286]

GILLAM, Benjamin¹ (c1608-by 1669/70) & Anne _____ (-1673/4-74); m by 1634 Boston [GM 3:62]

GILLAM, Benjamin² (c1634-) & Hannah SAVAGE; m Boston 26 Oct 1660 [GM 3:63]

GILLAM, Joseph² (1644-) & Martha KNIGHT; m by 1673 Boston [GM 3:63]

GILLAM, Zachary² (1636-); m Phoebe PHILLIPS; m Boston 26 July 1659 [GM 3:63]

GILLETT, Cornelius (c1636-) & Priscilla² KELSEY (c1640-); m by Jan 1659[/60?] Windsor [GMB 2:768, 1119]

GILLETT, Elias (bp 1649-) & 1/wf Sarah GRIFFEN; Simsbury 29 Oct 1676 [GMB 2:772]

GILLETT, Elias (bp 1649-) & 2/wf Rebecca (Kelsey) MESSENGER; m1 Nathaniel MESSENGER; by 1699 [GMB 2:772]

GILLETT, John (aft 1640-) & Mercy² BARBER (bp 1651-); m Windsor 8 July 1669 [GM 1:156; TAG 45:225]

GILLETT, Jonathan & Mary² KELSEY (c1644-); m Windsor 23 Apr 1661 [GMB 2:1119]

GILLETT, Jonathan (c1609-1677) & Mary DOLBIAR (bp. 1607-1685/6); m Colyton, Devonshire 29 Mar 1634; Windsor [GMB 2:768]

GILLETT, Joseph & Elizabeth² HAWKES (1646[/7]-); m2 Nathaniel DICKINSON; m Hadley 24 Nov 1663 [GM 3:259]

GILLETT, Nathan (c1613-1689) & _____ _____ (-1670/1); by 1639 Windsor [GMB 2:771]

GILMAN, Edward & Elizabeth² SMITH, ?m2 Samuel DUDLEY [AMacE]

GILMAN, John & Elizabeth² GODDARD (c1643-); m by 1663 [GM 3:87]

GILMAN, John & Hannah ?ROBINSON; m 9 Jan 1684/5 Hampton [TAG 55:18]

GILSON, William (c1610-1639/40) & Frances _____; by 8 Jan 1634/5 Scituate [GMB 2:775]

GIRLING, Richard¹ (c1599-1636) & Abigail CASSON; m 28 Feb 1623/4 "Of St Mary Quay, Ipswich, Suffolk"/Cambridge [GM 3:67]

GLADDING, John (c1641-1726) & 1/wf Elizabeth² ROGERS (1647/8-1696+); m Newbury 17 July 1667 Bristol [TAG 77:208]

GLADDING, John¹ (c1641-1726) & 2/wf Sarah _____; m Newbury 19 Oct 1696 [TAG 77:208]

GLADDING, John[2] (1670-1754) & 1/wf Alice WARDELL (1670-1729); m Bristol 31 Oct 1693 [TAG 77:212]

GLADDING, William[2] (1673-1759) & Mary _____ (-1751); Newbury/Bristol [TAG 77:213, 271]

GLASS, James & Mary[2] PONTUS (1622-); m2 Philip DELANO; m Plymouth 31 Oct 1645 [GMB 3:1492]

GLOVER, Habakuck[2] (bp 1628-) & Hannah ELIOT, dau. of John; m Boston 4 May 1653 [GM 3:75]

GLOVER, Henry (1610-1689) & Ellen RUSSELL; m bef 1652 [TAG 48:214]

GLOVER, John[1] (bp 1600-1653/4) & Anna _____; m by 1626 Boston/Dorchester [GM 3:75]

GLOVER, John[2] (bp 1629-) & Elizabeth (FRANKLIN) MAY; m c1680 [GM 3:75]

GLOVER, Nathaniel[2] (c1633-) & Mary SMITH; m by 1653 [GM 3:75]

GLOVER, Pelatiah (1665/6-1737) & Hannah PARSONS (1663-1739); m Springfield 7 Jan 1686/7 [REG 148:221]

GLOVER, Pelatiah[2] (1637-) & Hannah CULLICK; m Boston 20 May 1660 [GM 3:76]

GLOVER, Thomas[2] (bp 1626[/7?]-) & Rebecca BOUCHER; m St Mary the Virgin Aldermanbury, London 25 May 1652 [GM 3:75]

GOARD, Joseph[2] (bp 1651-) & Ann CHAPLIN; m Roxbury 23 Mar 1680/1 [GM 3:80]

GOARD, Richard[1] (c1618-1683) & Phebe HEWES (-1678/9); m Roxbury 30 Nov 1639 [GM 3:79]

GOBLE, Daniel (bp 1641-) & Hannah BREWER; m Sudbury 25 Feb 1663/4 [GM 3:83]

GOBLE, Thomas[1] (c1604-1657) & Alice _____; m by 1629 [GM 3:83]

GOBLE, Thomas[2] (c1631-) & Mary _____ [GM 3:83]

GODBERTSON, Godbert (c1592-1633) & 1/wf Elizabeth KENDALL (-by 1621); m Leiden 27 May 1617 [NS] Plymouth [GMB 2:778]

GODBERTSON, Godbert (c1592-1633) & 2/wf Sarah (ALLERTON)(VINCENT) PRIEST; m1 John VINCENT; m2 Degory PRIEST; m Leiden Nov 1621 Plymouth [GMB 2:778]

GODBERTSON, Samuel (c1622-) & _____ _____; m c1657 Middleborough [GMB 2:778]

GODDARD, John[1] (c1608-1666) & Welthean _____; m2 John SIMMONS; m c1641 Dover [GM 3:87]

GODDARD, Joseph (c1655-1728) & Deborah TREADWAY (1657-1714); m Watertown 25 Mar 1680 [AEBK 1:450]

GODDARD, William (-1702/3) & Leah FISHER (1656-1720); m Sherborn 10 Dec 1685 [AEBK 4:263]

GODDARD, William[1] (bp 1627/8-1691) & Elizabeth MILES (c1631-); Inglesham, Wiltshire/Watertown [REG 156:139]

GODFREY, Edward (1584-1663/4) & 1/wf Elizabeth OLIVER; by 1629 Ludgate Prison/Wilmington, Kent/York [GMB 2:780]

GODFREY, Edward (1584-1663/4) & 2/wf Anne MESSANT (-by 1683); between 1640-1651 York [GMB 2:780]

GODFREY, Oliver (c1624-) & Mary SMITH; by 20 Jan 1648/9 Seale, Kent [GMB 2:781]

GODFREY, Peter (c1632-1697) & Mary[2] BROWN (c1636-1716); m Newbury 13 May 1656 [REG 152:350; GM 1:437]

GODFREY, William[3] (1672-1741-3) & Priscilla[2] ANNIS (1677-1768); m 17 Jan 1699/1700 Hampton [ASBO, p.125]

GOFFE, Edward[1] (c1604-1658) & 1/wf Joyce (-1638); m c1629 Cambridge [GM 3:97]

GOFFE, Edward[1] (c1604-1658) & 2/wf Margaret WILKINSON; m2 1662 John WITCHFIELD; m 1639 Cambridge [GM 3:97]

GOFFE, John (-1641) & Amy _____; Newbury [TAG 77:282]

GOFFE, Moses ~ Margaret[2] TAYLOR (1663-1714+); Wethersfield [TAG 76:183]

GOFFE, Samuel (c1629-) & 1/wf Hannah BARNARD, dau. of John; m Cambridge 25 June 1655 [GM 3:97; GM 1:164]

GOFFE, Samuel[2] (c1629-) & 2/wf Mary (_____) SAXTON; m1 Thomas SAXTON; m Cambridge 9 Nov 1682 [GM 3:97]

GOLD, Edward & Mary _____; m bef 1677 [Suffolk Deed 11:50-51]

GOLDSTONE, Henry[1] (bp 1591-1638) & Anne _____ (c1590-1670); m2 John GEORGE; m by 1616 Watertown [GM 3:100]

GOLDTHWAIT, Thomas (by 1613-1682/3) & 1/wf Elizabeth _____ (-1642+); by 1637 Salem [GMB 2:785]

GOLDTHWAIT, Thomas (by 1613-1682/3) & 2/wf Rachel (Leach) SIBLEY; m1 John SIBLEY; between 1661-1678 Salem [GMB 2:785]

GOODALE, Isaac[2] (1633-) & Patience COOK; m Salem 25 Jan 1668[/9?] [GM 3:105]

GOODALE, Robert[1] (c1604-1682-3) & 1/wf Katherine _____; m by 1630 [GM 3:105]

GOODALE, Robert[1] (c1604-1682-3) & 2/wf Margaret LAZENBY; m "about" 30 Aug 1669 [GM 3:105]

GOODALE, Zachariah[2] (bp 1640-) & Elizabeth BEACHAM; m Salem 31 Dec 1666 [GM 3:106]

GOODENOW, Edmund[1] (c1611-1688) & Anne _____ (-1675[/6]); m c1635 Sudbury [AEBK 3]

GOODENOW, Edmund[3] (1661-1727) & 1/wf Dorothy MANN (-1689), dau of Robert; m Sudbury 6 June 1686 [AEBK 3]

GOODENOW, Edmund[3] (1661-1727) & 2/wf Rebecca _____ [AEBK 3]

GOODENOW, John[1] (c1596-1654) & Jane _____ (-by 1674); m c1631 Sudbury [AEBK 3]

GOODENOW, John[2] (c1635-1721) & 1/wf Mary[2] AXTELL (bp 1639-1704); m Sudbury 19 Sept 1656 [AEBK 3]

GOODENOW, John[3] (1670-1723+) & 1/wf Ruth WILLIS (-bef 1701); m Sudbury 28 Feb 1689/90 [AEBK 3]

GOODENOW, Thomas[1] (c1608-1665+) & Jane _____; m c1630s Marlborough [AEBK 3]

GOODHUE, Joseph[2] (c1635-) & 1/wf Sarah WHIPPLE, dau. of John; m Ipswich 13 July 1661 [GM 3:113]

GOODHUE, Joseph[2] (c1635-) & 2/wf Rachel (_____) TODD; m1 Thomas TODD; m Ipswich 15 Oct 1684 [GM 3:114]

GOODHUE, Joseph[2] (c1635-) & 3/wf Mercy (BOYNTON) CLARKE, dau. of John; m1 Josiah CLARKE; m Ipswich 4 July 169[ ] [GM 3:114]

GOODHUE, Nicholas[1] & Jane _____; m by 1635 [GM 3:108]

GOODHUE, William[1] (c1612-1694-) & 1/wf Margery WATSON (-1668); m c1635 Ipswich [GM 3:113]

GOODHUE, William[1] (c1612-1694-) & 2/wf Mary (_____) (FAIRWEATHER) EVERARD alias WEBB; m1 Thomas FAIRWEATHER; m2 John EVERED alias WEBB; m Ipswich 7 Sept 1669 [GM 3:113]

GOODHUE, William[1] (c1612-1694+) & 3/wf Bethiah (RAY)(LOTHROP) GRAFTON (-1688); m1 Daniel RAY; m2 Thomas LOTHROP; m3 Joseph GRAFTON; m aft 1680 Ipswich [GM 3:113]

GOODHUE, William[1] (c1612-1694+) & 4/wf Remember (_____) FISKE (-1701/2); m1 John FISKE; m by 1691 Ipswich [GM 3:113]

GOODHUE, William[2] (c1645-) & Hannah DANE; m Ipswich 14 Nov 1666 [GM 3:114]

GOODMAN, John (1661-) & Hannah NOBLE; m c1685 Deerfield [GMB 2:788]

GOODMAN, Richard (c1609-1676) & Mary[2] TERRY (-1692/3); m Windsor 8 Dec 1659 [GMB 2:788, 3:1806]

GOODMAN, Thomas (1673-) & Grace MARSH; m by 1699 Hadley [GMB 2:789]

GOODRIDGE, Daniel[3] (1570-1747) & Mary[2] ORDWAY (1673-1754); m int 16 Nov 1698 Newbury [ASEO, p.90]

GOODSPEED, Nathaniel & Elizabeth BURSLEY (bp 1649-1706/7); m Barnstable Nov 1666 [AEBK 4:138]

GOODWIN, Daniel (c1656-1726) & Amy THOMPSON; m Berwick 17 Dec 1682 [CG, 35]

GOODWIN, Daniel[1] (1617-by 1712/3) & Margaret[3] SPENCER (c1632-by 1673); m bef Mar 1653 Kittery [CG, 19]

GOODWIN, James (c1658-1697) & Sarah THOMPSON (-bef 1714); m2 William HEARL; m 9 Dec 1686 Berwick [CG, 41]

GOODWIN, Moses (c1665-1726) & Abigail TAYLOR; m South Berwick 7 Sept 1694 [CG, 44]

GOODWIN, Thomas (c1657-bef 1714) & Mehitable PLAISTED (c1670-1740+); m 1685 Berwick [CG, 39]

GOODWIN, William (c1591-1673) & 1/wf Elizabeth WHITE (-by 1669/70); m Shalford, Essex 7 Nov 1616 Hartford [GMB 2:792]

GOODWIN, William (c1591-1673) & 2/wf Susanna (GARBRAND) HOOKER (-1676); m1 Rev. Thomas HOOKER; m by 1669/70 Farmington [GMB 2:793]

GOODWIN, William (c1662-1714) & Deliverance TAYLOR (c1670-) ; m Kittery Oct 1687 [CG, 41]

GORDING, Abraham & _____ SUNDERLAND; m by May 1677 Boston [Boston TR 2:99]

GORE, John[1] (c1606-1657) & Rhoda _____ (c1610-) (kinswoman of John Weld of Roxbury); m2 John REMINGTON; m3 Edward PORTER, m4 Joshua TIDD; m by 1632 probably near Ippollitts, Hertfordshire/Roxbury [DR; REG 148:61; GM 3:118]

GORE, John[2] (1634-) & Sarah[2] GARDNER (1662-), dau. of Peter; m Roxbury 31 May 1683 [GM 3:15, 118]

GORE, Samuel[2] (c1647-) & Elizabeth WELD; m Roxbury 28 Aug 1672 [GM 3:119]

GORGES, William[1] (bp 1605/6-1658/9) & 1/wf _____ _____ [GM 3:119]

GORGES, William[1] (bp 1605/6-1658/9) & 2/wf _____ _____ [GM 3:119]

GORHAM, John & Desire[2] HOWLAND (c1624-); m by 1644 [GMB 2:1022]

GORTON, Benjamin & Sarah[2] CARDER; m Warwick 5 Dec 1672 [GM 2:9]

GOSNALL, Henry & Mary _____; Boston bef 1630 [GMSP]

GOSSE, John (c1600-1643/4) & Sarah _____; m2 Robert NICHOLS; m by 1625 Watertown [GMB 2:796]

GOTT, Charles (c1600-1667/8) & Gift PALMER (c1602-1667/8+); m St. Andrew the Great, Cambridge 30 Oct 1625 Salem [GMB 2:800; TAG 12:134-5]

GOULD, Daniel & Dorcas[2] BELCHER (c1656-1730; m by 1684 Reading [GM 1:235]

GOULD, Edward[1] (c1607-1684/5) & Margaret (_____) BACON (-1682/3); m1 George BACON; m by 1643 Hingham [GM 3:122]

GOULD, Jarvis[1] (c1605-1656) & Mary _____; m by 1646 Boston [GM 3:124]

GOULD, John & Abigail[2] BELCHER; m c1671 Reading [GM 1:235]

GOULD, John & Elizabeth CUMMINGS; m2 William BRUCE; m Dunstable 2 July 1686 [REG 153:68]

GOULD, John[1] (c1610-1635+) & Grace _____; m by 1635 [GM 3:125]

GOULD, John[2] (bp 1646-) & Mary CROSSMAN, dau. of Robert; m Taunton 24 Aug 1673 [GM 3:124]

GOZZARD, Nicholas & Elizabeth[2] GILLETTE (1639-1699+); m c1671 Simsbury [TAG 56:130; GMB 2:771]

GRANGER, John & Grace _____ delete

GRANGER, Thomas & Grace _____; m bef 1626 [RCA]

GRANNIS, Edward & Elizabeth[2] ANDREWS; m Hartford 3 May 1655 [GM 1:66]

GRANT, Benjamin[2] (1641-by 1671) & Mary BECKWITH (1643-1692/3+), dau. of Matthew; m2 Samuel DANIEL; m c1664 Lyme [AEJA; GM 3:130]

GRANT, Caleb[2] (1639-) & Mary _____; m by 1671 Watertown [GM 3:130]

GRANT, Christopher[1] (c1610-1685) & Mary _____ (-1692/3); m by 1634 Watertown [GM 3:130]

GRANT, James & Elizabeth[2] EVERILL (1641-); m2 Edward TOOGOOD; Kittery [GM 2:475]

GRANT, Joseph[2] (1646-) & Mary GRAFTON; m Watertown 24 Dec 1684 [GM 3:131]

GRANT, Joshua[2] (1637-1676) & Sarah BECKWITH (c1650-bef 1674), dau. of Matthew; m c1670 Watertown/Lyme [AEJA; GM 3:130]

GRANT, Matthew (1601-1681) & 1/wf Priscilla _____ (1600-1644); m 16 Nov 1625 Dorchester/Windsor [GMB 2:803]

GRANT, Matthew (1601-1681) & 2/wf Susanna (CAPEN) ROCKWELL (1602-1666); m1 William Rockwell; m Windsor 29 May 1645 [GMB 2:803]

GRANT, Seth (c1610-1646/7) & _____ _____; probably Elizabeth who m2 Richard WEBB; by c1635 Cambridge/Hartford [GMB 2:805]

GRANT, Thomas & Sarah[2] BROOKS; m2 Samuel LYON; m by 1668 Rehoboth [GM 1:410]

GRAVES, Benjamin[2] (bp 1645-) & Mary HOARE; m Concord 21 Oct 1668 [GM 3:138]

GRAVES, John (c1664-1718+) & Sarah BANKS (1668-1718+); m Chelmsford 25 Oct 1686 [AEBK 4:63]

GRAVES, John[1] (c1599-1644) & 1/wf Sarah FINCH; m by 1624 All Saints, Hertfordshire/Roxbury [GM 3:134]

GRAVES, John[1] (c1599-1644) & 2/wf _____ _____; m by 1628 Roxbury [GM 3:135]

GRAVES, John[1] (c1599-1644) & 3/wf Judith ALWARD; m2 1646 William POTTER; m3 1654 Samuel FINCH; m Roxbury Dec 1635 [GM 3:135]

GRAVES, John[2] (c1640-) & Mary CHAMBERLAIN; m Concord 1 Dec 1671 [GM 3:138]

GRAVES, Joseph[2] (bp 1642-) & 1/wf Elizabeth MAYNARD; m Sudbury 15 Jan 1665[/6?] [GM 3:138]

GRAVES, Joseph[2] (bp 1642-) & 2/wf Mary _____; m by 1680 [GM 3:138]

GRAVES, Richard[1] (c1612-by 1669) & Dorothy _____; m by 1636 Salem [GM 3:138]

GRAVES, Thomas & _____ _____; m by 1629 Gravesend, Kent/Charlestown [GMB 2:806]

GRAVES, Thomas (-1662) & Sarah SCOTT (-1666); by 1623 Thundridge, Hertfordshire/Hartford [LMM]

GRAVES, William (-1679) & 2/wf Sarah (_____) DIBBLE (-1656); m1 John DIBBLE; m Springfield 7 Nov. 1647 [REG 155:274]

GRAY, Edward & Mary[2] WINSLOW; m Plymouth 16 Jan 1650/1 [GMB 3:2029]

GRAY, John (-bef 1663) & Elizabeth[2] (FROST) WATSON (bp 1614-bef 1682); m1 John WATSON; m bet 1634-9 CT [TAG 64:163]

GRAY, Robert & Hannah[2] HOLT (c1648-); m Salem 8 Mar 1668[/9?] [GM 3:400]

GREEN, Bartholomew (c1590-1635/6) & Elizabeth _____ (c1589-1677, age 88); m by 1615 Cambridge [GMB 2:810]

GREEN, Henry[2] (bp 1638/9-1717) & Esther HASEY (1650/1-1747/8); m Malden 11 Jan 1671/2 [AEBK 4:305]

GREEN, Jacob (c1623-) & Elizabeth _____; m by 11 Oct 1654 Charlestown [GMB 2:813]

GREEN, John (c1593-1658) & 2/wf Joanna (TAYLOR)(TUTTLE) SHATSWELL; m1 Richard TUTTLE; m2 John SHATSWELL; m after Mar 1647 Ipswich [GMB 2:813]

GREEN, John (c1593-1658, age 65) & 1/wf Perseverance _____; probably m by 1620 Charlestown; perhaps dau of Rev. Francis Johnson [GMB 2:813]

GREEN, John[2] (bp 1632-1707) & Sarah WHEELER (c1643-1717); m Malden 18 Dec 1660 [AEBK 4:304]

GREEN, Ralph & Elizabeth[2] (or Ann) BLOTT (bp 1613/4-); m2 _____ TOZIER [GM 1:336]

GREEN, Samuel & Hannah BUTLER; m by 2 Apr 1677 Hartford [GMB 1:287; TAG 46:11]

GREEN, Samuel (c1615-) & 1/wf Jane[2] BANBURY/BANBRIDGE; m by 1640 Cambridge [GMB 2:810; GM 1:153]

GREEN, Samuel (c1615-) & 2/wf Sarah CLARK; m Cambridge 22 Feb 1662 [GMB 2:810]

GREEN, Samuel[2] (c1645-1724) & 1/wf Mary COOKE (c1649-1715); m about 1666 Malden [AEBK 4:305]

GREEN, Samuel[3] (1670-1717-36) & Elizabeth UPHAM (-1714+); m Malden 28 Oct 1691 [AEBK 4:310]

GREEN, Thomas[1] (bp 1599/1600-1667) & 1/wf Mary SMITH (bp 1606/7-1625); m Toppesfield, Essex 28 June 1624 [AEBK 4:300]

GREEN, Thomas[1] (bp 1599/1600-1667) & 2/wf Elizabeth _____ (c1610-1658); m c1630 Malden [AEBK 4:300]

GREEN, Thomas[1] (bp 1599/1600-1667) & 3/wf Frances (_____)(WHEELER) COOK (c1608-1667+); m Malden 5 Sept 1659 [AEBK 4:300]

GREEN, Thomas[2] (c1630-1671/2) & Rebecca HILLS (bp 1634-1674); m say 1652 Malden [AEBK 4:307]

GREEN, William & Mary CRISP; m by 21 May 1661 Cambridge [GMB 1:494]

GREEN, William[2] (bp 1636-1705) & 1/wf Elizabeth WHEELER (-1671-95); m Malden 13 Sept 1659 [AEBK 4:304]

GREENE, James & Elizabeth SLOAKUM; m 1695 RI [TAG 67:20]

GREENE, James[2] (bp 1626-) & 1/wf Deliverance POTTER; m by 1658 St. Thomas, Salisbury, Wiltshire/Warwick [GM 3:145]

GREENE, James[2] (bp 1626-) & 2/wf Elizabeth ANTHONY; m Warwick 3 Aug 1665 St. Thomas, Salisbury, Wiltshire [GM 3:145]

GREENE, John & Annis[2] ALMY (bp 1626/7-1709); m by 1649 Warwick [GM 1:44]

GREENE, John & Mary[2] JEFFREYS (1642-); m c1665 [GMB 2:1084]

GREENE, John[1] (c1594-1658-9) & 1/wf Joane TATARSOLE; m St Thomas, Salisbury,
Wiltshire 4 Nov 1619 [GM 3:144]

GREENE, John[1] (c1594-1658-9) & 2/wf Alice (_____) BEGGARLY (c1610-1643[/4]); m
by 14 Dec 1638 Providence [GM 3:144; GMB 1:148]

GREENE, John[1] (c1594-1658-9) & 3/wf Phillip _____ (-1668+); m after 1644 [GM
3:144]

GREENE, John[2] (1636-) & Ruth MITCHELSON, dau. of Edward; m Cambridge 20 Oct
1656 [GM 3:149]

GREENE, John[2] (bp 1620-); m Ann ALMY, dau. of William; m by 1649 St. Thomas,
Salisbury, Wiltshire/Warwick [GM 3:144]

GREENE, Percival[1] (c1603-1639) & Ellen _____ (c1603-1682); m2 Thomas FOX; m by
1635 Cambridge [GM 3:149]

GREENE, Peter[2] (bp 1621/2-) & Mary GORTON, dau. of Samuel; m2 1672 John
SANFORD; m by 1659 St. Thomas, Salisbury, Wiltshire/Warwick [GM 3:145]

GREENE, Thomas[2] (bp 1628-) & Elizabeth GREENE; m Warwick 30 June 1659 St.
Thomas, Salisbury, Wiltshire [GM 3:145]

GREENFIELD, Peter & Hannah DEVEREUX; m2 Richard KNOTT; m3 Joseph SWETT;
bef 1672 [GMB 1:533]

GREENHILL, Samuel[1] (c1603-by 1637) & Rebecca (TAYLOR) BASEDEN; m by 1637
[GM 3:152]

GREENLAND, David & Elizabeth BALLENTINE (1659-); m2 Roger YELLINGS, m3
John COOMBS [TAG 46:130]

GREENLEAF, Edmund & Sarah (JURDAIN) (HILL) SOWTHER; m1 William HILL; m2
Nathaniel SOWTHER [TAG 42:218]

GREENLEAF, Edmund[1] (-1671) & 1/wf Sarah MOORE; m 2 July 1611 Langford,
Essex/Salisbury [TAG 56:107, REG 122:28]

GREENMAN, John & Elizabeth[2] DYER; m c1693 [GM 2:383]

GREENOUGH, William & Elizabeth[2] RAINSFORD (bp 1648/9-); m c1681 Boston
[GMB 3:1547]

GREENOUGH, William & Elizabeth[2] UPSALL (1637/8-); m Boston 4 July 1652 [GMB
3:1868]

GREENWAY, John[1] (c1575-1650/1-2) & Mary _____ (-1658[/9]); m 1601? 1620?
perhaps second wife Mildenhall, Wiltshire/Dorchester [TAG 74:194; GMB
2:816]

GREET, John[1] (c1640-bef 1687/8) & Mary[2] HART (c1640s-1687/8+); m by 1668
Wethersfield/Southold, L I. [TAG 72:47; GMB 2:868]

GREGG, James (c1674-1758) & Janet CARGILL (c1660s-1674); m c1695
Ireland/Londonderry, NH [AEJA]

GREGGS, Humphrey (bp 1612-by 1657) & Grizzell[2] (FLETCHER) JEWELL (c1619-
1669); m Braintree 1 Nov 1655 [AEBK 4:277]

GREGORY, _____ (c1638-40-c1720) & Sarah (MESSENGER) PALMER (c1648-); m
bef 15 Oct 1699 [REG 152:363]

GREGORY, John[2] & Elizabeth MOULTHROP (c1638-); m New Haven 18 Oct 1663
[TAG 74:223]

GRIDLEY, Believe (1640-) & Ann _____; by 1664 Boston [GMB 2:821]

GRIDLEY, Richard (c1602-1674) & Grace SURREY (-1674/5+); Groton, Suffolk 25
July 1627 Boston [GMB 2:820]

GRIDLEY, Tremble (1642-) & Elizabeth BATEMAN; by c1671 Boston [GMB 2:821]

GRIFFIN, Jonathan (-1685) & Mary LONG (c1650s-1720/1+); m2 Daniel[1]
MUSSILLOWAY; m 25 Oct 1676 Sudbury [ASBO, p.165]

GRIGGS, George (c1593-1660) & Alice SIBTHORPE (c1593-1662); m Lavendon,
Buckinghamshire. 11 May 1618 Boston [GM 3:157]

GRIGGS, Joseph & Mary CRAFTS (1632-); by 1653 Roxbury [GMB 1:491]

GRINNELL, Matthew & Rose FRENCH, m2 Anthony PAINE, m3 James WEEDEN; m
Leyden, Essex 27 Aug 1615/Newport, RI [REG 147:71]

GRISWOLD, Francis[2] (c1629-1671) & Sarah _____; m by 1653 [REG 155:247-50]

GRISWOLD, Mathew & Anne[2] WOLCOTT; m Windsor 16 Oct 1646 [GMB 3:2051]

GRISWOLD, Thomas & NOT Mary[2] HAYWARD [GM 3:284]

GROSS, Clement[2] (bp 1620-) & 1/wf Mary _____; m by 1647 King's Lynn St Margaret,
Norfolk/Boston [GM 3:161]

GROSS, Clement[2] (bp 1620-) & 2/wf Anna _____; m by 1669 King's Lynn St Margaret,
Norfolk/Boston [GM 3:161]

GROSS, Edmund[2] (c1617-) & 1/wf Catherine COLE; m by 1644/5 Boston [GM 3:161]

GROSS, Edmund[2] (c1617-) & 2/wf Ann _____; m2 1658 Samuel SHEERES; m by 1647
Boston [GM 3:161]

GROSS, Edmund[3] (-1727/8) & Martha DAMON (not BACON)(-1730+); m 21 Apr
__ Boston [REG 127:116]

GROSS, Isaac[1] (c1588-1649) & Ann LOBLEY (-1653); m King's Lynn St Margaret,
Norfolk 5 Aug 1613 Boston [GM 3:161]

GROSS, Matthew[2] (c1630-) & 1/wf Mary TROTT; m Boston 5 Oct 1652 [GM 3:162]

GROSS, Matthew[2] (c1630-) & 2/wf Eleanor _____; m by 1670 [GM 3:162]

GROUT, John & Mary CAKEBREAD (c1620-); by 1640 Watertown/Sudbury [GMB
1:303]

GROUT, Martin & Dorothy[2] ROSSITER (c1608-); m Combe St. Nicholas, Somerset 12
Feb 1629/30 [GMB 3:1601]

GROVER, Andrew (c1650-1674) & Hannah HILLS (1656/7-1674); m Malden 7 Feb
1673/4 [TG 10:118]

GROVER, Edmund (c1600-1682) & 1/wf _____ _____; by c1628 Salem/Beverly [GMB
2:825]

GROVER, Edmund (c1600-1682) & 2/wf Margaret _____; by c1640 Salem/Beverly
[GMB 2:825]

GROVER, Lazarus[2] (1642-1715) & 1/wf Ruth[2] ADAMS (1642-1674); m bef 1655 Charlestown/Weymouth/Malden [TG 10:116; GM 1:10]

GROVER, Lazarus[2] (1642-1715) & 2/wf Elizabeth _____ (-1667/8); m bef 1678 Charlestown/Malden [TG 10:116]

GROVER, Lazarus[2] (1642-1715) & 3/wf Mercy _____ (-1715+); m bef 1692 Charlestown/Malden [TG 10:116]

GROVER, Matthew[2] (c1655-bef 1680) & Mary DAVIS (1657/8-1727); m2 Samuel Damon; m bef 1675 Malden [TG 10:119]

GROVER, Simon[2] (c1654-1717) & Sarah BARRETT (-1725/6); m bef 1687 Malden [TG 10:118]

GROVER, Stephen (c1660-1694) & Sarah _____ (-1695+); m bef 1681 Malden [TG 10:120]

GROVER, Thomas[1] (bp 26 Nov 1615-1661) & Elizabeth SMITH (bp 28 May 1620-1688); m bef 1642 Charlestown [TG 10:115]

GROVER, Thomas[2] (c1644-1711) & Sarah CHADWICK (1650-1711+); m Malden 23 May 1668 [TG 10:117]

GRUBB, Thomas (c1598-1673/4) & Ann SALTER; m St. Margaret, Kings Lynn, Norfolk 4 Mar 1621/2 Boston [GMB 2:828]

GUNN, Abel[2] (bp 1643-) & Mary SMITH, dau. of John; m Milford 29 Oct 1667 [GM 3:168]

GUNN, Daniel[2] (bp 1645-) & Deborah COLEMAN [GM 3:168]

GUNN, Jasper[1] (c1606-1670/1) & Christian _____ (-1690); m by 1637 Milford/Hartford [GM 3:168]

GUNN, Jobamah[2] (c1639-) & 1/wf Sarah LANE; m Milford 30 Oct 1663 [GM 3:168]

GUNN, Jobamah[2] (c1639-) & 2/wf Mary BRISTOL; m c1689 Milford [GM 3:168]

GUNN, John[2] (1647-) & Mary WILLIAMS; m Westfield 22 Jan 1678/9 [GM 3:172]

GUNN, Nathaniel[2] & Sarah[2] DAY, dau of Robert; m2 Samuel KELLOGG; m Springfield 17 Nov 1658 [GM 2:328, 3:168]

GUNN, Samuel[2] (c1648-) & Hannah SANFORD [GM 3:169]

GUNN, Thomas[1] (c1605-1680/1) & _____ _____ (1605-1678); m by 1638 Windsor/Westfield [GM 3:171]

GUNNISON, Elihu[2] (1649/50-) & 1/wf Martha TRICKEY, dau. of Thomas; m Dover 10 Nov 1674 [GM 3:177]

GUNNISON, Elihu[2] (1649/50-) & 2/wf Elizabeth (INGERSOLL) SKILLINGS, dau. of George; m1 John SKILLINGS; m by 1690 [GM 3:177]

GUNNISON, Hugh[1] (c1612-by 1660) & 1/wf Elizabeth _____ (-1645/6); m by 1637 Boston [GM 3:177]

GUNNISON, Hugh[1] (c1612-by 1660) & 2/wf Sarah (TILLEY) LYNN; m1 Henry LYNN; m3 John MITCHELL; m4 Francis MORGAN; m by 15 May 1647 Boston [GM 3:177]

GURNEY, John (c1615-by 1662/3) & 2 or 3/wf Grizzell[2] (FLETCHER)(JEWELL) (GREGGS) KIBBY (c1619-1669); m Braintree 12 Nov 1661 [AEBK 4:277]

GURNEY, Samuel & Sarah (ATKINS) STAPLES (c1651/2-c1724); m1 John[2] STAPLES; m3 Richard WILLIAMS [REG 121:243]

GUY, Nicholas & Jane (_____) TAINTER; m license Upton Grey, Hampshire 30 Oct 1629 [TAG 65:22]

GWIN, John & Mary[2] BUNKER (bp 1625-); m2 Eleazer LUSHER; m by 1646 Charlestown [GM 1:486]

GWINN, Thomas & Elizabeth[2] GILLAM (1641/2-); m by 1661 Boston [GM 3:63]

HACKETT, William[1] & 2/wf Mary[2] ATKINS (b c1642-); m bef 1666 Dover [REG 121:242]

HACKLETON, Francis (-1662) & Hannah[2] WAKEMAN (c1637-9-1694+); m2 Edward WHITTAKER; m bet 18 Mar 1656/7-7 July 1658 Hartford/Northampton/L.I. [NYGBR 127:73; GMB 3:1901]

HACKLETON, William[3] (c1658-1685) & Sarah[3] ROGERS; m2 John CAMPBELL; m bef 1 Sept 1683 Southampton [NYGBR 127:74]

HADDON, Garrett (c1605-by 1689/90) & Margaret _____ (-1672/3); by c1637 Boston/Salisbury/Amesbury [GMB 2:833]

HADEN, John & Joan[2] GREENE (bp 1630-); m early 1650s Warwick/ St. Thomas, Salisbury, Wiltshire [GM 3:145]

HADLOCK, John & Sarah[2] PASCO (1671-); m Salem 16 Jan 1694/5 [REG 150:133]

HAES, Jan & Janne (SCHABUELS) FISHCOCK, m1 Edward FISHCOCK; m New Amsterdam 12 Mar 1645 [Records of the Reformed Dutch Church, Marriages, p. 13]

HAFFIELD, Richard[1] (c1581-1639) & 1/wf Judith _____ (-c1627); m c1618 [GM 3:185]

HAFFIELD, Richard[1] (c1581-1639) & 2/wf Martha _____ (-1667/8) Wenham [GM 3:185]

HAGGETT, Henry (c1594-8-1677/8) & Ann _____ (-1677/8+); m bef 1644 Salem [50 GMC]

HAILSTONE, William[1] (c1611-1675+) & 1/wf _____ _____; m by 1639 Taunton [AEBK 4:313]

HAILSTONE, William[1] (c1611-1675+) & 2/wf Joan _____ (-1670+); m by 9 Nov 1670 Taunton [AEBK 4:313]

HAINES, Matthias[2] (c1650-) & Jane BRACKETT; m 28 Dec 1671 [GM 3:190]

HAINES, Richard & Mary[1] (____) PEASE; m1 Robert PEASE [TAG 70:207]

HAINES, Samuel[1] (c1603-1684+) & Eleanor NEATE; m Dilton, Wiltshire 1 Apr 1638 Greenland [GM 3:190]

HAINES, Samuel[2] (c1646-) & Mary FIFIELD; m Portsmouth 9 Jan 1672/3 [GM 2:524, 3:190]

HALE, Francis & Alice[2] THORNDIKE (c1647-); m (lic) St Mary's Church, Savoy, London 17 Nov 1675 [REG 154:475; GMB 3:1813]

HALE, Robert (c1607-1659) & Joanna _____; m2 Richard JACOB; m bef 14 Oct 1632 Ipswich/Charlestown [GMB 2:837]

HALE, Samuel[2] (1644/5-1711) & Ruth[3] EDWARD (c1651-1682); m Wethersfield 20 June 1670 [REG 145:325]

HALE, Thomas (bp 15 June 1606-1682) & Thomasine DOUCETT (c1610-1682/3); m St Helen's, Bishopsgate, London 11 Dec 1632 Newbury [50 GMC]

HALE, Thomas (c1613-by 1678/9) & 1/wf Jane LORD (-by 1659); m Roxbury Feb 1639/40 [GMB 2:839]

HALE, Thomas (c1613-by 1678/9) & 2/wf Mary NASH; m Charlestown 14 Dec 1659 [GMB 2:839]

HALL, _____ & Mary BENSON (c1637-); m bef 1700 Hull [REG 142:270]

HALL, Benjamin (1668-1726) & Sarah FISHER (1668-1756); m Wrentham 9 Jan 169- [AEBK 4:265]

HALL, Elisha (c1655-) & Lydia (_____); m by 20 Nov 1680 Yarmouth [GMB 2:843]

HALL, George (c1610-1669) & Mary _____ (c1615-1669+); m say 1635 Taunton [AEBK 4:320]

HALL, Gershom (bp 1647/8-) & 1/wf Bethia BANGS; m by 1669 Barnstable [GMB 2:842]

HALL, Gershom (bp 1647/8-) & 2/wf Martha BRAMHALL; m Hingham 9 Dec 1698 [GMB 2:842]

HALL, Isaac & Lydia[2] KNAPP (c1647-); m Fairfield 16 Jan 1666/7 [GMB 2:1137]

HALL, John & 2/wf Elizabeth[2] LEARNED (bp 1621-1683?); m by 1642 Charlestown [AEBK 4:432; GMB 2:1165]

HALL, John & Elizabeth[2] GREENE (1639-); m Cambridge Apr 1639 [GM 3:150]

HALL, John (1651/2-) & Elizabeth CORNWALL; m by 25 Oct 1670 Middleton [GMB 1:483]

HALL, John (bp 1638-) & Priscilla _____; perhaps daughter of Augustine BEARSE; by c1661 Charlestown/Barnstable [GMB 2:842]

HALL, John (c1611-1696) & Bethia _____ (-1683/4); by c1636 Boston/Charlestown/Barnstable/Yarmouth [GMB 2:841]

HALL, John[2] (c1641-by 1693) & Hannah[2] PENNIMAN (1648-1702+); m2 Samuel HASKINS; m Taunton 4 Feb 1671 [GMB 3:1429; TAG 71:17; AEBK 4:326]

HALL, John[3] (1666-c1735) & 1/wf Esther[2] BELL (1672-by 1714/5); m Taunton 14 Dec 1692 [AEBK 4:94, 335]

HALL, Joseph[2] (bp 1642-1716) & 2/wf Mary JOYCE (c1644-1717/8); m by 1675 Barnstable/Mansfield, CT [TAG 43:3; GMB 2:842]

HALL, Nathaniel (bp 1645/6-) & Anne[2] THORNTON; m by 1675 Barnstable [GMB 2:842, 3:1816]

HALL, Richard & Elizabeth COLLICOTT (bp 1628/9-); m by 12 Aug 1648 Dorchester [GMB 1:443]

HALL, Richard & Elizabeth[2] (HEMINGWAY) HOLBROOK (1645-); m1 John HOLBROOK; m Roxbury 22 May 1679 [GMB 2:910]

HALL, Samuel & Abigail PRATT; m Taunton 3 Jan 1683 [NGSQ 81:19]

HALL, Samuel (1665-1750) & Hannah SAWTELL (1670-1753); m bef 1698 Stow/Groton/Concord [REG 126:6]

HALL, Samuel (c1610-by 1680/1) & Sarah COCKING (by 1680/1); m by Nov 1645 Ipswich/Salisbury/Langford, Essex [GMB 2:846]

HALL, Samuel (c1636-) & Elizabeth FOLLAND; by 1686 Yarmouth [GMB 2:842]

HALL, Samuel[2] (c1644-1688/9) & Elizabeth WHITE (c1644-by 1707); m c1664 Taunton [AEBK 4:328]

HALL, Samuel[3] (1664-1699+) & Elizabeth BOURNE (-1699+); m Taunton 7 Apr 1686 [AEBK 4:331; NGSQ 81:19]

HALL, Stephen & Ruth[2] DAVIS (bp 1643/4-); m Concord 3 Dec 1663 [GM 2:296]

HALL, Thomas & Martha (DAVIES) (RUSSELL) BRADSHAW (-1695); m1 William RUSSELL; m2 Humphrey BRADSHAW [TAG 44:83]

HALL, Timothy & Sarah[2] BARBER (bp 1646-); m Windsor 26 Nov 1663 [GM 1:156]

HALL, William (bp 1651-) & Esther _____; m by 1683 Barnstable [GMB 2:842-3]

HALLETT, Andrew[1] (bp 1607-by 1684) & 1/wf _____ _____; m by 1642 Symondsbury, Dorsetshire/Dorchester/Sandwich/Yarmouth [GM 3:198]

HALLETT, Andrew[1] (bp 1607-by 1684) & 2/wf Ann[2] BESSEY, dau. of Anthony; m by 1663 Yarmouth [GM 1:268, 3:198]

HALLETT, John[2] (1650-) & Mary HOWES; m Yarmouth 16 Feb 1681/2 [GM 3:198]

HALLETT, Jonathan[2] (1647-) & Abigail DEXTER; m Yarmouth 30 Jan 1683/4 [GM 3:198]

HALLOOME, Isaac & Mary (FAIRFIELD) PARKER; m1 John PARKER; m bef 1684 Boston [SD 13:162-3]

HALLOWELL, Joseph[1] (c1646-1692) & 1/wf _____ _____; m c1673 Lynn [TEG 11:217]

HALLOWELL, Joseph[1] (c1646-1692) & 2/wf Mary HITCHINS (c1660-); m c1682 Lynn [TEG 11:217]

HALSEY, George & Joan[2] (RUCK) SWAN; m1 Henry SWAN; m3 Henry[1] FARNHAM [TAG 62:35]

HAMILTON, James & perhaps Christian[2] EDWARDS, dau of Robert; m by 1671[/2] Concord [GM 2:412]

HAMILTON, William & Mary RICHARDSON; m Boston 7 Aug 1654 [Boston VR]

HAMLIN, Giles & 1/wf Bridget HARRIS; m bef 1655 [TAG 46:138]

HAMLIN, Giles (1622-1689) & 2/wf Esther CROW (-1700); m bef 1663 Hartford [TAG 46:138]

HAMMOND, _____ & Abigail SOMES (1655-1700+); m bef 1700 Boston [TAG 53:13]

HAMMOND, _____ (-bef 1630) & Philip _____; m2 Robert HARDING; m bef 1630? 1639? Boston [GMSP; REG 149:219]

HAMMOND, John (bp 1626-) & 1/wf Abigail SALTER; m by 3 Feb 1653/4 Watertown [GMB 2:852]

HAMMOND, John (bp 1626-) & 2/wf Sarah NICHOLS; m Charlestown 2 Mar 1663/4 [GMB 2:852]

HAMMOND, Richard/Edward & Susannah BRADLEY; m 5 Jan 1684[/5?] Bristol [REG 142:221]

HAMMOND, Thomas (bp 1618-1655) & Hannah[2] CROSS (bp 1638-1656/7); m by 1655 Lavenham, Suffolk/Ipswich/Watertown [GMB 2:239, 852]

HAMMOND, Thomas[2] (c1630-1678) & Elizabeth[2] STEDMAN (bp 24 Nov 1637-1679+); m Cambridge 17 Dec 1662 [TAG 69:157]

HAMMOND, William (-d. London) & Elizabeth PENN; m by 1621 Boston [REG 142:218]

HAMMOND, William (1648-1675) & Elizabeth BARTRAM (c1654-by 1713); m2 1677 Joseph FISKE; m Rehoboth 9 July 1672 Swansea [REG 149:211, 223, 230]

HAMMOND, William (1675-1729/30) & 1/wf Elizabeth COLE; m Swansea 10 Jan 1695[/6?] [REG 149:224]

HAMMOND, William (bp 1575-1662) & Elizabeth PAINE (bp 1586-1670); m Lavenham, Suffolk 9 June 1605 Watertown [GMB 2:852]

HANCOCK, Nathaniel[1] (c1609-1648) & Joan _____; m by 1634 Cambridge [GM 3:204]

HANCOCK, Nathaniel[2] (1639-) & 1/wf Mary PRENTICE; m Cambridge 8 Mar 1663/4 [GM 3:204]

HANCOCK, Nathaniel[2] (1639-) & 2/wf Sarah GREEN; m Cambridge 26 Dec 1699 [GM 3:204]

HANFORD, Jeffrey & Eglin[1] (HANFORD) DOWNE (bp 1586-1653[/4?]+); m1 _____ DOWNE; m3 Richard[1] SILLIS; m Fremington, Devonshire 31 Mar 1611 [GM 3:206]

HANFORD, Thomas[2] (c1623-) & 2/wf Mary (MILES) INCE; m1 Jonathan INCE; m by 1662 [GM 3:206]

HANFORD, Thomas[2] (c1623-) & 1/wf Hannah NEWBERRY, dau. of Thomas [GM 3:206]

HANMER, Isaac[2] (c1653-) & Lydia _____; m by 1678 [GM 3:209]

HANMER, John[1] (c1614-1676-7) & Hannah _____ (-1676/7+); m by 1639 [GM 3:209]

HANMER, John[2] (c1645-) & _____[2] SAMSON (c1648-), dau. of Henry; m by 1682 [GM 3:209; GMB 3:1623]

HANMER, Joseph[2] (c1649-) & Bethiah TUBBS; m Marshfield 24 June 1674 [GM 3:209]

HANNUM, John[2] (c1637-) & 1/wf Sarah WELLER, dau. of Richard; m Northampton 20 Nov 1662 [GM 3:212]

HANNUM, John[2] (c1637-) & 2/wf Hester LANGTON, dau. of George; m Northampton 20 Apr 1675 [GM 3:212]

HANNUM, William[1] (c1612-1677) & Honor CAPEN (-1680), dau. of Bernard; m by 1637 Northampton [GM 3:212]

HANSETT, John[1] (c1614-1683/4) & 1/wf Elizabeth _____ (-by 1644); m by 1639 [GM 3:216]

HANSETT, John[1] (c1614-1683/4) & 2/wf Elizabeth PERRY; m1 John PERRY (probably); m Roxbury 2 Apr 1644 [GM 3:216]

HANSETT, Peter[2] (bp 1651-) & Mary _____; m by 1680 Roxbury [GM 3:216]

HAPGOOD, Nathaniel (1665-1735) & Elizabeth WARD (c1674-1748); m Marlborough 14 Aug 1695 [AEBK 1:330]

HAPGOOD, Shadrack[1] (c1642-1675) & Elizabeth TREADWAY (1646-1691+); m2 1676/7 Joseph HAYWARD; m Sudbury 21 Oct 1664 [AEBK 1:327; REG 150:156]

HAPGOOD, Thomas (1669/70-1763) & Judith[3] BARKER (1671-1759); m bef 1694 Concord/Marlborough [AEBK 1:330-31; AEBK 3]

HARDING, _____ & Martha _____ (c1612-1633); sister of John Doane?; by c1632 Plymouth [GMB 2:854]

HARDING, Philip & Susannah (_____) HAVILAND; m1 Edward HAVILAND; m Boston 23 Aug 1659 [GMB 2:857]

HARDING, Robert (c1610-1657/8) & 3/wf _____ _____; m by 24 July 1649 England [GMB 2:856]

HARDING, Robert (c1610-by 1657/8) & 1/wf Philip (_____) HAMMOND (-by 1645); m by 1 Sept 1639 Newport/Boston [GMB 2:856]

HARDING, Robert (c1610-by 1657/8) & 2/wf Esther WYLLYS; m Hartford 17 Oct 1645 [GMB 2:856]

HARDY, Jacob[2] (c1649-1706) & Lydia[2] EATON (1662-1737); m c1690 Bradford [ASBO, p.288; GMB 2:860]

HARDY, John[1] (c1591-1652) & Elizabeth _____ (-1654); m by 1616 Salem [GM 3:220]

HARDY, Joseph[2] (c1622-) & Martha _____; m by 1648 Salem [GM 3:220]

HARDY, Richard (-1684) & Ann[2] HEUSTIS (c1626-); m c1644 Stamford [NYGBR 129:20; GM 3:450]

HARDY, Thomas (c1605-1677/8) & Ann _____ (-1689); m by c1635 Ipswich/Rowley/Bradford [GMB 2:859]

HARDY, William[2] (c1644-c1722) & 1/wf Ruth TENNY (1653/4-1689); m 3 May 1678 Bradford [ASBO, p.287]

HARDY, William[2] (c1644-c1722) & 2/wf Sarah SAVORY, perhaps dau of Robert SAVORY (c1666-1762); m c1689 Bradford [ASBO, p.287; GMB 2:860]

HARKER, Anthony (c1608-by 1675) & Mary _____; m by 1638 Boston [GMB 2:863]

HARLACKENDEN, Roger[1] (bp 1611-1638) & 1/wf Emelen _____ (-1634); m by 1634 Earl's Colne, Essex [GM 3:224]

HARLACKENDEN, Roger[1] (bp 1611-1638) & 2/wf Elizabeth BOSVILLE; m2 Herbert PELHAM; m Earl's Colne, Essex, 4 June 1635 [GM 3:224]

HARLOCK, Thomas & Bethiah[2] MAYHEW (1636-); m2 Richard WAY; m by 1658 Martha's Vineyard [GMB 2:1245; TAG 61:256]

HARLOW, William & Mary[2] SHELLEY (bp 1639-); m Plymouth 25 Jan 1665[/6] [GM 3:27]

HARMAN, Francis[1] (c1592-1635+) & _____ _____; m by 1623 [GM 3:225]

HARMON, Nathaniel & Mary BLISS; Braintree [REG 142:216]

HARRIMAN, John[1] (by 1523-1683) & Elizabeth _____; m by 26 Jan 1646/7 New Haven [REG 150:44]

HARRIMAN, John[2] (1650-1675) & _____ _____; m by Oct 1674 Hampton [REG 150:43]

HARRIMAN, John[2] (bp 1646/7-1705) & Hannah BRIAN (1654-); m Milford 20 Nov 1672 [REG 150:47]

HARRIMAN, Jonathan[2] (1657-1741/2) & 1/wf Sarah PALMER (1661/2-1688); m bef 19 Aug 1686 [REG 150:44]

HARRIMAN, Jonathan[2] (1657-1741/2) & 2/wf Margaret (ELITHORP) WOOD (1672-1754); m1 Samuel WOOD; m Rowley 19 Aug 1691 [REG 150:44]

HARRIMAN, Leonard (c1621-1691) & Margaret _____; m by 1650 Rowley [REG 150:40]

HARRIMAN, Mathew[2] (1652-1732/3) & 1/wf Elizabeth SWAN (1653-1699+); m Haverhill 22 Dec 1673 [REG 150:44]

HARRIS, ?Joseph (c1630-) & _____ CHUBB, dau. of Thomas; m bef 24 Nov 1669 [EQC 4:216; GMB 1:355]

HARRIS, Anthony[2] (c1622-) & Elizabeth _____; m by 1651 [GMB 2:865]

HARRIS, Daniel[2] (c1626-) & Mary WELD, dau of Joseph; m by 1651 Roxbury [GMB 2:865]

HARRIS, Gabriel[2] (bp 1628/9-1683/4) & Elizabeth ABBOTT (-1702); m Guilford 3 Mar 1653/4 [REG 156:152]

HARRIS, George & Joan _____, m2 Thomas TUCK; m bef 1650 [EIHC 7:25]

HARRIS, John & Amie _____ (probably not HILLS); m c1656-61 Charlestown [REG 120:74, 152:344]

HARRIS, John & Joanna _____; m Boston by 17 Sept 1671 [REG 152:345]

HARRIS, John & Mary HOUGHTON (1660/1-); m after 1684 Lancaster [REG 152:345]

HARRIS, John & Sarah (NETTLETON) MILLER; m Middletown May 1684 [REG 152:346]

HARRIS, John & Susannah BRECK (c1654-); m 1674/5 Dorchester [REG 152:345]

HARRIS, John (-by 1664) & Hannah BRIGGS; m Boston 10 Sept 1657 [REG 152:344]

HARRIS, John (1640s-1679) & Elizabeth PERRY (1647/8-1692); m by 1669 Boston [REG 152:330]

HARRIS, John (1663-1739/40) & Hannah MANWARING (c1662-1732); m by 1688 New London [REG 156:273]

HARRIS, John (1674/5-) & Margaret ELSON; m2 Clement SUMNER; m Salem 22 May
   1695 [REG 152:328]

HARRIS, John (bp 1647-c1690) & Mary SANGER; m Watertown 2 Sept 1670 [REG
   152:344]

HARRIS, John[2] & 1/wf _____ _____; m aft 1684 [TAG 72:342]

HARRIS, John[2] & 2/wf Mehitable DANKS; m by 1693-5 Springfield [TAG 72:343]

HARRIS, John[2] (c1616-) & 1/wf Bridget _____; m by 1645 Rowley [GMB 2:864]

HARRIS, John[2] (c1616-) & 2/wf Elizabeth (ROWLANDSON) WELLS; m Rowley 24
   Oct 1677 [GMB 2:864]

HARRIS, John[2] (c1616-) & 3/wf Alice _____ [GMB 2:864]

HARRIS, Joseph (1672/3-1737) & 1/wf Mary STEVENS (1677-1718); m New London 1
   Dec 1696 [REG 156:363]

HARRIS, Peter[3] (1660-1718[/9]) & Elizabeth MANWARING (c1663-1720); m New
   London 7 July 1686 [NYGBR 133:13; REG 156:262]

HARRIS, Richard (-1697) & 2/wf Elizabeth BLACKLEACH (1659-1712+); m c1679
   Boston [REG 148:28]

HARRIS, Richard (1618-28-1666) & _____ SMITH (c1618-23 -), dau. of Richard[1]; m
   Hartford [TAG 46:137]

HARRIS, Richard (c1651-1713/4) & 1/wf Hannah DOVE (1652-1695+); m Salem 10 Mar
   1670[/1?] [REG 152:325]

HARRIS, Robert (1670s-1743+) & 1/wf Experience CHAPPELL (bp 1675-1747+); m2
   John COWLES; m c1700 Wethersfield; div. 1728 Wethersfield/East Hampton
   [NYGBR 130:184; NGSQ 78:194; Harris]

HARRIS, Samuel (1665-1724/5) & Elizabeth GIBSON (c1665-1745); m New London 5
   Aug 1687 [REG 156:357]

HARRIS, Thomas (-by 1681) & _____ _____ (-1681+); Boston/Southold [NYGBR
   128:15]

HARRIS, Thomas (1658-1691) & Mary WETHERELL (1668-1711); m by 1690 New
   London/Barbados [REG 156:156]

HARRIS, Thomas (1677-1725) & Miriam WILLIE (1677-1725); c1698-99 New Shoreham
   [NYGBR 84:138-39; Saybrook Deeds 1:238; Harris]

HARRIS, Thomas (c1630s-1682-88) & Sarah[2] WRIGHT (-1691+); m c1664 East
   Hartford /Glastonbury/Boston [NGSQ 78:190; TAG 67:39 Harris; GMB 3:2073;
   NYGBR 130:184]

HARRIS, Thomas (c1650s-by 1697) & Ruth JAMES (c1664-); m2 Joseph MOORE; m
   by 9 Mar 1682/3 East Hampton/Killingworth [NYGBR 128:24]

HARRIS, Thomas[1] (c1590-by 1634) & Elizabeth _____ (-1669/70); m2 William
   STITSON; m by 1613 Winnissimmett/Boston [GMB 2:864]

HARRIS, Thomas[2] (c1618-) & Martha LAKE; m Ipswich 15 Nov 1647 [GMB 2:865]

HARRIS, Walter[1] (c1590s-1654) & Mary FRY (-1655/6); m by 1621 Honiton, Devonshire/New London. [REG 156:145-6]

HARRIS, William & Elizabeth INNES; m2 Richard SMITH; m3 Roger ALGER; m by 1672 New Shoreham/Lyme/Block Island [NYGBR 133:3; Saxbe]

HARRIS, William (1667/8-1759) & Elizabeth BRUNSON (c1676-1733); m by 1695 Hartford [NGSQ 78:191]

HARRIS, William (c1640s-by 1691) & Hannah STACKHOUSE (bp 1648-1704/5+); m by 1672 Boston [REG 152:316]

HARRIS, William (c1644-1684) & 1/wf _____ _____; m by 1667 Boston [REG 152:336]

HARRIS, William (c1644-1684) & 2/wf Sarah (PIERCE) COLEPOT (-1702); m by June 1674 Boston [REG 152:336]

HARRIS, William (c1667-1721) & Sarah CRISP (1672-); m2 1722 John LEVERETT; m 11 Apr 1695 Boston [REG 152:342]

HARRIS, William[2] & ?Sarah ELIOT (bp 1647-); Boston [GMB 1:629]

HARRIS, William[2] (1675-1762) & Elizabeth BROCKWAY (1676-1754+); m Block Island 30 Nov 1697 [TAG 70:233]

HARRIS, William[2] (c1620-) & 1/wf Edith _____; m by 1645 Rowley [GMB 2:865]

HARRIS, William[2] (c1620-) & 2/wf Lydia (WRIGHT) SMITH, dau of Thomas; m1 Joseph SMITH [GMB 2:865]

HART, Edmund[1] (c1610-c1672) & _____ _____ (-1659) perhaps a PHELPS, sister of George; m c1638 Westfield [GMB 2:868-69]

HART, John[1] (c1595-by 1655/6) & 1/wf Mary _____ (-by 1639); m by 1635 [GM 3:229]

HART, John[1] (c1595-by 1655/6) & 2/wf Florence[2] NORMAN (c1619-suicide 1672), dau. of Richard; m2 Thomas WHITTRIDGE; m by 1639 Salem [TAG 77:103; GMB 2:1335; GM 3:229]

HART, John[2] (c1627-) & Sarah _____; m by 1652 Farmington [GMB 2:871]

HART, Jonathan[2] (c1645-) & Lydia NEALE, dau. of John; m Salem Nov 1671 [GM 3:229]

HART, Nicholas & Joane[2] ROSSITER (c1616-1691); Plymouth [GMB 3:1601]

HART, Samuel & Sarah[2] NORTON (bp 1646/7-); m Ipswich Feb 1678 [GMB 2:1338]

HART, Stephen[1] (c1599-1682/3-3) & 1/wf _____ _____ (-c1678); m by 1624 Farmington [GMB 2:871]

HART, Stephen[1] (c1599-1682/3-3) & 2/wf Margaret (_____) (SMITH) NASH (-1691/2-3/4); m1 Arthur SMITH; m2 Joseph NASH; m aft 1678 Farmington [GMB 2:871]

HART, Stephen[2] (c1634-1689) & Ann FITCH, dau of Thomas; m by 1662 [GMB 2:871]

HART, Thomas & Freeborn[2] WILLIAMS (1635-); m2 Walter CLARKE; m c1661 Newport [GMB 3:2009]

HART, Thomas & Mary[2] NORTON (1643-); m Ipswich 14 Oct 1664 [GMB 2:1338]

HART, Thomas[2] (c1640-   ) & 1/wf Mary SMITH, dau of Arthur; m by 1665 Farmington [GMB 2:872]

HART, Thomas[2] (c1640-   ) & 2/wf Ruth HOWKINS, dau of Anthony; m bet 1675/6 - 1678 Farmington [GMB 2:872]

HARTWELL, John[3] (1673-1746) & 1/wf Deborah THOMPSON (c1676-1744); Concord/Bedford [TAG 76:39]

HARTWELL, Samuel & Ruth[2] WHEELER (c1647-1713); m Concord 26 Oct 1665 [AEBK 3]

HARVEY, Peter & Elizabeth (CLEEVE) MITTON, m 1st Michael Mitton [JP]

HARVEY, Richard & Jehoadan[2] HORNE (c1638-   ); m c1656 [GMB 2:992]

HARVEY, Richard[1] (bp 1612-1686-9) & 1/wf Margaret _____ (-1639); m by 1639 Ilkeston, Derbyshire/Concord [GM 3:232]

HARVEY, Richard[1] (bp 1612-1686-9) & 2/wf _____ _____; m by 1644 Ilkeston, Derbyshire/Concord [GM 3:232]

HARWOOD, Henry[1] (c1605-1637) & 1/wf Elizabeth _____; m by 1630 Boston/Charlestown [GMB 2:874]

HARWOOD, Henry[2] (c1605-1637) & 2/wf Winifred _____; m by 1636/7 Charlestown [GMB 2:874]

HARWOOD, John[1] (c1625-1685/6) & Elizabeth USHER (-1687/8); m by 1649 Boston [AEBK 3]

HARWOOD, Nathaniel (1669-1751) & Mary BARRON (c1663-1758); m c1695 Concord/Chelmsford [AEBK 3]

HARWOOD, Nathaniel[1] (c1640-1715/6) & Elizabeth CHEEVERS (bp 1639-1715); m c1665 Concord [AEBK 3]

HARWOOD, Peter[2] (1671[/2?]-1740) & Mary FOX (1673-1742); m Concord 7 Nov 1700 [AEBK 3]

HARWOOD, Robert[1] (c1644-by 1678) & Joanna _____ (-1696); m c1673 Boston [AEBK 3]

HARWOOD, Thomas[1] (c1627-1707/8) & Rachel (SMITH) WOODWARD (-1695), dau of John; m1 Robert WOODWARD; m Boston 7 July 1654 [AEBK 3]

HARWOOD, William[2] (1665-1740) & Esther PERRY (1674-1747); m Concord 11 May 1692 [AEBK 3]

HASKELL, John & Patience[2] SOULE; m Middleboro Jan 1666[/7] [GMB 3:1707]

HASKELL, Roger & Elizabeth[2] HARDY; m2 Edward BERRY; m by 1643 [GM 3:220]

HASKINS, Samuel & 3/wf Rebecca[2] BROOKS (bp 1657-   ); m Taunton 12 May 1692 [GM 1:411]

HASSELL, John[1] (c1603-by 1668) & Margaret _____ (-1660[/1?]); m by 1628 Ipswich [GM 3:234]

HASTINGS, Benjamin[2] (1659-   ) & 1/wf Elizabeth GRAVES, dau. of Isaac; m c1682 Watertown [GM 3:239]

HASTINGS, Benjamin[2] (1659-   ) & 2/wf Mary (CLARK) PARSONS, dau. of Nathaniel; m1 Jonathan PARSONS; m by 1699 Watertown [GM 3:239]

HASTINGS, John & Lydia[2] CHAMPNEY; m Cambridge 20 May 1668 [GM 2:45]

HASTINGS, John[2] (1653/4-   ) & Abigail HAMMOND; m Watertown 18 June 1679 [GM 3:239]

HASTINGS, Joseph[2] (1657-   ) & 1/wf Ruth RICE; m Watertown 21 Nov 1682 [GM 3:239]

HASTINGS, Joseph[2] (1657-   ) & 2/wf Martha SHEPARD; m Watertown 8 Jan 1684[/5?] [GM 3:239]

HASTINGS, Nathaniel[2] (1661-   ) & Mary NEVINSON, dau. of John; m c1690 [GM 3:239]

HASTINGS, Samuel[2] (1665/6-   ) & 1/wf Lydia CHURCH; m Watertown 4 Jan 1686/7 [GM 3:239]

HASTINGS, Samuel[2] (1665/6-   ) & 2/wf Elizabeth NEVINSON; m Watertown 24 Apr 1694 [GM 3:239]

HASTINGS, Thomas[1] (c1605-1682-5) & 1/wf Susan _____ (-1651); m by 1634 Watertown [GM 3:238]

HASTINGS, Thomas[1] (c1605-1682-5) & 2/wf Margaret CHENEY (c1625-1685+), dau. of William; m Watertown cApr 1651 [GM 3:238; AEBK 1:231]

HASTINGS, Thomas[2] (1652-   ) & 1/wf Anna[2] HAWKES (1648-   ); m Hadley 10 Nov 1672 [GM 3:239, 259]

HATCH, Israel ~ Elizabeth _____ [Plymouth Court Mar 1699/1700]

HATCH, Jeremiah & Mary[2] HEWES (c1637-   ); m Scituate 29 Dec 1657 [GMB 2:920]

HATCH, Jonathan[2] (c1621-   ) & Sarah[2] ROWLEY (c1630-   ), dau of Henry; m Barnstable 11 Apr 1646 [GMB 2:376, 1603]

HATCH, Samuel & Mary DOTY; after 10 July 1677 [GMB 1:576]

HATCH, Thomas & Sarah[2] ELMES (1645-   ); m Scituate 4 Feb 1662[/3]? [GM 2:425]

HATCH, Thomas[1] (c1596-1661) & Grace _____ (-1661+); m by 1621 Barnstable [GMB 2:876]

HATCH, Walter[2] (c1623-   ) & 1/wf Elizabeth[2] HOLBROOK (c1634-   ), dau. of Thomas; m Scituate 6 May 1650 [GM 3:242, 353]

HATCH, Walter[2] (c1623-   ) & 2/wf Mary _____; m Marshfield 1 Aug 1674 [GM 3:242]

HATCH, William[1] (c1599-1651) & 1/wf _____ _____; m c1623 [GM 3:242]

HATCH, William[1] (c1599-1651) & 2/wf Jane YOUNG; m2 Thomas KING; m 9 July 1624 Scituate [GM 3:242]

HATCH, William[2] (bp 1629-   ) & Abigail[2] HEWES (c1633-   ); m2 John KING; m by 1653 Wye, Kent/Scituate [GM 3:243; GMB 2:920]

HATHAWAY, Jacob (1675-   ) & Philip CHASE (1679-   ); m Taunton 28 Jan 1696/7 [TAG 75:111]

HATHAWAY, John & Joanna[2] POPE (c1658-   ); m Dartmouth 5 Mar 1682 [GMB 3:1498]

HATHAWAY, John[3] (c1650-bef 1730) & 1/wf Hannah[2] BURT (c1655-1705+); m c1670s
    Freetown [TAG 75:110]

HATHERLY, Timothy[2] (bp 1588-1666) & 1/wf Alice COLLARD (-by 1634); m St
    Olave, Southwark, Surrey 26 Dec 1614 [GMB 2:879]

HATHERLY, Timothy[2] (bp 1588-1666) & 2/wf Susan _____ (-1640[/1]+); m by 11 Jan
    1634/5 Scituate [GMB 2:879]

HATHERLY, Timothy[2] (bp 1588-1666) & 3/wf Lydia (_____) TILDEN; m1 Nathaniel
    TILDEN; m aft 1641 [GMB 2:880]

HATHORNE, Eleazer[2] (1637-) & Abigail CURWEN (1637-); m Salem 28 Aug 1663
    [GMB 2:885; REG 150:195]

HATHORNE, John[1] (bp 20 Apr 1621-1676) & Sarah _____ (-bef 1702); c1643 Salem
    [TEG 12:86]

HATHORNE, John[2] (1641-) & Ruth GARDNER; m Salem 22 Mar 1674/5 [GMB
    2:885]

HATHORNE, William[1] (c1606-1681) & Ann _____ (-1681+); m by 1634 Salem [GMB
    2:885]

HATHORNE, William[2] (1645-) & Sarah _____ [GMB 2:885]

HAVEN, Richard (c1616-by 1703) & Susannah NEWHALL (bp 1624-1682/3]; m by
    1645/6 [AEBK 4:507]

HAWES, Daniel[2] (1651/2-1738/9) & Abiel GAY (1649-1718); m Dedham 23 Jan 1677/8
    [AEBK 3; GM 3:41]

HAWES, Edmund[1] (bp 1612-1693) & _____ _____; m by 1636 Solihull,
    Warwickshire/Yarmouth [GM 3:249]

HAWES, Edward[1] (by 1628-1687) & Eliony LUMBER; m Dedham 15 Apr 1648 [AEBK
    3]

HAWES, Eleazer[2] (bp 1644/5-) & Ruth HAYNES; m Dorchester 23 Feb 1669/70 [GM
    3:252]

HAWES, John[2] (1656-c1741/2) & Sarah DEERING; m Dedham 27 May 1683 [AEBK 3]

HAWES, John[2] (c1636-) & Desire GORHAM, dau. of John; m Barnstable 7 Oct 1661
    [GM 3:249]

HAWES, Joseph[2] (1664-1756) & Deborah DEWING (1668-1752); m c1692
    Dedham/Needham [AEBK 3]

HAWES, Nathaniel[2] (1660-1714) & Sarah NEWELL (1665[/6]-1758); m Dedham 29 Mar
    1688 [AEBK 3]

HAWES, Obadiah[2] (bp 1635-) & 1/wf Mary HUMPHREY; m by 1663 [GM 3:252]

HAWES, Obadiah[2] (bp 1635-) & 2/wf Sarah (_____) HOLMES; m1 John HOLMES; m
    by 7 Oct 1678 [GM 3:252]

HAWES, Richard[1] (bp 1606-by 1656/7) & Anne _____; m by 1632 Great Missenden,
    Buckinghamshire/Roxbury [GM 3:252]

HAWKES, Adam[1] (bp 1604/5-1671/2) & 1/wf Anne (_____) HUTCHINSON (-1669); m
    c1631 Hingham, Norfolk/Lynn [GM 3:254]

HAWKES, Adam[1] (bp 1604/5-1671/2) & 2/wf Sarah HOOPER; m2 Samuel
WARDWELL; m Lynn June 1670 [GM 3:255]

HAWKES, Eleazer (1655-) & Judith SMEAD; m Deerfield 30 Apr 1689 [GM 3:260]

HAWKES, Gershom[2] (1659-) & Elizabeth PRATT; m by 1691 Windsor [GM 3:260]

HAWKES, John[1] (c1613-1662) & Elizabeth _____ (-1685); m2 Robert HINSDALE; m3
Thomas DIBBLE; m by 1643 Hadley [GM 3:259]

HAWKES, John[1] (c1631-) & 1/wf Rebecca MAVERICK, dau. of Moses; m Lynn 3 June
1658 [GM 3:255]

HAWKES, John[1] (c1631-) & 2/wf Sarah CUSHMAN, dau. of Thomas; m Lynn 11 Apr
1661 [GM 3:255]

HAWKES, John[2] (1643-) & 1/wf Martha BALDWIN; m Hadley 26 Dec 1667 [GM
3:259]

HAWKES, John[2] (1643-) & 2/wf Alice ALLIS; m Deerfield 20 Nov 1696 [GM 3:259]

HAWKINS, James & Mary[2] MILLS (c1625-); m c1645 [GMB 2:1261]

HAWKINS, James[1] (c1603-1669/70) & Mary MILLS, dau. of John[1]; m by 1636 Boston
[GM 3:264]

HAWKINS, James[2] (1653[/4]-) & Lydia[2] RICE, dau. of Edmund; m by 1679 Boston
[GM 3:264]

HAWKINS, Job[1] (c1620-1681/2+) & Frances _____; m by 1646 Boston [GM 3:268]

HAWKINS, Joseph[2] (bp 1642-) & Abigail HOLBROOK, dau. of Richard; m Milford 8
Apr 1668 [GM 3:274]

HAWKINS, Narias[1] (c1609-1640+) & _____ _____; by 1634 Richmond Island [GM
3:270]

HAWKINS, Robert[1] (c1610-c1650) & Mary _____; m by 1635 Charlestown [GM 3:274]

HAWKINS, Timothy[1] (c1612-c1651) & Anna HAMMOND (bp 1616-1685); m2 Ellis
BARRON; m by 1637 Watertown/Lavenham, Suffolk [GMB 2:852, 889]

HAWKINS, Timothy[2] (1639-) & 1/wf Mary SHERMAN; m Watertown 18 Jan 1666/7
[GMB 2:889]

HAWKINS, Timothy[2] (1639-) & 2/wf Grace _____ (-1674[/5]); m by 1674 Watertown
[GMB 2:889]

HAWKINS, Timothy[2] (1639-) & 3/wf Mary (TREADWAY) FISHER; m Watertown 21
July 1675 [GMB 2:889; AEBK 1:459]

HAWKINS, Timothy[2] (1639-) & 4/wf Ruhamah JOHNSON; m 13 June 1680 Watertown
[GMB 2:889]

HAWKINS, Zechariah[2] (bp 1639-) & Mary BIGGS, dau. of Thomas; m c1665
Charlestown [GM 3:274]

HAWKSWORTH, Thomas[1] (c1612-1642) & Mary _____ (-1675); m by 1641 Salisbury
[GM 3:276]

HAWTHORNE, Nathaniel (-bef 1710) & Sarah HIGGINSON (1682-1750); m2
Nathaniel[3] SAWTELL; m 22 June 1699 Salem [REG 126:11]

HAYDEN, Ebenezer[2] (1645-) & Hannah _____; m by 1673 Milton/Braintree [AEBK 3; GMB 2:892]

HAYDEN, James[1] (c1608-1665) & Elizabeth _____(-1680); m by 1637 Charlestown/Barbados [GM 3:279]

HAYDEN, John & Hannah[2] AMES (1641-); m Braintree 6 Apr 1660 [AEBK 3]

HAYDEN, John[1] (c1609-1678-81/2) & Susanna _____ (c1614-by 1684); m c1634 Braintree [AEBK 3; GMB 2:891]

HAYDEN, John[2] (1639-) & Hannah MEINER; m Charlestown 14 Oct 1669 [GM 3:279]

HAYDEN, John[2] (c1634-) & Hannah AMES; m Braintree 6 April 1660 [GMB 2:892]

HAYDEN, John[3] (c1665-1718+) & Elizabeth _____ (-1694); m c1690 [AEBK 3]

HAYDEN, Jonathan[2] (1640-1718) & Elizabeth LADD; m Braintree 20 Apr 1669 [AEBK 3; GMB 2:892]

HAYDEN, Joseph[3] (c1672-1720+) & Elizabeth WALES; m c1696 Braintree [AEBK 3]

HAYDEN, Josiah & Elizabeth[3] GOODENOW (1672-); m Sudbury 6 Mar 1691[2?] [AEBK 3]

HAYDEN, Nehemiah[2] (1647/8-1717/8) & Hannah NEALE (c1663-1720); m Braintree Mar 1678 [AEBK 3; GMB 2:892]

HAYDEN, Samuel[2] (c1639-c1676) & Hannah THAYER; m Braintree 28 Oct 1664 [AEBK 3; GMB 2:892]

HAYES, George & Abigail DIBBLE; m by 1679 [REG 155:275]

HAYNE, Jonathan & 1/wf Mary MOULTON delete [TAG 23:110]

HAYNES, Hezekiah[2] (bp 1621-) & Anne SMITHSBY [GMB 2:896]

HAYNES, John[1] (1594-1653/4) & 1/wf Mary THORNTON, dau of Robert (-1624+); m Hingham, Norfolk 11 Apr 1616 [GMB 2:896]

HAYNES, John[1] (1594-1653/4) & 2/wf Mabel[1] HARLAKENDEN (bp 1614-1655), dau of Richard; m2 1654 Samuel EATON; m c1636 Earl's Colne, Essex/Hartford [GMB 2:896; GM 3:224]

HAYNES, John[2] (c1638-) & _____ _____; Cambridge/England [GMB 2:897]

HAYNES, Joseph[2] (1642-) & Sarah[2] LORD (c1649-), dau. of Richard; m by 1669 [GMB 2:897, 1200]

HAYNES, William & Sarah[2] INGERSOLL (bp 1627-); m2 Joseph HOLTON; m by 1644 [GMB 2:1062]

HAYWARD, Henry[1] (c1627-1708/9) & Sarah STONE (-1716+); m Hartford 28 Sept 1648 [GM 3:284]

HAYWARD, James[1] (c1613-1642) & Judith PHIPPEN; m2 William SIMONS; m by 1642 Woburn [GM 3:287]

HAYWARD, John & Sarah[2] MITCHELL (c1641-); m by Apr 1661 [GMB 2:1272]

HAYWARD, John (c1593-1672) & Mary (_____) (ALDRICH) JUDSON (c1616-1684); m1 Henry ALDRICH, m2 Samuel JUDSON; m after 11 July 1657 Watertown/Dedham/Charlestown [GMB 2:899]

HAYWARD, John[2] (1660-) & 1/wf Mary _____; m Wethersfield 1 June 1687 [GM 3:284]

HAYWARD, John[2] (c1626-) & Sarah MITCHELL, dau. of Experience; m by 1661 [GM 3:291]

HAYWARD, Jonathan[2] (c1640-1689) & Sarah THAYER (-1690), dau of Richard; m Braintree 6 May 1663 [AEBK 3]

HAYWARD, Joseph (1643-1713) & 1/wf Hannah HOSMER (1644-1675); m Concord 26 Oct 1665 [AEBK 1:327; GM 3:422]

HAYWARD, Joseph (1643-1713) & 2/wf Elizabeth (TREADWAY) HAPGOOD; m Concord 23 Mar 1676/7 [AEBK 1:327]

HAYWARD, Joseph[2] (c1646-) & 3/wf Hannah[2] MITCHELL (c1662-), dau. of Experience; m by 1682 [GM 3:292, 1272]

HAYWARD, Joseph[2] (c1646-) & 1/wf Alice BRETT, dau. of William; m by 1673 Bridgewater [GM 3:292]

HAYWARD, Nathaniel[2] (c1639-) & Hannah WILLIS, dau. of John; m by 1664 Bridgewater [GM 3:292]

HAYWARD, Samuel & Sarah[2] STOWERS; m c1646 Charlestown [GMB 3:1782]

HAYWARD, Samuel[2] (1665-) & Susanna BUNCE; m Hartford 18 Feb 1696/7 [GM 3:285]

HAYWARD, Samuel[2] (c1642-1713) & Mehitable THOMPSON (c1646-bef 1700/1); m Medfield 28 Nov 1666 [AEBK 3]

HAYWARD, Thomas[1] (c1599-1678) & Susanna _____; m c1624 [GM 3:291]

HAYWARD, Thomas[2] (c1624-) & Sarah _____ [GM 3:291]

HAYWARD, William[2] (c1646-1717) & 1/wf Sarah BUTTERWORTH (1653-by 1708); m c1671 Rehoboth/Swansea [AEBK 3]

HAYWARD, William[3] (1669-1728/9-29) & Hesther (HARBOUR) WARFIELD (1663-1729+); m c1692 [AEBK 3; TAG 73:16]

HAZARD, Lawrence & Mary FOXE (c1613-1669/70); m St Dunstan, Stepney, Middlesex 21 Oct 1633 [REG 156:217]

HAZARD, Robert[2] (c1628-) & Mary BROWNELL, dau. of Thomas; m c1660 [GM 3:296]

HAZARD, Thomas[1] (c1610-1677+) & 1/wf Martha _____; m c1628 [GM 3:296]

HAZARD, Thomas[1] (c1610-1677+) & 2/wf Martha (_____) SHREIVE; m1 Thomas SHREIVE; m3 Lewis HUES; m after 29 May 1675 [GM 3:296]

HEALD, John & Dorothy ROYLE; m Alderley, Cheshire 3 Dec 1636 Concord [50 GMC]

HEALEY, William & Grace[2] BUTTRY (c1634-); m Cambridge 14 Oct 1653 [GM 1:526]

HEARD, John & Elizabeth[2] HULL (c1628-); m c1643 [GM 3:455]

HEARD, John & Mary[2] CURTIS (1659-); m2 Jonathan LOOKE; m by 1677 [GM 2:263]

HEARLE, William (-1730) & 1/wf Patience ETHERINGTON (c1656-c1697); m after Feb 1675 Berwick [CG, 46]

HEATH, Isaac (1665-1684) & Ann FISHER (1661-1712+); m Roxbury 2 Feb 1680/1 [AEBK 4:264]

HEATH, Isaac[1] (bp 1586/7-1660/1) & Elizabeth MILLER, dau. of Thomas; m Ware, Hertfordshire 14 Jan 1628/9 Roxbury [GM 3:302]

HEATH, Isaac[2] (bp 1621-   ) & Mary DAVIS; m Roxbury 16 Dec 1650 [GMB 2:902]

HEATH, John[2] (1643-1706) & Sarah[2] PARTRIDGE (1647-1718); m 14 Nov 1666 Haverhill [ASBO, p.313]

HEATH, John[3] (1676-1731+) & Hannah[2] HAINES (-1731+); m 16 Dec 1697 Haverhill/Norwich [ASBO, p.316]

HEATH, Joseph[2] (c1645-1672) & Martha[2] DOW (1649-1707+); m2 Joseph[2] PAGE; m 27 June 1672 Haverhill [ASBO, p.314]

HEATH, Josiah[2] (1651-1731+) & 1/wf Mary[3] DAVIS (1647-1691+); m 19 Jul 1671 Haverhill [ASBO, p.315]

HEATH, Peleg[2] (bp 1624/5-   ) & Susanna _____; m by 1652 Nazeing/Weymouth [GMB 2:903]

HEATH, Richard & Mercy _____; m2 1692 Cornelius SALISBURY; m bef 1686 Swansea [JHO]

HEATH, William[1] (c1591-1652) & 1/wf Mary CRAMPTHORNE (bp 1591/2-1621); m Great Amwell, Hertfordshire 10 Feb 1616/7 Roxbury [REG 132:20; GMB 2:902]

HEATH, William[1] (c1591-1652) & 2/wf Mary PERRY (?1602-1659); m Gilston, Hertfordshire 29 Jan 1622/3 Roxbury [GMB 2:902; REG 132:20]

HEATON, Jabez[2] (bp 1632-dropped dead in the street in Boston 16 May 1676) & Experience MEAD (c1645-1674+); m Dorchester 4 Dec 1663 [Sewall's Diary 1:16; AEBK 4:391; GM 3:305]

HEATON, James (bp 1605-1631) & Elizabeth[1] TENNEY (bp 1607-   ); m2 Benjamin WILMOT; m3 William JUDSON; m Stallingborough, Lincolnshire 17 Aug 1630 [AEBK 4:379; DR]

HEATON, Nathaniel[1] (bp 1602-1648+) & Elizabeth WIGHT (bp 1606-1671/2-82/3); m2 Joseph PELL; m3 John MAYNARD; m Alford, Lincolnshire 21 Apr 1630 Boston [AEBK 4:380, 579; GM 3:305]

HEATON, Nathaniel[2] (1639-1714) & Mary _____; m by 1675 Wrentham [AEBK 4:391; GM 3:305]

HEATON, Samuel[2] (bp 1631-by 1660) & Mary _____; Boston [AEBK 4:391]

HEDGES, Elisha (c1642-1732) & Mary _____; m by 1666 Yarmouth [GMB 2:905]

HEDGES, William (c1612-1670) & 1/wf _____ _____; m by 1640 [GMB 2:905]

HEDGES, William (c1612-1670) & 2/wf Blanche (_____) HULL; m1 Tristram HULL; m aft 1667 Yarmouth [GMB 2:905]

HEDGES, William (c1651-   ) & Elizabeth _____; m by 1682/3 [GMB 2:906]

HEFFERNAN, William & Susannah GROSSE; Newport [REG 146:296]

HELGASON, Ingerman (-1683) & Mary PAYNE (1655-1702+); m2 _____ SMALL; m bef. 3 Nov 1683 Boston [SD 19:347, 350; Harris]

HELWISE, Edward & Sarah² HATHORNE (1634/5-); div 9 Sept 1664 [GMB 2:885]

HEMINGWAY, John² (1641-) & Mary TRESCOTT; m Dorchester 6 Oct 1665 [GMB 2:909]

HEMINGWAY, Joshua² (bp 1643-) & 1/wf Joanna EVANS; m Roxbury 16 Jan 1667[/8] [GMB 2:909]

HEMINGWAY, Joshua² (bp 1643-) & 2/wf Mary _____ (-1703); Roxbury [GMB 2:910]

HEMINGWAY, Ralph¹ (c1609-1673) & Elizabeth HEWES (-1684/5); m Roxbury 5 July 1634 [GMB 2:909, 3:79]

HEMINGWAY, Samuel² (1636-) & Sarah COOPER; m New Haven 23 Mar 1661/2 [GMB 2:909]

HENDRICK, Daniel & 1/wf Dorothy² PIKE (-1659); m bef 1645 Haverhill/Hampton/Newbury [REG 121:162; 50 GMC]

HENLEY, George & Hannah BURTON (bp 1641-); by 1670 Boston [GMB 1:284]

HEPBURN, George¹ (c1592-1665/6) & Hannah _____ (c1589-1638+); m by 1625 Charlestown [GM 3:310]

HERBERT, John¹ (bp 1612-1658) & Mary _____ (-1660+); m by 1639 [GM 3:312]

HERBERT, John² (bp 1643-) & 1/wf Elizabeth HOUGH, dau. of Samuel; m by 1679 [GM 3:312; REG 156:389]

HERBERT, John² (bp 1643-) & 2/wf Elizabeth (RUSSELL) GRAVES, dau. of Richard; m1 Nathaniel GRAVES; m Charlestown 15 Oct 1684 [GM 3:312]

HERRICK, Ephraim² (bp 1637[/8]-) & Mary CROSS (1640-), dau of Robert; m Beverly/Salem 3 July 1651 [GMB 2:912; GM 2:243]

HERRICK, Henry¹ (c1598-1670-71) & Edith LASKIN (c1612-1677+); m by 1634 Beverly [GMB 2:912]

HERRICK, Henry² (-1702) & Lydia ?GROVER, dau. of Edmund¹; Beverly [AMacE]

HERRICK, Henry² (bp 1639/40-) & 1/wf Lydia _____; m c1663 Salem [GMB 2:912]

HERRICK, Henry² (bp 1639/40-) & 2/wf Sarah (ALCOCK) GIDDINGS, dau of John; m1 John GIDDINGS; WOODBURY connection?; m c1692 Salem/York/Ipswich [GMB 2:912]

HERRICK, John² (bp 1650-) & Mary REDDINGTON; m2 Robert CUE; m Beverly 25 May 1674 [GMB 2:913]

HERRICK, Joseph² (bp 1645-) & 1/wf Sarah LEACH; m Beverly 7 Feb 1665 [GMB 2:912]

HERRICK, Joseph² (bp 1645-) & 2/wf Mary _____; m by 1686 Beverly [GMB 2:912]

HERRICK, Thomas² (c1634-) & Hannah ORDWAY; div 1673 [GMB 2:912]

HERRICK, Zachariah² (bp 1636-) & Mary DODGE, dau of Richard; m by 1654 Beverly/Salem [GMB 2:912]

HERRIS, John (bef 1650-1715+) & Sarah (NETTLETON) MILLER (c1642-1727/8); m
    Middletown 16 May 1684 [NGSQ 80:45]

HERRIS, Thomas (1620s-1713) & 1/wf _____ _____ (-by 1678) England/London/
    Boston [NGSQ 80:44; Harris]

HERRIS, Thomas (1620s-1713) & 2[last]/wf Rebecca (SHEAFE?) WILLIS; m1 William
    WILLIS; 26 June 1678 (contract) Boston/Hartford/Philadelphia [NGSQ 80:37,
    44; Harris]

HERRIS, Thomas (c1620s-1713) & 1/wf _____ _____; m bef 1660 Boston [NGSQ 80:44]

HERSEY, William & Rebecca[2] CHUBBOCK (bp 1641-); m Hingham 1 Sept 1656 [GM
    2:75]

HERSEY, William & Ruhama[2] (HALLETT) BOURNE; m1 Job BOURNE; m by 1689
    [GM 3:198]

HESKEYES, Henry & Ruth[2] GRAVES (c1636-); m Boston 7 Aug 1656 [GM 3:138]

HETT, Eliphalet[2] (bp 1639-) & Ann DOUGLAS, dau of Henry; m Boston 1 Sept 1660
    [GMB 2:917]

HETT, Thomas (bp 1611-1668) & _____ _____; Cambridge/Charlestown [REG 155:358]

HETT, Thomas[1] (c1612-1668) & Anne[1] NEEDHAM (-1688); m by 1637 Charlestown
    [GMB 2:916, 1326]

HETT, Thomas[2] (c1644-1692) & Dorothy EDMUNDS; m Charlestown 3 Oct 1666/7
    [GMB 2:917]

HEUSTIS, Angell[2] (c1624-) & 1/wf _____ _____; m by 1645 [GM 3:450]

HEUSTIS, Angell[2] (c1624-) & 2/wf Rebecca (_____) REYNOLDS; m1 Jonathan
    REYNOLDS; m aft 1673 [GM 3:450]

HEUSTIS, Robert[1] (c1595-1652-4) & 1/wf Anne MOON (-1621/2); m Bridport,
    Dorsetshire [GM 3:449]

HEUSTIS, Robert[1] (c1595-1652-4) & 2/wf Elizabeth _____ (-1654); m aft 1622 [GM
    3:449]

HEUSTIS, Robert[2] (c1628-) & Elizabeth BUXTON; m Stamford 7 Jan 16[55/6] [GM
    3:450]

HEWES, John[1] (c1608-1671-4) & Joan _____ (-1671+); m c1632 Scituate [GMB 2:919]

HEWES, John[2] (c1653-1721) & Ruth SAWTELL (c1650-1720); m Watertown 9 Mar
    1676/7 Lexington [REG 126:5; GMB 2:920]

HEWES, Joshua[1] (c1612-1675/6) & 1/wf Mary[2] GOLDSTONE (bp 1620-1655) dau of
    Henry; m Roxbury 8 Oct 1634 [GMB 2:922; GM 3:100]

HEWES, Joshua[2] (1644-) & 1/wf Hannah NORDEN; m by 1667 [GMB 2:922]

HEWES, Joshua[2] (1644-) & 2/wf Elizabeth _____; m by 1697 [GMB 2:923]

HEWES, Joshua[2] (c1612-1675/6) & 2/wf Alice (_____) CRABTREE (-1676+); m1 John
    CRABTREE; m Boston 11 Feb 1656[/7] [GMB 2:922]

HEWITT, Ephraim (1676-1733) & Katharine/Keturah ACRES (1675-1733); m int 8 Oct
    1698 Newbury/Easton [MD 44:132]

HEWITT, Thomas & Hannah[2] PALMER (bp 1634-); m2 Roger STERRY; m3 John FISH; m 26 Apr 1659 [GMB 3:1382]

HEYLETT, Edmund & Lydia[2] PALGRAVE (1635[/6]-); m aft 8 June 1651 [GMB 3:1375]

HIBBERT, _____ & Hannah[2] GIBBONS (c1668-); m2 c1700 Robert MACE; m c1689 [GM 3:48]

HICKS, Daniel & Rebecca[2] HANMER (c1639-); m Scituate 19 Sept 1659 [GM 3:209]

HICKS, Ephraim[2] (c1625-) & Elizabeth[2] HOWLAND (c1631-), dau of John; m2 John DICKENSON; m Plymouth 13 Sept 1649 [GMB 2:927, 1022]

HICKS, Gabriel & Mary ___; m bef 8 Oct 1661 [TAG 71:146]

HICKS, John & Mary[2] CARR; m2 Ralph EARLE; m c1682 Newport [GM 2:26]

HICKS, Michael (-1688) & Lucy[3] (CHADBOURNE) LANDALL (c1659-1702); m1 _____ LANDALL, m3 Peter LEWIS; m bef 1688 Kittery [CG, 28]

HICKS, Robert[1] (c1578-1647) & Margaret _____ (-1665-6); m by 1603 St Mary Magdalen, Bermondsey, Surrey/Plymouth [GMB 2:927]

HICKS, Samuel[2] (bp 1611-) & Lydia DOANE, dau of John; m Plymouth 11 Sept 1645 [GMB 2:927]

HICKS, Thomas & Mary[2] ALBRO; m c1673 Portsmouth [GM 1:19]

HIDE, John & Elizabeth[2] HARVEY (1644-); m by 1668 [GM 3:232]

HIDE, Jonathan & Mary[2] FRENCH (c1632-); m by 1651 Cambridge [GM 2:591]

HIGGINS, Benjamin[2] (1640-) & Lydia BANGS; m Eastham 24 Dec 1691 [GMB 2:930]

HIGGINS, Eliakim[2] (1654-) & Alice NEWBOLD; m Piscataway 15 May 1684 [GMB 2:930]

HIGGINS, Jadiah[2] (1656/7-) & Mary NEWBOLD; m 12 May 1684 [GMB 2:930]

HIGGINS, Jonathan[2] (1637-) & 1/wf Elizabeth ROGERS; m Eastham 9 Jan 1660 [GMB 2:930]

HIGGINS, Jonathan[2] (1637-) & 2/wf Hannah ROGERS; m by 1680 (a rare case of sisters marrying one man) [GMB 2:930]

HIGGINS, Richard[1] (c1609-1674+) & 1/wf Lydia CHANDLER (-1640+); m Plymouth 11 Dec 1634 [GMB 2:930]

HIGGINS, Richard[1] (c1609-1674+) & 2/wf Mary (_____) YATES (-1702+); m1 John YATES; m3 Isaac WHITEHEAD; m Eastham Oct 1651 [GMB 2:930]

HIGGINS, Thomas[2] (1661-) & Elizabeth HULL; m Piscataway 9 July 1690 [GMB 2:930]

HIGGINS, Zera[2] (1658-) & Elizabeth OLIVER; m Piscataway 25 Dec 1680 [GMB 2:930]

HIGGINSON, Francis[1] (bp 1586-1630) & Anne HERBERT (-1639/40); m St Peter's, Nottinghamshire 8 Jan 1615/6 [GMB 2:934]

HILL, Charles & Rachel[2] MASON (1648-); m New London 12 June 1678 [GMB 2:1228]

HILL, Ebenezer[3] (c1656-1734) & Mary[3] WHITE (c1674-); m2 1742 Seth CHAPIN; m c1691 Sherborn [AEBK 1:513]

HILL, James[2] (c1628-) & Hannah HENCHMAN; m Boston 10 Apr 1662 [GMB 2:940]

HILL, John & 1/wf Miriam GARDNER (c1635-); by 1657 Salem [GMB 2:734]

HILL, John & Abigail[2] WOODBURY (bp 1637-); m Salem 12 Oct 1657 [GMB 3:2055]

HILL, John (-1690) & Thankful[3] STOW (1646-1711); m c1671 Guilford [AEBK 3]

HILL, Jonathan[2] (1646-1710+) & Mary HARTWELL (c1643-1694/5); m 11 Dec 1666 Billerica [NGSQ 72:10]

HILL, Nathaniel[2] (1659/60-) & Sarah NUTTER, dau. of Anthony; m c1685 [GM 3:326]

HILL, Nathaniel[2] (c1642-1706) & 1/wf Elizabeth HOLMES (1644-1685); m 21 June 1667 Billerica [NGSQ 72:8]

HILL, Nathaniel[2] (c1642-1706) & 2/wf Lydia (FLETCHER) FISKE (1646/7-1730); m1 John FISKE; m after 1685 Billerica [NGSQ 72:8]

HILL, Peter[1] (c1610-by 1667) & _____ _____; m c1635 Saco [GMB 3:2081]

HILL, Ralph (-1663) & 2/wf Margaret (____) TOOTHAKER (aft 1597-1683); m 21 Dec 1638 Plymouth Colony [NGSQ 72:6]

HILL, Ralph (bef 1633-1695) & Martha TOOTHAKER (c1636-1703/4); m 15 Nov 1660 Billerica [NGSQ 72:6]

HILL, Roger[1] (c1640s-bef 1710) & 1/wf Ann _____ (-1682/3); m bef 1676 Bedminster, Somersetshire\Beverly [ASBO, p.334]

HILL, Roger[1] (c1640s-bef 1710) & 2/wf Elizabeth _____ (-aft 1721); m bef 1689 Beverly [ASBO, p.334]

HILL, Roger[2] (c1635-) & Mary CROSS, dau of John; m by 1661 [GMB 3:2081]

HILL, Samuel (c1654-1723[/4?]) & Hannah[3] TWITCHELL (1660-1703+); m Medfield 4 Nov 1679 [AEBK 3]

HILL, Samuel[3] (1671/2-1762) & Sarah PAGE (-1758); m claimed 7 Jan 1698/9 Billerica [NGSQ 72:17]

HILL, Valentine[1] (c1603-1660-1) & 1/wf Frances FREESTONE (-164[4/]5); m by 1638 Boston [GM 3:324]

HILL, Valentine[1] (c1603-1660-1) & 2/wf Mary EATON, dau. of Theophilus; m2 Ezekiel KNIGHT; m by 1646 Boston [GM 3:324]

HILL, William[1] (c1594-1649) & Sarah JURDAIN (-1671+); m2 Nathaniel SOWTHER; m3 Edmund GREENLEAF; m St Mary Arches, Exeter, Devonshire 28 Oct 1619 [GMB 2:939; TAG 42:218]

HILL, William[2] (c1622-) & Elizabeth JONES, dau. of John; m by 1661 [GMB 2:940]

HILLIARD, William[1] (c1614-1646/7+) & _____ _____; m by 1640 [GM 3:330]

HILLS, Benjamin[2] (c1653-) & Mary BRONSON; m Wethersfield 11 Jan 1688[/9] [GMB 2:944]

HILLS, Gershom (1639-1687+) & Elizabeth CHADWICK (1648-); m Malden 11 Nov 1667 [AEBK 4:417]

HILLS, John[2] (c1644-) & Mary _____; m c1678 [GMB 2:944]

HILLS, Jonathan[2] (c1664-) & Dorothy HALE, dau of Samuel; m by 1688 [GMB 2:945]

HILLS, Joseph[1] (bp 1601/2-1687/8) & 1/wf Rose CLARKE (c1604-1650); m Great Burstead, Essex 22 July 1624 [AEBK 4:399]

HILLS, Joseph[1] (bp 1601/2-1687/8) & 2/wf Hannah (SMITH) MELLOWS (bp 1612-say 1655); m1 Edward MELLOWS; m Malden 24 June 1651 [AEBK 4:399,]

HILLS, Joseph[1] (bp 1601/2-1687/8) & 3/wf Helen (____) ATKINSON (say 1623-1663/4); m1 Hugh ATKINSON; m Malden Jan 1655/6 [AEBK 4:399]

HILLS, Joseph[1] (bp 1601/2-1687/8) & 4/wf Ann (____) LUNT (c1621-3-1695+); m1 Henry LUNT; m Newbury 8 Mar 1664/5 [AEBK 4:399, Abel Lunt, p.5]

HILLS, Joseph[2] (bp 1629-1674) & Hannah SMITH (c1633-1674); m Malden Nov 1653 [AEBK 4:416]

HILLS, Joseph[2] (bp 1649-) & 1/wf Hannah EDWARDS; m c1676 [GMB 2:944]

HILLS, Joseph[2] (bp 1649-) & 2/wf Mehitable (HINSDALE) DICKINSON; m c1699 [GMB 2:944]

HILLS, Samuel (1652-1732) & Abigail WHEELER (1655/6-1742); m Newbury 20 May 1679 [AEBK 4:417]

HILLS, William[1] (c1607-1683) & 1/wf Phyllis[2] LYMAN (bp 1611-), dau of Richard; m c1638 [GMB 2:943, 1219]

HILLS, William[1] (c1607-1683) & 2/wf Mary (____) RISLEY; m1 Richard RISLEY; m late 1648 Hockanum [GMB 2:943]

HILLS, William[1] (c1607-1683) & 3/wf Mary (WARNER) STEELE, dau. of Andrew; m1 John STEELE; m late 1655-early 1656 [GMB 2:943]

HILLS, William[2] (c1640-) & Sarah ____; m c1665 [GMB 2:944]

HILTON, Edward[1] (bp 1596-1670+) & 1/wf _____ _____ (-by 1642); m by 1629 [GMB 2:949]

HILTON, Edward[1] (bp 1596-1670+) & 2/wf Katherine (SHAPLEIGH) TREWORGY (-1676), dau of Alexander, m1 James TREWORGY; m after 6 July 1650 Northwich, Cheshire/Dover [GMB 2:949]

HILTON, Edward[2] (c1629-) & Anne DUDLEY; m by 1658 [GMB 2:949]

HILTON, Mainwaring[2] (c1646-) & Mary MOULTON, dau of Thomas; m2 -----; m by 1670 York [GMB 2:954]

HILTON, William[1] (c1591-by 1656) & 1/wf _____ _____; m by 1616 Northwich, Cheshire/Plymouth [GMB 2:953]

HILTON, William[1] (c1591-by 1656) & 2/wf Frances _____ (c1618-1688+); m2 Richard WHITE; m by 1642 Plymouth [GMB 2:953]

HILTON, William[2] (bp 1617-) & 1/wf Sarah GREENLEAF, dau of Edmund; m by 1641 [GMB 2:953]

HILTON, William[2] (bp 1617-) & 2/wf Mehitable[2] NOWELL, dau of Increase; m2 John CUTLER; m Charlestown 16 Sept 1659 [GMB 2:953, 1345]

HILTON, William[2] (c1631-) & Rebecca SIMMONS, dau of John; m c1662 [GMB 2:949]

HILTON, William[2] (c1653-) & Ann _____; m by 1678 [GMB 2:954]

HINCKLEY, Samuel & Sarah[2] POPE (c1656-); m2 Thomas HUCKINS; m Barnstable 13 Nov 1676 [GMB 3:1498]

HINCKLEY, Samuel[1] (bp 1589-1662) & 1/wf Sarah SOOLE (bp 1600-1656); m Hawkhurst, Kent 7 May 1617 Harrietsham, Kent/Barnstable [GM 3:333]

HINCKLEY, Samuel[1] (bp 1589-1662) & 2/wf Bridget (_____) BOTFISH; m1 Robert[1] BOTFISH; m Barnstable c15 Dec 1657 [GM 3:333]

HINCKLEY, Samuel[2] (1642-) & 1/wf Mary GOODSPEED; m Barnstable 14 Dec 1664 [GM 3:335]

HINCKLEY, Samuel[2] (1642-) & 2/wf Mary FITZRANDOLPH; m Barnstable 15 Jan 1668[/9?] [GM 3:335]

HINCKLEY, Thomas[2] (bp 1619/20-) & 1/wf Mary[2] RICHARDS (bp 1620-); m Barnstable 4 Dec 1641 [GM 3:333; GMB 3:1577]

HINCKLEY, Thomas[2] (bp 1619/20-) & 2/wf Mary (SMITH) GLOVER; m Barnstable 16 Mar 1659/60 [GM 3:333]

HINDE, Francis & Esther[2] CANE (-by 1694/5); m aft 1682 [GM 2:5]

HINGSTON, George[1] (bp 1631-1667) & Alice GREENSLADE; m 25 Oct 1660 Newton Ferrers, Devonshire/Boston [REG 125:202]

HINKSON, Thomas & Martha[2] WALFORD; m2 John WESTBROOK; m c1662 [GMB 3:1904]

HINSDALE, Experience & Mary[2] HAWKES (1652-); m2 John EVANS; m Hadley 10 Oct 1672 [GM 3:260]

HINSDALE, Robert[1] & Ann _____; m bef 1635/6 [TAG 68:159]

HINSDALE, Samuel[2] (bp 1636/7-) & Mehitable JOHNSON; m Medfield 31 Oct 1660 [TAG 68:159]

HITCHCOCK, Eleazer/Eliakim[2] (c1642-) & Sarah MIRICK; m New Haven 4 Nov 1667 [GM 3:338]

HITCHCOCK, John[2] (c1649-) & 1/wf Abigail MERIMAN; m New Haven 8 Jan 1670/1 [GM 3:338]

HITCHCOCK, John[2] (c1649-) & 2/wf Mary (THOMPSON) LINES [GM 3:338]

HITCHCOCK, Matthew[1] (c1610-1669) & Elizabeth _____; m c1642 New Haven [GM 3:338]

HITCHCOCK, Nathaniel[2] (c1645-) & Elizabeth MOSS; m New Haven 8 Jan 1670/1 [GM 3:338]

HITCHCOCK, Richard[1] (c1608-1671) & Lucretia WILLIAMS, dau. of Thomas; m by 1653 Saco [GM 3:340]

HITCHINGS, Daniel (c1632-1731) & 1/wf Elinor _____ (-1694); m c1656 Lynn [TEG 11:205]

HITCHINGS, Daniel (c1632-1731) & 2/wf Sarah (CUSHMAN) HAWKES (c1639-);
Lynn 7 Nov 1695 [TEG 11:205]

HOAG, John & Ebenezer[2] EMERY (1648-); m Newbury 21 Apr 1669 [GM 2:449]

HOAR, Hezekiah[1] (bp 1608-c1692) & Rebecca _____ (c1630-1679+); m c1653 Taunton
[REG 141:32; GM 3:345]

HOAR, Nathaniel[2] (1656-) & Sarah WILBORE, dau. of Shadrach; m Taunton 2 Feb
1681[/2?] [GM 3:345]

HOAR, William (c1661-) & Sarah ROSS (1667[/8]-1704+); m Beverly 3 June 1685
[REG 157:44]

HOARE, William & Dorcas[2] GALLEY (c1635-); m c1655 Beverly [GM 3:3]

HOBART, Edmund[1] (c1575-1646[/7]) & 1/wf Margaret DEWEY (-by 1634); m
Hingham, Norfolk 7 Sept 1600 [GMB 2:959]

HOBART, Edmund[1] (c1575-1646[/7]) & 2/wf Sarah (____) (LYFORD) OAKLEY
(c1586-1649); m1 Rev. John LYFORD; m Charlestown 10 Oct 1634 Hingham
[GMB 2:959]

HOBART, Edmund[2] (bp 1602/3-) & Elizabeth ELMER; m Hingham, Norfolk 18 Oct
1632 [GMB 2:959]

HOBART, Enoch (bp 1654-) & Hannah HERRIS (-1697+); m Hingham 7 Aug 1676
[NGSQ 80:47]

HOBART, Joshua & Margaret[2] VASALL (c1633-); m St. Michael Parish, Barbados 25
Apr 1656 [GMB 3:1873]

HOBART, Joshua[2] (bp 1614-) & Ellen IBROOK, dau of Richard; m Cambridge Mar
1637/8 [GMB 2:960]

HOBART, Peter[2] & Elizabeth IBROOK; m Covehithe, Suffolk 12 Oct 1628 [TAG 67:28]

HOBART, Peter[2] (bp 1604-) & 1/wf Rebecca IBROOK, dau of Richard; m Covehithe,
Suffolk 12 Oct 1628 [GMB 2:959]

HOBART, Peter[2] (bp 1604-) & 2/wf Rebecca PECK, dau of Joseph; m c1646 [GMB
2:959]

HOBART, Samuel & Hannah[2] GOULD (c1653-); m Hingham 26 Feb 1673/4 [GM
3:122]

HOBART, Thomas[2] (bp 1605/6-) & 1/wf Anne PLOMER; m Wymondham, Norfolk 2
June 1629 [GMB 2:959]

HOBART, Thomas[2] (bp 1605/6-) & 2/wf Jane _____; Hingham [GMB 2:959]

HOBBS, Henry & Hannah CANNEY (1641-1720+); m bef 1661 Dover [NHGR 20:7]

HOBBY, John & Sarah GRAY (c1642-); m c1662 [TAG 64:167]

HOBSON, William (-1659) & Ann REYNER (c1632-1693); m Rowley 12 Nov 1652
[REG 156:317]

HODGE, Nicholas & Seaborn REYNOLDS [GMB 3:1842]

HODGES, John[1] (c1610-1654+) & Mary MILLER; m2 John ANDERSON; m
Charlestown 3 Jan 1654/5 [GMB 2:963]

HOLBIDGE, Arthur[1] (c1613-by 1648) & Susanna _____; m2 John JONES; m by 1638 [GM 3:349]

HOLBROOK, Abel (c1663-1747) & Hannah MERWIN (1667-1740); m Milford 20 Dec 1683 [REG 149:308]

HOLBROOK, John & Elizabeth[2] HEMINGWAY (1645-); m Dorchester 24 Nov 1663 [GMB 2:910]

HOLBROOK, John[2] (bp 1618-) & 1/wf Sarah _____; m by 1643 St. Johns Glastonbury, Somersetshire/Weymouth [GM 3:352]

HOLBROOK, John[2] (bp 1618-) & 2/wf Elizabeth STREAM; m by 1645 [GM 3:352]

HOLBROOK, John[2] (bp 1618-) & 2/wf Mary (JACOB) OTIS [GM 3:352]

HOLBROOK, Thomas & Hannah SHEPARD (1630/1-); m Medfield 26 May 1656 [TAG 68:145]

HOLBROOK, Thomas[1] (c1589-1673-7) & Jane POWYS (-by 1677); m St. Johns, Glastonbury, Somersetshire 12 Sept 1616 [GM 3:352]

HOLBROOK, Thomas[2] (c1624-) & Joan KINGMAN; m c1651 [GM 3:353]

HOLBROOK, William (1657-1714) & Margaret[3] FAIRBANKS (c1664-1731+); m Sherborn 23 Jan 1683[/4?] [AEBK 3]

HOLBROOK, William[2] (bp 1620-) & 1/wf Elizabeth PITTS; m by 1655 [GM 3:352]

HOLBROOK, William[2] (bp 1620-) & 2/wf Abigail (WRIGHT) (SHARP) CLAPP (c1623-1702-8), dau. of Richard; m1 Robert SHARP; m2 Thomas CLAPP; m by 1696 [AEBK 4:132; GM 3:353]

HOLCOMBE, Benajah[2] (1644-) & Sarah ENO; m Windsor 11 Apr 1667 [GMB 2:966]

HOLCOMBE, Joshua[2] (bp 1640-) & Ruth SHERWOOD; m Windsor 4 June 1663 [GMB 2:966]

HOLCOMBE, Nathaniel (1648-) & 1/wf Mary BLISS; m Springfield 27 Feb 1670[/1] [GMB 2:966]

HOLCOMBE, Thomas[1] (c1609-1657) & Elizabeth _____ (c1617-1679); m2 James ENO; m c1634 Windsor [GMB 2:966]

HOLDEN, John[2] (1650[/1?]-) & 1/wf Abigail ____; Woburn [GM 3:366]

HOLDEN, John[2] (1650[/1?]-) & 2/wf Sarah PIERCE; m Woburn 19 June 1690 [GM 3:366]

HOLDEN, John[2] (1675-) & Grace JENNISON; m Watertown 7 Nov 1699 [GM 3:360]

HOLDEN, Justinian & perhaps Elizabeth[2] ONGE (bp 1616-); m by 1642 [GMB 2:1361]

HOLDEN, Justinian[1] (bp 1611-1691) & 1/wf Elizabeth _____ (-1672/3) [GM 3:360]

HOLDEN, Justinian[1] (bp 1611-1691) & 2/wf Mary RUTTER, dau. of John; m by 1674 [GM 3:360]

HOLDEN, Justinian[2] (c1644-) & 2/wf Susanna (DUTTON) DURANT, dau. of Thomas; m1 John DURANT; m Billerica 6 Dec 1693 [GM 3:365]

HOLDEN, Justinian[2] (c1644-) & Mary _____; m by 1680 [GM 3:365]

HOLDEN, Richard[1] (c1609-1690/-3/4) & Martha[2] FOSDICK (c1621-1681), dau. of Stephen; m by 1642 [GM 2:548, 3:365]

HOLDEN, Samuel[2] (1674-) & Susanna SHATTUCK; m by 1697 [GM 3:360]

HOLDEN, Samuel[2] (c1655-) & Anna ____; m by 1682 Groton [GM 3:366]

HOLDEN, Stephen[2] (c1660-) & Hannah LAWRENCE, dau. of Nathaniel; m c1685 [GM 3:366]

HOLDRED, William[1] (c1610-1676+) & Isabel ____ (-killed by 1689); m by 1640 [GM 3:370]

HOLDRED, William[2] (1647[/8]-) & Lydia QUIMBY; m 10 Apr 1674 [GM 3:370]

HOLDRIDGE, John & Elizabeth[2] PERRY (1637[/8?]-); possibly the two who m Dedham 16 Sept 1663 [GMB 3:1443]

HOLGRAVE, John[1] (c1590-by 166E) & Elizabeth ____; m by 1636 or 1615 Salem [GMB 2:968]

HOLGRAVE, Joshua[2] (c1615-) & Jane ____; m by 1640 Salem [GMB 2:968]

HOLLAND, Adam & Rebecca[2] BISHOP (1652-); m by 1687 Boston [GM 1:305]

HOLLAND, John[1] (bp 1602-1652) & Judith STEPHENS; m2 John KENDRICK; m St Andrew, Plymouth, Devonshire 18 Nov 1629 Dorchester [GM 3:375; TAG 68:177-78]

HOLLAND, Samuel & Mary COLLER (c1675-)(perhaps); m Marlboro 9 Jan 1695/6 [AEBK 1:255]

HOLLARD, Angel[1] (bp 1614-1670) & Katherine RICHARDS; m2 John[1] UPHAM; m Beaminster, Dorsetshire 12 Aug 1635 Boston [GM 3:379]

HOLLINGSWORTH, Richard (c1594-5-1654) & 1/wf ____; m bef 1626 Eng [TAG 40:77]

HOLLINGSWORTH, Richard (c1594-5-1654) & 2/wf Susan ?HUNTER; m c1626/7 Eng [GM 3:474; TAG 40:77]

HOLLINGSWORTH, Richard[1] (c1595-1653+) & Susanna (____) HUNTER; m by 1628 Salem [GM 3:382]

HOLLINGSWORTH, Richard[2] (c1631-) & Elizabeth POWELL; m Boston 23 Aug 1659 [GM 3:382]

HOLLINGSWORTH, William[2] (c1628-) & Eleanor ____; m by 1655 Salem [GM 3:382]

HOLLOWAY, John[1] (c1613-1684) & Mary ____ (perhaps REEVE); m by 1663 [GM 3:385]

HOLLOWAY, Joseph & ____[2] BENNETT; m by 18 July 1670 Lynn [EQC 4:304; GM 1:258]

HOLLOWAY, Joseph[3] (c1668-1732) & Ann JENNINGS (1670-1732+); m c1693 Sandwich [NGSQ 64:20]

HOLMAN, Abraham[2] (bp 1634/5-) & Sarah PITTS; m Hingham 27 Feb 1662/3 [GM 3:390]

HOLMAN, Edward (1647?-) & Richard[2] (female) BRIMBLECOM (1646-) (not HOOPER); m c1665 Marblehead [DCD]

HOLMAN, Edward[1] (c1605-1675+) & Amy (GLASS) WILLIS, dau of James; m1 Richard WILLIS; m by 1644 [GMB 2:971]

HOLMAN, Jeremiah[2] (bp 1629-) & 1/wf Mercy[2] PRATT; m c1665 [GMB 3:1517; GM 3:390]

HOLMAN, Jeremiah[2] (bp 1629-) & 2/wf Susanna _____; m c1700 [GM 3:390]

HOLMAN, John[1] (bp 1602/3-1652-3) & 1/wf Anne _____ (-1639); m by 1637 Dorchester [GMB 2:974]

HOLMAN, John[1] (bp 1602/3-1652-3) & 2/wf Anne BISHOP (bp 1616-by 1673), dau of Thomas; m2 Henry BUTLER; m by 1641 Dorchester [GMB 2:974]

HOLMAN, John[2] (1637[/8]-) & Mary BLANTON (bp 1645-); m by 1667 [GMB 2:974]

HOLMAN, Samuel[2] (bp 1646-) & Rachel BATEMAN; m by 1671 [GMB 2:975]

HOLMAN, Thomas[2] (1641-) & Abigail RIGBY; m Dorchester 19 Feb 1663[/4] [GMB 2:975]

HOLMAN, William[1] (c1595-1652[/3]) & Winifred _____ (-1671); m by 1627 All Saints, Northampton, Northamptonshire/Cambridge [GM 3:389]

HOLMES, Abraham[2] (c1640-) & 1/wf Elizabeth ARNOLD; m by 1666 Scituate/Marshfield [GM 3:393]

HOLMES, Abraham[2] (c1640-) & 2/wf Abigail (_____) NICHOLS; m1 Ephraim NICHOLS; m Hingham 19 Apr 1695 [GM 3:393]

HOLMES, Francis (c1670s-1726) & Rebecca WHARF (c1670s-1730/1); m 11 Feb 1693/4 Boston [TG 3:57]

HOLMES, Isaac[2] (c1653-) & Anne ROWSE, dau. of John; m Marshfield Apr 167- [GM 3:394]

HOLMES, Israel[2] (c1650-) & Desire (DOTY) SHERMAN, dau. of Edward; m1 William SHERMAN; m Marshfield 24 Nov 1681 [GM 3:394]

HOLMES, John & 1/wf Elizabeth[3] GATES (1671-1726); m c1690 Stow [REG 120:164]

HOLMES, John & Sarah[2] FARR; m by 1672 [GMB 3:2079]

HOLMES, John[1] (c1611-1651+) & Sarah _____ (-1650); m c1636 Plymouth [GMB 2:978]

HOLMES, John[2] (c1636-1697) & 1/wf Patience FAUNCE (c1640-bef 1681), dau of John; m Plymouth 20 Nov 1661 [NGSQ 74:87; GMB 2:978]

HOLMES, John[2] (c1636-1697) & 2/wf Patience (BONHAM) WILLIS (c1647-1724+); m1 Richard WILLIS; m c1681 Plymouth [NGSQ 74:87; GMB 2:978]

HOLMES, Josiah[2] (c1638-) & Hannah[2] SAMSON (c1646-), dau. of Henry; m Duxbury 20 Mar 1665[/6?] [GM 3:393; GMB 3:1623]

HOLMES, Nathaniel[2] (c1648-) & Mercy FAUNCE, dau of John; m Plymouth 29 Dec 1667 [GMB 2:978]

HOLMES, Richard & Sarah GRANT (c1637-); Hartford/Norwalk [GMB 2:805]

HOLMES, Samuel[1] (bef 1651-1690/1) & 2/wf Mary _____ (c1655-1722+); m2 Peter CHENEY Jr.; m c1678-81 Boston [ASBO, p.341]

HOLMES, Thomas & Joan[2] FREETHY; m by 1671 [GM 2:585]

HOLMES, William[1] (c1592-1678) & Elizabeth _____ (-1698[/9?]); m c1638 Marshfield [GM 3:393]

HOLOWAY, Elisha? & Mary DEERING (1653-1678+); by Nov. 1678 Braintree/Taunton? [REG 106:30; Harris]

HOLT, Henry[2] (c1643-) & Sarah BALLARD; m Andover 24 Feb 1669[/70?] [GM 3:400]

HOLT, James[2] (c1650-) & Hannah ALLEN, dau. of Andrew; m Andover 12 Oct 1675 [GM 3:400]

HOLT, John[2] (1663[/4]-) & Sarah GEARY; m Andover 3 July 1685 [GM 3:400]

HOLT, Nicholas[1] (c1608-1685[/6]) & 1/wf Elizabeth _____ (-1656); m by 1636 Andover [GM 3:399]

HOLT, Nicholas[1] (c1608-1685[/6]) & 2/wf Hannah (BRADSTREET) ROLFE, dau. of Humphrey; m1 Daniel ROLFE; m Ipswich 12/20 June 1658 [GM 3:399]

HOLT, Nicholas[1] (c1608-1685[/6]) & 3/wf Martha (_____) PRESTON (-1702/3); m1 Roger PRESTON; m Andover 21 May 1666 [GM 3:399]

HOLT, Nicholas[2] (c1645-) & Mary RUSSELL; m Andover 8 Jan 1679[/80?] [GM 3:400]

HOLT, Samuel[2] (1641-) & Sarah ALLEN, dau. of Andrew; m by 1670 Andover [GM 3:400]

HOLWAY, Joseph & Mary HULL; m Sandwich Quaker Meeting 11 July 1657 [TAG 67:31]

HOLWAY, Joseph & Rose[2] ALLEN; m2 William NEWLAND; m c1639 Sandwich [GM 1:29]

HOLYOKE, Edward (bp 1585/6-1660) & 1/wf Prudence STOCKTON (bp 1584-by 1648); m Kimcote & Walton, Leicestershire 17 June 1612 Lynn [REG 147:170; NGSQ 69:11]

HOLYOKE, Edward[1] (bp 1585/6-1660) & 2/wf Anne (TAYLOR) TUTTLE, m1 Richard TUTTLE; m by 1648 Chelsea [REG 147:20]

HOLYOKE, Eliezer & Mary[2] PYNCHON (c1622-); m Springfield 20 Nov 1640 [GMB 3:1538]

HOMER, Michael & Mary (_____) BURROUGHS; m1 George BURROUGHS; m3 Christopher HALL [TAG 56:43]

HOOKE, William[1] (bp 1612-1652) & Eleanor (_____) NORTON; m1 Walter[1] NORTON; m c1636 St Stephens, Bristol, Gloucestershire/Charlestown [GM 3:406]

HOOKE, William[2] (c1638-) & Elizabeth DYER; m St Stephen's, Bristol 27 Dec 1660 [GM 3:406]

HOOKER, Samuel[2] (c1633-) & Mary[2] WILLETT (1637-), dau of Thomas; m Plymouth 22 Sept 1658 [GMB 2:984, 3:2000]

HOOKER, Thomas[1] (c1586-1647) & Susannah GARBRAND; m2 William GOODWIN; m Amersham, Buckinghamshire 3 Apr 1621 Hartford/Farmington [TAG 75:225; GMB 2:984]

HOOMERY, John[1] (by 1652-1675+) & Mary JENNINGS; Portsmouth [TAG 77:310]

HOOMERY, John[2] & Sarah WODELL; m by 1700 [TAG 77:311]

HOPKINS, Giles[2] (bp 1607/8-) & Catherine[1] WHELDEN; m Plymouth 9 Oct 1639
    [TAG 73:170; GMB 2:988]

HOPKINS, John[1] (c1606-1653-4) & Jane _____; m2 Nathaniel WARD; m3 Gregory
    WOLTERTON; m by 1631 [GM 3:413]

HOPKINS, Samuel & Hannah[2] TURNER (bp 1639-); m New Haven 5 Dec 1667 [GMB
    3:1850]

HOPKINS, Stephen[1] & Mary _____; m bef 1604 Hursley, Hampshire/Plymouth [TAG
    73:170]

HOPKINS, Stephen[1] (c1582-1644) & 1/wf _____ _____; m c1607 [GMB 2:988]

HOPKINS, Stephen[1] (c1582-1644) & 2/sf Elizabeth FISHER (-1640s); m St. Mary
    Matfellon, Whitechapel, London 19 Feb 1617/8 [GMB 2:988]

HOPKINS, Stephen[2] (c1633-) & Dorcas BROWNSON; m by 1657 [GM 3:413]

HOPKINS, William & Hannah[2] ANDREWS; m c1656 Roxbury [GM 1:60]

HORNE, Benjamin[2] (bp 1654/5-) & Sarah ABORNE, dau of Samuel; m by 1699 [GMB
    2:993]

HORNE, John[1] (c1602-1684) & 1/wf Anne _____ (-by 1649); m by 1636 Salem [GMB
    2:992]

HORNE, John[1] (c1602-1684) & 2/wf Frances (STONE) GREENE, dau of Simon; m1
    Henry GREENE; m by 1649 [GMB 2:992]

HORNE, John[2] (c1645-) & Mary CLARKE; m Salem 30 Oct 1667 [GMB 2:993]

HORNE, Joseph[2] (c1652-) & Anna TOMSON; m Salem 12 July 1677 [GMB 2:993]

HORNE, Simon[2] (bp 1649-) & Rebecca (RAY) STEVENS; m1 Samuel STEVENS; m
    Salem 28 Feb 1675 [GMB 2:993]

HORNE, William & Elizabeth[2] CLOUGH (1642-); m by 1662 Salisbury [GM 2:113]

HORSINGTON, John[1] (1640s-1703) & 2/wf Mary (STANBOROUGH) EDWARDS (-
    1728); m c1688-93 CT [REG 141:40]

HORSINGTON, John[1] (c1640s-1703) & 1/wf _____ (-c1688-93); m c1680 Wethersfield
    [REG 141:40]

HORTON, Jeremiah & Ruth[2] ELY; m Springfield 3 Oct 1661 [GM 2:438]

HOSFORD, John[2] (bp 1627-) & Phillip THRALL; m Windsor 5 Nov 1657 [GMB
    2:997]

HOSFORD, William[1] (c1595-1655+) & 1/wf Florence HAYWARD (bp 1594-1641); m
    Beaminster, Dorsetshire 14 Apr 1594 [GMB 2:996]

HOSFORD, William[1] (c1595-1655+) & 2/wf Jane (_____) FOWKES (-1671+); m1
    Henry FOWKES; m aft 1641 [GMB 2:997]

HOSIER, Samuel[1] (c1610-1665) & Ursula (ADAMS) STREETER, dau of Henry; m1
    Stephen STREETER; m3 William ROBINSON; m4 Griffin CRAFTS; m
    Charlestown 13 Oct 1657 [GMB 2:999]

HOSKINS, Anthony & Mary (GRIFFEN) WILSON; m1 Samuel WILSON; m bef 7 Mar 1700/1 Windsor, CT [TAG 52:80]

HOSKINS, John[1] (c1588-1648) & Ann _____ (-1662[/3]); m c1613 Windsor [GMB 2:1001]

HOSKINS, John[2] (c1650-) & 1/wf Elizabeth _____; m c1680 [GM 4:418]

HOSKINS, Richard[2] (c1661-) & 1/wf Jane FLUSTER; m Taunton 2 Aug 1686 [GM 3:418]

HOSKINS, Richard[2] (c1661-) & 2/wf Mary TISDALE; m c1694 [GM 3:418]

HOSKINS, Samuel[2] (1654-) & 1/wf Abigail STACY, dau. of Richard; m c1679 [GM 3:418]

HOSKINS, Samuel[2] (1654-) & 2/wf Mary AUSTIN, dau. of Jonah; m Taunton 5 Feb 1684[/5?] [GM 3:418]

HOSKINS, Samuel[2] (1654-) & 3/wf Rebecca BROOKS, dau. of Gilbert; m Taunton 12 May 1692 [GM 3:418]

HOSKINS, Thomas[2] (c1614-) & Elizabeth (GAYLORD) BIRGE, dau of William; m1 Richard BIRGE; m Windsor 20 Apr 1653 [GMB 2:1001]

HOSKINS, William[1] (c1611-1695) & 1/wf Sarah CUSHMAN; m 2 Nov 1636 [GM 3:416]

HOSKINS, William[1] (c1611-1695) & 2/wf Ann HYNES (c1617-1670+); m 21 Dec 1638 [GM 3:417]

HOSKINS, William[1] (c1611-1695) & 3/wf Elizabeth (_____) KNAPP; m1 Aaron KNAPP; m 1674+ [GM 3:417]

HOSKINS, William[2] (c1647-) & Sarah CASWELL, dau. of Thomas; m Taunton 3 July 1677 [GM 3:417]

HOSMER, James[1] (bp 1605-1685[/6?] & 1/wf Ann _____; m by 1633 Hawkhurst, Kent/Concord [GM 3:421]

HOSMER, James[1] (bp 1605-1685[/6?] & 2/wf Mary _____ (-1641); m c1637 Concord [GM 3:422]

HOSMER, James[1] (bp 1605-1685[/6?] & 3/wf Alice _____ (-1664/5); m by 1642 Concord [GM 3:422]

HOSMER, James[2] (c1637-) & Sarah WHITE; m Concord 13 Oct 1658 [GM 3:422]

HOSMER, Stephen[2] (1642-) & Abigail WOOD; m Concord 24 May 1667 [GM 3:422]

HOSMER, Stephen[2] (c1645-) & Hannah[2] BUSHNELL, dau of Francis; m by June 1668 [GMB 2:1004; GM 1:511]

HOSMER, Thomas[1] (bp 1602/3-1687) & 1/wf Frances _____ (-1675); m by 1636 [GMB 2:1004]

HOSMER, Thomas[1] (bp 1602/3-1687) & 2/wf Catherine (_____) WILTON (-1685[/6]+); m1 David WILTON; m Hartford 6 May 1679 [GMB 2:1004]

HOUCHIN, Jeremiah & Hester PIGEON; m Pulham St Mary the Virgin, Norfolk 16 Aug 1636 [TAG 67:54]

HOUGH, Atherton[1] (c1593-1650) & 1/wf Elizabeth (BULKELEY) WHITTINGHAM, dau of Edward; m1 Richard WHITTINGHAM; m Boston, Lincolnshire 9 Jan 1617/8 [GMB 2:1007]

HOUGH, Atherton[1] (c1593-1650) & 2/wf Susannah (HUTCHINSON) STORRE (-by 1651); m1 Augustine STORRE; m c1645 [GMB 2:1007]

HOUGH, Samuel & Ann[2] RAINSFORD (1651/2-); m by 1675 Boston [GMB 3:1547]

HOUGH, Samuel (1653-1718) & 1/wf Hannah ORVIS (1655-c1678); m c1676 Wallingford [TAG 41:46]

HOUGH, Samuel (1653-1718) & 2/wf Susanna WROTHAM [TAG 41:46]

HOUGH, Samuel (1653-1718) & 3/wf Mary BATES [TAG 41:46]

HOUGH, Samuel[2] (c1620-) & Sarah SYMMES, dau of Zachariah; m by 1650 [GMB 2:1008]

HOUGHTON, John (c1640s-1712) & Abigail FISHER (1648/9-1718); m Dedham 1 Mar 1666/7 [AEBK 4:256]

HOULTON, Robert[1] (c1613-1636-7) & Ann _____; m2 Richard WALKER; m by 1634 [GMB 2:1010]

HOUSE, Samuel[1] (bp 1610-1661) & Elizabeth HAMMOND (c1619-), dau. of William[1]; m cApr 1636 Eastwell, Kent/Watertown/Scituate [GMB 2:852; GM 3:426]

HOUSE, Samuel[2] (c1639-) & Rebecca NICHOLS; m Scituate 15 Mar 1664[/5?] [GM 3:426]

HOVEY, Daniel & Abigail[2] ANDREWS; m by 1643 [GM 1:54]

HOVEY, Nathaniel & Sarah[2] FULLER; m Ipswich Nov 1679 [GM 2:600]

HOWARD, John & Martha[2] HAYWARD (c1634-); m c1655 [GM 3:292]

HOWARD, William (-1709) & Tabitha[2] (perhaps KINSMAN); m bef Dec 1667 Ipswich [TAG 66:112]

HOWCHEN, Jerimy & Hester PIGEON; 16 Aug 1636 Pulham St Mary the Virgin, Norfolk [RCA] see Houchin

HOWD, Anthony & Elizabeth[2] HITCHCOCK (1651-); m New Haven Jan 1672[/3?] [GM 3:338]

HOWE, Abraham[1] (bp 1635-1694/5) & Hannah WARD (-1717); m Watertown 26 Mar 1657 [AEBK 3]

HOWE, Abraham[2] (1670-killed 1704) & Mary HOWE (1674-1751), dau of Josiah; m Marlborough 14 Nov 1695 [AEBK 3]

HOWE, Abraham[2] (c1650-) & Sarah PEABODY; m Ipswich 26 Mar 1678 [GM 3:434]

HOWE, Daniel[1] (c1608-1656+) & _____ _____; m say 1633 Southampton/Easthampton/New Haven [GMB 2:1012; GM 3:429]

HOWE, Daniel[2] (c1657-1718) & Elizabeth KERLEY (by 1731), dau of Henry; m Marlborough 12 Oct 1686 [AEBK 3]

HOWE, Edward (bp 12 June 1573-) & 1/wf _____ _____; m c1598/9 Ivinghoe, Buckinghamshire [26 GMC]

HOWE, Edward[1] (bp 1587/8-1644) & Margaret WELLS (bp 1590-bef 1660); m2 George
BUNKER; m Boxted, Essex 16 Aug 1610 Watertown [TAG 70:177; GMB
2:1015; AEBK 1:342]

HOWE, Edward[1] (c1575-1639) & Elizabeth _____; m by 1608 Lynn [GM 3:429]

HOWE, Eleazer[2] (1662[/3?]-1736/7) & Hannah[2] HOWE (1663-1735); m Marlborough 9
Nov 1684 [AEBK 3]

HOWE, Ephraim[2] (c1626-   ) & Ann HOUGH; m c1653 New Haven [GM 3:430]

HOWE, Isaac[2] (1648-1724) & Frances WOODS (1645-1718), dau of John; m Marlborough
17 Jan 1671[/2] [AEBK 3]

HOWE, Isaac[2] (c1628-   ) & _____ _____ Greenwich [GM 3:430]

HOWE, James[1] (c1603-1702) & Elizabeth DANE (-1693/4), dau. of John; m Bishop's
Stortford, Hertfordshire/Ipswich [GM 3:433]

HOWE, James[2] (bp 1633[/4?]-   ) & Elizabeth JACKSON; m Ipswich 13 Apr 1658 [GM
3:433]

HOWE, Jeremiah[2] (c1614-   ) & Elizabeth _____; m c1641 [GM 3:429]

HOWE, John[1] (bp 1617-1680) & Mary _____ (c1620-by 1698); m by 1640 Marlborough
[AEBK 3]

HOWE, John[2] (1640-killed 1676) & Elizabeth WARD (1642-1710); m 22 Jan 1662
[AEBK 3]

HOWE, John[2] (c1637-   ) & 1/wf Mary (COOPER) DORMAN; m by 1665 Topsfield [GM
3:434]

HOWE, John[2] (c1637-   ) & 2/wf Sarah TOWNE, dau. of Edmund; m by 1678 [GM 3:434]

HOWE, Joseph[2] (1661[/2]-1701) & Dorothy MARTIN (-1718+); m Marlborough 29 Dec
1687 [AEBK 3]

HOWE, Joseph[2] (c1621-   ) & Mary NEEDHAM, dau. of Edmund; m c1646 [GM 3:429]

HOWE, Josiah[2] (-bef 1710) & Mary HAYNES (-1711+); m 18 May 1671 [AEBK 3]

HOWE, Samuel[2] (1642-1713) & 1/wf Martha BENT (-1680); m Sudbury 5 June 1663
[AEBK 3]

HOWE, Samuel[2] (1642-1713) & 2/wf Sarah (LEAVITT) CLAPP (1659-1726); m Sudbury
1 Sept 1685 [AEBK 3]

HOWE, Thomas[2] (1656-1733[/4]) & 1/wf Sarah HOSMER (c1663-1724); m Marlborough
21 June 1681 [AEBK 3]

HOWE, William[2] (c1629-   ) & Mary _____; m by 1654 Concord [GM 3:430]

HOWELL, Arthur & Elizabeth[2] GARDINER (1641-   ); m by 1657 Lynn [GM 3:11]

HOWES, Jeremiah & Sarah[2] PRENCE (c1648-1706); m c1669 Yarmouth [GMB 3:1524]

HOWLAND, Arthur & Elizabeth[2] PRENCE (c1647-   ); m Marshfield 9 Dec 1667 [GMB
3:1523]

HOWLAND, Arthur[1] (-1675) & Margaret (   ) WALKER (-1683); m "possibly long
before" 6 June 1643 Fen Stanton, Huntingdonshire/Plymouth/ Marshfield
[NGSQ 71:84]

HOWLAND, Henry¹ (c1603-1670/1) & Mary _____ (-1674); m by say 1628 Duxbury [GMB 2:1018]

HOWLAND, Isaac² (1649-) & Elizabeth VAUGHN, dau of George; m by 1677 [GMB 2:1023]

HOWLAND, Jabez² (c1644-) & Bethiah THATCHER, dau of Anthony; m by 1669 [GMB 2:1023]

HOWLAND, John¹ (c1592-1672/3) & Elizabeth² TILLEY (bp 1607-1687); m Plymouth c1624 [GMB 2:1022, 3:1822]

HOWLAND, John² (1627-) & Mary LEE; m Plymouth 26 Oct 1651 [GMB 2:1022]

HOWLAND, John² (c1641-) & Mary WALKER; m Duxbury 29 Jan 1684/5 [GMB 2:1018]

HOWLAND, Joseph² (c1640-) & Elizabeth² SOUTHWORTH, dau of Thomas; m Plymouth 7 Dec 1664 [GMB 2:1023, 3:1714]

HOWLAND, Joseph² (c1649-) & Rebecca HUSSEY; m Hampton 4 May 1683 [GMB 2:1019]

HOWLAND, Samuel² (c1638-) & Mary SAMPSON, dau of Abraham; m by say 1673 [GMB 2:1018]

HOWLAND, Sarah ~ Plymouth [Plymouth Court Aug 1692]

HOWLAND, Sarah ~ Plymouth [Plymouth Court Mar 1698/9]

HOWLAND, Zoeth² (c1631-) & Abigail _____; m by 1657 [GMB 2:1018]

HOWLETT, John (-1679+) & Abigail POWELL (c1651-); m bef 1671 Boston [REG 131:174]

HOWLETT, John² (c1643-) & Susanna HUDSON, dau of Francis; m2 Edmund PERKINS; m by 1670 [GMB 2:1027]

HOWLETT, Samuel² (c1646-) & Sarah CLARK; m Topsfield 3 Jan 1670[/1] [GMB 2:1027]

HOWLETT, Thomas¹ (c1606-1677-8) & 1/wf Alice FRENCH (bp 1610-); m by 1637 Assington, Suffolk/Newbury [GMB 2:1026]

HOWLETT, Thomas¹ (c1606-1677-8) & 2/wf Rebecca (_____) SMITH (-1680); m1 Thomas SMITH; m aft 1666 [GMB 2:1027]

HOWLETT, Thomas² (c1637-) & Lydia PEABODY; m c1662 [GMB 2:1027]

HOWLETT, William² (c1650-) & Mary PERKINS; m Topsfield 27 Oct 1671 [GMB 2:1027]

HOWSON, Peter¹ (c1604-) & Ellen _____; m by 1635 London [GM 3:435]

HOXIE, Gideon² & Grace GIFFORD (1671-1714+); m c1695 Sandwich [REG 128:254]

HOYT, Benjamin (1644[/5]-) & Hannah² WEED (c1651-); m Stamford 5 Jan 1670[/1] [GMB 2:1031, 3:1958]

HOYT, John² (c1625-) & 1/wf _____ _____; m by 1650 [GMB 2:1030]

HOYT, John² (c1625-) & 2/wf Mary (BRUNDISH) PURDY; m1 Francis PURDY; m c1659 [GMB 2:1030]

HOYT, John[3] (1663-1691) & Elizabeth[2] CHALLIS (bef 1671-1744+); m2 John[3] BLAISDELL; m c1685 Amesbury [ASBO, p.151]

HOYT, Joshua[2] (c1639-) & Mary BELL; m by 1664 [GMB 2:1030]

HOYT, Moses[2] (c1634-) & Elizabeth _____; m by 1659 [GMB 2:1030]

HOYT, Nicholas[2] (bp 1620-) & Susanna (_____) JOYCE; m1 William JOYCE; m Windsor 12 June 1646 [GMB 2:1030]

HOYT, Samuel[2] (c1643-) & 1/wf Hannah HOLLY; m Stamford 16 Nov 1670 [1671?] [GMB 2:1030]

HOYT, Simon[1] (c1593-1657) & 1/wf _____ _____; m by 1618 [GMB 2:1029]

HOYT, Simon[1] (c1593-1657) & 2/wf Susannah [no proof for SMITH] (-by 1674); m2 Robert BATES; m c1632 [GMB 2:1030]

HOYT, Walter[2] (bp 1618-) & 2/wf Rhoda (_____) TAYLOR; m1 John TAYLOR; m c1652 [GMB 2:1030]

HOYT, Walter[2] (bp1618-) & 1/wf _____ _____; m by 1642 [GMB 2:1030]

HUBBARD, Benjamin (c1608-) & Alice _____; m by 1633 [GMB 2:1033]

HUBBARD, Jeremiah & Elizabeth WHITING, dau. of Samuel; m c1620s Eng [TAG 40:81]

HUBBARD, Nathaniel[2] (c1629-) & _____ _____; m c1668 [GM 3:441]

HUBBARD, Philip (1666-bef 1713) & Elizabeth (GOODWIN) EMERY, m1 Zachariah EMERY; m Berwick 22 Dec 1692 [CG, 45]

HUBBARD, Richard[2] (c1631-) & Sarah BRADSTREET, dau. of Simon; m c1658 [GM 3:441]

HUBBARD, William[1] (c1585-1670) & 1/wf _____ _____; m c1613 [GM 3:440]

HUBBARD, William[1] (c1585-1670) & 2/wf Judith _____ (-1657); m c1629 [GM 3:440]

HUBBARD, William[2] (c1622-) & 1/wf Mary ROGERS, dau. of Nathaniel; m c1650 [GM 3:440]

HUBBARD, William[2] (c1622-) & 2/wf Mary[2] (GIDDINGS) PIERCE (c1652-), dau. of George; m1 Samuel PIERCE; m 1694 [GM 3:55, 440]

HUBBARD/HOBART, Peter & Elizabeth IBROOK; m 12 Oct 1628 Covehithe, Suffolk [RCA]

HUBBELL, Ebenezer (-1698) & Mary HARRIS (1667-1723/4); m2 1702/3 Ebenezer GRIFFIN; m bef 20 June 1692 New London [REG 156:154-5]

HUDSON, Francis[2] (c1616-) & 1/wf Mary _____; m by 13 Oct 1640 [GMB 2:1036]

HUDSON, Francis[2] (c1616-) & 2/wf Elizabeth WATKINS; m Boston int 20 Aug 1695 [GMB 2:1036]

HUDSON, John & Abigail[2] TURNER; m New Haven 2 Sept 1651 [GMB 3:1850]

HUDSON, John ~ Mary CHANDLER; c1645 [GM 3:444]

HUDSON, Jonathan[1] (c1616-21-1698-1706) & 1/wf Elizabeth _____ (-1698); Salem [TEG 14:87]

HUDSON, Nathaniel & Elizabeth[2] ALFORD; m Boston 1 Dec 1659 [GM 1:25]

HUDSON, Ralph[1] (c1593-1638-9) & Mary WATTS, m c1621 [GM 3:447]

HUDSON, William[1] (c1588-1661[/2]) & Susan _____; m c1613 [GMB 2:1036]

HUDSON, William[2] (c1613-) & 1/wf Ann _____; m by 25 Apr 1641 [GMB 2:1036]

HUDSON, William[2] (c1613-) & 2/wf Mary (BROWNE) FOUNELL (c1611-1696); m1
      John FOUNELL; m Charlestown 23 Feb 1676[/7] [GMB 2:1036; TAG 40:29]

HUFF, Ferdinando & Mary[2] MOSES (c1645-); m by 1 Mar 1664/5 [GMB 2:1301]

HULBIRD, John[2] (c1640-) & 1/wf Ann _____; m by 1669 [GMB 2:1039]

HULBIRD, John[2] (c1640-) & 2/wf Mary BAKER; m Northampton 1 Mar 1671 [GMB
      2:1039]

HULBIRD, William[1] (c1606-1694) & 1/wf _____ _____ (-by 1649); m c1639
      Dorchester/ Windsor/Hartford/Northampton [GMB 2:1038]

HULBIRD, William[1] (c1606-1694) & 2/wf Ann (_____) ALLEN (c1608-1687); m1
      Samuel ALLEN; m by 1649 [GMB 2:1038]

HULBIRD, William[2] (c1653-) & 1/wf Ruth SALMON [no evidence] [GMB 2:1039]

HULBIRD, William[2] (c1653-) & 2/wf Hanah WHITAKER [no evidence] [GMB
      2:1039]

HULBIRD, William[2] (c1653-) & 2/wf Mary HOWARD [no evidence] [GMB 2:1039]

HULING, Walton (-1710+) & Martha PALMER (-1718+); Newport, RI [TAG 60:159]

HULL, Andrew[1] (c1606-c1641) & Katherine _____; m2 Richard BEECH; m by 1635 New
      Haven [GM 3:452]

HULL, Benjamin[2] (bp 1638/9-) & Rachel YORK, dau. of Richard; m by 1669 [GM
      3:456]

HULL, Dodovah[2] (c1643-) & Mary SEWARD, dau. of Richard; m c1680 [GM 3:456]

HULL, Edward[2] (c1627-) & Eleanor NEWMAN; m Boston 20 Jan 1652/3 [GM 3:461]

HULL, George[1] (c1589-1658) & 1/wf Thomasine MITCHELL (-by 1654); m Crewkerne,
      Somersetshire 27 Aug 1614 [GMB 2:1042]

HULL, George[1] (c1589-1658) & 2/wf Sarah (_____) PHIPPEN (-1659); m1 David
      PHIPPEN; m aft 11 July 1654 [GMB 2:1042]

HULL, Hopewell[2] (c1636-) & Mary MARTIN, dau. of John; m by 1669 [GM 3:456]

HULL, John & Abigail[2] KELSEY (1645-); m Killingworth 3 Dec 1668 [GMB 2:1119]

HULL, John (1662-1714) & Mary MERWIN (1665/6-); m c1690 Derby [REG 149:308]

HULL, John[2] (1624-) & Judith[2] QUINCY (bp 1626-), dau. of Edmund; m Boston 11
      May 1647 Market Harborough, Leicestershire [GMB 3:1540; GM 3:461]

HULL, Joseph[1] (bp 1596-1665) & 1/wf _____ _____; m by 1620 Crewkerne,
      Somersetshire [GM 3:455]

HULL, Joseph[1] (bp 1596-1665) & 2/wf Agnes _____ (-1666+); m by 1635 [TAG
      68:149; GM 3:455]

HULL, Josias[2] (bp 1616-) & Elizabeth LOOMIS; m Windsor 20 May 1641 [GMB 2:1042]

HULL, Phineas[2] (c1657-) & 1/wf Jerusha[2] HITCHCOCK (1653-), dau. of Richard; m c1675 [GM 3:341, 456]

HULL, Phineas[2] (c1657-) & 2/wf Mary (RISHWORTH) (WHITE) SAYWARD, dau. of Edward; m1 William? WHITE; m2 John SAYWARD; m aft 1689 [GM 3:456]

HULL, Reuben[2] (bp 1648/9-) & Hannah FERNISIDE; m by 1673 [GM 3:457]

HULL, Robert[1] (c1599-1666) & 1/wf Elizabeth (_____) STORER (-1646); m by 1624 [GM 3:461]

HULL, Robert[1] (c1599-1666) & 2/wf Judith (PARES) (QUINCY) PAINE; m1 Edmund QUINCY; m2 Moses PAINE; m 1646 [GM 3:461]

HULL, Samuel[2] (c1645-) & 1/wf Mary MANNING; m Piscataway, New Jersey, 16 Nov 1677 [GM 3:456]

HULL, Tristram[2] (c1624-) & Blanche ____; m by 1645 [GM 3:455]

HULLING, Josiah/Jesse? & ____ ____; m 11 Jan 1675 New Shoreham, RI [TAG 60:159]

HUMPHREY, John[1] (c1597-1651+) & 1/wf Isabel WILLIAMS, dau. of Bruen [GM 3:464]

HUMPHREY, John[1] (c1597-1651+) & 2/wf Elizabeth PELHAM (-1628), dau. of Herbert; m St Thomas, Salisbury, Wiltshire 4 Sept 1621 [GM 3:464]

HUMPHREY, John[1] (c1597-1651+) & 2/wf Susan FIENNES, dau. of Thomas; m c1632 [GM 3:464]

HUMPHREY, Jonas[1] (c1587-1661/2) & 1/wf Frances COLEY (-1617/8); m Wendover, Buckinghamshire 11 June 1607 [TAG 68:19]

HUMPHREY, Jonas[1] (c1587-1661/2) & 2/wf Elizabeth (SEAMER) FOSTER, m1 Thomas FOSTER; m Turville, Buckinghamshire. 8 Nov 1619 [TAG 68:19]

HUMPHREY, Jonas[1] (c1587-1661/2) & 3/wf Jane (CLAPP) WEEKS, m1 George WEEKS; m Dorchester aft 1650 [TAG 68:19]

HUMPHREY, Thomas & Hannah LANE (bp 1638/9-); m Hingham 23 Dec 1665 [REG 156:148]

HUNKING, Mark & Sarah[2] SHERBORN (1651-) [GMB 3:1668]

HUNN, George[1] (c1601-1640) & Anne ____; m2 William PHILPOT; m by 1626 [GM 3:469]

HUNN, Nathaniel[2] (c1626-1702) & Sarah KEENE; m c1649 Wethersfield [GM 3:469]

HUNNEWELL, John (-by 1706) & 1/wf Lydia[3] EDWARDS (1650-1683); m Wethersfield 1 Jan 1679/80 [REG 145:339]

HUNNEWELL, John (-by 1706) & 2/wf Elizabeth HARRIS (-by 1710); m by 1689 Wethersfield [REG 145:339]

HUNT, Edmund[1] (c1613-1656-7) & _____ _____; m c1640 [GM 3:470]

HUNT, Ephraim & Ann[2] RICHARDS (bp 1626-); m c1643 [GMB 3:1577]

HUNT, Jonathan & Clemence[2] HOSMER (c1642-); m2 John SMITH; m Northampton 3 Sept 1662 [GMB 2:1004]

HUNT, Josiah & Abigail HUSTIS (c1670-1743); m lic 24 Dec 1695 [NYGBR 129:206]

HUNT, Richard & Jane _____ (-1652); m2 William[1] TING [NGSQ 69:115]

HUNT, Samuel & Elizabeth[2] REDDING (c1635-1706/7); m by 1657 Ipswich [GMB 3:1568]

HUNT, Samuel[2] (c1640-) & Mary _____ [GM 3:471]

HUNTER, William & Rebecca[2] BESSEY; m Barnstable 17 Feb 1670[/1?] [GM 1:269]

HUNTER, William[1] (c1624-by 1667) & 1/wf Scissilla CORISH; m Boston 30 Jan 1656/7 [GM 3:476]

HUNTER, William[1] (c1624-by 1667) & 2/wf Mary CARTER, dau. of Richard; m2 Joseph COWELL; m aft 29 Apr 1673 [GM 3:476]

HUNTING, John (bp 1601/2-1689) & Hester SEABORNE; m Wramplingham, Norfolk 28 June 1624 Dedham [NGSQ 74:4, 78:92]

HUNTING, John (bp 1636-1718) & Elizabeth PAINE (1647/8-); m Dedham 18 Apr 1671 [NGSQ 78:94]

HUNTING, Samuel (1640-1701) & Hannah HAGBURNE (bp 1642-); m Dedham 24 Dec 1662 [NGSQ 78:94]

HUNTINGTON, Christopher[2] (bp 1624-) & Ruth[2] ROCKWELL (c1633-), dau of William; m Windsor 7 Oct 1652 [GMB 2:1045, 3:1596]

HUNTINGTON, Simon (bp 1629-) & Sarah CLARK; m Saybrook Oct 1653 [GMB 2:1045]

HUNTINGTON, Simon[1] (c1598-1633) & Margaret BARRETT; m2 Thomas STOUGHTON; m St Andrew's, Norwich, Norfolk 11 May 1623 Roxbury [GMB 2:1044]

HUNTINGTON, Thomas[2] (c1626-) & Hannah CRANE, dau of Jasper; m by 1660 [GMB 2:1045]

HUNTINGTON, William[1] & Joan[2] BAYLY (bp 1622-); m c1642 [TAG 77:245]

HUNTLEY, Moses (1652-) & Abigail (CHAPPELL) COMSTOCK (1644-1713/4+); m Lyme 18 Jan 1680/1 [REG 150:56]

HURD, Adam[1] & _____ _____ (-bef 1671) not Hannah BARTRAM; m bef 1640 Stratford, CT [TAG 50:5]

HURD, John (c1613-1681) & 2/wf Sarah THOMPSON (-1717/8); m2 Thomas BARNUM; m 10 Dec 1662 Stratford [TAG 50:3]

HURD, John, Jr. & Anna[2] (TUTTLE) JUDSON; m1 Joshua[2] JUDSON [TAG 50:7]

HURD, Joseph[2] (1644-by 1693) & Sarah ?LONG (-1693); m bef 1667 Boston [REG 132:86]

HURRY, William & Hannah[2] HETT (c1637-); m by 1662 Charlestown/Malden [GMB 2:917]

HURST, James[1] (c1582-1657) & Gertrude BENNISTER (-by 1670); m Amsterdam, Holland 4 Oct 1608 [GMB 2:1047]

HUSSEY, Christopher[1] (bp 1598/9-1685/6) & 2/wf Ann (CAPON) MINGAY (-1680); m1 Jeffrey MINGAY; m Hampton 9 Dec 1658 [GMB 2:1050]

HUSSEY, Christopher[1] (bp1598/9-1635/6) & 1/wf Theodate BACHILER (c1610-1649), dau of Stephen; m by 1635 Lynn/Ipswich/Newbury/Hampton [GMB 2:1050]

HUSSEY, John[2] (bp1635[/6]-   ) & Rebecca PERKINS; m Hampton 21 Sept 1659 [GMB 2:1050]

HUSSEY, Richard[2] & Jane[3] CANNEY; m c1691 Dover [AMacE]

HUSSEY, Stephen[2] (c1643-   ) & Martha BUNKER; m Nantucket 8 Oct 1676 [GMB 2:1051]

HUSTIS, Robert[1] (c1595-1652+) & 1/wf Anne MOON; m Bridport, Dorsetshire 6 Apr 1616 Stamford [NYGBR 129:197]

HUSTIS, Robert[1] (c1595-1652+) & 2/wf Elizabeth _____ (-1654) Stamford [NYGBR 129:197]

HUSTIS, Robert[2] (c1628-1704 & Elizabeth BUSTON (c1639-by 1711); m Stamford 9 Jan 1655/6 [NYGBR 129:201]

HUSTIS, Samuel[3] & Elizabeth PELL; m by 1 May 1700 Westchester [NYGBR 129:278]

HUTCHINS, Daniel & 1/wf Eleanor _____; Lynn [TAG 67:30]

HUTCHINS, Daniel & 2/wf Sarah (CUSHMAN) HAWKES; m int Lynn 7 Nov 1695 [TAG 67:30]

HUTCHINS, Joseph & Mary[2] EDMONDS; m Boston 1 Sept 1657 [GM 2:410]

HUTCHINS, Joseph[2] (1641-1689) & Joanna[2] CORLISS (1650-1734); m2 Stephen[2] DOW; m 29 Dec 1669 Haverhill [ASBO, p.210]

HUTCHINS, Nicholas & Elizabeth[2] FARR; m Lynn 4 Apr 1666 [GMB 3:2079]

HUTCHINS, William[2] (1638-by 1691) & 1/wf Sarah[2] HARDY (c1637-1684); m 1 Jul 1661 Haverhill [ASBO, p.287]

HUTCHINSON, Edward & Mary _____ (not Cushman); Lynn [TAG 67:31]

HUTCHINSON, Edward (op 1613-1675) & 2/wf Abigail (FIRMAGE) BUTTON; m c1650 Boston [REG 145:258]

HUTCHINSON, Edward[1] (bp1607-1669+) & Sarah _____ (-1669+); m by 1633 [GMB 2:1053]

HUTCHINSON, Edward[2] (bp 1613-1675) & 1/wf Katherine HAMBY (bef 1615-c1650); dau. of Robert; m lic. Lawford, Essex 19 Oct 1636 [REG 145:258; GM 3:480]

HUTCHINSON, Edward[2] (bp 1613-   ) & 2/wf Abigail (FERMAYES) BUTTON, dau. of Alice; m1 Robert[1] BUTTON; m by 1651 [GM 3:480]

HUTCHINSON, Elisha (1641-1717) & 1/wf Hannah HAWKINS (bp 1644-1676); m Boston 19 Nov 1665 [REG 145:261]

HUTCHINSON, Elisha (1641-1717) & 2/wf Elizabeth (CLARK) FREAK (1642-1702+); m Boston 12 Sept 1677 [REG 145:261]

HUTCHINSON, Francis & Mary CUSHMAN; m c1676 Reading [TAG 67:30]

HUTCHINSON, George[1] (c1608-1660) & Margaret _____ (-1660+); m by 1633 [GMB 2:1055]

HUTCHINSON, Joseph (c1633-1716) & 1/wf Bethiah CLARKE/PRINCE? (bp 1638-bef 1678); m bef 1660, Salem [TAG 39:111]

HUTCHINSON, Nathaniel[2] (bp1633-   ) & Sarah BAKER, dau of William; m Charlestown 16 Mar 1658/9 [GMB 2:1055]

HUTCHINSON, Richard & Alice BOSWORTH; m bef 1633 Salem [TAG 39:111]

HUTCHINSON, Samuel[2] (bp 1624-   ) & ____ ____ [GM 3:481]

HUTCHINSON, William[1] (bp 1586-1641+) & Anne MARBURY (bp 1591-killed 1643); m St Mary Woolnoth, London 9 Aug 1612 Alford, Lincolnshire/Westchester Co., N.Y. [GM 3:479]

HUXLEY, Thomas & Sarah[2] SPENCER (c1646-   ); m c1667 Hartford [GMB 3:1720]

HYDE, Samuel (1637-1677) & Jane LEE (bp 1640-1722/3); m2 John BURCHARD; m June 1659 Norwich, CT [AEJA]

HYDE, Samuel[2] (1653-1725) & Hannah[2] STEDMAN (c1644-1727); m Cambridge 20 Jan 1673/4 [TAG 69:159]

HYLAND, John & Elizabeth JAMES (1673-1748+); m Scituate 3 Jan 1694/5 [REG 155:68]

ILSLEY, John[1] & Sarah[2] HAFFIELD (c1621-   ); m by 1642 Salisbury [GM 3:185]

ILSLEY, William (1612-1681) & Barbara STEVENS (1611-1681+); m 6 Mar 1637/8 Caversham, Oxfordshire/Newbury [TAG 50:61]

INES, Matthew (say 1613-by 1661) & perhaps Hannah (BROWNE?) OKLYE? (bp 1604/5-   ); m by 1638 Boston [AEBK 1:178-9]

INGALLS, Edmund (c1588-1648) & Annis TELBE (-1649+); m 7 June 1618 Church of St Nicholas, Skirbeck, Lincolnshire/Ipswich [TAG 52:242]

INGERSOLL, George[2] (bp 1618-   ) & Elizabeth ____; m by 1646 [GMB 2:1061]

INGERSOLL, John & Abigail[2] BASCOMB (1640-   ); m Northampton 12 Sept or Dec 1657 [GM 1:188]

INGERSOLL, John[2] (bp 1620[/1?]-   ) & Judith FELTON; m by 1644 [GMB 2:1061]

INGERSOLL, Nathaniel[2] (c1633-   ) & Hannah[2] COLLINS; m Salem 25 Mar 16-- [fragment] [GMB 2:1062; GM 2:168]

INGERSOLL, Richard[1] (bp1587-1644) & Agnes LANGLEY; m2 John KNIGHT; m St Swithins, Sandy, Bedfordshire 10 Oct 1611 Salem [26 GMC; GMB 2:1061]

INGERSON, John & Elizabeth (SYMONDS?) NEWHALL; m Lynn 8 Jan 1696/7 [AEBK 4:514]

INGHAM, Ebenezer (c1668-70-   ) & Dorothy STONE [TAG 68:138]

INGHAM, Joseph[1] (c1630-1710) & 1/wf Sarah[2] BUSHNELL (c1639-1683); m Saybrook, CT 20 June 1655 [TAG 68:131; GM 1:511]

INGHAM, Joseph[1] (c1630-1710) & 2/wf Mary (____) ATWELL (c1640s-1714/5); m1 Benjamin ATWELL; m c1684 Saybrook [TAG 68:131-2]

INGHAM, Samuel[2] (c1661-   ) & Rebecca WILLIAMS [TAG 68:138]

INION, John, & Question? TYLER (c1665-72-   ); m bef 1697, Portsmouth, RI [TAG 52:221]

INMAN, Edward (c1620-by 1706) & 1/wf _____ _____ (-bef 1676); m bef 1646 Braintree/Providence [AEJA]

INMAN, Edward (c1620-by 1706) & 2/wf Barbara (____) PHILLIPS (c1620s-1706+); m1 Michael PHILLIPS; m aft 1668 Providence/Newport [AEJA]

INMAN, Edward (c1654-1735) & Elizabeth BENNETT (-1721+); m c1680 Smithfield [AEJA]

INMAN, John (1648-1712) & Mary WHITMAN (1652-1720); m c1672 Providence [AEJA]

INNES, Alexander[1] (-1679) & Katherine _____ "an Irish woman" ; m by 1656 Lynn/Taunton/ New Shoreham [Saxbe; TAG 73:314]

INNES, John[2] (1638-) & Elizabeth _____ [GMB 2:1058]

INNES, Matthew (c1613-by 1661) & Anne _____ perhaps BROWNE; m by 1638 [GMB 2:1058]

INNES, Samuel[2] (bp 1650-) & Sarah BELCHER; m Braintree 13 Nov 1677 [GMB 2:1058]

IRESON, Benoni[2] (1645-) & Mary LEACH; m Lynn 1 Aug 1680 [GMB 2:1065]

IRESON, Edward[1] (c1601-1675) & Alice _____ (-1681); m by 1637 Lynn [GMB 2:1064]

IRISH, Elias[2] (c1649-) & Dorothy WITHERILL; m Taunton 26 Aug 1674 [GMB 2:1067]

IRISH, John[1] (c1611-1677/8) & Elizabeth _____ (-1659+); m by 1644 [GMB 2:1066]

IRISH, John[2] (c1647-) & 1/wf Elizabeth _____ (perhaps SAVORY); m c1672 [GMB 2:1067]

IRONS, Matthew (bef 1615-1657-61) & Anne _____ (-1655+); m bef 1638 Boston [GMSP]

IVY, John & Mercy BARTLETT (he was John JOY of Plymouth) [TAG 67:31]

JACKLIN, Edmund & Susan[2] PEASE (c1620-); m c1640 Boston [GMB 3:1416]

JACKSON, John & Elizabeth SEAMAN (c1647-) Hempstead [NYGBR 131:8]

JACKSON, John[1] (bp 1608-1666) & 1/wf Elinor MILCOME; m 10 Aug 1629 Dartmouth, St. Saviour/Portsmouth [REG 144:33]

JACKSON, John[1] (bp 1608-1666) & 2/wf Joane LURFETE (c1612-bef 1680); m 30 Mar 1633 Portsmouth [REG 144:33]

JACKSON, John[1] (bp 1624-1682+) & Sarah PALMER; m 27 Apr 1654 Dartmouth, Eng [REG 144:37]

JACKSON, Robert[1] & NOT Agnes WASHBURN; Hempstead, L.I. [NYGBR 131:3]

JACKSON, Robert[1] (c1615-20-c1683) & 1/wf _____ _____; m probably in England/Hempstead [NYGBR 131:10]

JACKSON, Robert[1] (c1615-20-c1683) & 2/wf _____ WASHBURN (-1656) Hempstead [NYGBR 131:10]

JACKSON, Robert[1] (c1615-20-c1683) & 3/wf Agnes (____) PUDDINGTON (c1615-1683+); m1 Robert PUDDINGTON [NYGBR 131:10]

JACKSON, Samuel (-1683+) & _____ _____ [NYGBR 131:8]

JACKSON, Walter & 1/wf Jane _____; m bef 1666, Dover [TAG 53:134]

JACKSON, Walter (-1697/8) & 2/wf Ann _____; m aft 1666, Dover [TAG 53:134]

JACOB, John² (bp 1629/30-) & 1/wf Margery² EAMES (bp 1630-); m Hingham 20 Oct 1653 [GMB 2:1070; GM 2:390]

JACOB, John² (bp 1629/30-) & 2/wf Mary RUSSELL; m Hingham 3 Oct 1661 [GMB 2:1070]

JACOB, Joseph² (bp 1646-) & Hannah BOSWORTH; m c1672 [GMB 2:1070]

JACOB, Nicholas¹ (c1604-1657) & Mary GILMAN (-1681); m2 John BEAL; m by 1629 [GMB 2:1070]

JACOBS, George¹ & 1/wf or 2/wf Mary JACOBS; m bef 12 Jan 1673/4 Salem [TAG 58:71]

JAMES, Edmund (c1610-1639/40+) & Reana _____ (-1672+); m 2 William ANDREWS; m3 Robert DANIEL; m4 Edmund FROST; Watertown [GMB 2:1071]

JAMES, Thomas¹ (bp 1595-1682[/3]-4) & 1/wf Olive INGOLDSBY; m Fishtoft, Lincolnshire, 20 Apr 1620 [GMB 2:1074]

JAMES, Thomas¹ (bp 1595-1682[/3]-4) & 2/wf Elizabeth _____; m by 1632 Charlestown/Providence/New Haven/Nansemond [GMB 2:1074]

JAMES, Thomas² (c1622-) & 1/wf Ruth JONES, dau of John; m by 1648 [GMB 2:1074]

JAMES, Thomas² (c1622-) & 2/wf Katharine (_____) BLUX; m 2 Sept 1669 [GMB 2:1074]

JAMES, William¹ (c1639-1697) & Susannah MARTIN (-1726); m2 Joseph KELLEY, m3 Benjamin THAYER; m Newport 10 Dec 1677 [REG 126:247, 147:331]

JAMES, William¹ (c1641-1722+) & Mehitable (_____) _____; m c1672 Scituate/Boston [REG 155:36-68]

JAQUITH, Abraham & Anna JORDAN [TAG 70:178]

JARVIS, John & Rebecca² PARKMAN (c1640-); m Boston 18 Sept 1661 [GMB 3:1401]

JAY, Joseph & Mary PRINCE; m bef 1689 Hingham [TAG 56:246]

JAY, William & Mary HUNTING (bp 1625/6-); m2 Charles BUCKNER; m 1653 Boston [NGSQ 78:94]

JEFFREY, Thomas & Mary² HARVEY (1647-); m Stratford 1 May 1674 [GM 3:233]

JEFFREY, Thomas¹ (c1613-1661) & _____ _____; m by 1640 [GMB 2:1081]

JEFFREYS, William¹ (c1590-1675) & Mary GOULD, dau of Jeremy; m by 1642 [GMB 2:1083]

JEFFRIES, Aaron (-1695+) & Mary² BLACKLEACH (bp 7 Sep 1651-1688+); m bef Dec 1672 Boston/Wethersfield/Salem [REG 148:21; GM 1:317]

JEGGLES, Thomas & Abigail² SHARP (c1630-); m c1648 [GMB 3:1654]

JENKINS, Edward¹ & Lettice² (HANFORD) FOSTER; m1 Edward¹ FOSTER; m c1650 [GM 3:206]

JENKINS, Ezekiel² (bp 1649-1705) & Sarah GOWING (-1705+); Boston [AEBK 4:426]

JENKINS, Joel (-1688) & Sarah² GILBERT (-1663/4+); m c1640 Braintree [TAG 67:165; AEBK 4:421]

JENKINS, John & Sarah² HAWKINS (1656-); m by 1684 Boston [GM 3:264]

JENKINS, John & Susannah COOKE; m bef 1648 Boston [TAG 67:135]

JENKINS, Lemuel (c1644-1713) & 1/wf Elizabeth OAKES (1650-); m Malden 12 July 1670 [AEBK 4:425]

JENKINS, Lemuel (c1644-1713) & 2/wf Mercy (TUFTS) WAITE (-1736); m1 Joseph WAITE; m Malden 11 June 1694 [AEBK 4:425]

JENKINS, Obadiah² (bp 1650-by 1720) & Mary (JONES) LEWIS (-by 1720); m1 Joseph LEWIS; m Malden 11 Jan 1676/7 [AEBK 4:426]

JENKS, Joseph & Hester² BALLARD; m c1652 Lynn [GM 1:148]

JENNINGS, John (-bef 1723) & Ruhama TURNER (c1645-bef 1723); m 29 Aug 1667 Sandwich [NGSQ 64:19]

JENNY, John¹ (c1589-1643) & Sarah CARY (-1655-65/6); m Leiden 1 Nov 1614 [GMB 2:1092]

JENNY, Mark & Elizabeth BARLOW; m bef 1701 [TAG 67:31]

JENNY, Samuel² (c1616-) & 1/wf Susanna WOOD (-1654); m aft 1637 Plymouth/Dartmouth [TAG 60:159; GMB 2:1092]

JENNY, Samuel² (c1616-) & 2/wf Anne LETTICE; m by 1657 [GMB 2:1093]

JEWELL, Thomas (about 1608-1654) & Grizzell² FLETCHER (c1619-1669); m say 1639 Concord/Braintree/Chelmsford [AEBK 4:277]

JEWETT, _____, did not marry Mary³ HALE (1661-1747+) [TAG 68:83]

JEWETT, John & Elizabeth _____ (c1637-1679); m Ipswich [REG 145:240]

JOHNS, Samuel & Sarah² FOSTER; m by 1673 Southampton [GM 2:553]

JOHNSON, Davy¹ (-by 1 Mar 1635/6) & _____ _____; m bef 1635/6 Dorchester [GMB 2:1095]

JOHNSON, Edward (bp 16 Sept 1598-) & Susan MUNTER (bp 5 Oct 1597-); Canterbury, Kent/Charlestown/Woburn [26 GMC]

JOHNSON, Edward¹ (c1593-1687[/8]) & Priscilla _____ (c1618-1706+); m by 1646 [GMB 2:1097]

JOHNSON, Elkanah ~ Dinah² SILVESTER (1642-); in court 1 June 1669 [GMB 3:1680]

JOHNSON, Francis & Sarah² HAWKES (1671-); m Andover 1 Feb 1693[/4?] [GM 3:255]

JOHNSON, Francis¹ (c1607-1690/1) & 1/wf Joan _____ (-1653/4+); m by 1636 Boston [GMB 2:1101]

JOHNSON, Francis¹ (c1607-1690/2) & 2/wf Hannah (____) HANBURY (not Madbury); m1 William HANBURY; m Boston 24 Oct 1656 [GMB 2:1101]

JOHNSON, Humphrey[2] (bp 1620-1678+) & 1/wf Ellen[2] CHENEY (c1620-1678); m Roxbury 20 Mar 1641/2 or 42/3 [REG 146:275; GMB 2:1108; AEJA; AEBK 1:231]

JOHNSON, Humphrey[2] (bp 1620-1678+) & 2/wf Abigail (STANSFIELD) MAY; m1 Samuel MAY; m Roxbury 6 Dec 1678 [REG 146:275; GMB 2:1108; AEBK 1:231; AEJA]

JOHNSON, Isaac[1] (bp 1601-1630) & Arbella FYNES (-1630); m lic 5 Apr 1623 [GMB 2:1104]

JOHNSON, Isaac[2] (bp 1615/6-1674) & Elizabeth PORTER (bp 1610/11-1675-85); m Roxbury 20 Jan 1636/7 [REG 146:274; AEJA; GMB 2:1108; REG 148:50]

JOHNSON, Jacob (-1673+) & Elizabeth (_____) _____ (-1668+); m bef. 2 Mar 1664/5 Wethersfield/Glastonbury [Harris]

JOHNSON, James & Abigail[2] OLIVER (c1625-); m by 1644 Boston [GMB 2:1356]

JOHNSON, John[1] (c1590-1659) & 1/wf Mary[1] HEATH (bp 1593/4-1629); m Ware, Hertfordshire 21 Sept 1613 [REG 146:274; GMB 2:903, 1108; AEJA]

JOHNSON, John[1] (c1590-1659) & 2/wf Margery _____ (-1655); m 1630s Roxbury [REG 146:274; GMB 2:1108; AEJA]

JOHNSON, John[1] (c1590-1659) & 3/wf Grace (NEGUS) FAWER (-1671); m1 Barnabus FAWER; m bet Nov 1655 - Oct 1656 Roxbury [REG 146:274; TG 6:196; AEJA; GMB 2:1108]

JOHNSON, Joseph (1637-1714) & 1/wf Mary SAWTELL (1640-1664/5); m 19 Apr 1664 Charlestown [REG 126:5]

JOHNSON, Joseph (c1675-1756) & Anna BELCHER; m Boston int 26 Jan 1696/7 [REG 156:221]

JOHNSON, Marmaduke & 1/wf _____ _____; bef 1670 Boston [Suffolk Probate 6:180]

JOHNSON, Marmaduke & 2/wf Ruth[2] CANE (1647-); m Cambridge 28 Apr 1670 [GM 2:5; SPR 6:180]

JOHNSON, Matthew & Hannah[2] PALFREY (c1634-); m Woburn 12 Nov 1656 [GMB 3:1371]

JOHNSON, Samuel & Mary[2] COLLINS; m Lynn 22 Jan 1663[/4?] [GM 2:168]

JOHNSON, Samuel (-c1656) & Mary (FOXE) HAZARD (1613-1669/70); m St Dunstan, Stepney, Middlesex 1 Apr 1646 Boston [REG 156:217]

JOHNSON, Samuel (bp 1646/7-by 1716) & Hannah COLE (-1717+); m by 24 Jan 1670/1 Boston [REG 156:220]

JOHNSON, Solomon & Hannah[2] HOLMAN (bp 1627-); m by 1654 [GM 3:389]

JOHNSON, Thomas & Mary[2] HOLT (1638-); m Andover 5 July 1657 [GM 3:400]

JOHNSON, William & Elizabeth[2] BUSHNELL (bp 1633/4-); m by 1654 Guilford [GM 1:511]

JONES, _____ & Joanna[2] CUDWORTH (bp 1643-); m by 1681 Barnstable [GM 2:254]

JONES, Alexander & Hannah[2] WALFORD; m c1649 [GMB 3:1904]

JONES, Benjamin (-by 1717) & Johanna _____; m by 1670 [NYGBR 128:170]

JONES, Edward & Ann _____ (not Griggs); m bef 1636/7 Charlestown/Southampton [GMSP]

JONES, Edward[1] (c1610-1644+) & Anna _____; m by 1636 [GMB 2:1112]

JONES, Isaac & Hannah[2] HEATH; m by 1658 Dorchester [GMB 2:903]

JONES, John & Abigail _____; by 1698/9 Barnstable [TAG 67:30]

JONES, John & Mary _____ Hempstead [NYGBR 128:108]

JONES, John[1] & Sarah _____; m bef 1612/20 Abbot's Ripton, Huntingdonshire/St Stephens Coleman St., London [TAG 71:54]

JONES, Joseph & Patience[2] LITTLE (c1637-); m Weymouth 11 Nov 1657 [GMB 2:1191]

JONES, Josiah (c1643-1714) & Lydia TREADWAY (c1649-1743); m Watertown 2 Oct 1667 [AEBK 1:350]

JONES, Josiah (c1660-) & Joanna _____; m by 1685 Huntington/Brookhaven [NYGBR 128:175]

JONES, Lewis[1] (c1600-1684) & Anna _____ (c1602-1680); m England 1635 Watertown [AEBK 1:345]

JONES, Rice & Anne[2] GRIGGS (c1629-); m2 Robert LATTIMORE; m by 1651 Boston [GM 3:157]

JONES, Richard (-1670) & Elizabeth CARPENTER (1644-1694+); m2 John CHAPPELL div; m3 _____ HILL; m c1662 Haddam [TAG 41:42]

JONES, Robert (c1596-c1691) & 1/wf Margaret GARNFORD; m Caversham, Oxfordshire 30 Apr 1621 Hingham [50 GMC]

JONES, Robert (c1596-c1691) & 2/wf _____ (ALEXANDER?) CURTIS (-1657); Hingham [50 GMC]

JONES, Robert (c1596-c1691) & 3/wf Elizabeth _____ (c1616-1712); m Hingham [50 GMC]

JONES, Samuel & Mary[2] BUSHNELL; m Saybrook 1 Jan 1663[/4] [GM 1:511]

JONES, Thomas & Ann (PRIDDETH) WOOD; m1 Richard WOOD; m3 Paul WHITE [REG 139:141]

JONES, Thomas[1] (-1671) & Mary[2] NORTH (bp 1612-1681/2); m c1638 Gloucester [TAG 68:70]

JONES, Thomas[1] (-1669/70) & 2/wf Katherine (ESTEY) SCUDDER; m1 Henry SCUDDER; m aft 1661 Fairfield/Huntington [NYGBR 128:103]

JONES, Thomas[2] (-by 1723/4) & Abigail ROWLAND; m Fairfield 5 Mar 1670/1 [NYGBR 128:106]

JONES, William & Abigail (MORSE) EVERETT (1645/6-737); m Watertown 18 Oct 1687 [AEBK 4:215]

JORDAN, _____ & Susannah _____; m bef 1693 Marblehead [LB]

JORDAN, Robert & Sarah[2] WINTER; m cJan 1643/4 [GMB 3:2037]

JOSE, Christopher & Jane COMINS; m by 19 June 1679 Portsmouth [REG 153:53]

JOSSELYN, Henry[1] (c1606-1682) & Margaret (_____) CAMMOCK (-1680+); m1 Thomas CAMMOCK; m aft 18 Oct 1643 [GMB 2:1114]

JOY, Ephraim (1674/5-bef 1714) & _____ GOFFE; m bef 1699 Kittery [CG, 51]

JOY, Ephraim[2] (1646/7-bef 1699) & Susanna[3] (SPENCER) GATTENSBY (c1636-1684+); m1 John GATTENSBY; m bef 1673 Kittery [CG, 20]

JOY, Jacob (c1645-by 1690/1) & Elizabeth (SPENCER) WELLMAN; m1 William WELLMAN; m Killingworth 23 May 1672 [REG 154:333]

JOY, John & Mercy BARTLETT; m Plymouth 25 Dec 1668 [see Ivy] [TAG 67:30]

JOY, Thomas[1] & Joan[2] GALLUP (bp 1618-1690); m c1637 Boston [GMB 2:726; TAG 68:13]

JOY, Walter (-by 1667) & Deborah[2] WATHEN (bp 1624/5-1679+); m2 Thomas FRENCH; m by 1652 Salem/Guilford [REG 154:329]

JUDD, Thomas & Sarah[2] STEELE; m c1663 Waterbury [GMB 3:1759]

JUDD, William & Mary[2] STEELE; m Farmington 31 Mar 1657 [GMB 3:1759]

JUDKINS, Job[1] (1609/10-1672+) & Sarah _____ (c1612-1657); m bef 1637 Southam, Warwickshire/Boston [AEBK 1:359]

JUDKINS, Joel[2] (1643-1714+) & Mary BEAN (1655-1743); m 25 Apr or June 1674 Exeter [AEBK 1:361]

JUDKINS, Samuel[2] (1638-1676) & Elizabeth LEAVITT (bp 28 Apr 1644-1697); m2 Richard DRAKE; m Boston 25 Mar 1667 [AEBK]

JUDSON, Jeremiah & Sarah[2] FOOTE (c1632-); m by 1653 Stratford [GM 2:543]

JUDSON, Joshua[2] & Anna[2] TUTTLE (1632/3-); m2 John HURD Jr.; m bef 1655 Stratford [TAG 50:7]

JUDSON, William (-1662) & Elizabeth[1] (TENNEY) (HEATON) WILMOT (bp 1607-) [AEBK 4:379]

KEAYNE, Benjamin & Sarah DUDLEY (bp 1620-); m2 Thomas PACY; by 1639 Boston [GMB 1:585]

KEAYNE, Robert (c1593-1656) & Ann MANSFIELD (bp c1596/7-1667); m2 Samuel COLE; m by 1617 London/Boston [REG 155:24-29]

KEELER, John & Mehitable ROCKWOOD/ROCKWELL (c1656-); m2 Zerubbabel HOYT; m Norwalk 18 June 1679 [TAG 77:109]

KEENE, John (c1621-c1675) & Hannah STEBBINS (1640-by 1685); m bef 1660 Boston [TAG 41:95]

KEENE, Josiah & Abigail[2] LITTLE (c1635-); m c1656 [GMB 2:1191]

KEENEY, John[2] & Sarah DOUGLAS (1643-); m New London Oct 1661 [TAG 74:280]

KELLAM, Augustine[1] & Alice GORBALL; m Wrentham, Suffolk 8 Sep 1619 [TAG 67:54]

KELLEY, John (c1603-1663) & Bethiah WAKEMAN (-1670+); m2 David PHILLIPS; by 1653 Hartford [TAG 68:212; Harris; GMB 3:1901]

KELLOGG, John & perhaps RUTH WARNER [GMB 3:1931]

KELLOGG, Joseph & Abigail[2] TERRY (1646-); m Hadley 9 May 1667 [GMB 3:1806]

KELLY, James & Susanna CLARK; m2 Nathaniel SANFORD; m3 John BUTTOLPH [TAG 58:136]

KELLY, Roger & Mary[2] HOLDRED (1656-); m Exeter 29 Sept 1681 [GM 3:371]

KELSEY, Daniel[2] (1650-) & 1/wf Mary STEVENS; m Killingworth 27 Mar 1672 [GMB 2:1119]

KELSEY, Daniel[2] (1650-) & 2/wf Jane CHALKER; m by 1693 [GMB 2:1119]

KELSEY, John[2] (c1638-) & Hannah (not Phebe) DESBOROUGH; m bef 1670 Hartford [TAG 38:210; GMB 2:1119]

KELSEY, Mark[2] (c1634-) & 1/wf Rebecca HOSKINS; m Windsor 8 Mar 1658/9 [GMB 2:1119]

KELSEY, Mark[2] (c1634-) & 2/wf Abigail (____) ATWOOD; m1 Thomas ATWOOD; m Windsor 26 Dec 1683 [GMB 2:1119]

KELSEY, William[1] & ____ ____ Hartford [TAG 71:95]

KELSEY, William[1] (c1609-1675-6) & ____ ____ (perhaps Hester); m by 1634 [GMB 2:1118]

KEMBALL, Henry & Susanna (STONE) CUTTING (bp 1597-1684); m Great Bromley, Essex 27 Nov 1528 [AEBK 1:258; TAG 55:26 (wrong)]

KEMBLE, Henry & Mary[2] BRIGDEN; m c1660 Boston [GM 1:399]

KEMPTON, Ephraim[1] (bp 26 Oct 1591-b7 1645) & Elizabeth WILSON (c1590s-1620/1+); m Holy Trinity the Less, London 12 Apr 1617 Scituate [AEBK 1:67; TAG 67:132-5]

KEMPTON, Ephraim[2] (1620/1-1655) & Joanna[2] RAWLINGS (c1625-1656); m Scituate 28 Jan 1644/5 [AEBK 1 72; GMB 3:1559]

KEMPTON, Ephraim[3] (bp 1649-by 1714) & Mary REEVES (c1650s-by 1712/3); m Scituate 7 Nov 1673 [AEBK 1:78]

KEMPTON, Manasseh[1] (bp 20 Feb 1589/90-1662/3) & Juliana (CARPENTER) MORTON (bp 1584/5-1664/5); m1 George MORTON; m say 1627 Scituate [AEKB 1:65; GMB 2:1123]

KENDRICK, George & Ruth[2] BOWEN (c1626-1688); m Rehoboth 23 Apr 1647 [TAG 76:277]

KENDRICK, John[1] & Lydia[2] CHENEY (c1637-); m Newbury 12 Nov 1657 [TAG 76:247; GM 2:52]

KENNICUT, Roger & Joanna[2] SHEPARDSON (bp 1641/2-); m Malden Nov 1661 [GMB 3:1665]

KENRICK, John & 1/wf Anna ?SAWTELL (-1656); m bef 1651 Muddy River [REG 126:1]

KENT, Oliver & Dorothy[2] HULL (c1632-); m2 Benjamin MATHEWS; m by c1660 [GM 3:455]

KETTLE, John[2] (1639-) & Sarah[2] GOODENOW (1642[/3?]-1671+); m c1661 [GMB 2:1125; AEBK 3]

KETTLE, Jonathan[2] (c1646-) & Abigail CONVERSE; m Charlestown 30 Mar 1676 [GMB 2:1126]

KETTLE, Joseph[2] (1640/1-) & 1/wf Hannah FRODINGHAM, dau of William; m Charlestown 5 July 1665 [GMB 2:1125]

KETTLE, Joseph[2] (1640/1-) & 2/wf Dorothy (EDMONDS) HETT; m1 Thomas HETT; m Charlestown 15 Mar 1693/4 [GMB 2:1125]

KETTLE, Nathaniel[2] (1644-) & 2/wf Hannah KIDDER; m Sudbury 30 Oct 1672 [GMB 2:1126]

KETTLE, Nathaniel[2] (1644-1723) & 1/wf Hannah EVELETH (bp 1643-1670); m Charlestown 13 Jan 1669[/70] Boston/Gloucester [REG 134:309; GMB 2:1126]

KETTLE, Richard[1] (c1614-1680) & Esther WARD; m by 1637 [GMB 2:1125]

KETTLE, Samuel[2] (1642-) & 2/wf Mary (HETT) FROTHINGHAM; m1 Nathaniel FROTHINGHAM; m Charlestown 3 May 1694 [GMB 2:1126]

KETTLE, Samuel[2] (1642-) & Mercy[2] HAYDEN (c1645-); m Charlestown 11 July 1665 [GM 3:280; GMB 2:1126]

KEYES, Elias[2] (1643-) & Sarah BLANFORD; m Sudbury 11 Sept 1665 [GMB 2:1129]

KEYES, Peter[2] (c1635-) & Elizabeth _____; m by 1667 Sudbury [GMB 2:1129]

KEYES, Robert[1] (c1606-1647) & Sarah _____; m2 John GAGE; m by 1633 Newbury/Watertown [GMB 2:1128]

KEYES, Solomon[2] (c1631-) & Frances GRANT; m Newbury 2 Oct 1653 [GMB 2:1129]

KEYSER, George & Rebecca (AYER) ASLEBEE (-bef 1702); m1 John ASLEBEE; m after 1671 [TAG 40:231]

KIBBY, Henry (-1661) & 2/wf Grizzell[2] (FLETCHER)(JEWELL) GREGGS (c1619-1669); m Dorchester 8 Oct 1657 [AEBK 4:277]

KILBORN, John & Susannah[2] HILLS (c1651-1701); m Wethersfield 4 Mar 1673[/4] [GMB 2:944]

KILBORN, Thomas & Hannah[2] HILLS (c1658-); m c1677 [GMB 2:945]

KILLAM, John & Anna[2] PICKWORTH (c1635-); m c1660 Wenham [GMB 3:1463]

KILLAN, Lot & Hannah[2] GOODALE (bp 1645-); m Wenham 21 May 1666 [GM 3:106]

KIMBALL, Charles & _____ _____ Plymouth [TAG 71:146]

KIMBALL, John & Mary[2] BRADSTREET (c1633-); m c1655-65 [GM 1:387]

KIMMING, John (-by 1708) & _____ _____; Exeter [REG 153:56]

KIND, Arthur (c1611-1686/7) & Jane _____ (c1624-1710); m bef 1646 Boston [REG 126:17]

KINDE, John[2] (c1646-1690) & Rachel _____ (-1690); m bef 1674 Boston [REG 126:19]

KING, Daniel & Tabitha[2] WALKER (1647-); m Lynn 11 Mar 1663 [GMB 3:1909]

KING, Hezekiah[3] & Mary[3] SHAW (1659/60-   ); m bef 1679 Weymouth [TAG 68:23]

KING, James & Elizabeth[2] FULLER; m Ipswich 23 Mar 1674[/5?] [GM 2:600]

KING, John & Abigail[2] (HEWES) HATCH (c1633-   ), dau of John; m1 William HATCH; m Weymouth 14 Oct 1658 [GMB 2:920]

KING, Ralph & Elizabeth[2] WALKER; m2 John LEWIS; m Lynn 2 Mar 1664 [GMB 3:1909]

KING, Thomas & Mary[2] SPRAGUE (bp 1652-   ); m by 1670 Weymouth [GMB 3:1738]

KING, Thomas (1645-1711) & Elizabeth CLAPP (c1649-1698/9); m Scituate 20 Apr 1669 [AEBK 4:139]

KING, William & Deborah PRINCE, m2 Robert SMITH [TAG 59:232]

KING, William & Sarah[2] GRIGGS (1637-   ); m2 Roger BURGESS; m by 1655 Boston [GM 3:158]

KINGMAN, John ~ _____ _____ [Plymouth Court Mar 1690/1]

KINGSBURY, Henry[1] (1596-1636+) & Margaret ALABASTER; m Assignton, Suffolk 18 May 1621 [GMB 2:1132]

KINGSBURY, Samuel[2] (c1649/50-1698) & Huldah[2] CORLISS (1661-   ); m2 Abraham[2] WHITTAKER; m 5 Nov 1679 Haverhill [ASBO, p.212]

KINGSLEY, Eldad (1638-1679) & Mehitable[2] MOWRY (c1640s-1712+); m2 Timothy Brooks; m Providence 9 May 1662 [AEJA; GMB 2:1314]

KINGSTON, Thomas & Mary[2] MUNT (c1647-   ); m by 1666 Boston [GMB 2:1318]

KINSMAN, Robert & Mary[2] BOREMAN; m bef 1657 Ipswich [GM 1:354]

KIRTLAND, Philip (bp 1611-   ) & Rose _____; Olney, Buckinghamshire/Lynn [TAG 65:66-7]

KNAPP, Aaron & Rachel[2] BURT (c1666-1724+); m Taunton 8 Dec 1686 [TAG 75:115]

KNAPP, Caleb[2] (1636/7-   ) & Hannah SMITH; m by 1661 Watertown/Stamford [GMB 2:1136]

KNAPP, James[2] (bp 1626-1698+) & Elizabeth WARREN (bp 1629-1667+); m c1654 Watertown [AEBK 1:473]

KNAPP, Moses[2] & Abigail WESTCOTT; m by 1669 [GMB 2:1137]

KNAPP, Nicholas[1] (c1606-1670) & 1/wf Elinor _____ (-1658); m by 1631 Stamford [GMB 2:1136]

KNAPP, Nicholas[1] (c1606-1670) & 2/wf Unica (_____) (BUXTON) BROWN (-by 1670); m1 Clement BUXTON; m2 Peter BROWN; m Stamford 9 Mar 165[8/]9 [GMB 2:1136]

KNAPP, Timothy & Bethiah[2] BROWN? [GM 1:447]

KNAPP, Timothy[2] (1632-   ) & Bethia _____ (perhaps BRUNDISH); m by 1658 Watertown/Stamford [GMB 2:1136]

KNAPP, William[1] (bp 1580/1-1658) & 1/wf Judith TUE (bp 1589-bef 1651); m Wormingford, Essex 11 Jan 1606/7 Watertown [REG 147:324 & 26 GMC {wrong}]

KNEELAND, John & Mary[2] HAWKINS (c1636-   ); m by 1659 Boston [GM 3:264]

KNIGHT, Alexander[1] & Anne[1] TUTTY (bp 1616-); m2 Robert[1] WHITMAN; m by Oct 1640 Ipswich [TAG 76:10]

KNIGHT, John & Abigail[2] STOWERS (1636-); m c1663 Charlestown [GMB 3:1782]

KNIGHT, John & Bathsheba[2] INGERSOLL (c1629-); m Newbury [date fragment] [GMB 2:1062]

KNIGHT, Philip & Margaret[2] WILKINS (bp 1648[/9]-); m by 1669 Topsfield [GMB 3:1993]

KNIGHT, Richard & Johanna[2] DAVIS (bp 163[1/]2-), dau of James; m by 1652 Boston [GM 2:300; Boston VR 1:36]

KNIGHT, Richard[1] (-by 1680) & 2/wf Sarah _____ [TAG 76:249]

KNIGHT, Roger[1] (c1596-1672/3) & Ann _____ (-1662+); m by 1630 [GMB 2:1139]

KNIGHT, Walter[1] (1605-1643+) & _____ _____ (likely not Ruth GRAY); m by 1642 Piscataqua [GMB 2:1140]

KNOPP, James[2] (bp 1626-) & Elizabeth[2] WARREN (bp 1629-), dau of John; m by 1655 Watertown [GMB 2:1145, 3:1934] see KNAPP

KNOPP, John[2] (bp 1622/3-) & Sarah YOUNG; m Watertown 21 May 1660 [GMB 2:1145]

KNOPP, William[1] (bp 1580/1-1658) & 1/wf Judith TUE (-by 1651); m Wormingford, Essex 11 Jan 1606[/7] Watertown [GMB 2:1144] see KNAPP

KNOPP, William[1] (bp 1580/1-1658) & 2/wf Priscilla (____) AKERS; m1 _____ AKERS; m soon after 20 June 1651 Watertown [GMB 2:1144]

KNOPP, William[2] (bp 1610/1-) & 1/wf Mary _____; m by 1642 Watertown [GMB 2:1144]

KNOPP, William[2] (bp 1610/1-) & 2/wf Margaret _____; m by 1652 Watertown [GMB 2:1144]

KNOWER, George[1] (c1611-1674/5) & Elizabeth _____ (-1674+); m by 1645 Malden [GMB 2:1147]

KNOWER, Jonathan[2] (c1645-) & Sarah WINSLEAD, dau of John; m by 1685 Malden [GMB 2:1147]

KNOWER, Thomas[1] (c1602-1641) & Noll _____; m c1628 Charlestown [GMB 2:1149]

LADD, Samuel[2] (1649-1697/8) & Martha[2] CORLISS (1652/3-1697+); m 1 Dec 1674 Haverhill [ASBO, p.211]

LAKE, William & Anne[2] STRATTON, dau of John; m2 William STEVENS; m by 1660 [GMB 3:1783]

LAKIN, Abraham (1667-by 1747) & Abigail[3] SNOW; m c1700 Groton [TAG 70:147; AEBK 3]

LAKIN, John (c1660-bef 1696/7) & Sarah[2] WHEELER (1666/7-); m2 1699 William TAYLOR [TAG 70:148]

LAKIN, John[1] (bp 1628-1697/8) & Mary[3] BACON (c1635-1701+); m c1656 Ruddington, Nottinghamshire/Groton/Woburn [TAG 70:147-8]

LAKIN, Joseph[2] & Abigail[-] LAKIN (c1671-bef 1753); first cousins; m c1695 [TAG 70:147]

LAKIN, William[1] (c1624-1700/1) & Lydia[2] BROWNE (1631/2-1693/4); by 1649 Reading/Groton/Watertown [AEBK 1:185; TAG 70:147]

LAKIN, William[2] (1655-1735) & Elizabeth ROBERTSON; m Chelmsford 4 Jan 1685/6 [TAG 70:147]

LAMB, Abiel[2] (1646-) & Elizabeth (CLARK) BUCKMINSTER; m by 28 Feb 1674[/5] [GMB 2:1155]

LAMB, Caleb[2] (1641-) & Mary WISE; m Roxbury 30 June 1669 [GMB 2:1155]

LAMB, Edward[1] (c1608-1648-50) & Margaret _____; m2 Samuel ALLEN; m by 1633 Watertown/Boston [GMB 2:1151]

LAMB, John[2] (bp 1628-) & 1/wf Joanna _____; m by 1653 Springfield [GMB 2:1154]

LAMB, John[2] (bp 1628-) & 2/wf Lydia (WRIGHT) (BLISS) NORTON, dau of Samuel; m1 Lawrence BLISS; m2 John NORTON; m Springfield 26 Jan 1687/8 [GMB 2:1154]

LAMB, John[2] (c1642-) & 1/wf Mary (FRENCH) POOLE; m by 1677 [GMB 2:1152]

LAMB, John[2] (c1642-) & 2/wf Lydia _____; m by 1690 Braintree [GMB 2:1152]

LAMB, Joshua[2] (1642-) & Mary ALCOCK, dau of John; m by 1675 Roxbury [GMB 2:1155]

LAMB, Thomas[1] (c1599-1646) & 1/wf Elizabeth _____ (-1639); m by 1624 Roxbury [GMB 2:1154]

LAMB, Thomas[1] (c1599-1646) & 2/wf Dorothy HARBITTLE; m2 Thomas HAWLEY; m Roxbury 16 July 1640 [GMB 2:1154]

LAMB, William & Mary[2] HEWES (1641-); m by 14 Apr 1680 Roxbury [GMB 2:922]

LANCASTER, John (c1670-1717) & Sarah (_____) BANKS (c1660-5-1740/1); m c1697 Eng [TAG 50:_1]

LANCASTER, Joseph & Mary[2] CARTER (1641-); m by 1665 Salisbury [GM 2:28]

LANDALL, _____ & Lucy[3] CHADBOURNE (c1659-1702); m2 Michael HICKS, m3 Peter LEWIS; m c1680s Kittery [CG, 28]

LANDERS, Joseph[2] (c1666-c1750) & Rebecca (_____) ALLEN; m1 John[4] ALLEN [REG 124:45]

LANDERS, Richard[2] (c1660-c1750) & Sarah[3] FREEMAN (1662-1732/3); m 6 Jan 1695/6 Sandwich [REG 124:49]

LANDERS, Thomas[2] (c1658-1730/1) & Deborah FREEMAN (1665-1732+); m c1688 Sandwich [REG 124:46]

LANE, Ebenezer (bp 1650-1726) & Hannah HERSEY; m Hingham Dec 1688 [REG 156:148]

LANE, George[2] (c1613-1689) & Sarah HARRIS (bp 1624/5-1695); m by 1638 Hingham [REG 156:147]

LANE, Isaac & Hannah[2] BROWN (1651-); m Middletown 5 Nov 1669 [GM 1:430]

LANE, John (c1652-1738) & Dorcas WALLIS (c1658-1751); m by 1682 Falmouth [REG 152:290]

LANE, Josiah (bp 1641-1714) & 1/wf Mary _____ (-1671) [REG 156:148]

LANE, Josiah (bp 1641-1714) & 2/wf Deborah GILL; m Hingham 9 May 1672 [REG 156:148]

LANGDON, Tobias & Elizabeth² SHERBORN (1638-); m2 Tobias LEAR; m3 Richard MARTYN; m 10 June 1656 [GMB 3:1667]

LANGFORD, Thomas (bp 1634-1670 & Mary COOK (c1650-1670/1); m bef 1670 Portsmouth, RI [Fiske 1:32]

LANGSTAFF, Henry¹ (c1610-1705) & _____ _____; m by 1640 Dover [GMB 2:1158]

LANGSTAFF, John² (c1640-) & Martha _____; m by 1675 Piscataway, NJ [GMB 2:1158]

LARGE, John & Phoebe LEE (bp 1642-); m Saybrook 1 Nov 1659 [AEJA]

LARKIN, Edward¹ (c1611-by 1651/2) & Joanna _____ (c1616-1685[/6]); m2 John PENTICOST; m by Jan 1638/9 Charlestown [AEBK 3]

LARKIN, John² (1640/1-1655[/8]) & Joanna HALE (c1646-1693), dau of Robert; m Charlestown 9 Nov 1664 [AEBK 3]

LARKIN, Thomas² (1644-1677) & 1/wf Hannah REMINGTON (-1673); m Charlestown 13 Sept 1666 [AEBK 3]

LARKIN, Thomas² (1644-1677) & 2/wf Elizabeth DOWSE (1647[/8]-1732+); m Charlestown 18 June 1674 [AEBK 3]

LATHAM, Robert & Susanna² WINSLOW; m by 1650 Plymouth [GMB 3:2029]

LATHROP, Thomas & 2/wf Sarah² (LEARNED) EWER (c1607-); m Boston 11 Dec 1639 [AEBK 4:431]

LATTIMORE, Robert & Anne² (GRIGGS) JONES (c1629-); m1 Rice JONES; m Charlestown 1 Sept 1662 [GM 3:157]

LATTING, Richard¹ (1608/9-1673) & 1/wf Joan CHADD Concord/Fairfield/Oyster Bay [TAG 74:123]

LAWES, William & Mary² CHENEY (bp 1625-); m Rowley 3 Sept 1645 [TAG 76:246; GM 2:62]

LAWRENCE, Isaac & Abigail² BELLOWS (1661-); m Cambridge 19 Apr 1682 [GM 1:251]

LAWRENCE, John & Susanna² BACHELOR; m Charlestown 2 Nov 1664 [GM 1:125]

LAWRENCE, Nicholas (-1684/5) & Mary HARRIS (bp 1626/7-1685+); m by 1652 Dorchester [REG 156:149]

LAWRENCE, Nicholas (1662-1711/2) & 1/wf Mary HARICE; m Dorchester 3 Nov 1681 [REG 156:145-50]

LAWRENCE, Nicholas (1662-1711/2) & 2/wf Abigail (LAWRENCE) WYER; m Charlestown 25 Dec 1689 [REG 156:150]

LAWRENCE, Thomas & Joan² ANTROBUS (bp 1592-); m2 John TUTTLE; m St Albans, Hertfordshire 23 Oct 1609 [GM 1:68]

LAWRENCE, William & Anna[2] SPRAGUE; m c1644 [GMB 3:1727]

LAWRENCE, William (br 28 July 1522-bef 1680) & 1/wf _____ _____; St Albans Abbey, Hertfordshire/N.Y. [TG 10:22]

LAWRENCE, William (br 28 July 1522-bef 1680) & 2/wf Elizabeth SMITH; St Albans Abbey, Hertfordshire/Smithtown, NY [TG 10:22]

LAWTON, George & Elizabeth[2] HAZARD (c1630-); m c1650 [GM 3:297]

LEACH, John & Sarah CONANT [GMB 1:454]

LEACH, Lawrence[1] (c1583-1662) & Elizabeth _____ (-1662+); m by 1636 Salem [GMB 2:1162]

LEACH, Peter & Hannah RAINSFORD (1671-1721+); m c1693 Boston [REG 139:304]

LEACH, Richard[2] (c1619-) & Sarah FULLER, dau of Anne; m by 1645 [GMB 2:1163]

LEACH, Robert[2] (c1615-) & ?Alice _____ (-1674+); m bef 1674 [GMB 2:1162]

LEADBETTER, Henry & Relief[2] (HOLLAND) (DOWSE) FOSTER, m1 John DOWSE, m2 1680/1 Timothy FOSTER; m Dorchester 9 Mar 1691/2 [TAG 68:181]

LEARNED, Benoni (1657-1738) & 1/wf Mary FANNING (-1688); m Sherborn 10 June 1680 [AEBK 4:441]

LEARNED, Benoni (1657-1738) & 2/wf Sarah WRIGHT (1664/5-1736/7); m c1689 Sherborn [AEBK 4:441]

LEARNED, Isaac (1655-1737) & Sarah BIGELOW (bp 1659-); m Sherborn 23 July 1679 [AEBK 4:440]

LEARNED, Isaac[2] (bp 1623/4-1657) & Mary STEARNS (bp 1626/7-1663/4), dau of Isaac; m Woburn 9 July 1646 [AEBK 4:433; GMB 2:1165; 3:1749]

LEARNED, William (c1581-1645/6) & 1/wf Godethe GILLMAN (c1586-c1640s); m St Olave, Southwark, Surrey 22 Apr 1606 Malden [AEBK 4:430; SB; GMB 2:1165]

LEARNED, William[1] (c1581-1645[/6]) & 2/wf Jane _____ (-1660[/1]); m c1640s Malden/Woburn [AEBK 4:430; GMB 2:1165]

LeBLOND, James & Ann GRAY; bef 1690 Boston [TAG 67:31]

LEE, _____ & Rebecca[2] SMITH (1550-), dau of Henry; m by 1681 [GMB 3:1692]

LEE, John & Mary[2] HART (c1638-); m2 1691[/2] Jedediah STRONG; m by 1657 [GMB 2:872]

LEE, John (1670-1715/6) & Elizabeth SMITH (c1673-1761?); m2 John BAILEY; m Lyme 8 Feb 1692/3 [AEJA]

LEE, Peter & Ann MOSHER; m bef 1690 E. Greenwich, RI [TAG 59:239]

LEE, Thomas (1672-1749/50) & Elizabeth GRAHAM (c1670s-1750+); m Lyme 24 Jan 1695 [AEJA]

LEE, Thomas (bp 1644-1704/5) & 1/wf Sarah KIRTLAND (c1648-1676); m c1668 Lyme [AEJA]

LEE, Thomas (bp 1644-1704/5) & 2/wf Mary DeWOLFE (c1656-1724); m Lyme 13 July 1676 [AEJA]

LEE, Thomas (c1610s-1645) & Phebe BROWNE (bp 1620-1664); m2 Greenfield
    LARRIBEE, m3 James CORNISH; m by 1640 Rusper, Sussex/New London
    [AEJA]

LEGGE, John (c1645-) & Elizabeth PEACH, dau of John; m c1668 [GMB 2:1167]

LEGGE, John[1] (c1608-1672-4) & Elizabeth _____ (1609-1672+); m by 5 June 1638
    Lynn/Marblehead [GMB 2:1167]

LEGGE, Samuel[2] (c1642-) & Deliverance _____; m by 1669 Boston [GMB 2:1167]

LEGROVE, Nicholas & Hannah[3] SALLOWS (1654-1703/4+); m bef 1672 Salem [TAG
    72:6]

LEIGHTON, Thomas[2] & 1/wf Elizabeth[2] NUTTER (-1670/1+) [TAG 72:276]

LEIGHTON, Thomas[2] & 2/wf Elizabeth _____ [TAG 72:276]

LEIGHTON, William & Catherine FROST (c1634-); m2 Joseph HAMMOND; by 1655
    Kittery [GMB 1:707]

LELAND, Henry[1] (c1625-1680) & Margaret _____ (c1630-1705); m c1650 Sherborn
    [AEBK 4:453]

LELAND, Hopestill[2] (1655-1729) & 1/wf Abigail HILL (c1660-1689); m Medfield 5 Nov
    1678 [AEBK 4:459]

LELAND, Hopestill[2] (1655-1729) & 2/wf Patience RICE (1671/2-1720); m c1694
    Sherborn/Medfield [AEBK 4:461]

LEONARD, Isaac & Mary (_____) RANDALL not Bailey, m1 Samuel RANDALL [TAG
    33:140]

LEONARD, James & perhaps Hannah[2] HAYDEN (1642-by 1678); Taunton [AEBK 3]

LEONARD, Thomas & Mary[2] WATSON; m Plymouth 21 Aug 1662 [GMB 3:1946]

LEONARD[SON], Solomon & Sarah CHANDLER; bef 1643 Duxbury/ Bridgewater
    [TAG 67:31; GMB 1:331]

LETHERLAND, William[1] (c1608-1684+) & Margaret _____; m bet 1634-47 Boston
    [GMB 2:1171]

LETHERLAND, Zebulon[2] (c1650-) & Rachel _____; m bef 4 July 1670 Boston [GMB
    2:1171]

LETTIN, Richard[1] (bp 1608/9-1673) & 1/wf Joan CHADD; m 3 Nov 1634 Salford,
    Bedfordshire/Oyster Bay [NYGBR 117:222]

LETTIN, Richard[1] (bp 1608/9-1673) & 2/wf Joan (_____) IRELAND; m license 24 Aug
    1670 Oyster Bay [NYGBR 117:222]

LEVENS, John[1] (c1582-1647) & 1/wf Elizabeth _____ (-1638); m by 1632 Roxbury
    [GMB 2:1174]

LEVENS, John[1] (c1582-1647) & 2/wf Rachel WRITE; m Roxbury 5 July 1639 [GMB
    2:1174]

LEVENS, John[2] (1640-) & 1/wf Hannah WOODS (called Sarah at death) (-1666); m
    Roxbury 7 June 1665 [GMB 2:1175]

LEVENS, John[2] (1640-) & 2/wf Elizabeth PRESTON; m New Haven 23 Nov 1674
    [GMB 2:1175]

LEVERETT, John[2] (bp 1616-) & 1/wf Hannah[2] HUDSON (c1621-); m by 1640 [GMB 2:1177; GM 3:447]

LEVERETT, John[2] (bp 1616-) & 2/wf Sarah SEDGWICK; m by 1645 [GMB 2:1177]

LEVERETT, Thomas[1] (c1585-1650) & Anne FITCH (-1656); m Boston, Lincolnshire 29 Oct 1610 [GMB 2:1177]

LEVERICH, Caleb[2] (c1638-) & Martha (____) SWAINE; m by 1669 Newtown [GMB 2:1179]

LEVERICH, Eleazer[2] (c1640-) & Rebecca WRIGHT, dau of Nicholas; m by 1662 Oyster Bay; div. 1670 [GMB 2:1179]

LEVERICH, William[1] (c1603-1677) & _____ _____; m say 1638 [GMB 2:1179]

LEWIS, George[1] (bp 1600-1663/4) & Mary ____; m bef 1625 Benchley, Kent/Barnstable [TAG 68:25]

LEWIS, George[1] (bp 1600-bef 1663/4) & Mary[1] DOGGET (bp 1600-1676+); Barnstable [TAG 72:328]

LEWIS, James (bp 1632-1713) & Sarah LANE (bp 1637/8-); m Hingham 31 Oct 1665 [REG 156:148]

LEWIS, John (-1657) & 2/wf Mary BROWNE (bp 1623/4-by 1693/4); m Malden 10 April 1650 [AEBK 1:185]

LEWIS, Joseph (-1675) & Mary JONES (-by 1720); m Swansea 13 June 1671 [AEBK 4:426]

LEWIS, Peter[2] (c1669-bef 1739) & Lucy[3] (CHADBOURNE)(LANDALL) HICKS (c1659-1702); m after 1688 Kittery [CG, 28]

LEWIS, Thomas & Mary[2] DAVIS (c1631-); m Barnstable 15 June 1653 [GM 2:296]

LEWIS, Thomas[1] (c1590-1637) & Elizabeth MARSHALL, dau of Roger (-by 1640); m St. Chad, Shrewsbury, Shropshire 29 Aug 1618 [GMB 2:1182]

LEWIS, William[1] (c1595-1683) & Felix _____ (-1671); m by 1620 Hadley [GMB 2:1186]

LEWIS, William[2] (c1620-) & Mary HOPKINS, dau of William; m by 1645 Hartford [GMB 2:1186]

LEYOUGE, James & Amy[2] BULL; m2 Edward RICHMOND; m by 1668 Little Compton [GM 1:468; TAG 77:283]

LILLE, John & Hannah[2] BASSETT; m c1691 Woburn [GM 1:193]

LINCOLN, Samuel & Martha[2] LYFORD (c1628-); m by 1650 [GMB 2:1215]

LINCOLN, Thomas & Mary[2] CHUBBOCK (bp 1642-); m Hingham 18 Feb 1662/3 [GM 2:75]

LINCOLN, Thomas[1] (bp 1601-1675) & 1/wf Susanna _____ (-1641[/2]); m by 1641 Hingham [GMB 2:1188]

LINCOLN, Thomas[1] (bp 1601-1675) & 2/wf Mary _____ (-1683); m aft Mar 1641/2 [GMB 2:1188]

LINDE, Simon & Hannah[2] NEWGATE (1635-); m Boston 22 Feb 1652/3 [GMB 2:1332]

LINDLEY, John & 1/wf Ellen DAYTON (bp 1626-1654); m c1644-5 New Haven [REG 128:148]

LINDSAY, Eleazer & Sarah² ALLEY (1651-); m Lynn Aug 1668 [GM 1:41]

LINDSAY, John & Mary² ALLEY (1641[/2]-); m Lynn 6 June 1667 [GM 1:41]

LINNELL, David & Hannah² SHELLEY (bp 1637-); m Barnstable 9 Mar 1652/3 [GM 3:27]

LINNELL, Robert & 1/wf _____ _____; Barnstable [TAG 51:35]

LINNELL, Robert & 2/wf Peninah HOWES; m bet 1623-1638 Barnstable [TAG 51:35]

LISCOMB, Ebenezer & Mehitable CURTICE; m Boston 18 Oct 1694 [REG 156:219]

LISCOMB, John (c1633-1680) & Hannah HAZARD (bp 1642-1701/2+); m bef 2 Jan 1666/7 Boston [REG 156:218]

LITCHFIELD, Josiah & Sarah² LITCHFIELD; m Scituate 22 Feb 1671[/2] [GM 1:144]

LITTEN, Edward (-1691/2) & Katherine³ CHADBOURNE (c1665-1727+); m2 James WEYMOUTH; m bef 1691/2 [CG, 30]

LITTLE, Ephraim² (1650-) & Mary STURTEVANT, dau of Samuel; m Scituate 22 Nov 1672 [GMB 2:1191]

LITTLE, Isaac² (c1646-1699) & Bethia THOMAS, dau of Nathaniel; m by 1674 Marshfield [GMB 2:1191]

LITTLE, Samuel² (c1656-) & Sarah GRAY, dau of Edward; m Marshfield 18 May 1682 [GMB 2:1191]

LITTLE, Thomas¹ (c1608-1671[/2]) & Ann² WARREN (c1612-1675/6+), dau of Richard; m Plymouth 19 Apr 1633 [GMB 2:1190, 3:1936]

LITTLEFIELD, Anthony² & Mary PAGE [TAG 75:19]

LITTLEFIELD, Francis & Meribah² WARDWELL (1637-); m c1658 [GMB 3:1923]

LIVERMORE, John (1606-1684) & _____ _____; REG 150:435]

LOBDELL, Nicholas (-1648+ & Jane _____ (-1641); m bef 1631 probably near Northam, Devon/Hingham, MA [TAG 54:35-37]

LOCKERMANS, Baultus Jacobus (-1661+) & _____ _____ (-1661+) Springfield/Hartford [TAG 67:40; Harris]

LOCKWOOD, Edmund¹ (c1600-1632-5) & 1/wf _____ _____; m c1625 [GMB 2:1193]

LOCKWOOD, Edmund¹ (c1600-1632-5) & 2/wf Elizabeth² MASTERS (c1612-), dau of John; m2 Cary LATHAM; m by 1632 Cambridge [GMB 2:1193, 1236]

LOCKWOOD, Edmund² (c1625-) & Hannah SCOTT, dau of Thomas; m Stamford 7 Jan 1655[/6] [GMB 2:1193]

LOCKWOOD, Jonathan & Mary² FERRIS; m2 Thomas MERRITT [GM 2:520]

LOCKWOOD, Robert¹ & Susanna² NORMAN (bp 1617-); m by 1635 Watertown [TAG 77:103; GMB 2:1335]

LOMBARD, Benjamin² (1642-) & 1/wf Jane WARREN; m Barnstable 19 Sept 1672 [GMB 2:1197]

LOMBARD, Benjamin[2] (1542-) & 2/wf Sarah WALKER; m Barnstable 19 Nov 1685
[GMB 2:1197]

LOMBARD, Benjamin[2] (1542-) & 3/wf Hannah (_____) WHETSTONE; m Barnstable
24 May 1694 [GMB 2:1197]

LOMBARD, Bernard[2] (c1608-) & _____ _____; m c1633 [GMB 2:1197]

LOMBARD, Caleb[2] (c1635-) & _____ _____ [GMB 2:1197]

LOMBARD, Jedediah[2] (1640-) & Hannah WING; m Barnstable 20 May 1668 [GMB
2:1197]

LOMBARD, Joshua[2] (bp 1620-) & Abigail LINNETT; m Barnstable 27 May 1651
[GMB 2:1197]

LOMBARD, Thomas[1] (bp 1581/2-1663-4/5) & 1/wf _____ _____; m by 1602
Thorncombe, Dorsetshire [GMB 2:1196]

LOMBARD, Thomas[1] (bp 1581/2-1663-4/5) & 2/wf _____ _____; m by 1617
Thorncombe, Dorsetshire [GMB 2:1196]

LOMBARD, Thomas[1] (bp 1581/2-1663-4/5) & 3/wf _____ _____; m c1635 Plymouth
[GMB 2:1196]

LOMBARD, Thomas[1] (bp 1581/2-1563-4/5) & 4/wf Joyce (_____) WALLEN (-1683+);
m1 Ralph WALLEN; m aft 1644/5 Plymouth [GMB 2:1196]

LONDON, Ambrose (-1694+) & Mary GOOR (-1694+); m New Amsterdam, NY 4
June 1644 Gravesend, L.L/Northampton Co., VA/Annemessex, Somerset Co.,
MD [TAG 58:160-163; 54:75-78]

LONG, Abiel (1648/9-1743) & Hannah[2] HILLS (c1655-169+); m Newbury 27 Oct 1682
[AEBK 4:418]

LONG, Thomas & Sarah ELMER (c1664-); by 1685 Hartford [GMB 1:637]

LONGHORNE, Thomas & Sarah GREEN (c1626-); by 26 Aug 1647 Cambridge [GMB
2:810]

LONGLEY, William Jr. (-1694) & Deliverance CRISPE (c1650-1694); m bef Apr 1674
Watertown/Groton [TAG 62:27; GMB 1:495]

LOOMIS, John & Mary[2] TRASK (bp 1636/7-); m by 1659 [GMB 3:1836]

LOOMIS, Joseph & Sarah[2] HILL (c1620-); m Windsor 17 Sept 1646 [GMB 2:940]

LOOMIS, Nathaniel & Elizabeth[2] MOORE (c1635-); m Windsor 24 or 27 Nov 165[3]
[GMB 2:1277]

LORD, Richard[1] (bp 1611/2-1662) & Sarah _____ (-1676); m c1636 Hartford [GMB
2:1200]

LORD, Richard[2] (c1636-) & Mary SMITH (1642/3-), dau of Henry; m2 Thomas
HOOKER; m Springfield 25 Apr 1665 [GMB 2:1200, 3:1692]

LORESEN, Cornelius & Abiel PAIGE; m 25 Oct 1697 Boston [TAG 132:38]

LORING, John & Mary[2] BAKER (bp 1639-); m Hingham 16 Dec 1657 [GM 1:138]

LORING, Thomas & Hannah[2] JACOB (bp 1639/40-); m2 Stephen FRENCH; m 16 Dec
1657 [GMB 2:1070]

LOTHROP, John[1] & Hannah HOUSE [TAG 70:250; REG 142:218]

LOTHROP, Samuel & Abigail DOANE (-1735); by 1690s Norwich [GMB 1:562]

LOTHROP, Samuel[2] (c1623-1699/1700) & Elizabeth[1] SCUDDER (bp 1625-); m Barnstable 28 Nov 1644 [TAG 72:297]

LOTHROP, Thomas[1] (c1613-1675) & Bethia[2] RAY, (c1630-by 1686) dau of Daniel; m2 Joseph GRAFTON; m3 William GOODHUE; m aft 1637 [GMB 2:1204, 3:1562]

LOUNSBURY, Richard[2] (c1672-1715) & Abigail THOMAS (1674-bef 1733), dau. of John; m c1690s New Haven/NYC [NYGBR 99:65]

LOVELAND, Thomas & Charity[2] HART (c1646-); m by 1677 [GMB 2:868]

LOVELL, John & Elizabeth[2] SILVESTER (1643/4-); m Scituate 24 Jan 1658[/9] [GMB 3:1680]

LOVELL, John & Jane[2] HATCH (bp 1631-); m by 1651 Wye, Kent/Scituate [GM 3:243]

LOVELL, Thomas[1] & _____ HASSELL (c1628-); m by 1648 [GM 3:234]

LOVELL, William[1] (c1585-1638+) & Wybro _____; m by 1610 or 1637 Dorchester/Marblehead [GMB 2:1207]

LOVETT, Daniel & Joanna[2] BLOTT (bp 1620-); m c1644 [GM 1:336]

LOVETT, Thomas & Bethiah STANDLY; m bef 26 Dec 1693 Beverly [REG 144:54]

LOW, John (bp 1633-1695) & Sarah[2] THORNDIKE; m Ipswich 10 Dec 1661 [GMB 3:1812]

LOW, Thomas & Martha[2] BOREMAN (c1641-1720/1); m Ipswich 4 July 1660 [GM 1:354]

LOW, Thomas & 3/wf Susanna (STONE) (CUTTING) KIMBALL (bp 1597-1684); m1 Richard CUTTING; m2 Henry KIMBALL; m aft 1648 Ipswich [TAG 55:26; AEBK 1:258]

LOWDEN, Richard & Mary COLE (c1621-); by 10 May 1641 Charlestown [GMB 1:429]

LOWE, Thomas & 1/wf Margaret TODD; m Polstead, Suffolk 22 June 1630 [AEBK 1:258]

LUDDINGTON, William (c1655-) & 1/wf Martha[3] ROSE; m c1678 [TAG 74:216]

LUDDINGTON, William (c1655-) & 2/wf Mercy[2] WHITEHEAD; m c1690 Branford [TAG 74:216]

LUDDINGTON, William[1] (c1607-by 1661) & Ellen NICHOL (bp 1614-); m2 John ROSE; m Wrawby, Lincolnshire 7 Apr 1635 New Haven [TAG 74:82, 215]

LUDLAM, Charles, did not m. Henry[2] Townsend's daughter [NYGBR 131:115]

LUDLAM, Joseph[2] (1646-1691+) & Elizabeth (TOWNSEND) WRIGHT; m1 Gideon WRIGHT; m aft 1685 Oyster Bay [NYGBR 131:109]

LUDLOW, George[1] (bp 1596-1655) & Elizabeth _____; m by 1629 Dorchester [GMB 2:1209]

LUDLOW, Roger[1] (bp 1590-c1666) & Mary COGAN (-1664), dau of Philobert; m aft 1623 Dinton, Wiltshire/Dublin/Dorchester/Windsor [GMB 2:1212; NGSQ 51:233]

LUGG, John[1] (bp 1595-1646) & Jane DEIGHTON (bp 1609-1671+); m2 Jonathan NEGUS; m St Nicholas, Gloucester, Gloucestershire 3 Jan 1627/8 Boston [AEBK 4:492; TG 6:195]

LUM, John & _____[2] STRICKLAND; m c1645 [GMB 3:1786]

LUMBART, Thomas (bp 1581-1663-4) & 2/wf Joyce _____ (-1683+); m bef 1630 Dorchester/Barnstable [TAG 52:136]

LUNT, Daniel & Hannah[2] COKER; m Newbury 16 May 1664 [GM 2:143]

LUNT, Henry[1] (c1610-1662) & Ann _____ (c1620-1688+); m2 Joseph HILLS; m c1638 Newbury [Abel Lunt, p.5; AEBK 4:400]

LUNT, Henry[2] (1652-1709) & Jane BROWNE (c1657-1737+); m2 Joseph MAYO; m c1676 Newbury [Abel Lunt, p.13]

LUSHER, Eleazer & Ann BANCROFT; m St Pulham Mary the Virgin, Norfolk 8 July 1628 [TAG 67:54]

LYFORD, John[1] (c1590-1628) & Sarah _____ (c1586-1649); m2 _____ OAKLEY (perhaps); m by 1617 Hingham/Virginia [GMB 2:1214]

LYMAN, John[2] (1623-) & Dorcas PLUMB, dau of John; m Branford 12 Jan 1654[/5] [GMB 2:1219]

LYMAN, Richard[1] (bp 1580-1640-1) & Sarah _____ (-by 1642[/3]); m by 1611 High Ongar, Essex/Hartford [GMB 2:1218]

LYMAN, Richard[2] (bp 1617/8-) & Hepzibah FORD (bp 1625-), dau of Thomas; m2 John MARSH; m by 1644 Windsor/Northampton [GMB 1:689, 2:1219]

LYMAN, Robert[2] (1629-) & Hepzibah[2] BASCOMB (1644-); m Northampton 5 Nov 1662 [GMB 2:1219; GM 1:188]

LYNDE, Samuel (1653-1721) & 2/wf Mary (BRECK) RICHARDSON (1655-1700); m1 John Richardson; m Boston 15 Sept 1698 [DR]

LYNN, Ephraim[2] (1639/40-) & Anne LOCKWOOD; m by 1667 [GMB 2:1221]

LYNN, Henry[1] (c1611-by 1643) & Sarah TILLEY, dau of William; m2 Hugh GUNNISON; m3 John MITCHELL; m4 Francis MORGAN; m by 1636 Boston/York [GMB 2:1221]

LYON, Thomas & Abigail[2] GOULD (c1650-); m Roxbury 10 Mar 1669[/70?] [GM 3:122]

LYON, Thomas & Martha Johanna WINTHROP, dau of Henry [GMB 2:1030]

LYON, Thomas & Mary[2] HOYT (c1632-); m c1652 [GMB 2:1030]

MacCALLUM, John[1] (-1693/4) & Elizabeth (_____) GUTTERSON (-1694+); m1 William GUTTERSON; m Haverhill 17 Nov 1670 [TAG 70:1]

MacCARWITHY, James (c1630-1702+) & Mary EVERETT (1638-1670); m Dedham Nov 1662 [AEBK 4:214, 497]

MacCARWITHY, James[2] (1666-1742-3) & Bethiah LEWIS (c1674-1715); m by 1694/5 Needham/Dedham [AEBK 4:499]

MacCAULLUM, Mackum[1] & Martha _____; m by 1657 Lynn [TAG 70:2-3]

MACKUM, Duncan & Mary[2] HOAR (1669-); m Boston 2 Dec 1698 [GM 3:345]

MACOMBER, William (1610-1670) & Ursula COOPER; m 16 Jan 1633/4 St Mary's, Bridport, Dorsetshire [TG 2:170]

MACOONE, John & Deborah BUSH (-1664/5); m Cambridge 8 Nov 1656 [TAG 76:232]

MACOONE, John (-1705) & Sarah WOOD; m Cambridge 14 June 1665 [TAG 76:232]

MACREASE, Benoni & Lydia[2] FIFIELD (1654/5-); m Salisbury 12 Sept 1681 [GM 2:524]

MAGOUN, James (1666-bef 1705) & 1/wf Sarah FORD (1672-1735+); m c1695 Duxbury [REG 119:14]

MAHURIN, Hugh[1] (-1718) & Mary ?CAMPBELL; m2 William BASSETT; m bef 1691 Taunton [REG 136:18]

MAINE, Hannah ~ Scituate [Plymouth Court Mar 1698/9]

MAINWARING, Oliver & Hannah[2] RAYMENT (bp 1642/3-); m c1665 [GMB 3:1564]

MAINWARING, Oliver[1] & _____ _____; New London [TAG 76:46]

MAKER, James & Rachel _____; m bef 15 Apr 1692 Eastham [Higgins]

MAN, Richard (-1655/6) & Rebecca SHORT; m2 1656 John CORWIN; m St Julians, Norwich, Norfolk 21 July 1637 Scituate [TAG 70:222]

MANCHESTER, Job & Hannah ARCHER (c1662-); m c1683 Tiverton [REG 157:113]

MANLEY, William & Phebe[2] BROOKS (bp 1652-); m by 1686 Boston [GM 1:410]

MANN, Thomas[2] (1650-by 1732) & Sarah[2] ENSIGN; m c1678 Scituate [TAG 61:48, 73:248]

MANN, William[3] (1671-1735/6) & Rebecca[2] BURNHAM (c1660-1702+); m c1689 Wethersfield/Boston/Hartford [TAG 68:83,74:37]

MANNING, John & Abigail[2] MAVERICK (bp 1613/4-); m by 1643 [GMB 2:1243]

MANNING, Samuel & Elizabeth[2] STEARNS; m Watertown 13 Apr 1664 [GMB 3:1749]

MANSFIELD, John[1] (c1597-1674) & Mary (SHRAD) GOVE (-1681/2); m by 1648 Charlestown [REG 155:24]

MANSFIELD, John[2] (1648-1726/7) & Sarah (PINNEY) PHELPS (1648-1732); m Windsor 13 Dec 1683 [REG 155:33-35]

MARABLE, Thomas (c1647-1714) & Sarah BELL (1666-1708+); m Charlestown 30 Aug 1689 [AEBK 4:93]

MARCH, Hugh (1673-1695) & Sarah COKER (1676-1717/8); m2 Archelaus ADAMS; m c1694 [Abel Lunt, p.48]

MARE, Robert & Hannah HOWARD (1657-); m2 John SHAW, m3 Hugh AIRE [TAG 67:27]

MARION, John & Sarah EDDY (c1628-); by 1651 Boston [GMB 1:612]

MARKS, Roger & Sarah[2] HOLT (c1655-); m by 1680 [GM 3:400]

MARRIET, Thomas & Susanna SHANKE; m Filby, Norfolk 29 May 1627 Cambridge
[RCA]

MARSH, John & Susanna² SKELTON (bp 1625-); m2 Thomas RIX; m c1646 Salem
[GMB 3:1686]

MARSH, Jonathan³ (1672-1750/1) & 1/wf Mary VERRY (1668/9-); m Salem 20 or 24
May 1697 [REG 157:159]

MARSHALL, John & 1/wf Sarah WEBB [TAG 77:108]

MARSHALL, John & 2/wf Hannah.? ROCKWELL; Greenwich [TAG 77:180]

MARSHALL, John & 3/wf Elizabeth LYON; Greenwich [TAG 77:180]

MARSHALL, John & Ruth² HAWKINS (c1638-); m2 Daniel FAIRFIELD; m by 1659
Boston [GM 3:264]

MARSHALL, Richard & Hester (LUGG) BELL (bp 1632/3-1713/4+); m Taunton 11 Feb
1676/7 [AEBK 4:87]

MARSHALL, Samuel & Mary² WILTON; m Windsor 6 May 1652 [GMB 3:2021]

MARSHALL, Samuel (c1646-1742) & Ruth³ KEMPTON (bp 1654-1714); m by 1676
Boston [AEBK 1:76]

MARSHALL, Thomas & Ann² CROSS; m2 Ephraim FELLOWS; m by 1678 Ipswich
[GM 2:244]

MARSHALL, Thomas (by 1675-1700) & Mary CHANTRELL (1672-1698+); m Boston
18 June 1697 [AEBK 1:221]

MARSHFIELD, Thomas (-1642/9) & _____ _____ (not Priscilla) (-1649+); m bef
1633 probably near Exeter, Devonshire/Dorchester/ Windsor/Springfield [TAG
63:161-163]

MARTIN, Christopher¹ (c1582-1620/1) & Mary (____) PROWER; m1 _____ PROWER;
m Great Burstead, Essex 26 Feb 1606/7 Plymouth [GMB 2:1224]

MARTIN, George & 1/wf Hannah _____; Salisbury [REG 154:339]

MARTIN, George (-1686) & 2/wf Susanna NORTH (bp 1621-1692); m Salisbury 11
Aug 1626 [TAG 68:70 REG 154:339]

MARTIN, Richard & Elizabeth² BORDON (c1632-); m Salem 1660 [GM 1:351]

MARTIN, Robert & Joanna UPHAM; m 16 Nov 1618 Ottery St Mary, Devonshire [REG
127:28]

MARTIN, Samuel & Abigail² NORTON (c1651-); m Andover 30 Mar 1676 [GMB
2:1338]

MARTIN, Thomas & Rebecca² HIGGINS; m Piscataway 28 Apr 1683 [GMB 2:931]

MARTYN, Richard & Elizabeth SALTER; m 9 June 1630 Ottery St Mary, Devonshire
[REG 127:28]

MARVIN, Reinold (1669-1737) & 1/wf Phebe LEE (1677-1707); m c1696 Lyme [AEJA]

MASKELL, Thomas (-1671) & Bethia PARSONS (1642-1708+); m2 John WILLIAMS,
m Windsor 10 May 1660 [REG 148:230]

MASON, Arthur & Joanna² PARKER (1635-); m Boston 5 July 1655 [GMB 3:1395]

MASON, Daniel[2] (1652-) & 1/wf Margaret DENISON (-1679), dau of Edward; m by 8 Feb 1673/4 [GMB 2:1228]

MASON, Daniel[2] (1652-) & 2/wf Rebecca HOBART; m Hingham 10 Oct 1679 [GMB 2:1228]

MASON, John & Mary[2] EATON (bp 1630/1-); m Dedham 5 May 1651 [GM 2:405]

MASON, John (-1698) & Hannah[2] HAWES (1654/5-1727+); m Dedham 5 Jan 1676[/7] [AEBK 3]

MASON, John[1] (c1605-1672) & 1/wf _____ _____ (-by 1638[/9]); m by 1638 Norwich [GMB 2:1227]

MASON, John[1] (c1605-1672) & 2/wf Ann PECK, dau of Robert (-c1672); m Hingham July 1639 [GMB 2:1227]

MASON, John[2] (1646-) & Abigail FITCH (1650-); m by 1670 [GMB 2:1228; TAG 40:54]

MASON, Robert & Abigail[2] EATON (1639/40-); m Dedham 10 Nov 1659 [GM 2:405]

MASON, Robert (-1667) & 1/wf Mary WISE (-1637); m All Saints, Sudbury, Suffolk 15 Apr 1624 Roxbury/Dedham [TAG 55:149-150]

MASON, Samuel & Mary[2] HOLMAN (c1639-); m Boston 29 May 1662 [GMB 2:974]

MASON, Samuel[2] (1644-) & 1/wf Judith SMITH; m Rehoboth 26 June 1670 [GMB 2:1228]

MASON, Samuel[2] (1644-) & 2/wf Elizabeth PECK; m Rehoboth 4 July 1694 [GMB 2:1228]

MASSEY, Jeffery[1] (c1591-1676) & Ellen FOX (-by 1680); m Wybenbury Hunsterson, Cheshire 25 May 1625 [GMB 2:1233]

MASSEY, John[2] (c1631-) & Sarah WELLS, dau of Thomas; m Salem 27 Apr 1658 [GMB 2:1233]

MASTERS, John[1] (c1581-1639) & Jane _____ (-1639); m c1606 Cambridge [GMB 2:1235]

MASTERS, Nathaniel & Ruth[2] PICKWORTH (c1633-); m by 1654 [GMB 3:1463]

MASTERSON, Nathaniel[2] (c1620-) & Elizabeth[2] COGSWELL (bp 1616-); m Ipswich 31 July 1657 [GMB 2:1237; GM 2:138]

MASTERSON, Richard[1] (c1594-1633) & Mary GOODALL (c1590-1659); m2 Ralph SMITH; m Leiden, Holland 23 Nov 1619 [GMB 2:1237]

MATHER, Eleazer & Esther[2] WARHAM (bp 1644-); m2 Solomon STODDARD; m Windsor 29 Sept 1659 [GMB 3:1927]

MATHEWSON, James & Elizabeth CLEMENCE (1673-); m Providence 5 Apr 1696 [REG 155:138]

MATSON, John[2] (bp 1636-) & 1/wf Mary COTTON, dau of William; m Boston 7 Mar 1659/60 [GMB 2:1241]

MATSON, John[2] (bp 1636-) & 2/wf Jane _____; m by 1672 Boston [GMB 2:1241]

MATSON, Joshua[2] (1640-1686) & Elizabeth[3] THOMAS (1646-1716+), dau of Nathaniel; m bef 28 Feb 1677/8 Boston/Braintree/Marshfield [TAG 70:139; GMB 2:1241]

MATSON, Nathaniel (-1686) & _____ THOMAS; m bef. 1684 Lyme delete [TAG 71:146]

MATSON, Thomas[1] (c1602-1676-7) & Amy CHAMBERS (c1613-1678), dau of Thomas; m by 1633 Boston/Braintree [GMB 1:325-26, 2:1241]

MATSON, Thomas[2] (bp 1633-) & Mary (_____) READ; m Boston 14 Aug 1660 [GMB 2:1241]

MATTHEWS, James & Sarah[2] HEDGES (c1645-); m c1668 [GMB 2:906]

MATTOON, Philip & 1/wf Sarah[2] HAWKES (1657-); m2 1704+ Daniel BELDEN; m Springfield 10 Sept 1677 [GM 3:260]

MAVERICK, Antipas[2] (c1619-) & _____ _____; m c1648 [GMB 2:1243]

MAVERICK, Elias[2] (c1604-1684) & Anna[2] HARRIS (c1613-1697), dau of Thomas; m by 1635 Charlestown/Reading [GMB 2:864, 1242]

MAVERICK, John[1] (bp 1578-1635[/6]) & Mary GYE (-1666+); m Ilsington, Devonshire 28 Oct 1600 [GMB 2:1242]

MAVERICK, John[2] & Jane ANDREWES (c1621-); m All Hallows London Wall, London 15 Apr 1649 [GMB 2:1243]

MAVERICK, Moses[2] (bp 1611-) & 1/wf Remember ALLERTON, dau of Isaac; m by 6 May 1635 [GMB 2:1242]

MAVERICK, Moses[2] (bp 1611-) & 2/wf Eunice (_____) ROBERTS; m1 Thomas ROBERTS; m Boston 22 Oct 1656 [GMB 2:1243]

MAVERICK, Samuel[2] (c1602-) & Amias (COLE) THOMSON; m1 David THOMSON; m bet 1628-30 [GMB 2:1242]

MAY, George & Elizabeth[2] FRANKLIN (1638-); m Boston 6 Oct 1656 [GM 2:570]

MAYHEW, Thomas[1] (bp 1593-1682) & 1/wf _____ _____ (-by 1635); m by 1620 [GMB 2:1244]

MAYHEW, Thomas[1] (bp 1593-1682) & 2/wf Jane (GALLION) PAINE (-1666+); m1 Thomas PAINE; Wantage, Berkshire/London/Martha's Vineyard [GMB 2:1244; TAG 76:98; LMM]

MAYHEW, Thomas[2] (c1620-) & Jane _____; m by 1648 [GMB 2:1245]

MAYNARD, John (-1672) & 1/wf Elizabeth CARTER; m Bures St Mary, Suffolk 13 Apr 1632 Sudbury [DR]

MAYNARD, John[1] & 1/wf Mary STARR, dau. of Comfort [AEBK 4:381]

MAYNARD, John[1] & 2/wf Elizabeth (WIGHT)(HEATON) PELL (bp 1606-1671/2-82/3); m1 Nathaniel HEATON; m2 Joseph PELL; m aft 30 Aug 1650 Boston [AEBK 4:381, 579; GM 3:305]

MAYO, John & Hannah[2] GRAVES (1636-); m Roxbury 24 May 1654 [GM 3:135]

MAYO, Nathaniel & Hannah[2] PRENCE (c1629-); m2 Jonathan SPARROW; m Eastham 13 Feb 1649/50 [GMB 3:1523]

MAYO, Nathaniel (?1667-1716) & 1/wf Mary BROWN; m by 1697 Eastham [MF5G 6:359]

McALLISTER, Angus (c1670-1737+) & Margaret _____; m bef 1698 Northern Ireland/Londonderry, NH [NGSQ 68:165]

McCARTHY, Thaddeus & Elizabeth[2] JOHNSON (bp 1642-); m by 1667 [GMB 2:1101]

MEAD, John (c1628-1698/9) & Hannah perhaps POTTER; m c1655 Stamford [TAG 73:9]

MEAD, Joseph (bp 1624-1690) & Mary BROWN; m Stamford 4 Dec 1654 [TAG 73:9]

MEAD, William[1] (bp 1592-) & Philip _____ (-1657); m bef 1621/2 Watford, Hertfordshire/Stamford [TAG 73:8]

MEADS, David (-1724+) & Hannah[3] WARREN (-bef 1707/8); m Watertown 24 Sept 1675 [AEBK 1:479]

MEAKINS, Thomas[1] & Katherine GREENE; m Thorpe Achurch, Northamptonshire 27 Jan 1607[/8] [REG 157:32]

MEAKINS, Thomas[1] (c1589-1641-51) & Katherine BELL (-1650/1), sister of Thomas; m c1614 Boston/Braintree [GMB 2:1247]

MEAKINS, Thomas[2] (c1614-) & 1/wf Sarah ____; m by 1639 Roxbury/Boston [REG 157:33; GMB 2:1247]

MEAKINS, Thomas[2] (c1614-) & 2/wf Elizabeth TULSTON; m Roxbury 14 Feb 1650[/1] [GMB 2:1247]

MEIGS, John (bp 1613-1672) & Thomasine FRY (-1671+); m probably near Axminster, Devonshire c1634 Weymouth/New Haven/Guilford [DR]

MEIGS, Vincent (-1658) & Emm ____; m probably near Chardstock, Dorset bef 1610 Weymouth/New Haven/Guilford [DR]

MEKUSETT, Mordecai & Sarah SCANT; m c1690 Braintree [BTR, 720]

MELLOWS, John & Martha ____; Boston [AEBK 1:217]

MELLOWS, Abraham[1] (c1570-1638) & Martha BULKELEY, dau of Edward; m by 1595 [GMB 2:1249]

MELLOWS, Edward[2] (bp 1609-) & Hannah SMITH (bp 1612-c1655); m2 Joseph HILLS; m c1636 [GMB 2:1249; AEBK 4:399]

MELLOWS, Oliver[2] (c1595-) & 1/wf Mary JAMES; m Boston, Lincolnshire 3 Aug 1620 [GMB 2:1249]

MELLOWS, Oliver[2] (c1595-) & 2/wf Elizabeth (HAWKREDD) CONEY; m Boston, Lincolnshire 1 Jan 1633[/4] Charlestown [GMB 2:1249; AEBK 1:217]

MENDALL, John & ____ (HEWES) BURROUGHS; m1 Jeremiah BURROUGHS; m bef 1663 Marshfield [TAG 40:33]

MENDUM, Jonathan[2] (c1650-) & Mary RAYNES; m2 John WOODMAN; m c1675 [GMB 2:1253]

MENDUM, Robert[1] (c1602-1682) & 1/wf Mary ____ (-by 1658); m by 1639 Duxbury [GMB 2:1253]

MENDUM, Robert[2] (c1602-1682) & 2/wf Judith (____) ____; m perhaps c1658 [GMB 2:1253]

MERCER, Thomas & Elizabeth[2] HAWKINS (c1650-   ); m by 1671 Boston [GM 3:264]

MERRIAM, John & Mary[2] WHEELER (1673-   ); m Concord 14 Nov 1688 [AEBK 3]

MERRIAM, John (1666-1713+) & 1/wf Sarah[3] WHEELER (1666-1692); m Concord 22 July 1691 [AEBK 3]

MERRIAM, Joseph (-1702) & Sarah[2] JENKINS (c1652-1688+); m Lynn 19 Aug 1675 [AEBK 4:426]

MERRICK, William & Rebecca[2] TRACY (c1625-   ); m c1645 [GMB 3:1833]

MERRILL, Abel[2] (1643/4-1689) & Priscilla[2] CHASE (1648/9-1697+); m 10 Feb 1670/1 Newbury [ASBO, p.173]

MERRILL, Daniel & Sarah[2] CLOUGH (1646-   ); m Newbury 14 May 1667 [GM 2:113]

MERRILL, John[1] & Elizabeth VINCENT; m 15 July 1633 Little Wenham, Suffolk/Newbury [HQ 24:38]

MERRITT, Henry ~ Deborah _____; Scituate [Plymouth Court Mar 1686/7]

MERRITT, John (1661-1740) & Elizabeth PINCEN (1663/4-1746) not HYLAND; m c1686 Scituate [TAG 50:98]

MERRITT, John ~ Elizabeth _____; Scituate [Plymouth Court Mar 1687/8]

MERRY, Walter[1] (c1608-1657) & 1/wf Rebecca _____ (-1653); m by 1633 [GMB 2:1257]

MERRY, Walter[1] (c1608-1657) & 2/wf Mary DOLING; m2 Robert THORNTON; m Boston 18 Aug 1653 [GMB 2:1257]

MERRY, Walter[2] (1656-   ) & 1/wf Martha COTTRILL; m Taunton 17 Jan 1682[/3] [GMB 2:1257]

MERRY, Walter[2] (1656-   ) & 2/wf Elizabeth CUNNILL; m Taunton 21 Jan 1685/6 [GMB 2:1257]

MERWIN, John (1649/50-1727/8) & 1/wf Mary (WELCH) HOLBROOK; m1 Israel HOLBROOK; m Milford 12 Apr 1683 [REG 149:307]

MERWIN, Miles (bp 1623/4-1697) & 1/wf Elizabeth POWELL (bp 1630-1664); m c1648 Windsor [REG 149:305]

MERWIN, Miles (bp 1623/4-1697) & 2/wf Sarah (PLATT) BEACH (1639-1670); m c1665 Windsor/Milford [REG 149:306]

MERWIN, Miles (bp 1623/4-1697) & 3/wf Sarah (YOUNGS) SCOFIELD; m1 Daniel SCOFIELD; m Stamford 30 Nov 1670 [REG 149:306]

MERWIN, Miles[2] (1658-1724) & Hannah (WILMOT) MILES; m1 Samuel MILES; m New Haven 20 Sept 1681 [REG 149:307]

MERWIN, Samuel (1656-1705/6) & Sarah WOODEN; m New Haven 13 Dec 1682 [REG 149:307]

MERWIN, Thomas (c1652-1716+) & Abigail CLAPHAM; m Fairfield Mar 1678/9 [REG 149:307]

MESSENGER, Andrew (by 1618-by 1681) & Rachel _____; m c1641 New Haven/Jamaica, L.I. [REG 152:358]

MESSENGER, Andrew (c1651-1730) & 1/wf Rebecca (PICKETT) St. JOHN (-1684); m c1675 Norwalk [REG 152:363]

MESSENGER, Andrew (c1651-1730) & 2/wf Rachel HAYES; m aft 1684 [REG 152:363]

MESSENGER, Edward (c1630-1685+) & _____ _____; m by 1650 [REG 152:363]

MESSENGER, Samuel (c1642-1685/6) & Susanna _____ (not MILLS); m 20 Apr 1669 Long Island [REG 152:362]

METCALF, Michael (-1654) & Mary^2 FAIRBANKS (bp 1622-1668+); m2 Christopher SMITH; m Dedham 2 Apr 1644 [AEBK 3]

METCALFE, Thomas & Sarah^2 PIDGE (c1637-); m Dedham 12 Sept 1656 [GMB 3:1466]

MEW, Ellis^1 & _____ _____; New Haven [TAG 76:15]

MICHELL, John ~ Hannah^2 BONNEY; in court 27 Oct 1685 [GM 1:342]

MIGHILL, John & Sarah^2 BATT (1640-); m Rowley 6 July 1659 [GM 1:203]

MILES, John (bp 1644-1704) & 1/wf Elizabeth^2 HARRIMAN (bp 1648-1675); m New Haven 11 Apr 1665 [REG 150:47]

MILES, John (bp 1644-1704) & 2/wf Mary^2 ALSOP (1654-); m New Haven 2 Nov 1680 [REG 150:47; GM 1:50]

MILES, Joseph & Exercise^2 FELTON; m Salem 7 Nov 1664 [GM 2:515]

MILES, Richard & 2/wf Experience COLLICUTT (1641-); by 1664 [GMB 1:443]

MILLARD, Nathaniel (1672-1740/1) & Susannah^2 GLADDING (1668-1727) [TAG 77:212-3]

MILLER, John & Margaret^2 WINSLOW (1640-); m Marshfield 24 Dec 1659 [GMB 3:2033]

MILLER, Joseph & Mary^2 POPE (c1640-); m c1660 [GMB 3:1499]

MILLETT, Thomas^1 (bp 1604-1675-6) & Mary^2 GREENWAY (bp 1605-bef 1682); m c1633 Dorchester [TAG 74:195, 75:93; GMB 2:816]

MILLS, Isaac & Elizabeth _____; m bef 1670s East Hampton [RCA]

MILLS, James & Martha^2 ALLEY (1649-); m Lynn 1 Apr 1671 [GM 1:41]

MILLS, John^1 (c1597-1678) & Susanna _____ (-1675); m c1622 Braintree [GMB 2:1261]

MILLS, John^1 (c1610-by 1664) & Sarah _____; m c1642 Scarborough [GMB 3:2082]

MILLS, John^2 & Joanna (ALGER) OAKMAN, dau of Andrew; m1 Elias OAKMAN; m by 1686 [GMB 3:2082]

MILLS, John^2 (bp 1632-) & Elizabeth SHOVE; m Braintree 26 Apr 1653 [GMB 2:1261]

MILLS, Richard & Ann _____, not widow of Vincent SIMPKINS; m bef 1662 Stamford [RCA]

MILLS, Richard^1 & Sarah NICHOLS (bp 1615-); m c1641 Wethersfield [TAG 75:279]

MILLS, Samuel & Susannah (PALMER) MILLS; Jamaica, L.I. [REG 156:113]

MILLS, Samuel[3] (c1673-1751+) & Sarah DENTON; m c1693 Jamaica, L.I. [REG 156:113]

MILLS, Zachariah & Abigail (MESSENGER) DARLING; m bet 1674-86 [REG 152:362]

MINGAY, Jeffrey[1] (bp 24 July 1608-1658) & Anne CAPON (c1610-1680); m Denton, Norfolk 30 Sept 1630 Hampton [NHGR 8:154]

MINOR, Clement[2] (bp 1637/8-) & 1/wf Frances (BURCHAM) WILLEY; m Stonington 26 Nov 1662 [GMB 2:1264]

MINOR, Clement[2] (bp 1637/8-) & 2/wf Martha WELLMAN; m 20 Feb 1672/3 Stonington? [GMB 2:1264]

MINOR, Clement[2] (bp 1637/8-) & 3/ wf Joanna _____; m 1681+ New London [GMB 2:1264]

MINOR, Ephraim[2] (bp 1642-) & Hannah AVERY; m 20 June 1666 [GMB 2:1264]

MINOR, John[2] (bp 1635-) & Elizabeth BOOTH; m Stratford 19 Oct 1658 Charlestown [GMB 2:1264]

MINOR, Joseph[2] (bp 1644-) & 1/wf Mary AVERY; m 23 Oct 1668 [GMB 2:1264]

MINOR, Joseph[2] (bp 1644-) & 2/wf Bridget (CHESEBOROUGH) THOMPSON; m1 William THOMPSON; Stonington [GMB 2:1264]

MINOR, Manasseh (1647-) & Lydia MOORE; m 26 Sept 1670 [GMB 2:1265]

MINOR, Samuel[2] (1652[/3]-) & Mary LORD; m 15 Dec 1681 [GMB 2:1265]

MINOR, Thomas[1] (bp 1608-1690) & Grace PALMER (c1614-1684/5+), dau of Walter; m Charlestown 23 Apr 1634 [GMB 2:1264, 3:1381]

MINOT, George[1] (bp 1592-1671) & Martha STOCKE (c1597-1657); m Epping, Essex 6 Sept 1623 Dorchester [AEBK 3; GMB 2:1268]

MINOT, James[2] (1653-1735) & Rebecca WHEELER (c1666-1734), dau of Timothy; m c1684 Concord [AEBK 3]

MINOT, James[2] (bp 1628/9-) & 1/wf Hannah STOUGHTON (c1637-), dau of Israel; m Dorchester 9 Dec 1653 [GMB 2:1268, 3:1775; AEBK 3]

MINOT, James[2] (bp 1628/9-) & 2/wf Hepzibah CORLETT; m Cambridge 21 May 1673 [GMB 2:1268; AEBK 3]

MINOT, John[2] (bp 1626-1699) & 1/wf Lydia BUTLER; m 19 May 1647 [GMB 2:1268; AEBK 3]

MINOT, John[2] (bp 1626-1699) & 2/wf Mary (DASSETT) BIGG; m1 John BIGG; m 1667+ [GMB 2:1268; AEBK 3]

MINOT, John[3] (1647[/8]-1690/1) & Elizabeth BRECK (-1690); m Dorchester 11 Mar 1670[/1] [AEBK 3]

MINOT, Samuel[2] (1635-1690) & Hannah HOWARD, dau of Robert; m 23 June 1670 Dorchester [GMB 2:1258; AEBK 3]

MINOT, Stephen[2] (bp 1631-1671) & Truecross DAVENPORT (c1634-1692), dau of Richard; m 10 Nov 1654 [GMB 2:1268; AEBK 3]

MINOT, Stephen[3] (bp 1662-1732) & Mercy CLARK (-1732+), dau of Christopher; m 1 Dec 1686 Dorchester/Boston [AEBK 3]

MITCHELL, Andrew & Abigail[2] ATWOOD (1662-); m Charlestown 12 Nov 1686 [GM 1:106]

MITCHELL, Edward[2] (c1645-) & 1/wf Mary[2] HAYWARD (c1648-); m c1668 [GMB 2:1272; GM 3:292]

MITCHELL, Experience[1] (c1603-c1689) & 1/wf Jane COOKE, dau of Francis; m c1628 [GMB 2:1271]

MITCHELL, Experience[1] (c1603-c1689) & 2/wf Mary _____ (-c1662); m c1641 [GMB 2:1272]

MITCHELL, Jacob[2] (c1643-) & Susanna[2] POPE (c1647-); m Plymouth 7 Nov 1666 [GMB 2:1272; 3:1498]

MITCHELL, John[2] (c1650-) & 1/wf Mary[2] BONNEY; m Duxbury 14 Dec 1675 [GMB 2:1272; GM 1:341]

MITCHELL, John[2] (c1650-) & 3/wf Mary PRIOR; m Duxbury 24 May 1682 [GMB 2:1272]

MITCHELL, John[2] (c1650-) & 2/wf Mary LATHRUP; m Duxbury 14 Jan 1679[/80] [GMB 2:1272]

MITCHELL, Thomas & Mary[2] MOULTON (c1635-1711/2); m Malden Nov 1655 [GMB 2:1308]

MITTON, Michael & 1/wf _____ _____; Falmouth [JP]

MITTON, Michael & 2/wf Elizabeth CLEEVE; m England c1636 [JP]

MIX, Thomas & Rebecca[2] TURNER; m by 4 Sept 1649 [GMB 3:1850]

MIXER, Isaac & 1/wf Mary[2] BARKER (1637-1659/60); m Watertown 19 Sept 1655 [AEBK 3]

MIXER, Isaac & Mary[2] COOLIDGE (1637-); m Watertown 19 Sept 1655 [GM 2:196]

MIXER, Isaac[2] & 2/wf Rebecca[2] GARFIELD (1640/1?-1682/3); m 10 Jan 1660/1 Watertown [GM 3:20; AEBK 3; REG 156-332]

MONK, Henry & Margaret CHANDLER; Roxbury [TAG 73:51]

MONROE, John (-1691) & Sarah _____; m bef 1667, Bristol [TAG 40:201]

MONTAGUE, Richard[1] & Abigail DOWNING (bp 1617-1694) [TAG 74:302]

MOODY, Caleb & Judith[2] BRADBURY (1638-); m Newbury 9 Nov 1665 [GM 1:379]

MOODY, John[1] (bp 1593-1655) & Sarah COX (bp 1598-1671); m Bury St. Edmonds St. James, Suffolk 8 Sept 1617 [GMB 2:1275]

MOODY, John[3] & Hannah DOLE (1665-); m Newbury 18 May 1692 [TAG 74:57]

MOODY, Samuel[2] (c1634-) & Sarah _____; m c1659 [GMB 2:1275]

MOON, Ebenezer[2] (1645-1707-12) & Rebecca[2] PEABODY (c1657-bef 1712); m say 1686 Newport [AEBK 1:371; REG 117:97]

MOOR, John & Elizabeth[2] HART (c1638-); m Weymouth 26 June 1661 [GMB 2:868]

MOOR, Sampson & Elizabeth (THOMAS) MATSON; m1 Joshua MATSON; m 15 Dec. 1687 Charlestown/Boston [TAG 71:146]

MOORCOCK, Nicholas (-1727) & Amy BURNHAM (1662-1721); m bef 1688 Boston [TAG 74:37]

MOORE, John[1] (c1602-1673/4) & 2/wf Elizabeth RICH (bp 1612-1690); m Little Gaddesden, Hertfordshire 27 Nov 1633 Sudbury [TAG 66:76; TG 6:139]

MOORE, John[1] (c1602-1673/4) & perhaps 1/wf Elizabeth _____; m c1625 perhaps area of Henham, Essex [TAG 66:76]

MOORE, John[1] (c1603-1677) & _____ _____; m c1628 Windsor [GMB 2:1277]

MOORE, John[1] (c1611-1643/4+) & _____ _____ perhaps Hannah; m by 1636 Salem [GMB 2:1279]

MOORE, John[2] (1645-) & 1/wf Hannah[2] GOFFE (1643[/4?]-); m Windsor 21 Sept 1664 [GMB 2:1277; Gm 3:97]

MOORE, Samuel & Sarah[2] HIGGINS; m Woodbridge 26 Oct 1693 [GMB 2:931]

MOORE, Samuel[1] (c1610-c1638) & _____ _____; m by 1636 Salem [GMB 2:1280]

MOORES, Samuel & 1/wf Hannah[2] PLUMMER (c1633-); m Newbury 3 May 1653 [GMB 3:1484]

MOORES, Samuel & 2/wf Mary ILSLEY; m Newbury 12 Sept 1656 [GMB 3:1485]

MORE, Richard[1] (bp 1614-by 1696) & 1/wf Christian[1] HUNTER (c1615-1676); m Plymouth 20 Oct 1636 Shipton, Shropshire/Salem [TAG 40:79; GM 3:473; GMB 2:1285]

MORE, Richard[1] (bp 1614-by 1696) & 2/wf Jane (_____) CRUMPTON (not Hollingsworth); m1 Samuel CRUMPTON; m aft 1676 Salem [TAG 67:31; GMB 2:1285]

MORE, William & Mary (?CROWELL) ALLEN (-1727); m1 Joshua ALLEN; nd [REG 125:232-4]

MORELY, Ralph[1] (-1630) & _____ _____; m by 1630 Charlestown [GMB 2:1288]

MOREY, John & Constance[2] BRACY; m c1660 Wethersfield [GM 1:373]

MOREY, Jonathan[3] (-c1733) & Hannah BOURNE (1667-1732); m 24 Jan 1689 Plymouth [REG 118:199]

MORGAN, Joseph & Deborah[2] HART (c1649-); m Lynn 12 July 1669 [GM 3:230]

MORGAN, Richard & Rebecca[2] HOLDRED (1643-); m Andover 21 May 1660 [GM 3:370]

MORGAN, Robert[1] (-c1673) & Margaret[2] NORMAN (bp 1614/5-); m2 Samuel FOWLER perhaps; m c1633 [GMB 2:1335; TAG 77:103]

MORRILL, Isaac[1] (c1588-1662) & Sarah _____ (-1672/3); m c1625 Roxbury [GMB 2:1291]

MORRIS, John & Sarah[2] JOHNSON (bp 1653/4-); m bef 6 Mar 1683[/4] [GMB 2:1102]

MORRIS, Rice[1] (c1609-1647) & Hester _____; m2 Henry EVANS; m c1634 Charlestown [GMB 2:1293]

MORRIS, Richard[1] (c1600-1665+) & 1/wf ___ ___ (-by 1628); m c1625 [GMB 2:1293]

MORRIS, Richard[1] (c1600-1665+) & 2/wf Leonora (PAWLEY) UNDERHILL; m1 John UNDERHILL; m The Hague 28 Nov 1628 [GMB 2:1295]

MORRIS, Richard[1] (c1600-1665+) & 3/wf Mary ___; m by 18 Dec 1658 [GMB 2:1295]

MORRISON, Edward (bp 1631//2-1690) & Grace BETT (-1705); m Boston 20 Nov 1655 [REG 146:277]

MORSE, Daniel (1613-1688) & Lydia FISHER (bp 1620/1-1690/1); m c1638 Dedham/Medfield [AEBK 4:242]

MORSE, Jeremiah (-bef 1724/5) & Mehitable CHENEY (1680-1727); m Medfield 19 Nov 1699/1700 [AEBK 1:236]

MORSE, John & Abigail[2] STEARNS; m Watertown 25 Apr 1666 [GMB 3:1749]

MORSE, John (c1670-1727) & 1/wf Sarah ___ (perhaps Tucker) (1670-1723-6); m c1693 Salisbury/prob. Dartmouth/N. Kingstown [DR]

MORSE, Joseph (1667-1733) & Grace WARREN (1671/2-1753); m Watertown 20 Jan 1690/1 [AEBK 1:480]

MORSE, Joseph (1671-1709) & Elizabeth SAWTELL (1671-1713/4+); m2 Benjamin NOURSE; m 25 Aug 1691 Watertown [REG 126:7]

MORSE, Obadiah & Elizabeth[2] RAWLINS (c1649-); m c1670 [GMB 3:1553]

MORTON, Ephraim[2] (c1623-) & Ann COOPER; m Plymouth 18 Nov 1644 [GMB 2:1297]

MORTON, Ephraim[4] (1671-) & Hannah[3] FAUNCE (1678-); m2 John COOK; m c1698 Plymouth [REG 116:119]

MORTON, George[1] (c1587-1624) & Juliana CARPENTER (-1664), dau of Alexander; m2 Manasseh KEMPTON; m Leiden 22 July 1612 [GMB 2:1297]

MORTON, George[3] (c1645-1727) & Joanna[3] KEMPTON (bp 1645-1728); m Plymouth 22 Dec 1664 [AEBK 1:75]

MORTON, John[2] (c1617-) & Lettice ___; m2 Andrew RING; m c1649 [GMB 2:1297]

MORTON, Nathaniel (c1613-) & Lydia COOPER; m Plymouth 25 Dec 1635 [GMB 2:1297]

MORTON, Richard (-1710) & Ruth[2] EDWARDS (1643-1714); m by 26 Feb 1665/6 Windsor/Hatfield [REG 145:333]

MORTON, Richard[3] (c1668-1692/3) & Mehitable GRAVES (1671-1742); m2 1693/4 William WORTHINGTON; m Hatfield 21 Jan 1689/90 [REG 145:334]

MORTON, Thomas[1] (c1592-c1627) & ___ ___; m by 1617 [GMB 2:1298]

MORTON, Thomas[2] (c1617-) & Rose ___ (-1685); m c1645 Plymouth [GMB 2:1298]

MORTON, William[1] (-by 1711/2) & Mary[2] BURNHAM (1650-1719/20); m by 1674 [TAG 74:36]

MOSES, Aaron[2] (c1651-) & 1/wf Ruth[2] SHERBORN (probably) (1660-); m 1 June 1676 [GMB 2:1301, 3:1668]

MOSES, Aaron[2] (c1651-) & 2/wf Mary _____ [GMB 2:1301]

MOSES, Henry & Remember GILES (bp 1638/9-); m Salem 1 Apr 1659 [TAG 72:300]

MOSES, John[1] (c1616-1693/4+) & 1/wf Alice _____ (-by 1667); m by 1648 Casco/Portsmouth [GMB 2:1301]

MOSES, John[1] (c1616-1693/4+) & 2/wf Anne (_____) JONES (-1679/80+); m1 John JONES; m by 17 Sept 1667 [GMB 2:1301]

MOSHER, Hugh[1] (c1613-by 1666) & _____ _____; m c1638 Casco [GMB 2:1303]

MOSHER, John[2] (c1640-) & Elizabeth _____; m c 1683 Brookhaven [GMB 2:1303]

MOSLEY, Richard & Maria[2] EYRE (1652-); m by 1675 Boston [GM 2:488]

MOULTHROP, Mathew[1] (bp 1607[/8]-1668] & Jane[1] NICHOL; m Wrawby, Lincolnshire 13 May 1633 [TAG 74:223]

MOULTHROP, Mathew[2] (bp 1603/4-) & Hannah[2] THOMPSON; m New Haven 26 June 1662 [TAG 74 223]

MOULTON, Henry & Sobriety[2] HILTON (c1632-); m 20 Nov 1651 [GMB 2:949]

MOULTON, Jacob[2] (c1639-) & Ruhamah[2] HAYDEN (1641-); m Charlestown 3 July 1663 [GMB 2:1308; GM 3:280]

MOULTON, Robert[1] (c1587-1654/5-5) & Alice _____; m c1612 [GMB 2:1305]

MOULTON, Robert[2] (c1616-) & Abigail GOAD; m c1641 [GMB 2:1305]

MOULTON, Thomas[1] (c1609-1657) & Jane _____ (c1610-1682[/3]+); m c1631 Malden [GMB 2:1307]

MOUSALL, John[2] (c1628-) & 1/wf Elizabeth RICHARDSON, dau of Samuel; m by 1659 Charlestown [GMB 2:1311]

MOUSALL, John[2] (c1628-) & 2/wf Eleanor HOW; m Charlestown 26 Mar 1686 [GMB 2:1311]

MOUSALL, John[2] (c1628-) & 3/wf Mercy MIRICK; m Charlestown 24 Apr 1695 [GMB 2:1311]

MOUSALL, Ralph[1] (c1603-1657) & Alice _____ (-c1674/5); m c1628 Charlestown [GMB 2:1310]

MOUSALL, Thomas[2] (bp 1633-) & 1/wf Mary RICHARDSON, dau of Samuel; m by 1655 Charlestown [GMB 2:1311]

MOUSALL, Thomas[2] (bp 1633-) & 2/wf Mary MOORE; m Charlestown 21 Apr 1679 [GMB 2:1311]

MOWRY, Benjamin (1649-1719+) & Martha (HAZARD) POTTER, m1 Ichabod POTTER; m c1676 [AEJA; GMB 2:1314]

MOWRY, John (c1640s-1690) & Mary _____ (-1690); m by 1674 Providence [AEJA; GMB 2:1314]

MOWRY, Jonathan[2] (bp 1637-1708) & 1/wf Mary (BARTLETT) FOSTER (c1634-1692); m1 Richard FOSTER; m Plymouth 8 July 1659 [AEJA; GMB 2:1313]

MOWRY, Jonathan[2] (bp 2:2:1637-1708) & 2/wf Hannah (PINCEN) (YOUNG) WITHERELL (1642-1720+); m1 George YOUNG, m2 John WITHERELL; m c1694 Plymouth [AEJA; GMB 2:1313]

MOWRY, Joseph (1647-1716) & Mary WILBUR (-1720); m bef 1672 [AEJA; GMB 2:1314]

MOWRY, Nathaniel (c1644-1718) & Joanna INMAN (-1717/8); m 1666 Providence [AEJA; GMB 2:1314]

MOWRY, Roger[1] (c1600s-1668) & Mary[2] JOHNSON (bp 31 July 1614-1678/9); m2 John KINGSLEY; m c1630s perhaps Roxbury/Salem/Providence [REG 146:274; GMB 2:1108, 1313; AEJA]

MOWRY, Thomas (1652-1717) & Susanna NEWELL (bp 6 April 1656-1729); m Roxbury 6 Sept 1673 [AEJA; GMB 2:1314]

MOYCE, Joseph (-1669+) & Hannah _____ (-1655); perhaps Dennington, Suffolk 2 Nov 1609 thus Anna FOLCARD Salisbury [Pillsbury Ancestry, 507-508]

MUCHMORE, James & Sarah[2] MENDUM (c1647-); m by 1667 [GMB 2:1253]

MULFORD, John (1670-1730) & 1/wf Jemima HIGGENS (-1723); m 1 Nov 1699 Eastham [TAG 40:197]

MULFORD, Thomas (c1640-1706) & 1/wf Elizabeth BARNS (bp 1644-by 1678/9); m bef 1670 Hingham [TAG 40:193]

MULLINEX, Worseman & Elizabeth HUSTIS (c1674-); m 30 Nov 1692 [NYGBR 129:206]

MULLINS, William[1] (c1572-1621) & Alice _____ (not Atwood, not Poretiers] (-1621); m by 1600 Plymouth [MD 44:43-4; GMB 2:1315]

MULLINS, William[2] (c1593-) & 1/wf _____ _____; m by 1618 [GMB 2:1316]

MULLINS, William[2] (c1593-) & 2/wf Ann (_____) BELL; m1 Thomas BELL; m Boston 7 May 1656 [GMB 2:1316]

MUMFORD, Thomas & Sarah[2] SHERMAN (c1636-); m c1656 [GMB 3:1672]

MUNGER, Samuel (-1717) & Sarah HAND (1665-1751) [she did not marry second Caleb Woodworth]; by 1689 Guilford [Higgins]

MUNJOY, George & Mary[2] PHILLIPS (c1638-); m2 Robert LAWRENCE; m3 Stephen CROSS; m say 1653 Boston [GMB 3:1456]

MUNN, John (1652/3-1684) & Abigail PARSONS (1662/3-1686+); m2 John RICHARDS; m Springfield 23 Dec 1680 [REG 148:224]

MUNROE, John[1] & Sarah _____ (-1692/3); m bef 1670 Scotland/Bristol, RI [TAG 61:181]

MUNSELL, Thomas (-1711-12) & Lydia WAY (c1653-1733); m c1675 New London [AEJA]

MUNT, Thomas[1] (c1616-1664) & 1/wf Dorothy _____ (-1639[/40]); m by 1639 [GMB 2:1318]

MUNT, Thomas[1] (c1616-1664) & 2/wf Elinor _____; m2 Thomas HILL; m by 1645 [GMB 2:1318]

MURDOCK, Robert & Hannah[3] STEDMAN (c1667-1737); m Roxbury 28 Apr 1692 [TAG 71:85]

MUSSILLOWAY, Daniel[1] (c1645-1710/11) & 2/wf Mary (LONG) GRIFFIN (c1650s-1720/1+); m1 Jonathan GRIFFIN; m 7 Sept 1687 Newbury [ASBO, p.165]

MUSTE, Edward[1] (c1609-1634-5) & Hester _____; m2 William RUSKEW; m by 1634 [GMB 2:1319]

MUZZEY, Joseph[2] & Esther[2] JACKMAN; m2 Samuel[2] FRENCH; m3 John SWEET [AMacE]

MYCALL, James & Mary[2] FARR; m2 Matthias FARNSWORTH; m Braintree 11 Dec 1657 [GMB 3:2078]

MYLAM, Humphrey & Mary[2] GORE (bp 1632-); m by 1652 Boston [GM 3:118]

NASH, Isaac[2] & Phebe _____ [TAG 76:250]

NASH, Isaac[3] & 1/wf Dorothy[3] LITTLEFIELD (-bef 1723) [TAG 76:250]

NASH, James & Sarah[2] SIMONSON (c1649-); m by 1669 Weymouth [GMB 3:1683]

NASH, John & Elizabeth[2] (HITCHCOCK) HOWD (1651-); m Branford 22 Aug 1677 [GM 3:338]

NASH, Samuel did not marry Esther DELANO [GMB 1:520]

NASH, Samuel[1] (c1602-1682+) & _____ _____; m c1625 Plymouth [GMB 2:1323]

NASH, Timothy & Rebecca[2] STONE; m by 1657 [GMB 3:1771]

NEALE, Edward & Martha[2] HART (1640-); m Weymouth 24 Jan 1662[/3] [GMB 2:868]

NEALE, Francis[1] (c1626-bef 1697) & Jane[2] ANDREWS (1629/30-1686+); m bef 28 Mar 1658 St James, Garlickhithe, London/Saco [TG 3:51; GM 1:58]

NEEDHAM, Anthony[1] & Ann POTTER; m Salem 10 Jan 1655 [TAG 73:26]

NEFF, William[1] (c1639-42-1688/9) & Mary[2] CORLISS (1646-1722); m 23 Jan 1665/6 Haverhill [ASBO, p.210]

NEGUS, Benjamin (c1612-by 1693/4) & Elizabeth WILLIAMSON (c1612-1681/2); m St Faith the Virgin, London aft 22 Feb 1637/8 [TG 6:198]

NEGUS, Jabez (bp 1648-1723) & 1/wf Hannah PHILLIPS (1643-by1693/4); m bef 28 Sept 1674 Boston [TG 6:201]

NEGUS, Jabez (bp 1648-1723) & 2/wf Sarah BROWN (-1737+); m 9 Jan 1693/4 Boston [TG 6:201]

NEGUS, Jonathan (c1601-c1675/6) & Jane (DEIGHTON) LUGG (bp 1609-1671+); m1 John LUGG; m bef 27 Oct 1647 [AEBK 4:492; TG 6:195]

NELSON, Thomas[1] (c1600-c1650) & 1/wf Dorothy STAPLETON (bp 11 Aug 1608-1637); m All Saints, York 27 Jan 1626/7 Rowley [REG 128:82, 148:132]

NELSON, Thomas[1] (c1600-c1650) & 2/wf Joan DUMMER; m Rowley Feb 1641/2 [REG 148:133]

NELSON, William & Ruth[2] FOXWELL (1641-); m by 1668 Barnstable [GM 2:567]

NELSON, William¹ (c1635-bef 1694) & Elizabeth² CROSS (1636-1694+); m by 1658 Ipswich [ASBO, p.229; GM 2:243]

NETTLETON, John² (c1644-1690/1) & Martha HULL (1650-1691+); m Killingworth 10 June 1650 [TAG 71:183]

NETTLETON, John³ (1670/1-1714/5) & Sarah² WOODMANSEE (1672/3-1723); m Killingworth 21 Jan 1691/2 [TAG 71:183; REG 147:40]

NEWCOMB, John² (1634-1722) & Ruth MARSHALL (-1697); m bef 1659 Braintree [TAG 61:113]

NEWCOMB, Peter (c1648-1725) & Susannah CUTTING (1650s-by 1703); m Braintree 26 June 1672 [AEBK 1:264; GM 2:274]

NEWCOMBE, Francis (?1592-1692) & Rachel BRACKETT (1615-); m 27 May 1630 Sudbury/Boston [TAG 52:92, 55:215]

NEWELL, Jacob & Martha² GIBSON (1639-); m Roxbury 3 Nov 1657 [GM 3:51]

NEWELL, James (negro) ~ Mary _____ [Plymouth Court Mar 1688/9]

NEWELL, John (c1634-1704) & Hannah² LARKIN (1643[/4?]-1704); m Charlestown 15 Feb 1664[/5] [AEBK 3]

NEWGATE, John¹ (c1588-1665) & 1/wf Lydia _____ (-1620); m c1613 [GMB 2:1330]

NEWGATE, John¹ (c1588-1665) & 2/wf Thomasine HAYES (-1625); m All Hallows London Wall, London 1 Nov 1620 [GMB 2:1330]

NEWGATE, John¹ (c1588-1665) & 3/wf Ann (_____) (HUNT) DRAPER (-1676+); m by 1627 Boston [GMB 2:1331]

NEWHALL, Anthony & Mary WHITE; m 6 Nov 1632 Olney, Buckinghamshire/ Lynn [TAG 65:66]

NEWHALL, John² (bp 1631/2-1711/2+) & 1/wf Elizabeth LAIGHTON (-1677); m Lynn 3 Feb 1657/8 [AEBK 4:507]

NEWHALL, John² (bp 1631/2-1711/2+) & 2/wf Sarah FLANDERS (1654-1717/8); m Lynn 17 July 1679 [AEBK 4:507]

NEWHALL, John³ (1655/6-) & Esther BARTRAM (1658-1728); m Lynn 18 June 1677 [AEBK 4:513; REG 149:232]

NEWHALL, Joseph³ (1658-1704/5) & Susanna FARRAR (1659-1707/8+); m c1678 Lynn [AEBK 4:514]

NEWHALL, Nathaniel (1660/1-1695) & Elizabeth SYMONDS?; m2 John INGERSON; m by 1684/5 Lynn [AEBK 4:514]

NEWHALL, Samuel (1672/3-bef 1719/20) & Abigail LINDSEY (1677-); m int Lynn 31 Dec 1695 [AEBK 4:515]

NEWHALL, Samuel (1672/3-bef 1719/20) & Mary HALLEWELL; m int (probably did not marry) Lynn 25Aug 1695 [AEBK 4:515]

NEWHALL, Thomas¹ & _____ _____ [TAG 74:51]

NEWHALL, Thomas¹ (c1589-1674) & Mary WOODLAND (c1598-1665); m Clifton Reynes, Buckinghamshire. 12 July 1618 [AEBK 4:505; TAG 65:66 (not Woodard); TAG 73:120]

NEWHALL, Thomas[2] (bp 1629-1687) & Elizabeth POTTER (bp 1634-1686/7); m Lynn 29 Dec 1652 [AEBK 4:509]

NEWHALL, Thomas[3] (1653-1728) & Rebecca[3] GREEN (c1653-1725); m 9 Nov 1674 (deed) Malden [AEBK 4:309, 516]

NEWLAND, William & Catherine[2] MELLOWS (c1607-); m Boston, Lincolnshire 17 Jan 1627/8 [GMB 2:1249]

NEWMAN, Noah & Joanna[2] FLINT (1648[/9?]-); m Braintree 30 Dec 1669 [GM 2:536]

NEWTON, John (c1641-1723) & Elizabeth[2] LARKIN (1641-1719); m Charlestown 5 June 1666 [AEBK 3]

NEWTON, Moses (c1646-1736) & 1/wf Joanna[2] LARKIN (c1649-1713); m Charlestown 28 Oct 1668 [AEBK 3]

NEWTON, Richard[1] & Anna LOKER; m 1636 Bures St. Mary, Suffolk [TAG 55:87]

NEWTON, Roger & Mary[2] HOOKER (c1624-); m c1646 [GMB 2:984]

NICHOLS, ____ & Mercy[2] HOLBIDGE (c1638-); m by 1670 [GM 3:349]

NICHOLS, Caleb (c1623-1690/1) & Anne[2] WARD (-1718) [TAG 75:271]

NICHOLS, Francis[1] (1575-bef 1650/1) & 1/wf Francis WIMARKE (bp 1577-); m Sedgeborrow, Worcestershire 24 Jan 1599/1600 [TAG 75:269]

NICHOLS, Francis[1] (1575-bef 1650/1) & 2/wf Ann[2] WINES (c1632-1693/4+); m c1649 [TAG 75:269]

NICHOLS, Isaac (c1620-1694/5); m Margery ____ [TAG 75:270]

NICHOLS, John & Lydia[2] WILKINS (bp 1644-); m by 1663 Topsfield [GMB 3:1993]

NICHOLS, John & Susan[2] DAWES (bp 1652-); m c 1675 [GM 2:322]

NICHOLS, John[2] (bp 1601-1655) & 1/wf ____ ____ [TAG 75:269]

NICHOLS, John[2] (bp 1601-1655) & 2/wf Grace ____ [TAG 75:269]

NICHOLS, Thomas & Sarah[2] WHISTON; m Scituate 25 May 1663 [GMB 3:1975]

NICHOLS, Walter & Elizabeth CATLYN [RCA, DCD]

NILES, Joseph[2] (1640-) & Mary (FARR) MYCALL; m1 1657 James[1] MYCALL; Braintree [TAG 75:18, 149]

NILES, Nathaniel[3] (c1680-) & 1/wf & Jane LITTLEFIELD; m by 1700 [TAG 75:18]

NOBLE, John & Mary GOODMAN (1665-); by 1685 Hadley [GMB 2:789]

NORCROSS, Nathaniel & Mary[2] GILBERT (c1625-); m by 1654 [GM 3:59]

NORCUTT, William & Sarah[2] CHAPMAN (1645-); m by 1671 [GM 2:53]

NORMAN, John[2] (bp 1605/7-) & Arabella ____ ; m by May 1637 Salem [GMB 2:1335; TAG 77:103]

NORMAN, Richard & Florence ____ [LMM]

NORMAN, Richard (c1587-1653+) & Arabella ____ ; m by 1612 Salem/ Marblehead [GMSP]

NORMAN, Richard[1] (-1653+) & Florence ____ ; m by 1606/7 Charminster, Dorsetshire/Salem [TAG 77:103]

NORMAN, Richard[1] (c1587-1653+) & _____ _____; m c1612 Salem/Marblehead [GMB 2:1335]

NORMAN, Richard[2] (c1623-) & Margaret _____; m c1650 Salem [TAG 77:103; GMB 2:1335]

NORTH, Richard[1] (bef 1590-1667/8?) & 1/wf? Joan BARTRAM; m Olney, Bucks. 29 Nov 1610 Salisbury [TAG 68:70]

NORTH, Richard[1] (bef 1590-1667/8?) & 2/wf? Ursula _____ (-1670/1); m aft 1621 Salisbury [TAG 68:70]

NORTHEY, John & Sarah[2] EWELL (bp 1645-); m by 1675 Scituate [GM 2:478]

NORTHWAY, John & Susanna (BRIGGS) PALMER; m bef 1684 Portsmouth, RI [TAG 60:159]

NORTON, Freegrace[2] (c1635-) & Lydia SPENCER; m Ipswich 3 Aug 1658-62 [GMB 2:1337]

NORTON, George[1] (c1610-1659) & Mary _____; m2 Philip FOWLER; m by 1635 Salem [GMB 2:1337]

NORTON, George[2] (bp 1641-) & 1/wf Sarah HART; m Ipswich 7 Oct 1669 [GMB 2:1338]

NORTON, George[2] (bp 1641-) & 2/wf Mercy (BARBER) GILLETT, dau of Thomas; m1 John GILLETT; m Windsor 14 June 1683 [GMB 2:1338]

NORTON, John[2] (bp 1637-) & Mary[2] SHARP (bp 1640-); m Salem 3 Apr 1660 [GMB 2:1337, 3:1654]

NORTON, Joseph & Susanna[2] GATCHELL (c1642-); m Salisbury 10 Mar 1662[/3?] [GM 3:34]

NORTON, Nathaniel[2] (bp 1639-) & Mary MILLS, dau of Richard; m c1665 Salem [GMB 2:1338]

NORTON, Thomas (-1648) & Grace WELLS (bp 1608-1669+), m2 Francis BUSHNELL; m Shelton, Bedfordshire 5 May 1631 Guilford [DR]

NORTON, Walter[1] (c1580-1633) & 1/wf Jane (REEVE) REYNOLDS; m by 1605 [GMB 2:1340]

NORTON, Walter[1] (c1580-1633) & 2/wf Eleanor _____; m2 William HOOKE; m c1618 [GMB 2:1340]

NORTON, William[1] & Lucy DOWNING (c1625-1697/8); m c1649 Ipswich [TAG 74:174]

NOWELL, Increase[1] (c1603-1655) & Parnell (GRAY) PARKER (-1687); m Holy Trinity Minories, London 8 July 1628 [GMB 2:1345]

NOWELL, Samuel (1634-) & Mary (ALFORD)(BUTLER) USHER, dau of William; m1 Peter BUTLER; m2 Hezekiah USHER; m 1676+ [GMB 2:1345]

NOYES, Peter (bp 1590-1657) & Elizabeth _____ (-1635/6); m England c1621/2 Weyhill, Hampshire [REG 150:152, 152:283]

NUTT, Miles (bp 7 May 1598-1671) & 1/wf Sarah BRANSON (-bef 1659); m Barking, Suffolk 16 July 1623 Watertown/Charlestown [50 GMC; TAG 52:21]

NUTT, Miles (bp 7 May 1598-1671) & 2/wf Sybil (TICKNELL) BIBLE (bp 2 Aug 1607-1690); m1 John BIBLE, m3 John DOOLITTLE; m cJan 1658/9 Malden [50 GMC]

NUTTER, Anthony[2] (c1630-1685/6) & Sarah[2] LANGSTAFF (c1643-1704+); m c1662 Dover/Newington [TAG 72:276; GMB 2:1158]

NUTTER, Hatevil[1] (c1598+ -1674) & Anne _____ (-1674+); m by 1630 Dover [TAG 72:276]

NUTTING, John[2] & Mary[2] LAKIN; m 11 Dec 1674 [TAG 70:147]

NYSSEN, Theunis & Phebe[2] SALES (bp 1626-); m2 Jan Cornelison BUYS; m New Amsterdam 11 Feb 1640 [GMB 3:1617]

ODDYN, William & Margaret _____; m2 John[1] PORTER; m by 1610 [TAG 73:180]

ODLIN, Elisha[2] (1640-) & Abigail BRIGHT (1637-), dau of Henry; m c1666 [GMB 1:241, 2:1349]

ODLIN, John[1] (c1602-1685) & Margaret _____ (-1667+); m by 1635 Boston [GMB 2:1348]

ODLIN, John[2] (1641/2-) & Martha HOLMES, dau of Obadiah; m c1666 [GMB 2:1349]

ODLIN, Peter[2] (1646-) & Hannah SHARP, dau of Samuel; m by 1672 Boston [GMB 2:1349]

OGLETREE, _____ & Martha[2] COBBETT (1643-); m by 1697 [GM 2:117]

OLCUTT, John & Mary (BLACKLEACH) WELLES (c1665-1729); m1 Thomas WELLES; m bef 1696 Hartford [REG 148:30]

OLDHAM, John[1] (bp 1592-1636) & _____ (_____) BRIDGES; m1 _____ BRIDGES; m by 1623 Plymouth/Nantasket/Watertown [GMB 2:1351]

OLIVER, James[2] (c1619-) & Mary (DEXTER) FRIEND, dau of Thomas; m1 John FRIEND [GMB 2:1356, 1:543]

OLIVER, John[2] (c1613-) & Elizabeth[2] NEWGATE (bp 1617/8-), dau of John; m2 Edward JACKSON; m by 1638; m by 1638 Boston [GMB 2:1331, 1355]

OLIVER, Peter[2] (c1616-) & Sarah[2] NEWGATE (bp 1621-), dau of John; m by 1643 Boston [GMB 2:1331, 1355]

OLIVER, Samuel[2] (c1627-1652) & Lydia _____; m by 1647 Boston [GMB 2:1356; REG 157:36]

OLIVER, Thomas & Bridget (PLAYFER) WASSILBE (-1692); m1 Samuel WASSILBE; m3 Edward BISHOP; m 26 July 1666 Salem [TAG 57:129-38; TAG 64:207]

OLIVER, Thomas (c1575-) & 1/wf Agnes (_____) HENSON (-by 1617); m Lilford, Northamptonshire 24 Jan 1599/1600 [REG 157:34]

OLIVER, Thomas (c1575-) & 2/wf Elizabeth _____ (-1624); m by 26 Dec 1617 Thorpe Achurch, Northamptonshire [REG 157:34]

OLIVER, Thomas (c1575-) & 3/wf Anne _____ (-1635); m by 1632 [REG 157:35; GMB 2:1355]

OLIVER, Thomas[1] (c1580-1657/8) & 4/wf Anne (SQUIRE) PURCHASE (-1662); m1 Aquila PURCHASE; m by 1642 Boston [GMB 2:1355; REG 157:35]

OLMSTEAD, James[1] (bp 1580-1640) & Joyce CORNISH (-1621); m Great Leighs, Essex 26 Oct 1605 [GMB 2:1359]

OLMSTEAD, Nehemiah[2] (bp 1618-) & Elizabeth BURR, dau of Jehu; m c1655 [GMB 2:1359]

OLMSTEAD, Nicholas[2] (bp 1612/3-) & Sarah LOOMIS, dau of Joseph; m c1645 [GMB 2:1359]

OLNEY, Epenetus (bp 14 Feb 1633/4-1698) & Mary[2] WHIPPLE (bp 1648-1698+); m Providence 9 Mar 1665/6 [AEJA; GMB 3:1973]

OLNEY, Thomas (bp 6 Jan 1631/2-1722) & Elizabeth MARSH (c1640s-1675+); m Providence 3 July 1660 [AEJA]

OLNEY, Thomas (by 1605-1682) & Marie ASHTON (bp 25 Aug 1605-bet 1645-1659); m St Albans Abbey, Hertfordshire 16 Sept 1629 Providence [AEJA]

OLNEY, William (1663-) & Catharine SAYLES; m Providence 20 Dec 1692 [AEJA]

ONGE, Edmund (bp 1568-1630) & Frances READ (c1583-1638); m Brent Eleigh, Suffolk 8 Apr 1602, Watertown [GMB 2:1360]

ONGE, Jacob[2] (c1630-) & Sarah _____; m2 Abraham BYAM; m by 1671 [GMB 2:1361]

ORDWAY, Edward[2] (1653-1714) & 1/wf Mary[2] WOOD (1653-1704); m 12 Dec 1678 Newbury [ASBO, p.91]

ORDWAY, Hannaniah[2] (1665-1758) & 1/wf Abigail MERRILL (1665-1708); m bef 1690 Newbury [ASBO, p.89]

ORDWAY, James[1] (bp 1621-c1710) & 1/wf Ann[2] EMERY (bp 1632/3-1686/7); m Newbury 25 Nov 1648 [ASBO, p.77; GM 2:449]

ORDWAY, James[1] (bp 1621-c1710) & 2/wf Joanna (DAVIS) CORLISS (c1620s-1690s); m1 George CORLISS; m 4 Oct 1687 Newbury [ASBO, p.77]

ORDWAY, James[2] (1651-1721/2) & 2/wf Sarah CLARK (1675-); m 19 June 1696 Rowley [ASBO, p.87]

ORDWAY, Samuel[1] (-1692-4) & Sarah[2] ORDWAY (1655/6-1715+); m 25 Feb 16[78] Ipswich [ASBO, p.68]

ORTON, Ebenezer & Abigail[2] FURBER; m Charlestown 28 Oct 1687 [GM 2:611]

ORTON, Thomas & Mary EDDY (bp 1625/6-); by 27 Aug 1648 Charlestown [GMB 1:612]

OSBORN, John[2] (-1705/6) & 1/wf Abigail EGGLESTON (-1689); m by 1689 Windsor [REG 156:333]

OSBORN, John[2] (-1705/6) & 2/wf Martha[2] ELLSWORTH (-1718+); m by 1692/3 [REG 156:333]

OSGOOD, Christopher & Margery[2] FOWLER (bp 1615-); m2 Thomas ROWELL; m3 Thomas COLEMAN; m4 Thomas OSBORNE; m St Mary, Marlborough, Wiltshire 28 July 1633 [GM 2:562]

OSGOOD, William (c1648-1729) & Abigail AMBROSE (1654-1714/5); m Oct 1672 Salisbury [NHGR 9:55]

OTIS, John & Mary[2] JACOB (bp 1632-); m c1649 [GMB 2:1070]

OTIS, Stephen[3] & Hannah[3] ENSIGN (c1565-); m Scituate 16 Jan 1685[/6] [TAG 73:250]

OTLEY, Adam & _____ HUMPHREY, dau. of John Humphrey; by 1662 Salem [DR]

OWEN, Josias & Sarah _____ [GMB 2:966]

OWEN, William & Elizabeth[2] DAVIS (c1634-); m Braintree 29 Sept 1650 [GM 2:304]

PABODIE, William (1664-1744) & 1/wf Judith TILDEN (1669/70-1714); m 27 June 1693 Little Compton RI [TAG 53:246-8]

PADDOCK, Zachariah & Deborah[2] SEARS (c1639-1732); m c1661 Yarmouth [GMB 3:1643]

PADDON, _____ & Elizabeth[2] WRIGHT (c1644-1666+); m Twelve Mile Island c May-July 1666 [TAG 67:39+; Harris; GMB 3:2073]

PADDY, Thomas & Deborah[2] WAIT (bp 1643/4-) [GMB 3:1898]

PADDY, William & Alice[2] FREEMAN (bp 1619-); m 24 Nov 1639 [GM 2:579]

PAGE, Cornelius & Martha[2] CLOUGH (1654-); m Haverhill 13 Nov 1674 [GM 2:113]

PAGE, Edward & Elizabeth BUSHNELL (bp 1632-); m by 1653 Boston [GM 1:508]

PAGE, Isaac (-1680) & Damaris SHATTUCK; m Boston 30 Sept 1653 Salem/Albemarle Co., NC [DR]

PAGE, John (-1686+) & _____ _____ (-1686+); Saybrook [NGSQ 80:40, 42; Harris]

PAGE, John[1] (bp?1586-1676) & Phebe PAINE (bp 1594-1677), dau of William; m Lavenham, Suffolk 5 June 1621 Watertown [GMB 3:1366]

PAGE, John[2] (c1629-) & Faith DUNSTER; m Groton 12 May 1664 [GMB 3:1366]

PAGE, Joseph[2] & Martha[2] (DOW) HEATH (1649-1707+); m1 Joseph[2] HEATH [ASBO, p.314]

PAGE, Onesiphorus & Mary[2] HAWKSWORTH (1641-); m Salisbury 22 Nov 1664 or 1665 [GM 3:276]

PAGE, Robert[1] (1604-1679) & Lucy WARD (bp 1604/5-1665); m 8 Oct 1629 St Marys, So Walsham, Norfolk [REG 141:120]

PAGE, Samuel[2] (1633-) & Hannah _____; m by 1667 Watertown [GMB 3:1367]

PAGE, Thomas & Mary[3] HUSSEY (bp 1638-); m2 Henry GREEN; m Hampton 21 Jan 1664[/5] [GMB 2:1050]

PAGE, Thomas[1] & Elizabeth[1] FELKIN (bp 1606-); m St. Martin Ludgate, London 20 Aug 1628 Saco [TAG 71:219]

PAINE, John & Jemima[2] ALSOP (1670/1-); m New Haven 24 Mar 1691/2 [GM 1:50]

PAINE, Samuel & Mary[2] PENNIMAN (1653-); m Braintree 4 Apr 1678 [GMB 3:1429; TAG 71:18]

PAINE, Stephen[1] (c1602-7-1679) & 1/wf Neele ADCOCKE (bp 1602/3-1660); m bef 1629 Norfolk/Hingham [TAG 62:107; REG 143:299]

PAINE, Thomas & Hannah[2] BRACY (c1640-); m Boston 25 Aug 1659 [GM 1:374]

PAINE, Thomas & Mercy[2] CARR (1661-) [GM 2:15]

PAINE, Thomas (-by 1632) & Jane[1] GALLION (bp 1602-1666+); m2 Thomas[1] MAYHEW; Wantage, Berkshire/London [TAG 78:98]

PAINE, Thomas (c1656-1721) & 2/wf Hannah SHAW (c1661-1713); m Eastham 5 Aug 1678 [REG 151:417]

PALFREY, Peter[1] (c1605-1663) & 1/wf Edith _____; m by 1636 Salem [GMB 3:1371]

PALFREY, Peter[1] (c1605-1663) & 2/wf Elizabeth (_____) FAIRFIELD; m1 John FAIRFIELD; m by 1660 [GMB 3:1371]

PALFREY, Peter[1] (c1605-1663) & 3/wf Alice _____ (-1677[/8?]); m say 1662 Reading [GMB 3:1371]

PALGRAVE, John[2] (1633/4-) & Mary MAVERICK, dau of Samuel; m Boston 8 Feb 1655[/6] [GMB 3:1375]

PALGRAVE, Richard[1] (c1593-1651) & Anne _____ (-1668/9); m c1618 Roxbury [GMB 3:1375]

PALMER, Abraham[1] (c1605-by 1653) & Grace _____ (-by 1660); m by 1630 [GMB 3:1379]

PALMER, Benjamin[2] (1642-) & _____ _____; m Antigua by 8 May 1681 [GMB 3:1382]

PALMER, Christopher & Susanna[2] HILTON (c1633-); m Hampton 7 Nov 1650 [GMB 2:949]

PALMER, Ephraim & Sarah MESSENGER (c1648-); m c1668 [REG 152:363]

PALMER, George & Appiah MOWRY [GMB 2:1314]

PALMER, George (-1669) & Bethiah MOWRY (bp 17:4:1638-); m 30 Sept 1662 Providence [AEJA]

PALMER, Gershom[2] (c1644-) & 1/wf Ann DENISON; m c26 Nov 1667 [GMB 3:1382]

PALMER, Jonah[2] (c1621-) & 1/wf Elizabeth GRISELL; m Rehoboth 3 May 1655 [GMB 3:1382]

PALMER, Jonah[2] (c1621-) & 2/wf Abigail (CARPENTER) TITUS, dau of William; m1 John TITUS; m Rehoboth 9 Nov 1692 [GMB 3:1382]

PALMER, Moses[2] (bp 1640-) & Dorothy GILBERT; m c1672 [GMB 3:1382]

PALMER, Nehemiah[2] (bp 1637-) & Hannah STANTON; m Stonington 20 Nov 1662 [GMB 3:1382]

PALMER, Samuel & Elizabeth BOND, m2 Ephraim[1] CHILD [TAG 62:29]

PALMER, Walter[1] (c1589-1661) & 1/wf _____ _____ (-by 1633); m by 1614 [GMB 3:1381]

PALMER, Walter[1] (c1589-1661) & 2/wf Rebecca SHORT (-1671); m by 1633 Charlestown/Rehoboth/Stonington [GMB 3:1381, 3:1675]

PALMER, William & Susanna BRIGGS; m2 John NORTHWAY; Plymouth/Little Compton [TAG 60:160]

PALMER, William[1] (c1581-1637) & 1/wf Frances _____; m c1606 [GMB 3:1385]

PALMER, William[1] (c1581-1637) & 2/wf Mary _____; m2 Robert PADDOCK; m3 Thomas ROBERTS; m by 1537 Duxbury [GMB 3:1385]

PALMER, William[2] (1634-) & Susanna _____; m c1662 Duxbury [GMB 3:1385]

PALMER, William[2] (c1612-) & Elizabeth HODGEKINS; m Plymouth 27 Mar 1634 [GMB 3:1385]

PALMES, William & Ann[2] HUMPHREY (bp 1625-); m c1642 Fordington, Dorsetshire [GM 3:465]

PALSGRAVE, Richard & Anne _____ (-1669); m 1620s Charlestown [GMSP]

PARIS, John & Elizabeth[2] VINES; m by 1650 [GMB 3:1879]

PARISH, Thomas & Mary[2] DANFORTH; m by 1637 [GM 2:283]

PARKE, William[1] (bp 1607-1685) & Martha[2] HOLGRAVE (c1617-1708), dau of John; m by 1637 [GMB 2:968, 3:1389]

PARKER, _____ & Thankful WEEKES (1660-); perhaps [REG 156:151]

PARKER, Abraham (bp 1619-1685) & Rose WHITLOCK (-1691); m Woburn 18 Nov 1644 [REG 153:91]

PARKER, Benjamin[2] (1636-) & Sarah HARTWELL; m Billerica 18 Apr 1661 [GMB 3:1398]

PARKER, Ebenezer (1675/6-1749) & Rebecca NEWHALL (1675-1737); m Reading 22 May 1697 [AEBK 4:515]

PARKER, Elisha & Elizabeth[2] HINCKLEY (bp 1635-); m Barnstable 15 July 1657 [GM 3:334]

PARKER, Jacob[1] (bp 1626-1668/9) & Sarah _____ (c1627-); m2 John WAITE; Billerica [REG 153:92]

PARKER, James[1] (c1605-by 1652) & Mary[2] MAVERICK (bp 1609/10-), dau of John; m c1630 Portsmouth/Weymouth/Barbados [GMB 2:1242, 3:1392]

PARKER, James[1] (c1617-1700) & 2/wf Eunice (BROOKS) CARTER (1655-); m1 Samuel[2] CARTER; m3 John KENDALL; m bet 1693-97 Woburn/Chelmsford/Groton [REG 153:90; TEG 13:146]

PARKER, James[1] (c1617-1700+) & 1/wf Elizabeth LONG (bp1621-); m Woburn 23 May 1643 [TEG 13:146; REG 153:90]

PARKER, John & Elizabeth FITCH d/o James; m bef 26 Apr 1659 Boston [JEA]

PARKER, John (bp 1615-1667) & Mary (?POPE) (POULTER) AYLETT (c1605-1692/3); m1 John POULTER; m2 John AYLETT; m4 Thomas CHAMBERLAIN; m Great Burstead, Essex 23 June 1642 [REG 141:217, 153:89]

PARKER, John (c1665-1744) & 1/wf Sarah VERIN (c1665-1711); m bef 1695 Boston [REG 131:110]

PARKER, John[1] (bp 1603/4-1646) & Jane/Joan HELLYER (bp 1607/8-1656+); m2 Richard THAYER; m St. Mary Marlborough, Wiltshire [TAG 76:187]

PARKER, John[2] (bp 1629/30-1684/5) & Sarah CURTIS?; m by 1658 Roxbury [TAG 76:188]

PARKER, Joseph[1] (bp 1622-1690) & 1/wf Margaret PUTTOW; m Great Burstead, Essex 16 Apr 1650 [REG 153:90]

PARKER, Joseph[1] (bp 1622-1690) & 2/wf Hannah (JENKINS) BALKE (-1716); m1 John BALKE; m Chelmsford 19 Nov 1683 [REG 153:91]

PARKER, Nathaniel ~ Lois ROGERS; Scituate [Plymouth Court June 1688]

PARKER, Nicholas[1] (c1606-1659+) & Ann _____; m c1631 Roxbury/Boston [GMB 3:1395]

PARKER, Peter (c1668-1727) & Hannah _____ (-1760); m2 Joseph CARPENTER; Westerly, RI [Fiske 1:45]

PARKER, Peter[2] & Sarah[3] COOK (c1646-aft 1675); m c1664 Portsmouth RI/Shrewsbury, NJ [Fiske 1:45]

PARKER, Robert (c1603-1684/5-5) & Judith (_____) BUGBY (-1682); m1 Richard BUGBY; m by 6 Dec 1635 Cambridge [GMB 3:1398]

PARKER, Samuel & Sarah[2] HOLMAN, (bp 1632/3-); m Dedham 9 Apr 1657 [GM 3:390]

PARKER, Samuel[2] & Abigail[2] LAKIN (1666/7-1722+); m2 1721/2 Robert DIXON; Groton [TAG 70:148]

PARKER, William (-1684) & 1/wf Mary[2] RAWLINGS (c1619-1651); m Scituate Apr 1639 [AEBK 1:382; GMB 3:1559]

PARKER, William (-1684) & 2/wf Mary[2] TURNER (bp 1634/5-1703-6); m Scituate 13 Nov 1651 [AEBK 1:382; GMB 3:1845]

PARKHURST, George & 2/wf Sarah[2] GARFIELD (bp 1616-); m by 1649 (possibly) [GM 3:20, 22]

PARKHURST, George (c1588-1675) & 1/wf Phebe LEETE (bp 20 Dec 1585-bef 1643); m Ipswich, Suffolk/Eversden, Cambridgeshire/Watertown [50 GMC; TAG 52:113]

PARKHURST, George (c1588-1675) & 2/wf Susanna (_____) SIMSON; m c1644 Watertown [50 GMC]

PARKHURST, George[2] (bp 1621-1698/9) & 1/wf Sarah BROWNE (bp 1620-c1649), dau of Abraham (possibly); m Watertown 16 Dec 1643 [GM 3:22; AEBK 1:184]

PARKHURST, George[2] (bp 1621-1698/9) & 2/wf Mary VEASEY; m Watertown 24 Sept 1650 [AEBK 1:184]

PARKHURST, John & Abigail[2] GARFIELD (1646-); m by 1671 probably Watertown [GM 3:21; REG 156:332]

PARKMAN, Deliverance[2] (1651-) & 1/wf Sarah VEREN; m Salem 9 Dec 1673 [GMB 3:1401]

PARKMAN, Deliverance[2] (1651-) & 2/wf Mehitable WAITE; m aft 14 Jan 1681/2 [GMB 3:1401]

PARKMAN, Deliverance[2] (1651-   ) & 3/wf Margaret GARDNER; m Marblehead 3 June 1683 [GMB 3:1402]

PARKMAN, Deliverance[2] (1651-   ) & 4/wf Susanna (CLARK) GEDNEY; m aft 25 Mar 1689 [GMB 3:1402]

PARKMAN, Elias[1] (c1611-by 1662) & Bridget _____ (-1682+); m2 Sylvester EVELETH; m c1636 Dorchester/Boston [GMB 3:1401]

PARKMAN, Elias[2] (c1636-   ) & Sarah[2] TRASK, dau of William; m Salem 13 Oct 1656 [GMB 3:1401, 1835]

PARKMAN, Nathaniel[2] (1655-   ) & Hannah HETT, dau of Eliphalet; m by 1686 Boston [GMB 3:1402]

PARKS, Harry & Johan _____; m be? 3 June 1651 [Aspinwall, 385]

PARKS, Richard & Mary[2] CUTLER (1643-   ); m c1668 [GM 2:270]

PARMENTER, John & Elizabeth[2] CUTLER (1646-   ); m c1671 [GM 2:270]

PARMENTER, John (c1611-1666) & Amy _____; Sudbury [REG 147:382]

PARMENTER, John[1] (c1588-1671) & 1/wf Bridget READE (-1660); m Bures St Mary, Suffolk 27 Apr 1597 Sudbury [BB; REG 147:361]

PARMENTER, John[1] (c1588-1671) & 2/wf Annis (BAYFORD) (CHANDLER) DANE (bp 1603-   ); m1 William CHANDLER; m2 John DANE [REG 147:382]

PARROTT, John & Sarah CROCKETT; by 1675 [GMB 1:497]

PARSEVAL, James (1671-1728) & 1/wf Abigail ROBINSON (1674-   ); m 27 Feb 1696 or 18 Feb 1695/5 Falmouth delete Parseuah [TAG 60:160; MD 30:59]

PARSONS, Benjamin[1] (bp 1 May 1625-1689) & 1/wf Sarah VORE (c1635-1675/6); m Windsor 6 Oct 1653 Springfield [REG 148:222]

PARSONS, Benjamin[1] (bp 1 May 1625-1689) & 2/wf Sarah (HEALD) LEONARD (-1711); m1 John LEONARD, m3 Peter TILTON; m Springfield 21 Feb 1676/7 [REG 148:222]

PARSONS, Benjamin[2] (1658-1728) & Sarah KEEP (1666-1729); m Enfield 17 Jan 1683/4 [REG 148:223]

PARSONS, Ebenezer[2] (1668-1752) & Margaret MARSHFIELD (1670-1758); m Springfield 10 Apr 1690 [REG 148:224]

PARSONS, John (1650-1728) & Sarah CLARK (1658/9-1728); m Northampton 23 Dec 1675 [REG 148:219]

PARSONS, Jonathan (1657-1694) & Mary CLARK (1663/4-1712+); m Northampton 5 Apr 1682 Hatfield [REG 148:219]

PARSONS, Joseph[1] (bp 25 June 1620-1683) & Mary BLISS (c1628-1711/2); m Hartford 26 Nov 1646 [REG 148:216]

PARSONS, Joseph[2] (1675-1733) & Abigail PHELPS (1679-1736/7); m2 Pelatiah MORGAN; m Northampton 1697 [REG 148:225]

PARSONS, Joseph[2] (c1647-1729) & Elizabeth STRONG (1647/8-1736); m Northampton 17 Mar 1668/9 [REG 148:218-9]

PARSONS, Samuel (1666-1735/6) & Hannah HITCHCOCK (1668-1748); Springfield [REG 148:224]

PARSONS, Samuel[2] (1652/3-1734) & 1/wf Elizabeth COOKE (1653-1690); m c1677 Springfield/Durham, CT [REG 148:219]

PARSONS, Samuel[2] (1652/3-1734) & 2/wf Rhoda TAYLOR (1669-1759); m c1691 Northampton/Durham [REG 148:219]

PARSONS, Thomas & Lydia BROWN [GM 1:429]

PARSONS, Thomas[1] (bp 8 Feb 1608/9 [probably]-1661) & Lydia BROWN (c1616-1671+); m2 Eltweed POMEROY; m Windsor 28 June 1641 [REG 148:226]

PARSONS, Thomas[2] (1645-1680) & Sarah DARE (-1674); m Windsor 24 Dec 1668 [REG 148:235]

PARTRIDGE, George & Sarah[2] TRACY (c1623-); m Plymouth Nov 1638 [GMB 3:1833]

PARTRIDGE, John (-1706) & Magdalin BULLARD (bp 1635-1676); m Medfield 18 Dec 1655 [AEBK 1:209]

PARTRIDGE, William & Anne SPIGON?, m2 Anthony STANYON; m 5 Oct 1635? Olney, Buckinghamshire/Lynn [TAG 65:68]

PARTRIDGE, William[1] & Ann SPICER; m Olney, Bucks. 6 Oct 1636 [NHGR 9:180]

PASCO, Hugh (c1640-1706) & 1/wf Sarah WOOLAND (-1676); m Salem 20 Apr 1670 [REG 150:132]

PASCO, Hugh[1] & 2/wf Mary[2] PEASE (bp 1643 or 1658-1737), dau of Robert[1]; m Salem 16 Dec 1678 [REG 150:132; TAG 70:206]

PASCO, John & Elizabeth LOFT; m Boston 20 May 1691 [REG 150:137]

PASCO, John & Rachel _____ ; m by 1672 England [REG 150:137]

PATRICK, Daniel (c1605-killed 1643) & Aneken VAN BEYEREN (c1610-1656), dau of Albert; m2 Tobias FEAKE; m The Hague, Neth., 17 Mar 1630 [GMB 3:1405]

PATRICK, Daniel[2] (c1638-) & 1/wf Dorcas IRWIN; m int Flushing 6 Apr 1693 [GMB 3:1405]

PATRICK, Daniel[2] (c1638-) & 2/wf Dianah YATES; m Flushing 25 Apr 1696 [GMB 3:1405]

PATTEE, Peter[1] (c1644-1724) & 1/wf _____ _____ ; Haverhill [REG 146:316]

PATTEE, Peter[1] (c1644-1724) & 2/wf Sarah GILL (1654-1719); m Haverhill 8 Nov 1682 [REG 146:316]

PAUL, John (c1624-1692/3+) & Lydia[2] JENKINS (1640-1692/3+); m Malden 3 May 1657 [AEBK 4:421]

PAULING, Matthew (-1708) & Sarah (HUNTER) WALKER (1663-1704-8); m1 Samuel WALKER; m 15 June 1698 Boston [TAG 40:82]

PAYNE, John[3] (1640s-bef 1708) & Sarah (RISLEY) CROOKE (1640-1716); m1 Samuel CROOKE; m c1680 Southold, L.I. [TAG 70:162-70, 71:146; Harris]

PAYSON, Giles[1] (bp 14 May 1609-1688/9) & Elizabeth ALLOTT (bp 10 Dec 1609-1677); m Roxbury Apr 1637 [REG 148:57]

PEABODY, John (1654-1710) & Rachel NICHOLSON (1658-1711); m bef 1680 Newport [AEBK 1:371]

PEABODY, John[1] (c1611-1687) & 1/wf _____ _____ (not Dorothy); m say 1639 Newport [AEBK 1:365]

PEABODY, John[1] (c1611-1687) & 2/wf Mary (_____) ROGERS (-c1678); m1 James ROGERS; m after 1676 Newport [AEBK 1:365]

PEACH, William & Emme DEVEREUX (c1657-1737); [GMB 1:534]

PEAKE, Christopher[1] (c1612-1666) & Dorcas FRENCH (-1697); m2 Griffin CRAFTS; m Roxbury 3 Jan 1636[/7] [GMB 3:1414]

PEAKE, Jonathan[2] (1637-) & Sarah[2] FRENCH; m Roxbury 15 Aug 1660 [GMB 3:1414; GM 2:592]

PEARCE, Robert[1] & Abigail SYMONDS (c1622-1680) [TAG 74:116]

PEARSON, John[1] (c1616-1679) & possibly 2/wf Maudlin _____ (c1616-1690); Lynn [REG 155:354; TEG 13:200]

PEASE, Henry[1] (c1591-1648) & 1/wf Susan _____ (-1645); m c1616 [GMB 3:1416]

PEASE, Henry[1] (c1591-1648) & 2/wf Bridget _____ (-by 1683/4); m by 15 May 1647 Boston [GMB 3:1416]

PEASE, Henry[2] (c1618-) & Gartred _____; m c1643 [GMB 3:1416]

PEASE, John & Anne CUMMINGS (bp 1634/5-1689); m Enfield, CT [REG 145:240]

PEASE, John & Mary[2] GOODALE (c1630-); m c1654 Salem [GM 3:105]

PEASE, John[2] (c1616-) & 1/wf Ruth _____; m c1665 Boston [GMB 3:1416]

PEASE, John[2] (c1616-) & 2/wf Hannah _____; m by 1677 Boston [GMB 3:1416]

PECK, Benjamin[2] (bp 1647-1730) & Mary SPERRY (1650-); m 29 Mar 1670 New Haven [REG 121:83]

PECK, Eleazer (bp 1648/9-1736) & 1/wf Mary BUNNELL (1650-1724); m 31 Oct 1671 New Haven/Wallingford [REG 121:84]

PECK, Joseph & Elizabeth HUNTING (bp 1634-1667); m bef 1657 Dedham [NGSQ 78:94]

PECK, Joseph (bp 30 Apr 1587-1663) & 1/wf Rebecca CLARK (-1637); m Hingham, Norfolk 21 May 1617 [50 GMC]

PECK, Joseph (bp 30 Apr 1587-1663) & 2/wf _____ _____; m c1637 England/Rehoboth [50 GMC]

PECK, Joseph[2] (bp 1647-1720) & Sarah ALLING (bp 1649-1734); m 28 Nov 1672 New Haven [REG 121:83]

PECK, Robert (c1580-) & 1/wf Ann LAWRENCE (-1648); m 1605 [50 GMC]

PECK, Robert (c1580-) & 2/wf Martha (_____) BACON; m1 James BACON; m 1648+ Hingham, England/Burgate, Suffolk/Hingham [50 GMC]

PECK, Samuel (-1734/5) & Elizabeth LEE (1681-1731); m Lyme 28 Dec 1699 [AEJA]

PECK, Simon & Prudence[2] CLAPP (1637-); m Dorchester 13 Feb 1659/60 [GM 2:78]

PECKHAM, John & Dorothy[3] GOODENOW (-by 1723); m Sudbury 9 Dec 1687 [AEBK 3]

PECKHAM, John & Mary CLARKE (bp 17 Jul 1607-); m c1648 Newport [ITC]

PEDRICK, John (c1624-1686) & Miriam _____ (c1637-1717); m2 Richard GROSSE; m by 1655 Marblehead [TEG 14:143]

PEGGY, Edward ~ Ruth[2] HEMINGWAY (1638-); child b. 1674 [GMB 2:909]

PEIRCE, John & Ruth[2] BISHOP (1639-); m2 William FULLER; m c1684 [GM 1:304]

PEIRCE, William & Sarah KIND (1646-c1704/5); m2 William ROUSE; m 13 Jul 1666 Charlestown [REG 126:18]

PELL, Joseph[1] (bp 1598-by 1650) & 1/wf Elizabeth TAYLOR (bp 1600-by 1637); m Great Hale, Lincolnshire 5 Nov 1619 Lynn/Boston [AEBK 4:380]

PELL, Joseph[1] (bp 1598-by 1650) & 2/wf Johanna COCKETT; m Boston, Lincolnshire 5 Oct 1637 Lynn [AEBK 4:380]

PELL, Joseph[1] (bp 1598-by 1650) & 3/wf Elizabeth (WIGHT) HEATON; m1 Nathaniel HEATON; m c1648-50 Boston [AEBK 4:380, 579; GM 3:305]

PELTON, John & Susanna[2] WAY (bp 1621-) [GMB 3:1952]

PEMBERTON, James[1] (c1608-1661/2) & 1/wf Alice _____ (-1642+); m c1633 Charlestown [GMB 3:1420]

PEMBERTON, James[1] (c1608-1661/2) & 2/wf Margaret _____; m by 1653 [GMB 3:1420]

PEMBERTON, John[1] (c1608-1653-4) ~ Elizabeth MARSON (-1645[/6?]); ordered whipped 11 June 1633 [GMB 3:1422]

PEMBERTON, John[2] (bp 1642-) & Deborah BLAKE; m c1668 [GMB 3:1420]

PENDLETON, James & 1/wf Mary PALMER (-1655); m Sudbury 22 Oct 1647 [AEBK 3]

PENDLETON, James & 2/wf Hannah[2] GOODENOW (1639-1725+); m Sudbury 29 Apr 1656 [AEBK 3]

PENN, James[1] (c1601-1671) & Katherine _____ (-1679+); m by 1630 Boston [GMB 3:1425]

PENNELL, John & Sarah PUDDINGTON; m aft 5 July 1658 [GM 1:493]

PENNIMAN, James[1] (bp 1599-164) & Lydia ELIOT (bp 1610-bef 1676), dau of Bennet; m2 1665 Thomas WIGHT; m High Laver, Essex 26 July 1631 Braintree [TAG 71:14; GMB 3:1429]

PENNIMAN, James[2] (bp 1633-1679) & Mary CROSS; m Boston 10 May 1659 [TAG 71:16; GMB 3:1429]

PENNIMAN, John[2] (bp 1636[/7]-) & Hannah[2] BILLINGS; m Braintree 24 Feb 1664/5 [TAG 71:17; GMB 3:1429]

PENNIMAN, Joseph[2] (1639-1705) & 1/wf Waiting[2] ROBINSON; m Braintree 25 Sept 1666 [TAG 71:17; GMB 3:1429]

PENNIMAN, Joseph[2] (1639-1705) & 2/wf Sarah[2] (BASS) STONE; m1 John STONE; m Braintree 10 May 1693 [TAG 71:17; GMB 3:1429]

PENNIMAN, Samuel[2] (1645-1704/5) & Elizabeth[2] PARMENTER; m Dorchester 6 Jan 1673/4 [TAG 71:17; GMB 3:1429]

PENNOYER, Samuel & Rose HOBSON (c1616-1698); m2 Samuel DESBOROW [NGSQ 60:248]

PENTICOAST, John[1] & 1/wf Joane (MILES) SMYTH; m1 Richard SMYTH; m 27 Nov 1632 Cranbrook, Kent/Charlestown [TAG 62:118]

PEPPER, Robert (c1620-1684) & Elizabeth JOHNSON (bp 1619-1683/4); m Roxbury 14 Mar 1642/3 [REG 146:275; GMB 2:1108]

PERHAM, John[1] (1632-1720/1) & Lydia[2] SHEPLEY (c1641-1710); m Chelmsford 15 Dec 1664 [AEBK 4:533]

PERHAM, John[2] (1667/8-1743) & Lydia FLETCHER (1669-1742); m Chelmsford 27 Dec 1692 [AEBK 4:539]

PERHAM, Joseph (1669-1724/5+) & Dorothy _____ ; m by 1691 Chelmsford [AEBK 4:536]

PERKINS, Jacob[2] (bp 1624-) & 1/wf Elizabeth _____ ; m by 1649 [GMB 3:1432]

PERKINS, Jacob[2] (bp 1624-) & 2/wf Damaris (_____) ROBINSON; m1 Nathaniel ROBINSON; m aft 12 Feb 1685 [GMB 3:1432]

PERKINS, John (bp 1609-) & Elizabeth _____ ; m c1636 Ipswich [GMB 3:1432]

PERKINS, John[1] (bp 1583-1654) & Judith GATER (bp 1588/9-), dau of Michael; m Hillmorton, Warwickshire 3 Oct 1608 [GMB 3:1432]

PERKINS, John[2] & Elizabeth ?WESTLY; m c1635 Ipswich? [AMacE]

PERKINS, John[2] (1655-) & Anna HUTCHINSON; m Lynn 29 Aug 1695 [GMB 3:1436]

PERKINS, Thomas[2] (bp 1622-) & Phebe GOULD, dau of Zacheus; m c1644 [GMB 3:1432]

PERKINS, Timothy[2] (1658-) & Edna HAZEN; m Topsfield 2 Aug 1686 [GMB 3:1436]

PERKINS, Tobijah (1646-) & Sarah DENISON; m Topsfield 4 Nov 1680 [GMB 3:1436]

PERKINS, William[1] (1607-1682) & Elizabeth WOOTON; m Roxbury 30 Aug 1636 [GMB 3:1435]

PERKINS, William[2] (1640[/1]-) & Elizabeth CLARKE, dau of Daniel; m Topsfield 24 Oct 1669 [GMB 3:1435]

PERLEY, John & Mary[2] HOWLETT (c1645-); m c1665 [GMB 2:1027]

PERRY, Arthur & Elizabeth[2] CROW; m2 John GILLETT; m3 William WARDWELL; m c1637 Boston [GM 2:247]

PERRY, Edward & Mary[2] FREEMAN; m by 1653 [GM 2:580]

PERRY, Francis[1] (c1608-1659) & 1/wf _____ _____ ; m by 1635 [GMB 3:1439]

PERRY, Francis[1] (c1608-1659) & 2/wf Jane (CASH) VERIN (-1659); m1 Robert VERIN; m by 1638 Salem/Barbados [GMB 3:1439]

PERRY, Henry[2] & 1/wf Susanna _____ (-by 1700); m c1690 [TAG 70:46]

PERRY, Henry[2] & 2/wf Mary (_____) PRATT; m1? Joshua PRATT; m Plymouth 26 Nov 1700 [TAG 70:46]

PERRY, John & 1/wf Phebe CRAMPHORNE (bp c1588-1627); m Sawbridgeworth, Hertfordshire 10 Nov 1614 [AEBK 1:195]

PERRY, John[1] (c1612-1642) & Elizabeth _____; m2 John HANSETT; m by 1637 Roxbury [GMB 3:1442]

PERRY, John[2] (1639-) & Bethia MORSE, dau of Daniel; m c1667 Medfield [GMB 3:1443]

PERRY, John[2] (1657-) & Elizabeth ?WILLIAMSON; dau. of Timothy[1]; m bef 1684 Sandwich [REG 126:279]

PERRY, Samuel[2] (1640-1706) & Sarah[2] STEDMAN (c1648-1727); m Roxbury 28 Jan 1668/9 [TAG 69:159; GMB 3:1443]

PERRY, Seth & Mehitable ELIOT (1645-1662/3); by 14 Oct 1662 Boston [GMB 1:629]

PERRY, Seth[2] & 2/wf Dorothy POWELL (1643-); m bef 1665 Dedham [REG 131:174]

PERRY, Thomas[2] (c1645-1719) & Susanna[2] WHISTON (-1715); m Scituate 2 May 1671 [TAG 70:43; GMB 3:1975]

PERRY, Thomas[3] (1671/2-1715) & Ruth RIPLEY (-1719); m Boston 29 Jan 1699/1700 Rehoboth [TAG 70:44]

PERRY, William (-1695) & Susan BARSTOW (1618-); m c1641 Watertown/Scituate [RCA]

PERRY, William[1] & Susanna[2] CARVER; Scituate [TAG 70:42]

PERRY, William[2] (c1655-1716) & Elizabeth[2] LOBDELL; m2 Benjamin PIERCE; m Scituate 31 May 1681 [TAG 70:44-5]

PESTER, William & Dorothy STRATTON (living 1641); Salem [REG 156:43]

PETERSON, John & Mary[2] SOULE (c1642-); m by 1667 [GMB 3:1707]

PETTINGILL, Nathaniel[2] (1654-c1717/8) & 1/wf Mary _____ (-bef 1703); m bef 1694 Newbury [Abel Lunt, p.53]

PETTINGILL, Richard & Joan[2] INGERSOLL (bp 1624[/5?]-); m by 1644 [GMB 2:1061]

PETTINGILL, Samuel[2] (1644/5-1711) & Sarah POORE (-1716+); m 13 Feb 1673/4 Newbury [Abel Lunt, p.53]

PEVERLY, Thomas & Jane[2] WALFORD; m2 Richard GOSS; m c1644 [GMB 3:1903]

PHELPS, Abraham & Mary[2] PINNEY (bp 1644-); m Windsor 6 July 1663 [GMB 3:1480]

PHELPS, Christopher & Experience[2] SHARP (bp 1641-); m Salem 9 July 1658 [GMB 3:1654]

PHELPS, George & Philura[2] RANDALL (c1617-); m c1638 [GMB 3:1549]

PHELPS, Henry (-1670s) & 2/wf Hannah (BASKEL) PHELPS (bef 1630-1695+); m1 Nicholas PHELPS; m c1664 Salem [NGSQ 75:296]

PHELPS, John & Sarah[2] BUCKLAND (1648[/9]-); m by 1675 Windsor [GM 1:452]

PHELPS, Joseph[2] (bp 1628-) & 1/wf Hannah NEWTON, dau of Anthony; m Windsor 20 Sept 1660 [GMB 3:1446; TAG 65:13-16]

PHELPS, Joseph[2] (bp 1628-) & 2/wf Mary (_____) SALMON; m Northampton 19 Dec 1676 [GMB 3:1446]

PHELPS, Nathaniel[2] (bp 1624[/5]-) & Elizabeth (_____) COPLEY; m Windsor 17 Sept 1650 [GMB 3:1446]

PHELPS, Nicholas (-c1664) & Hannah BASKEL (bef 1630-1695+); m Salem c1650 [NGSQ 75:296]

PHELPS, Samuel[2] (bp 1621-) & Sarah GRISWOLD; m Windsor 10 Nov 1650 [GMB 3:1445]

PHELPS, Timothy[2] (1639-) & Mary GRISWOLD; m Windsor 19 Mar 1661[/2?] [GMB 3:1446]

PHELPS, William[1] (c1593-1672) & 1/wf Mary _____ (-1626); m by 1618 Crewkerne, Somersetshire/Windsor [GMB 3:1445; TAG 65:163]

PHELPS, William[1] (c1593-1672) & 2/wf Anne DOVER (-1689); m Crewkerne, Somersetshire 14 Nov 1626 [GMB 3:1445; TAG 65:163; 75:26]

PHELPS, William[2] (bp 1618-) & 1/wf Isabel WILSON; m Windsor 4 June 1645 [GMB 3:1445]

PHELPS, William[2] (bp 1618-) & 2/wf Sarah[2] PINNEY (1648-); m Windsor 20 Dec 1676 [GMB 3:1445, 1480]

PHETTIPLACE, Philip (bp 1621-1687+) & _____; m bef 1682, RI [REG 123:252]

PHILBRICK, James[3] (c1679-bef 1707/8) & Sarah SILVER (1682-1770); m2 Benjamin[3] EMERSON; m c1700 Hampton [TAG 40:20]

PHILBRICK, John & Anne[2] KNOPP (bp 1618-); m by 1650 Hampton [GMB 2:1145]

PHILBRICK, Thomas[1] (bp 1584-1667) & Elizabeth KNAPP (bp 1593-1663/4); m Bures St Mary, Suffolk 4 June 1615 Hampton [REG 147:327]

PHILLIPS, George[1] (c1592-1678) & Sarah _____ (-1662); Windsor [GMB 3:1451]

PHILLIPS, George[1] (c1593-1644) & 1/wf _____ SERGEANT (-1630/1), dau of Richard; m c1626 [GMB 3:1448]

PHILLIPS, George[1] (c1593-1644) & 2/wf Elizabeth (_____) WELDEN (-1681); m1 Robert WELDEN; Watertown [GMB 3:1448]

PHILLIPS, Henry & Mary[2] DWIGHT (1635-); m aft 24 June 1653 [GM 2:376]

PHILLIPS, John[1] (c1605-1682) & 1/wf Joanna _____ (-1675); m by 1633 Boston [GMB 3:1455]

PHILLIPS, John[1] (c1605-1682) & 2/wf Sarah (_____) MAYNARD; m by 1676 Boston [GMB 3:1455]

PHILLIPS, Jonathan[2] (1633[/4]-) & Sarah HOLLAND; m Watertown 26 Jan 1680/1 [GMB 3:1449]

PHILLIPS, Samuel[2] (c1626-) & Sarah APPLETON, dau of Samuel; m Oct 1651 [GMB 3:1448]

PHILLIPS, Theophilus² (1636-   ) & 1/wf Bethiah KEEDELL; m Watertown 3 Nov 1666 [GMB 3:1449]

PHILLIPS, Theophilus² (1636-   ) & 2/wf Mary BENNETT; m Watertown 21 Nov 1677 [GMB 3:1449]

PHILLIPS, Thomas & Mary (___) JEFFERSON; m Newport 26 Feb 1684 [NYGBR 7:40]

PHILLIPS, Zorobabel² (1632-   ) & 1/wf Ann (COOPER) WHITE, dau of John; m1 John WHITE; m aft 1662 [GMB 3:1449]

PHILLIPS, Zorobabel² (1632-   ) & 2/wf Martha (TAPPING) HERRICK, dau of Thomas; m1 James HERRICK; m c1686-7 [GMB 3:1449]

PHIPPEN, Gamaliel & Sarah² PURCHASE (bp 1626-   ); m c1649 [GMB 3:1528]

PHIPPS, Solomon (c1619-1671) & Elizabeth WOOD (bp 1620-1688); m bef 15 May 1642 Charlestown [TG 9:91]

PICKERAM, John¹ (c1580-1630) & Esther _____ (-1646+); m c1610 Watertown [GMB 3:1457]

PICKERING, _____ & _____ CHAMBERS, dau. of Rev. Thomas Chambers; m bef 1640 [may not have come] [RCA]

PICKERING, John¹ (c1609-1668/9) & _____ _____ (-c1656); m c1643 [GMB 3:1460]

PICKERING, John² (c1645-   ) & Mary STANYAN, dau of Anthony; m 10 Jan 1665/6 [GMB 3:1460]

PICKERING, Thomas² (c1656-   ) & Mary GEE, dau of John; m c1686 [GMB 3:1460]

PICKMAN, Samuel & Lydia² PALFREY (c1632-   ); m by 1659 [GMB 3:1371]

PICKWORTH, Benjamin (bp 1648-   ) & Elizabeth _____; perhaps out of New England [GMB 3:1464]

PICKWORTH, John¹ (c1606-1663) & Anne _____ (-1682-3); m by 6 Feb 1631/2 Salem [GMB 3:1463]

PICKWORTH, Samuel² (c1640-   ) & Sarah MARSTON; m Salem 3 Nov 1667 [GMB 3:1463]

PIDGE, John² (c1640-   ) & Mary FARRINGTON; m Dedham 27 Apr 1667 [GMB 3:1466]

PIDGE, Thomas¹ (c1594-1643) & Mary SOTHY; m2 Michael METCALF; m Saffron Walden, Essex 1 Nov 1619 [GMB 3:1465]

PIERCE, Abraham¹ (c1605-by 1673) & Rebecca _____; m by 1638 Plymouth/Duxbury [GMB 3:1467]

PIERCE, Abraham² (1638[/9?]-   ) & 1/wf Hannah BAKER, dau of Francis; m c1665 Barnstable [GMB 3:1468]

PIERCE, Abraham² (1638[/9?]-   ) & 2/wf Hannah [perhaps GLASS]; m Scituate 29 Oct 1695 [GMB 3:1468]

PIERCE, John¹ (c1606-1661) & 1/wf Parnell _____ (-1637 or 39); m by 1631 [GMB 3:1471]

PIERCE, John¹ (c1606-1661) & 2/wf Mary _____ (-1647); m by 1638 Dorchester [GMB 3:1471]

PIERCE, John[1] (c1606-1661) & 3/wf Rebecca (_____) WHEELER; m1 Thomas WHEELER; m Boston 10 Aug 1654 [GMB 3:1471]

PIERCE, Michael & Persis EAMES (bp 1621-); m by 1645 Hingham [GM 2:389]

PIERCE, Nehemiah (1641-) & 1/wf Phebe BLANTIN, dau of William; m by 1663 Boston [GMB 3 1471]

PIERCE, Nehemiah (1641-) & 2/wf Anne (ADDINGTON) MOSELEY, dau of Isaac; m1 Samuel MOSELEY/MAUDSLEY; m aft 18 Sept 1684 [GMB 3:1472]

PIERCE, Robert[1] (-1664/5) & Ann[2] GREENWAY (c1601-1695?); m c1635 Dorchester [TAG 74:195; GMB 2:816]

PIERCE, Samuel & Mary[2] GIDDINGS (c1652-); m2 1694 William HUBBARD; m by 1681 [GM 3:55]

PIERCE, Samuel[2] (c1650-) & Mary _____; m by 1673 Boston [GMB 3:1472]

PIERCE, Thomas & Elizabeth COLE (c1619-); by 17 June 1639 Charlestown [GMB 1:429]

PIERCE, William[1] (c1591-1641) & Bridget _____ (1647[/8]+); m c1624 Boston [GMB 3:1474]

PIERCE, William[2] (c1624-) & Hester _____ (possibly WEBB); m c1656 [GMB 3:1474]

PIERPONT, John (c1618-1682) & Thankful[2] STOW (bp 1629-1705); m 1646-48 Roxbury [AEBK 3]

PIGGOT, Christopher & _____ _____; m bef 27 Apr 1655 Boston [RCA]

PIKE, John[1] & Dorothy DAY; m Whiteparish, Wiltshire 17 Jan 1612/3 [TAG 73:256]

PIKE, John[2] (bp 1613-1689/90) & 1/wf Mary TURVELL (bp 1615/16-1680-5); m bef 1638 Hampshire/Wiltshire/Woodbridge [REG 121:162]

PIKE, John[2] (bp 1613-1689/90) & 2/wf Elizabeth (BLOSSOM) FITZ-RANDOLPH (-1690+); m 30 June 1685 Piscataway, NJ [REG 121:162]

PIKE, Moses[3] (1658-1741/2) & Susanna WORCESTER (1671-1710+); m bef 1688 Salisbury [REG 121:167]

PIKE, Robert & Grace _____; m Ottery St Mary, Devonshire bef 1642 [Loyal Dissenter, pp. 37-44]

PIKE, Thomas[3] (1657-1730) & 3/wf Mary (HUNT) PHILLIPS (-1730+); m1 Ephraim PHILLIPS; m 30 June 1699 Woodbridge, NJ [REG 121:165]

PINCIN, Ebenezer ~ Martha WRIGHT alias STETSON; Scituate [Plymouth Court June 1700]

PINDER, Henry (-1661) & 1/wf Mary ROGERS (1582-1647-55); m 22 May 1614 Church of St. Mary the Great, Cambridge, Eng. 22 May 1614 Ipswich [TAG 52:175; 50 GMC]

PINDER, Henry (c1580-1661) & 2/wf Elizabeth (_____) ANDREWS (c1590-1671); m bef 1655 Ipswich [50 GMC]

PINE, Charles & Grace BALSTER; m c1698 Honiton, Devonshire/ Scarborough [JP]

PINE, James & _____[2] ARMITAGE; m c1650 [GM 1:79]

PINNEY, Humphrey[1] (bp 1605-1683) & Mary[2] HULL (bp 1618-), dau of George; m by 1636 Dorchester [GMB 2:1042, 3:1480]

PINNEY, Isaac[2] (1663[/4?]-) & Sarah CLARK, dau of Daniel; m by 1686 Windsor [GMB 3:1480]

PINNEY, Nathaniel[2] (1641-) & Sarah (GRISWOLD) PHELPS, dau of Edward; m1 Samuel PHELPS; m Windsor 21 July 1670 [GMB 3:1480]

PINNEY, Samuel[2] (c1636-) & Joyce BISSELL; m Windsor 17 Nov 1665 [GMB 3:1480]

PINSON, Thomas[1] & Joan (____) STANLEY; m1 Daniel[1] STANLEY; m 4 Nov 1639 Scituate [TAG 50:97]

PINSON, Thomas[2] (1640-1714) & Elizabeth WHITE (1642-1714+) (only wife); m 18 Sep 1662 Scituate [TAG 50:98]

PINSON, Thomas[3] (1665-1733) & Sarah (STOCKBRIDGE) TURNER (1665-); w? of Israel; m 23 Feb 1691/2 or 26 Dec 1693 Scituate [TAG 50:99; 38:186]

PITCHER, John[2] (1650-) & 1/wf Hannah ____ (-c1690); m bef 1683 Boston [TAG 59:204]

PITCHER, John[2] (1650-) & 2/wf Mary ____ (-1703); m bef 1695 Boston [TAG 59:205]

PLAISTED, James & Lydia[2] HITCHCOCK (1658-); m c1680 [GM 3:341]

PLAISTED, Roger & Hannah[2] FURBER; m 1671 [GM 2:610]

PLUMB, John (c1634-) & Elizabeth GREEN (1640-); m bef 1666 Hartford [TAG 46:10]

PLUMB, John[1] (1594-1648) & Dorothy ____; Wethersfield/Blanford [TAG 70:65, 152]

PLUMMER, Francis[1] (c1594-1672/3) & 1/wf Ruth ____ (-1647); m c1619 Newbury [GMB 3:1484]

PLUMMER, Francis[1] (c1594-1672/3) & 2/wf Ann (____) PALMER (-1665); m1 William PALMER; m Newbury 31 Mar 1648 [GMB 3:1484]

PLUMMER, Francis[1] (c1594-1672/3) & 3/wf Beatrice (BURT) CANTLEBURY; m1 William CANTLEBURY; m3 Edward BERRY; m Newbury 29 Nov 1665 [GMB 3:1484]

PLUMMER, Joseph[2] (c1627-) & Sarah[2] CHENEY (bp 1635-), dau of John; m Newbury 23 Dec 1652 [GMB 3:1484; TAG 76:247]

PLUMMER, Samuel[2] (c1619-) & Mary BITFIELD; m c1646 [GMB 3:1484]

POLLEY, John & Susannah[2] BACON; m c1647 Roxbury [GM 1:128]

POMEROY, Caleb[2] (bp 1641[/2]-) & Hepzibah BAKER; m Windsor 8 Mar 1664 [GMB 3:1488]

POMEROY, Eltweed[1] (bp 1585-1673) & 1/wf Johana KEECH, dau of John (bp 1586-1620); m Beaminster, Dorsetshire 4 May 1617 [GMB 3:1487]

POMEROY, Eltweed[1] (bp 1585-1673) & 2/wf Margery ROCKET (-1655); m Crewkerne, Somersetshire 7 May 1629 [GMB 3:1487]

POMEROY, Eltweed[1] (bp 1585-1673) & 3/wf Lydia (BROWN) PARSONS (-1671+); m1 Thomas PARSONS; m Windsor 30 Nov 1664 [GMB 3:1488; GM 1:429]

POMEROY, Joseph[2] (bp 1652-) & Hannah LYMAN; m Westfield 20 Jun 1677 [GMB 3:1489]

POMEROY, Joshua[2] (bp 1646-) & 1/wf Elizabeth LYMAN, dau of Richard; m Northampton 22 Aug 1672 [GMB 3:1488]

POMEROY, Joshua[2] (bp 1646-) & 2/wf Abigail COOK; m Northampton 9 Jan 1678 [GMB 3:1488]

POMEROY, Medad[2] (bp 1638-) & 1/wf Experience WOODWARD; m Northampton 21 Nov 1661 [GMB 3:1488]

POMEROY, Medad[2] (bp 1638-) & 2/wf Abigail (STRONG) CHAUNCY; m Northampton 14 Sept 1686 [GMB 3:1488]

POND, Ephraim (1656-1704) & Deborah[2] HAWES (1666-1704+); m2 Thomas BACON; m Wrentham 6 Jan 1685[/6?] [AEBK 3]

POND, William (c1636-) & Mary DYER; by 1657 Dorchester [GMB 1:605]

PONDER, John & Temperance[2] BUCKLAND (1642-); m Hartford 26 June 1668 [GM 1:452]

PONTUS, William[1] (c1585-1652/3) & Wybra HANSEN (-1633+); m Leiden 4 Dec 1610 Plymouth [GMB 3:1492]

POOLE, John[1] (c1609-1667) & Margaret _____ (-1662); m c1631 [GMB 3:1495]

POOLE, Jonathan[2] (c1631-) & Judith _____ [not JACOBS]; m2 William HASEY; m3 Robert GOULD; m by 1656 [GMB 3:1495]

POOR, Daniel & Mary[2] FARNHAM (bp 1628-); m Boston 20 Oct 1650 St. Nicholas, Kent [GM 2:493]

POOR, Walter (c1645-) & Elizabeth LANE (1646-1672+); m by 1672 [REG 156:148]

POPE, Isaac[2] (c1664-) & Alice FREEMAN (1658-1755), dau of Edmund; m by 1687 Dartmouth [GMB 3:1498; TAG 40:110]

POPE, John & Jane CLAP; m c1630 Venn Ottery, Devonshire [JP]

POPE, Seth[2] (1648/9-) & 1/wf Deborah PERRY; m c1675 Dartmouth [GMB 3:1498]

POPE, Seth[2] (1648/9-) & 2/wf Rebecca _____ (-1741); Dartmouth [GMB 3:1498]

POPE, Thomas[1] (c1612-1683) & 1/wf Anne FALLOWELL (-by 1646), dau of Gabriel; m Plymouth 28 July 1637 [GMB 3:1498]

POPE, Thomas[1] (c1612-1683) & 2/wf Sarah[2] JENNY (-by 1683), dau of John; m Plymouth 29 May 1646 [GMB 2:1093, 3:1498]

POPE, Walter[1] (c1609-by 1640) & Eleanor _____; m2 Richard MILLER; m3 Henry HERBERT/HARBERD; m c1640 Charlestown [GMB 3:1499]

PORTER, Edward[1] (bp 5 Mar 1608/9-1677) & 1/wf Anne ELLIOTT (-1674+); m Chelmsford, Essex 1 Oct 1632 [REG 148:51]

PORTER, Edward[1] (bp 5 Mar 1608/9-1677) & 2/wf Rhoda (_____) (GORE) REMINGTON (c1610-1693); m1 John GORE, m2 John REMINGTON, m4 Joshua TIDD; Roxbury [REG 148:51-2]

PORTER, Israel & Elizabeth[2] HATHORNE (1649-); m Salem 20 Nov 1672 [GMB 2:885]

PORTER, John[1] (c1608-aft 1674) & 1/wf Margaret (____) ODDYN; m c1630 Portsmouth [GMB 3:1503; TAG 73:180]

PORTER, John[1] (c1608-aft 1674) & 2/wf Horrod (LONG) (HICKS) GARDINER; m1 John HICKS; m2 George GARDINER; m bet 1665-1671 Portsmouth [GMB 3:1503]

PORTER, John[3] (1667-1723) & 1/wf Mercy CARVER (1672/3-1708/9); m c1693 Weymouth [REG 119:94]

PORTER, Joseph & Anna[2] HATHORNE (1643-); m Salem 27 Jan 1664/5 [GMB 2:885]

PORTER, Samuel & Hannah DODGE (bp 1642-); m2 Thomas WOODBURY; m by 1658/9 Salem [GMB 1:566]

PORTER, Thomas & Sarah[2] HART (c1624-); m Hartford 20 Nov 1644 [GMB 2:871]

POST, Abraham[1] (c1640-) & 1/wf Mary JORDAN (c1640-1683/4); m c1663 Saybrook [REG 146:213]

POST, Abraham[2] (c1640-) & 2/wf Lydia (BUCKLAND) (BROWN)(LORD) DUNK (-by 1700); m1 John BROWN; m2 William LORD; m3 Thomas DUNK; Saybrook [REG 146:213]

POST, Abraham[3] (1669-1747/8) & Elizabeth STEVENS (-1755); m Saybrook 7 Apr 1692 [REG 146:221]

POST, Daniel[3] (1673-1742+) & Mary RUTTY (1679-by 1754); m Saybrook 29 Aug 1699 [REG 146:225]

POST, Stephen[1] (-1659) & Elinor PANTON (-1670); Otham, Kent/Saybrook, CT [REG 146:212-213]

POST, Stephen[3] (1664-1753) & Hannah HOSMER (bp 1670-1750/1); m Saybrook 14 June 1692 [REG 146:217]

POST, Thomas & Rebecca BRUEN (-1721); m 1663 Norwich [REG 156:152]

POTTER, Ichabod & Martha[2] HAZARD (c1642-); m2 Benjamin MOWRY; m c1662 [GM 3:297]

POTTER, Nicholas & Eme CARTER; m Newport-Pagnall, Buckinghamshire 22 Apr 1628 Lynn [parish register]

POTTER, Robert & Ruth[2] DRIVER; m Lynn 25 Jan 1659/60 [GM 2:366]

POULTER, John[1] (c1596-1638) & Mary ?POPE (c1596-1692/3); m2 John AYLETT; m3 John PARKER; m4 Thomas CHAMBERLAIN; m c1630 Rayleigh, Essex/Chelmsford [REG 141:217]

POWELL, Arthur & Sarah (SCANT) MEKUSETT, m1 Mordecai MEKUSETT; m Braintree 17 Jan 1693 [BTR, 720]

POWELL, Michael[1] (c1605-bef 1672/3) & Abigail BEDLE (bp 1608-bef 1677); m c1630 Eng/Dedham [REG 131:173]

POWELL, Thomas (1641-1721/2) & _____[2] WOOD (c1644-c1685-8); m c1665 Huntington/Bethpage, L.I. [NYGBR 123:144]

POWERS, Isaac (c1665-1731+) & Mary (POULTER) WINSHIP (-1745); m Concord 14 Apr 1701 [AEBK 4:8]

POWERS, Thomas (c1667-1719+) & 1/wf Elizabeth GOULD (1664/5-1698); m say 1692 Concord/Littleton [AEBK 4:9]

POWERS, Walter[1] (c1635-1707/8) & Trial[2] SHEPPARD (1641/2-1708+); m Malden 11 Mar 1660/1 [AEBK 4:2]

POWERS, Walter[2] (1674-1738) & Rebecca BARRETT (1673-1753); m Chelmsford 16 Dec 1696 [AEBK 4:10-11]

POWERS, William[2] (c1661-1710/1) & Mary[2] BANKS (1670/1-1719/20+); m say 1688 Concord [AEBK 4:13]

PRATT, Aaron[2] (c1654-) & 1/wf Sarah PRATT, dau of Joseph; m c1684 [GMB 3:1517]

PRATT, Abraham[1] (c1580-1645) & Jane CHARTER (-1645); m Amsterdam, Holland 14 Apr 1612 Charlestown [GMB 3:1505]

PRATT, Benajah[2] (c1630-) & Persis DUNHAM, dau of John; m Plymouth 29 Nov 1655 [GMB 3:1512]

PRATT, Daniel & Anna _____; Plymouth/Providence [TAG 67:31]

PRATT, Daniel[2] (c1635-) & Hannah[2] WARNER, dau of Andrew; m c1660 [GMB 3:1510, 1931]

PRATT, Daniel[2] (c1641-) & Anna _____; m c1680 [GMB 3:1517]

PRATT, John & Margaret KIMBALL; m c1686 Plymouth [TAG 71:76]

PRATT, John[1] (c1608-1655) & Elizabeth _____ (-1654+); m c1633 [GMB 3:1509]

PRATT, John[2] (c1633-) & 1/wf Hannah BOOSEY; m c1658 Hartford [GMB 3:1509]

PRATT, John[2] (c1633-) & 2/wf Hepsibah WYATT; m c1677 Hartford [GMB 3:1510]

PRATT, John[2] (c1635-) & Ann BARKER, dau of John; m c1664 Kingstown [GMB 3:1516]

PRATT, Jonathan[2] (c1637-) & 1/wf Abigail WOOD; m Plymouth 2 Nov 1664 [GMB 3:1512]

PRATT, Jonathan[2] (c1637-) & 2/wf Elizabeth (WHITE) HALL (c1644-by 1707), dau of Nicholas; m1 Samuel HALL; m Taunton 3 Mar 1689/90 [GMB 3:1512; AEBK 4:328]

PRATT, Joseph[2] (1639-1720) & Sarah JUDKINS (1645-1726); m Weymouth 7 May 1662 [AEBK 1:362]

PRATT, Joseph[2] (c1647-) & Dorcas FOLGER, dau of Peter; m Charlestown 12 Jan 1674/5 [GMB 3:1517]

PRATT, Joshua[1] (c1605-1652-56) & Bathsheba _____; m2 John DOGGETT; m c1630 Plymouth [GMB 3:1512]

PRATT, Macute (Matthew) & Elizabeth KINGHAM; m Aston Clinton, Bucks. 9 Nov 1619 [TAG 65:89]

PRATT, Nathaniel & Sarah[2] BEAMON; m Saybrook 2 May 1688 perhaps [GM 1:222]

PRATT, Peter[2] (c1643-) & Elizabeth (GRISWOLD) ROGERS, dau of Matthew; m1 John ROGERS; m Lyme 5 Aug 1679 [GMB 3:1517]

PRATT, Phineas[1] (c1593-1680) & Mary[2] PRIEST (c1612-1689), dau of Degory; m c1633 Charlestown [GMB 3:1516, 1526; TAG 60:160, 74:123]

PRATT, Samuel[2] (1636/7-1679) & 1/wf Hannah RAWLINGS (c1644-1721); m Weymouth 19 Sept 1660 [AEBK 1:404]

PRATT, Samuel[2] (c1637-) & Mary BARKER, dau of John; m2 Francis COOMBS; m c1668 [GMB 3:1517]

PRATT, Timothy & Deborah[2] COOPER (bp 1634-); m Boston 9 Nov 1659 [GM 2:199]

PRAY, Ephraim (c1661-1709/10) & Elizabeth[3] HAYDEN (c1663-1718+); m c1681 Braintree [AEBK 3]

PRENCE, Thomas[1] (c1600-1673) & 1/wf Patience BREWSTER (-1634), dau of William; m Plymouth 5 Aug 1624 [GMB 3:1522]

PRENCE, Thomas[1] (c1600-1673) & 2/wf Mary COLLIER, dau of William; m Plymouth 1 Apr 1635 [GMB 3:1523]

PRENCE, Thomas[1] (c1600-1673) & 3/wf Apphia (QUICK) FREEMAN, dau of William; m1 Samuel FREEMAN; m bet 1 July 1644 - 8 Dec 1662 [GMB 3:1523]

PRENCE, Thomas[1] (c1600-1673) & 4/wf Mary (____) HOWES (-1695); m1 Thomas HOWES; m bet 26 Feb 1665[/6] - 1 Aug 1668 [GMB 3:1523]

PRENCE, Thomas[2] (c1627-) & _____ _____ [GMB 3:1523]

PRENTICE, Thomas & Grace BULL; m Earls Colne, Essex 6 July 1647 [LMM]

PRENTICE, Valentine (bp 1599/1600-by 1634) & Alice BREDDA; m2 John WATSON m probably Chelmsford, Essex 29 June 1626 Roxbury [TAG 77:175; GMB 3;1525]

PRENTICE, Valentine/John[2] (bp 1628-) & 1/wf Hester NICHOLS; m c1651 [TAG 77:175; GMB 3:1525]

PRENTICE, Valentine/John[2] (bp 1628-) & 2/wf Esther NICHOLS; m by 1683 [TAG 77:175; GMB 3:1525]

PRENTICE, Valentine/John[2] (bp 1628-) & 3/wf Rebecca PARKER; m contract 12 June 1685 [TAG 77:175; GMB 3:1525]

PRESCOTT, Jonas (1678-1750) & Thankful[3] WHEELER (1682-1716); m Concord 5 Oct 1699 [AEBK 3]

PRESCOTT, Samuel & Esther[3] WHEELER (1678-1723+); m Concord 5 May 1698 [AEBK 3]

PRESTON, Samuel & Abigail THOMAS delete [NYGBR 99:65]

PRICE, Richard & Grace[2] WAIT (1638/9-); m Boston 6 May 1662 [GMB 3:1898]

PRICE, Theodore & Anne WOOD; m2 Dudley BRADSTREET [REG 139:139]

PRIEST, Degory[1] (c1579-1620/1) & Sarah (ALLERTON) VINCENT; m1 Jan VINCENT; m3 Godbert GODBERTSON; m Leiden 4 Nov 1611 Plymouth [GMB 3:1526]

PRIME, James (bp 1660-1736) & Martha MERWIN (1665/6-1693); m Milford 20 Sept 1685 [REG 149:308]

PRINCE, Samuel & Martha² BARSTOW (bp 1655-); m 9 Dec 1674 [GM 1:178]

PROCTER, John & Elizabeth² BASSETT; m2 Daniel RICHARDS; m Salem 1 Apr 1674 [GM 1:193]

PROCTOR, John & Elizabeth² THORNDIKE; m Ipswich Dec 1662 [GMB 3:1812]

PUFFER, Matthias (c1637-1717) & 1/wf Rachel FARNSWORTH (-killed 1675); m Braintree 18 Mar 1662/3 [AEBK 4:215]

PUFFER, Matthias (c1637-1717) & 2/wf Abigail EVERETT (1647-1685); m Dedham 11 Apr 1677 [AEBK 4:214]

PUFFER, Richard (1657/8-1723) & Ruth EVERETT (1653/4-1727+); m Dorchester 23 Mar 1681 Dedham [AEBK 4:215]

PURCHASE, Abraham² (c.667-) & Ruth WILLIAMS, dau of John; m c1695 Salem [GMB 3:1532]

PURCHASE, Aquila¹ (c1589-1633) & Anne SQUIRE, dau of Henry; m2 Thomas OLIVER; m Kingweston, Somersetshire 28 Jan 1612/3 [GMB 3:1528]

PURCHASE, Oliver² (c1614-) & 1/wf Sarah _____; m c1638 [GMB 3:1528]

PURCHASE, Oliver² (c16.4-) & 2/wf Mary² PERKINS (1651[/2?]-), dau of William; m Lynn 17 Sept 1672 [GMB 3:1436, 1528]

PURCHASE, Thomas (c1660-1681/2) & Elizabeth WILLIAMS (-1727+); m2 Jonathan FELT; m 3 Dec 1679 Salem [TG 3:53]

PURCHASE, Thomas¹ (c1577-1678) & 1/wf Mary GROVE (-1655/6); m Boston bet 21 Apr 1631 - 30 Aug 1631 Lynn [GMB 3:1531]

PURCHASE, Thomas¹ (c1577-1678) & 2/wf Elizabeth (ANDREWS) PIKE (c1633-), dau of Samuel; m1 Richard PIKE; m3 John BLANEY; m c1657 [GMB 3:1532]

PURCHASE, Thomas² (c1657-) & Elizabeth WILLIAMS; m Salem 3 Dec 1679 [GMB 3:1532]

PURDY, Francis & Mary² BRUNDISH; m2 John HOYT; m c1645 [GM 1:447]

PURRIER, William & Alice KNIGHT; m 21 Feb 1621/2 Olney, Buckinghamshire/ Ipswich/Southold [TAG 65:69]

PURTON, _____ & Elizabeth¹ _____ (c1608-1649/50-50); m c1628 Boston [GMB 3:1535]

PUTNAM, Edward³ & Mary³ HALE (1660-); m 1681 Salem [TAG 68:77; 69:212-8]

PUTNAM, John & Priscilla GOULD; m bef 1605 Eng/Salem [REG 119:174]

PUTNAM, Thomas & Ann² CARR (1661-); m Salem 25 Nov 1678 [GM 2:21]

PYNCHON, John² (c1620-) & Amy WYLLYS; m Hartford 6 Nov 1645 [GMB 3:1538]

PYNCHON, William¹ & _____ _____ [TAG 76:216]

PYNCHON, William¹ (c1590-1662) & 1/wf Anne ANDREW (-1630/1); m c1618 [GMB 3:1537]

PYNCHON, William¹ (c1590-1662) & 2/wf Frances (_____) (SMITH) SANDFORD (-1657); m by 1632 [GMB 3:1537]

QUINCY, Edmund[1] (bp 1602-c1639) & Judith PARES (-1654); m2 Moses PAINE; m3 Robert HULL; m Lilford, Northamptonshire 14 July 1623 [GMB 3:1539]

QUINCY, Edmund[2] (c1628-) & 1/wf Joanna HOAR; m Braintree 26 July 1648 [GMB 3:1540]

QUINCY, Edmund[2] (c1628-) & 2/wf Elizabeth (GOOKIN) ELIOT, dau of Daniel; m1 John ELIOT; m Braintree 8 Dec 1680 [GMB 3:1540]

RACKETT, John[1] (c1650-by 1686) & Anna _____ (c1654/5-1724/5); m by 1681 Southold, L.I. [NYGBR 126:234]

RAINSFORD, David[2] (1644-) & 1/wf Abigail _____; m c1674 Boston [GMB 3:1547]

RAINSFORD, David[2] (1644-1691) & 2/wf Hannah[2] GRIGGS (not Abigail)(1659-), dau of John; m2 Joshua FULLER; m bef 1674 Boston [TAG 56:174, REG 139:307; GMB 3:1547]

RAINSFORD, Edward[1] (bp 1609-1680) & 1/wf _____ _____ (-1632); m bef 1632 [GMB 3:1546]

RAINSFORD, Edward[1] (bp 1609-1680) & 2/wf Elizabeth _____ (-1688); m by 1633 Boston [GMB 3:1546]

RAINSFORD, Edward[2] (1641-) & Mary ALLEN; m Charlestown 28 Nov 1665 [GMB 3:1547]

RAINSFORD, Edward[2] (bp 1654-) & Huldah DAVIS, dau of William; m c1686 Boston [GMB 3:1547]

RAINSFORD, John[2] (1634-) & 1/wf Susanna VERGOOSE, dau of Peter; m c1661 Boston [GMB 3:1546]

RAINSFORD, John[2] (1634-) & 2/wf Sarah _____; m bef 1688 [GMB 3:1546]

RAINSFORD, John[3] (1661/2-1710/11) & Rebecca _____; m2 1712 John NICHOLLS; m bef 1695 Boston [REG 139:311]

RAINSFORD, Jonathan[2] (1636-) & Mary SUNDERLAND; m Boston 29 Nov 1656 [GMB 3:1546]

RAINSFORD, Solomon[2] (1646-) & Priscilla[2] GETCHELL (1648[/9]-), dau of Samuel; m c1670 Boston [GMB 3:1547; GM 3:34]

RAMSDELL, Daniel & 1/wf _____ _____; by 1677 Plymouth [MD 36:187-9]

RAMSDELL, John & Elizabeth[2] _____ (1643-); m Salem 31 May 1671 [GMB 3:1436]

RAMSDELL, John (c1602-1688) & Priscilla _____ (-1675/6); m bef 1632 Lynn [50 GMC]

RAMSDEN, John & Elizabeth[2] (FROST) (WATSON) GRAY (bp 1614-bef 1682); m1 John WATSON; m2 John GRAY; m bef 1663 Newtown, LI [TAG 64:163]

RANDALL, Abraham[2] (c1615-) & 1/wf Mary WARE (not PHELPS); m Windsor 8 Dec 1640 [GMB 3:1549]

RANDALL, Abraham[2] (c1615-) & 2/wf Elizabeth (_____) KIRBY; m Windsor 27 Oct 1681 [GMB 3:1549]

RANDALL, Philip[1] (c1590-1662) & _____ _____ (-1665); m c1615 Windsor [GMB 3:1549]

RANDALL, Richard & Elizabeth[2] INNES (1641-); m by 28 Sept 1676 [GMB 2:1058; SD 9:416]

RANDALL, Samuel (1675-) & Mary GURNEY? not Bailey [TAG 33:139]

RANDALL, Stephen[2] (c1628-1707/8) & Susannah[2] BARRON (c1635-1684+); m Watertown 14 Dec 1653 [AEBK 1:129]

RANDALL, William (-1682+) & Elizabeth _____ (-murdered 5 June 1682); Wethersfield [REG 145:340-41; Harris]

RANDALL, William (-1693) & Elizabeth BARSTOW (1618-); m c1639 Watertown/Scituate [RCA]

RANES, John (c1630s-1677/8) & Mary ROGERS (c1641-1684+); m Weymouth 24 Nov 1659 [AEBK 1:404]

RAVENSCROFT, Samuel[1] & Dyonisia SAVAGE (1649-); m2 Thomas HADLEY; returned to England; m by 1681 Boston [Suffolk Deed 39: 54, 15:173, 23:162, 37:108]

RAWLINGS, Caleb[2] (1645-1693) & Elizabeth _____; m bef 1678 Boston [AEBK]

RAWLINGS, Ichabod[2] (c1645-) & Mary TIBBETTS; m c1675 [GMB 3:1553]

RAWLINGS, James[1] (c1613-1685-7) & Hannah _____ (-1685+); m c1643 Dover [GMB 3:1553]

RAWLINGS, Jasper[1] (c1575-1665/5-7) & 1/wf Joan HUNSDEN (-by 1651); m Ingatestone, Essex 14 Dec 1600 Roxbury [MLS; GMB 3:1556]

RAWLINGS, Jasper[1] (c1575-1665/6-7) & 2/wf Mary (GREEN) GRIGGS (-1665/6+); m1 Thomas GRIGGS; m Roxbury 8 June 1651 [GMB 3:1556]

RAWLINGS, Nathaniel[2] (bp 1627-1662) & Lydia SYLVESTER (1633-), dau of Richard; m2 1664 Edward WRIGHT; m Scituate 4 Sept 1652 [AEBK 1:383; GMB 3;1559, 1679]

RAWLINGS, Samuel[2] (c1651-) & Rebecca perhaps PICKERING, dau of John; m c1676 [GMB 3:1553]

RAWLINGS, Thomas[1] (by 1583-1659/60) & 1/wf Mary _____ (c1600-c1639); m bef 1622 Scituate [AEBK 1:375; GMB 3:1558]

RAWLINGS, Thomas[1] (by 1583-1659/60) & 2/wf Em _____ (-1655); m c1640s Boston [AEBK 1:375; GMB 3:1559]

RAWLINGS, Thomas[1] (c1580s-1660) & 3/wf Sarah (_____) MATTOCKS (-1660+); m1 David MATTOCKS; m Boston 2 May 1656 [AEBK 1:375; GMB 3:1559]

RAWSER, Richard (-by 1664) & Exercise[2] BLACKLEACH (bp 24 Jan 1636-1684+); m2 Thomas HODGES; m Boston 24 Aug 1660 [REG 148:17; GM 1:316]

RAWSON, Edward[1] (1615-1693) & Rachel PERNE (-1677); he called "cousin" [possibly nephew] by Rev. John Wilson; m England say 1635 Newbury/Boston [REG 125:263]

RAY, Daniel[1] (c1597-by 1662) & Bethiah _____ (-1662+); m by 1637 Plymouth/Salem [GMB 3:1561]

RAY, Joshua (c1627-) & Sarah WALTERS; m Salem 26 Feb 1651/2 [GMB 3:1562]

RAYMENT, John[2] (c1635-) & Mary BETTS, dau of Thomas; m Norwalk 10 Dec 1664 [GMB 3:1564]

RAYMENT, Joshua[2] (bp 1638/9-) & Elizabeth SMITH, dau of Nehemiah; m New London 10 Dec 1659 [GMB 3:1564]

RAYMENT, Richard[1] (c1602-1692) & Judith _____; m by 1635 Saybrook [GMB 3:1564]

RAYMENT, Samuel[2] (bp 1645-) & Mary SMITH, dau of Nehemiah; New London [GMB 3:1564]

RAYMOND, Daniel[2] (bp 1653-) & 1/wf Elizabeth HARRIS (1656-1683), dau of Gabriel; m c1675 [REG 156:153; GMB 3:1565]

RAYMOND, Daniel[2] (bp 1653-) & 2/wf Rebecca LAY; m Lyme 15 Apr 1684 [REG 156:153; GMB 3:1565]

RAYMOND, John & Martha[2] WOODIN (1654/5-); m bef 1677 Beverly [TAG 64:73]

READ, Thomas[1] (bp 1612-1662) & Priscilla BANKS; m by 1642 [GMB 3:1566]

READE, Esdras (1600-1680) & 1/wf Elizabeth WATSON (-1629); m St Michael's Crooked Lane, London 18 Oct 1621 Brookline [50 GMC]

READE, Esdras (1600-1680) & 2/wf Sarah DICKINSON; m St Katherine by the Tower, London 22 Feb 1630/1 Brookline [50 GMC]

RECKARD, John ~ Grace _____; Scituate [Plymouth Court Dec 1688]

REDDING, Joseph[1] (c1613-1674/5) & Annis/Agnes _____ (-by 1693); m by 25 Mar 1662 Ipswich [GMB 3:1568]

REDMAN, John[1] & 1/wf Margaret KNIGHT (-1658); m by 1658 Hampton [NHGR 15:150]

REDMAN, John[1] & 2/wf _____ (_____) WEEKS?; m perhaps 1660s Hampton [NHGR 15:150]

REDMAN, John[1] & 2/wf or 3/wf Sabina (_____) MARSTON; m1 William MARSTON; m 23 July 1673 [NHGR 15:150]

REED, John & Elizabeth[2] HOLDEN (c1662-); m Woburn 21 Mar 1682 [GM 3:366]

REED, John (-1721/2) & Hannah PEABODY (c1643-1727); m say 1665 Freetown [AEBK 1:370]

REEVE, Robert[1] & Anne SKINNER; m by 1659 [TAG 74:99]

REEVES, John[1] (bp 30 Aug 1612-1681) & Jane _____ (c1620-bef 1677); m c1630s Salem [AEBK 1:390]

REEVES, William[1] (bp 29 Mar 1609-) & Hannah ROOTES (c1619-1670+); m c1635 Salem/Kittery [AEBK]

REEVES, William[2] (c1645-1717/8) & Elizabeth COLLINS (c1650-1717/8+); m Salem 14 Mar 1669/70 [AEBK 1:396]

REMINGTON, Daniel (1661-1690s) & Sarah[3] PARKER (c1670-1686); m c1685 RI [TAG 57:22; Fiske 1:46]

REMINGTON, Stephen (c1659-1738) & Penelope PARKER (1666-1740+); m c1685 Portsmouth, RI [TAG 57:20; Fiske 1:45]

REWSE, Simon (-1620) & Anne DALTON (1588-); m2 Henry BOAD; m3 Samuel WINSLEY; m West Wratting, Cambridgeshire, 26 Dec 1611 [REG 154:262]

REYNER, Humphrey (-1660) & Mary MIDDLEBROOK (-1672); m by July 1631 Rowley [REG 156:316, 323]

REYNER, John (-1669) & 1/wf Anna BOYSE [REG 156:322]

REYNER, John (-1669) & 2/wf Frances CLARK [REG 156:322]

REYNOLDS, Alexander/Electious (-1738) & Mary[3] PEASE (1667-), dau. of Robert[2]; m Salem 16 July 1686 [TAG 70:208]

REYNOLDS, John & Anne[2] HOLBROOK (c1630-) [GM 3:353]

REYNOLDS, Jonathan (1676/7-1704) & Elizabeth[2] COLTMAN (1677-1732+); m2 Stephen HOLLISTER; m Wethersfield 4 Nov 1697 [TAG 77:257]

REYNOLDS, Jonathan[3] & Nevill RI[ ]; m 7 Dec 1682 [TAG 73:203]

REYNOLDS, Nathaniel & Sarah[2] DWIGHT (1638-); m Boston 30 Dec 1657 [GM 2:376]

REYNOLDS, Nathaniel (c1627-1708) & 2/wf Priscilla BRACKETT (c1646-1688+); m by 1664/5 Boston/Bristol [REG 155:286]

RHOADES, Malachi & Mary[2] CARDER; m Warwick 27 May 1675 [GM 2:9]

RHODES, Henry[1] (c1608-1703+) & Elizabeth COLDHAM (-1700); m bef 1640 Salem [TEG 14:156]

RHODES, Zachariah & Joanna[2] ARNOLD (1617-); m2 Samuel REAPE; m by 7 Mar 1646[/7?] [GM 1:88]

RICE, Peter (-1753) & Rebecca[2] HOWE (1668[/9]-1749); m c1690 Marlborough [AEBK 3]

RICE, Samuel & Mary (DIX) BROWNE; m1 Abraham BROWNE; Watertown [GMB 1:552]

RICE, Thomas & Mary[2] WITHERS (c1660-); m c22 July 1674 [GMB 3:2046]

RICH, Obadiah & Bethia[2] WILLIAMS (bp 1642-); m Salem 6 July 1661 [GMB 3:2005]

RICHARD, Thomas[1] (c1604-1681-1/2) & 1/wf _____ _____ [GMB 3:1574]

RICHARD, Thomas[1] (c1604-1681-1/2) & 2/wf Rosamond (____) LINDALL (-1682+); m1 Henry LINDALL; m New Haven 15 Mar 1663/4 [GMB 3:1574]

RICHARDS, Benjamin[2] (c1638-) & Hannah HUDSON; m Boston 10 Oct 1661 [GMB 3:1578]

RICHARDS, David & Elizabeth RAYMOND (bp 1676-1744/5); m New London 14 Dec 1698 [REG 156:154]

RICHARDS, Edward[1] (-1689/90) & 1/wf _____ _____; Lynn [TEG 12:142]

RICHARDS, Edward[1] (-1689/90) & 2/wf Ann KNIGHT; m c1649 Lynn [TEG 12:142]

RICHARDS, Humphry & Mehitable[2] RUGGLES (1650-); m c1666/7 [GMB 3:1607]

RICHARDS, James[2] (bp 1632-) & Sarah GIBBONS; m c1655 [GMB 3:1577]

RICHARDS, John & Mary FULLER; m2 Boaz BROWN [REG 140:317]

RICHARDS, John (c1655-1718) & Abigail (PARSONS) MUNN (1662/3-); m
    Springfield 7 Oct 1686 Whippany, NJ [REG 148:224]

RICHARDS, John[2] (bp 1625-) & 1/wf Elizabeth (HAWKINS) (LONG) WINTHROP; m
    Boston 3 May 1654 [GMB 3:1577]

RICHARDS, John[2] (bp 1625-) & 2/wf Ann WINTHROP; m Boston 1 Sept 1692 [GMB
    3:1577]

RICHARDS, Nathaniel (c1604-1681) & 1/wf _____ (_____) HAYES;
    Cambridge/Hartford/ Norwalk [GMSP]

RICHARDS, Nathaniel (c1604-1681) & 2/wf Rosamond (_____) LINDALL; m 15 Mar
    1663/4 [GMSP]

RICHARDS, Richard & Rebecca WILLIAMS; m Plymouth, Devonshire 1 Apr 1644 [JP]

RICHARDS, Richard (-1687) & Elizabeth REEVES (c1642-1687+); m Salem 16 Jan
    1660/1 [AEBK 1:396]

RICHARDS, Thomas (c1666-1749) & Mary PARSONS (1670-1758); m Hartford 1 or 21
    Oct 1691 [REG 148:225]

RICHARDS, Thomas[1] (bp 1596-1650-1) & Welthian _____ (-1679); m by 1620 [GMB
    3:1577]

RICHARDSON, Amos (c1618-1683) & Mary _____ (-1683) (possibly sister of John
    Witherden, millwright); m bef 1645 Boston/Stonington [DR]

RICHARDSON, Ezekiel[1] (c1604-1647) & Susanna ____; m2 Henry BROOKS; m by 1632
    Woburn [GMB 3:1582]

RICHARDSON, James[2] (bp 1641-) & Bridget HENCHMAN; m Chelmsford 28 Nov
    1660 [GMB 3:1582]

RICHARDSON, John & Martha MEAD (c1630-by 1695); m by Jan 1653/4 Westchester
    Co., N.Y. [TAG 73:9]

RICHARDSON, Joshua (c1651-bef 1724/5) & 2/wf Jane[2] ORDWAY (1663-1705+); m 4
    Jan 1687/8 Newbury [ASBO, p.88]

RICHARDSON, Josiah[2] (bp 1635-) & Remembrance UNDERWOOD; m Concord 6
    June 1659 [GMB 3:1582]

RICHARDSON, Theophilus[2] (bp 1633-) & Mary[2] CHAMPNEY (1635-); m Woburn 2
    May 1654 [GMB 3:1582; GM 2:39]

RICHARDSON, Thomas & 1/wf Hannah[2] COLBURN; m Chelmsford 28 Sept 1682 [GM
    2:148]

RICHARDSON, William? & Ann (SOULBY) BURDEN; m c1660s Barbados/Newport
    [REG 155:91+]

RICHMOND, Edward & 2/wf Amy (BULL) LEYOUGE; m1 James LEYOUGE [TAG
    77:283]

RICHMOND, John & Susanna[2] HAYWARD (c1632-); m by 1654 [GM 3:292]

RIDDLESDALE, Edward (c1592-1630/1) & Mary _____, m2 John WYATT, m3 James BARKER; m c1519 Assington, Suffolk/Ipswich [50 GMC]

RIDLAND, William & Patience[2] DAVIS (bp 1636-); m c1663 Charlestown [GM 2:289]

RIGGS, Edward[1] (c1593-1671/2) & 1/wf Elizabeth HOLMES (-1635); m Nazeing, Essex 16 Sept 1618 [GMB 3:1584]

RIGGS, Edward[1] (c1593-1671/2) & 2/wf Elizabeth ROOSA (-1669); m Roxbury 5 Apr 1635 [GMB 3:1584]

RIGGS, Edward[2] (bp 1619-) & _____ _____; m by 1662 [GMB 3:1584]

RING, Andrew[2] (c1618-1692/3) & 1/wf Deborah[2] HOPKINS (c1626-), dau of Stephen; m Plymouth 23 Apr 1646 [TAG 73:171; GMB 2:988, 3:1587]

RING, Andrew[2] (c1618-1692/3) & 2/wf Lettice (_____) MORTON; m1 John MORTON; m c1674 [GMB 3:1587]

RING, Eleazer (c1663-1749) & Mary SHAW (c1665-1730); Lakenham, Norwich/North Carver 11 Jan 1687/8 [REG 151:424]

RING, William (-1620-29) & Mary _____ (c1589-1631); m c1609 Leiden/Plymouth [GMB 3:1587]

RING, William (-c1620s) & Mary DURRANT? (-1631); m 21 May 1601 Ufford, Suffolk/Plymouth [TAG 42:193]

RISEING, James & Elizabeth HINSDALE; m Boston 7 July 1657 [TAG 68:159]

RISLEY, Richard[1] (-c1648) & Mary _____; Hartford [TAG 70:162]

ROBBARTS, William & Susannah LANE (bp 1644-); m 23 Dec 1665 [REG 156:148]

ROBBINS, George (c1640-1689) & 1/wf Mary _____ (-1672); m by 1667 Chelmsford [REG 151:388]

ROBBINS, George (c1640-1689) & 2/wf Alice _____ (-1686); m c1672 Chelmsford [REG 151:388]

ROBBINS, George (c1640-1689) & 3/wf Mary BARRETT (1658-); m Chelmsford 21 Jan 1686/7 [REG 151:388]

ROBBINS, George (c1675-1747) & 1/wf Elizabeth WOOD (1678-1717/8); m Concord 19 Oct 1697 [REG 151:392]

ROBBINS, John (1672-1762) & Dorothy HILDRETH (c1674-1757); m Chelmsford 30 Nov 1699 [REG 151:391]

ROBERTS, John[2] (-1694/5) & Abigail NUTTER (-1674+) [TAG 72:276]

ROBERTS, Simon & Christian[2] BAKER; m Boston 18 July 1654 [GM 1:131]

ROBERTS, Thomas & Parnell HARRIS (-1676) [GM 3:227]

ROBERTS, William & Anna CROCKETT; by 1673 [GMB 1:497]

ROBERTS, William & Mary[2] ABBOTT (165[6/]7-); m by 1681 probably [GM 1:4]

ROBINSON, George & Mary[2] BUSHNELL (1636-); m2 Thomas DENNIS; m Boston 3 Oct 1657 [GM 1:508]

ROBINSON, Increase[2] & Sarah[2] PENNIMAN (1641-); m Dorchester 19 Jan 1663/4 [TAG 71:17; GMB 3:1429]

ROBINSON, Isaac[1] (c1610-1704) & 1/wf Margaret[2] HANFORD (c1619-1649), dau of Eglin; m Scituate 26 Sept 1636 [GMB 3:1592; GM 3:206]

ROBINSON, Isaac[1] (c1610-1704) & 2/wf Mary _____ (-1669+); m by 1651 [GMB 3:1592]

ROBINSON, Israel[2] (bp 1651-) & Anne COTTLE; Martha's Vineyard [GMB 3:1593]

ROBINSON, Jacob[2] (bp 1653-) & 1/wf Mary _____ [GMB 3:1593]

ROBINSON, James & Lucretia FOXWELL (c1644-); by 1668 Boston/Piscataqua [GMB 1:695]

ROBINSON, John (1611/12-1675) & Elizabeth PEMBERTON (-1645); m by 1641 Newbury [REG 143:151]

ROBINSON, John[2] (bp 1640-) & Elizabeth WEEKS; m Barnstable mid-May 1667 [GMB 3:1592]

ROBINSON, Joseph (-1647/8) & Dorothy _____, m2 Edmund FAULKNER; m after 1637 Salem [50 GMC]

ROBINSON, Peter[2] (c1655-) & 1/wf Mary MANTER, dau of John; m c1688 Martha's Vineyard [GMB 3:1593]

ROBINSON, Peter[2] (c1655-) & 2/wf Experience _____; m c1698 [GMB 3:1593]

ROBINSON, Thomas & Rebecca LAWRENCE (1664-); m Dorchester 23 Feb 1686/7 [REG 156:150]

ROBINSON, Thomas & Silence BOYES; m Halifax, Yorkshire 8 Dec 1630 Boston [DR]

ROCK, Joseph & Elizabeth COGGAN; by 1651 Boston [GMB 1:404]

ROCKETT, Josiah (c1652-1719-27) & 1/wf Mary[3] TWITCHELL (165[8/]9-1699); m Medfield 9 May 1677 [AEBK 3]

ROCKWELL, John & Deliverance[2] HAWES (1640-); m2 Robert WARNER; m Windsor 18 Aug 1662 [GM 3:252]

ROCKWELL, John (bp 1621-by 1677) & 1/wf Mehitable _____ (-1656) [TAG 77:104-6]

ROCKWELL, John[1] (?bp 1621-by 1677) & 2/wf Elizabeth[2] WEED (-1677+) [TAG 77:104-6; GMB 3:1958]

ROCKWELL, John[2] (bp 1627-) & 1/wf Sarah[2] ENSIGN; m Windsor 6 May 1651 [GMB 3:1596; GM 2:456]

ROCKWELL, John[2] (bp 1627-) & 2/wf Deliverance HAYES; m Windsor 18 Aug 1662 [GMB 3:1596]

ROCKWELL, Jonathan (c1665-) & Abigail CANFIELD [TAG 77:109]

ROCKWELL, Samuel[2] (1631-) & Mary NORTON; m Windsor 7 Apr 1660 [GMB 3:1596]

ROCKWELL, William[1] (bp 1590/1-1640) & Susanna CAPEN (-1666), dau of Bernard; m2 Matthew GRANT; m Holy Trinity, Dorchester, Dorsetshire 14 Apr 1624 [GMB 3:1595]

ROCKWOOD, Joseph (-1718[/9] & Mary[3] HAYWARD (c1667-1714+); m c1689 Mendon [AEBK 3]

ROGERS, Ezekiel & Elizabeth[2] WILSON; m c1650 [GMB 3:2015]

ROGERS, Henry & Ann (____) WOOD; m1 George WOOD; m after 1664 LI [TAG 39:131]

ROGERS, Jeremiah & Abigail[2] PIERCE (1633-); m by 1653 Dorchester [GMB 3:1471]

ROGERS, John[1] (c1610-1660/1) & Judith ____ (-1660+); m bef 1639 Weymouth [AEBK 1:399]

ROGERS, John[2] (bp 1606-) & Anna CHURCHMAN; m Plymouth 16 Apr 1639 [GMB 3:1598]

ROGERS, John[2] (c1639-1709/10) & 1/wf Mary BATES (-bef 1683?); m Weymouth 8 Jan 1662/3 [AEBK 1:403]

ROGERS, John[2] (c1639-1709/10) & 2/wf Judith ____ (-1710+); m Weymouth [AEBK 1:403]

ROGERS, Joseph[2] (bp 1602/3-) & Hannah ____; m by 1633 [GMB 3:1598]

ROGERS, Robert (c1617-1663) & Susanna ____ (-1677); m2 William THOMAS; m bef 1647/8 Newbury [REG 140:204]

ROGERS, Samuel & Sarah[2] WADE; m Ipswich 13 Nov 1661 [GMB 3:1886]

ROGERS, Samuel (1640-1713) & 1/wf Mary STANTON; m New London 17 Nov 1662 [Hempstead Diary, 432]

ROGERS, Thomas & Elsgen ____; bef 1610 Holland/Plymouth [TAG 67:31]

ROGERS, Thomas[1] (-1538) & Grace (RAVENS) SHERMAN; m1 John SHERMAN; m bef 1634 Essex/Watertown [TAG 62:76]

ROGERS, Thomas[1] (c1572-1620/1) & Alice COSFORD, dau of George; m Watford, Northamptonshire 24 Oct 1597 [GMB 3:1598]

ROGERS, Thomas[3] & Elizabeth[2] SNOW (c1640-); m Eastham 13 Dec 1665 [GMB 3:1703]

ROGERS, William & Sarah[2] LYNN (1636-); m by 14 Mar 1658/9 Boston [GMB 2:1221]

ROICE, Joshua[2] (1637-) & Bathsheba[2] PRATT (c1639-); m Charlestown Dec 1662 [GMB 3:1513, 1599]

ROICE, Robert[1] (c1613-by 1668) & Elizabeth ____; m2 Michael TEARN; m by 1637 Boston [GMB 3:1599]

ROLAND, Hugh & Hannah SMITH (1651-bef 1618); m2 ____ Andrews; m c1670s Lyme [AEJA]

ROLFE, Daniel & Hannah[2] BRADSTREET (c1625-); m2 Nicholas HOLT; m by 1655 [GM 1:386]

ROLFE, John[2] (1634-1681) & Mary[2] SCULLARD (1641[/2?]-); m Newbury 4 Dec 1656 [TAG 75:185]

ROLLINS, Samuel & Rebecca[2] PICKERING (c1651-); perhaps [GMB 3:1460]

ROOD, Micah & Sarah (PEAKE) DAYNS, m1 Abraham DAYNS; m Norwich 15 Jan 1692 [BB]

ROOT, Thomas & Mary[2] SPENCER (1655-); m Westfield 7 Oct 1675 Hartford [GMB 3:1721]

ROOTS, Jurrian (-1697) & Willmet ( ) ALBERTSON; Oyster Bay [NYGBR 109:205]

ROSE, Jabez ~ Abigail STANDLAKE; Scituate [Plymouth Court June 1700]

ROSE, John[2] (-by 1676) & 1/wf Ellen (NICHOL) LUDDINGTON (1614-1665+); m1 William LUDDINGTON [TAG 74:215]

ROSE, John[2] (-by 1676) & 2/wf Phebe (BRACY) DICKINSON [TAG 74:215]

ROSE, Roger & Abigail[2] GRANT (1634[/5]-); m c1660 Providence [GM 3:130]

ROSEMORGAN, Richard & _____ _____ [REG 156:389]

ROSS, John[1] (-1707/8+) & Mary HAGGETT (c1646-) [REG 157:38]

ROSS, Killecross & Mary[2] GALLEY (c1641-); m Ipswich 9 May 1661 [GM 3:3]

ROSS, Thomas & Seeth[2] HOLMAN (c1642-); m Cambridge 16 Jan 1661[/2] [GM 3:390]

ROSSITER, Bryan/Bray[2] (-1672) & Elizabeth ALSOP (bp 1614-1669); m bef 1640 Dorchester/Windsor/Guilford [DR; GMB 3:1601]

ROSSITER, Edward[1] (c1575-1630) & _____ COMBE; m c1599 Combe St. Nicholas, Somersetshire/Dorchester [GMB 3:1600; REG 138:12]

ROSSITER, Hugh[2] (c1615-) & Dorothy (COMBE) NORRIS; m c1641 [GMB 3:1601]

ROSSITER, Nicholas (c1599-) & Anne _____ [GMB 3:1601]

ROUND, John[1] (c1620-) & Ruth _____ (-1658/9); m c1646 Yarmouth [TAG 54:37]

ROUND, John[2] (c1646-1716) & Elizabeth ?CHASE; m c1669 Yarmouth [TAG 54:37]

ROUSE, William (c1640-1704/5) & Sarah (KIND) PEIRCE (1646-c1704/5); m1 William PEIRCE; m bef 1676 Charlestown [REG 126:18]

ROWE, John & Abigail[2] (1656-); m New Haven 14 July 1681 [GM 1:50]

ROWE, Matthew & Sarah[2] ABBOTT; m by 1650 New Haven [GM 1:3]

ROWLANDSON, Thomas & Martha[2] BRADSTREET (c1632-); m2 William BEALE; m by Mar 1648 div c1651 [GM 1:387]

ROWLEY, Henry & _____[2] PALMER, dau of William; m by 1630 [GMB 3:1385]

ROWLEY, Henry[1] (c1605-1670-73) & 1/wf _____ _____ (perhaps dau of William PALMER); m c1630 Plymouth [GMB 3:1603]

ROWLEY, Henry[1] (c1605-1670-73) & 2/wf Anne (ELDSON) BLOSSOM; m1 Thomas BLOSSOM; m Plymouth 17 Oct 1633 [GMB 3:1603; TAG 63:74]

ROWLEY, Moses[2] (c1632-) & Elizabeth FULLER, dau of Matthew; m Barnstable 22 Apr 1652 [GMB 3:1603]

RUDDUCK, John[1] (c1609-1692/3) & Dorothy[1] GOODENOW (-1686); m aft 1633/4 [AEBK 3]

RUGG, John (-1697) & 1/wf Martha PRESCOTT (1632-1656); m bef 1656 Lancaster [Stevens-Miller Ancestry, pp. 54-59]

RUGG, John (-1697) & 2/wf Hannah _____ (not Prescott) (-1697); m Lancaster 4 May 1660 [DR]

RUGGLES, George[1] (c1608-1669) & Elizabeth _____ (-1681); m by 1633 Boston [GMB 3:1606]

RUGGLES, John & Mary[2] GIBSON (1637-); m Roxbury 3 Apr 1655 [GM 3:51]

RUGGLES, John[1] (c1594-1656/7) & Frances _____; m by 1630 Boston [GMB 3:1609]

RUGGLES, John[2] (bp 1637-) & Rebecca FARNSWORTH; m Braintree 18 Mar 166[1/]2 [GMB 3:1606]

RUGGLES, Samuel[2] (1648[/9]-) & Sarah _____ (no evidence for surname HOWARD); m by 1673 Boston [GMB 3:1607]

RUSS, John (1671-1717) & Hannah ROSS (1669[/7]-1704+); m Andover 6 May 1695 South Carolina [REG 157:45]

RUSSELL, James & Mabel[2] HAYNES (1645[/6]-); m by 1665 Hartford/Charlestown [GMB 2:897]

RUSSELL, John & Mary[2] TALCOTT; m Hartford 28 June 1649 [GMB 3:1797]

RUSSELL, John & Sarah[2] CHAMPNEY (1638-); m Woburn 31 Oct 1661 [GM 2:39]

RUSSELL, Joseph & Mary[2] BELCHER; m Cambridge 23 June 1662 [GM 1:235]

RUSSELL, Philip & Elizabeth[2] TERRY (1641[/2]-); m Hadley 10 Jan 1665 [GMB 3:1806]

RUSSELL, Philip & Joanna[2] CUTLER (c1661-1703); m Cambridge 19 June 1680 [GM 2:270]

RUSSELL, William[1] (-1661/2) & Martha DAVIES (-1695); m2 Humphrey BRADSHAW; m3 Thomas HALL; m 26 May 1636 Abbotts Langley, Hertfordshire [TAG 44:83]

RUST, Nathaniel & Mary[2] WARDWELL (bp 1644-); m bef 1664 Ipswich [GMB 3:1923]

RYALL, Isaac[2] (c1644-) & 1/wf Ruth TOLMAN, dau of Thomas; m c1668 Dorchester [GMB 3:1611]

RYALL, Isaac[2] (c1644-) & 2/wf Waitstill SPURR; m c1682 [GMB 3:1611]

RYALL, John[2] (c1655-) & Elizabeth DODD, dau of George; m c1680 [GMB 3:1612]

RYALL, Joseph[2] (c1646-) & Mary _____; m by 1673 Charlestown [GMB 3:1612]

RYALL, Samuel[2] (c1648-) & Sarah MARSHALL, dau of John; m c1663 Boston [GMB 3:1612]

RYALL, William[1] (c1608-1676) & Phebe GREEN; m c1640 Salem/Casco/Dorchester [GMB 3:1611]

RYALL, William[2] (c1640-1724) & Mary _____; m c1672 Dorchester [GMB 3:1611]

SABEERE, Stephen (-1688+) & Deborah ANGELL (c1648-1694+); m Providence 24 Nov 1668 [AEJA]

SABIN, Nehemiah (1647-) & Elizabeth FULLER; m 1 Aug 1672 [TAG 76:275]

SACKET, John[2] (c1630-) & 2/wf Sarah (STILES) STEWART; m Westfield 14 Jan 1690[/1] [GMB 3:1616]

SACKETT, John[2] (c1630-) & 1/wf Abigail[2] HANNUM (bp 1640-); m Northampton 23 Nov 1659 [GM 3:212; GMB 3:1616]

SACKETT, Simon[1] (c1602-1635) & Isabel PEARCE; m2 William BLOOMFIELD; m St. John Margate, Isle of Thanet, Kent 6 Aug 1627 Cambridge [GMB 3:1615]

SACKETT, Simon[2] (c1628-) & Sarah[2] BLOOMFIELD (c1633-); m2 Lambert WOODWARD; m c1652 Hartford [GM 1:332; GMB 3:1615]

SADLER, Anthony[1] (-by 1650) & Martha[2] CHENEY (bp 1626-); m2 Thomas BURKBY; m c1649 [TAG 76:247; GM 2:62]

SAFFIN, John & Martha[2] WILLET (1639-); m Plymouth 2 Dec 1658 [GMB 3:2000]

SAGE, David (1665-1712 or 13) & Mary[2] COLTMAN (1672-); m Wethersfield 3 May 1693 [TAG 77:257]

SALES, John[1] (c1600-1645) & 1/wf Phillip SOALES (-by 1644); m Little Waldingfield, Suffolk 11 Aug 1625 Charlestown/Boston/New Amsterdam [NYGBR 123:65-73; GMB 3:1617]

SALES, John[1] (c1600-1645) & 2/wf Maria (____) SLOOFS, m1 Jan SLOOFS; m3 Thomas GRYDY; m New Netherland 21 Aug 1644 New Amsterdam [NYGBR 123:65-73; GMB 3:1617]

SALLOWS, John & 1/wf Hannah WOLFE [TAG 72:3]

SALLOWS, John & 2/wf Elizabeth _____ [TAG 72:3]

SALLOWS, John[3] (1656-1690) & Katherine _____; by 1690 Salem [TAG 72:115]

SALLOWS, Michael[1] (-1646) & Ann _____ (-1643+); m bef 1627 Salem [TAG 72:2]

SALLOWS, Robert & Freeborn WOLFE; m2 1664 John BLACK; m bef 1654 [GMB 3:2068; TAG 72:3]

SALLOWS, Robert[3] (bp 1676-1756) & 1/wf Mary THISTLE (c1674-1714); m Beverly 14 Dec 1697 [TAG 72:121]

SALLOWS, Thomas[2] (-drowned 1663) & Grace LEMON (-1663) [TAG 72:3]

SALLOWS, Thomas[3] (1665-1747) & Abigail _____; m by 1693 Salem [TAG 72:116]

SALLY, Manus & Hannah[2] HEPBURN (c1631-); m2 c1651 Aaron LUDKIN; m by 1648 [GM 3:310]

SALMON, George & Remember[2] FELTON (bp 1643-); m Salem Oct 1664 [GM 2:515]

SALMON, William[1] & 1/wf _____ _____; m Southold by 1648 [TAG 76:296]

SALMON, William[1] & 2/wf Sarah HORTON [TAG 76:296]

SALTONSTALL, Richard[1] & Elizabeth _____; m bef 5 Nov 1628 All Saints Barking, London/Isleworth, Middlesex [TAG 76:173]

SALTONSTALL, Richard[1] (bp 1586-1661) & 1/wf Grace KAYE (-1625), dau of Robert; m Almondbury, Yorkshire 28 Nov 1609 [GMB 3:1619]

SALTONSTALL, Richard[1] (bp 1586-1661) & 2/wf Elizabeth WEST, dau of Thomas; m by 1632 [GMB 3:1619]

SALTONSTALL, Richard[1] (bp 1586-1661) & 3/wf Martha (CAMMOCK) WILSFORD, (-by 1662), dau of Thomas; m1 Francis WILSFORD; m c1640 Watertown [GMB 3:1619]

SAMPSON, Abraham & _____[2] NASH (c1625-); m c1645 Duxbury [GMB 2:1323]

SAMPSON, George (c1653-1739) & Elizabeth SPRAGUE (c1657-1727); m c1678 Plympton [TAG 41:189, 63:209]

SAMPSON, Isaac & Lydia STANDISH, m c1686 Plymouth [MD 39:127]

SAMPSON, John & Sarah PEASE; m Beverly 22 Oct 1667 [TAG 70:207]

SAMSON, Caleb[2] (c1654-) & 1/wf Mercy STANDISH, dau of Alexander; m c1686 [GMB 3:1623]

SAMSON, Henry[1] (bp 1603/4-1684-4/5) & Anne PLUMMER (-1668+); m Plymouth 6 Feb 1635/6 [GMB 3:1623]

SAMSON, James[2] (c1644-) & Hannah (_____) WAIT; m1 Samuel WAIT; m by 1679 [GMB 3:1623]

SAMSON, Stephen[2] (c1638-) & Elizabeth _____; m by 1686 [GMB 3:1623]

SAMUEL, John & Lucy (_____) WIGHT; m Boston 1652 [AEBK 4:579]

SAMWAYS, Richard & Hester[2] HOSFORD (bp 1621-); m2 _____ WILLIAMS; m by 1643 [GMB 2:997]

SANDERS, Martin (c1595-1658) & Rachel (_____) BRACKETT (-1651); m1 Peter BRACKETT; m probably near Sudbury, Suffolk c1618 Boston/Braintree [TAG 55:215-217]

SANDERSON, Edward (c1614-) & Mary EGGLESTON (not Sarah LYNN); m 16 Oct 1645 Watertown [REG 127:181]

SANDERSON, Jonathan[3] (1673-1743) & Abigail FISKE (1675-1759); m 14 July 1699 [REG 127:185]

SANDIN, Ephraim & Miriam[2] BASSETT (1655-); m c1681 [GM 1:193]

SANDS, James & Sarah[2] WALKER; m c1648 [GMB 3:1907]

SANFORD, Esbon[2] (1646-) & Sarah _____ [GMB 3:1629]

SANFORD, John[1] (c1608-1653) & 1/wf Elizabeth WEBB; m by 1633 Portsmouth [GMB 3:1628]

SANFORD, John[1] (c1608-1653) & 2/wf Bridget[2] HUTCHINSON (bp 1619-c1698), dau of William; m2 William PHILLIPS; m by 1637 Portsmouth/Boston [GM 3:480; GMB 3:1628]

SANFORD, John[2] (bp 1633-) & 1/wf Elizabeth SPATCHURST, dau of Henry; m Portsmouth 8 Aug 1654 [GMB 3:1628]

SANFORD, John[2] (bp 1633-) & 2/wf Mary (GORTON) GREENE, dau of Samuel; m1 John GREENE; m Portsmouth 17 Apr 1663 [GMB 3:1628]

SANFORD, Nathaniel & Susanna (CLARK) KELLY; m1 James KELLY; m3 John[2] BUTTOLPH [TAG 58:136]

SANFORD, Peleg[2] (1639-) & 1/wf Mary BRENTON, dau of William; m c1665 [GMB 1:22, 3:1628]

SANFORD, Peleg[2] (1639-) & 2/wf Mary CODDINGTON, dau of William; m 1 Dec 1674 Newport/Portsmouth [GMB 3:1628]

SANFORD, Robert & Elizabeth[2] SKELTON (c1630-); m by 1652 Boston [GMB 3:1686]

SANFORD, Samuel[2] (bp 1635-) & Sarah WODELL, dau of William; m Portsmouth 1661 [GMB 3:1628]

SANFORD, Samuel[2] (bp 1635-) & Susanna SPATCHURST, dau of William; m Portsmouth 13 Apr 1686 [GMB 3:1628]

SAPATTA, Philip (negro) & _____[2]_____ (-1680/1), dau of Angola[1] [Boston TR]

SARGENT, Thomas[2] (1643-) & Rachel BARNES; m Salisbury 2 Mar 1667[/8] [GMB 3:1632]

SARGENT, William & Elizabeth[2] PERKINS (bp 1611-); m c1636 [GMB 3:1432]

SARGENT, William (c1624-1715/6) & Abigail CLARK; m Ipswich 10 Sept 1651 [REG 148:78]

SARGENT, William[1] (c1611-1673[/4]-5) & 1/wf Elizabeth PERKINS, dau of John; m by 1636 Amesbury [GMB 3:1632]

SARGENT, William[1] (c1611-1673[/4]-5) & 2/wf Joanna (PINDER) ROWELL (c1621-1690); m1 Valentine ROWELL; m3 Richard CURRIER; m Amesbury 18 Sept 1670 [GMB 3:1632]

SARGENT, William[2] (1645[/6]-) & Mary COLBY, dau of Anthony; m Amesbury 23 Sept 1668 [GMB 3:1632]

SATTERLY, John & Phebe PIERCE (1663-1684+); bef 8 July 1684 Boston [RC 9:89; DS 13:180, 15:161; Harris]

SAUNDERS, Tobias & Mary PECKHAM; Newport, RI [ITC]

SAVAGE, Ephraim & Sarah HAUGH [REG 156:389]

SAVAGE, Henry & Elizabeth[2] WALFORD; m c1663 [GMB 3:1904]

SAVAGE, Thomas & Faith[2] HUTCHINSON (bp 1617-); m by 1638 [GM 3:480]

SAVORY, Samuel[2] (1651-) & _____ _____; m by 1678 Plymouth [GMB 3:1636]

SAVORY, Thomas[1] (c1617-1674-75/6) & Ann/Annis _____ (-1677+); m by 1645 [GMB 3:1636]

SAWDY, John[1] (c1619-bef 1670) & Ann HOLMES (-by 1693/4); m2 John HALLEDAY, perhaps m3 _____ GRIFFETH; m Boston 7 July 1653 [REG 148:142]

SAWDY, John[2] (1658-1681) & Elizabeth PETERS (c1662-1703); m2 Walter WRIGHT; m Ipswich "but one day before he was to be married to Mary Starkwether to whome he had been legally published" 25 Nov 1678 [REG 148:143]

SAWDY, Joseph[2] (1660-1718) & Bethia LUCAS; m Bristol 18 Oct 1682 [REG 148:147]

SAWTELL, John[2] (-bef 1700) & (only wife) Elizabeth POST (-1700); m bef 1691 Cambridge [REG 126:5]

SAWTELL, Jonathan[2] (1639-1690) & Mary TARBELL (-1676); m 3 July 1665 Groton [REG 126:5]

SAWTELL, Obadiah (1648-1740) & Hannah LAWRENCE (1661/2-1726+); m c1680 Watertown/Groton [REG 126:8]

SAWTELL, Richard (bp 7 Apr 1611-1694) & Elizabeth _____ (-1694); Aller, Somersetshire/Watertown [50 GMC]

SAWYER, John & 1/wf Mercy[2] LITTLE; m Marshfield Nov 1666 [GMB 2:1191]

SAWYER, John & 2/wf Rebecca (BARKER) SNOW, dau of Robert; m1 Josiah SNOW; m Marshfield 23 [blank] 169✗ [GMB 2:1191; REG 124:118]

SAWYER, Nathaniel[2] (1670-) & 1/wf Mary ?CARTER (-1709+); m by 1693 Lancaster [TAG 75:51]

SAYLES, John & Mary[2] WILLIAMS (1633-); m by 1652 [GMB 3:2009]

SAYLES, John (1654-1727) & Elizabeth OLNEY (1666/7-1699); m bef 1689 [AEJA]

SAYRE, Daniel & Hannah[2] FOSTER; m c1663 [GM 2:553]

SAYRE, Daniel[2] (-1708) m 2/wf Hannah (WHITE) TOPPING; m1 Thomas TOPPING; m Southampton. LI [TAG 38:226]

SAYWELL, David & Abigail[2] BUTTOLPH (1642[/3]-); m2 Thomas BINGLEY; m Boston 15 Aug 1660 [GM 1:520]

SCALES, James & Sarah[2] CURTIS, m Rowley 7 Nov 1677 [GM 2:263]

SCARLETT, George & Jane BENDALL; m Kersey, Suffolk 16 Jan 1615/6 [RCA]

SCARLETT, Samuel & perhaps Mary ELLIS; m Boston bef 1650s [RCA]

SCOFIELD, Daniel (c1650-1714) & Abigail MERWIN; m Stamford 12 July 1677 [REG 149:307]

SCONE, John & Sarah[2] HART (c1653-); m2 John BURBANK; m by 25 July 1673 Westfield [GMB 2:868]

SCOTT, John & Hannah[2] DUNKIN (1651-); m Roxbury 29 May 1672 [GM 2:370]

SCOTT, Robert & Elizabeth _____; m2 John SWEET; m by 1668 Boston [Suffolk Deed 5:531]

SCOTT, Robert[1] (c1613-1653/4) & Elizabeth _____ (c1616-); m c1638 Boston [GMB 3:1639]

SCOTT, Stephen & Sarah[2] LAMB (c1644-); m Braintree 27 July 1664 [GMB 2:1152]

SCOTT, Thomas & Margaret[2] HUBBARD (c1636-); m2 Ezekiel ROGERS; m c1656 [GM 3:441]

SCOTTOW, John & Rebecca ( ); m2 Caleb CHURCH [TAG 60:135]

SCOTTOW, Thomas (-1660-61) & Sarah[1] HARWOOD (c1635-1684+); m by 1655 [AEBK 3]

SCUDDER, Henry[2] (c1626-30-1661/2+) & Katherine[2] ESTY; m c1655 Southold [TAG 72:295]

SCUDDER, John & _____ _____ (perhaps Hannah); m by 1650 Barnstable [GMB 3:1468]

SCUDDER, John (c1616-20-) & Mary[2] KING [TAG 72:294]

SCUDDER, John[1] (bp 1618-) & Hannah _____ [TAG 72:297]

SCUDDER, Thomas[1] (c1586-1657) & Elizabeth _____ (-1665); m c1610 Horton Kirkby, Kent/Salem [TAG 72:293]

SCUDDER, Thomas[2] (c1622-6-1690) & Mary[2] LUDLAM; m c1650s Salem/Southold [TAG 72:294]

SCUDDER, William[2] (c1612-15-by 1657) & Penelope _____; Salem [TAG 72:294]

SCULLARD, Samuel[1] (c1616-c1647) & Rebecca[2] KENT; m 1641 Newbury [TAG 75:183]

SEALEY, William & Elizabeth[2] LYNN (1638-); m 2 Thomas COWELL; m by 14 Mar 1658/9 [GMB 2:1221]

SEARING, John & Susan PINE; m 10 May 1671 [GM 1:79]

SEARLE, Philip & Hannah SALTER; m Ottery St Mary, Devonshire 28 Sept 1657 [JP]

SEARLE, Robert & Deborah SALTER; m Ottery St Mary, Devonshire 26 Aug 1661 [JP]

SEARLE, Samuel (1668-1720+) & Sarah[2] PERHAM (c1679-1720+); m Chelmsford 26 Sep 1699 [AEBK 4:537]

SEARLE, William & Grace COLE; m Ottery St Mary, Devonshire 12 Apr 1659 [JP]

SEARS, Paul[2] (c1637-1707/8) & Deborah _____ (perhaps dau of George WILLARD); m by 1659 Yarmouth [GMB 3:1643]

SEARS, Richard (not Robert) & Bathsheba HARLOW; m 21 Oct 1696 Plymouth [TAG 60:160]

SEARS, Richard[1] (c1595-1676) & Dorothy JONES (c1603-1678[/9]), dau of George; m by 1637 Plymouth/Marblehead/Yarmouth [GMB 3:1643]

SEARS, Silas[2] (c1641-) & Anna _____ (perhaps dau of James BURSELL); m c1665 Yarmouth [GMB 3:1643]

SEAVER, Caleb[2] (1641-) & Sarah INGLESBY; m Charlestown 15 Dec 1671 [GMB 3:1645]

SEAVER, Joshua[2] (1641-) & Mary (____) PEPPER; m1 Joseph PEPPER; m Roxbury 28 Feb 1677[/8] [GMB 3:1645]

SEAVER, Nathaniel[2] (bp 1645/6-) & Sarah _____; m c1671 Roxbury [GMB 3:1645]

SEAVER, Robert[1] (c1609-1683) & 1/wf Elizabeth BALLARD (-1657); m Roxbury 10 Dec 1635 [GMB 3:1645]

SEAVER, Robert[1] (c1609-1683) & 2/wf Sarah (____) BURRELL (-1669); m1 John BURRELL; m aft 1657 [GMB 3:1645]

SEAVER, Shubael[2] (1639[/40]-) & Hannah WILSON; m Roxbury 7 Feb 1668[/9] [GMB 3:1645]

SEAVERNS, Samuel & Sarah[2] GRANT (1642[/3]-); m Charlestown 23 Feb 1665[/6] [GM 3:130]

SEDGWICK, William & Elizabeth[2] STONE; m2 John ROBERTS; m by 1666 [GMB 3:1771]

SEELEY, Nathaniel[2] (bp 1627-) & 1/wf Mary TURNEY, dau of Benjamin; m c Oct 1649 [GMB 3:1649]

SEELEY, Nathaniel[2] (bp 1627-) & 2/wf Elizabeth (BURR) (OLMSTEAD) GILBERT, dau of Jehu; m1 Nehemiah OLMSTEAD; m2 Obadiah GILBERT; m c1674 [GMB 3:1649]

SEELEY, Robert[1] (bp 1602-by 1668) & 1/wf Mary (_____) (HEATH) MASON (-bef 1651); m1 William HEATH; m2 Walter MASON; m St. Stephen, Coleman St., London 15 Dec 1626 [GMB 3:1649]

SEELEY, Robert[1] (bp 1602-by 1668) & 2/wf Mary (MANNING) WALKER (-1669+); m by lic 22 Dec 1666 NY [GMB 3:1649]

SELMAN, John & Mary WATERS (c1633-1717); m2 John DOLLING; m bef 1684 Boston [TAG 47:160]

SENDALL, Samuel[1] & Elizabeth (DANSON) WARREN (c1643-1727); m1 John[1] WARREN; m3 John HAYWARD; m4 Phineas WILSON [TAG 47:19]

SERGEANT, John & Deborah[2] TILLEY (1643-); m Barnstable 19 Jan 1662/3 [GMB 3:1821]

SEWARD, Obed & Bethia[2] HAWES (1637-); m Milford 31 Oct 1660 [GM 3:252]

SEXTON, George & Hannah[2] SPENCER (unproven) [GMB 3:1720]

SEYMOUR, Zachariah & Mary GREET; m2 Joseph HOLLISTER; m Wethersfield 9 Feb 1687/8 [TAG 72:42]

SHAPLEIGH, John & Sarah[2] WITHERS; m shortly aft 25 Apr 1671 [GMB 3:2046]

SHARP, John & Elizabeth[2] GIBBONS (1652-); m Saco 14 Nov 1667 [GM 3:47]

SHARP, Nathaniel[2] (bp 1544-) & Rebecca MARSHALL; m Salem 30 Dec 1668 (not 1658) [GMB 3:1654]

SHARP, Richard & Hannah[2] GILLAM (1639/40-); m by 1671 Boston [GM 3:63]

SHARP, Robert (-1654/5) & Abigail[2] WRIGHT (c1623-1702-8); m2 Thomas CLAPP; m2 William HOLBROOK; m bef 1640 Rehoboth [GMB 3:2073; AEBK 4:132]

SHARP, Robert & Mary[2] FRENCH (1670-); m2 Nathaniel DUNCKLEE; m 20 June 1687 [GM 2:592]

SHARP, Samuel[2] (c1593-c1656) & Alice STILEMAN (c1625-1667), dau of Robert; m by lic 4 Apr 1629 Salem [GMB 3:1654]

SHARP, Thomas[1] (c1587-1636+) & Tabitha _____; m c1612 Boston [GMB 3:1655]

SHATSWELL, John[1] (c1597-1646/7-7) & 1/wf _____ _____; m c1627 [GMB 3:1657]

SHATSWELL, John[1] (c1597-1646/7-7) & 2/wf Joanna _____; m2 John GREEN; m c1642 [GMB 3:1657]

SHATSWELL, Richard[2] (c1627-) & Rebecca TUTTLE, dau of Richard; m c1647 [GMB 3:1657]

SHATTUCK, Philip & Deborah[2] BARSTOW (bp 1650-); m Watertown 9 Nov 1670 [GM 1:178]

SHAW, Abraham (1589/90-1638) & Bridget BEST; m Halifax, Yorkshire 24 June 1616 Dedham [TG 10:92 & 50 GMC]

SHAW, Benoni (c1672-1750/1) & Lydia WATERMAN (1678-1757); m say 1696 Plymouth [REG 151:433]

SHAW, Daniel (c1654-bef 1708) & Ruth WILLIAMS (-1695+); m Stonington 17 Sept 1678 [TG 10:103]

SHAW, Fearnot (c1647-1698+) & Bethia LEAGER (-1696/7+); m by 4 Apr 1671 Boston [TG 10:108]

SHAW, George (c1661-1720) & Constant DOANE (1669/70-1741/2); m Eastham 8 Jan 1690/1 [REG 151:427]

SHAW, James[2] (c1626-) & Mary[2] MITCHELL (c1632-), dau of Experience; m2 John JENNY; m Plymouth 24 Dec 1652 [GMB 2:1272, 3:1661]

SHAW, John & Alice PHILLIPS; m bef 24 Apr 1674 Weymouth [TAG 38:72]

SHAW, John (-by 1691) & Martha KEENE; Boston [TG 10:99]

SHAW, John (1646-by 1677/8) & Sarah BRACKETT (c1651-1704/5+); m2 John[3] BENJAMIN; m3 James? JIMMERSON/JEMPSON; m bef 1672 Boston [TG 10:100; REG 155:287-8]

SHAW, John (1647/8-1709+) & Susannah WEST (-1709+); m Stonington 4 Oct 1677 [TG 10:101]

SHAW, John (1667-1696) & Hannah (HOWARD) MARE (?1656-1720/1); m1 Robert MARE, m3 Hugh AIRE (-1717); m 1690s Rehoboth [TAG 67:27 & TG 10:110]

SHAW, John (c1645-1688+) & 1/wf Hannah GROVER (c1646-1674); m bef 1667 Malden [TG 10:108]

SHAW, John (c1645-1688+) & 2/wf Elizabeth RAMSDELL; m Malden 12 Aug 1674 [TG 10:108]

SHAW, John[1] (c1597-1663[/4]) & Alice _____ (-1654/5); m by 3 Nov 1653 Plymouth [GMB 3:1661]

SHAW, Jonathan (c1663-1729/30) & 1/wf Mehitable PRATT (c1667-1712); m Plymouth 29 Dec 1687 [REG 151:419]

SHAW, Jonathan[2] (c1631-) & 1/wf Phebe[2] WATSON; m Plymouth 22 Jan 1656/7 [GMB 3:1661, 1946]

SHAW, Jonathan[2] (c1631-) & 2/wf Persis (DUNHAM) PRATT, dau of John; m1 Benajah PRATT; m Aug 1683 [GMB 3:1661]

SHAW, Joseph (1643-1701) & 1/wf Sarah POTTERTON (-1672/3+); m Charlestown 16 Dec 1664 [TG 10:107]

SHAW, Joseph (1643-1701) & 2/wf Ruth _____ (c1658-1683+); m by 1680 Weymouth/Boston/Charlestown [TG 10:107]

SHAW, Joseph (1643-1701) & 3/wf Elizabeth _____ (-1701+); m after 1683 Weymouth/Boston/Charlestown [TG 10:107]

SHAW, Joseph (bp 14 Mar 1618/9-1653) & 1/wf _____ _____; m bef 1643 Halifax, Yorkshire/Weymouth [TG 10:104]

SHAW, Joseph (bp 14 Mar 1618/9-1653) & 2/wf Mary SOUTHER, m2 John BLAKE; m Boston 1 Dec 1653 [TG 10:104]

SHAW, Nathaniel (1677-by 1712) & Margaret JACKSON; m Boston 12 July 1698 [REG 155:292]

SHAW, Thomas (c1625-1700/1) & Mary _____ (-1675+); m bef 1 July 1645 Charlestown/Stonington [TG 10:101]

SHELDON, Isaac & Mary[2] WOODFORD; m c1654 [GMB 3:2059]

SHELDON, Isaac & Mehitable[2] (GUNN) ENSIGN (1644-); m1 David ENSIGN; m by 1687 Windsor/Hartford [GM 3:172]

SHELDON, John (-1690) & Mary (CONVERSE) THOMPSON; m Billerica 1 Feb 1659/60 [REG 153:95]

SHELLEY, Robert[1] (c1587-by 1637) & _____ _____; m c1612 Boston/Roxbury [GMB 3:1662]

SHELLEY, Robert[2] (c1612-) & 1/wf Judith[1] GARNETT (c1608-by 1668); m Scituate 26 Sept 1636 [GMB 3:1662; GM 3:27]

SHELLEY, Robert[2] (c1612-) & 2/wf Susanna _____ (perhaps dau of Thomas DIMOCK); m c1668 [GMB 3:1663; GM 2:349]

SHEPARD, Israel[2] (c1650s-1719+) & _____ _____; m bef 1682 Taunton/Nansemond Co., VA [ASBO, p.372]

SHEPARD, John & Rebecca[2] GREENHILL (bp 1630-); m Cambridge 4 Oct 1649 Staplehurst, Kent [GM 3:152]

SHEPARD, John & Sarah[2] GOBLE (bp 1638-); m by 1661 Concord [GM 3:83]

SHEPARD, John[1] & Margaret SQUIRE; m Kingweston, Somerset 29 Apr 1630 [TAG 68:145]

SHEPARD, Ralph[1] & Thankslord PERKINS; m St Bride on Fleet St., London 21 May 1632 [TAG 67:29]

SHEPARD, Samuel & Dorothy[2] FLINT (1642-); m Braintree 30 Apr 1666 [GM 2:536]

SHEPARD, Samuel[2] (by 1650-1707) & Mary (PAGE) DOW (bp 1646-1717/18); m 14 July 1673 Haverhill [ASBO, p.372]

SHEPARD, Solomon[2] (c1650s-1731) & Sarah (EASTMAN) FRENCH (1655-1748); m1 Joseph FRENCH; m 4 Aug 1684 Salisbury [ASBO, p.374]

SHEPARD, Thomas & 1/wf Hannah ENSIGN (c1638-1697/8); m Malden 19 Nov 1658 [TAG 73:248]

SHEPARD, Thomas & 1/wf Margaret TUTVILLE; m 23 Jul 1632 Bossall, North Riding, Yorkshire [RCA]

SHEPARD, Thomas & 2/wf Joanna[2] HOOKER (c1622-); m c1638 [GMB 2:984]

SHEPARD, Thomas[2] & 2/wf Joanna _____; m by 1700 [TAG 73:249]

SHEPARD, William[1] & Experience[2] HART (c1650-); div 1677 Westfield/Conn. [TAG 70:83, 71:146; GMB 2:868]

SHEPARDSON, Daniel[1] (c1612-1644) & Joanna _____ (-1660[/1]; m2 Thomas CALL; m by 1637 Charlestown [GMB 3:1665]

SHEPARDSON, Daniel[2] (bp 1640-) & Elizabeth (CALL) TINGLEY, dau of Thomas; m1 Samuel TINGLEY. m Malden 11 Apr 1667 [GMB 3:1665]

SHEPLEY, John[1] (c1587-1678) & Anne _____ (-1685); m by 1637 Chelmsford/Salem [AEBK 4:563]

SHEPLEY, John[2] (c1637-killed 1694) & Susannah WHEELER (164x-killed 1694?); m Chelmsford 23 Sept 1672 [AEBK 4:565]

SHERBORN, Henry[1] (bp 1611-by 1680) & 1/wf Rebecca GIBBONS (-1667), dau of Ambrose; m 13 Nov 1637 Piscataqua [GMB 3:1667]

SHERBORN, Henry[1] (bp 1611-by 1680) & 2/wf Sarah (____) ABBOTT; m1 Walter ABBOTT; m by 30 June 1668 Piscataqua [GMB 3:1667]

SHERBORN, John[1] (1647-) & Mary COWELL; m c 29 Jan 1677[/8] Newbury [GMB 3:1667]

SHERBORN, Samuel[2] (1638-) & Love HUTCHINS; m 15 Dec 1668 [GMB 3:1667]

SHERLY, Robert & Sarah[2] EASTON (c1645-); m by 1687[/8] [GM 2:395]

SHERMAN, Benjamin[2] (1650-1719) & Hannah[2] MOWRY (1656-bef 1718), dau of Roger; m Portsmouth, RI 3 Dec 1674 [AEJA; GMB 2:1314, 1672]

SHERMAN, Eber[2] (c1634-) & Mary _____, NOT dau of Edward WILCOX [GMB 3:1672]

SHERMAN, Edmund (1572-1641) & Joan _____ (not MAKIN); m c1598 Eng [TAG 61:79]

SHERMAN, Edmund[2] (1641-) & Dorcas HICKS, dau of Samuel; m c1674 [GMB 3:1672]

SHERMAN, John (bp 1585-1615/6) & Grace RAVENS (c1591-1662); m2 Thomas ROGERS; m 26 Sep 1611 Wattisfield, Suffolk [TAG 62:76]

SHERMAN, John[2] (1644-) & Sarah SPOONER, dau of William; m c1674 [GMB 3:1672]

SHERMAN, John[2] (1646-1723) & Jane HATCH, dau of Walter; m Boston 25 Oct 1677 [GMB 3:1674]

SHERMAN, Peleg[2] (c1637-) & Elizabeth LAWTON, dau of Thomas; m Portsmouth 26 July 1657 [GMB 3:1672]

SHERMAN, Philip & Mary ANTHONY; m 1699 Portsmouth [TAG 67:21]

SHERMAN, Philip[1] (bp 1610/1-1686/7) & Sarah ODDING; m c1633 Roxbury [GMB 3:1671]

SHERMAN, Samson[2] (1642-) & Isabel TRIPP, dau of John; m Portsmouth 4 Mar 1674/5 [GMB 3:1672]

SHERMAN, Samuel & Naomi[2] JOHNSON (bp 1638-); m by 1661 [GMB 2:1101]

SHERMAN, Samuel[2] & Sarah MITCHELL; Wethersfield [TAG 77:257]

SHERMAN, Samuel[2] (1648-) & Martha TRIPP; m Portsmouth 23 Feb 1680/1 [GMB 3:1672]

SHERMAN, Samuel[2] (c1644-) & 1/wf Sarah DOGGETT, dau of Thomas; m c1674 [GMB 3:1674]

SHERMAN, Samuel[2] (c1644-) & 2/wf Hannah _____; m by 1688 Marshfield [GMB 3:1674]

SHERMAN, William[1] (c1613-1679) & Prudence HILL; m 23 Jan 1638[/9] Marshfield [GMB 3:1674]

SHERMAN, William[2] (c1642-) & Desire DOTY, dau of Edward; m Marshfield 25 Dec 1667 [GMB 3:1674]

SHERWOOD, Matthew & Mary FITCH (1643-1730), dau. Thomas [REG 155:246]

SHORE, Sampson & Abigail[2] PURCHASE (bp 1624-); m c1643 Boston [GMB 3:1528]

SHORT, Clement & Faith[2] MUNT (1645-); m Boston 21 Nov 1660 [GMB 2:1318]

SHRIMPTON, Samuel & Elizabeth ROBERTS; m 12 May 1670 Boston [NGSQ 63:200]

SHUTE, George & Elizabeth[2] GILBERT (c1607-); m by 1626 [GM 3:59]

SHUTE, Michael (-1706) & Mary RAINSFORD (not VERMAY) (1662/3-1707+); m bef 1681 Boston [REG 139:304]

SIBLEY, John & Rachel[2] LEACH (c1622-); m2 Thomas GOLDTHWAIT; m c1642 [GMB 2:1163]

SIBLEY, John & Rachel[2] PICKWORTH (bp 1646-); m c1675 Manchester [GMB 3:1463]

SILLIS, Richard[1] & Eglin[1] (HANFORD) DOWNE (bp 1586-1653[/4?]+); m1 _____ DOWNE; m2 Jeffrey HANFORD; m Scituate 15 Dec 1637 [GM 3:206]

SILSBY, Ephraim & Rachel[2] BASSETT (1666-); m Salem 23 Jan 1693[/4] [GM 1:193]

SILVESTER, Benjamin[2] (bp 1657-) & Mary STANDLAKE, dau of Richard; m c1687 Scituate [GMB 3:1680]

SILVESTER, Israel[2] (c1640-) & Martha _____; m by 1674 Scituate [GMB 3:1680]

SILVESTER, John[2] (1634/5-) & Sarah _____; m c1659 Marshfield [GMB 3:1679]

SILVESTER, Joseph[2] (1638-) & Mary[2] BARSTOW (1641-); m by 1664 Scituate [GMB 3:1680; GM 1:177]

SILVESTER, Richard[1] (c1608-1663) & Naomi _____ (-by 1668); m c1633 Weymouth [GMB 3:1679]

SILVESTER, Thomas & Sarah[2] (GRANT) SEAVERNS; m1 Samuel SEAVERNS; m by 27 Nov 1696 [GM 3:131]

SIMMONS, Aaron & Mary[2] WOODWORTH (1650/1-); m Scituate 24 Dec 1677 [GMB 3:2066]

SIMMONS, John & Hannah HATHAWAY; m Taunton 14 Dec 1697 [TAG 75:112]

SIMMONS, John & Mary _____, m2 John BUTTON; m bef 1663 Boston [RCA]

SIMMONS, John & Welthean (_____) GODDARD; m1 John[1] GODDARD; m by 10 May 1670 Dover [GM 3:87]

SIMONDS, Benjamin[2] (1654-) & 1/wf Rebecca HEYWOOD (not Tidd) (1660-bef 1713); m c1680s Woburn [REG 148:239]

SIMONDS, William & Mary[2] WADE; m2 Francis LITTLEFIELD; m by 1669 Charlestown [GMB 3:1386]

SIMONS, William (-1664-84) & Mary _____ (-1657-85); m bef 1654 East Hampton, L.I./Isle of Wight/Albemarle Co., NC [DR]

SIMONSON, Aaron[2] (c1653-) & Mary WOODWORTH, dau of Walter; m Scituate 24 Dec 1677 [GMB 3:1683]

SIMONSON, John[2] (c1644-) & Mercy PABODIE; m Duxbury 16 Nov 1669 [GMB 3:1683]

SIMONSON, Moses[1] (c1605-1689-91) & Sarah _____; m c1635 or 1660 [GMB 3:1683]

SIMONSON, Moses[2] (c1639-) & Patience[2] BARSTOW (1643-), dau of William; m2 Samuel BAKER; m c1664 [GM 1:177; GMB 3:1683]

SIMPSON, Henry & Jane[2] NORTON (c1618-); m2 Nicholas BOND; m c13 Mar 1638 [GMB 2:1341]

SKELTON, Samuel[1] (bp 1592/3-1634) & Susanna TRAVIS (bp 1597-1630/1), dau of William; m Sempringham, Lincolnshire, 27 Apr 1619 [GMB 3:1685]

SKERRY, Henry[1] & Elizabeth MOULTON; m c1633 Deanery of Flegg/Salem [REG 147:146]

SKINNER, John & Mary[2] EASTON; m c1664 Hartford [GM 2:395]

SKINNER, John (1673-1751) & 2/wf Sarah WILSON (1675/6-), dau of Michael; Norton [Wilson]

SLASON, John[3] & Mary[3] HOLMES (delete CLASON entry); m 12 Jan 1692 Stamford [TAG 43:41]

SLAWSON, Eleazer & Mary CHAPMAN; by 1672 Stamford [GMB 1:334]

SLOAN, Thomas & Elizabeth[2] PALMER (c1617-); m2 William CHAPMAN; m bef 29 Mar 1656 [GMB 3:1381]

SLOPER, Richard & Mary[2] SHERBORN (1640-); m 21 Oct 1658 [GMB 3:1667]

SMALL, Daniel[3] & probably Abigail[3] SNOW; Truro/Provincetown [TAG 71:135]

SMALLEY, Isaac[2] (1647-) & 1/wf Esther WOOD; m Piscataway 20 Feb 1683/4 [GMB 3:1689]

SMALLEY, John[1] (c1613-1692) & Ann WALDEN (-1693/4); m Plymouth 29 Nov 1638 Piscataway [GMB 3:1689]

SMALLEY, John[2] (1644-) & Lydia MARTEN; m Piscataway 18 Oct 1676 [GMB 3:1689]

SMEDLEY, Baptiste (bp 31 July 1609-1675) & Katherine SHORTHOSE (-1679); m Derbyshire/Charlestown 27 Mar 1645 [50 GMC]

SMITH, Adam[2] (c1649-) & Elizabeth BROWN; m bef 1688 Smithtown [Smith, p.48]

SMITH, Andrew & Mary[2] BUNDY (1653-); m Taunton 5 Jan 1673 [GM 1:481]

SMITH, Benjamin & Jehoidan[2] PALFREY (bp 1636-); m Reading 27 Mar 1661 [GMB 3:1371]

SMITH, Benjamin (-1713) & Lydia CARPENTER (-1711); m c1660 Pawtuxet, RI [AEJA]

SMITH, Benjamin (c1672-1751) & 1/wf Mercy ANGELL (c1675-1719+); m Providence, RI 12 Apr 1693 [AEJA]

SMITH, Christopher & Sarah _____; m bef Oct 1655 Northampton [Pynchon Court Book, pp. 389-90]

SMITH, Christopher (c1600s-1676) & Alice _____ (c1600s-1679+); m c1623 Providence [AEJA]

SMITH, Daniel & Hannah³ COOLIDGE (1671-1750); m 3 Nov 1693 Watertown [AEBK 3]

SMITH, Daniel² & Mary² GRANT (c1648-); m Watertown 27 Jan 1667[/8?] [GM 3:131]

SMITH, Daniel² (bp 1646/7-) & Mary YOUNG; m Eastham 3 Mar 1676[/7?] [GMB 3:1698]

SMITH, Ebenezer³ & Abigail³ BOLTON; m 27 Oct 1691 Hadley [TAG 67:246]

SMITH, Edward (c1630s-1693) & Amphillis ANGELL (c1644-1694+); m Providence 9 May 1663 [AEJA]

SMITH, Francis¹ (c1578-1667+) & _____ _____ (-1667); m by 1627 or earlier Roxbury [GMB 3:1690]

SMITH, Henry¹ (c1610-1681-2) & Ann² PYNCHON (c1618-), dau of William; m c1635 Dorchester/Springfield/England [GMB 3:1538, 1691]

SMITH, Henry³ (c1673-) & Rebecca _____; m c1698 [RCA]

SMITH, Isaac & Elizabeth² UNDERHILL (1669-); m by 1690 [GMB 3:1862]

SMITH, James & 1/wf Hannah³ GOODENOW (1657-1691); m Sudbury 25 Mar 1680 [AEBK 3]

SMITH, James & 2/wf Hannah (PENDLETON) (BUSH) RUTTER, dau of James; m 5 May 1693 [AEBK 3]

SMITH, James & Sarah² COKER (1643-); m Newbury 26 July 1667 [GM 2:143]

SMITH, James² & Martha _____ Newtown [NYGBR 134]

SMITH, James² (1637-1687) & Martha MILLS (1653-); m2 1689/90 Christopher GRANT; m c1673 Berwick [AEBK 1:434]

SMITH, John "Blue" & _____² STRICKLAND; m c1650 [GMB 3:1786]

SMITH, John & Anne² MELLOWS (c1611-); m Boston, Lincolnshire 26 Nov 1631 [GMB 2:1249]

SMITH, John & Catherine² MORRILL (c1627-); m Roxbury 1 Aug 1647 [GMB 2:1291]

SMITH, John & Elizabeth² GOODALE; m by 1658 [GM 3:105]

SMITH, John & Hannah² PARKE (bp 1658-); m Hingham 6 Apr 1680 [GMB 3:1390]

SMITH, John & Huldah² HUSSEY (c1646-); m Hampton 26 Feb 1666[/7] [GMB 2:1051]

SMITH, John & Lydia² ELIOT (bp 1631-); m by 1658 Dedham [GM 2:416]

SMITH, John & Mary² HORNE (c1657-); m Charlestown 22 Oct 1677 [GMB 2:993]

SMITH, John & Sarah² WHIPPLE (bp 1641[/2]-); m c1662 Providence [GMB 3:1973]

SMITH, John & Susanna[2] HINCKLEY (bp 1625-); m by 1644 Barnstable/Tenterden, Kent [GM 3:333]

SMITH, John (-1672/3) & Sarah (perhaps CONVERSE) (-1687); m by 1659 Charlestown [REG 153:96]

SMITH, John (1655/6-by 1736) & Mary _____ (not Tinker); m Lyme 26 Oct 1685 [AEJA wrong]

SMITH, John (c1600-1669) & Mary _____ (c1600-1659); m bef 1621 Lancaster [AEJA]

SMITH, John (1669-1737+) & Susanna KEMBALL (1673-by 1727?); m by 1695 Concord /Watertown/Weston/Leicester/Worcester [Watertown VR 435; TAG 61:242]

SMITH, John[1] (1659-1727) & Mary ELLINGWOOD (1664-1750); m bef 1686 Beverly [TAG 61:7; GM 2:423]

SMITH, John[1] (bp 31 July 1618-1683) & Anne TREADWAY (c1617-perhaps 1719); m c1639 Sudbury [AEBK]

SMITH, John[2] "Nan" & 1/wf Anna GILDERSLEEVE [NYGBR 134]

SMITH, John[2] "Nan" & 2/wf Elizabeth (WICKES) TOWNSEND [NYGBR 134]

SMITH, John[2] (1641-1718?) & Mary[2] BEECH (1641-); m Watertown 19 Apr 1665 [AEBK 1:435]

SMITH, John[2] (bp 1644-) & Hannah WILLIAMS; m Eastham 24 May 1670 [GMB 3:1698]

SMITH, Jonathan & Martha[2] BUSHNELL; m Saybrook 1 Jan 1663[/4] [GM 1:511]

SMITH, Jonathan & Mehitable[2] HOLDRED (1652-); m Haverhill 25 Jan 1669[/70?] [GM 3:371]

SMITH, Jonathan[2] (c1659-1724) & Jane PEABODY (c1660-1726); m Watertown 16 Mar 1682/3 [AEBK 1:372]

SMITH, Joseph & Ruth[2] BEARDSLEY; m c1668 Jamaica [GM 1:226]

SMITH, Joseph (-1735) & Elizabeth (GIBSON) HARRIS (c1665-1745) [REG 156:357]

SMITH, Joseph (1643-1712) & Hannah TIDD (1652-1735/6); m2 _____ CUTLER; m Watertown 1 Dec 1674 [AEBK 1:435]

SMITH, Joseph (1655-1718) & 1/wf Lydia _____ (-bef 1692); m by 1682 Middletown/ Hartford/Farmington [Hist. of N.B., 390; Manwaring 2:433; Stanley 28; GBS]

SMITH, Joseph (1655-1718) & 2/wf Joanna LOOMIS; m by 1692 Farmington [Desc. by the Female Branches of Joseph Loomis 1:279; GBS]

SMITH, Joseph (c1674-1736) & Esther PARSONS (1672-1760); m Springfield 15 Sept 1698 [REG 148:221]

SMITH, Martin (-1704) & 2/wf Sarah _____ (-executed 25 Aug 1698); c1693 Deerfield/Northampton [Harris]

SMITH, Matthew[1] (-by 1681) & Jane _____; Sandwich, Kent/ Charlestown [TG 10:120]

SMITH, Philip & Rebecca[2] FOOTE (c1634-); m2 Aaron COOKE; m by 1659 Wethersfield [GM 2:543]

SMITH, Ralph[1] (c1590-1660/1) & 1/wf _____ _____ (-by 1633); m by 1629 [GMB 3:1696]

SMITH, Ralph[1] (c1590-1660/1) & 2/wf Mary (GOODALL) MASTERSON; m1 Richard MASTERSON. m by 1 July 1633 [GMB 3:1696]

SMITH, Ralph[1] (c1616-1685) & Grace _____ (-1685+) (NOT the widow of Thomas HATCH); m c1640 Hingham/Eastham [GMB 3:1698]

SMITH, Richard & 2/wf Elizabeth WADE; m c1691 Lyme [TAG 49:209]

SMITH, Richard & Hannah[2] CHENEY (1642-); m Newbury 16 Nov 1659 [GM 2:62; TAG 76:247]

SMITH, Richard (c1621-by 1682) & 1/wf Mary KERLEY (-1654); m Sudbury 6 Oct 1647 [AEJA]

SMITH, Richard (c1621-by 1682) & 2/wf Joanna QUARLES (-1682+); m Boston 2 Aug 1654 Lancaster [AEJA]

SMITH, Richard[1] (-1692) & Sarah ?HAMMOND (not FOLGER) (-1707+); m bef 1641 Smithtown, L.I. [NYGBR 121:19, 21; GMB 2:852]

SMITH, Robert & Deborah (PRINCE) KING; m1 William KING; m 12 Jul 1694 Boston [TAG 59:232]

SMITH, Robert (c1626-1693) & Mary FRENCH (bp 2 Mar 1633/4-1720); m c1655 Boston/Ipswich [50 GMC; GMB 1:705]

SMITH, Samuel & Mary[2] ENSIGN (c1641-); m c1662 Wethersfield [GM 2:456]

SMITH, Samuel & Rebecca[2] HOAR (c1671-); m Taunton 20 Feb 1690[/1?] [GM 3:345]

SMITH, Samuel (c1575-80-) & Sarah _____, m2 Daniel RUMBALL; Wenham [50 GMC]

SMITH, Samuel[2] (bp 1641-) & Mary HOPKINS, dau of Giles; m Eastham 3 Jan 1665[/6] [GMB 3:1698]

SMITH, Samuel[2] (c1654-) & Hannah PERRING [RCA]

SMITH, Seth (-1682) & Mary[2] THURSTON (1642/3-1683+); m Medfield 27 Dec 1660 [AEBK 3]

SMITH, Stephen & Decline[2] LAMB (1637-); m Charlestown 7 Dec 1663 [GMB 2:1155]

SMITH, Thomas & Sarah[2] BOYLSTON (1642-); m by 1664 Charlestown [GM 1:371]

SMITH, Thomas (-1681/2) & Joannah _____; m bef 1635 Bradford [50 GMC]

SMITH, Thomas (c1635-1670) & Ruth WICKENDEN (-1670/1); m c1660 Providence [AEJA]

SMITH, Thomas[1] (c1601-1692/3) & Mary[2] KNAPP (bp 1613-1697+); m bef 1637 Watertown [AEBK 1:425; GMB 2:1145]

SMITH, Thomas[2] (1640-1727) & Mary[2] HOSMER (1645/6-1719); m Concord 19 Jan 1663 [AEBK 1:435; GM 3:422]

SMITH, Thomas[2] (c1651-) & Mary _____; m by 1682 Eastham [GMB 3:1698]

SMITH, William (c1632-) & Rebecca[2] KEYES (1637/8-1696); m2 Daniel KILLUM; m Topsfield 6 July 1657 [50 GMC; GMB 2:1129]

SNOW, Anthony & Abigail[2] WARREN; m Plymouth 8 or 9 Nov 1639 [GMB 3:1936]

SNOW, Jabez[2] (c1642-) & Elizabeth _____; m c1670 [GMB 3:1703]

SNOW, James[2] (c1643-1709) & Sarah JAQUITH (c1640s-1708/9+); m c1670 Lancaster [AEBK 3]

SNOW, John & Mary[2] SMALLEY (1647-); m Eastham 19 Sept 1667 [GMB 3:1689, 1703]

SNOW, John[2] (bp 1641-1706) & Mary GREEN (1644[/5]-1707+), dau of William; m c1667 Woburn [AEBK 3]

SNOW, Joseph (c1634-) & Mary _____; m c1670 [GMB 3:1703]

SNOW, Josiah[3] (-1692) & Rebecca BARKER (-1711); m2 1694 John SAWYER; m c1669 Marshfield [REG 124:118]

SNOW, Mark[2] (1628-) & 1/wf Anna COOKE, dau of Josiah; m Eastham 18 Jan 1654[/5] [GMB 3:1703]

SNOW, Mark[2] (1628-) & 2/wf Jane[2] PRENCE (1637-), dau of Thomas; m Eastham 9 Jan 1660[/1] [GMB 3:1523, 1703]

SNOW, Nicholas (not PRENCE) (1663-1754) & Lydia SHAW (c1670-1714); m Harwich 4 Apr 1689 Eastham [TAG 60:160; MD 3:180, 4:207; REG 151:430]

SNOW, Nicholas[1] (1599/1600-1676) & Constance[2] HOPKINS (-1677), dau of Stephen; m by 1627 [GMB 2:988, 3:1703; TAG 73:17]

SNOW, Richard[1] (bp 1608-1677) & 1/wf Mary WYNPENNIE; m Barnstaple 31 July 1633 Woburn [AEBK 3]

SNOW, Richard[1] (bp 1608-1677) & 2/wf Avis _____ (-1677+); m by 1676 [AEBK 3]

SNOW, Samuel[2] (1647-1717) & 1/wf Sarah WILSON (-1686); m 1668 Woburn [AEBK 3]

SNOW, Samuel[2] (1647-1717) & 2/wf Sarah PARKER (c1660-1695[/6?]); m Woburn 9 Aug 1686 [AEBK 3]

SNOW, Stephen[2] (c1636-) & Susanna (DEANE) ROGERS, dau of Stephen; m1 Joseph ROGERS; m Eastham 28 Oct 1663 [GMB 3:1703]

SNOW, Zerubbabel & Jemima[2] CUTLER; m Woburn 22 Sept 1697 [GM 2:271]

SOAN, William (-1671) & Dorothy _____; m bef 1668 Scituate [TAG 59:83]

SOLACE, John & Hannah[2] WOOLFE; m Salem 9 Dec 1655 [GMB 3:2068]

SOMES, Morris (c1603-4-1688/9) & 1/wf Marjorie JOHNSON (-1646/7); m 4 June 1635 Cranfield, Bedfordshire/Gloucester [TAG 53:12]

SOULE, George[1] (c1602-1677-80) & Mary BUCKETT (-1672); m by 1627 Plymouth [GMB 3:1706]

SOULE, George[2] (c1639-) & Deborah _____; m by 1671 [GMB 3:1707]

SOULE, John (-1707) & 2/wf Hester ( ) SAMPSON; m 1675-8 Duxbury [TAG 60:160; TG 1:233]

SOULE, John did not marry Esther DELANO [GMB 1:520]

SOULE, John[2] (c1632-) & 1/wf Rebecca SIMONSON (c1635-), dau of Moses; m c1656 [GMB 3:1683, 1707]

SOULE, Nathaniel[2] & Rose _____; m by 1681 Dartmouth [GMB 3:1707]

SOULE, Nathaniel[2] ~ _____ _____ (Indian woman); bef 4 Mar 1673/4 [GMB 3:1707]

SOULE, Zachariah[2] (c1627-) & Margaret _____; m by 163 [GMB 3:1706]

SOUTHWICK, Lawrence[1] & Cassandra[1] BURNELL (c1598-); m Kingswinford, Staffordshire 25 Jan 1623/4 [TAG 71:197]

SOUTHWICK, Samuel (1658-by 1709/10) & Mary[2] ROSS (1666-1704+); m Ipswich 24 June 1686 [REG 157:40]

SOUTHWORTH, Constant[1] (c1612-1678/9) & Elizabeth COLLIER (-1678/9+), dau of William; m Plymouth 2 Nov 1637 [GMB 3:1711]

SOUTHWORTH, Edward[2] & Mary PABODIE, dau of William; m Duxbury 16 Nov 1671 [GMB 3:1711]

SOUTHWORTH, Nathaniel[2] & Desire GRAY; m Plymouth 10 Jan 1672 [GMB 3:1711]

SOUTHWORTH, Thomas (c1617-1669) & Elizabeth REYNOR (-1679); m Plymouth 1 Sept 1641 [GMB 3:1714]

SOUTHWORTH, William[2] (c1659-) & 1/wf Rebecca PABODIE (-1702), dau of William; m by 1681 Little Compton [GMB 3:1711]

SOWTHER, Nathaniel (c1592-1655) & 1/wf Alice DEVONPORT (-1651); m 28 Mar 1613 St. Peters, Derbyshire/Boston [TAG 42:218]

SOWTHER, Nathaniel (c1592-1655) & 2/wf Sarah (JURDAIN) HILL; m1 William HILL; m3 Edmund GREENLEAF; m Boston 5 Jan 1653 [TAG 42:218]

SPARKS, John & Dorothy COLT (c1667-1712); m2 John PARSONS; m by 1694 Windsor [REG 145:330]

SPARROW, Jonathan[2] & 1/wf Rebecca BANGS, dau of Edward; m Eastham 26 Oct 1654 [GMB 3:1717]

SPARROW, Jonathan[2] & 2/wf Hannah (PRENCE) MAYO, dau of Thomas; m1 Nathaniel MAYO; m by 1671 [GMB 3:1717]

SPARROW, Jonathan[2] & 3/wf Sarah (LEWIS) COBB, dau of George; m1 James COBB; m Barnstable 23 Nov 1693 [GMB 3:1717]

SPARROW, Richard[1] (c1605-1660/1) & Pandora _____; m c1629 Eastham [GMB 3:1717]

SPEAR, George & Mary[2] HEATH (bp 1627-); m by 1644 [GMB 2:903]

SPECK, Gerard (Dutchman) & Mary PURCHASE; m by 22 June 1667 Hartford [WMJ 741]

SPENCER, Abraham & Abigail[2] ATKINSON (1657-); m c1676 Boston [GM 1:102]

SPENCER, Humphrey[3] (c1638-1700) & 1/wf Elizabeth SHEARS; m c1673 Berwick [CG, 21]

SPENCER, Humphrey[3] (c1638-1700) & 2/wf Grace _____ (-1686+); m bef 1676 Berwick [CG, 21]

SPENCER, Jared[2] & Hannah PRATT, dau of John; m Hartford 22 Dec 1680 [GMB 3:1720]

SPENCER, Moses[3] (c1642-1693) & Elizabeth (FREETHY) BOTTS, m1 Isaac BOTTS; m bef 1679 Berwick [CG, 23]

SPENCER, Obadiah[2] & Mary DISBOROUGH, dau of Nicholas; m c1666 [GMB 3:1720]

SPENCER, Samuel & Sarah _____; m c1668 [GMB 3:1724]

SPENCER, Samuel[2] (c1639-) & Sarah _____; m c1684 [GMB 3:1720]

SPENCER, Thomas[1] (bp 1607-1687) & 1/wf Anne DORRYFALL (-by 1645); m aft 2 Nov 1634 Hartford [GMB 3:1720]

SPENCER, Thomas[1] (bp 1607-1687) & 2/wf Sarah BEARDING, dau of Nathaniel; m Hartford 11 Sept 1645 [GMB 3:1720]

SPENCER, Thomas[1] (c1596-1681) & Patience[2] CHADBOURNE (bp 8 Nov 1612-1683); m England bef 1629 Berwick/Kittery [GM 2:33, CG, 5]

SPENCER, Thomas[2] & Esther ANDREWS (1641-), dau of William; m c1666 [GMB 3:1720; GM 1:66]

SPENCER, William[1] (bp 1601-1640) & Agnes HARRIS (bp 1604-1680+); m2 William EDWARDS; m c1633 Barnstaple, Devonshire/Stotfold, Bedfordshire/ Hartford/Cambridge [GMB 3:1724; TAG 63:41]

SPOFFORD, John (bp 21 Apr 1611-1678) & Elizabeth SCOTT (bp 18 Nov 1623-1678+); m 1646 Ipswich [50 GMC]

SPOONER, William & Hannah[2] PRATT (c1632-); m Plymouth 18 Mar 1651[/2?] [GMB 3:1512]

SPRAGUE, Anthony[2] (bp 1636-) & Elizabeth BARTLETT, dau of Robert [GMB 3:1737]

SPRAGUE, Francis[1] & 2/wf _____ _____; by 1630 Plymouth/ Duxbury [GMSP]

SPRAGUE, Francis[1] (c1590-1670+) & 1/wf _____ _____; m c1614 England/Plymouth/Duxbury [GMB 3:1726]

SPRAGUE, John (c1635-1677) & Ruth BASSETT (1635-1693/4+), dau of William; m2 _____ THOMAS; m c1655 Plymouth [TAG 41:179; GMB 3:1727]

SPRAGUE, John[2] (bp 1624-) & Lydia[2] GOFFE (c1631-); m Malden 2 May 1651 [GMB 3:1730; GM 3:97]

SPRAGUE, John[2] (bp 1638-) & Elizabeth HOLBROOK, dau of William; m2 James BICK; m Hingham 6 Dec 1666 [GMB 3:1737]

SPRAGUE, Jonathan[2] (bp 1648-) & Mehitable HOLBROOK; m c1670 Hingham [GMB 3:1737]

SPRAGUE, Phineas (bp 1637-) & Mary CARRINGTON; m Malden 11 Dec 1666 [GMB 3:1730]

SPRAGUE, Ralph[1] (c1595-1650) & Johane/Joan WARREN (-1680), dau of Richard; m2 Edward CONVERSE; m Fordington St. George, Dorsetshire 15 Aug 1623 Woburn [GMB 3:1730]

SPRAGUE, Richard[1] (c1605-1668) & Mary _____ (-1672-4); m c1632 Charlestown [GMB 3:1735]

SPRAGUE, Richard[2] & 1/wf Eunice CHESTER, dau of Leonard; m Charlestown 25 Feb 1672[/3] [GMB 3:1730]

SPRAGUE, Richard[2] & 2/wf Katharine (RICHARDSON) ANDERSON, dau of Amos; m1 David ANDERSON; Charlestown [GMB 3:1730]

SPRAGUE, Samuel[2] (bp 1632-) & Rebecca CRAWFORD; m Boston 23 Aug 1655 [GMB 3:1730]

SPRAGUE, Samuel[2] (bp 1640-) & Sarah CHILLINGWORTH; m c1666 Marshfield [GMB 3:1737]

SPRAGUE, William[1] (c1611-1675) & Millicent[2] EAMES (-1695/6), dau of Anthony; m by 1635 Hingham/Charlestown [GM 2:389; GMB 3:1737]

SPRAGUE, William[2] (bp 1650-) & 1/wf Deborah LANE; m Hingham 30 Dec 1674 [GMB 3:1738]

SPRING, Henry & Lydia[2] CUTTING (1666-); m c1686 Watertown [GM 2:274]

SPROUT, Robert & Elizabeth[2] SAMSON (c1642-); m c1662 Scituate [GMB 3:1623]

SPURR, John & Mercy[2] HOAR (1654[/5?]-); m Dorchester 26 Dec 1676 [GM 3:345]

SQUIRE, Luke & Margaret STUBBS (c1660s-1709/10); Hull [REG 143:333]

SQUIRE, Philip & Rachel[2] RUGGLES (1642[/3]-); m by 1665 Braintree [GMB 3:1606]

SQUIRE, Thomas[1] (by 1613-1663[/4]+) & Bridget _____ (perhaps GYVER); m by 1633 Charlestown [GMB 3:1740]

ST. JOHN, Matthias/Matthew[1] (-1669?) & Mary _____ (-c1714); m by 1633 Eng/Dorchester/Windsor [TAG 60:160; 53:241]

STANDISH, Alexander[2] (c1626-) & 1/wf Sarah ALDEN; m c1660 [GMB 3:1743]

STANDISH, Alexander[2] (c1626-) & 2/wf Desire (DOTY) (SHERMAN) HOLMES, dau of Edward; m1 William SHERMAN; m2 Israel HOLMES; m by 1689 [GMB 1:575, 3:1743]

STANDISH, Josiah & Sarah CARY?; m by 1690 Stafford [TAG 67:30]

STANDISH, Josias[2] & Mary DINGLEY; m Marshfield 19 Dec 1654 [GMB 3:1744]

STANDISH, Josias[2] & Sarah ALLEN, dau of Samuel; m aft 1655 [GMB 3:1744]

STANDISH, Miles[1] (c1593-1656) & 1/wf Rose _____ (-1620/1); m by 1618 [GMB 3:1743]

STANDISH, Miles[1] (c1593-1656) & 2/wf Barbara _____ (-1659+); m by 1624 [GMB 3:1743]

STANDISH, Miles[2] & Sarah[2] WINSLOW, dau of John; m2 Tobias PAYNE; m3 Richard MIDDLECOTT; m Boston 19 July 1660 [GMB 3:1744, 2030]

STANFORD, Robert ~ Lydia (_____) HANMORE; in court 8 Mar 1678/9 [GM 3:209]

STANLEY, Daniel[1] & Joan _____, m2 Thomas[1] PINSON [TAG 50:97]

STANLEY, Nathaniel & Sarah[2] BOOSY (1643-); m Hartford 2 June 1659 [GM 1:349]

STANNARD, Samuel & Elizabeth[3] NETTLETON (c1680-1753+); m2 1717 Joseph[3] POST; m by 1699 New London [TAG 71:184]

STANYAN, John (1642-) & Mary[2] BRADBURY (1642/3-); m Salisbury 17 Dec 1663/ m Hampton 15 Dec 1663 [50 GMC; GM 1:379]

STAPLES, Abraham & Mehitable[3] HAYWARD (c1670-1714+); m c1689 Mendon [AEBK 3]

STAPLES, John[2] (1647-1692) & Sarah ATKINS (c1651/2-c1724); m2 Samuel GURNEY; m3 Richard WILLIAMS; m c1670 Weymouth/Boston [REG 121:243]

STARK, Aaron (-1709/10+ and probably 1726+) & Mehitable SHAW (c1651-); m Stonington 27 Nov 1676 [TG 10:102]

STARK, Aaron ~ Mary HOLT; ordered to marry 11 Apr 1639 but probably didn't [PRC 1:28]

STARKEY, George & Susanna?[2] STOUGHTON; m by 1650 [GMB 3:1775]

STARR, Comfort & Martha[2] BUNKER (bp 1627-); m c1652 Charlestown [GM 1:486]

STARR, Robert & Susanna[2] HOLLINGSWORTH (c1633-); m Salem 24 Nov 1650 [GM 3:382]

STEARNS, Charles & Rebecca[2] GIBSON (c1634-); m Cambridge 22 June 1654 [GM 3:51]

STEARNS, Isaac[1] (c1600-1671) & Mary BARKER (-1677), dau of John; m by 1625 Watertown [GMB 3:1748]

STEARNS, Isaac[2] (1632/3-) & Sarah BEERS; m Cambridge 28 June 1660 [GMB 3:1749]

STEARNS, John[2] & 1/wf Sarah MIXER, dau of Isaac; m by 1654 [GMB 3:1749]

STEARNS, John[2] & 2/wf Mary LOTHROP, dau of Thomas; m Barnstable 20 Nov 1656 [GMB 3:1749]

STEARNS, Samuel[2] (1638-) & Hannah MANNING; m Cambridge 1 Feb 1662[/3] [GMB 3:1749]

STEBBINS, Edward[1] (perhaps bp 1594/5-1663-8) & Frances (TOUGH) (CHESTER) SMITH (-1673), dau of Ralph; m1 Sampson CHESTER; m2 Thomas SMITH; m c1629 [GMB 3:1753]

STEBBINS, John (c1611-1681) & 1/wf Ann MUNKE (c1630-1680); m 17 Apr 1644 Roxbury [TAG 41:95]

STEBBINS, Martin (c1589-1657) & 2/wf Jane GREEN (-1659); m 25 Dec 1639 Roxbury [TAG 41:95]

STEDMAN, Isaac[1] (bp 21 Apr 1605-1678) & 1/wf Elizabeth _____; m England/Boston [TAG 69:156]

STEDMAN, Isaac[1] (bp 21 Apr 1605-1678) & 2/wf Pilgrim[2] (EDDY) BAKER (1634-1709); m1 William BAKER, m3 Sylvester EVELETH; m bet 1676 and 11 Jan 1677/8 Boston/Cranbrook, Kent/Nayland, Suffolk/Watertown [GMB 1:613; TAG 69:156]

STEDMAN, John (-1675) & 2/wf Elizabeth[2] BLACKLEACH (1644-1678); m2 Thomas
DUNK; m bef 6 Mar 1664/5 Hartford/Wethersfield/Saybrook [REG 148:18;
Harris; GM 1:317]

STEDMAN, Nathaniel[2] (bp 9 Sept 1632-1678) & 1/wf Sarah[2] HAMMOND (bp 13 Sept
1640-); m c1650s Boston [TAG 69:157, 71:85]

STEDMAN, Nathaniel[2] (bp 9 Sept 1632-1678) & 2/wf Temperance _____ (-1679+); m
bef 1678 Boston [TAG 69:157, 71:85]

STEDMAN, Nathaniel[3] (1665-1705) & Hannah _____; m c1690 Muddy River/Brookline
[TAG 71:86, 146]

STEDMAN, Robert (1657-1735/6) & 1/wf _____ (not Mary[2], probably Lydia) FITCH
(-c1715); East Windsor & Lebanon [TAG 68:97-98]

STEDMAN, Thomas[2] (c1640-1706/7) & 1/wf Mary[2] WATSON (1644-1703/4); m by 1667
Roxbury [TAG 69:158; GMB 3:1949]

STEELE, George[1] (c1583-1663-4) & Margery SORRELL (-by 1663); m Fairstead, Essex
12 Oct 1608 Cambridge/Hartford [GMB 3:1755]

STEELE, James[2] (bp 1622-) & 1/wf Bethia BISHOP, dau of John; m perhaps at Guilford
18 Oct 1651 [GMB 3:1755]

STEELE, James[2] (bp 1622-) & 2/wf Bethia (HOPKINS) STOCKING; m1 Samuel
STOCKING; m by 1685 [GMB 3:1755]

STEELE, John & Mary[2] WARNER; m2 William HILLS; m Hartford 22 Jan 1645/6
[GMB 3:1930]

STEELE, John[1] (bp 1591-1664[/5?]) & 1/wf Rachel TALCOTT (-1653); m Fairstead,
Essex 10 Oct 1622 Farmington [GMB 3:1758]

STEELE, John[1] (bp 1591-1664[/5?]) & 2/wf Mercy (RUSCOE) SEYMOUR (-1668+);
m1 Richard SEYMOUR; m Farmington 25 Nov 1655 [GMB 3:1758]

STEELE, John[2] & Mary WARNER, dau of Andrew; m Hartford 22 Jan 1645[/6] [GMB
3:1758]

STEELE, Samuel & Mary[2] BOOSEY; m by 1652 Farmington [GMB 3:1759; GM 1:349]

STEPHENS, Edward & _____[2] SHERMAN (c1648-); m c1666 Marshfield [GMB
3:1674]

STEPHENS, Thomas (1576/7-1711) & Hannah PIERSON; m2 James COOPER; m after
1698 Southampton, L.I. [NYGBR 121:73]

STERLING, Daniel & Elizabeth SAWTELL (1638-bef 1692); m bef 1665
Watertown/Groton [REG 126:4]

STETSON, Robert (1615-1702/3) & Honour TUCK; m Plymouth, Eng. 2 May 1635
[REG 151:438]

STETSON, Robert ~ Elizabeth[2] WOODWORTH, dau of Walter; in court 27 Oct 1675 so
m c1675-6 [GMB 3:2066; GM 1:414]

STEVENS, Francis & Elizabeth[2] BROOKS (bp 1646-); m by 1663 Rehoboth [GM
1:410]

STEVENS, John[2] (1650-1725) & Mary[2] CHASE (1650/1-1724/5+); m 9 Mar 1669/70
Newbury [ASBO, p.173]

STEVENS, Joseph & Sarah SALLOWS (c1660-1735); m bef 1698 Beverly [TAG 72:8]

STEVENS, Joseph (1642-1677) & Sarah[3] THAYER (1654-1678+); m Mendon 2 July 1671 [AEBK 3]

STEVENS, Thomas & Mary GREEN (1634-); by 1658 Charlestown [GMB 2:813]

STICKNEY, Thomas & Mehitable DALTON (1658-); Haverhill [NHGR 10:70]

STICKNEY, William[1] (1592-1665) & Elizabeth DAWSON (1608-1678+); m 29 Nov 1628 Cottingham, Yorkshire/Rowley [REG 139:319]

STILEMAN, Elias[1] (bp 1587-c1662) & Judith ADAMS (bp 1585-1663+), dau of William; m St. Andrew Undershaft, London 28 Aug 1614 Wantage, Berkshire/East Lockinge, Berkshire/Salem [GMB 3:1761]

STILEMAN, Elias[2] (bp 1615-) & 1/wf Mary _____; m c1639 Salem [GMB 3:1761]

STILEMAN, Elias[2] (bp 1615-) & 2/wf Lucy (TREWORGYE)(CHADBOURNE) WILLS (c1632-bef 1708), dau of James; m1 Humphrey CHADBOURNE; m2 Thomas WILLS; m aft 14 Mar 1687/8 [GMB 3:1761]

STITSON, William[1] (c1601-1691) & 1/wf Elizabeth (_____) HARRIS (-1669/70); m1 Thomas HARRIS; c1634 [GMB 3:1765]

STITSON, William[1] (c1601-1691) & 2/wf Mary (_____) NORTON (-1677[/8?]+); m1 Francis NORTON; m Charlestown 22 Aug 1670 [GMB 3:1766]

STOCKBRIDGE, Charles (c1634-1683) & Abigail EAMES (-1709/10); m2 Nathaniel TURNER; m c1657 Scituate [TAG 38:186]

STOCKBRIDGE, John[1] (c1608-1657) & Anne KENDALL (c1613/14-); m 16 Jan 1631/2 Rayleigh, Essex/Scituate [NGSQ 74:111]

STOCKING, Samuel[2] (-1691/2) & Bethia[2] HOPKINS (c1632-); m2 James STEELE; m Hartford 27 May 1652 [TAG 77:25-27; GM 3:413]

STOCKWELL, Quinton (-1714/5) & Abigail BULLARD (1641-1730); m Medfield 11 Apr 1666 [AEBK 1:210]

STODDARD, Anthony & Christian[2] EYRE (c1628-); m by 1656 [GM 2:487]

STODDARD, Anthony (-1686/7) & Barbara (CLAPP) WELD (c1614-1655); m 24 July 1647 agreement Boston [AEBK 4:130]

STODDARD, Anthony[1] & Mary DOWNING (c1615-8-1647); m c1639 Boston [TAG 74:173; GMB 1:579]

STODDARD, John & Mary[2] FOOTE; m2 John GOODRICH; m3 Thomas TRACY; m by 1643 Wethersfield [GM 2:542]

STODDARD, Samson (1645-) & Susanna CLARKE; by 1670 [GMB 1:580]

STOERS, Joseph[2] (1632/3-) & Mary BLAISDELL, dau of Ralph; m c1661 [GMB 3:1782]

STOKES, Isaac & Rebecca[2] RAWLINS (c1643-); m c1663 [GMB 3:1553]

STONE, Daniel (1643-1712) & Patience[3] GOODWIN (1653-1715/6); m Kittery 19 Sept 1670 [CG, 33]

STONE, John & Abigail DIXEY; by 1654 Salem [GMB 1:556]

STONE, John[2] (bp 1618-1683) & Anne TREADWAY (c1617-1719?); m c1639 Watertown/Cambridge/Nayland, Suffolk [TAG 70:178]

STONE, Peter (1671/2-1725) & Elizabeth SHAW (1675-1704+); m Warwick, R.I. 25 June 1696 [TG 10:111]

STONE, Samuel & Sarah[2] STEARNS (1635-); m Cambridge 7 June 1655 [GMB 3:1749]

STONE, Samuel[1] (bp 1602-1663) & 1/wf _____ _____ (-c1640); m by 1634 [GMB 3:1770]

STONE, Samuel[1] (bp 1602-1663) & 2/wf Elizabeth ALLEN; m2 George GARDNER; m by 25 July 1641 Hartford [GMB 3:1771]

STORRER, William & Sarah _____ (not Sarah [STARBUCK]) [SPC]

STORY, William & Susanna[2] FULLER (c1650-); m Ipswich 25 Oct 1671 [GM 2:600]

STOUGHTON, Israel[1] (bp 1602/3-1644) & Elizabeth KNIGHT (-1681); m Rotherhithe, Surrey 27 Mar 1627 Dorchester [GMB 3:1775]

STOUGHTON, John[3] (1657-1712) & 1/wf Elizabeth[3] BISSELL (-1688); m Windsor 11 Aug 1682 [TAG 68:103]

STOUGHTON, John[3] (1657-1712) & 2/wf Sarah[2] FITCH (c1670-1731+); m2 probably Joseph Drake; m Windsor 23 Jan 1689 [TAG 68:103]

STOUGHTON, Nicholas & Sarah[2] HOAR; m Taunton 25 Feb 1691/2 [GM 3:345]

STOUGHTON, Samuel & Dorothy (BISSELL) WATSON (1665-1712+); m1 Nathaniel[2] WATSON [REG 123:279]

STOUGHTON, Thomas[1] (bp 1592[/3]-1661) & 1/wf Elizabeth TOMPSON (-1627); m Great Totham, Essex 5 May 1612 [GMB 3:1778]

STOUGHTON, Thomas[1] (bp 1592[/3]-1661) & 2/wf Margaret (BARRETT) HUNTINGTON (-1665/6+); m1 Simon HUNTINGTON; m c1634 Windsor [GMB 3:1778]

STOUGHTON, Thomas[2] (bp 1625-) & Mary[2] WADSWORTH; m Windsor 30 Nov 1655 [GMB 3:1778, 1895]

STOW, John[1] (bp 1582/3-1648) & Elizabeth[2] BIGG (bp 1590-1638); m Biddenden, Kent 13 Sept 1608 [AEBK 3; GM 1:287]

STOW, John[3] (1641[/2?]-1688) & Mary WHITMORE, dau of Thomas; m Middletown 13 Nov 1668 [AEBK 3]

STOW, Nathaniel[2] (bp 1621-1684) & 1/wf Elizabeth _____ (-1661); m bef 1653 Concord [AEBK 3]

STOW, Nathaniel[2] (bp 1621-1684) & 2/wf Martha (METCALF) (BIGNELL) SMITH (-1717); m1 William BIGNELL; m2 Christopher SMITH; m Concord 20 Aug 1662 [AEBK 3]

STOW, Nathaniel[3] (-1704/5) & Hannah WHITMORE (-1704); m Middletown Apr 1677 [AEBK 3]

STOW, Samuel[2] (bp 1623/4-1704) & Hope FLETCHER (-by 1702) dau of William; m c1649 Middletown [AEBK 3]

STOW, Samuel[3] (c1645-1720/1) & Elizabeth STONE (c1649-1736/7); m 16 Nov 1669 Marlborough [AEBK 3]

STOW, Thomas[2] (bp 1615-1680/1) & Mary GRIGGS (c1619-1680); m Roxbury 4 Dec 1639 [AEBK 3]

STOW, Thomas[3] (c1650-1729/30) & Bethia STOCKING (-1732); m Middletown 16 Oct 1675 [AEBK 3]

STOWELL, David[2] & Mary[3] STEDMAN (c1670-); m Cambridge 7 Apr 1692 [TAG 71:85]

STOWELL, Samuel & Mary[2] FARROW (bp 1633-); m2 Joshua BEAL; m Hingham 25 Oct 1649 [GM 2:500]

STOWERS, Joseph & Mary[2] BLAISDELL (1641[/2?]-); m2 William STERLING; m c1661 [GM 1:322]

STOWERS, Nicholas[1] (c1585-1646) & Amy _____ (-1667/8); m by 1630 Charlestown [GMB 3:1781]

STOWERS, Richard[2] (c1617-) & Hannah FROST, dau of Henry; m by 15 Oct 1647 [GMB 3:1781]

STRANGE, John & Alice FEERE; m 2 Feb 1643 Ware, Hertfordshire [TAG 56:149]

STRANGE, John & Sarah[2] COBBETT (1646-); m 1681 Boston [GM 2:117]

STRATTON, Bartholomew & Eliphal[2] SANFORD (bp 1637-); m c1656/7 Boston [GMB 3:1628]

STRATTON, John (-1627) & Anne[1] DEREHAUGH (c1584-1640-42); m c1603 Shotley, Suffolk/Badingham, Suffolk/Salem [REG 155:367, 156:42-3]

STRATTON, John (c1642-1691) & Mary[2] SMITH (c1645-1719); m Watertown 29 Nov 1667 [AEBK 1:435-6]

STRATTON, John[1] (1606-1641+) & _____ _____; m c1637 Salem [GMB 3:1783]

STRATTON, Joseph (c1667-1732) & Sarah[2] HOWE (1672-1746); m Marlborough 14 Nov 1695 [AEBK 3]

STRATTON, Samuel[1] (c1592-1672) & 1/wf Alice _____ (-1649-57); m probably near Podington, Bedfordshire c1624 Watertown/Boston [TAG 65:200-202 & DR]

STRATTON, Samuel[2] (c1592-1672) & 2/wf Margaret (BOWLINS) PARKER, m1 William Parker; m bef 27 June 1657 Boston [TAG 65:202]

STREET, Robert & Elizabeth HARKER, bef 1680s Boston [Suffolk Deed 12:282]

STRICKLAND, John[1] (c1595-1672) & _____ _____; m c1620 [GMB 3:1786]

STRICKLAND, Peter (c1646-1718/9-1723) & Elizabeth COMSTOCK (c1656-1734); m bef 1675 Ipswich/Flushing, NY/New London [AEJA]

STRONG, John & 2/wf Abigail FORD (bp 1619-); by 1637 Windsor [GMB 1:689]

STRONG, Return & Sarah[2] WARHAM (1642-); m Windsor 11 May 1664 [GMB 3:1927]

STRONG, Samuel & Esther[2] CLAPP (bp 1656-); m 19 June 1684 Dorchester [GM 2:78]

STUARD, Hugh & Watestill DENNE; m c1672? Falmouth/Yarmouth [TAG 60:160]

STUART, Duncan & Ann WINCHEST; m c1654 Ipswich [50 GMC]

STUDLEY, Joseph & Sarah[2] BROOKS (bp 1650-); perhaps [GM 1:414]

STURGES, Samuel & Mary[2] HEDGES; m by 1667 Yarmouth [GMB 2:906]

SUMMERS, John & Mary[2] SAMSON (c1650-); m c1684 [GMB 3:1623]

SUMNER, Clement & Margaret (ELSON) HARRIS; m Boston 18 May 1698 [REG 152:328]

SUMNER, William & Elizabeth[2] CLEMENT (bp 1633/4-); m c1652 Dorchester [GM 2:104]

SUTTON, Daniel & Mary[2] COLE (bp 1638/9-); m Charlestown 15 Apr 1667 [GM 2:156]

SUTTON, John & Elizabeth[2] HOUSE (bp 1636-); m Scituate 1 Jan 1661[/2] [GM 3:426]

SUTTON, Sarah ~ Scituate [Plymouth Court Sept 1690]

SUTTON, William & Mary JOHNSON (1672/3-); m Boston 31 Jan 1694 [REG 156:221]

SWAINE, Francis (bp 1620/1-by 1665) & Martha ____; m2 Caleb LEVERICH [TAG 74:248]

SWAINE, John[2] (bp 1634-bef 1717/8) & Mary[2] WEARE; m Hampton 15 Nov 1660 [TAG 74:249]

SWAINE, Richard[1] (bp 1595-1682) & 1/wf Basil ____; m by 1634 if 1st wife Easthamstead, Berkshire/Hampton [TAG 74:245]

SWAINE, Richard[1] (bp 1595-1682) & 2/wf Jane (____) BUNKER (-1662); m1 George BUNKER; m Hampton 15 Sept 1658 Nantucket [TAG 74:245]

SWAINE, William[2] (c1619-1657) & Prudence MARSTON; m2 Moses[1] COX; m c1642 [TAG 74:248]

SWAN, Gershom & Sarah[2] HOLDEN (c1657-); m Cambridge 20 Dec 1677 [GM 3:366]

SWAN, Henry & Joan[2] RUCK, m2 George HALSEY, m3 Henry[1] FARNHAM [TAG 62:35]

SWAN, John & Mary[2] PRATT (c1633-1702[/3]); m Cambridge 1 Mar 1655[/6] [GMB 3:1516]

SWAN, Thomas & Mary[2] LAMB (bp 1644-); m2 James BAYLEY; m by 1665 Boston [GMB 2:1155]

SWEET, Henry[3] (-1728) & Mary ANDREW (1664-1752); m 1681 East Greenwich [TAG 52:20]

SWEET, James[2 or 3] (?1623-1698) & Mary GREENE (1633-); m 1653 Providence/Warwick [TAG 53:29; 67:177; GMB 3:1790]

SWEET, John[1] (c1603-1637) & 2/wf Mary ____; m2 Ezekiel HOLLIMAN; m c1628 Providence [TAG 53:29; GMB 3:1790]

SWEET, John[2] & 2/wf Elizabeth ____; m2 ____ WILSON; m bef 1635 Warwick [TAG 53:29]

SWEET, John[2] & Elizabeth ____; m c1655 [GMB 3:1790]

SWEETSER, Benjamin (c1632-1718) & Abigail WIGGLESWORTH (bp 1640-1722); m2
  1719 Ellis CALLENDER; m by 1663 [REG 156:317]

SWIFT, William[1] (by 1596-by 1642/3) & 1/wf Sarah _____ (-1625); m bef 1625 St Mary
  Magdalene, Bermondsey, Surrey [TAG 77:168-9]

SWIFT, William[1] (by 1596-by 1642/3) & 2/wf Joane (_____) DIMBLEBY (-1663); m St
  Mary Magdalene, Bermondsey, Surrey 3 Jan 1625/6 Sandwich [TAG 77:169]

SWIFT, William[2] (bp 1627-1705/6) & Ruth _____; Sandwich [TAG 77:171]

SYLVESTER, Nathaniel[1] (c1620-1680) & Grizzell BRINLEY (bp 6 Jan 1635/6-1687); m
  bef 1652 Shelter Island [NYGBR 125:16]

SYMONDS, Mark[1] (c1584-1659) & 2/wf Joanna _____ (-1666) [TAG 74:115]

SYMONDS, Mark[1] (c1584-1659) & probably 1/wf Susan EDGAR; m Great Birch, Essex
  24 Apr 1609 [TAG 74:115]

SYMONDS, Samuel[1] (bp 1595-1678) & 1/wf Dorothy HARLAKENDEN; m Great
  Yeldham, Essex 2 Apr 1617 Ipswich [TAG 70:65, 152-3]

TABOR, Joseph & Hannah _____; m c1680-1 Little Compton [LCF]

TABOR, Joseph[2] (-1700+) & Hannah _____ (-1700+); Providence/Tiverton [TAG
  72:330]

TABOR, Philip[1] (c1605-1671-82) & 1/wf Lydia MASTERS, dau of John; m c1639 [GMB
  2:1236, 3:1792]

TABOR, Philip[1] (c1605-1671-82) & 2/wf Jane _____; m by 1669 [GMB 3:1792]

TABOR, Philip[2] & Mary COOKE, dau of John; m by 1668 Dartmouth [GMB 3:1792]

TABOR, Thomas[2] & 1/wf Esther COOKE, dau of John; m by 1668 Dartmouth [GMB
  3:1792]

TABOR, Thomas[2] & 2/wf Mary THOMPSON, dau of John; m by 1673 Dartmouth [GMB
  3:1792]

TAILER, William & Rebecca[2] STOUGHTON (bp 1641-); m Dorchester 25 Aug 1664
  [GMB 3:1775]

TAINTER, Jonathan (1654-c1712) & 1/wf Elizabeth WARREN (1660-1692); m
  Watertown 6 Dec 1681 [AEBK 1:479]

TAINTER, Joseph & Mary[2] EYRE (bp 1619-); m c1642 Watertown [TAG 65:21; GM
  2:487]

TALBY, John[1] (c1595-by 1644/5) & Dorothy RAWLINSON (bp. 5 Nov 1598-hanged
  1638); m Threckingham, Lincolnshire 14 Oct 1619 Spalding/Whaplode,
  Lincolnshire/Salem [TAG forthcoming]

TALBY, Samuel[3] (1665-) & Priscilla SOUTHWORTH; m Bristol 1 Mar 1689 (as
  Talbot) [TAG forthcoming; GMB 3:1711]

TALBY, Stephen[2] (bp 1632-by 1673/4) & Hannah PLACE, dau of Peter; m by 1662
  Boston [TAG forthcoming]

TALCOTT, John[1] (c1594-1659/60-60) & Dorothy MOTT (1669/70), dau of John; m c1625
  Hartford [GMB 3:1797]

TALCOTT, John[2] (c1625-) & 1/wf Helena WAKEMAN; m 29 Oct 1650 from secondary source [GMB 3:1797]

TALCOTT, John[2] (c1625-) & 2/wf Mary[2] COOKE (1646[/7?]-); m 9 Nov 1676 from secondary source Cambridge [GM 2:181; GMB 3:1797]

TALCOTT, Samuel[2] (c1635-1691) & 1/wf Hannah HOLYOKE, dau of Eleazer; m Springfield 7 Nov 1661 [GMB 3:1797]

TALMADGE, Thomas & Elizabeth[2] ALSOP (1650-); m by 1677 New Haven [GM 1:50]

TALMAGE, Robert[2] & Sarah NASH, dau of Thomas; m c1649 [GMB 3:1799]

TALMAGE, Simon[2] & Katharine HAY, dau of Bartholomew; m by 1638 [GMB 3:1798]

TALMAGE, Thomas[1] (c1580-by 1653) & _____ _____; m c1605 Barton Stacey, Hampshire/Lynn [GMB 3:1798]

TALMAGE, Thomas[2] & Elizabeth _____; m by 1643 [GMB 3:1799]

TALMAGE, William[2] & Elizabeth _____; m by 1632 Roxbury [GMB 3:1798]

TANKERSLEY, George & perhaps Tabitha[2] ABDY (1652-); m by 1673 [GM 1:7]

TAPP, Edmund[1] (c1592-by 1653) & Anne _____ (-1673); m by 1614 Great Haddam, Hertfordshire/New Haven/Milford [TAG 72:77]

TAPPAN, James (1665-) & Ann WARD; m Middletown 4 Feb 1691/2 [TAG 71:98]

TAPPAN, James[2] (bp 1642-3-1712) & Hannah[2] GARRETT (c1637-40-1731/2); m Guilford 5 Mar 1656/7? [TAG 71:97]

TAPPIN, John & Mary WOODMANSEE (c1629-1707); m2 William AVERY; m Boston 20 Aug 1654 [REG 147:45]

TATMAN, Jabez[2] (1641-) & 2/wf Elizabeth DAVIS, dau of William; m by 1695 Roxbury [GMB 3:1801]

TATMAN, Jabez[2] (1641-) & 1/wf Deborah TURNER (-1689); m Roxbury 18 Nov 1668 [GMB 3:1801]

TATMAN, John[1] (c1615-1670) & _____ _____ (-1668) (perhaps Joanna); m by 1640 Roxbury [GMB 3:1801]

TAYLOR, Edward (-1701) & Mary MERKS (-1705); m 19 Feb 1663 Barnstable [TAG 47:229]

TAYLOR, Gregory[1] (c1605-1657) & 1/wf _____ _____; m by 1630 Haverhill, Suffolk/Boston [GMB 3:1802]

TAYLOR, Gregory[1] (c1605-1657) & 2/wf Alice (_____) WATERBURY (-by 1657); m1 William WATERBURY; m 1631 Boston/Watertown/Stamford [GMB 3:1802]

TAYLOR, Henry & Lydia[2] HATCH (c1625-); m Barnstable 19 Dec 1650 [GMB 2:876]

TAYLOR, Henry[1] (-1719) & 1/wf Mary _____ [NYGBR 120:27]

TAYLOR, Henry[1] (-1719) & 2/wf Sarah PALMER (1666-); m2 Benjamin FIELD; m 1686 Boston/NYC [NYGBR 120:27]

TAYLOR, Jacob[2] (1670-bef 1750/1) & Rebecca WEEKS (-1716+); m 29 May 1693 Barnstable [NGSQ 61:110]

TAYLOR, John[2] (1649-1728+) & Sarah SCONE (1677/8-1713+); m Wethersfield 2 Mar 1698/9 [TAG 76:180]

TAYLOR, Joseph & Bethiah[2] BROWN? [GM 1:447]

TAYLOR, Samuel (1656-) & Mary ROBBINS (1667-); m Concord 9 Dec 1685 [REG 151:390]

TAYLOR, Samuel[2] (1649-51-1711) & Sarah (COLE) PEARSON (1654-1712); m1 John PEARSON; m Wethersfield 9 Dec 1678 [TAG 76:181]

TAYLOR, Stephen & Sarah[2] HOSFORD (bp 1623/4-); m Windsor 1 Nov 1642 [GMB 2:997]

TAYLOR, Stephen & Sarah[2] WHITE (c1641-); m2 Barnabas HINSDALE; m3 Walter HICKSON; m c1664 [GMB 3:1979]

TAYLOR, William[1] (c1620s-1686/7+) & Mary _____ (-1671/2+); m by 1649 Wethersfield/New London [TAG 76:179]

TAYLOR, William[2] (1659/60-1695+) & Elizabeth[3] BIGGS (c1673-1695); m Wethersfield 18 Dec 1693 [TAG 76:183]

TED, John & Elizabeth[2] FIFIELD (1657-); m Hampton 12 June 1678 [GM 2:524]

TEMPLE, Richard & Mary[3] BARKER (1677-1718+); m Concord 2 May 1699 [AEBK 3]

TERRILL, Roger & Abigail[2] UFFORD; m by 3 Nov 1644 [GMB 3:1858]

TERRY, John[2] (1637[/8]-) & Elizabeth WADSWORTH, dau of William; m Windsor 27 Nov 1662 [GMB 3:1806, 1895]

TERRY, Robert & Sarah[2] FARRINGTON [GM 2:496]

TERRY, Stephen[1] (1608-1668) & 1/wf Jane HARDEY (-1647); m Symondsbury, Dorsetshire 13 Mar 1633/4 [GMB 3:1806]

TERRY, Stephen[1] (1608-1668) & 2/wf Elizabeth _____ (-1683); m aft 1647 Hadley [GMB 3:1806]

THATCHER, John & Rebecca[2] WINSLOW (1643-); m by 1665 Marshfield [GMB 3:2033]

THATCHER, Judah & Mary[2] THORNTON (-1708); m Yarmouth c1666 [GMB 3:1815]

THAXTER, John & Elizabeth[2] JACOB (c1634-); m2 Daniel CUSHING; m Hingham 4 Dec 1648 [GMB 2:1070]

THAYER, Benjamin[3] (c1680-bef 1729) & 1/wf Sarah[3] HAYWARD (c1679-1711); m Mendon 15 Sept 1699 [AEBK 3]

THAYER, Cornelius (1670-1738) & Abigail[3] HAYDEN (c1674-1730/1); m c1694 Braintree [AEBK 3]

THAYER, Ebenezer[3] (c1674-1723) & Martha THOMPSON (c1675-1715+); m bef 9 July 1696 [AEBK 3]

THAYER, Ferdinando (1625-1712) & 2/wf Ann (_____) FREEBERY (c1648-1700+); perhaps widow of Richard Freebery of Pemaquid; m bet 1692-1696 Mendon [Sprague; AEBK 3]

THAYER, Ferdinando (c1620-1713) & 1/wf Huldah[2] HAYWARD (c1633-1690); m Braintree 14 Jan 1652[/3] [AEBK 3]

THAYER, Isaac[3] (c1672-1755) & 1/wf Marcy ROCKWOOD (-1700); m 1 Apr 1691/2 Mendon [AEBK 3]

THAYER, Jonathan[3] (1658[/9]-1690) & Elizabeth FRENCH (-1690+); m Medfield 13 July 1680 [AEBK 3]

THAYER, Jonathan[3] (1658[/9]-1690) ~ Sarah DARLING; c1686 [AEBK 3]

THAYER, Josiah[3] (c1666-1728/9) & 1/wf Sarah _____; m Mendon 7 Feb 1690[/1]; no evidence she was a BASS [AEBK 3]

THAYER, Nathaniel (1657['8]-1728) & Hannah[3] HAYDEN (1661/2-1743); m Braintree 27 May 1679 [AEBK 3]

THAYER, Samuel[3] (1666[/7?]-1721) & Mary BUTTERWORTH, dau of John; m by 1691 [AEBK 3]

THAYER, Shadrack[2] (bp 1629-1678) & 1/wf Mary BARRETT (-1659); m Braintree 1 Jan 1655 [AEBK 3]

THAYER, Shadrack[2] (bp 1629-1678) & 2/wf Deliverance PRIEST (c1645-172[2/]3); m Weymouth 12 July 1661 [AEBK 3]

THAYER, Thomas[1] (bp 1596-1665) & Margery WHEELER (bp 1600-1672[/3]); m Thornbury, Gloucestershire 13 Apr 1618 [AEBK 3]

THAYER, Thomas[2] (bp 1622-1692) & Hannah _____ (c1625-1697/8); m c1647 Braintree [AEBK 3]

THAYER, Thomas[3] (1664[/5?]-1738) & Mary POOLE (1668-); m Milton 28 Oct 1687 [AEBK 3]

THOMAS, _____ & Ruth (BASSETT) SPRAGUE (1635-1693/4+); m1 John SPRAGUE [TAG 41:179]

THOMAS, Elizabeth, ~ dau. of John; Marshfield [Plymouth Court Mar 1690/1]

THOMAS, Francis & Rebecca[2] INNES (1644/5-); m by 1665 [GMB 2:1058]

THOMAS, James & Martha[2] GODDARD (c1647-); m2 1717 Elias CRITCHET; m c1670 [GM 3:87]

THOMAS, Nathaniel & Deborah[2] JACOB (bp 1643-); m Hingham 19 Feb 1663/4 [GMB 2:1070]

THOMAS, William & Susanna (_____) ROGERS (-1677); m1 Robert ROGERS [REG 140:204]

THOMPSON, Simon (-1558) & Mary CONVERSE; m Woburn 19 Dec 1643 [REG 153:95]

THOMSON, David[1] (bp 1592-by 1628) & Amias COLE (-1672+), dau of William; m2 Samuel MAVERICK; m St. Andrew, Plymouth, Devonshire 18 July 1613 Boston [NHGR 9:113; GMB 3:1808]

THOMSON, James[1] (bp 1592-1681/2-2) & 1/wf Anne _____ (-1625); m c1618 [TAG 74:103]

THOMSON, James[1] (bp 1592-1681/2-2) & 2/wf Elizabeth _____; m by 1628 [TAG 74:103]

THOMSON, James[1] (c1593-1681/2-2) & 1/wf Elizabeth _____ (-1643); m by 1618
[GMB 3:1810]

THOMSON, James[1] (c1593-1681/2-2) & 2/wf Susanna (____) BLODGETT (-1660/1);
m1 Thomas BLODGETT; m Woburn 15 Feb 1643/4 [GMB 3:1810]

THOMSON, Jonathan[2] (bp 1628-) & Susanna[2] BLODGETT (1637-); m Woburn 28
Nov 1655 [TAG 74:104; GM 1:325; GMB 3:1811]

THOMSON, Simon[2] (bp 1619-) & Mary[2] CONVERSE, dau of Edward; m Woburn 19
Dec 1643 [TAG 74:103; GMB 3:1811]

THORNDIKE, John[1] (bp 1611-1668) & Elizabeth STRATTON (c1614-by 1668) dau of
John; m by 1637 Shotley, Suffolk/Ardleigh, Essex/ Salem/Ipswich/London
[REG 154:467+, 155:367, 156:43; GMB 3:1812]

THORNDIKE, Paul[2] (c1642-) & Mary PATCH, dau of James; m Beverly 28 Apr 1668
[GMB 3:1813]

THORNTON, Theophilus[2] (1651-) & Hannah _____; m by 1677 Boston [GMB 3:1816]

THORNTON, Thomas[1] (c1608-1699/1700) & 1/wf Ann TINKER (bp 1616-), dau of
Robert; m St. Margaret Moses, London 23 Apr 1633 [GMB 3:1815]

THORNTON, Thomas[1] (c1608-1699/1700) & 2/wf _____ (____) MORE; m1 _____
MORE; m Yarmouth 10 June 1683 [GMB 3:1815]

THORNTON, Timothy[2] (-1726) & 1/wf Experience HOLLARD; m c1673 [GMB
3:1815]

THORNTON, Timothy[2] (-1726) & 2/wf Sarah (____) GREENOUGH; m1 William?
GREENOUGH; m Braintree 9 Aug 1694 [GMB 3:1815]

THORPE, John[1] (c1608-1633) & Alice _____; m by 1633 [GMB 3:1817]

THRALL, Timothy & Deborah[2] GUNN (1641/2-); m Windsor 10 Nov 1659 [GM
3:172]

THREENEEDLE, Bartholomew & Damaris[2] HAWKINS (c1640-); m by 1660 Boston
[GM 3:264]

THRESHER, Samuel & Bethia[2] BROOKS (1662-); m Taunton 5 Dec 1683 [GM 1:411]

THROCKMORTON, John[1] & Rebecca[1] FARRAND (c1610-) (NOT COVELL); m by
1635 [TAG 77:234; LMM]

THURSTON, Benjamin[2] (1640-by 1668) & Elishua[2] WALKER (1635/6-); m Boston 12
Dec 1660 [GMB 3:1913; AEBK 3]

THURSTON, Daniel[2] (1646-1682) & 1/wf Mary[2] STEDMAN (1645-1680), dau of Robert;
m Cambridge 1 Apr 1674 [AEBK 3]

THURSTON, Daniel[2] (1646-1682) & 2/wf Hannah MILLER; m Rehoboth 16 Dec 1681
[AEBK 3]

THURSTON, Daniel[3] (1676-1745) & 1/wf Experience WARREN (-1704); m Medfield
28 Dec 1699 [AEBK 3]

THURSTON, Edward & Susannah[2] JEFFREYS (c1656-); m c1688 [GMB 2:1084]

THURSTON, John[1] (bp 1601-1685) & Margaret _____ (c1605-1662); m by 1633 [AEBK 3]

THURSTON, John[2] (bp 1635-1711/2) & Mary WOOD; m Medfield 4 Oct 1660 [AEBK 3]

THURSTON, Joseph[2] (c1636-1688-91) & Anne _____ (-by 1721); m c1662 [AEBK 3]

THURSTON, Thomas (c1610/11-) & Margaret _____; m c1631 Wrentham, Eng/Dedham [TAG 54:177]

THURSTON, Thomas[2] (bp 1633-1704) & Sarah THAXTER (-1678); m Dedham 13 Dec 1655 [AEBK 3]

TIBBETTS, Jeremiah & Mary[2] CANNEY (c1635-1706); m c1655 [NHGR 20:7]

TILDEN, Stephen & Hannah[2] LITTLE (c1641-); m Scituate 25 Jan 1661[/2] [GMB 2:1191]

TILDEN, Stephen (1659-1732) & Abigail CLAPP (1659/60-1735/6); m 1685 Marshfield [AEBK 4:139]

TILDEN, Thomas & Mary[2] HOLMES (c1644-); m Marshfield 24 Jan 1664[/5?] [GM 3:393]

TILLEY, Edward (1588-1621) Agnes COOPER (-1621); m 20 June 1614 Henlow, Bedfordshire/Plymouth [TAG 52:198]

TILLEY, Hugh (c1613-1647/8) & Rose _____ (c1616-1687); m2 Thomas HUCKENS; m by 1643 Salem/Yarmouth [GMB 3:1821]

TILLEY, John & Joan (HURST) ROGERS (not Elizabeth Comyngs); m1 Thomas ROGERS; m Henlow, Bedfordshire 20 Sept 1596 [TAG 67:31; GMB 3:1822]

TILLEY, John[1] (c1600-killed 1636) & _____ _____ (-1637/8+); Cape Ann/Dorchester [GMB 3:1823]

TILLEY, Samuel[2] (1646-) & Mary _____; m c1679 perhaps m Oyster Bay by lic 26 Sept 1678 Mary SIMPKINS [GMB 3:1821]

TILLINGHAST, Pardon & Lydia[2] TABOR; m2 1718 Samuel MASON; m Providence 16 Apr 1664 [GMB 3:1793]

TILLOTSON, John & Dorcas[2] COLEMAN (bp 1626-); m Newbury 4 July 1648 [GM 2:160]

TILLY, William & Alice (FROST) BLOWER; m1 Thomas BLOWER Boston [TAG 71:113]

TILSON, Ephraim & Elizabeth[2] HOSKINS (c1645-); m Plymouth 7 July 1666 [GM 3:417]

TILTON, Samuel & Hannah MOULTON; m Hampton 17 Dec 1662 [REG 155:415]

TING, William (-1653) & 2/wf Elizabeth COYTMORE (-bet 1642/3-6); m by 1638 Boston/Braintree [NGSQ 69:115]

TING, William[1] & 3/wf Jane (_____) HUNT (-1652); m1 Richard HUNT; m bet 1643-6 Eng [NGSQ 69:115]

TINGLEY, _____ & Hannah[2] FOSDICK (c1616-); m2 James BARRETT; m c1638 Charlestown [GM 2:548]

TINKER, _____ & _____ _____ (mother of John Tinker); probably m2 _____ _____; in New England bef 26 Feb 1639/40 [DR; Winthrop Papers 4:205-206]

TIPPETT, George & Mehitable[2] BETTS;m2 Lewis VITTREY; m3 Samuel HITCHCOCK; m c1670 [GM 1:280]

TIPPING, Bartholomew & _____ DEAN; m bef 1685/6 Taunton [TAG 59:229]

TITUS, Edmund[2] (c1630-1706+) & Martha WASHBURN (-1706+) Hempstead/L.I. [NYGBR 133:182]

TITUS, John[2] & Abigail[3] CARPENTER (bp 1629-); m2 1692 Jonah PALMER; m c1649/50 [TAG 70:203-4]

TOLMAN, John & Elizabeth[2] COLLINS; m Lynn 30 Nov 1666 [GM 2:168]

TOMKINS, Ralph[1] & Katherine FOSTER; m Wendover, Bucks 6 Nov 1608 [TAG 68:19]

TOMLINS, Edward[1] (c1604-1661+) & possibly Jane BASSALL; m St. Bennet, Paul's Wharf, London 31 Oct 1621 [GMB 3:1827]

TOMLINS, Timothy[1] (bp 1606/7-1645/6) & Elizabeth SPENCER, dau of Gerrard; m bef 1645/6 [GMB 3:1829; TAG 41:111]

TOOTHAKER, Roger[1] (c1612-bef 1638) & Margaret _____ (c1607-1683); m2 Ralph[1] HILL; m England c1633 Plymouth/Billerica [TAG 69:1]

TOOTHAKER, Roger[2] (c1634-1692) & Mary[2] ALLEN (c1644-1695); m Billerica 9 June 1665 [TAG 69:2]

TOPPING, John[2] (c1629-) & Mary WOODMANSEY; m Boston 20 Aug 1654 [GMB 3:1831]

TOPPING, Josiah (1663-1726) & Hannah SAYRE; m Southold, LI [TAG 38:227]

TOPPING, Richard[1] (c1598-1657-8) & 1/wf Judith _____ (-1635); m by Nov 1633 Boston [GMB 3:1831]

TOPPING, Richard[1] (c1598-1657-8) & 2/wf Alice _____; m by 1645 Boston [GMB 3:1831]

TOPPING, Thomas & Hannah WHITE; m2 Daniel[2] SAYRE [TAG 38:226]

TORREY, James & Anne[2] HATCH (bp 1626-); m Scituate 2 Nov 1643 Wye, Kent [GM 3:243]

TOTMAN, Stephen ~ Scituate [Plymouth Court Sept 1691]

TOWERS, William & Leah[2] WARDWELL (1646-); m c1668 [GMB 3:1923]

TOWNSEND, Henry & Ann _____; by 1653 [GMB 1:438]

TOWNSEND, Henry & Deborah[2] UNDERHILL (1659-); m by 1676 [GMB 3:1862]

TOWNSEND, Richard & Deliverance COLES; by 1652 [GMB 1:438]

TOWNSEND, Thomas & Sarah COLES (c1646-) [GMB 1:438]

TOWNSEND, Thomas[1] (?bp 8 Jan 1594/5-1677) & 1/wf _____ _____; Bracon-Ash, Norfolk/Lynn [TEG 13:153]

TOWNSEND, Thomas[1] (?bp 8 Jan 1594/5-1677) & 2/wf _____ _____; Bracon-Ash, Norfolk/Lynn [TEG 13:153]

TOWNSEND, Thomas[1] (?bp 8 Jan 1594/5-1677) & 3/wf Mary ?NEWGATE (-1692/3); Lynn [TEG 13:153]

TRACY, John & Mary[2] WINSLOW; m Marshfield 10 June 1670 [GMB 3:2033]

TRACY, John[2] & Mary[2] PRENCE (c1639-), dau of Thomas; m c1661 [GMB 3:1523, 1833]

TRACY, Stephen (bp 1596-1654/5) & Tryphosa LEE (c1597-); m Leiden, Holland 3 Jan 1621 [NS] [GMB 3:1833]

TRANTOR, Thomas & Ann (BOURNE) BAILEY; m1 John BAILEY; m bef 1688 Freetown [TAG 40:33]

TRASK, John & Florence[2] HART (c1651-); m by 1672 [GM 3:230]

TRASK, John[2] (bp 1642-) & 1/wf Abigail PARKMAN, dau of Elias; m Salem 19 Feb 1662[/3] [GMB 3:1401]

TRASK, Osmund & Elizabeth[2] GALLEY (c1643-); m2 John GILES; m Salem 22 May 1663 [GM 3:3]

TRASK, William (1674-1746) & Ann[3] WHITE (c1678-); m by 1698 Weymouth [AEBK 1:513]

TRASK, William[1] (bp 1585-1666) & Sarah _____ (-1666+); m c1634 Salem [GMB 3:1835]

TRASK, William[2] (bp 1640-) & 1/wf Ann PUTNAM (-1676); m Salem 18 Jan 1666 [GMB 3:1836]

TRASK, William[2] (bp 1640-) & 2/wf Hannah _____; m c1678 Salem [GMB 3:1836]

TREADWAY, Jonathan (1640-1710) & Judith THURSTON (c1648-1726); m Medfield 1 Mar 1666/7 [AEBK 1:459; AEBK 3]

TREADWAY, Josiah (c1650-1731/2) & 1/wf Sarah SWEETMAN (1654-1696/7); m Watertown 9 June 1674 [AEBK 1:460]

TREADWAY, Josiah (c1650-1731/2) & 2/wf Dorothy (BELL) CUTLER (1661-1740/5); m Charlestown 3 Feb 1697/8 [AEBK 1:460]

TREADWAY, Nathaniel[1] (c1614/5-1689) & Sufferanna[2] HAYNES (c1618-1682); m c1639 Watertown [TAG 70:178; AEBK 1:453]

TREAT, Robert[2] & 1/wf Jane[2] TAPP (bp 1624+-1703); m Milford by 1649 [TAG 72:80]

TREAT, Samuel & Elizabeth MAYO; m 16 Apr 1674 not 16 Mar 1674 [Sewall's Diary 1:4]

TREBBY, Peter[1] (c1638-1713/14) & 1/wf Bethiah[2] SHEPARD (c1650-1675); m c1668 Newport [ASBO, p.372]

TRENT, Mathias & Mary SMITH (1627-) dau. of Richard[1]; m after 1645 [TAG 46:137]

TRESCOTT, William & Elizabeth DYER; by 1646 Dorchester [GMB 1:605]

TROOP, William & Mary[2] CHAPMAN (1643-); m Barnstable 14 May 1666 [GM 2:53]

TROWBRIDGE, James & Lydia[2] ALSOP (1665-); m New Haven 8 Nov 1688 [GM 1:50]

TROWBRIDGE, John (1557-) & Mary ROSE; m bef 1690/1 Marshfield [TAG 67:155]

TROWBRIDGE, Thomas (c1598-1673) & 1/wf Elizabeth MARSHALL; m St Mary
    Arches, Exeter, Devon 26 Mar 1627 New Haven [REG 59:291-297; TG 9:3-38]

TROWBRIDGE, Thomas (c1598-1673) & 2/wf Frances (GODSALL) SHATTOCK; m St
    David's, Exeter, Devon 10 Feb 1640/1 New Haven [REG 59:291-297; TG 9:3-
    38]

TRUANT, John[2] (c1655-1730) & Silence _____ (c1643-1718) [GMB 3:1840]

TRUANT, Joseph[2] & Hannah BARNES; m Marshfield 6 Jan 1674[/5] [GMB 3:1840]

TRUANT, Morris[1] (c1606-1685) & Jane _____ (-1678+); m Plymouth 16 Oct 1639
    [GMB 3:1839]

TRUE, Henry & Jane[2] BRADBURY (1645-); m Hampton 16 Mar 1667/8 [GM 1:380]

TRUE, Henry[1] & Israel[2] PIKE (bp 1623-); m c1644 Salem/Salisbury [TAG 73:256]

TRUESDALE, Richard[1] & Mary[1] HOOD (c1607-1674); m by 1646 Boston [GM 3:401]

TRUSTEANE, Robert & Martha[2] HERBERT (c1645-); m c1665 [GM 3:312]

TUBBS, William & Mercy[2] SPRAGUE; m Plymouth 9 Nov 1637 [GMB 3:1727]

TUCKER, Andrew[1] (c1642-1691) & Mary[2] BRIMBLECOM (bp 1646/7-); m c1663
    Marblehead [DCD]

TUCKER, Lewis & Sarah[2] GUNNISON (c1653-); m by 1673 [GM 3:178]

TUCKER, Richard[1] (perhaps bp 1594-by 1679) & Margaret _____ (-1693+); m by 6 Apr
    1646 Portsmouth [GMB 3:1842]

TUELL, Richard & Martha _____; m by 1660 Boston [ITC]

TULLY, John & Mary[2] BEAMON (1647-); m Saybrook 3 Jan 1671/2 [GM 1:221]

TUPPER, Thomas & Martha[2] MAYHEW (c1641-); m Sandwich 27 Dec 1661 [GMB
    2:1245]

TURBET, Nicholas (c1648-1707/8+) & Elizabeth[3] (SPENCER) CHICK (c1640-); m1
    Thomas CHICK; m bef 1687 Kittery [CG, 22]

TURLAND, _____ & Ann[2] GARFORD (c1615-); m by 1635 Essex co. [GM 3:24]

TURNER, Daniel & Hannah RANDALL, dau of William; m Scituate 20 June 1665 or
    1666 [GMB 3:1845]

TURNER, Ephraim[2] (1639-) & Sarah _____, possibly dau of William PHILLIPS; m
    c1663 Boston [GMB 3:1853]

TURNER, Ezekiel & Elizabeth STARTER; m St Mary Magdalen, Bermondsey, Surrey 30
    Sept 1698 London/Boston [REG 141:151]

TURNER, Humphrey[1] (c1595-1672-3) & Lydia _____ (-1668+); m c1620 [GMB
    3:1845]

TURNER, Increase & Mehitable[2] HETT (bp 1648-); m Charlestown 3 Oct 1673 [GMB
    2:917]

TURNER, Isaac & Mary WINSOR; m 15 Sept 1673 [TAG 67:30]

TURNER, Isaac[2] (bp 1640-) & Mary TODD; m New Haven 19 Aug 1668 [GMB
    3:1850]

TURNER, Israel[3] & Sarah STOCKBRIDGE; m2 Thomas[3] PINSON [TAG 50:99]

TURNER, John[1] & ____; m bef 1612 Eng/Lynn [REG 123:33]

TURNER, John[1] (c1590-1620/1) & ____ ____; m c1615 Plymouth [GMB 3:1846]

TURNER, John[2] & Ann JAMES; m Scituate 25 Apr 1649 [GMB 3:1845]

TURNER, John[2] & Mary BREWSTER, dau of Jonathan; m 10 or 12 Nov 1645 Plymouth [GMB 3:1845]

TURNER, John[2] (1642-) & Lucy GARDNER, dau of Thomas; m2 George MONK [GMB 3:1854]

TURNER, John[2] (c1655-65-1728) & Hannah BRETT (-1728); m c1685 Bridgewater [TAG 61:131]

TURNER, Nathaniel[1] (c1601-1645/6) & ____ ____; m2 Samuel VANGOODENHAUSEN; m by 1626 Lynn [GMB 3:1849]

TURNER, Nathaniel[2] & 1/wf Mehitable RIGBY, dau of John; m Scituate 29 Mar 1664/5 [GMB 3:1845]

TURNER, Nathaniel[2] (1638-1715) & 2/wf Abigail (EAMES) STOCKBRIDGE (- 1709/10); m1 Charles STOCKBRIDGE; m after 1680/1 Scituate [TAG 38:186; GMB 3:1845]

TURNER, Robert & Nazareth[2] HOBART (bp 1601-); m2 John BEAL; m Hingham, Norfolk 9 Nov 1626 [GMB 2:959]

TURNER, Robert[1] (c1613-1664) & Penelope DARLOE (-1675+); m by 1639 Boston [GMB 3:1853; GM 2:286]

TURNER, Thomas[2] & Sarah HILAND; m Scituate 6 Jan 1651[/2] [GMB 3:1845]

TURNING, William & Elizabeth DEANE; by 1650 Eastham [GMB 1:516]

TURPIN, John & Mary[2] BELL (bp 1645-); Roxbury [GM 1:241]

TURPIN, William & Elizabeth[2] HOAR (1660-); m by 1690 [GM 3:345]

TUTTLE, Simon & Sarah[2] COGSWELL (c1645-); m c1664 [GM 2:139]

TUTTLE, Simon (-1630) & Isabel WELLS (c1565-1635+); m probably near Ringstead, Northampton c1592 [TAG 59:211-215]

TWELVES, Robert (c1620-1696/7) & Martha[2] BRACKETT (bp 1636-1716; m Boston 22 Nov 1655 (also recorded Braintree) [TAG 77:74; REG 155:284]

TWISS, Peter[1] & Ann[2] CALLUM (1659-); m Salem 20 Oct 1680 [TAG 70:3]

TWITCHELL, Benjamin[2] (c1627-1681) & Mary[2] RIGGS (bp 1632-1694), dau of Edward; m c1652 [GMB 3:1584, 1856; AEBK 3]

TWITCHELL, Benjamin[3] (c1657-1730) & Mary WHITE (c1663-1730+); m Medfield 5 Apr 1683 [AEBK 3]

TWITCHELL, John (c1669-) & Sarah PIERSON (c1678-1738/9); m Derby 21 Jan 1698/9 [AEBK 3]

TWITCHELL, Joseph[1] (bp 1582-1657) & Elizabeth LOVETT (bp 1589-1633[/4?]+); m Chesham, Buckinghamshire 12 May 1614 [AEBK 3; GMB 3:1856]

TWITCHELL, Joseph[3] (c1654-1710) & Lydia[2] GOARD (bp 1652/3-1725), dau of Richard; m bef 29 Apr 1679 Sherborn/Roxbury [AEBK 3; GM 3:80]

TYLER Lazarus (c1661-6-) & Mary _____ (-1732); m c1687 Portsmouth, RI/Preston [TAG 52:221; 60:160]

TYLER, George[2] & Hannah LUDDINGTON Branford [TAG 74:216]

UFFORD, John[2] (bp 1626-) & 1/wf Hanah HAWLEY; m by 1654 [GMB 3:1858]

UFFORD, John[2] (bp 1626-) & 2/wf Martha NETTLETON, dau of Samuel; m 1657 [GMB 3:1858]

UFFORD, Thomas[1] (c1596-by 1660) & 1/wf Isabel _____; m c1621 [GMB 3:1858]

UFFORD, Thomas[1] (c1596-by 1660) & 2/wf Elizabeth (_____) THEALE (-1660); m1 Nicholas THEALE; m by 1659 Stamford [GMB 3:1858]

UFFORD, Thomas[2] (bp 1623-) & Frances KILBOURNE (bp 1621-), dau of Thomas; m c1650 [GMB 3:1858]

UMFREVILLE, John[1] (bp 1630-1720+) & _____ _____; m c1660 New Haven [TAG 72:18]

UNDERHILL, David[2] (1672-) & Hannah _____; m by 1700 Oyster Bay [GMB 3:1862]

UNDERHILL, John (c1608-1672) & _____ _____ [NYGBR 127:22]

UNDERHILL, John[1] (c1609-1672) & 1/wf Helena DeHOOCH, dau of William; m The Hague, Netherland 12 Dec 1628 [GMB 3:1861]

UNDERHILL, John[1] (c1609-1672) & 2/wf Elizabeth FEAKE (c1633-by 1675); m by 1659 Watertown [GMB 1:658, 3:1862]

UNDERHILL, John[2] (bp 1642-) & Mary PRIOR; m 11 Oct 1668 Flushing [GMB 3:1862]

UNDERHILL, Nathaniel & Mary[2] JACKSON [NYGBR 131:7]

UNDERHILL, Nathaniel[2] (1663-) & Mary FERRIS; m aft 27 Feb 1685/6 [GMB 3:1862]

UPHAM, Phinehas (c1635-1676) & Ruth WOOD (c1638-1696/7); m Malden 14 Apr 1658 [AEBK 3]

UPSALL, Nicholas[1] (c1596-1666) & Dorothy CAPEN (c1608-), dau of Bernard; m Holy Trinity, Dorchester, Dorsetshire 17 Jan 1629/30 Boston [GMB 1:310, 3:1867]

USSELL, Richard & Abigail[2] DAVIS; m2 Edward RICHMOND; m c1655 against her will [GM 2:318]

VAIL, Jeremiah (-1687) & m2 Mary (?FOLGER) PAINE; m 24 May 1660 Southold [TAG 38:183]

VARLETT, Casper (-by 1662) & Judith _____ (-by 1662); Hartford [Manwaring 1:158; NYGBR 9:54-55; Harris]

VASSALL, William[1] (bp 1592-1655-7) & Anna KING, dau of George; m Cold Norton, Essex by lic 9 June 1613 Barbados [GMB 3:1872]

VAUGHAN, Daniel (1653-1715) & Susanna JENNEY (1657-1715+) (not Grimes) [TAG 35:72]

VAUGHAN, John & Elizabeth BULL; m Portsmouth, RI 24 Nov 1698 [RCA]

VEASEY, George & Mary[2] WIGGIN; m2 William MOORE; m c1664 [GMB 3:1984]

VERIN, Philip (-c1649) & Dorcas _____ (-1668+); m by 1605 Eng/Salem [REG 131:100]

VERIN, Robert[2] (bp 1606-bef 1639) & Jane CASH; m?2 Francis PERRY; m 15 July 1626 St Thomas, Wilts/Salem [REG 131:102]

VERNON, Daniel (1643-1715) & Anne (HUTCHINSON) DYRE (1643-1716/7); m Kingstown, RI 22 Sep 1679 [REG 145:262]

VIALL, Jonathan[2] (c1675-1724) & Mercy SYLVESTER (-1724+); m c1699 Barrington, RI [TAG 42:158]

VINAL, John & Elizabeth[2] BAKER (bp 1644-); m Scituate 2 Feb 1663/4 or4[/5] [GM 1:144; TAG 39:41; REG 142:123]

VINAL, John[3] & Mary WOODWORTH; m bef 19 Dec 1691 Plymouth [REG 142:123 & TAG 39:41]

VINAL, Stephen & Mary[2] BAKER (bp 1640-); m Scituate 26 Feb 1661/2 [GM 1:143]

VINES, Richard[1] (c1600-1651) & Joan _____ (-1669+); m by 1625 Saco/Barbados [GMB 3:1878]

VINSON, Nicholas & Elizabeth _____; m bef 1657 Manchester [EQC 2:50; 4:216]

VINTON, Blaise[2] (c1660s-1716) & Lydia[3] HAYDEN (c1670-1756); m c1690 Hingham [AEBK 3]

VINTON, John (-1700+) & Hannah GREEN (1659/60-1700+); m Malden 16 Aug 1677 [AEBK 4:310]

VITTUM/VITTOON, John (-1712/13) & Jane _____ (-1788); m bef 1693 Scarborough/Greenland [GFS]

WADE, Jonathan[1] (c1612-1683) & Susanna _____ (-1678); m by 1633 Ipswich [GMB 3:1885]

WADE, Jonathan[2] (c1637-1689) & 1/wf Dorothy BUCKLEY; m Ipswich 9 Dec 1660 [GMB 3:1886]

WADE, Jonathan[2] (c1637-1689) & 2/wf Deborah DUDLEY (1644/5-), dau of Thomas; m by 1665 [GMB 1:585, 3:1886]

WADE, Jonathan[2] (c1637-1689) & 3/wf Elizabeth DUNSTER; m c1687 [GMB 3:1886]

WADE, Joseph[2] & Sarah[2] ENSIGN (c1650-) [TAG 73:248]

WADE, Nathaniel[2] (c1648-) & Mercy BRADSTREET, dau of Simon; m Andover 31 Oct 1672 [GMB 3:1886]

WADE, Nicholas[1] & Elizabeth[2] HANFORD (not ENSIGN); m by 1646 Scituate [GM 3:206; TAG 73:251]

WADE, Robert & Susanna BIRCHARD (bp 1626-); Norwich/Saybrook/Martha's Vineyard [TAG 51:18]

WADE, Thomas[2] & Hannah[2] ENSIGN (c1652-); m c1670 Scituate [TAG 73:253]

WADE, Thomas[2] (c1650-) & Elizabeth COGSWELL; m Ipswich 22 Feb 1670 [GMB 3:1886]

WADE, William & Sarah[2] PHELPS (c1632-); m Windsor 9 June 1658 [GMB 3:1446]

WADLIN, William (-1725) & 2/wf Elizabeth GATTENSBY (c1660s-); m after 1690 Berwick [CG, 50]

WADSWORTH, Christopher[1] (c1609-1677-80) & Grace _____, perhaps COLE; m c1634 [GMB 3:1890]

WADSWORTH, John[2] & Sarah STANLEY, dau of Thomas; m c1658 [GMB 3:1895]

WADSWORTH, John[2] (c1638-1700) & Abigail ANDREWS, dau of Henry; m Duxbury 25 July 1667 [GMB 3:1891]

WADSWORTH, Joseph & 1/wf Elizabeth TALCOTT; m c1682 [GMB 3:1895]

WADSWORTH, Joseph[2] & Mary _____ [GMB 3:1891]

WADSWORTH, Samuel[2] & Abigail LINDALL, dau of James; m c1660 [GMB 3:1891]

WADSWORTH, Thomas[2] (c1651-) & Elizabeth Barnard; m by 1677 [GMB 3:1896]

WADSWORTH, William[1] (c1601-1675) & 1/wf Sarah TALCOTT, dau of John; m by 1626 [GMB 3:1895]

WADSWORTH, William[1] (c1601-1675) & 2/wf Elizabeth STONE; m Hartford 2 July 1644 [GMB 3:1895]

WAIT, Gamaliel[1] (bp 1605[/6]-1685) & Grace _____ (-1687); m by 1637 Boston [GMB 3:1898]

WAIT, John (bp 1645-) & 1/wf Mary _____; m by 1673 [GMB 3:1898]

WAIT, John (bp 1645-) & 2/wf Eunice _____, perhaps dau of Thomas ROBERTS; m by 1677 Boston [GMB 3:1898]

WAIT, John (c1618-1693) & Mary[2] HILLS (bp 1625-1674); m by 1650 Malden [AEBK 4:415]

WAIT, Richard & Rebecca[2] HEPBURN (c1625-); m by 1653 Boston [GM 3:310]

WAITE, Thomas & Sarah[2] CUTLER (c1653-1743/4); m by 1674 Watertown/Weston [GM 2:270]

WAKEMAN, Ezbon[2] (c1636-) & Hannah JORDAN, dau of John; m Stratford 28 June 1666 [GMB 3:1901]

WAKEMAN, Samuel[1] (bp 1603-1641) & Elizabeth _____; m2 Nathaniel WILLETT; m by 1630 Roxbury [GMB 3:1900]

WALCOTT, John & Mary WRENTMORE; m St John's Glastonbury, Somerset 18 Jan 1621 [RCA; Robin Bush]

WALCOTT, William & Alice[2] INGERSOLL (bp 1612-); m c1634 [GMB 2:1061]

WALDO, Cornelius & Hannah[2] COGSWELL (bp 1626-); m bef 2 Jan 1651/2 [GM 2:139]

WALDREN, Edward & Tamesin _____; by June 1671 Essex County [EQC 4:416; JHO]

WALES, Jonathan & Sarah[2] BAKER (bp 1651-), dau of Alexander; m by 1684/5 Boston [GM 1:132]

WALES, Nathaniel[1] & Susanna GREENWAY (c1620-); m by 5 Feb 1650[/1] Dorchester [TAG 74:195; GMB 2:816]

WALFORD, Jeremiah[2] & Mary _____; m c1654 [GMB 3:1903]

WALFORD, Thomas[1] (c1599-1666) & Jane _____ (c1598-by 1681); m c1624 Charlestown/Portsmouth [GMB 3:1903]

WALKER, Francis & Elizabeth[2] SOULE (c1644-); m by 23 July 1668 [GMB 3:1707]

WALKER, Jacob[2] (1643/4-) & Elizabeth (WHEELER) BLACKMAN; m Stratford 6 Dec 1670 [GMB 3:1914]

WALKER, James & Bathsheba[2] BROOKS (bp 1655-); m Taunton 23 Dec 1673 [GM 1:410]

WALKER, John & Lydia[2] COLBURN (1666-); m c1686 Chelmsford [GM 2:149]

WALKER, John[1] (c1603-1647[/8]+) & Katharine _____ (-by 1654); m c1628 Roxbury/Boston/Portsmouth [GMB 3:1907]

WALKER, John[2] (1656-) & Hannah LEAGER; m c1676 [GMB 3:1914]

WALKER, Joseph & Elizabeth[2] MOSES (c1642-); m c1662 [GMB 2:1301]

WALKER, Joseph[2] (1646-) & Abigail PRUDDEN; m Milford 14 Nov 1667 [GMB 3:1914]

WALKER, Obadiah[2] & Sarah HOUGH, dau of Samuel; m c1673 [GMB 3:1910]

WALKER, Peter (c1650-1711) & Hannah HUTCHINSON (1658-1704); m c1689 Taunton [REG 145:265]

WALKER, Richard & Jane[2] TALMAGE (-by 1640); m c1638 [GMB 3:1799]

WALKER, Richard & Sarah HUSTON; m bef 29 Mar 1698 Newbury [REG 144:54]

WALKER, Richard[1] (c1611-1687) & 1/wf Jane TALMAGE, dau of Thomas; m by 1637 Lynn/Reading/Boston [GMB 3:1909]

WALKER, Robert[1] (perhaps bp 1607/8-1687) & 2/wf? Sarah _____ (-1695); perhaps Sarah Leager, dau of Jacob; m by 1635 Boston [GMB 3:1909, 1913]

WALKER, Samuel (-1696) & Sarah[2] HUNTER (1663-1704-8); m2 Matthew PAULING; m c1678 Boston [TAG 40:82; GM 3:477]

WALKER, Shubal[1] (c1639-) & Patience JEWETT; m Lynn 29 May 1666 [GMB 3:1909]

WALKER, William & Sarah[2] SNOW (c1632-); m Eastham 25 Feb 1654 [GMB 3:1703]

WALKER, William (-1732) & Sarah[3] GOODENOW (1666-1723+); m Sudbury 6 May 1686 [AEBK 2]

WALKER, Zachary (1637-) & 1/wf Mary PRUDDEN; m c1669 [GMB 3:1913]

WALKER, Zachary (1637-) & 2/wf Susannah ROSSITER; m aft 1673/4 [GMB 3:1913]

WALL, John & Susan[2] BELL; m2 John BELL [GM 1:241]

WALLEN, Ralph[1] (c1595-by 1644) & Joyce _____ (-1665+); m2 Thomas LUMBARD; m by 1623 [GMB 3:1916; TAG 67:47-53]

WALLER, John (c1654-1685/6) & Mary DURANT (c1668-1712+); m2 Samuel SHEATHER; m3 Robert CHAPMAN; m Lyme 28 Dec 1678 [AEJA]

WALLER, Samuel (c1658-1741/2) & 1/wf _____ _____ (-bef 1685); m c1679 New London [AEJA]

WALLER, Samuel (c1658-1741/2) & 2/wf Mary DANIELS; m New London 26 Dec 1685 [AEJA]

WALLER, Samuel (c1658-1741/2) & 3/wf Hannah (HAMPSTEAD) MOORE (1652-1729); m c1690 New London [AEJA]

WALLER, Thomas (-by 1657) & Sarah[1] WOLTERTON (bp 1582-1658+); m c1603 probably Norfolk, England [TAG 68:170; AEJA]

WALLER, William (c1610s-1674) & Elizabeth MARVIN (1627-1679); m c1651 Lyme [AEJA]

WALLEY, John[2] & Sarah[3] BLOSSOM (1646-50-); m c1671 Boston [TAG 63:239]

WALLING, Thomas[2] (-1674) & Margaret (WHITE) COLWELL; m1 Robert COLWELL div [TAG 73:100]

WALLING, Thomas[2] (-1674) & Mary[2] ABBOTT; m 1651 Providence [TAG 73:100]

WALLIS, Benjamin (c1675-1724/5) & 1/wf Elizabeth MORGAN (c1678-1703); m Beverly 23 Mar 1695/6 [REG 152:300]

WALLIS, James (c1670-by 1744) & Martha STANDFORD (c1672-1731+); m by 1693/4 Gloucester [REG 152:299]

WALLIS, John (c1627-1690) & Mary PHIPPEN (bp 1643/4-1691+); m c1650s Falmouth [REG 152:288]

WALLIS, Josiah (c1660s-1740/1) & 1/wf Elizabeth _____ (-1693/4); m by 1693/4 Beverly/Gloucester [REG 152:296]

WALLIS, Josiah (c1660s-1740/1) & 2/wf Mary STANDFORD (-1703); m by 1696 Beverly/Gloucester [REG 152:298]

WANNERTON, Thomas[1] (c1600-killed 1644) & Ann _____; m2 Thomas WILLIAMS; m by 1643 Piscataqua [GMB 3:1916]

WANTON, Edward (-1716) & 2/wf Mary PHILLIPS; m 25 Sept 1676 Scituate [TAG 60:160]

WARD, Andrew[1] (c1603-1659) & Hester SHERMAN (-1665-5/6), dau of Edmund; m c1628 [GMB 3:1920]

WARD, Andrew[2] & Trial MEIGS, dau of John; m c1669 [GMB 3:1920]

WARD, Henry & Remember[2] FARROW (bp 1642-); m Hingham 3 Feb 1659/60 [GM 2:500]

WARD, Henry (bef 1647-1683/4) & 1/wf Mary[2] DYRE (bef 1650-bet 1679-84); m bet 1670-78 Newport/NY/Delaware [REG 145:22-8; GM 2:383]

WARD, John & Sarah[2] HILLS (c1638-); m2 Stephen DAVIS [GMB 2:944]

WARD, John[2] & Mary HARRIS, dau of William; m Middletown 18 Apr 1664 [GMB 3:1920]

WARD, Samuel & Sarah[2] HOWE (1644-1707); m Marlborough 6 June 1667 [AEBK 3]

WARD, Samuel[2] & 1/wf _____ OGDEN, dau of Richard; m c1671 [GMB 3:1920]

WARD, Samuel[2] & 2/wf Hannah (HOWKINS) NICHOLS, dau of Anthony; m1 Jonathan NICHOLS [GMB 3:1920]

WARD, Thomas & Hannah TAPPAN (1662-); m Middletown 6 Dec 1683 [TAG 71:98]

WARD, William[2] & Deborah LOCKWOOD, dau of Robert; m c1664 [GMB 3:1920]

WARDWELL, Elihu[2] (1642-) & Elizabeth[2] WADE, dau of Jonathan; m Ipswich 26 May 1665 [GMB 3:1886, 1923]

WARDWELL, Uzall[2] (1639-) & 1/wf Mary (KINSMAN) RINDGE, dau of Robert; m1 Daniel RINDGE; m Ipswich 3 May 1664 [GMB 3:1923]

WARDWELL, Uzall[2] (1639-) & 2/wf Grace _____ [GMB 3:1923]

WARDWELL, William[1] (bp 1606/7-1670) & 1/wf Alice _____ perhaps sister of John PYCE; m by 1636 Alford, Lincolnshire/Boston [GMB 3:1923]

WARDWELL, William[1] (bp 1606/7-1670) & 2/wf Elizabeth (CROW)(PERRY) GILLETT (-1696/7); m Boston by contract 4 Dec 1657 [GMB 3:1923]

WARE, John & Joanna (GAY) WHITING (1644/5-); m1 Nathaniel WHITING; m Dedham 24 Mar 1678/9 [GM 3:40]

WARE, Nathaniel & Mary WHEELOCK; m Wrentham 12 Oct 1696 [AEBK 4:264]

WARE, Nicholas & Anna[2] VASSALL (bp 1628-); m by 1651 [GMB 3:1873]

WARE, Robert & Margaret HUNTING (bp 1628-); m Dedham 24 Mar 1645/6 [NGSQ 78:94]

WARFIELD, John[1] (c1631-1714-9) & 1/wf Elizabeth[2] SHEPARD (-1669); m Medfield 3 Aug 1661 [TAG 73:11]

WARFIELD, John[1] (c1631-1714-9) & 2/wf Peregrina[2] WHELOCK (-1671); m Medfield 26 Oct 1669 [TAG 73:11]

WARFIELD, John[1] (c1631-1714-9) & 3/wf Hannah[2] RANDALL (-1714/5-18/9); m Medfield 26 Dec 1671 [TAG 73:11]

WARFIELD, John[2] (1662-1692) & Hester HARBOUR (1663-); m2 William HAYWARD; m by 1688 Mendon [TAG 73:15]

WARHAM, John (bp 1595-1670) & 3/wf Abigail (SEARLE) BRANKER (bp 1612-1684); m1 John BRANKER; m Windsor 9 Oct 1662 [DR; REG 149:305]

WARHAM, John[1] (bp 1595-1670) & 1/wf Susanna GOLLOP (-1634); m Stoke Abbot, Dorsetshire 8 June 1625 [GMB 3:1926]

WARHAM, John[1] (bp 1595-1670) & 2/wf Jane (____) NEWBERRY (-1655); m1 Thomas NEWBERRY; m c1637 [GMB 3:1927]

WARMAN, William (c1650-c1741) & Abigail LAY (c1650-bef 1721); m 3 Aug 1687 Lyme [TAG 48:13; 60:160]

WARNER, Andrew[1] (c1599-1684) & 1/wf Mary HUMFREY (bp 1602[/3?]-), dau of Robert; m Thaxted, Essex 5 Oct 1624 [GMB 3:1930]

WARNER, Andrew[1] (c1599-1684) & 2/wf Esther (WAKEMAN) SELDEN (-by 1693); m1 Thomas SELDEN; m by 1657 [GMB 3:1930]

WARNER, Andrew[2] & Rebecca FLETCHER, dau of John; m Milford 10 Oct 1653 [GMB 3:1930]

WARNER, Daniel[2] & 1/wf Mary _____; m c1667 [GMB 3:1931]

WARNER, Daniel[2] & 2/wf Martha BOLTWOOD; m Hatfield 1 Apr 1674 [GMB 3:1931]

WARNER, Isaac[2] & Sarah BOLTWOOD; m Hadley 31 May 1666 [GMB 3:1931]

WARNER, Jacob[2] (c1658-) & 1/wf Rebecca _____ [GMB 3:1931]

WARNER, Jacob[2] (c1658-) & 2/wf Elizabeth GOODMAN, dau of Richard; m c1690 Deerfield [GMB 2:789, 3:1931]

WARNER, John[2] & Anna NORTON; m Hartford 1649 [GMB 3:1930]

WARNER, John[2] & Priscilla SYMONDS (c1620-) [TAG 74:116]

WARNER, Robert[2] & 1/wf Elizabeth GRANT; m Middletown Feb 1654[/5?] [GMB 3:1930]

WARNER, Robert[2] & 2/wf Deliverance[2] (HAWES) ROCKWELL; m Windsor 2 Feb 1674[/5] [GMB 3:1931; GM 3:252]

WARREN, Daniel (1653-1735) & Elizabeth WHITNEY (1656-1735+); m Watertown 19 Dec 1678 [AEBK 1:478]

WARREN, Daniel[2] (bp 1626/7-1706/7) & Mary[2] BARRON (c1630-1715/6); m Watertown 10 Dec 1650 [AEBK 1:128, 475; GMB 3:1934]

WARREN, James & _____ _____, probably not Griselda HULL [GM 3:455]

WARREN, John & 1/wf Deborah[2] WILSON (1634-); m Exeter 21 Oct 1650 [GMB 3:2018]

WARREN, John[1] (-1677) & 3/wf Elizabeth DANSON (c1643-1727); m2 Samuel[1] SENDALL; m3 John HAYWARD; m4 Phineas WILSON; m early 1670s Boston [TAG 47:19]

WARREN, John[1] (bp 1 Aug 1585-1667) & Margaret _____ (-1662); m bef 1615 Nayland, Suffolk/Watertown [AEBK 1:470; GMB 3:1933]

WARREN, John[2] (bp 1622-1702/3) & Micaell (JENNISON) BLOIS (1640-1713), dau of Robert; m1 Richard BLOIS; m Watertown 11 July 1667 [GMB 3:1934; AEBK 1:473]

WARREN, John[3] (1665/6-1703) & Mary[3] BROWNE (1662-1711+); m2 1703/4 Samuel HARRINGTON; m Watertown 22 Mar 1682/3 [AEBK 1:190, 481]

WARREN, Joseph (c1633-) & Priscilla FAUNCE, dau of John; m by 1653 Plymouth [GMB 1:652-53, 3:1936]

WARREN, Joshua[3] (1668-1760) & Rebecca CHURCH (1678-1760+); m by 1696 Watertown/Waltham [AEBK 1:479]

WARREN, Nathaniel[2] & Sarah WALKER; m Plymouth 19 Nov 1645 [GMB 3:1936]

WARREN, Nathaniel[3] & Phebe[2] PECKHAM; m2 1708/9 Thomas[2] GRAY; m bef 26 Apr 1688 Plymouth [TAG 71:151]

WARREN, Richard[1] (c1578-1628) & Elizabeth _____ (-1673); m c1609 Plymouth [GMB 3:1936]

WASHBURN, John[1] (bp 1597-1671) & Margery MOORE; m Bengeworth, Worcestershire 23 Nov? 1618 [GMB 3:1938]

WASHBURN, John[2] (bp 1620-) & Elizabeth[2] MITCHELL (c1628-), dau of Experience; m Plymouth 6 Dec 1645 [GMB 2:1272, 3:1939]

WASHBURN, John[3] & Rebecca[2] LAPHAM [TAG 71:135]

WASHBURN, Philip (c1624-) & Elizabeth[2] IRISH (c1644-), dau of John; m c1664 [GMB 2:1066, 3:1939]

WASHBURN, William[1] (bp 1601-by 1659) & Jane[2] NICHOLS (bp1603-1666/7+); m c1625 Bengeworth, Worcestershire [TAG 75:270]

WASSILBE, Samuel & Bridget PLAYFER, m2 Thomas OLIVER; m 13 Apr 1660 St. Mary-in-the-Marsh, Norwich, Norfolk [TAG 64:207]

WATERBURY, John[2] & Rose _____; m2 Joseph GARNSEY; m by 1639 [GMB 3:1940]

WATERBURY, William[1] & Alice _____; m by 1630 Boston [GMB 3:1939]

WATERMAN, John (c1666-1728) & Anne OLNEY (1669-1745); m c1691 Providence [AEJA]

WATERMAN, Nathaniel (bp 1637-) & Susanna[2] CARDER; m Providence 14 Mar 1662/3 [GMB 3:1942; GM 2:9]

WATERMAN, Resolved & Mercy[2] WILLIAMS (1640-), dau of Roger; m c1660 [GMB 3:1942, 2009]

WATERMAN, Richard[1] (c1605-1673) & Bethia _____ (-1680); m c1630 Providence [GMB 3:1942]

WATERS, Josiah & 1/wf Mary (not Elizabeth) WATERS; m bef 1688 Woburn [REG 146:57]

WATHEN, Ezekiel (bp1636-1716) & Hannah MARTIN (1643/4-1730); m Salisbury 1 Feb 1661 [REG 154:339]

WATHEN, George (1669-1745) & 1/wf Anne ANNIS (1681-1732); m 1699 [REG 154:347]

WATHEN, George (c1595-by 1642) & Margery HAYWARD (bp 1593-by 1644); m Trowbridge, Wiltshire 15 Apr 1624 Salem [REG 154:325+]

WATHEN, Thomas (1667-1702) & Hannah ANNIS (1679-); m2 1704 Ephraim WEED; m Amesbury 11 May 1700 [REG 154:346]

WATKINS, Thomas & Elizabeth[2] BAKER; m by 1652 Boston [GM 1:131]

WATKINS, Thomas & Margaret[2] RYALL; m2 Thomas STEVENS [GMB 3:1612]

WATSON, Caleb[2] (1641-) & Mary HIDE; m Roxbury 15 Dec 1665 [GMB 3:1949]

WATSON, Elkanah & perhaps Mercy HEDGE (1656-), dau of William [GMB 3:1946]

WATSON, George (1602-1688/9) & Phebe HICKS (bp 1614/5-1663), dau of Robert; m c1635 St Mary Magdalen, Bermondsey, Surrey/Plymouth [GMB 2:927, 3:1946]

WATSON, John & 2/wf Elizabeth² FROST (bp 1614-bef 1682); m 24 June 1634 St. Peter's Church, Nottingham [TAG 64:163]

WATSON, John¹ (c1605-10-1671/2) & Alice (BREDDA) PRENTICE; m1 Valentine PRENTICE; m Roxbury 3 Apr 1634 [GMB 3:1948; TAG 77:175]

WATSON, John² (1634/5-) & Mary ECCLES, dau of Richard; Roxbury [GMB 3:1948]

WATSON, Nathaniel² (1663/4-1690) & Dorothy³ BISSELL (1665-1712+); m2 Samuel STOUGHTON; m 21 Jan 1685 Windsor [REG 123:279]

WATSON-CHALLIS, Philip & Mary² SARGENT (c1636-); m c1652 [GMB 3:1632]

WATTS, Henry¹ (bp 1602-1687+) & Cicely (_____) BARLOW; m1 George BARLOW; m c1653-65 Cockfield, co. Durham/Black Point [GMB 3:1950]

WATTS, Thomas & Elizabeth² STEELE (bp 1628-); m Hartford 1 May 1645 [GMB 3:1755]

WAY, Aaron² (bp 1613-) & Joan SUMNER [GMB 3:1952]

WAY, George (c1610s-c1684) & Elizabeth _____ (c1630-1713); m bef 1651 Boston [AEJA]

WAY, George (c1655-1716/7) & Sarah NEAST (-1708); m c1687 Lyme [AEJA]

WAY, Henry¹ (c1573-1667) & Elizabeth _____ (-1665); m c1606 Dorchester [GMB 3:1952]

WAY, Richard (bp 1624-1697) & 2/wf Bethia (MAYHEW) HARLOCK, dau. Thomas & Jane; m1 Thomas HARLOCK; m bef 1689 Boston [TAG 61:256; GMB 3:1952]

WAY, Richard² (bp 1624-) & 1/wf Hester JONES [GMB 3:1952]

WAY, Richard² (bp 1624-) & 3/wf Katharine _____ [GMB 3:1952]

WAY, Richard² (bp 1624-) & 4/wf Hannah (TOWNSEND) (HULL) (ALLEN) KNIGHT; m Boston 13 Aug 1689 [GMB 3:1952]

WEARE, Nathaniel² & Elizabeth² SWAINE (bp 1638-1712/3); m Newbury 3 Dec 1656 [TAG 74:249]

WEAVER, Clement & Mary² FREEBORN (bp 1626/7-); m c1650 [GM 2:574]

WEAVER, Thomas & Mary SPRINGER; m bef 1682 RI [NGSQ 73:38]

WEBB, John & Bethiah ADAMS; m 1680 Braintree [TAG 71:21]

WEBB, Richard (c1611-1665) & Elizabeth (_____) GRANT (-1680[/1]); m1 Seth GRANT; m bef 1665 [GMB 3:1956]

WEBB, Thomas & Marah² FOSDICK; m by 1663 [GM 2:549]

WEBSTER, Israel & perhaps Elizabeth² BROWN; m Newbury 3 Jan 1665[/6] [GM 1:434]

WEBSTER, James² & Mary DAWES; Boston [TAG 77:220-25]

WEBSTER, John & Ann² BATT; m Newbury 13 June 1653 [GM 1:203]

WEED, Daniel² & Ruth _____; m by 1675 [GMB 3:1957]

WEED, George (1661-1732) & Margerite WATHEN (1674-1742+); m c1699 Amesbury/Salisbury [REG 154:349]

WEED, John² & 1/wf Joanna WESTCOTT, dau of Richard; m by 1664 [GMB 3:1957]

WEED, John² & 2/wf Mary _____; m aft 1678 Fairfield [GMB 3:1957]

WEED, Jonas¹ & _____ _____ [TAG 77:106]

WEED, Jonas¹ (c1610-1672-6) & Mary _____ (-by 1689/90); m c1637 Watertown/Wethersfield/Stamford [GMB 3:1957]

WEED, Jonas² & Bethia HOLLY; m 16 Nov 1670 Stamford [GMB 3:1958]

WEED, Samuel² & Mary _____ (-1708+); m c1680 [GMB 3:1958]

WEEDEN, Edward & Elizabeth COLE (c1624-); by Aug 1644 Boston [GMB 1:433]

WEEKES, Amiel (1662-) & Abigail TRESCOTT; m Dorchester 2 Mar 1682 [REG 156:151]

WEEKES, Joseph (1667-1745/6) & Sarah (SUMNER) TURELL [REG 156:151]

WEEKES, Supply (1671-1755) & 1/wf Susannah BARNES; m Marlborough 22 Sept 1755 [REG 156:151]

WEEKS, Amiel (bp 1631-1679) & Elizabeth HARRIS (bp 1631-1723); m bef 19 Jan 1655/6 Dorchester [REG 156:150]

WEEKS, Daniel & Mary² ALLING ; m bef 1691 Oyster Bay [NYGBR 129:80, 185]

WEEKS, Ebenezer (1665-) & Deliverance SUMNER; m Milton 8 May 1689 [REG 156:151]

WEEKS, Henry & Susannah² ALLING; m bef 1697/8 Oyster Bay [NYGBR 129:80, 186]

WEEKS, John² (1668-by 1710/11) & Elizabeth (PACKER) STARK (c1669-1719/20+); m c1691-93 New London [NHGR 19:102]

WEEKS, Leonard¹ (c1633-1706-07) & 1/wf _____ HAYNES; m c1657 Portsmouth [NHGR 19:101]

WEEKS, Leonard¹ (c1633-1706-07) & 2/wf Mary² REDMAN (1649-by 1693/4); m c1667 Portsmouth/Greenland [NHGR 19:101]

WEEKS, Leonard¹ (c1633-1706-07) & 3/wf Elizabeth _____ (-1727+); m aft 1693/4 Greenland/Portsmouth [NHGR 19:101; GM 3:190]

WEEKS, William & Mercy² ROBINSON (bp 1647-); m Falmouth 16 Mar 1669 [GMB 3:1593]

WELD, Joseph (-1646) & 1/wf Elizabeth WISE (-1638); m All Saints, Sudbury, Suffolk 11 Oct 1620 Roxbury [TAG 55:145-150; AEBK 4:130]

WELD, Joseph (-1646) & 2/wf Barbara¹ CLAPP (c1614-1655); m2 Anthony STODDARD; m Roxbury 20 Apr 1639 [AEBK 4:130]

WELD, Thomas¹ (bp 1595-1660[/1]) & 1/wf Margaret _____; m c1625 Roxbury [GMB 3:1962]

WELD, Thomas¹ (bp 1595-1660[/1]) & 2/wf Judith _____ (-1656); m c1636 Roxbury [GMB 3:1962]

WELD, Thomas¹ (bp 1595-1660[/1]) & 3/wf Margaret _____ (-by 1671); m aft 1656 [TAG 55:147; GMB 3:1962]

WELD, Thomas² (bp 1626-) & Dorothy WHITING, dau of Samuel; m Roxbury 4 June 1650 [GMB 3:1963]

WELDEN, Robert[1] (-1630/1) & Elizabeth _____; m by 1631 Charlestown [GMB 3:1964]

WELLES, Joshua & Hannah[2] BUCKLAND (1654-); m Windsor 11 Aug 1681 [GM 1:453]

WELLES, Thomas & perhaps Mary[2] BEARDSLEY (c1631-); m by 1651 Wethersfield [GM 1:225]

WELLES, Thomas (1595-1637) & Frances[1] ALBRIGHT (c1600-1678); m2 by 1638 Thomas Coleman; m c1625 England [REG 146:31]

WELLES, Thomas[3] (c1657-1695) & Mary BLACKLEACH (c1665-1729+); m bef 1687 Hartford [REG 148:29]

WELLINGTON, Benjamin (1676-1738) & Lydia BROWNE (1677-1711); m Lexington 16 Jan 1698/9 [AEBK 1:192]

WELLINGTON, Roger & Mary[2] PALGRAVE (c1618-); m by 1638 Watertown [GMB 3:1375]

WELLMAN, Isaac & Hannah[2] ADAMS (1662-); m Lynn 13 Mar 1678/9 [GM 1:10]

WELLMAN, William & Elizabeth[2] SPENCER; m2 Jacob JOY; m c1650 [GMB 3:1724]

WEST, Bartholomew & Catherine[2] ALMY; m c1652 [GM 1:44]

WEST, Francis & Susanna[2] SOULE; m c1660 [GMB 3:1707]

WESTON, Elnathan[2] (c1657-1729) & Jane _____ (-1735); m by 1688 Duxbury [NGSQ 71:43]

WESTON, Francis[1] (c1611-by 1645) & Margaret _____ [GMB 3:1966]

WESTON, John[2] (c1662-1736) & 1/wf Deborah ?DELANO (c1672-bef 1717); m c1695-7 Duxbury/Plympton [NGSQ 71:44]

WESTON, Thomas[1] (bp 1584-1646+) & Elizabeth WEAVER, dau of Christopher; m by 17 Oct 1623 Rugeley, Staffordshire/Weymouth [GMB 3:1968]

WETHERBY, John & Mary[2] HOWE (1653[/4]-1680-84); m Marlborough 18 Sept 1672 [AEBK 3]

WETHERELL, William ~ Rebecca NICHOLS; Scituate [Plymouth Court June 1700]

WEYMOUTH, James (c1662-) & Katherine[3] (CHADBOURNE) LITTEN (c1665-1727); m1 Edward LITTEN; m after 1693 [CG, 30]

WEYMOUTH, Robert & Rebecca[2] EMERY; m2 Thomas SADLER; m3 Daniel EATON [GM 2:444]

WHALE, Philemon (bp 1599-1675/6) & 1/wf Elizabeth (FROST) RICE (c1585-1647); m1 Henry RICE; m 24 Jan 1621/2 St Mary's Bury St Edmonds, Suffolk/Sudbury [TG 6:131]

WHAPLES, Thomas[2] & 1/wf Rebecca GILLETTE (1657-bef 1698); m bef Mar 1687/8 Simsbury/Windsor [TAG 56:134; GMB 2:772]

WHARFE, Nathaniel[2] (c1661-1733+) & Anna RIGGS (1664-1701); m Gloucester 30 Jan 1683/4 [TEG 14:150]

WHARTON, Philip & Mary GRIDLEY (1632-); by 1650 Boston [GMB 2:820]

WHEATLEY, Lionel & 2/wf Abigail² MATSON (c1642-); m by 1671 Boston [GMB 2:1241]

WHEATON, Robert¹ & Alice² BOWEN (c1620-); m c1640 Salem [TAG 76:273-77]

WHEELER, Edward³ (1669-1733/4) & Sarah MERRIAM (1675-1738); m Concord 23 Nov 1697 [AEBK 3]

WHEELER, George¹ (bp 1605/6-1684/5) & Catherine PIN (c1610-1684/5); m Cranfield, Bedfordshire 8 June 1630 Concord [AEBK 3]

WHEELER, John (1642/3-1713) & Sarah² LARKIN (1647[/8?]-1727); m Charlestown 25 Mar 1663 [AEBK 3]

WHEELER, Joseph (-by 1698) & Mary² POWERS (c1663-1697+); m Concord 1 Mar 1681/2 [AEBK 4:8]

WHEELER, Roger & Mary WILSON (-1658); m Newbury 7 Dec 1653 [REG 155:217]

WHEELER, Samuel² & Elizabeth² HERRIS (c1656-1725); m2 Hugh NEWBITT; m3 Edward POISSON; m4 Richard BLACKLEACH; m Stratford 29 May 1678 [NGSQ 80:48]

WHEELER, Samuel³ (1664-1717) & Mary HOSMER; m Concord 27 Jan 1689/90 [AEBK 3]

WHEELER, Thomas² (c1632-1687) & Hannah¹ HARWOOD (c1632-1707+); m Concord 10 Oct 1657 [AEBK 3]

WHEELER, Timothy (1667-1718) & Lydia³ WHEELER (1675-); m Concord 19 May 1692 [AEBK 3]

WHEELER, William² (-1683) & Hannah BUSS (1641[/2?]-), dau of William; m Concord 30 Oct 1659 [AEBK 3]

WHEELOCK, Ralph¹ & Rebecca CLARKE; m 17 May 1630 Wramplingham, Norfolk/Dedham [NGSQ 74:4; REG 152:312]

WHELDEN, Jonathan³ (1658-1742) & Mercy TAYLOR (1671-1742); m 1 Dec 1698 Yarmouth [TAG 48:8; 60:160]

WHIPPLE, Benjamin² (bp 1654-) & Ruth MATTHEWSON; m 1 Apr 1686 [GMB 3:1973]

WHIPPLE, David² (bp 1656-) & 1/wf Sarah HEARNDON; m Providence 15 May 1675 [GMB 3:1973]

WHIPPLE, David² (bp 1656-) & 2/wf Hannah TOWER; m Hingham 11 Nov 1677 [GMB 3:1973]

WHIPPLE, Eleazer (c1646-1719) & Alice ANGELL (c1649-1743); m Providence 26 Jan 1669/70 [AEJA; GMB 3:1973]

WHIPPLE, John & Lydia² HOAR (1665[/6?]-); m Taunton 16 Nov 1688 [GM 3:345]

WHIPPLE, John (1625-1683) & Martha REYNER (c1632-1679/80); m say 1656 Ipswich [REG 156:317]

WHIPPLE, John (c1639-1700) & 1/wf Mary OLNEY (c1643-c1676); m 4 Dec 1663 Providence [AEJA; GMB 3:1973]

WHIPPLE, John¹ (c1617-1685) & Sarah _____ [HAWKINS?]; m c1640 Providence [GMB 3:1972]

WHIPPLE, John² (c1640-) & 2/wf Rebecca SCOTT; m Providence 15 Apr 1678 [GMB 3:1973]

WHIPPLE, Jonathan & 2/wf Anne _____ [GMB 3:1974]

WHIPPLE, Jonathan (c1664-1721) & 1/wf Margaret ANGELL (c1660-1702/3+); m c1680 Providence, RI [AEJA; GMB 3:1974]

WHIPPLE, Joseph² & Alice SMITH; m Providence 20 May 1684 [GMB 3:1973]

WHIPPLE, Matthew & Anna [HAWKINS?] [DCS]

WHIPPLE, Matthew & Mary² BARTHOLOMEW; m2 Jacob GREEN; m Gloucester 24 Dec 1657 [GM 1:183]

WHIPPLE, Samuel² (bp 1643/4-) & Mary HARRIS, dau of Thomas; m c1669 [GMB 3:1973]

WHIPPLE, William² (bp 1652-) & Mary _____ [GMB 3:1973]

WHISTON, John & Susanna DOWNE [not Hanford]; m2 William BROOKS   [TAG 30:154; GM 3:206; GMB 3:1975]

WHISTON, John² (c1648-) & Abigail LOMBARD, dau of Joshua; m c1678 Scituate [GMB 3:1975]

WHITAKER, Edward (-1694) & Hannah² (WAKEMAN) HACKLETON; m1 Francis HACKLETON; m 1672 Ulster Co. [NYGBR 127:73]

WHITCOMB, Robert & Mary² CUDWORTH (bp 1637-); m 9 Mar 1660/1 [GM 2:254]

WHITE, Daniel² & Sarah CROW; m Hadley 1 Nov 1661 [GMB 3:1979]

WHITE, Ebenezer² (c1649-1703) & Hannah PHILLIPS (1654-by 1727); m by 1670 [AEBK 1:506]

WHITE, Jacob (1645-) & Elizabeth BUNCE, dau of Thomas; m by 1669 [GMB 3:1979]

WHITE, John & Ann² COOPER (bp 1619-); m2 Zorobabel PHILLIPS; m c1640 Watertown [GM 2:203]

WHITE, John & Elizabeth² GOBLE; m2 1682 Thomas CARTER; m by 1653 Sudbury [GM 3:83]

WHITE, John (-1633) & Elizabeth¹ HERBERT (bp 1611-1668); m c1630 Salem [REG 150:193]

WHITE, John (c1649-1726) & Hannah SMITH (1662-); m Taunton 24 Feb 1679/80 [AEBK 4:573]

WHITE, John¹ (c1597-1683/4) & Mary LEVIT; m Messing, Essex 26 Dec 1622 Hartford [GMB 3:1978]

WHITE, John² (c1636-) & Sarah BUNCE, dau of Thomas; m by 1659 [GMB 3:1979]

WHITE, Joseph (c1632-1706) & Lydia RAWLINGS (1642-1704-25); m Weymouth 19 Sept 1660 [AEBK 1:404]

WHITE, Joseph² (c1651-by 1724) & Mary _____ (c1660-1724); m 1681 Taunton [AEBK 4:573]

WHITE, Joseph³ (1661-1757) & Lydia COPELAND (1661-1727); m by 1683 Mendon [TAG 67:91; AEBK 1:512]

WHITE, Nathaniel² & 1/wf Elizabeth _____; m by 1653 [GMB 3:1979]

WHITE, Nathaniel[2] & 2/w Martha (COIT) MOULD, dau of John; m1 Hugh MOULD; m aft 1692 [GMB 3:1979]

WHITE, Nicholas[1] (c1611-1697) & Susannah FOSTER (bp 1616-1661/2+); m c1643 Taunton/Wendover, Buckinghamshire [AEBK 4:569]

WHITE, Nicholas[2] (c1646-1727/8) & Ursula MACOMBER (c1653-by 1724); m Taunton 9 Dec 1673 [AEBK 4:573]

WHITE, Paul (-1679) & Ann (PRIDDETH) (WOOD) JONES; m1 Richard WOOD; m2 Thomas JONES; m 14 Mar 1664/5 Newbury [REG 139:141]

WHITE, Peregrine[2] (1620-) & Sarah BASSETT, dau of William; m by 6 Mar 1648/9 [GMB 3:1980]

WHITE, Resolved[2] & Judith[2] VASSALL (c1619-); m Scituate 8 Apr 1640 [GMB 3:1872, 1980]

WHITE, Samuel & NOT Rebecca[2] LAPHAM [TAG 71:134]

WHITE, Samuel[2] (c1642-1699) & Mary DYER (1641-1716); Weymouth [AEBK 1:503]

WHITE, Samuel[3] (1666/7-) & Anna BINGLEY (-1737/8); m Milton 6 Dec 1687 [AEBK 1:512]

WHITE, Sylvanus[3] (-1688) & Deborah[2] CHURCH? (1657-); m bef 1683 Scituate [TAG 40:101, 60:131]

WHITE, Thomas & Ruth[1] HAFIELD (c1632-); m by 1659 [GM 3:186]

WHITE, Thomas[1] & 1/wf or only wife _____ _____; m bef 1636 Weymouth [TAG 68:29-30]

WHITE, Thomas[1] (c1599-1679) & _____ _____; m say 1635 Weymouth [AEBK 1:493]

WHITE, Thomas[2] & Mary[2] PRATT (c1640s-); m c1669 Weymouth [TAG 68:29-30]

WHITE, Thomas[2] (c1643-1706) & Mary _____ (c1640-1722/3); m c1670 Braintree [AEBK 1:505]

WHITE, Thomas[3] (1665-1748) & Mehitable THORNTON (1666-1704): m Boston 5 Dec 1687 [AEBK 1:515]

WHITE, William[1] (c1590-1620[/1]) & Susanna _____ (-1680); m2 Edward WINSLOW (not husband of Ann FULLER) m c1615 Plymouth [TAG 60:160]

WHITE, William (c1666-1750/1) & Judith (MEALES) HAYES, m1 Richard HAYES; m c1690 Salisbury, CT/Kingston [NYGBR 123:1-9]

WHITEHAND, George[1] (c1608-1646+) & Alice _____; m c1633 Charlestown [GMB 3:1981]

WHITEHEAD, Daniel[1] (1603-) & 1/wf _____[2] ARMITAGE, dau. of Thomas [NYGBR 131:263; GM 1:79]

WHITEHEAD, Daniel[1] (1603-) & 2/wf Jane IRELAND Newtown, L.I. [NYGBR 131:263]

WHITEHORNE, George[1] (1661/2-1722) & poss 1/wf Ann WILLIS; m St Marylebone Church, London 9 Feb 1683 [REG 146:4]

WHITEHORNE, George[1] (1661/2-1722) & poss 2/wf Katherine HOE (-1722); m St James Duke's Place, Aldgate, London 19 Jan 1689/90 [REG 146:4]

WHITING, Nathaniel & Hannah[2] DWIGHT (bp 1626-); m Dedham 4 Nov 1643 [GM 2:376]

WHITING, Nathaniel & Joanna[2] GAY (1644/5-); m2 John WARE; m Dedham 29 Mar 1664 [GM 3:40]

WHITMAN, Robert[1] & Anne[1] (TUTTY) KNIGHT (bp 1616-); m1 Alexander[1] KNIGHT; m Ipswich Nov 1664 [TAG 76:10]

WHITNEY, Benjamin (1643-1723) & 1/wf Jane _____ (-1690); m May 1669 Watertown/York [AEBK 1:535]

WHITNEY, Benjamin (1643-1723) & 2/wf Mary POORE; m Marlborough 13 Apr 1696 [AEBK 1:535]

WHITNEY, John (1662-by 1735) & Mary[2] HAPGOOD (1667-1692/3); m Watertown 10 Apr 1688 [AEBK 1:330]

WHITNEY, John[1] (bp 20 July 1592-1673) & 1/wf Elinor _____ (c1600-1659); m c1623 England [AEBK 1:528]

WHITNEY, John[1] (bp 20 July 1592-1673) & 2/wf Judah CLEMENT (-bef 1670); m Watertown 29 Sept 1659 [AEBK 1:528]

WHITNEY, John[2] (bp 1621-1692) & Ruth REYNOLDS (c1620s-1695+); m c1643 Watertown [AEBK 1:533]

WHITNEY, Jonathan[2] (c1634-1702/3) & Lydia[2] JONES (c1636-1701/2); m Watertown 30 Oct 1656 [AEBK 1:350, 536]

WHITNEY, Joshua[2] (1635/6-1719) & 1/wf Lydia _____ [AEBK 1:534]

WHITNEY, Joshua[2] (1635/6-1719) & 2/wf Mary _____ (-1671) [AEBK 1:534]

WHITNEY, Joshua[2] (1635/6-1719) & 3/wf Abigail TARBELL; m Watertown 30 Sept 1672 [AEBK 1:535]

WHITNEY, Josiah[3] (1664-1717) & 1/wf Mary _____ (-1710); m by 1686 Wrentham [AEBK 1:540]

WHITNEY, Richard[2] (1623/4-1691+) & Martha COLDHAM (c1630s-1672+); m Watertown 19 Mar 1650/1 [AEBK 1:534]

WHITNEY, Thomas[2] (bp 1627-1719) & Mary KEDEL (c1630s-1673/4+); m Watertown 11 Jan 1654/5 [AEBK 1:534]

WHITNEY, William (1677/8-) & Lydia PERHAM (1673/4-1716); m Chelmsford 1699/1700 [AEBK 4:537]

WHITSON, Thomas (1652-1740) & Martha JONES (c1665-) [NYGBR 128:106]

WHITTAKER, Edward & Hilletje BURHANS; m Kingston 18 June 1700 [NYGBR 127:75]

WHITTAKER, James (bp 1675-) & Elizabeth TITSOORT; m Kingston 6 Dec 1696 [NYGBR 127:74]

WHITTAMORE, Lawrence[1] (-1644) & Elizabeth (_____) ADAM (-1643); m Great Amwell, Hertfordshire 25 Feb 1627/8 Roxbury [REG 132:23]

WHITTEMORE, Nathaniel & Mary[2] KNOWER (c1650); m2 John MARABLE; m by 1668 Charlestown [GMB 2:1147]

WHITTIER, Abraham (-1690) & Mary SALMON (1643-1690+); m 6 July 1665 Southold [Southold Town Records 1:464; 2:198-200; TAG 21:246-47; Harris]

WHITTINGHAM, John[1] & Martha[2] HUBBARD (c1613-); m2 Simon EYRE; m c1638 [GM 3:440]

WHITTON, Jeremiah[2] & Elizabeth[2] DOGGETT (c1636-) [TAG 72:100; GMB 1:570]

WHITTRIDGE, Thomas (-1672) & Florence (NORMAN) WHITTRIDGE [TAG 77:103]

WHOOD, Jonas[3] (c1657-1731) & Deborah SMITH; m by 1700 Hempstead/Jamaica, L.I. [NYGBR 132:121]

WIGGIN, Andrew[2] (c1635-) & Hannah BRADSTREET, dau of Simon; m Hampton 11 June 1659 [GMB 3:1983]

WIGGIN, James & Magdalene[2] HILTON (c1636-); m2 Henry KENNING; m by 1656 [GMB 2:954]

WIGGIN, James & Rachel[2] BROOKS (bp 1650-); m by 1672 Rehoboth [GM 1:410]

WIGGIN, Thomas[1] (c1592-1666+) & 1/wf _____ _____; m bef 1633 [GMB 3:1983]

WIGGIN, Thomas[1] (c1592-1666+) & 2/wf Catherine WHITEING (c1601-); m St. Margaret, New Fish St., London by lic 11 July 1633 [GMB 3:1983]

WIGGIN, Thomas[2] (c1640-) & Sarah BAREFOOT, sister of Walter; m by 1665 Hampton [GMB 3:1984]

WIGGLESWORTH, Edward (bp 1603-1653) & Esther MIDDLEBROOK (-1665+); m Wrawby, Lincolnshire 27 Oct 1629 [REG 156:309]

WIGGLESWORTH, Michael (1631-1705) & 1/wf Mary REYNER (c1632-1659); m Rowley 18 May 1655 [REG 156:316]

WIGGLESWORTH, Michael (1631-1705) & 2/wf Martha MUDGE (c1662-1690); m c1679 Malden [REG 156:318]

WIGGLESWORTH, Michael (1631-1705) & 3/wf Sybil (SPARHAWK) AVERY (c1655-1708); m Braintree 23 June 1691 [REG 156:318]

WIGHT, Thomas & Lydia (ELIOT) PENNIMAN (bp 1610-bef 1676); m1 James PENNIMAN; m Medfield 7 Dec? 1665 [TAG 71:14]

WIGHT, Thomas (-1690) & Mehitable CHENEY (bp 1643-1693); m by 1663 Medfield [AEBK 1:233]

WIGHT, Thomas[1] (bp 1607-1646+) & Lucy ____; m bef 1643 Exeter [AEBK 4:579]

WILBORE, Joseph[2] (bp 1629/30-) & Elizabeth FARWELL, dau of Henry; m c1651 [GMB 3:1988]

WILBORE, Samuel & Hannah[2] PORTER (c1630-); m c1650 [GMB 3:1503]

WILBORE, Samuel[1] (c1595-1656) & 1/wf Ann SMITH (-1633+); m Sible Hedingham, Essex 13 Jan 1619/20 [GMB 3:1988]

WILBORE, Samuel[1] (c1595-1656) & 2/wf Elizabeth (____) LECHFORD (-1656+); m1 Thomas LECHFORD. m by 1645 [GMB 3:1988]

WILBORE, Samuel[2] (bp 1622-) & Hannah PORTER, dau of John [GMB 3:1988]

WILBORE, Shadrack[2] (bp 1631-) & 1/wf Mary DEANE, dau of Walter; m c1659 [GMB 3:1988]

WILBORE, Shadrack[2] (bp 1631-) & 2/wf Ann (BASS) PAINE, dau of Samuel; m1 Stephen PAINE; m Taunton 13 Sept 1692 [GMB 3:1988]

WILCOCK, John & Katharine[2] STOUGHTON (bp 1622-); m Hartford 18 Jan 1649/50 [GMB 3:1778]

WILCOX, Daniel[2] (bp 1632/3-1720) & 1/wf _____ _____; Tiverton, MA [REG 147:191]

WILCOX, Daniel[2] (bp 1632/3-1720) & 2/wf Elizabeth COOK; m Tiverton 28 Nov 1661 [REG 147:191]

WILCOX, Edward[1] (bp 1603/4-1638-60) & 1/wf Mary _____ (-1630); Croft, Lincolnshire [REG 147:190]

WILCOX, Edward[1] (bp 1603/4-1638-60) & 2/wf Susan THOMSON; m Orby, Lincolnshire 12 May 1631 [REG 147:191]

WILCOX, John & Esther CORNWALL; m2 John STOW; by 9 July 1672 Middletown [GMB 1:483]

WILCOX, John & Sarah[2] WADSWORTH; m Hartford 17 Sept 1646 [GMB 3:1895]

WILCOX, Stephen[2] (bp 1634-c1690) & Hannah[2] HAZARD (bp 1637-); m c30 Jan 1658[/9?] Boston [GM 3:297; REG 147:191]

WILD, Thomas ~ Hannah (Indian); Marshfield [Plymouth Court June 1688]

WILDER, Edward & Elizabeth[2] EAMES (bp 1624-); m c1651 Hingham [GM 2:390]

WILDER, Thomas (1644-1716) & Mary HOUGHTON; m Lancaster 25 June 1668 [Lancaster Records, Middlesex register, 13]

WILKES, William[1] (c1608-1645[/6]) & Joan _____; m by 1633 [GMB 3:1990]

WILKINS, Benjamin[2] (c1665-) & Priscilla BAXTER; m Salem 3 June 1677 [GMB 3:1993]

WILKINS, Bray & Anna/Hannah[2] WAY (bp 1615[/6]-); m by 1636 [GMB 3:1952]

WILKINS, Bray[1] (1611-1702) & Hannah[2] ?WAY not GINGILL; m c1636 Salem [TAG 60:3]

WILKINS, Bray[1] (c1611-1701/2) & Hannah WAY, dau of Henry; m c1636 Salem [GMB 3:1993]

WILKINS, Henry[2] (bp 1651[/2]-) & 1/wf Rebecca _____; m by 1673 [GMB 3:1993]

WILKINS, Henry[2] (bp 1651[/2]-) & 2/wf Ruth (FULLER) WHEELER; m by 1 July 1691 [GMB 3:1993]

WILKINS, Henry[2] (c1651-1737) & 1/wf Rebecca ?BAXTER (?1648/9-); m c1672 Dorchester/Salem [TAG 60:103]

WILKINS, John[2] & Mary _____; m c1664 [GMB 3:1993]

WILKINS, Samuel[2] (c1636-1688) & Jane _____; m c1673 [GMB 3:1993]

WILKINS, Thomas[2] (bp 1647-) & Hannah NICHOLS; m Salem May 1667 [GMB 3:1993]

WILKINSON, _____ & Prudence _____ (c1595-1654/5-5); m c1615 England [GMB 3:1996]

WILKINSON, John² & _____ _____ [GMB 3:1997]

WILKINSON, Lawrence (c1620s-1692) & Susanna SMITH (c1625-1662/3+); m c1645-1650 Providence [AEJA]

WILLARD, Benjamin² & Sarah² LAKIN (1661/2-1740) Concord/Lancaster [TAG 70:148]

WILLARD, Henry² & Mary² LAKIN (c1658-1688); m 18 July 1674 [TAG 70;148]

WILLARD, John & Margaret³ WILKINS (c1667-1751); m2 William³ TOWNE; m c1687 Topsfield [TAG 60:16]

WILLARD, Josiah & Hannah² HOSMER (c1636-); m2 William MALTBY; m Concord 20 Mar 1656[/7] [GMB 2:1004]

WILLET, Andrew² (1655-) & Susannah HOLBROOK; m 6 Mar 1693/4 [GMB 3:2000]

WILLET, Hezekiah (1653-) & Anna BROWN, dau of John; m Swansea 7 Jan 1675[/6] [GMB 3:2000]

WILLET, James (1649-) & 1/wf Elizabeth HUNT, dau of Peter; m Rehoboth 17 Apr 1673 [GMB 3:2000]

WILLET, James² (1649-) & Grace FRINCK; m Swansea 2 Aug 1677 [GMB 3:2000]

WILLET, John² (1641-) & Abigail COLLINS, dau of Edward; m c1663 [GMB 3:2000]

WILLET, Nathaniel & 3/wf Eleanor WATTS; m aft 1677 Hartford [TAG 46:136]

WILLET, Samuel² (1658-) & _____ _____; Flushing, Long Island [GMB 3:2000]

WILLET, Thomas¹ (c1610-1674) & 1/wf Mary² BROWN (-1669[/70]), dau of John; m Plymouth 6 July 1636 [GMB 3:2000; GM 1:426]

WILLET, Thomas¹ (c1610-1674) & 2/wf Joanna (BOYSE) PRUDDEN; m1 Peter PRUDDEN; m Milford 19 Sept 1671 [GMB 3:2000]

WILLIAMS alias HARRIS, Thomas & Elizabeth _____; m2 William STITSON; Charlestown [REG 152:343]

WILLIAMS, Anthony (-bef 1698) & Mary SALLOWS (1658/9?-1698+); m2 1698 Daniel GOWING; m Beverly 25 Sept 1676 [TAG 72:7]

WILLIAMS, Charles & Mary² GLADDING (1678/9-) [TAG 77:213]

WILLIAMS, Daniel² & Rebecca (RHODES) POWER, dau of Zachariah; m Providence 2 Dec 1676 [GMB 3:2010]

WILLIAMS, Ebenezer & Sarah² BEAMON (1658/9-); m Dorchester 28 Dec 1680 [GM 1:218]

WILLIAMS, Ebenezer² (1649[/50]-) & Martha HALL; m Dorchester 18 Sept 1674 [GMB 3:2007]

WILLIAMS, George (c1605-1654) & Mary _____ (-1654); m c1630 Salem [GMB 3:2004]

WILLIAMS, Isaac & Deborah² PARKE (bp 1651-); Roxbury [GMB 3:1390]

WILLIAMS, Isaac & Margery² COLLINS (1633-); m c1656 [GM 2:167]

WILLIAMS, John (-1702-7) & Bethia (PARSONS) MASKELL (1642-1708+); m Windsor 8 Aug 1672 [REG 148:230-1]

WILLIAMS, John[2] (1656-1713) & 1/wf Sarah _____ (-c1699); by 1687 Hartford/East Hartford [TAG 69:93; Harris]

WILLIAMS, John[2] (c1630-) & Elizabeth _____; m by 1664 Salem [GMB 3:2004]

WILLIAMS, Joseph & Elizabeth[2] WATSON (1648[/9]-); m Plymouth 28 Nov 1667 [GMB 3:1946]

WILLIAMS, Joseph & Lydia OMES (1649-1689-90); m bef 1670 Boston [TAG 53:13]

WILLIAMS, Joseph (1643-1724) & Lydia OLNEY (c1645-1724); m 17 Dec 1669 Providence [AEJA]

WILLIAMS, Joseph[2] (bp 1640-) & Sarah BROWNING; m Salem 20 Nov 1661 [GMB 3:2005]

WILLIAMS, Mathew ~ Susan COLE, in court 10 July 1645 [PCR 1:129]

WILLIAMS, Nathaniel & Mary ( ); m2 Peter[1] BRACKETT [TAG 52:73]

WILLIAMS, Robert & Margery ROUND (1648-); m 2 June 1671 Yarmouth [TAG 54:37]

WILLIAMS, Roger[1] (c1606-1682/3) & Mary BERNARD (-1676+), dau of Richard; m High Laver, Essex 15 Dec 1629 Providence [GMB 3:2009]

WILLIAMS, Roger[1] (c1610-1650+) & 1/wf _____ _____; m by 1645 Windsor [GMB 3:2007]

WILLIAMS, Roger[1] (c1610-1650+) & 2/wf Lydia BATES (bp 1615-), dau of James; m by 1649 [GM 1:199]

WILLIAMS, Samuel & Theoda[2] PARKE (1637-); m Roxbury 2 Mar 1653[/4] [GMB 3:1389]

WILLIAMS, Samuel[2] (bp 1638-) & Mary VEREN; m Salem 2 Apr 1662 [GMB 3:2005]

WILLIAMS, Thomas & Martha MEAD (c1630-by 1695); m lic 24 July 1683 NY [TAG 73:9]

WILLIAMS, Thomas & Mary[2] HOLDEN (c1648-); m Groton 11 Aug/July 1666 [GM 3:366]

WILLIAMS, Thomas (c1644-1705) & Johanna _____ (c1654-1744); m bef 1672 New London [AEJA]

WILLIAMSON, Michael/Moyles (c1605-1645) & Ann PANKHURST (c1619-); m2 Henry PEARSALL; m c1638 Boston/Hempstead [NYGBR 119:81]

WILLIS, Henry (1628-1714) & Mary PEACE (c1632-1714); Warminster, Wiltshire/Westbury [NYGBR 118:65]

WILLIS, John[1] (c1607-1634) & Jane _____; m by 1632 Boston/Lynn [GMB 3:2011]

WILLIS, Richard & Patience BONHAM; m2 John[2] HOLMES [NGSQ 74:87]

WILLIS, Samuel & Ruth[2] HAYNES (c1636-); m by Mar 1653/4 [GMB 2:896]

WILLIS, William (-by 1678) & Rebecca SHEAFE? (-1685+); m2 Thomas HERRIS; England/Boston [NGSQ 80:37-38; Harris]

WILLOUGHBY, Francis (bp 1615-1671) & 1/wf Mary TAYLOR (-1640); m 26 Nov 1635 Blackwall, Middlesex [TAG 56:12; 60:160]

WILLS, Samuel & Rebecca² PIERCE (c1643-); m c1673 [GMB 3:1468]

WILMOT, Benjamin (-1651) & Elizabeth (TENNEY) HEATON (bp 1610-1685); m1 James HEATON, m3 William JUDSON; m c1644 New Haven [DR; AEBK 4:379]

WILMOT, John & Sarah² RUGGLES (1646-); m2 John SMITH; m c1669 [GMB 3:1607]

WILSON, Anthony & Elizabeth² HILL (c1630-); m c1650 [GMB 2:940]

WILSON, Anthony & Sarah² (JONES) BULKELEY; m1 Thomas² BULKELEY [TAG 71:54]

WILSON, Humphrey² & Judith HERSEY; m Exeter 21 Dec 1665 [GMB 3:2018]

WILSON, James (1673-1705/6) & Alice (SABEERE) HUBBARD (-1734), dau. of Stephen; m c1690s Kingstown, RI [REG 144:296]

WILSON, John & Sarah² HOOKER (bp 1629/30-); m by 1649 Boston [TAG 76:216; GMB 2:984]

WILSON, John (-by 1695) & Hester (CHANDLER) GAGE (1652-); m c1675 Newbury/Elizabeth, NJ/Bristol [REG 155:220-24]

WILSON, John (c1588-1667) & Elizabeth MANSFIELD (bp 3 Dec 1592-c1658), dau of John; m c1615 Boston [REG 155:24+; GMB 3:2014]

WILSON, John² (bp 164[3/]4-) & Sarah HOOKER, dau of Thomas; m by 1649 Boston [GMB 3:2014]

WILSON, Nathaniel & Thankful² BEAMON (1663-); m Charlestown 27 Sept 1683 [GM 1:219]

WILSON, Robert & Elizabeth² STEBBINS; m2 Thomas CADWELL; m c1650 [GMB 3:1753]

WILSON, Samuel & Mary GRIFFEN; m2 Anthony HOSKINS [TAG 52:80]

WILSON, Thomas¹ (c1595-1642[/3]) & 1/wf _____ _____; m by 1620 [GMB 3:2018]

WILSON, Thomas¹ (c1595-1642[/3]) & 2/wf Ann _____; m2 c1644 John LEGATE; m by 1633 Roxbury [GMB 3:2018]

WILSON, William¹ (-1646) & Patience TRUSTRAM; m Boston, England 6 Oct 1636 Boston [REG 155:219]

WILTON, David¹ (bp 1608-1677/3) & Katherine² HOSKINS (c1615-); m2 Thomas HOSMER; m c1634 Hartford/Windsor [GMB 2:1001, 3:2021]

WINCOLL, John (c1616-1694) & 2/wf Mary ETHERINGTON (c1658-bef 1679); m Watertown contract 29 Feb 1675/6 Portsmouth [CG; GMB 3:2023]

WINCOLL, John² & 1/wf Elizabeth _____; m by 1662 [GMB 3:2022]

WINCOLL, John² & 3/wf Olive (COLEMAN) PLAISTED; m1 Roger PLAISTED; m by 16 Sept 1682 [GMB 3:2023]

WINCOLL, Thomas¹ (c1587-1657) & 1/wf Elizabeth _____; m by 1622 Watertown [GMB 3:2022]

WINCOLL, Thomas[1] (c1587-1657) & 2/wf Beatrix _____ (-1656); m bef 1656 [GMB 3:2022]

WINDSOR, Robert (-1679) & Rebecca SCOTTOW (-1698) [JHO]

WING, Daniel & 1/wf Hannah[2] SWIFT (c1620-1664/5); m Sandwich 5 Nov 1642 [TAG 77:171]

WING, Daniel & 2/wf Anna EWER; m Sandwich June 1666 [TAG 77:171]

WING, Elisha (1669-1757) & Mehitable BUTLER (c1670-1731); m 12 Mar 1689 Sandwich [REG 127:24]

WING, John & Johoshabeath[2] DAVIS (bp 1642-); m c1660 Boston [GM 2:300]

WING, John & Miriam DEANE; m after 31 Jan 1692/3 Plymouth [GMB 1:516]

WINGATE, John[1] & 1/wf Mary[2] NUTTER [TAG 72:276]

WINGATE, John[1] & 2/wf Sarah (TAYLOR) CANNEY; m by 1678 [TAG 72:276]

WINNOCK, Joseph & Sarah[2] MILLS; m c1676 [GMB 3:2082]

WINSLEY, Samuel (-1663) & 2/wf Anne (DALTON)(REWSE) BOAD (-1676/7); m (contract) Salisbury 5 Oct 1657 [REG 154:265]

WINSLOW, Edward[1] (bp 1595-1655) & 1/wf Elizabeth BARKER (-1620/1); m Leiden, Holland aft 12 May 1618 Plymouth [GMB 3:2024]

WINSLOW, Edward[1] (bp 1595-1655) & 2/wf Susannah (_____) WHITE; m1 William WHITE; m Plymouth 12 May 1621 [GMB 3:2025]

WINSLOW, Edward[2] & 1/wf Sarah HILTON, dau of William; m c1661 Boston [GMB 3:2029]

WINSLOW, Edward[2] (c1635-1682) & Elizabeth HUTCHINSON (1639-1728) dau of Edward; m Boston 8 Feb 1688 [REG 145:261; GMB 3:2030]

WINSLOW, Gilbert (1673-) & Mercy SNOW (1675-); m 7 Feb 1698 Marshfield [REG 124:119]

WINSLOW, Isaac[2] & Mary[2] NOWELL (1643-), dau of Increase NOWELL; m2 John LONG; m Charlestown 14 Aug 1666 [GMB 2:1345, 3:2030]

WINSLOW, Job[2] & Ruth _____; m by 1674 Swansea [GMB 3:2036]

WINSLOW, John & Sarah[2] MOULTON (c1631-); m Malden 5 May 1652 [GMB 2:1307]

WINSLOW, John[1] (bp 1597-1673/4-4) & Mary CHILTON (-1676-9), dau of James; m Plymouth by 22 May 1627 [GMB 1:354, 3:2029]

WINSLOW, John[2] & 1/wf Elizabeth _____; m by 1664 Boston [GMB 3:2029]

WINSLOW, John[2] & 2/wf Judith _____; m aft 1644 [GMB 3:2029]

WINSLOW, Jonathan[2] (1639-) & Ruth SARGENT; m by 1664 Marshfield [GMB 3:2032]

WINSLOW, Josiah[1] (bp 1605/6-1674) & Margaret BOURNE (-1683), dau of Thomas; m by 1637 Marshfield [GMB 3:2032]

WINSLOW, Josiah[2] (1627+-) & Penelope PELHAM, dau of Herbert; m by 1658 Marshfield [GMB 3:2025]

WINSLOW, Kenelm[1] (bp 1599-1672) & Ellen (NEWTON) ADAMS (-1681); m1 John ADAMS; m Plymouth June 1634 [GMB 3:2035]

WINSLOW, Kenelm[2] & 1/wf Mercy WORDEN; m by 1668 Scituate [GMB 3:2035]

WINSLOW, Kenelm[2] & 2/wf Damaris EAMES, dau of Mark; m by 1693 [GMB 3:2035]

WINSLOW, Nathaniel[2] & Faith MILLER; m Marshfield 3 Aug 1664 {GMB 3:2035]

WINSLOW, Samuel & Hannah BRIGGS, dau of Walter; m by 1675 Boston [GMB 3:2030]

WINSOR, Samuel & Mercy[2] WILLIAMS; m Providence 2 Jan 1676/7 [GMB 3:2009]

WINTER, John & Posthume[2] BROWN?; Westchester [GM 1:447]

WINTER, John[1] (c1585-1645+) & Joane BOWDON; m Holbeton, Devonshire 29 Jan 1609/10 Casco [GMB 3:2037]

WINTHROP, Adam[2] (1620-) & 1/wf Elizabeth GLOVER; m by 10 Oct 1642 [GMB 3:2040]

WINTHROP, Adam[2] (1620-) & 2/wf Elizabeth (HAWKINS) LONG, dau of Thomas; m1 Nathaniel LONG; m 7 May 1649 [GMB 3:2041]

WINTHROP, Deane[2] (bp 1622/3-) & 1/wf Sarah GLOVER [GMB 3:2041]

WINTHROP, Deane[2] (bp 1622/3-) & 2/wf Martha (_____) MELLOWS; m1 John MELLOWS [GMB 3:2041]

WINTHROP, Henry[2] (1607/8-) & Elizabeth FONES; m2 Robert FEAKE; ~William HALLETT; m 25 Apr 1629 [GMB 3:2040]

WINTHROP, John[1] (bp 1587/8-1649) 3/wf Margaret TYNDAL (-1647); m Great Maplestead, Essex 29 Apr 1618 Boston [GMB 3:2039]

WINTHROP, John[1] (bp 1587/8-1649) & 1/wf Mary FORTH (-1615); m Great Stambridge, Essex 16 Apr 1605 [GMB 3:2039]

WINTHROP, John[1] (bp 1587/8-1649) & 2/wf Thomasine CLOPTON (-1616); m Groton 6 Dec 1615 [GMB 3:2039]

WINTHROP, John[1] (bp 1587/8-1649) & 4/wf Martha (RAINSBOROUGH) COYTMORE (-1660); m1 Thomas COYTMORE; m3 John COGGAN; aft 20 Dec 1647 Boston [GMB 3:2040]

WINTHROP, John[2] (1605/6-) & 1/wf Martha FONES; m Groton 8 Feb 1630/1 [GMB 3:2040]

WINTHROP, John[2] (1605/6-) & 2/wf Elizabeth READE; m St. Matthew, Friday Street, London 6 July 1635 [GMB 3:2040]

WINTHROP, Stephen[2] (1618/9-) & Judith RAINSBOROUGH; m by 1644 [GMB 3:2040]

WINTHROP, Waitstill & Mary[2] BROWN (bp 1656/7-); m bet 1678-79 Boston [GM 1:444]

WISE, _____ & Elizabeth[1] _____ (-1633+, by 1646); m bef 1600, Roxbury [TAG 55:149-50]

WISWALL, Ichabod[2] (-1700) & 2/wf Priscilla (PABODIE) WISWALL (-1724) [REG 155:245]

WISWELL, Thomas (bp 20 Sept 1601-1683) & 1/wf Elizabeth BURBAGE; m Great Packington, Warwickshire [50 GMC]

WISWELL, Thomas (bp 20 Sept 1601-1683) & 2/wf Isabell (MUSTON) FARMER (- 1686); m after 1669 [50 GMC]

WITCHFIELD, John[1] (c1612-1678[/9]) & 1/wf _____ _____ (-1659); Windsor [GMB 3:2043]

WITCHFIELD, John[1] (c1612-1678[/9]) & 2/wf Margaret (____) GOFFE (-1669); m1 Edward GOFFE; m Cambridge Dec 1662 [GMB 3:2043]

WITHERDEN, John (bp 1624-1664+) & Mary _____ (-1664+); m bef 1661 Scituate/Boston [DR]

WITHERS, Thomas[1] (c1606-1684-5) & Jane _____; m2 William GODSOE; m c1651 [GMB 3:2046]

WITHINGTON, Richard & Elizabeth[2] ELIOT (bp 1627-); m by 1649 Dorchester [GM 2:416]

WLLIS, Nicholas & Sarah[2] BRADSTREET (c1638-); m Ipswich 13 Apr 1657 [GM 1:387]

WOLCOTT, George[2] & Elizabeth _____ perhaps TREAT; m c1649 [GMB 3:2051]

WOLCOTT, Henry & Abiah[2] GOFFE (1646-); m Windsor 12 Oct 1664 [GM 3:98]

WOLCOTT, Henry[1] (bp 1578-1655) & Elizabeth SAUNDERS (-1655); m Lydyeard St. Lawrence, Somersetshire 19 Jan 1606 Windsor [GMB 3:2051]

WOLCOTT, Henry[2] & Sarah NEWBURY, dau of Thomas; m Windsor 8 Nov 1641 [GMB 3:2051]

WOLCOTT, Simon[2] & 1/wf Joanna COOKE (-1657), dau of Aaron; m Windsor 19 Mar 1656/7 [GMB 3:2051]

WOLCOTT, Simon[2] & 2/wf Martha PITKIN; m Windsor 17 Oct 1661 [GMB 3:2051]

WOLCOTT, William & Alice[3] INGERSOLL (bp 1612-1644+); m c1630 Sandy, Bedfordshire/Salem/Newfoundland [Abel Lunt, p.65]

WOLFORD, Hans & Mary[2] (GODDARD) (BENNETT) FIELD (c1645-); m1 Arthur BENNETT; m2 Joseph FIELD; m 1690+ [GM 3:87]

WOOD, Ebenezer[3] (1669-1736) & 1/wf Rachel NICHOLS (1677-1714+); m Rowley 5 Apr 1695 [AEBK 3]

WOOD, Edmund[1] (c1585-90-) & Martha (LOME) WOOD; m 21 May 1611 Halifax/Hempstead [NYGBR 120:6; 132:37]

WOOD, Edward[1] (bp 1598-1642) & Ruth LEE (c1600-1642); m 2 Feb 1619/20 Nuneaton, Warwickshire/Charlestown [TG 9:90; AEBK 3]

WOOD, Henry & Abigail[2] JENNY (c1621-); m Plymouth 28 Apr 1644 [GMB 2:1093]

WOOD, John (-1723+) & Hannah HACKLETON (c1661-1723+); m Kingston 12 Jan 1682 Hartford [NYGBR 127:74]

WOOD, John[2] (-1689+) & Mary PEABODY (c1640-1689+); m say 1662 Newport [AEBK 1:370]

WOOD, John[3] (c1653-5-by 1692) & _____ RHODES (-c1691); m c1680 Southampton, L.I./Hempstead [NYGBR 132:119]

WOOD, Jonas & Elizabeth[2] (probably) STRICKLAND; m c1640 [GMB 3:1786]

WOOD, Jonas[1] (bp 20 Feb 1613/4-1661) & Mary DRAKE; m Skipton, Yorkshire 20 Aug 1635 Watertown/Huntington [NYGBR 123:137]

WOOD, Josiah[2] (c1630-1691) & Lydia BACON (c1638-1712); m Charlestown 28 Oct 1657 [AEBK 3]

WOOD, Mark & Elizabeth[2] HANCOCK (1644[/5?]-); m Charlestown 2 Feb 1664/5 [GM 3:205]

WOOD, Nicholas & Mary[2] PIDGE (c1622-); m by 1642 [GMB 3:1465]

WOOD, Obadiah[2] (bp 1625-1694) & 1/wf Margaret SPARKS (-1667); m by 26 Mar 1650 Nuneaton, Warwickshire/Ipswich [AEBK 3]

WOOD, Obadiah[2] (bp 1625-1694) & 2/wf Hazelephony (WILLIX) GEE (c1636-1714), dau of Balthasar WILLIX; m1 John GEE; m aft 19 Nov 1671 Ipswich [AEBK 3]

WOOD, Obadiah[3] (1652/3-1712) & 1/wf Catherine KING; Hartford [TG 9:102]

WOOD, Richard & Ann PRIDDETH, m2 Thomas JONES, m3 Paul WHITE [REG 139:141]

WOOD, Thomas[2] (c1633-1687) & Ann _____ (c1637-1714) NOT HUNT; m Rowley 7 June 1654 [AEBK 3]

WOOD, Timothy[2] (bp 1622-1659/60) & _____[2] STRICKLAND, dau. of John; m2 Samuel MATTHEWS; m c1644 Huntington, L.I./Hempstead [NYGBR 132:38; GMB 3:1786]

WOOD, William & Abigail _____; m 1698 Hampstead, NY [TAG 39:140]

WOOD, William[1] (c1610-1650+) & Jane _____; m by 20 Aug 1644 Lynn/Sandwich [GMB 3:2053; TAG 71:146]

WOOD/ATWOOD, John & Sarah[2] MASTERSON (c1625-); m c1645 [GMB 2:1237]

WOODBERY, Andrew & Mary[2] COCKERILL; m by 1657 Salem [GM 2:122]

WOODBRIDGE, John & Mercy DUDLEY; by 7 June 1640 Newbury [GMB 1:585]

WOODBURY, Humphrey[2] & Elizabeth[1] HUNTER (c1617-); m c1637 Salem [GM 3:473; GMB 3:2055]

WOODBURY, John[1] (c1583-1641/2) & 1/wf _____ _____; m c1608 [GMB 3:2055]

WOODBURY, John[1] (c1583-1641/2) & 2/wf Agnes _____ (-1672[/3]); m by 1636 Salem [GMB 3:2055]

WOODBURY, John[2] & Elizabeth _____; m by 1654 Salem [GMB 3:2055]

WOODBURY, Peter[2] (bp 1640-) & 1/wf Abigail BATCHELDER, dau of John; m Beverly Sept 1666 or earlier [GMB 3:2055]

WOODBURY, Peter[2] (bp 1640-) & Sarah DODGE, dau of Richard; m Beverly July 1667 [GMB 3:2055]

WOODBURY, William & Johanna[3] WHEELER (1671-   ); m Beverly 29 Sept 1689 [AEBK 3]

WOODCOCK, William & Sarah[2] COOPER; m Hingham Oct 1648 [GM 2:198]

WOODFORD, Thomas & Mary[2] BLOTT (bp 1609-   ); m c1636 [GM 1:335]

WOODFORD, Thomas[1] (c1614-1666/7) & Mary BLOTT (bp 1609-   ), dau of Robert; m c1636 Harrold, Bedfordshire/Northampton [GMB 3:2059]

WOODIN, John[1] & 2/wf Mary[2] JOHNSON (-bef 1692); m bef 1653 Hampton [TAG 64:70]

WOODIN, John[1] & 3/wf Mary _____ (c1640-   ); m bef 1692 [TAG 64:70]

WOODMANSEE, Gabriel[1] & Sarah _____; m2 James? RIX; m c1665 New London [REG 147:35]

WOODMANSEE, James[3] & Abigail (MELYEN); m Boston 17 May 1686 [REG 147:47]

WOODMANSEE, John[2] (c1635-1684) & 1/wf Margaret _____ (-1660); m c1659 Boston [REG 147:46]

WOODMANSEE, John[2] (c1635-1684) & 2/wf Elizabeth CLARK; m Boston 1 May 1662 [REG 147:46]

WOODMANSEE, Robert[1] (c1595-1667) & 1/wf Anna _____; Boston [REG 147:44]

WOODMANSEE, Robert[1] (c1595-1667) & 2/wf Margaret _____; by 1644 Boston [REG 147:44]

WOODMANSEE, Thomas[2] (1670-1733) & 1/wf Hannah _____; m bef Oct 1699 N.J. [REG 147:38]

WOODMANSEY, John & Elizabeth[2] CARR (1642-   ); m Boston 1 May 1662 [GM 2:20]

WOODS, John (c1610-1678) & Mary[2] PARMENTER (c1610-1690); m Bures St Mary, Suffolk 10 Oct 1633 Sudbury/Framingham/ Marlborough [REG 147:382; DR]

WOODWARD, Israel[2] & Jane GODFREY; m Taunton 4 Aug 1670 [GMB 3:2062]

WOODWARD, James[2] & Hannah STACY, dau of Richard; m c1698 [GMB 3:2062]

WOODWARD, John[2] & Sarah CROSSMAN; m Rehoboth 11 Nov 1675 {GMB 3:2062}

WOODWARD, Nathaniel (-1661+) & Margaret _____ (-1661+); m probably near Podington, Bedfordshire bef 1615 Boston [DR]

WOODWARD, Nathaniel[1] (c1615-1686+) & 1/wf Mary JACKSON, dau of Edmund; m by 1640 [GMB 3:2062]

WOODWARD, Nathaniel[1] (c1615-1686+) & 2/wf Katherine _____ (-1686+); m c1664 [GMB 3:2062]

WOODWARD, Nathaniel[2] (bp 1646-   ) & Elizabeth _____; m c1667 Taunton [GMB 3:2062]

WOODWORTH, Benjamin[2] & 1/wf Deborah _____; m c1680 Scituate [GMB 3:2066]

WOODWORTH, Benjamin[2] & 2/wf Hannah _____; m by 1691 [GMB 3:2066]

WOODWORTH, Isaac[2] & Lydia STANDLAKE, dau of Richard [GMB 3:1681, 2066]

WOODWORTH, Joseph[1] & Sarah STOCKBRIDGE; m Scituate 6 Jan 1669[/70] [GMB 3:2066]

WOODWORTH, Thomas & Deborah DAMAN, dau of John; m Scituate 8 Feb 1666[/7] [GMB 3:2066]

WOODWORTH, Walter[1] (c1612-1685-5/6) & _____ _____; m by 1641 Scituate [GMB 3:2066]

WOODY, John & Mary COGGAN; m2 1652/3 Thomas ROBINSON; by 1648 Roxbury [GMB 1:404]

WOOLFE, Peter[1] (c1610-1675) & Martha _____ (-1675+); m by 1636 Beverly [GMB 3:2068]

WOOLRIDGE, John[1] (c1605-1640+) & Sarah _____; m2 William AYRE; m c1630 Charlestown [GMB 3:2070]

WORCESTER, William[1] & 1/wf Sarah _____; m bef 1630 Olney, Buckinghamshire [TAG 71:51]

WORKMAN, Samuel & Martha WHITE; m Boston 3 Aug 1693 [REG 153:59]

WORMALL, Joseph[1] (c1620s-1662) & Miriam _____ (-1662+); m by 1642 Scituate [MD 43:153]

WORMWOOD, _____ & Christian[2] TALMAGE; m2 Edward BELCHER; m c1636 [GMB 3:1799]

WORTHEN, George[3] (1669-1721+) & Anne[2] ANNIS (1681-1726+); m by 1699 Amesbury [ASBO, p.125]

WORTHEN/WATHEN, George[1] (c1597-1641-2) & Margery HAYWARD; m Trowbridge, Wiltshire 14 or 15 Apr 1624 Lynn/Salem/Salisbury [REG 148:75]

WRIGHT, James & Dorcas[2] WEED; m Wethersfield 20 Nov 1660 [GMB 3:1957]

WRIGHT, Richard & Hester COOKE (c1620-); Plymouth 1644 [GMB 1:470]

WRIGHT, Richard[1] & 1/wf _____ _____ [TAG 67:38]

WRIGHT, Richard[1] & 2/wf _____ _____ [TAG 67:38]

WRIGHT, Richard[1] (c1596-1667/8-) & 1/wf Margaret _____ (-by 1643); m c1621 Boston [GMB 3:2072]

WRIGHT, Richard[1] (c1598-1668+) & 2/wf _____ _____ (perhaps mother of William Sabin); by c1640 Saugus/Boston/Braintree/Rehoboth/Lyme/East Hartford [TAG 67:34-38; Harris; GMB 3:2073]

WRIGHT, William[1] (-c1633) & Priscilla CARPENTER; m2 John COOPER; m Plymouth by 1633 [GMB 3:2076]

WYER, Edward & Abigail LAWRENCE; m Cambridge 1 Sept 1684 [REG 156:150]

WYMAN, Francis & Elizabeth RICHARDSON; m 2 May 1617 West Mill, Hertfordshire/Woburn [50 GMC]

YALE, Thomas & Mary TURNER; m c1626 [GMB 3:1849]

YELLINGS, Roger & Elizabeth (BALLENTINE) GREENLAND; m1 David GREENLAND; m3 John COOMBS [TAG 46:130]

YORK, James[2] (1648-1676) & Deborah BELL (1650-1719/20+); m2 1678/9 Henry
     ELLIOT; m Stonington 17 Jan 1669 [TAG 74:285]

YOUNG, John & Abigail[2] HOWLAND (c1628-); m Plymouth 13 Dec 1648 [GMB
     2:1018]

YOUNGMAN, Francis (-1712) & Ann FISHER (1661-1712+); m Roxbury 2 Dec 1685
     [AEBK 4:264]

YOUNGS, Christopher[2] (1643/4-1698) & Ann NICHOLS (c1650-); m by 14 Feb 1677/8
     [TAG 75:271]

INDEX

287

ALEXANDER
— 163
ALFORD
Ann (___) 4
Charity (Dike) 4
Elisha 4
Elizabeth 153
John 4
Mary 46 194
Mary (Draper) 4
Nathaniel 4
William 4 194
ALGER
Agnes (___) 4
Allen 4
Elizabeth (Innes)
(Harris) (Smith)
129
Joanna 184
Roger 129
ALLEN
— 4
Alice (___) 6
Andrew 147
Ann (___) 154
Anna (Barnes) 5
Anne (___) 5
Benjamin 4
Bethiah (Penniman)
5
Caleb 4
Christian (___) 5
Deborah 40
Elizabeth 79 98
107 247
Elizabeth (Bacon) 5
Elizabeth
(Greenway) 4 6
Elizabeth (Howland)
5
Elizabeth (Sisson) 4
Elizabeth (Twitchell)
5
Esther (Swift) 5 41
George 4
Gideon 5
Hannah 147
Hannah (Bullard) 4
Hannah (Butler) 5
Hannah (Townsend)
(Hull) 268
Hannah (Woodford)
5
Hannah (___) 4
Henry 5
James 5
Jane 41
Jedediah 5
John 5
Joshua 5 187
Katharine (___) 4
Margaret (___)
(Lamb) 169
Martha 31
Mary 216 256
Mary (Baldwin) 5
Mary (Bourne) 5

Mary (Crowell) 5
187
Mary (Hannum) 5
Matthew 5
Mercy (Wright) 5
Nehemiah 5
Priscilla (Browne)
5
Ralph 5 41
Rebecca (Hazard) 5
Rebecca (___)
(Rose) 5
Rebecca (___) 5
169
Richard 5
Rose 147
Samuel 5 154 169
243
Sarah 147 243
Sarah (___) 4
Sarah (Hill) 5
Sarah (Kirby) 5
Sarah (Prudden) 5
Sarah (Woodford) 5
Susanna (___) 5
Thomas 5 41
William 4-6
ALLERTON
Elizabeth 11
Elizabeth
(Swinnerton) 6
Fear (Brewster) 6
Isaac 6 181
Joanna (Swinnerton)
6
Mary 72
Mary (Norris) 6
Remember 181
Sarah 113 214
ALLEY
Hugh 6
Joanna (Furnell) 6
John 6
Martha 184
Mary 174
Mary (___) 6
Rebecca (Hood) 6
Sarah 174
ALLIN
John 83
Katharine
(Deighton)
(Hagborn)
(Dudley) 83
ALLING
Abraham 6
Elizabeth (Weeks) 6
Mary 269
Mary (___) 6
Sarah 203
Susanna 269
Thomas 6
ALLIS
Alice 133
ALLOTT
Elizabeth 202

ALLYN
Abigail (Warham) 6
Ann 6
Hannah (Smith) 6
John 6
Margret (Wyot) 6
Matthew 6
Thomas 6 69
Winifred (___)
(Crawford)
(Wolcott) 69
ALMY
Ann 119
Annis 118
Audrey (Barlow) 6
Catherine 270
Christopher 6
Elizabeth (Cornell)
6
Job 6
John 6
Mary (Cole) 6
Mary (Unthank) 6
William 6 119
ALSOP
Abigail (Thompson)
6
Elizabeth 224 251
Elizabeth (Preston)
6
Hannah (Underhill)
6
Jemima 197
Joseph 6
Lydia 257
Mary 184
Richard 6
ALVORD
Benedict 6
Experience 25
Joan (Newton) 6
ALWARD
Judith 97 117
AMBROSE
Abigail 197
Henry 7
Hope (Lamberton)
7
Samuel 7
Susanna (___)
(Worcester) 7
Susanna (___) 7
AMES
Elizabeth (Hayward)
7
Hannah 134
Hannah (___) 7
John 7
Sarah (Willis) 7
William 7
ANDERSON
David 243
John 143
Katharine
(Richardson) 243
Mary (Miller)
(Hodges) 143

ANDREW
Anne 215
Elizabeth (White) 7
Hester (___) 7
Mary 249
Samuel 7
Seeth (Grafton) 7
William 7
ANDREWES
Jane 181
ANDREWS
— 223
____ (Lilly) 7
Abigail 150 262
Abigail (Graves) 8
Alice 102
Ann 25
Ann (___) 7
Anne (Tapp)
(Gibbard) 8 110
Christian 25
Deborah (Abbott) 7
Dorcas (Mitton) 7
Esther 242
Elizabeth 111 116
215
Elizabeth (Spencer)
7
Elizabeth (___) 7
209
Hannah 148
Hannah (Kirby) 7
Hannah (Smith)
(Roland) 223
Henry 7 262
James 7
Jane 191
Jane (___) 7
Jane (Jordan) 7
John 7
Joseph 7
Judith (Belcher) 7
Katharine (___) 26
Margaret (Phips)
(Halsey) 7
Martha (Baker)
(Antrum) 8
Mary 71
Mary (Belcher) 7
Mary (Wadsworth)
7
Nathan 7
Phebe (Goard) 8
Philippa 95
Reana (___) (James)
104 160
Rebecca 2 105
Robert 7 102
Samuel 7 215
Sarah (Holyoke) 7
Thomas 7 8
William 8 104 110
160 242
Alice 102
ANGELL
Abigail (Dexter) 8
Alice 271

288

Alice (Ashton) 8
Amphillis 237
Deborah 225
James 8
John 8
Margaret 272
Mary 9
Mercy 236
Ruth (Field) 8
Thomas 8
ANNABLE/
  ANNIBALL
  Ann (Elcock/Clark)
    8
  Anna (___) 55
  Anthony 8 92
  Jane (Moumford) 8
  Sarah 92
ANNIS
  Abraham 8
  Anne 267 285
  Anthony 8
  Cormac 8
  Hannah 267
  Hannah (Badger) 8
  Isaac 8
  Jane (Rundlett) 8
  Priscilla 114
  Rebecca (Bailey) 8
  Sarah (Chase) 8
ANTHONY
  Elizabeth 118
  John 8
  Mary 234
  Susanna (Albro) 8
ANTROBUS
  Alice (Denton) 8
  Jane (Arnold) 8
  Joan 170
  Walter 8
  William 8
ANTRUM
  Hannah 43
  Jane (Batter) 8
  Martha (Baker) 8
  Obadiah 8
  Thomas 8
APPLEGATE
  Annekin (Patrick) 8
  Avis (Goulding) 8
  Bartholomew 8
  Elizabeth (___) 8
  Hannah (Patrick) 8
  Helena 94
  Johanna (Gibbons)
    8
  John 8
  Thomas 8 94
APPLETON
  Samuel 207
  Sarah 207
ARCHER
  Alse (___) 9
  Elizabeth (Stow) 9
  Hannah 178
  Henry 9
  John 9

Mehitable (Shears)
    9
  Mercy 69
  Samuel 9
  Susanna (___) 9
ARMITAGE
  — 209 273
  Anne (Lillestone) 9
  Godfrey 9
  Martha (___) 9
  Mary (Cogswell) 9
  Thomas 9 273
ARMS
  Joanna (Hawkes) 9
  William 9
ARNOLD
  Benedict 9
  Christian (Peak) 9
  Damaris (Westcott)
    9
  Daniel 9
  Elizabeth 48 146
  Elizabeth (Osborn)
    9
  Elizabeth
    (Wakeman) 9
  Isaac 9
  Jane 8
  Joanna 219
  John 9
  Joseph 9
  Mary 40
  Mary (Angell) 9
  Richard 9
  Samuel 9
  Sarah (Cornell)
    (Washburn) 9
  Sarah (Holmes) 9
  Sarah (Smith) 9
  Stephen 9
  Susanna (___) 9
  William 9
ASHCRAFT
  Hannah (Osborn) 9
    27
  John 9 27
ASHLEY
  Jonathan 9
  Mary (Parsons) 9
  Sarah (Wadsworth)
    9
ASHTON
  Alice 8
  James 9
  Lucretia (Foxwell)
    9
  Marie 196
ASHWOOD
  Jone 109
ASLEBEE
  John 10 156
  Rebecca (Ayer) 10
    166
ASPINWALL
  Elizabeth
    (Goodyear) 10
  Peter 10

Remember (Palfrey)
    10
  William 10
ASTWOOD
  Dinis (Stallworth)
    10
  Hannah 103
  James 10
  John 10
  Martha (Carter) 10
  Sarah (___)
    (Baldwin) 10
  Sarah (Prudden) 10
ATKINS
  Mary 122
  Sarah 122 244
ATKINSON
  Abigail 241
  Abigail (Chambers)
    10
  Elizabeth
    (Mitchelson) 10
  Ellen (___) 10
  Helen (___) 141
  Hugh 10 141
  Jane 53
  Mary (Wheelwright)
    (Lyde) 10
  Theodore 10
ATWATER
  Ann 83
  Joshua 10
  Mary (Maverick)
    (Smith) 10
ATWELL
  Benjamin 158
  Mary (___) 158
ATWOOD
  Abigail 186
  Abigail (___) 165
  Alice 190
  Anna (Betts) 10
  Elizabeth 68
  Elizabeth (Grover)
    10
  Elizabeth (___) 10
  John 10
  Mary (Lucas) 10
  Nathaniel 10
  Oliver 10
  Philip 10
  Rachel (Bachelor)
    10
  Sarah (Masterson)
    10
  Sarah (Tenney) 10
  Thomas 165
AUGER
  Martha (___)
    (Carver) 10
  Matthew 10
AULGAR
  Hannah (Baker) 10
  John 10
AUSTIN
  ____ (Canney) 11

Abigail (Bachelor)
    11
  Constance (___)
    (Robinson) 11
  Esther (___) 11
  Frances (___) (Hill)
    11
  John 10
  Jonah 149
  Jonas 11
  Mary 149
  Mary (Davis)
    (Dodd) 80
  Matthew 11 80
  Richard 11
  Sarah (Hall) 10
AVERY
  Christopher 11
  Hannah 185
  Hannah (Minor) 11
  Jonathan 11
  Joseph 11
  Margery (Stephens)
    11
  Mary 185
  Mary (Woodmansee)
    (Tappin) 11 251
  Sibyl (Sparhawk)
    11 275
  Susanna (___) 11
  Thomas 11
  William 11 251
AWKLEY
  Mary (___) 11
  Miles 11
AXTELL
  Hannah (Merriam)
    11
  Henry 11
  Mary 114
  Mary (___) 11
  Sarah (Barker) 11
  Thomas 11
AYER
  Elizabeth (Chase)
    11
  Joseph 11
  Rebecca 10 166
  Sarah (Corliss) 11
  Zachariah 11
AYLETT
  John 199
  Mary (Pope)
    (Poulter) 199
AYRE
  Sarah (___)
    (Woolridge) 285
  William 285
AYRES/AYERS
  Abigail (Fellows)
    11
  Elizabeth (Allerton)
    (Starr) 11
  Elizabeth (Palmer)
    11
  John 11
  Judith (___) 11

Robert 11
Samuel 11
Sarah (Reynolds)
11
Simon 11
Susanna (Symonds)
11
Thomas 11
William 11
BACHELER/
BACHELOR/
BACHILER/
BATCHELDER
Abigail 11
Abigail 283
Agnes (Wadland)
(Gillingham) 12
Christian (Weare)
12
David 12
Hannah (___) 12
Hannah (Boynton)
(Warner) 12
Hannah (Plummer)
12
Helena (Mason) 12
Jane (___) 12
John 12
John 19 283
Mary 68
Mary (___) (Beedle)
12
Rachel 10
Rachel (Bate) 12
Rebecca (___) 12
Sarah (Goodale) 19
Sarah (Lunt) 12
Seaborn 70
Stephen 12 157
Susanna 170
Theodate 157
William 10 12
BACKHOUSE
Elizabeth 23
Samuel 23
BACON
Deborah (Hawes)
(Pond) 211
Elizabeth 5 27
George 12 116
James 203
Lydia 283
Margaret (___) 12
116
Martha 120
Martha (Foxwell)
12
Martha (Howland)
(Damon) 12
Martha (___) 203
Mary 168
Mary (Jacob) 12
Peter 12
Rebecca 109
Rebecca (Potter) 12
Robert 27
Samuel 12

Sarah (Jenkins) 12
Susanna 210
Thomas 211
William 12
BADGER
Elizabeth
(Greenleaf) 38
Elizabeth (Hayden)
13
Giles 38
John 13
BADGER
Hannah 8
BADLAM
Joan (___) 13
Mary (French) 13
William 13
BAGLEY
Orlando 13
Sarah (Sargent) 13
BAILEY
Ann (Bourne) 13
257
Ann (Emery) 13
Elizabeth (Smith)
(Lee) 171
Elizabeth (___)
(Dearing) 77
Guido 13 43
James 13
John 13 171 257
Jonas 77
Mary (Carr) 13
Rebecca 8 37 80
Ruth (___) (Gurney)
(Bundy) 43
Ruth (Ratchell)
(Gurney) (Bundy)
13
Sarah 53
BAKER
_____ (Lane) 13
_____ (Pequot
Woman) 14
Abigail (Lathrop)
(Huntington) 14
Alexander 13 262
Alice (Pierce) 13
Charity (___) 13
Christian 221
Cornelius 13
Deborah 54
Eleanor (___) 14
Elizabeth 13 261 267
Ellen (Winslow) 13
Experience (Collier)
13
Fear (Robinson) 14
Francis 208
Grace (___)
(Dipple) 13
Hannah 10 208
Hannah (Banks) 13
Hannah (Woodbury)
13
Hannah (___)
(Minter) 13

Hepzibah 210
Jeffrey 13
Joan (___) 14
Joan (Rockwell) 13
John 13
Joseph 13
Joshua 13
Josiah 13
Katharine (Perkins)
13
Martha 8
Mary 154 175 261
Mary (___) 13
Mary (Haugh) 14
Mary (Pierce) 13
Nathaniel 13
Nicholas 13
Patience (Barstow)
(Simonson) 236
Pilgrim (Eddy) 244
Samuel 13 14 236
Sarah 158 262
Sarah (___) 13
Sarah (Carr) 14
Sarah (Fitts) 14
Sarah (Snow) 14
Thomas 14
William 14 158 244
BALCH
Annia (___) 14
Benjamin 14
Grace (___)
(Mallott) 14
John 14
Margery (___) 14
Mary (Conant) 14
Sarah (Gardner) 14
BALCOM
Alexander 3 14
Jane (Holbrook)
(Albee) 3 14
BALDWIN
Elizabeth (Grover)
15
Elizabeth (___)
(Hitchcock)
(Warriner) 14
Elizabeth (___) 14
Hannah 99
Hannah (Birchard)
14
Hannah (Whitlock)
14
Henry 14
Isabel (Northam)
(Catlin) 14
James 14
John 14 53
Joseph 14 15
Josiah 19
Martha 133
Mary 5
Phebe (Richardson)
14
Rebecca (Palmer)
(Cheeseborough)
53

Sarah (___) 10
Sarah (Coley) 14
Sylvester 10
BALDWIN
Sarah 19
BALKE
Hannah (Jenkins)
200
John 200
BALLENTINE
Elizabeth 66 119
285
Hannah (Hollard)
15
William 15
BALLARD
Elizabeth 230
Elizabeth (___) 15
34
Hester 161
John 15
Nathaniel 15
Rebecca (___) 15
Rebecca (Hutson)
15
Sarah 147
William 15 34
BALLINE
Experience (Sabin)
15
Samuel 15
BALSTER
Grace 209
BAMFORT
Rebecca 54
BANBRIDGE
Guy 15
Justice (___) 15
BANBURY/
BANBRIDGE
Jane 118
BANCROFT
Ann 177
Elizabeth (___) 34
Roger 34
BANFIELD
John 15
Mary (Pickering) 15
BANGS
Bethiah 123
Edward 15 241
Hannah (Jenkins)
15
Hannah (Smalley)
15
John 15
Jonathan 15
Lydia 15 139
Lydia (Hicks) 15
Mary (Fisher) 15
Mary (Mayo) 15
Rebecca 241
BANKS
Hannah 13
Mary 213
Priscilla 218
Sarah 117

Sarah (___) 169
BARBER
Abigail (Loomis) 15
Anne (Chase) 15
Bathsheba (Coggins) 15
Elizabeth 74
Francis 15
Jane (___) 15
John 15
Josiah 15
Mary (Coggins) 15
Mary (Phelps) 15
Mercy 112 194
Ruth (Drake) 15
Samuel 15
Sarah 124
Thomas 15 194
BARDING
Abigail (Graves) (Andrews) 8
Nathaniel 8
BAREFOOT
Sarah 275
Walter 275
BARKER
Ann 213
Dorothy (Hayward) 16
Dorothy (Shepard) 16
Elizabeth 103 280
Isaac 16
James 16 221
John 16 214 244
Juda (Simonds) 16
Judith 126
Judith (Prence) 16
Lucy (___) 16
Mary 66 186 214 244 252
Mary (___) (Riddlesdale) (Wyatt) 221
Rebecca 229 240
Robert 16 229
Sarah 11
Sarah (Jeffreys) 16
William 16
BARLOW
Abigail 83
Audrey 6
Cicely (___) 268
Edward 16
Edmund 16
Elizabeth 161
Elizabeth (Royall) 66
George 24 268
Jane (___) (Bessey) 24
Mary (Pemberton) 16
Stafford 6
BARNAART
Casper 16

BARNABY
Elizabeth (Hughes) 16
James 16
BARNARD
Abigail (Bull) 16
Abigail (Phillips) 16
Bartholomew 16
Benjamin 16
Elizabeth 282
Elizabeth (Stone) 16
Frances (Foote) (Dickinson) 79
Francis 79
Hannah 114
James 16
John 16
Joseph 16
Lydia (Hayward) 16
Mary 17
Mary (Lugg) 16
Mary (Morse) 16
Mary (Pegram) 16
Mary (Stace) 16
Nathaniel 16
Phebe (Whiting) 16
Rebecca (Howe) 16
Sarah (Birchard) 16
Sarah (Cutting) 16
Sarah (Fleming) 16
Sarah (Wentworth) 16
Stephen 15
Thomas 15
BARNES/BARNS
Anna 5
Anna (___) 17
Elizabeth 42 190
Elizabeth (Heaton) 16
Elizabeth (Hedges) 17
Hannah 258
Joan (___) 17
John 16 17
Jonathan 17
Mary (Plummer) 17
Rachel 223
Rachel (___) 17
Sarah (Stone) 17
Susanna 259
Thomas 17
William 17
**BARNETT alias
BARBANT**
John 17
Mary (Bishop) 17
BARNEY
Anna (___) 17
Elizabeth (___) 17
Jacob 17
BARNUM
Sarah (Thompson) (Hurd) 17 156

Thomas 17 156
BARRETT
Abiel (Phillips) 17
Abigail (Eames) (Weston) 17
Anne (Lillestone) (Armitage) 9
Deborah (Howe) 17
Dorcas (Green) 17
Elizabeth 79
Esther 23
Hannah 58
Hannah (Betts) 17
Hannah (Fosdick) (Tingley) 255
James 17 255
John 17
Jonathan 17
Margaret 156 247
Mary 62 85 221 253
Mary (Barnard) 17
Rebecca 213
Samuel 9 17
Sarah 121
Sarah (Buttrick) 17
Sarah (Learned) 17
Sarah (Poole) (Champney) 17
William 17
BARRON
Anna (Hammond) 133
Anne (Hammond) (Hawkins) 18
Elizabeth (Hunt) 18
Ellis 17 18 66 133
Grace (___) 17
Hannah 66
John 18
Lydia (Prescott) (Fairbanks) 17
Mary 130 266
Mary (Learned) 18
Moses 18
Sarah 85
Susanna 217
BARROWS
Deborah 97
BARSHAM
Anabel (Smith Alias Bland) 18
William 18
BARSTOW
Ann (Hubbard) 18
Deborah 231
Elizabeth 217
George 18
Grace (Halstead) 18
Grace (Walker) (Carver) 18 50
Joseph 18
Margaret 108
Martha 215
Martha (___) 18
Mary 235
Mercy (___) 18

Mercy (Clark) 18
Michael 18 50
Patience 236
Sarah 54
Susan 206
Susanna (Lincoln) 18
Susanna (Marriott) 18
William 18 236
BARTHOLOMEW
Ann (___) 18
Elizabeth (Scudder) 18
Henry 18
Katharine (Hutchinson) 18
Mary 272
William 18
BARTLETT
Ann (___) 19
Benjamin 18
Bethiah (Devereux) 18
Elizabeth 242
Hannah (___) 19
Hannah (Pope) 18
Henry 18
John 18
Joseph 18
Lydia (Griswold) 18
Mary 81 190
Mary (Bush) 18
Mary (Warren) 18
Mercy 159 164
Robert 18 19 242
Sarah (Purchase) 19
Susanna (Jenny) 18
Thomas 19
William 19
BARTON
Elisha 19
Mary (Crockett) 19
BARTRAM
Eleanor 67
Ellen 67
Elizabeth 99 125
Esther 192
Hannah 156
Hannah (Johnson) (Burt) 19
Joan 194
Sarah (Johnson) (Burt) 19
William 19
BASCOMB
Abigail 158
Avis (___) 19
Hannah 37
Hepzibah 177
Mary (Newell) 19
Thomas 19
BASEDEN
Anna 24
Rebecca 2
Rebecca (Taylor) 119

292

Thomas 22 85
BEEDLE
Mary (___) 12
Robert 12
BEERE
Henry 36
Sarah (___) (Brock)
36
BEERS
Eliezer 22 73
Elizabeth (Firmin)
22
Richard 22
Sarah 244
Susanna (Harrington)
(Cutting) 22 73
BEGGARLY
Alice 119
Alice (___) 22 118
Richard 22
BELCHER
Abigail 116
Andrew 22
Ann 44
Anna 162
Christian (Talmage)
(Wormwood) 22
285
Dorcas 116
Edward 22 285
Elizabeth 29
Elizabeth (Danforth)
22
Jeremy 22
Josias 22
Judith 7
Mary 7 225
Mary (Cobbett) 22
Mary (Lockwood)
22
Mary (Simpson) 22
Mercy
(Wigglesworth)
(Brackenbury) 22
Ranis (Rainsford)
22
Richard 22
Samuel 22
Sarah 80 159
Sarah (Weeden)
(Senter) 22
BELDEN
Daniel 181
Margaret
(Ackrenden) 22
Richard 22
Sarah (Hawkes)
(Mattoon) 181
BELKNAP
Abraham 22
Mary (Stallon) 22
BELL
Ann (___) 190
Anna (___) 23
Anne (Essex) 23
Deborah 286
Dorothy 257

Esther 123
Hannah (Pray) 23
Hester (Lugg) 22
179
James 22 23
Jane (___) 23
John 263
Katharine 182
Mary 153 259
Sarah 20 178
Susan 263
Susan (Bell) (Wall)
263
Susanna (Brydon)
23
Thomas 23 182 190
BELLAMY
Bridget 30
Jeremiah 30
BELLINGHAM
Elizabeth
(Backhouse) 23
Elizabeth (Smith)
(Savage) 23
Lucy (___) 23
Penelope (Pelham)
23
Richard 23
Samuel 23
BELLOWS
Abigail 170
Eleazer 23
Esther (Barrett) 23
Hannah (Newton)
23
John 23
Mary (Wood) 23
BELLSIRE
Christian 76
BEMIS
Sarah 25
BENDALL
Edward 23
Jane 229
Jane (___) (Gower)
23
Mary (___) 23
BENEDICT
Mary (Messenger)
23
Thomas 23
BENFIELD
Mary 108
BENHAM
John 4 23
Margery (___)
(Alcock) 4
BENJAMIN
Daniel 23
Elizabeth (Browne)
23
Jemima (Lombard)
23
John 232
Joseph 23
Sarah (Brackett)

(Shaw) 232
BENNETT
— 145
Aphra (___)
(Adams) 24
Arthur 23 96 282
David 53
Deborah (Green) 24
Deliverance 71
Dorothy (___) 23
Elisha 23
Elizabeth 111 159
Elizabeth (Goodale)
(Smith) 23
Henry 23
James 24
Jane (___) 24
John 24
Lydia (Perkins) 23
Margaret (___) 24
Mary 208
Mary (Cobbett) 24
Mary (Goddard) 23
96 282
Mary (Joy) 24
Mary (Plummer)
(Cheney) 53
Priscilla 48
Samuel 24
Sarah (___) 24
Sarah (Hargrave) 24
Sarah (Harris) 24
William 24
BENNISTER
Gertrude 156
BENSON
Elizabeth (Marsh)
24
Isaac 24
John 24
Mary 123
Mary (Bumpus) 24
Mary (Williams) 24
BENT
Martha 151
BENTON
Andrew 24
Martha (Spencer)
24
BERNARD
Mary 24 278
Musachiell 24
Richard 278
BERRY
Beatrice (Burt)
(Cantlebury)
(Plummer) 210
Benjamin 24
Edward 24 130 210
Elizabeth (Hardy)
(Haskell) 24 130
Elizabeth (Withers)
24
BESBEECH
Alice 31
Anna (Baseden) 24
Mary 39

Thomas 24
BESSEY
Ann 124
Anthony 24 30 124
Elizabeth 30
Jane (___) 24
Mary (Ranson) 24
Nehemiah 24
Rebecca 156
BEST
Bridget 231
BESWICK
George 24
BETSCOMBE
Mary (Strong) 24
Richard 24
BETT
Grace 188
BETTS
Alice (___) 25
Anna 10
Elizabeth (Bridge)
24
Elizabeth (___)
(Lisley) 101
Hannah 17
Joanna
(Chamberlain) 25
John 24 101
Mary 218
Mehitable 256
Richard 25
Ruth (___) 25
Samuel 25
Sarah (Hustis) 25
Susanna (___) 24
Thomas 218
William 25
BETTYS
— 25
Miriam (Tyler) 25
BIAM
Abraham 25
Experience (Alvord)
25
BIBLE
John 195
Sibyl (Ticknell) 195
BICK
Elizabeth
(Holbrook)
(Sprague) 242
James 242
BICKFORD
Bridget (Furber) 25
John 25
Susanna (Furber)
25
Temperance (Hull)
25
Thomas 25
BICKNELL
Agnes (___) 25
Joanna 101
John 25
Mary (___) 25
Mary (Porter) 25

293

Zachary 25
BIDDLE
Joseph 77
Rachel (___)
(Deane) 77
BIDFORD
Samuel 25
Sarah (Joans) 25
BIDWELL
Elizabeth (Stow) 25
Samuel 25
BIGELOW
James 25
Mary (Warren) 25
Patience (Browne) 25
Sarah 171
Sarah (Bemis) 25
BIGG/BIGGE/BIGGS
Elizabeth 247 252
Ellen (___) 25
John 25 185
Mary 133
Mary (Dassett) 185
Mary (Williams) 25
Patience 101
Rachel (Martin) 25
Smallhope 25
Thomas 133
William 25
BIGNELL
Martha (Metcalf) 247
William 247
BILL
Anne (Tuttle) 25
Dorothy (___) 25
James 25
Mary (Holman) 27
Thomas 27
BILLINGS
Ann (Andrews) 25
Elizabeth (___) 25
Hannah 204
John 25
BILLINGTON
Christian (Penn) (Eaton) 86
Francis 86
BINGLEY
Abigail (Buttolph) (Saywell) 229
Anna 273
Elizabeth 52
Thomas 229
BIRCHARD
Christian (Andrews) 25
Deborah (___) 26
Hannah 14
Jane (Lee) (Hyde) 25
John 25
Katharine (___) (Andrews) 26
Mary (Robinson) 26

Sarah 16
Susanna 261
Thomas 26
BIRD
James 26
Joseph 26
Lydia (Steele) 26
Mary (___) 26
Mary (Clark) 26
Simon 26
BIRDSALL
Agnes (Kempe) 26
Henry 26
Judith 65
Nathan 26
BIRGE
Daniel 26
Deborah (Holcombe) 26
Elizabeth (Gaylord) 149
Richard 149
BISBY
Hannah 37
Joanna (Brooks) 26
John 26
Phebe 33
William 33
BISHOP
— 26
Abigail 29 58
Alice (___) 26
Anne 146
Anne (Douglas) (Geary) 109
Bethiah 245
Bridget (Playfer) (Wassilbe) (Oliver) 26 195
Dulsabel (___) (King) 26
Edward 26 59 195
Elizabeth 29 112
Elizabeth (Phillips) 26
James 29
Job 26
John 26 245
Lydia (Norman) 26
Mary 17 59
Mary (___) (Gault) 26
Mary (___) 26
Mary (Williams) 26
Nathaniel 26
Rebecca 145
Richard 26
Ruth 204
Sarah 40
Thomas 26 109 146
Townsend 26
BISSELL
Abigail (Holcombe) 26
Abigail (Moore) 26
Dorothy 247 268
Elizabeth 247

Israel (Mason) 26
John 26
Joyce 210
Mindwell (Moore) 26
Nathaniel 26
Samuel 26
Thomas 26
BITFIELD
Elizabeth (___) 26
Mary 210
Samuel 26
BIXBY
Joseph 27
Sarah (Riddlesdale) (Heard) 27
BLACK
Daniel 27
Deborah (___) 27
Faith (Bridges) 27
Freeborn (Wolfe) (Sallows) 27 226
John 27 29 226
Mary (Morgan) 27
Mary (Phippen) (Wallis) 27
Susanna (Selbee) 29
BLACKLEACH
Abigail (Hudson) 27
Benjamin 27
Benoni 27
Dorcas (Bowman) 27
Elizabeth 128 245
Elizabeth (Bacon) 27
Elizabeth (Harbert) 27
Elizabeth (Herris) (Wheeler) (Newbitt) (Poisson) 271
Elizabeth (Sheafe) 27
Exercise 217 218
Hannah (___) 27
John 27
Mary 160 195 270
Mary (Holman) (Bill) (Bucknell) 27
Mary (Milbury) (Freethy) 27
Nathaniel 27
Richard 27 271
Sindeniah (___) 27
Solomon 27
Susanna (Fenn) (Hooker) 27
BLACKMAN
Adam 10
Deliverance 27
Elizabeth (Wheeler) 263
Hannah (Osborn)

(Ashcraft) 27
BLACKWELL
Jane 110
BLAISDELL
Elizabeth (___) 27
Elizabeth (Challis) (Hoyt) 27 153
Henry 27
John 27 153
Martha 31 57
Mary 246 248
Mary (Haddon) 27
Ralph 27 57 246
BLAKE
Deborah 88 204
Deborah (Everett) 28
Elizabeth (Clapp) 28
James 28
Jasper 28 88
John 232
Mary 72
Mary (Souther) (Shaw) 232
BLANCHARD
Elizabeth (Hills) 28
Hannah (Brackett) (Kinsley) 28
Hannah (Everill) 28
John 28
Mary 37 66
William 28
BLAND
Isabel (Drake) 28
John 28
See also Smith
BLANEY
Elizabeth (Andrews) (Pike) (Purchase) 215
Elizabeth (Purchase) 28
Hannah 78
John 28 215
BLANFORD
Sarah 166
BLANTIN/BLANTON
Mary 146
Phebe 209
William 209
BLINMAN
Mary (Parke) 28
Richard 28
BLINN
Hannah (Crampton) 28
James 28
Margaret (Dennison) 28
Peter 28
BLISH
Abraham 28
Martha (Shaw) 28
BLISS
Jonathan 28
Lawrence 169

294

Lydia (Wright) 169
Margaret (Hulins)
28
Mary 127 144 201
Miriam (Harmon)
28
Thomas 28
BLODGETT
Daniel 28
Mary (Butterfield)
28
Ruth (Eggleton) 28
Samuel 28
Sarah (Underwood)
28
Susanna (___) 28
254
Thomas 28 254
BLOIS
Edmund 28
Mary (___) 28
Micaell (Jennison)
28 266
Richard 28 266
Ruth (Parsons) 28
BLOOD
Elizabeth 46
Hannah (Jenkins)
(Parker) 28
Joseph 28
Mary 46 76
Mercy (Butterworth)
28
Robert 28 46
Sarah 59
BLOOMFIELD
Isabel (Pearce)
(Sackett) 29 226
Sarah 226
Sarah (___) 29
William 29 226
BLOSSOM
Anne (Eldson/
Helsdon) 29 224
Elizabeth 209
Peter 29
Sarah 264
Sarah (Botfish) 29
Sarah (Ewer) 29
Thomas 29 224
BLOTT
Ann 118
Joanna 176
Mary 284
Robert 29 284
Sarah 89
Susanna (Selbee)
29
BLOWER
Alice 33
Alice (Frost) 29
255
Elizabeth (Belcher)
29
John 29
Pyam 29
Tabitha (___) 29

Thomas 29 255
BLUNDEN
— 29
Sarah (Mullins) 29
BLUX
Katharine (___) 160
BOAD
Anne (Dalton)
(Rewse) 29 219
280
Henry 29
BOARD
Henry 219
BOLLES
Hannah 21
Hopestill (Rose-
morgan)
(Chappell) 52
Joseph 21
Mary 104
Sarah 50
Thomas 52
BOLTWOOD
Martha 266
Sarah 266
BOND
Elizabeth 54 198
Esther 52
Hepzibah (Hastings)
29
Jane (Norton)
(Simpson) 236
Nicholas 236
Rachel 103
William 29
BONFIELD
George 29
Rebecca (Bradstreet)
29
BONHAM
George 29
Patience 146 278
Sarah (Morton) 29
BONNEY
Abigail (Bishop) 29
Ann 29
Dorcas (Samson)
29
Elizabeth (Bishop)
29
Hannah 1 184
James 29
John 29
Mary 186
Mary (___) 29
Mehitable (King)
29
Sarah 61
Sarah (Studley) 29
Thomas 29
William 29
BONYTHON
Agnes (___) 29
Elizabeth 71
John 29
Lucretia (Leigh) 30
Richard 30

Susanna 102
BOOMER
Mary 103
Matthew 103
BOOSEY/BOOSY
Alice (___) 30
Esther (Ward) 30
Hannah 213
James 30
Joseph 30
Mary 245
Sarah 243
BOOTH
Benjamin 30
Elizabeth 185
Elizabeth (Garrett)
(Elmore) 90
Elizabeth (Granger)
30
Elizabeth (Wilkins)
30
George 30
John 30
Joseph 30
Mary (Sutton) 30
Simeon 90
BORDEN/BORDON
Elizabeth 179
Hannah (Hough) 30
Joanna (___) 30
109
John 30 109
BORDMAN
Andrew 30
Ruth (Bull) 30
BOREMAN
Daniel 30
Elizabeth (Perkins)
30
Hannah
(Hutchinson) 30
Joanna 95
Margaret 95
Margaret (Offing)
30
Martha 176
Mary 167
Thomas 30
BORODELL
Ann 77
BOSTON
Ann (Devereux) 30
Walter 30
BOSVILLE
Elizabeth 126
BOSWORTH
Alice 158
Beatrice (Hampson)
(Josselyn) 30
Benjamin 30
Bridget (Bellamy)
30
Edward 30 40
Elizabeth (___) 30
Hannah 160
Hannah (Howland)
30

Jonathan 30
Mary 40
Mary (___) 30
Nathaniel 30
BOTFISH
Bridget (___) 30
142
Elizabeth (Bessey)
30
Joseph 30
Mary 69
Robert 30 142
Sarah 29
BOTSFORD
Hannah (___) 31
Samuel 31
BOTTS
Elizabeth (Freethy)
31 242
Isaac 31 242
BOUCHER
Rebecca 113
BOUDE
Elizabeth 108
BOUENTON
see Buffington
BOULTER
Grace (Swaine) 31
Nathaniel 31
BOURNE
Alice (Besbeech)
31
Ann 13 257
Bathsheba (Skiffe)
31
Elizabeth 124
Elizabeth (Brayton)
31
Hannah 187
Henry 31
Jared 31
Job 31 138
John 31
Margaret 280
Mary 5
Mary (___) 31
Ruhama (Hallett)
31 138
Sarah (___) 31
Shearjashub 31
Temperance (Swift)
31
Thomas 280
Timothy 31
BOUTON
Abigail 237
BOWDEN
Martha (Blaisdell)
31 57
Richard 31 57
BOWDISH
Nathaniel 31
BOWDITCH
Sarah (Beare) 31
William 31
BOWDON
Joan 281

295

BOWEN
Alice 271
Ann (___) 31
Elizabeth (Nichols)
31 106
Elizabeth (___)
(Marsh) 31
Esther (Sutton) 31
Griffith 31
Margaret (Fleming)
31
Martha (Allen)
(Saben) 31
Mary (___) 31
Obadiah 31
Richard 31
Ruth 165
Sarah 2 105
Thomas 31 106
(___) a Welsh
woman 31
BOWERMAN
Hannah 105
Mary (Harper) 31
Thomas 31
BOWKER
John 31
Mary (Howe) 31
BOWLES
Elizabeth (Heath)
32
John 32
BOWLINS
Margaret 248
BOWMAN
Dorcas 27
Nathaniel 27
BOWNE
Andrew 32
Anne (___) 32
Dorothy 94
Elizabeth (___) 32
James 32
John 32
Lydia (Holmes) 32
Mary (Stoute) 32
Thomas 94
William 32
BOYCE
Antipas 32
Dorothy 49
Hannah (Hill) 32
BOYDEN
Frances (___) 32
Hannah (Phillips)
(Morse) 32
Jonathan 32
Martha (Holden) 32
Mary 55
Mary (Clark) 32
Thomas 32
BOYES
Lydia (Beamon) 32
Samuel 32
Silence 222
BOYLSTON
Elizabeth 98

Mary (Gardner) 32
Sarah 239
Sarah (___) 32
Thomas 32
BOYNTON
Caleb 32
Hannah 12
Hannah (Harriman)
32
John 12 115
Joshua 32
Mercy 115
Sarah 75
Sarah (Brown) 32
Susanna 63
BOYSE
Anna 219
Joanna 277
BRABROOK
Rachel 105
BRACKENBURY
Alice (___) 32
Anne (___) 32
Ellen (___) 32
Mercy
(Wigglesworth)
22 32
Michael 22
Richard 32
Samuel 22 32
William 32
BRACKETT
Alice (Blower) 33
Eleanor 102
Hannah 28
Hannah (French) 32
Jane 122
John 32
Martha 259
Martha (Ray) 32
Mary (___)
(Williams) 33
278
Peter 32 33 102
227 278
Priscilla 219
Priscilla (___) 32
Rachel 70 192
Rachel (___) 227
Richard 33 70
Sarah 70 232
Sarah (Parker)
(Foster) 102
Sarah (Stedman) 32
BRACY
Anne (Pearce)
(Carmichael) 32
Constance 187
Hannah 198
Hannah (Hart) 32
John 33
Mary (Osborn) 33
Phebe 79 224
Phebe (Bisby) 33
Thomas 32
BRADBURY
Elizabeth 45

Jane 258
Judith 186
Mary 244
Mary (Perkins) 33
Rebecca
(Wheelright)
(Maverick) 33
Sarah (Pike) 33
Thomas 33
William 33
Wymond 33
BRADELL
Abigail 100
BRADFORD
Alice (Richards) 33
Anne (Fitch) 33
Joseph 33
Mary (Sherwood)
(Fitch) 33
Mary (Wood)
(Holmes) 33
Sarah (___)
(Griswold) 33
William 33
BRADHURST
Hannah (Gore) 33
Ralph 33
BRADISH
James 33
John 33
Joseph 33
Katharine (___) 33
Mary 110
Mary (___) 33
Mary (Frost) 33
Robert 33
Susanna (___) 33
Vashti (___)
(Morrill) 33
BRADLEY
Elizabeth (Brewster)
54
Susanna 125
BRADSHAW
Humphrey 33 124
225
Martha (Davies)
(Russell) 33 124
225
BRADSTREET
Anne (Downing)
(Gardner) 34 107
Anne (Wood) (Price)
33 214
Bridget (___) 34
Dudley 33 214
Elizabeth (Harris)
34
Hannah 147 223
275
Hannah (Peach) 34
Humphrey 34 147
John 34
Martha 224
Mary 166
Mercy 261
Moses 34

Rebecca 29
Sarah 153 282
Simon 34 107 153
261 275
BRAINERD
Daniel 34
Hannah (Spencer)
34
BRAMHALL
Martha 123
BRANKER
Abigail (Searle) 34
265
John 34 265
BRANSON
Ann (Shapleigh)
101
Henry 101
Sarah 194
BRATTLE
Catherine 92
Thomas 92
BRAY
Hannah 103
Richard 103
BRAYTON
Elizabeth 31
Francis 31
Sarah 108
BREAD
Allen 15
Elizabeth (___)
(Ballard) (Knight)
15
BRECK
Elizabeth 185
Isabel (___) (Rigby)
97
Mary 177
Susanna 127
BREDDA
Alice 214 268
BREED
Allen 34
Elizabeth (Wheeler)
34
Elizabeth (___)
(Ballard) (Knight)
34
BRENTON
Abigail 45
Catherine 65
Dorothy (___) 34
Hannah (Davis) 34
Martha 107
Martha (Burton) 34
Mary 227
Mehitable 38
Sarah 88
William 34 38 227
BRETT
Alice 135
Hannah 259
William 135
BREWER
Daniel 34
Hannah 113

Elizabeth (Shepard)
37
Francis 37 52
George 37
Grace (___) 38
Hannah 158 169
Hannah (Corwin)
39
Henry 37
Hugh 37
Isaac 37
James 38 39
Jane 177
Jeremiah 65
Joan (Shelton) 39
John 38 39 212 277
Jonathan 39
Joseph 38
Joshua 38
Josiah 38
Judith (___) 38
Lydia 169 202 211
270
Lydia (___) 39
Lydia (Buckland)
38 212
Lydia (Howland)
38
Martha 49
Martha (___) (Ford)
101
Martha (___)
(Lawrence)
(Chapman) 52
Martha (Hughes)
38
Mary 1 73 102 114
154 173 181 182
266 277 281
Mary (___) 38
Mary (Besbeech)
39
Mary (Dix) 39 219
Mary (Fellows) 38
Mary (Fuller) 37
Mary (Fuller)
(Richards) 220
Mary (Healy) 38
Mary (Hyde) 39
Mary (Jaques) 38
Mary (Johnson) 37
Mary (Linforth) 38
Mary (Morse) 37
Mary (Newhall) 39
Mary (Shattuck) 39
Mary (Shearman)
(Cook) 65
Mary (Winship) 37
Mehitable (Brenton)
38
Nathaniel 38
Nicholas 38
Patience 25
Persis (Bridges) 38
Peter 5 101 167
Phebe 172

Posthume 281
Priscilla 5
Rachel (Poulter) 38
Rebecca (Bailey)
37 39 80
Richard 38
Robert 39
Sarah 21 32 77 96
191 200
Sarah (Harker) 39
Sarah (Sawyer) 38
Sarah (Smith) 38
Thomas 38 39
Unica (___)
(Buxton) 167
Wait (Waterman)
37
William 38 39 49
BROWNELL
Martha 84
Mary 135
Sarah 103
Thomas 135
BROWNING
Nathaniel 39
Sarah 278
Sarah (Freeborn) 39
BROWNSON
Dorcas 148
Edith 86
BRUCE
Elizabeth
(Cummings)
(Gould) 39 116
Elizabeth (Forbush)
39
Magdalen (___) 39
Roger 39
Thomas 39
William 39 116
BRUEN
Rebecca 212
BRUFF
Damaris
(Threeneedles) 39
Stephen 39
BRUNDISH
Bethiah 167
Hannah (___) 39
John 39
Mary 152 215
Rachel (___) 39
BRUNING
Joseph 39
Marah (Cobbett) 39
BRUNSON
Elizabeth 129
BRUSHETT
Christabell 106
BRYANT
Abigail (Shaw) 39
Stephen 39
BRYDON
John 23
Susanna 23
BUCK
Elizabeth 46 51

Emmanuel 40
Mary (Arnold) 40
Rachel (Levens) 40
Roger 40
Samuel 40
Susan (___) 40
William 40
BUCKETT
Mary 240
BUCKINGHAM
Daniel 40
Esther (Hosmer) 40
Hester 21
Sarah (Lee) 40
Thomas 21 40
BUCKLAND
Abigail (Vore) 40
Benjamin 40
Deborah (Allen) 40
Elizabeth 2
Elizabeth (Drake) 40
Elizabeth (Williams)
40
Hannah 270
Hannah (Cook) 40
Hannah (Smith)
(Trumbull)
(Strong) 40
Joseph 40
Lydia 38 212
Martha (Wakefield)
40
Mary (Bosworth)
40
Nicholas 40
Rachel (Wheatley)
40
Sarah 206
Temperance 211
Temperance
(Denslow) 40
Thomas 40
Timothy 40
William 38 40
BUCKLEY
Dorothy 261
BUCKMASTER
Joanna (___) 108
Thomas 108
BUCKMINSTER
Elizabeth (Clark)
169
BUCKNAM
____ (Knower) 40
____ (Wilkinson)
40
Joses 40
William 40
BUCKNELL
Mary (Holman)
(Bill) 27
Samuel 27 40
Sarah (Bishop) 40
BUCKNER
Charles 160
Mary (Hunting)
(Jay) 160

BUFFINGTON
Benjamin 40
Hannah (Southwick)
40
Sarah (Southwick)
40
Thomas 40
BUGBEE/BUGBY
Abiel (Twitchell)
(Corbett) 67
Abigail (Holbrook)
40
Edward 40 41
Experience (Pitcher)
41
John 67
Joseph 41
Judith (___) 200
Rebecca (___) 41
Richard 200
Sarah 51
BULKELEY
Ann (Try) 41
Avis (___) 41
Edward 150 182
Elizabeth 150
Elizabeth (___)
(Okes) 41
Gershom 41
Grace (Chetwood)
41
Jane (Allen) 41
John 41
Margaret (___) 41
Martha 182
Peter 41
Sarah (Chauncy) 41
Sarah (Jones) 41
279
Thomas 41 279
BULL
Abigail 16
Amy 173 220
Ann (Clayton)
(Easton) 41 85
David 41
Elizabeth 260
Elizabeth (Goffe)
41
Elizabeth (___) 41
Esther (Cowles) 41
Esther (Swift)
(Allen) 41
Grace 214
Hannah (Chapman)
41
Hannah (Humphrey)
41
Henry 41 85
Isaac 41
Jonathan 41
Joseph 41
Mary (Cheever)
(Lewis) 41
Phebe (Gosse) 41
Robert 41
Ruth 30

298

Sarah (Manning) 41
Sarah (Parker) 41
Sarah (Whiting) 41
Susanna 42
Susanna (___) 41
Thomas 41
BULLARD
Abigail 246
Anne (Martyn) 42
Beatrice (Hall) 42
Benjamin 41
Elizabeth 62
Ellen (___)
(Dickerman) 42
George 42
Hannah 4
Jane (Lisham)
(Ellis) 42
John 42
Joseph 42
Magdalen (Martin)
42
Magdalin 202
Margaret (Cheney)
42
Margaret (___) 42
Martha (Pidge) 41
Mary 109
Mary (___)
(Griswold) 42
Mary (___) 42
Mary (Richards)
(Maplehead) 42
Robert 42
Sarah (___) 42
William 42
BULLOCK
— 42
Alice (Flint) 42
Edward 42
Elizabeth 57
Elizabeth (Barnes)
42
Elizabeth (___) 42
Henry 42
John 42
Susan (___) 42
BUMPAS/BUMPUS
Edward 42
John 42
Mary 24
Sarah (___) 42
BUMSTEAD
Hannah (Odlin) 42
Jeremiah 42
Mary 76
BUNCE
Elizabeth 272
Sarah 272
Susanna 135
Susanna (Bull) 42
Thomas 42 272
BUNDY
James 42
John 43
Martha (Chandler)
43

Mary 236
Mary (___) 42
Ruth (Ratchell)
(Gurney) 13 43
BUNKER
Ann 61
Benjamin 43
Elizabeth 44
George 43 61 151
249
Hannah (Mellows)
43
Jane (___) 249
John 43
Jonathan 43
Judith (Major) 43
Margaret (Wells)
(Howe) 43 151
Martha 157 244
Mary 122
Mary (Chickering)
43
Mary (Howard) 43
BUNNELL
Mary 203
BURBAGE
Elizabeth 282
BURBANK
John 229
Sarah (Hart) (Scone)
229
BURCHAM
Frances 185
BURCHARD
Jane (Lee) (Hyde)
158
John 158
BURDEN
Ann (Soulby) 43
220
George 43
BURDETT
George 43
Susan (___) 43
Susanna (Coocke)
43
BURGE
Grizzell
(Fletcher)(Kibby)
(Gurney) 43
Jane (___) (Gornell)
43
John 43
Mary (Stearns)
(Learned) 43
Rachel (___) 43
BURGES
Dorothy 57
BURGESS
Elizabeth 87
Joseph 43
Mary 89
Patience (Freeman)
43
Roger 43 167
Sarah (Griggs)
(King) 43 167

BURGETT
James 43
Lydia (Mead) 43
BURHANS
Hilletje 274
BURKBY
Martha (Cheney)
(Sadler) 43 226
Thomas 43 226
BURKE
Abigail (Sawtell) 43
Richard 43
BURMAN
Hannah (___) 43
Thomas 43
BURNAP
Ann (___) 43
Hannah (Antrum)
43
Isaac 43
Mary (Pearson) 44
Robert 43
Thomas 44
BURNELL
Cassandra 241
BURNHAM
Amy 187
Ann (Belcher) 44
Ann (Wright) 44
Elizabeth (Loomis)
44
Hannah 106
John 44
Marie (Lawrence)
44
Mary 56 188
Mary (Catlin) 44
Mary (Fitch) 44
Moses 44
Naomi (Hull) 44
Rebecca 178
Richard 44
Samuel 44
Sarah (Humphries)
44
Thomas 44 56
William 44
BURR
Elizabeth 196 230
Esther (Ward)
(Boosy) 30
Hester (Ward) 44
Jehu 30 44 230
John 44 196
Mary (Ward) 44
Nathaniel 44
Sarah (Ward) 44
BURRAGE
Joanna (Stowers)
44
John 44
BURRELL
John 44 230
Sarah 75
Sarah (___) 44 230
BURRIDGE
Hannah 104

BURRILL
Elizabeth 94
BURROUGHS
____ (Hewes) 44
182
George 44 147
Hannah (Colver) 44
Hannah (Fisher) 44
Jeremiah 44 182
John 44
Mary (___) 44 147
Rebecca 102
Sarah (Ruck)
(Hawthorne) 44
BURSELL
Anna 230
James 230
BURSLEY
Elizabeth 55 115
Joanna 79
Joanna (___) 44
Joanna (Hull) 44 75
John 44 79
Thomas 44
BURT
Ann (Holland)
(Bassett) 45
Anna (___) 45
Beatrice 210
Charity (Hall)
(Gallop) 45 106
Edward 44
Elizabeth (Bunker)
44
Hannah 132
Hannah (Johnson)
19
Hugh 19 45
James 45
Mary (Thayer) 45
Rachel 167
Richard 45 106
Sarah (Johnson) 45
Sarah (Johnson) 19
Ursula (___) 45
BURTON
Abigail (Brenton)
45
Boniface 24 45
Frances (___) 45
Hannah 137
Martha 34
Stephen 45
BURWELL
Deborah (Merwin)
45
Samuel 45
BUSBY
Abigail (Compton)
(Brisco) 36
Abraham 36
BUSCOTE
Mary (May) 45
Peter 45
BUSH
Abigail (Lee) 45
Deborah 178

Hannah (Pendleton)
237
Mary 18
Mary (Goodenow)
45
Samuel 45
BUSHNELL
Edmund 45
Elizabeth 162 197
Francis 45 149 194
Grace (Wells)
(Norton) 194
Hannah 149
Jane 91
Jane (___) 45
John 45
Martha 238
Martha (Hallor) 45
Mary 162 221
Mary (Grombridge)
45
Ruth (Sanford) 45
Samuel 45
Sarah 68 158
Sarah (Lovering)
(Place) 45
Sarah (Scranton) 45
BUSHROD
Elizabeth (Hannum)
45
Peter 45
BUSS
Elizabeth (Bradbury)
45
Elizabeth (Hill) 45
Hannah 271
John 45
William 271
BUSTON
Elizabeth 157
BUSWELL
Samuel 45
Sarah (Keyes) 45
Susanna (Perkins)
106
BUTLER
Anne (Bishop)
(Holman) 146
Daniel 45
Dorothy 109
Elizabeth (House)
45
Elizabeth (___) 46
Hannah 5 118
Henry 146
James 45
Lydia 185
Lydia (Snow) 45
Mary (Alford) 46
194
Mehitable 280
Nathaniel 3 46
Patience 110
Peter 46 194
Samuel 46
Sarah 76
Sarah (Cross) 46

Sarah (Green) 3 46
Sarah (Stone) 46
Thomas 46
William 46
BUTMAN
Jeremiah 46 62
Mehitable (Giles)
(Collins) 46 62
BUTTERFIELD
Mary 28
BUTTERWORTH
Benjamin 46
Hannah (Wheaton)
46
Huldah (Hayward)
46
John 46
John 253
Mary 253
Mercy 28
Sarah 135
Sarah (___) 46
BUTTOLPH
Abigail 229
Abigail (Fitch)
(Mason) 46
Ann (Harding) 46
Elizabeth (Buck) 46
George 46
Hannah (Gardner)
46
John 46 165 227
Mary (Baxter) 46
Mehitable 105
Susanna (Clark)
(Kelly) (Sanford)
46 165 227
Thomas 46
BUTTON
Abigail (Firmage)
157
John 46 235
Mary (___)
(Simmons) 46
235
Robert 157
BUTTRICK
Elizabeth (Blood)
46
Jane (___)
(Goodenow) 46
John 46
Mary (Blood) 46
Mary (Hastings) 46
Samuel 46
Sarah 17
Sarah (___) 46
William 46
BUTTRY
Grace 135
Martha (___) 46
Nicholas 46
BUXTON
Clement 167
Elizabeth 138
Unica (___) 167

BUYS
Jan Cornelison 195
Phebe (Sales)
(Nyssen) 195
BYAM
Abraham 196
Sarah (___) (Onge)
196
BYLEY
Mary 83
CABLE
John 47
Sarah (___) 47
CADE
James 47
Margaret (___) 47
CADMAN
Mary 61
CADWELL
Elizabeth (Stebbins)
(Wilson) 279
Mary 79
Thomas 279
CADY
Judith (Knopp) 47
Nicholas 47
CAIN
Arthur 47
Sarah (Gould) 47
CAINE
Christopher 51
CAKEBREAD
Mary 120
Sarah (___) 47
Thomas 47
CALDWELL
John 47
Sarah (Dillingham)
47
CALL
Elizabeth 233
Hannah (Kettle) 47
Joanna (___)
(Shepardson) 233
John 47
Lydia (Shepardson)
47
Thomas 47 233
CALLENDER
Abigail
(Wigglesworth)
(Sweetser) 250
Ellis 74 250
Mary (___) 47
CALLOW
Judith (___) (Clock)
47
Oliver 47
CALLUM
Ann 259
Caleb 47
Elizabeth (Beans) 47
Elizabeth (Dynn)
47 63
John 47
Martha 100
Sarah 100

CALY
Sarah 79
CAMMOCK
— 47
Margaret (___) 47
164
Martha 226
Martha (Smith) 47
Thomas 47 164 226
CAMP
Mehitable (Gunn)
(Fenn) 47 95
Nicholas 47 95
CAMPBELL
John 47 122
Mary 178
Sarah (Rogers)
(Hackleton) 47
122
CANE
Christopher 47
Deborah (Welch)
47
Elizabeth (___) 47
Esther 142
Jonathan 47
Margery (___) 47
Ruth 162
Sarah (Green) 47
CANFIELD
Abigail 222
Elizabeth (Merwin)
47
Nathaniel 47
Samuel 47
Sarah (Willoughby)
47
CANNEY
— 11
Hannah 143
Jane 157
Jane (___) 48
Joseph 47
Mary 255
Mary (___) 47
Mary (Clements)
47
Mary (Damm) 47
Sarah (Taylor) 48
280
Thomas 48
CANTLEBURY
Beatrice (Burt) 210
William 210
CAPEN
Ann 156 185
Bernard 48 126 222
260
Dorothy 260
Honor 126
Joan (Purchase) 48
John 48
Mary (Bass) 48
Radigon (Clapp)
48
Susan 222
Susanna 117

300

CARDER
Bethiah (___) 48
Hannah (___) 48
James 48
John 48
Joseph 48
Mary 219
Mary (___) 48
Mary (Holden) 48
Mary (Whipple) 48
Richard 48
Sarah 116
Susanna 267
CARGILL
David 48
Janet 119
Janet (Smith) 48
CARMAN
Abigail 58
Caleb 48
Elizabeth (___) 48
Florence (___) 48
John 48 58
CARMICHAEL
Anne (Pearce) 32
John 33
CARPENTER
Abiah 48
Abigail 198 256
Abigail (Briant) 48
Agnes 105
Alexander 188
Alice 48
Alice (Carpenter) 48
David 36 48
Elizabeth 52 163
Elizabeth (___) 36 48
Elizabeth (Arnold) 48
Hannah (___) (Parker) 200
Hannah (Smith) 48
John 48
Joseph 48 200
Juliana 165 188
Lydia 236
Margaret (Sutton) 48
Mary (Redway) 48
Miriam (Sale) 48
Priscilla 66 285
Priscilla (Bennett) 48
Samuel 37 48
Sarah (Redway) 37 48
William 48 198
CARR
Ann 215
Anne (Cotten) 49
Caleb 49 79
Deborah (___) 49
Dorothy (Boyce) 49
Edward 49
Elizabeth 39 284

Elizabeth (Lawton) 49
Elizabeth (Pike) 49
Elizabeth (___) 49
Ezek 49
George 49
Hannah (Stanton) 49
John 49
Mary 13 139
Mercy 198
Mercy (___) 49
Nicholas 49
Phillipa (Greene) 49 79
Rebecca (Nicholson) 49
Richard 49
Robert 49
Samuel 49
Sarah 14
Sarah (Clarke) (Pinner) 49
Susanna (___) 49
Wait (Easton) 49
William 49
CARRELL
Hannah (___) 49
Mary (Pease) 49
Nathaniel 49
CARRINGTON
Edward 49
Elizabeth (___) 49
Mary 242
CARTER
Abigail 99
Elizabeth 1 181
Elizabeth (Goble) (White) 49 272
Eme 212
Eunice (Brooks) 199
John 49
Martha (Brown) 49
Mary 156 159 229
Mary (___) 49
Richard 156
Samuel 199
Sarah 75
Thomas 49 272
CARTER
Martha 10
CARTHRICK
Michael 35 49
Mildred 35
Sarah (___) 49
CARTWRIGHT
Edward 49
Elizabeth (Morrison) 49
CARVER
Catherine (White) (Leggatt) 49
Elizabeth (___) 50
Grace (Walker) 18 50
John 49
Margaret (Skurrie) 50

Martha (___) 10
Mercy 212
Richard 18 50
Robert 10
Susanna 206
CARWITHE
Katharine 110
CARY
Abigail (Penniman) 50
John 50
Sarah 161 243
CASE
Henry 50
John 50
Martha (Curwin) 50
Sarah (Spencer) 50
Tabitha (Vail) 50
CASH
Jane 205 261
CASS
Joseph 50
Mary (Hobbs) 50
CASSON
Abigail 112
CASWELL
Benjamin 35
Elizabeth (Hall) 50
John 50
Mary (Hall) (Briggs) 35
Mary (Ramsden) 50
Sarah 149
Thomas 50 149
CATLIN/CATLYN
Elizabeth 193
Isabel (Northam) 14
Mary 44
Mary (___) (Elmer) 89
Thomas 89
CAVERLY
George 50
CAZNEAU
Margaret (Germaine) 50
Paix 50
CHADBOURNE
Alice 81
Elizabeth 3
Elizabeth (Heard) 50
Elizabeth (Sparry) 50
Humphrey 50 246
James 50
Katharine 174 270
Lucy 139 169 173
Lucy (Treworgye) 50 246
Mary 101
Mary (___) 50
Patience 242
Sarah (Bolles) 50
William 50
CHADD
Joan 170 172

CHADWELL
Barbara (___) (Davis) (Brimblecom) 36 50 75
Thomas 36 50 75
CHADWICK
Charles 50
Elizabeth 140
Elizabeth (___) 50
Sarah 121
CHAFFEE
Elizabeth (Hammond) (Franklin) (Hayward) 102
John 102
CHALKER
Abraham 50
Jane 165
Sarah (Ingham) 50
CHALLIS
Elizabeth 27 153
John 50
Lydia 52
Margaret (Fowler) 51
Mary 82
Mary (Colby) 50
Sarah (Frame) 50
Thomas 50
William 51
CHAMBERLAIN
Agnes (Haiden) 51
Eunice (Ewell) 51
Francis 51
Joanna 25
Mary 117
Mary (Pope) (Poulter) (Aylett) (Parker) 51 199 212
Richard 51
Sarah (Bugby) 51
Thomas 51 199 212
William 51
CHAMBERS
— 208
Abigail 10
Amy 181
Thomas 10 181 208
CHAMPNEY
Christopher 51
Daniel 51
Dorcas (Bridge) 51
Esther 64 73
Hepzibah (Corlet) (Minot) 51
Jane (___) 51
Joan (___) 51
John 51
Joseph 51
Lydia 131
Margaret (___) 51
Mary 103 220
Richard 51 73 103

Ruth (Mitchelson)
(Green) 51
Samuel 51
Sarah 225
Sarah (Hubbard) 51
Sarah (Poole) 17 51
CHANDLER
Agnes (Bayford) 51
Alice
(Thoroughgood)
51
Annis (Bayford)
201
Benjamin 51
Edmund 51
Elizabeth (Buck) 51
Elizabeth (Douglas)
51
Hester 279
John 51
Joseph 51
Lydia 139
Margaret 77 78 186
Martha 43
Mary 37 153
Mercy (___) 51
Roger 43
Samuel 75
Sarah 172
Sarah (Burrell)
(Davis) 75
William 51 201
CHANEY
Hannah (Thurston)
51
Joseph 51
CHANTRELL
Amie (Gardner) 51
John 51
Joseph 51
Mary 179
Mary (Mellowes)
51
CHAPIN
Mary (White) (Hill)
140
Seth 140
CHAPLIN
Ann 113
Clement 52
Sarah (Hindes) 52
CHAPMAN
Abigail (___) 52
Edward 52
Elizabeth (Beamon)
52
Elizabeth (Palmer)
(Sloan) 236
Elizabeth (Sherwin)
52
Hannah 41
Hannah (Spencer)
52
Isaac 52
John 52
Jonathan 52
Lydia (Wills) 52

Martha (___)
(Lawrence) 52
Mary 236 257
Mary (___) 52
Mary (Durant)
(Waller)
(Sheather) 264
Mary (Symonds) 52
Ralph 52
Rebecca (Leonard)
52
Robert 264
Sarah 193
William 236
CHAPPELL
Abigail 156
Alice (Way) 52
Caleb 52
Christian (___) 52
Elizabeth
(Carpenter)
(Jones) 52 163
Experience 128
George 52
Hopestill (Rose-
morgan) 52
John 52 163
Margaret (___) 52
Mary 74
Nathaniel 52
Rachel 69
Ruth (Royce) 52
CHARD
Elizabeth 101
CHARTER
Jane 213
CHASE
Anne 15
Aquila 52
Benjamin 52
Daniel 52
Elizabeth 11 224
Elizabeth (Bingley)
52
Esther (Bond) 52
Hannah (Sherman)
53
John 52
Lydia (Challis) 52
Martha (Kimball)
52
Mary 245
Mary (___) 53
Philip 131
Philip (Sherman)
52
Priscilla 183
Rebecca
(Follansbee) 52
Sarah 8
Thomas 52
William 53
CHATER
Alice (Emery) 53
John 53
CHAUNCY
Abigail (Strong)
211
Sarah 41

CHEAME
Mary (___) 3
CHECKLEY
Anna (Eyre) 53
John 53
CHEESEBOROUGH
Elisha 53
Hannah (Denison)
53
Nathaniel 53
Rebecca (Palmer)
53
CHEEVER
Ezekiel 41
Mary 41
CHEEVERS
Elizabeth 130
CHENERY
John 32
Sarah (___)
(Boylston) 32
CHENEY
Amy (___) 53
Daniel 53
Deborah (Wiswall)
53
Elizabeth 70
Ellen 162
Hannah 239
Hannah (Noyes) 53
Hannah (Thurston)
53
Hope (Lamberton)
(Ambrose)
(Herbert) 7
Jane (Atkinson) 53
John 53 70 210
Joseph 53
Lydia 165
Margaret 42 131
Margaret (___) 53
Martha 43 226
Martha (Smithe)
53
Mary 170
Mary (___)
(Holmes) 53 146
Mary (Plummer)
53
Mehitable 188 275
Mehitable
(Plimpton)
(Hinsdale) 53
Peter 53 146
Sarah 210
Sarah (Bailey) 53
Thomas 53
William 7 53 131
CHENNERY
Benjamin 55
Mary (___) (Clapp)
55
CHESEBOROUGH
Bridget 185
CHESHOLM
Isabel (___) 53
Thomas 53

CHESLEY
Philip 53
Sarah (Rawlins) 53
CHESTER
Dorothy (Hooker)
53
Eunice 243
Frances (Tough)
244
John 53
Leonard 53 243
Mary (___) 53
Sampson 244
Sarah (Welles) 53
CHETWOOD
Grace 41
Richard 41
CHICK
Elizabeth (Spencer)
53 258
Thomas 53 258
CHICKERING
Francis 43
Mary 43
CHILD
Abigail (Sanderson)
54
Elizabeth (Bond)
(Palmer) 54 198
Ephraim 54 198
Hannah (French) 54
John 54 99
Mary (Truant) 54
Mary (Warren) 54
99
Mehitable
(Dimmock) 54
Richard 54
Shubael 54
CHILDS
Elizabeth (Trouant)
54
Joseph 54
CHILLINGSWORTH
Mehitable 85
Sarah 243
CHILTON
James 280
Mary 280
CHIPMAN
Hope (Howland) 54
John 54
CHITTENDEN
Deborah (Baker) 54
Henry 54
Isaac 54
Israel 54
Martha (Vinall) 54
Rebecca (Bamfort)
54
Thomas 54
CHRISTOPHERS
Christopher 54
Elizabeth (Brewster)
(Bradley) 54
CHUBB
— 127 128

302

Mercy (Page) 57
Ruth (Connor) 57
Samuel 57
Sarah 183
Thomas 57
CLOVE
Hannah (___)
(Blackleach) 27
John 27
CLOYSE
Peter 22 73
Susanna
(Harrington)
(Cutting) (Beers)
22 73
COATS
Susanna 96
COBB
Edward 57
Henry 57
James 241
John 58
Mary (Hoskins) 57
Patience (Hurst) 57
Sarah (Hinckley)
57
Sarah (Lewis) 241
Susanna (Briggs)
58
COBBETT
Deborah (___) 58
Elizabeth (___) 58
Joshua 58
Josiah 58
Marah 39
Martha 195
Mary 22 24
Mary (Haffield) 58
Sarah 248
COCHRAN
Agnes 58
Agnes (Cochran)
58
Christian (Wallace)
58
Peter 58
William 58
COCKE
Joseph 58
Susanna (Upsall)
58
COCKERILL
Elizabeth 62
Elizabeth (___) 58
Mary 283
Susanna 55
William 55 58
COCKERUM
Christian (Ibrooke)
58
William 58
COCKETT
Johanna 204
COCKING
Sarah 124
CODDINGTON
Ann (Brinley) 58

Elizabeth 92
Mary 227
Mary (___) 58
Mary (Moseley) 58
Nathaniel 58
Priscilla (Jeffreys)
58
Susanna
(Hutchinson) 58
Thomas 58
William 58 227
COE
Abigail (Carman)
58
Benjamin 58
Hannah (Barrett)
(Jenner) 58
Hannah (Dearslay)
58
Hannah (Mitchell)
58
Jane (___) (Smith)
(Rouse) 58
John 58
Mary (___) 58
Robert 58
COFFIN
Apphia (Dole) 58
Peter 58
COGAN
Elizabeth 91
Mary 177
Philobert 177
COGGAN
Abigail 104
Abigail (Bishop) 58
Anne (___) 59
Henry 58 104
John 59 281
Martha
(Rainsborough)
(Coytmore)
(Winthrop) 59
281
Mary 285
Mary (___) 59
Mary (Jourdaine)
59
Mary (Long) 59
COGGESHALL
Ann 85
John 59 85
Mary (___) 59
Mary (Hedges)
(Sturges) 59
COGGIN
Elizabeth 222
COGGINS
Bathsheba 15
Mary 15
COGSWELL
Abigail 56
Abigail (Wise) 59
Adam 59
Elizabeth 180 262
Elizabeth
(Thompson) 59

Hannah 262
John 59
Mary 9
Sarah 259
Susanna (Hawkes)
59
William 59
COIT
John 273
Martha 273
COKER
Benjamin 59
Catherine (___) 59
Hannah 177
Joseph 59
Joseph (Hathorne)
(Helwise) 59
Martha (Perley) 59
Mary (Jones)
(Woodbridge) 59
Robert 59
Sarah 178 237
Sarah (Hathorne)
59
COLBORN
Mary (Brooks) 59
Nathaniel 59
COLBRON
Margery (___) 59
William 59
COLBURN
Alice (___) 59
Daniel 59
Edward 59
Ezra 59
Hannah 220
Hannah (___) 59
Hannah (Rouf)
60
Hannah (Varnum)
59
John 59
Joseph 59
Lydia 263
Marcy (Partridge)
59
Mary (Bishop) 59
Mary (Richardson)
60
Robert 59
Samuel 59
Sarah (Blood) 59
Susanna (Read) 59
Thomas 60
COLBY
Anthony 60 228
Elizabeth (Sargent)
60
James 60
Mary 50 228
Samuel 60
Susanna (___)
(Waterman) 60
COLCORD
Anne (Ward) 60
Edward 60
Mary 96

COLDHAM
Elizabeth 219
Joanna (___) 60
Martha 274
Thomas 60
COLE
Abraham 60
Amias 181 253
Ann 73
Ann (___) 61
Ann (Mansfield)
(Keayne) 61 164
Ann (Wallington)
60
Anne (___)
(Edwards) 60
Arrald (Dunnington)
61
Catherine 120
Damaris (Seabrook)
60
Daniel 60
Elizabeth 125 209
269
Elizabeth (Doughty)
61
Esther (___) 60
Frances (___) 60
Grace 230 262
Hannah 96 162
Henry 60
Hepsibah 80
Hugh 60
Isaac 60
Jacob 60
James 6 60 61
Jane (___)
(Eggleton)
(Britton) 60
Joan (Jones) 60
John 61
Margaret (___)
(Greene) 61
Martha (Jackson)
61
Mary 6 105 109
176 249
Mary (Cadman) 61
Mary (Foxwell) 60
Mary (Tibbes) 60
Mary (Tilson) 60
Mary (Wedgwood)
60
Mercy (Freeman)
60
Mercy (Fuller) 60
Nathaniel 61
Philip (___) 61
Rachel (Hart) 61
Rice 61
Robert 61
Ruth (___) 60
Ruth (Snow) 61
Samuel 61 164
Sarah 252
Sarah (Bonney) 61
Sarah (Train) 60

304

Sarah 200
Submit (Weekes)
64
Lydia (White) 64
COOKE
Aaron 65 101 238
282
Anna 240
Anne (___) 65
Catherine (Brenton)
65
Damaris (Hopkins)
65
Elisha 65
Elizabeth 81 202
Elizabeth (Chard)
101
Elizabeth (Haynes)
65
Elizabeth (Lettice)
(Shurtleff) 65
Elizabeth (Leverett)
65
Elizabeth (Nash) 65
Elizabeth (Ring)
(Deane) 77
Elizabeth (___)
(Deane) 65
Elizabeth (___) 65
Ellis 65
Esther 250
Francis 65 186
George 65
Hannah (Harris) 65
Henry 65
Hester 285
Hester (Mahieu) 65
Jacob 65
Jane 186
Joan (Denslow) 65
Joanna 282
John 65 250
Joseph 65
Josiah 240
Josias 65 77
Judith (Birdsall) 65
Martha (Cooper) 65
Martha (Stedman)
65
Mary 118 250 251
Mary (___) 65
Phebe (Weeden) 65
Rebecca (Foote)
(Smith) 65 238
Richard 65
Sarah (Warren) 65
Susanna 161
Thomas 65
Walter 65
COOKERY
Henry 65
Mary (Beamon) 65
COOLEY
Elizabeth (___) 68
John 68
COOLIDGE
Elizabeth (Rose) 66

Hannah 237
Hannah (Baron) 66
Hannah (Livermore)
65
John 65 66
Jonathan 66
Joseph 66
Martha (Rice) 66
Mary 36 186
Mary (Bright) 66
Mary (Ravens) 65
Mary (Wellington)
(Maddock) 66
Nathaniel 66
Obadiah 66
Priscilla (Rogers)
66
Rebecca (___) 66
Rebecca (Frost) 66
Simon 66
Stephen 66
COOMBS
Bathshuah
(Rayment) 66
Deborah (Morton)
66
Elizabeth
(Ballentine)
(Greenland)
(Yellings) 66 119
285
Elizabeth
(Messenger)
(Palmer) 120
Elizabeth
(Moulthrop) 120
Elizabeth (Royall)
(Barlow) 66
Francis 66 214
Humphrey 66
John 66 119 120
285
Mary (Barker)
(Pratt) 66 214
Sarah (Priest) 66
COOPER
Agnes 255
Ann 188 272
Anthony 66
Christian (___) 22
85
Deborah 214
Desire (Lamberton)
67
Elizabeth (Munson)
67
Elizabeth (___) 67
Frances (___) 66
Hannah (Pierson)
(Stephens) 245
James 245
John 66 208 285
Josiah 37 66 67
Lydia 188
Margaret (Clarke)
66
Martha 65

Mary 81 151
Mary (Blanchard)
37 66
Mary (Gardner) 67
Mary (Harriman)
67
Mary (Raynor) 67
Peter 81
Priscilla (Carpenter)
(Wright) 66 285
Rebecca 55
Samuel 67
Sarah 76 137 284
Sarah (Mew) 66
Sarah (Slye) 67
Thomas 22 67 76
85
Timothy 67
Ursula 178
Waitawhile
(Makepeace) 67
Wibroe (Griggs)
(Pierson) 66
COPELAND
Lydia 272
COPLEY
Elizabeth (___) 207
COPP
Aaron 67
Mary (Heath) 67
CORBETT
Abiel (Twitchell)
67
Eleanor (Bartram)
67
Ellen (Bartram) 67
Robert 67
William 67
CORBIN
Clement 107
Mary 107
COREY
Giles 56
CORISH
Scissilla 156
CORLETT
Hepzibah 51 185
CORLISS
George 67 196
Huldah 167
Joanna 82 157
Joanna (Davis) 67
196
John 67
Martha 168
Mary 191
Mary (Wilford) 67
Sarah 11
CORNELIS
Arent 67
Patience (Patrick)
67
CORNELL
Elizabeth 6
Elizabeth (Fishcock)
67
Elizabeth (___) 67

Grissell (Strange)
(Fish) 67 97
Samuel 67 97
Sarah 9
Thomas 6 67
CORNISH
James 172
Joyce 196
Katharine (___) 67
Phebe (Browne)
(Lee) (Larribee)
172
Richard 67
CORNWALL
Elizabeth 123
Esther 276
Joan (Ranke) 67
Mary (___) 67
William 67
CORWIN
Elizabeth (Herbert)
(White) 67
George 67
Hannah 39
John 67 178
Margaret (Winthrop)
67
Rebecca (Short)
(Man) 178
CORY
Mary (Earle) 68
William 68
COSFORD
Alice 223
George 223
COTTA
Joan (___) 68
John 68
Mary (Moore) 68
Robert 68
COTTEN
Anne 49
Mary 100
Mary (___) 100
COTTLE
Anne 222
COTTON
Abigail (Pickering)
68
Anne (Groves) 82
Elizabeth (Horrocks)
68
John 68
Marie (Stow) 68
Mary 180
Prudence (Wade)
(Crosby) 70
Sarah (___) (Story)
68
Seaborn 70
William 68 180
COTTRELL/
COTTRILL
Anna (Peabody)
68
Em (Peabody) 68
Jabez 68

306

Martha 183
Nicholas 68
COUNTS
Edward 68
Sarah (Adams) 68
COURSER
Joan (___) 68
John 68
Margaret (___) 68
William 68
COVELL
Elizabeth (Atwood) 68
Philip 68
Rebecca 254
Richard 68
Sarah (Bushnell) 68
COWDALL
Joan (___) 68
John 68 76
Mary (___) (Davis) 76
COWDREY
Mary (Bacheler) 68
Nathaniel 68
COWELL
Amy 106
Elizabeth (Lynn) (Sealey) 230
Joseph 156
Mary 234
Mary (Carter) (Hunter) 156
Thomas 230
COWEN
Israel 68
COWLES
Esther 41
Experience (Chappell) (Harris) 128
John 128
COX
Alice 2
Moses 68 249
Prudence (Marston) (Swaine) 68 249
Sarah 186
COY
Martha (Haffield) 68
Richard 68
COYTMORE
Elizabeth 255
Martha (Rainsborough) 59 281
Thomas 281
CRABTREE
Alice (___) 138
John 138
CRACKBONE
Benjamin 68
Elizabeth (___) (Cooley) 68
Elizabeth (Dutton) 68

Gilbert 68
Judith (Squire) 68
Mary (Eastwood) 58
CRACKSTONE
John 68
CRAFORD
John 69
Winifred (Longman) 69
CRAFTS
Alice (___) 63
Dorcas (French) (Peake) 69 203
Elizabeth (Seaver) 69
Griffin 68 69 148 203
Mary 120
Moses 69
Rebecca (Gardner) 69
Samuel 69
Ursula (Adams) (Streeter) (Hosier) (Robinson) 59 148
CRAM
Argentine (Cromwell) 69
Benjamin 69
Elizabeth (Weare) 69
Esther (White) 69
Hannah 96
John 69
Thomas 69
CRAMP[T]HORNE
Mary 136
Phebe 206
CRAMPTON
John 69
Sarah (Rockwell) 69
CRAMPTON
Hannah 28
CRANE
Hannah 156
Jasper 156
CRANSTON
Mercy (Archer) 69
William 69
CRAWFORD
— 69
Rebecca 243
CREBER
____ (Moses) 69
Thomas 69
CRISP/CRISPE
Benjamin 69
Bridget (___) 69
Deliverance 175
Eleazar 69
Elizabeth (___) 69
George 80
Hepsibah (Cole) 80
Joanna (Goffe) (Longley) 69

Mary 118
Sarah 129
CRITCHET
Elias 253
Martha (Goddard) (Thomas) 253
CRITCHLEY
Alice (Close) (Dinely) 79
Richard 79
CRITTENDEN
Abraham 69
Susanna (Gregson) 69
CROCKER
Agnes 77
Francis 69
John 69
Mary (Botfish) 69
Mary (Gaunt) 69
Rachel (Chappell) 69
Thomas 69
CROCKETT
Ann (___) 69 70
Anna 221
Elihu 69
Ephraim 69
Hannah (Clements) 69
Hugh 69
Joseph 69
Joshua 69
Margaret (___) 69
Mary 19
Mary (Winnock) 69
Sarah 201
Sarah (Trickey) 69
Thomas 70
CROMWELL
Argentine 69
Giles 69
John 70
Seaborn (Bachelor) 70
CROOKE
Joseph 70
Rebecca 107
Samuel 70 202
Sarah (Risley) 70
Susanna (Risley) 202
CROSBY
Ann (Brigham) 70
Anthony 70
Deborah (Fifield) 70
Eleanor (Veasey) (Paine) 70
Joseph 70
Prudence (Wade) 70
Rachel (Brackett) 70
Rachel (Fifield) 70
Sarah (___) 70
Sarah (Brackett) 70

Sarah (French) 70
Simon 70
Thomas 70
CROSS
Ann 95
Ann (___) 70
Anna 179
Anna (Jordan) 70
Elizabeth 192
Elizabeth (Cheney) 70
Hannah 125
John 70 140
Martha 79 84
Martha (Treadwell) 70
Mary 137 140 204
Mary (___) 70
Mary (Phillips) (Munjoy) (Lawrence) 190
Robert 70 95 137
Sarah 46
Stephen 70 190
CROSSMAN
Mary 116
Robert 116
Sarah 284
CROW
Elizabeth 205 265
Elizabeth (___) 71
Esther 124
Hannah (Winslow) 71
Sarah 272
William 71
Yelverton 71
CROWELL
Christopher 71
Deliverance (Bennett) 71
Margaret (___) 71
Mary 5 187
CROXON
Sicily 63
CRUMPTON
Jane (___) 187
Samuel 187
CUDWORTH
Israel 71
James 71
Joanna 162
Jonathan 71
Mary 272
Mary (Howland) 71
Mary (Parker) 71
Sarah (Jackson) 71
CUE
Mary (Reddington) (Herrick) 137
Robert 137
CULLICK
Hannah 113
CULLIMORE
Isaac 71
Margaret (___) 71
Margery (Page) 71

307

308

309

Sarah (Scullard) 78
Thomas 221
DENNISON
Alice (Parker) 78
Margaret 28
Margaret (Chandler)
78
William 78
DENSLOW
Elizabeth (___) 78
Joan 65
Nicholas 40 78
Temperance 40
DENTON
Alice 8
Mary (Smith) 78
Nathaniel 78
Samuel 78
Sarah 185
Sarah (___) 78
DEREHAUGH
Anne 248
DERRICK/RICH
Mary (Bassett) 78
Michael 78
DESBOROUGH/
DESBOROW/
DISBOROUGH/
DISBROW
Elizabeth (___) 78
Hannah 165
Henry 78
Isaac 78
Margaret (___) 78
Mary 242
Mercy (Holbidge)
(Nichols) 79
Nicholas 242
Peter 78
Phebe (Perry) 78
Rose (Hobson)
(Pennoyer) 78
205
Samuel 78 205
Sarah 87
Sarah (Knapp) 78
Thomas 79
Walter 78
DEVEREUX
Ann 30
Ann (___) 78
Bethiah 18
Elizabeth (___) 78
Emme 203
Hannah 119
Hannah (Blaney)
78
Humphrey 78
John 78
Robert 78
Susanna (Hartshorn)
78
DEVONPORT
Alice 241
DEWEY
Constant (Hawes)
78

Frances (___)
(Clark) 78
Jedediah 78
Margaret 143
Sarah (Orton) 78
Thomas 78
DEWING
Deborah 132
DEWOLFE
Mary 171
DEWSBERY
Hester 77
DEXTER
Abigail 8 124
Abigail (Whipple)
78
Anna (Sanders) 78
Elizabeth (___) 78
John 78
Mary 104 195
Mehitable (Hallett)
78
Stephen 78
Thomas 78 195
DIBBLE
Abigail 134
Abigail (Graves) 79
Elizabeth (___)
(Hawkes)
(Hinsdale) 133
Elizabeth (___)
(Hawks)
(Hinsdale) 79
John 117
Miriam (___) 79
Robert 78
Samuel 79
Sarah (___) 117
Thomas 79 133
DICKENSON
Elizabeth (Howland)
(Hicks) 139
John 139
Sarah 218
DICKERMAN
Eleanor
(Whitington) 79
Ellen (___) 42
Thomas 42 79
DICKERSON
Mary (___) 96
Thomas 96
DICKINSON
Charles 49 79
Elizabeth (Hawkes)
(Gillett) 112
Frances (Foote) 79
Hannah (Beardsley)
79
John 79
Joseph 79
Mehitable
(Hinsdale) 141
Nathaniel 79 112
Obadiah 79
Phebe (Bracy) 79
224

Phillipa (Greene)
(Carr) 49 79
Sarah (Beardsley)
79
DICKSEY
Elizabeth (Allen)
79
John 79
DIGGINS
Jeremiah 79 108
Mary (Cadwell) 79
DIKE
Anthony 79
Charity 4
Margery (___) 79
Tabitha (___) 79
DILLINGHAM
John 79
Sarah 47
Sarah (Caly) 79
DIMBLEBY
Joan (___) 250
DIMMOCK/DIMOCK
Ann (___) 79
Joanna (Bursley) 79
Mehitable 54
Shubael 79
Susanna 233
Thomas 79 233
DIMON
Abigail (___) 79
Moses 79
DINELEY
Fathergone 79
Hannah (Porter) 79
DINELY
Alice (Close) 79
John 79
William 79
DINGLEY
Mary 243
DIPPLE
Grace (___) 13
DIRKYE
Martha (Cross) 79
William 79
DISBOROUGH
see Desborough
DISBROW
see Desborough
DIVEN
Hester (___) 79
John 79
DIX
Edward 79
Elizabeth (Barrett)
79
Jane (___) 79
John 79 80
Mary 39 219
Rebecca (Goffe) 80
Susanna (___) 79
DIXEY
Abigail 246
Ann (___) 80
Sarah 106
William 80

DIXON
Abigail (Lakin)
(Parker) 200
Robert 200
DOANE
Abigail 176
Ann (___) 80
Constant 232
Daniel 80
Ephraim 80
Hepsibah (Cole)
(Crispe) 80
John 80 126 139
Lydia 139
Lydia (___) 80
Martha 126
Mary (Smalley)
(Snow) 80
DOBYSON
— 80
Sarah (Masters) 80
DODD
Elizabeth 225
George 80 225
Mary (Davis) 80
DODGE
Elizabeth (___)
(Woodbury) 80
Elizabeth (___) 80
Hannah 212
John 80
Mary 137
Mary (Conant)
(Balch) 14
Richard 137 283
Sarah 283
William 14 80
DODSON
Bethiah 89
DOGGET/DOGGETT
Alice (Broterton)
80
Amy 86
Anne (Sutton) 80
Bathsheba (___)
(Pratt) 80 213
Elizabeth 275
Hannah (Mayhew)
80
Hepzibah 86
John 37 80 213
Martha 97
Mary 173
Persis (Sprague) 80
Rebecca (Bailey)
(Brown) 37 80
Sarah 234
Sister of
Putuspaquin 80
Thomas 80 234
DOLBIAR
Mary 112
DOLE
Abner 80
Apphia 58
Hannah 186
Hannah (Rolfe) 80

Hannah (___)
(Brocklebank) 81
Henry 80
John 80
Mary (Brocklebank)
81
Mary (Gerrish) 80
Mary (Jewett) 80
Patience (Jewett)
(Walker) 81
Richard 80 81
Sarah (Belcher) 80
Sarah (Brocklebank)
80
Sarah (Greenleaf)
81
William 81
DOLING
Mary 183
DOLLING
John 231
Mary (Waters)
(Selman) 231
DOLLIVER
Mary (Elwell) 81
Samuel 81
DONNELL
Alice (Chadbourne)
81
Samuel 81
DOOLITTLE
John 195
Sibyl (Ticknell)
(Bible) (Nutt)
195
DORCHESTER
James 81
Sarah (Parsons) 81
DORMAN
Ellen (___) 81
Ephraim 81
John 81
Judith (Wood) 81
Mary (___) 81
Mary (Cooper) 81
151
Thomas 81
DORRYFALL
Anne 242
Barnaby 81
Elizabeth (___) 81
DOTEN
Martha 81
Thomas 81
DOTEY
Deborah (Ellis) 81
Joseph 81
DOTY
Deborah (Ellis) 81
Desire 146 235 243
Edward 81 146 235
243
Elizabeth (Cooke)
81
Elizabeth (England)
81
Faith (Clarke) 81

Isaac 81
John 81
Joseph 81
Mary 131
Mary (___) 81
Sarah (Rickard) 81
Thomas 81
DOUCETT
Thomasine 123
DOUD
Elizabeth (___) 81
Hannah (Salmon) 81
Henry 81
John 81
DOUG
John 81
Mary (Bartlett) 81
DOUGHTY
Anne (Groves)
(Cotton) (Eaton)
82
Bridget (___) 81
Elizabeth 61
Francis 81 82
James 82
Lydia (Turner) 82
DOUGLAS
Abiah (Hough) 82
Ann 138
Anne 109
Anne (Motley) 82
Elizabeth 51
Henry 138
Mary (Hempstead)
82
Robert 82
Sarah 164
William 82
DOVE
Hannah 128
DOVER
Anne 207
DOW
Joanna (Corliss)
(Hutchins) 32
157
Joseph 82
Martha 136 197
Mary (Challis) 82
Mary (Page) 233
Phebe (___) 86
Stephen 82 157
Susanna (Hill) 82
Thomas 82 86
DOWNE
— 82 125 235
Eglin (Hanford) 82
125 235
Susanna 37 272
DOWNES
Susanna (Eliot)
(Hobart) 82
Thomas 82
DOWNHAM
Elizabeth 74
DOWNING
Abigail 186

Anne 34 107
Anne (Ware) 82
Emanuel 82
Frances (Howard)
82
George 82
John 82
Joshua 82
Lucy 194
Lucy (Winthrop) 82
Mary 246
DOWSE
Deborah 62
Elizabeth 170
John 82 171
Relief (Holland) 82
102 171
DRAKE
— 82
Elizabeth 40
Elizabeth (Leavitt)
(Judkins) 164
Hannah (Moore) 82
Isabel 28
Jane (Holbrook) 82
Joan (___) 82
Job 82
John 82
Joseph 247
Mary 283
Mary (Wolcott) 82
Richard 164
Ruth 15
Sarah (Fitch)
(Stoughton) 247
Thomas 82
DRAPER
Ann (___) (Hunt)
192
Mary 4
DRINKER
Edward 82
Elizabeth (Richards)
83
Elizabeth (___) 82
John 82
Mary (Abraham) 82
Philip 82 83
Thomasine
(Shrubsole) 82
DRIVER
John 83
Phebe (___) 83
Robert 83
Ruth 212
Sarah (Salmon) 83
DUCY
Joan (Vines) 83
John 83
DUDLEY
Anne 141
Deborah 261
Dorothy (Yorke) 83
Elizabeth (Smith)
(Gilman) 83 112
Francis 83
Katharine

(Deighton)
(Hagborn) 83
Mary (Byley) 83
Mary (Leverett) 83
Mary (Winthrop)
83
Mercy 283
Paul 83
Samuel 83 112
Sarah 164
Sarah (Wheeler) 83
Thomas 83 261
DUERCANT
Mary 107
DUMBLETON
John 83
Mercy (Marshfield)
83
DUMMER
Ann (Atwater) 83
Frances (___) 83
Hannah 5
Jane (Mason) 83
Jeremiah 83
Joan 191
Lydia (Alcock) 83
Richard 83
Shubael 83
DUNCAN
Elizabeth
(Jourdaine) 83
Mary (Epes) 83
Nathaniel 83
Peter 83
DUNCKLEE
Mary (French)
(Sharp) 231
Nathaniel 231
DUNHAM
Abigail (Barlow)
83
Daniel 83
Hannah (___) 83
John 83 213 232
Mary (___) 83
Mary (Tilson) 83
Nathaniel 83
Persis 213 232
Susanna (Keno) 83
Thomas 83
DUNK
Elizabeth
(Blackleach)
(Stedman) 245
Lydia (Buckland)
(Brown) (Lord)
38 212
Thomas 38 212 245
DUNKIN
Deliverance (___)
83
Hannah 229
Mary (___) 83
Samuel 83
DUNNE
Grace (___) 84
Richard 84

311

313

314

315

Hannah (Leonard)
98
Isabel (___) (Rigby)
(Breck) 97
Joanna (Faxon) 97
John 98
Joshua 98
Judith (___) 98
Judith (Smith) 98
Leah 113
Leah (Heaton) 97
Lydia 188
Lydia (___) (Oliver)
98
Mary 15 20 55
Mary (Aldis) 98
Mary (Treadway)
98 133
Meletiah (Snow) 98
Nathaniel 84 98
Rebecca (Partridge)
98
Rebecca
(Woodward) 98
Samuel 98
Sarah 123
Sarah (Everett) 97
Thomas 98
Vigilance 98
FISKE
Abigail 227
Bridget (Matchet)
99
Elizabeth (Bartram)
(Hammond) 99
125
Hannah (Baldwin)
99
John 99 115 140
Joseph 99 125
Lydia (Fletcher) 99
140
Mary (Warren)
(Child) 54 99
Nathaniel 54 99
Rebecca (Perkins)
99
Remember (___)
115
Sarah 93
Thomas 99
William 99
FITCH
Abigail 46 180
Abigail (Munnings)
99
Ann 129
Ann (___) 99
Anne 33 173
Daniel 33
Elizabeth 199
Elizabeth (Mason)
99
James 33 99 199
Jeremiah 99
Joseph 99
Lydia 245

Mary 44 235 245
Mary (Sherwood)
33
Mary (Stone) 99
Priscilla (Mason)
99
Rebecca 89
Sarah 247
Sarah (Chubbock)
99
Thomas 129 235
FITHIAN
Margaret (___) 99
William 99
FITTS
Sarah 14
FITZ-RANDOLPH
Elizabeth (Blossom)
209
Isaac 99
Mary 142
Ruth (Higgins) 99
FLACK
Ann (Wormwood)
99
Cotton 99
Dorothy (Wright)
99
Jane (___) 99
Mary (___) 99
Samuel 99
FLANDERS
Abigail (Carter) 99
Sarah 192
Stephen 99
FLATMAN
Thomas 99
FLEMING
John 16
Margaret 31
Sarah 16
FLETCHER
Elizabeth 16
Elizabeth (Wheeler)
99
Francis 99
Grizzell 43 119 122
161 166
Hannah (Foster)
100
Hannah (Wheeler)
100
Hope 247
John 266
Lydia 99 140 205
Lydia (___) (Bates)
20 100
Margaret (Hailstone)
99
Mary (___) (Cotten)
100
Mary (Cotten) 100
Mary (Evans) 99
Moses 99
Rachel (___) 100
Rebecca 2 266
Robert 99

Samuel 99 100
Sarah (Denby) 99
William 20 100 247
FLINT
Abigail (Bradell)
100
Alice 42
Anna 84
Dorothy 233
Edward 100
Elizabeth (Hart)
100
Hannah 74
Henry 100
Hester (Willett) 100
Joanna 193
Josiah 100
Margery (Hoar)
(Matthews) 100
Thomas 100
William 42
FLOOD
Jane (West) 100
Joseph 100
FLOUNDERS
Sarah (Greene) 100
Thomas 100
FLUSTER
Jane 149
FOBES
Elizabeth
(Southworth) 100
Martha (___) 100
William 100
FOGG
Ann (___) 100
Ezekiel 100
Grace (___) 100
John 100
Ralph 100
Susanna (___) 100
FOLCARD
Anna 190
FOLGER
Dorcas 213
Joanna 61
Mary 260
Peter 213
Sarah 239
FOLLAND
Elizabeth 124
FOLLANSBEE
Rebecca 52
FOLLETT
Abraham 100
John 100
Martha (Callum)
100
Sarah (Callum) 100
FOLSOM
Hannah (Farrow)
100
Nathaniel 100
FONES
Elizabeth 95 281
Martha 281
FOOTE

Elizabeth 55
Elizabeth (Deming)
100
Elizabeth (Smith)
100
Elizabeth (___) 100
Frances 79
Joshua 100
Mary 246
Nathaniel 100
Rebecca 65 238
Robert 101
Sarah 164
Sarah (Potter) 101
FORBUSH
Elizabeth 39
FORD
— 101
Abiah (Pierce) 101
Abigail 248
Andrew 101
Ann (___) (Scott)
101
Elizabeth (Chard)
(Cooke) 101
Hepzibah 177
Joanna (Bicknell)
101
Martha (___) 101
Nathaniel 101
Sarah 178
Thomas 101 177
FORTH
Mary 281
FOSDICK
Ann (Shapleigh)
(Branson) 101
Anna (Harre) 101
Damaris (___) 101
Elizabeth (___)
(Lisley) (Betts)
101
Hannah 255
John 101
Marah 268
Martha 144
Sarah (Wetherell)
101
Stephen 101 144
Thomas 101
FOSKETT
Elizabeth (Leach)
101
Hannah (Hazard)
(Liscomb) 101
John 101
FOSS
Mary (Jackson) 101
Stephen 101
FOST
John 101
Mary (Chadbourne)
101
FOSTER
____ (Shaw) 101
Benjamin 101
Christopher 101

316

318

GARRETT
  Daniel 108
  Elizabeth 90
  Hannah 251
  Joseph 108
  Margaret (____) 108
  Maria (Usher) 108
  Mary (Elmore) 108
  Richard 108
GATCHELL/
  GETCHELL
  Bethiah (Evans)
    108
  Dorcas (____) 108
  Elizabeth (Boude)
    108
  Elizabeth (Jones)
    108
  Hannah (Saith) 108
  Jeremiah 108
  John 108
  Jonathan 108
  Joseph 108
  Judith (____) 108
  Mary (Tripp)
    (Wodell) 108
  Priscilla 216
  Samuel 108
  Samuel 216
  Sarah (Brayton)
    108
  Susanna 194
  Thomas 108
  Wyboro (____) 108
GATER
  Judith 205
  Michael 205
GATES
  Elizabeth 146
  Margaret (Barstow)
    108
  Simon 108
GATTENSBY
  Elizabeth 262
  John 108 164
  Moses 108
  Susanna (Spencer)
    108 164
GAULT
  Mary (____) 26
  William 26
GAUNT
  Dorothy (Butler)
    109
  Hannaniah 109
  Mary 69
GAWDREN
  — 109
  Mary (Cole) 109
GAY
  Abiel 132
  Daniel (Hawes) 109
  Eleazer 109
  Joanna 265 274
  Joanna (____)
    (Borden) 30 109
  John 30 109

Jonathan 109
Judith 105
Lydia (Hawes) 109
Lydia (Starr) 109
Mary (Bridge) 109
Mary (Bullard) 109
Mary (Curtis) 109
Nathaniel 109
Rebecca (Bacon)
  109
Samuel 109
GAYLORD
  Benjamin 109
  Elizabeth 149
  Elizabeth (Hull)
    109
  Jone (Ashwood)
    109
  Martha 89
  Mary 76
  Mary (Stebbins)
    109
  Ruth (Williams)
    109
  Samuel 109
  Sarah (Rockwell)
    109
  Walter 76 109
  William 109 149
GEARY
  Arne (Douglas)
    109
  Nathaniel 109
  Sarah 147
GEDNEY
  Susanna (Clark)
    201
GEE
  Hazelephony
    (Willix) 283
  Joan 109 208 283
  Joseph 109
  Mary 208
  Mary (____) 109
  Sarah (Lancaster)
    109
GEER/GEERE
  Daniel 109
  Dennis 109
  Elizabeth (Monk)
    109
  Sarah (Howard)
    109
GEORGE
  Ann (Swaddock)
    109
  Anne (____)
    (Goldstone) 109
    114
  John 109 114
  Mary (____) 86
GEREARDY
  John 109
  Renewed (Sweet)
    109
GERMAINE
  Margaret 50

GERRARD
  Elizabeth
    (Beckwith) 20
    110
  Robert 20 110
GERRISH
  Mary 80
GETCHELL
  see Gatchell
GIBBARD
  Anne (Tapp) 8 110
  William 110
GIBBINS/GIBBONS
  Ambrose 110 234
  Dorcas (Seeley)
    110
  Edward 110
  Elizabeth 231
  Giles 110
  Hannah 139
  James 110
  Johanna 8
  Jotham 110
  Judith (Lewis) 110
  Margaret (____) 110
  Rachel 86
  Rebecca 234
  Rebecca (____) 110
  Richard 8
  Sarah 220
  Susanna (____) 110
GIBBS
  Benjamin 110
  Giles 110
  Gregory 110
  Jane (Blackwell)
    110
  John 110
  Joyce (Smith)
    (Osborn) 110
  Katharine
    (Carwithe) 110
  Lydia (Scottow)
    110
  Mary 105
  Mary (Bradish) 110
  Matthew 110
  Mercy (Archer)
    (Cranston) 69
  Patience (Butler)
    110
  Samuel 69 110
GIBSON
  — 91
  Christopher 110
  Elizabeth 128 238
  Elizabeth (Cogan)
    91
  Elizabeth (Stedman)
    111
  Joanna (____)
    (Prentice) 110
  John 110
  Margaret (Bate)
    110
  Marie (____) 110
  Martha 192

Mary 225
Mary (Lewis) 110
Rebecca 244
Rebecca (Errington)
  110
Rebecca (____) 110
Richard 110
Samuel 11 111
Sarah (Pemberton)
  110
Sarah (Sale) 110
GIDDINGS
  Abigail 84
  Elizabeth (Andrews)
    111
  Elizabeth (Ross)
    111
  George 111 153
  Hannah (Martin)
    111
  James 111
  Jane (Lawrence)
    111
  John 111 137
  Joseph 111
  Mary 153 209
  Mary (Goodhue)
    111
  Samuel 111
  Sarah (Alcock) 111
    137
  Susanna (Ring)
    111
  Thomas 111
GIFFORD
  — 111
  Abigail (____) 111
  Grace 152
  Mary (Mills) 111
  William 111
GILBERT
  — 111
  ____ (Slocum) 111
  Alice (Hopkins)
    111
  Deborah (Beamon)
    111
  Dorothy 198
  Elizabeth 235
  Elizabeth (Bennett)
    111
  Elizabeth (Burr)
    (Olmstead) 230
  Frances (Collard)
    111
  Giles 111
  Jane (Rossiter) 111
  John 111
  Jonathan 111
  Joseph 111
  Lydia (____) 111
  Martha 63
  Mary 193
  Mary (____) (Heaton)
    111
  Mary (Street) 111
  Mary (White) 111

319

Mary (Wilmarth)
(Rockett) 111
Obadiah 230
Sarah 161
Sarah (___) (Parker)
111
Sarah (Gregson)
111
Thomas 111
Winifred (___)
(Combe) 111
GILDERSLEEVE
Anna 238
GILES
Bridget (___)
(Verry) 111
Edward 111
Eleazer 111 112
Elizabeth (Bishop)
112
Elizabeth (Galley)
(Trask) 112 257
John 112 257
Mary 73
Mehitable 46 62
Remember 189
Sarah (More) 111
GILL
Deborah 170
Hannah 55
John 112
Mary (MacCarwithy)
112
Sarah 202
GILLAM
Anne (___) 112
Benjamin 112
Elizabeth 122
Hannah 231
Hannah (Savage)
112
Joseph 112
Martha (Knight)
112
Phebe (Phillips)
112
Zachary 112
GILLETT
Cornelius 112
Elias 112
Elizabeth (Crow)
(Perry) 205 265
Elizabeth (Hawkes)
112
John 112 194 205
Jonathan 112
Joseph 112
Mary (Dolbiar) 112
Mary (Kelsey) 112
Mercy (Barber) 112
194
Nathan 112
Priscilla (Kelsey)
112
Rebecca (Kelsey)
(Messenger) 112
Sarah (Griffen) 112

GILLETTE
Elizabeth 116
Rebecca 270
GILLINGHAM
Agnes (Wadland)
12
William 12
GILLMAN/GILMAN
Edward 83 112
Elizabeth (Goddard)
112
Elizabeth (Smith)
83 112
Godethe 171
Hannah (Robinson)
112
John 112
Mary 21 160
GILSON
Frances (___) 112
William 112
GINGELL
Hannah 276
GINNUARIE
Rosamund 89
GIRLING
Abigail (Casson)
112
Richard 112
GLADDING
Alice (Wardell) 113
Elizabeth (Rogers)
112
John 112 113
Mary 277
Mary (___) 113
Sarah (___) 112
Susanna 184
William 113
GLASCOCK
Alice 105
GLASS
Amy 146
Hannah 208
James 77 113 146
Mary (Pontus) 77
113
GLOVER
Alice 19
Anna (___) 113
Elizabeth 281
Elizabeth (Franklin)
(May) 113
Ellen (Russell) 113
Habakuck 113
Hannah (Cullick)
113
Hannah (Eliot) 113
Hannah (Parsons)
113
Henry 113
John 113
Mary 72
Mary (Smith) 113
142
Nathaniel 113
Pelatiah 113

Rebecca (Boucher)
113
Sarah 281
Thomas 113
GOAD
Abigail 189
GOARD
Ann (Chaplin) 113
Joseph 113
Lydia 260
Phebe 8
Phebe (Hewes) 113
Richard 113 260
GOBLE
Alice (___) 113
Daniel 113
Elizabeth 49 272
Hannah (Brewer)
113
Mary 77
Mary (___) 113
Sarah 233
Thomas 113
GODBERTSON
Elizabeth (Kendall)
113
Godbert 113 214
Samuel 113
Sarah (Allerton)
(Vincent) (Priest)
113 214
GODDARD
Deborah (Treadway)
113
Elizabeth 112
Elizabeth (Miles) 113
John 113 235
Joseph 113
Leah (Fisher) 113
Martha 253
Mary 23 96 282
Welthean (___) 113
235
William 113
GODFREY
Anne (Messant)
114
Edward 113 114
Elizabeth (Oliver)
113
Jane 284
Mary (Brown) 114
Mary (Hoskins)
(Cobb) (Phillips)
57
Mary (Smith) 114
Oliver 114
Peter 114
Priscilla (Annis) 114
Richard 57
William 114
GODSALL
Frances 258
GODSOE
Jane (___) (Withers)
282
William 282

GOFFE
— 164
Abiah 282
Amy (___) 114
Edward 114 282
Elizabeth 41
Hannah 187
Hannah (Barnard)
114
Joanna 69
John 114
Joyce (___) 114
Lydia 242
Margaret (___) 282
Margaret
(Wilkinson) 114
Mary (___) (Saxton)
114
Moses 114
Rebecca 80
Samuel 114
GOLD
Edward 12 114
Margaret (___)
(Bacon) 12
Mary (___) 114
GOLDSTONE
Anne 36
Anne (___) 109
114
Henry 109 114 138
Mary 138
GOLDTHWAIT
Elizabeth (___) 114
Rachel (Leach)
(Sibley) 114 235
Thomas 114 235
GOLLOP
Susanna 265
GOOCH
John 43
Ruth (___) 43
GOODALE
Elizabeth 23 237
Elizabeth (Beacham)
114
Hannah 166
Isaac 114
Katharine (___) 114
Margaret (Lazenby)
114
Mary 92 203
Patience (Cook)
114
Richard 92
Robert 114
Sarah 19
Zachariah 114
GOODALL
Mary 180 239
GOODENOW
Anne (___) 114
Dorothy 204 224
Dorothy (Mann)
114
Edmund 114
Elizabeth 134

320

Hannah 204 237
Jane (___) 46 114
115
John 114
Mary 45
Mary (Axtell) 114
Rebecca (___) 114
Ruth (Willis) 114
Sarah 166 263
Thomas 46 115
GOODHUE
Bethiah (Ray)
(Lothrop)
(Grafton) 115
176
Hannah (Dane) 115
Jane (___) 115
Joseph 115
Margery (Watson)
115
Mary 111
Mary (___)
(Fairweather)
(Everard alias
Webb) 91 93 115
Mary (___) 92
Mercy (Boynton)
(Clarke) 115
Nicholas 115
Rachel (___) (Todd)
115
Remember (___)
(Fiske) 115
Richard 92
Sarah (Dalton) 92
Sarah (Whipple)
115
William 91 93 115
176
GOODMAN
Elizabeth 266
Grace (Marsh) 115
Hannah (Noble)
115
John 115
Mary 193
Mary (Terry) 115
Richard 115 266
Thomas 115
GOODRICH
John 246
Mary (Foote)
(Stoddard) 246
GOODRIDGE
Daniel 115
John 105
Mary (Gibbs) 105
Mary (Ordway)
115
GOODSPEED
Elizabeth (Bursley)
55 115
Mary 142
Nathaniel 115
GOODWIN
Abigail (Taylor)
115

Amy (Thompson)
115
Daniel 115
Deliverance (Taylor)
116
Elizabeth 91 153
Elizabeth (White)
115
James 115
Margaret (Spencer)
115
Mehitable (Plaisted)
115
Moses 115
Patience 246
Ruth 21
Sarah (Thompson)
116
Susanna (Gartrand)
(Hooker) 115 147
Thomas 21 115
William 115 116
147
GOODYEAR
Elizabeth 10
Thomas 10
GOOKIN
Daniel 20 215
Elizabeth 216
Mary 20
GOOLE
Elizabeth
(Cummings) 116
John 116
GOOR
Mary 175
GORBALL
Alice 164
GORDING
____ (Sunderland)
116
Abraham 116
GORE
Elizabeth 106
Elizabeth (Weld)
116
Hannah 33
John 116 211
Mary 191
Rhoda (___) 116
211
Samuel 116
Sarah (Gardner)
116
GORGES
William 116
GORHAM
Desire 132
Desire (Howland)
116
John 116 132
GORNELL
Jane (___) 43
GORTON
Benjamin 116
Mahershallalhashbaz
62

Mary 119 227
Samuel 119 227
Sarah (Carder) 116
GOSNALL
Henry 116
Mary (___) 116
GOSS
Jane (Walford)
(Peverly) 206
Richard 206
GOSSE
John 116
Phebe 41
Sarah (___) 116
GOTT
Charles 116
Gift (Palmer) 116
GOULD
Abigail 177
Abigail (Belcher)
116
Daniel 116
Dorcas (Belcher)
116
Edward 116
Elizabeth 213
Elizabeth
(Cummings) 39
Grace (___) 116
Hannah 143
Jarvis 116
Jeremy 160
John 116
Judith (___) (Poole)
(Hasey) 211
Margaret (___)
(Bacon) 116
Mary 160
Mary (___) 116
Mary (Crossman) 116
Phebe 205
Priscilla 215
Robert 211
Sarah 47
Zacheus 205
GOULDING
Avis 8
William 8
GOVE
Mary (Shrad) 178
GOWEN
Anne 91
GOWER
Jane (___) 23
GOWING
Daniel 277
Mary (Sallows)
(Williams) 277
Sarah 161
GOZZARD
Elizabeth (Gillette)
116
Nicholas 116
GRAFTON
Bethiah (Ray)
(Lothrop) 115
176

John 64
Joseph 64 115 176
Mary 117
Seeth 7
Seeth (Gardner)
(Conant) 64
GRAHAM
Elizabeth 171
GRANGER
Elizabeth 30
Grace (___) 116
John 116
Thomas 116
GRANNIS
Edward 116
Elizabeth (Andrews)
116
GRANT
Abigail 224
Benjamin 116
Caleb 116
Christopher 117
237
Elizabeth 266
Elizabeth (___) 117
268
Elizabeth (Everill)
117
Frances 166
James 117
Joseph 117
Joshua 117
Martha (Mills)
(Smith) 237
Mary 237
Mary (___) 116
117
Mary (Beckwith)
74 116
Mary (Grafton) 117
Matthew 117 222
Priscilla (___) 117
Sarah 146 230 235
Sarah (Beckwith)
117
Sarah (Brooks) 117
Seth 117 268
Susanna (Capen)
(Rockwell) 117
222
Thomas 117
GRANTHAM
Alice 90
Walter 90
GRAVES
Abigail 8 79
Benjamin 117
Dorothy (___) 117
Elizabeth 130
Elizabeth (Maynard)
117
Elizabeth (Russell)
137
Hannah 181
Isaac 130
John 97 117
Joseph 117

321

323

Mary 35
Mary (___)
  (Burroughs)
  (Homer) 44 147
Mary (___) 123
Mary (Benson) 123
Mary (Joyce) 123
Nathaniel 123
Priscilla (___) 123
Priscilla (Bearse)
  123
Richard 124
Ruth (Davis) 124
Samuel 124 213
Sarah 10
Sarah (Barber) 124
Sarah (Cocking)
  124
Sarah (Fisher) 123
Stephen 124
Thomas 33 124
  225
Timothy 124
William 124
HALLEDAY
Ann (Holmes)
  (Sawdy) 228
John 228
HALLETT
Abigail 4
Abigail (Dexter)
  124
Alice 56
Andrew 124
Ann (Bessey) 124
John 124
Jonathan 124
Mary (Howes) 124
Mehitable 78
Ruhama 31 138
William 281
HALLEWELL/
HALLOWELL
Joseph 124
Mary (Hitchins)
  124
Mary 192
HALLOOME
Isaac 124
Mary (Fairfield)
  (Parker) 124
HALLOR
Martha 45
HALSEY
George 93 124 249
Joan (Ruck) (Swan)
  93 124 249
Margaret (Phips) 7
HALSTEAD
Grace 18
HAMBY
Katharine 157
Robert 157
HAMILTON
Christian (Edwards)
  124
James 124

Mary (Richardson)
  124
William 124
HAMLET
Rebecca 104
William 104
HAMLIN
Bridget (Harris)
  124
Esther (Crow) 124
Giles 124
HAMMOND
— 124 125
Abigail 131
Abigail (Salter) 125
Abigail (Somes)
  124
Anna 133
Anne 18
Catherine (Frost)
  (Leighton) 172
Edward 125
Elizabeth 102 150
Elizabeth (Bartram)
  99 125
Elizabeth (Cole)
  125
Elizabeth (Paine)
  125
Elizabeth (Penn)
  125
Elizabeth (Stedman)
  125
Hannah (Cross) 125
John 70 125
Joseph 172
Philip (___) 125
  126
Prudence (Wade)
  (Crosby) (Cotton)
  70
Richard 125
Sarah 239 245
Sarah (Nichols) 125
Susanna (Bradley)
  125
Thomas 125
William 99 125
  150
HAMPSON
Beatrice 30
HAMPSTEAD
Hannah 264
HANBURY
Hannah (___) 161
William 161
HANCOCK
Elizabeth 283
Joan (___) 125
Mary (Prentice)
  125
Nathaniel 125
Sarah (Green) 125
HAND
Sarah 190
HANFORD
Downe 235

Eglin (Hanford)
  (Downe) 82 125
  222 235
Elizabeth 261
Hannah (Newberry)
  125
Jeffrey 37 82 125
  235
Lettice 101 160
Margaret 221
Mary (Miles) (Ince)
  125
Susanna 36 37
Thomas 125
HANMER
____ (Samson) 125
Bethiah (Tubbs)
  125
Hannah (___) 125
Isaac 125
John 125
Joseph 125
Lydia (___) 125
Rebecca 139
HANMORE
Lydia (___) 243
HANNUM
Abigail 226
Elizabeth 45
Hester (Langton)
  125
Honor (Capen) 126
John 125
Mary 5
Sarah (Weller) 125
William 126
HANSEN
Wybra 211
HANSET/HANSETT
Elizabeth (___) 126
Elizabeth (___)
  (Perry) 126 206
John 126 206
Mary (___) 126
Peter 126
HAPGOOD
Elizabeth
  (Treadway) 126
  135
Elizabeth (Ward)
  126
Judith (Barker) 126
Mary 274
Nathaniel 126
Shadrack 126
Thomas 126
HAPSCOTT
— 107
HARBERD
Eleanor (___)
  (Pope) (Miller)
  211
Henry 211
HARBERT
Elizabeth 27
HARBITTLE
Dorothy 169

HARBOUR
Hester 135 265
HARDING
— 126
Ann 46
Elizabeth 35
Esther (Wyllys) 126
Martha (Doane)
  126
Philip 126
Philip (___)
  (Hammond) 125
Robert 125 126
Susanna (___)
  (Haviland) 126
HARDY
Ann (___) 126
Ann (Heustis) 126
Elizabeth 24 130
Elizabeth (___) 126
Jacob 126
Jane 252
John 126
Joseph 126
Lydia (Eaton) 126
Martha (___) 126
Mary 71
Richard 126
Ruth (Tenny) 126
Sarah 157
Sarah (Savory) 126
Thomas 126
William 126
HARGRAVE
Sarah 24
William 24
HARICE
Mary 170
HARKER
Anthony 126
Elizabeth 248
Mary (___) 126
Mercy 91
Sarah 38 39
HARLA(C)KENDEN
Dorothy 250
Elizabeth (Bosville)
  126
Emelen (___) 126
Mabel 134
Richard 134
Roger 126
HARLOCK
Bethiah (Mayhew)
  127 268
Thomas 127 268
HARLOW
Bathsheba 230
Mary (Shelley) 127
William 127
HARMAN
Francis 127
HARMON
Deborah (Johnson)
  (Foxwell) 102
John 102

325

326

327

328

329

Judith (Stephens)
145
Mary (Coller) 145
Obedience 72
Rebecca (Bishop) 145
Relief 82 102 171
Samuel 145
Sarah 207
HOLLARD
Angel 145
Elizabeth 36
Experience 254
Hannah 15
Katharine (Richards)
145
HOLLIMAN
Ezekiel 249
Mary (___) (Sweet)
249
HOLLINGSWORTH
Eleanor (___) 145
Elizabeth (Powell)
145
Richard 145
Susan (Hunter) 145
Susanna 244
Susanna (___)
(Hunter) 145
William 145
HOLLISTER
Elizabeth (Coltman)
(Reynolds) 219
Joseph 231
Mary (Greet)
(Seymour) 231
Stephen 219
HOLLOWAY
____ (Bennett) 145
Ann (Jennings) 145
Hannah 35
John 145
Joseph 145
Mary (Reeve) 145
HOLLY
Bethiah 269
Hannah 153
HOLMAN
Abigail (Rigby)
146
Abraham 145
Amy (Glass)
(Willis) 146
Anne (___) 146
Anne (Bishop) 146
Edward 145 146
Elizabeth 2
Hannah 162
Jeremiah 146
John 146
Mary 27 180
Mary (Blanton) 146
Mercy (Pratt) 146
Rachel (Bateman)
146
Richard
(Brimblecom)
145

Samuel 146
Sarah 200
Sarah (Pitts) 145
Seeth 224
Susanna (___) 146
Thomas 146
William 146
Winifred (___) 146
HOLMES
Abigail (___)
(Nichols) 146
Abraham 146
Ann 228
Anne (Rowse) 146
Desire (Doty)
(Sherman) 146
243
Elizabeth 140 221
Elizabeth (Arnold)
146
Elizabeth (Gates)
146
Elizabeth (___) 147
Francis 146
Hannah (Samson)
146
Isaac 146
Israel 146 243
Joan (Freethy) 147
John 132 146 278
Josiah 146
Lydia 32
Martha 195
Mary 236 255
Mary (___) 53 146
Mary (Wood) 33
Mercy (Faunce)
146
Nathaniel 146
Obadiah 32 195
Patience (Bonham)
(Willis) 146 278
Patience (Faunce)
146
Rebecca (Wharf)
146
Richard 146
Samuel 53 146
Sarah 9 89
Sarah (___) 132
146
Sarah (Farr) 146
Sarah (Grant) 146
Thomas 147
William 147
HOLOWAY
Elisha 147
Mary (Deering) 147
HOLT
Elizabeth 93
Elizabeth (___) 147
Hannah 117
Hannah (Allen) 147
Hannah (Bradstreet)
(Rolfe) 147 223
Henry 147
James 147

John 147
Martha (___)
(Preston) 147
Mary 162 244
Mary (Russell) 147
Nicholas 147 223
Samuel 147
Sarah 178
Sarah (Allen) 147
Sarah (Ballard) 147
Sarah (Geary) 147
HOLTON
Joseph 134
Sarah (Ingersoll)
(Haynes) 134
HOLWAY
Joseph 147
Mary (Hull) 147
Rose (Allen) 147
HOLYOKE
Anne (Taylor)
(Tuttle) 147
Edward 7 147
Eleazer 251
Eliezer 147
Hannah 251
Mary (Pynchon)
147
Prudence (Stockton)
147
Sarah 7
HOMER
Mary (___)
(Burroughs) 44
147
Michael 44 147
HOOD
Mary 258
Rebecca 6
Sarah 19
HOOKE
Eleanor (___)
(Norton) 147
194
Elizabeth (Dyer)
147
William 147 194
HOOKER
Anne 3
Dorothy 53
Joanna 233
Mary 193
Mary (Smith) 1
Mary (Willett) 147
Samuel 147
Sarah 279
Susanna (Fenn) 27
Susanna (Garbrand)
115 147
Thomas 53 115 147
175 279
William 27
HOOMERY
John 148
Mary (Jennings)
148
Sarah (Wodell) 148

HOOPER
Richard 145
Sarah 133
HOPKINS
Abigail (Whipple)
(Dexter) 78
Alice 111
Bethiah 245 246
Catherine (Whelden)
148
Constance 240
Damaris 65
Deborah 221
Dorcas (Brownson)
148
Elizabeth (Fisher)
148
Giles 148 239
Hannah (Andrews)
148
Hannah (Turner)
148
Jane (___) 148
John 148
Mary 173 239
Mary (___) 148
Samuel 148
Stephen 148 221
240
William 78 148
HORNE
Ann 95
Anna (Tomson) 148
Anne (___) 148
Benjamin 148
Elizabeth 107
Elizabeth (Clough)
148
Frances (Stone)
(Greene) 148
Jehoadan 130
John 148
Joseph 148
Mary 237
Mary (Clarke) 148
Rebecca (Ray)
(Stevens) 148
Sarah (Aborne) 148
Simon 148
William 148
HORROCKS
Elizabeth 68
HORSINGTON
John 148
Mary (Stanborough)
(Edwards) 148
HORTON
Jeremiah 148
Ruth (Ely) 148
Sarah 64 226
HOSFORD
Florence (Hayward)
148
Hester 227
Jane (___) (Fowkes)
102 148
John 148

330

Philip (Thrall) 148
Sarah 252
William 102 148
HOSIER
Samuel 69 148
Ursula (Adams)
(Streeter) 69 148
HOSKINS
Abigail (Stacy) 149
Ann (___) 149
Ann (Hynes) 149
Anthony 149 279
Elizabeth 255
Elizabeth (Gaylord)
(Birge) 149
Elizabeth (___)
(Knapp) 149
Elizabeth (___) 149
Jane (Fluster) 149
John 149
Katharine 279
Mary 57
Mary (Austin) 149
Mary (Griffen)
(Wilson) 149 279
Mary (Tisdale) 149
Rebecca 35 165
Rebecca (Brooks)
149
Richard 149
Samuel 149
Sarah 85
Sarah (Caswell) 149
Sarah (Cushman) 149
Thomas 149
William 149
HOSMER
Abigail (Wood) 149
Alice (___) 149
Ann (___) 149
Catherine (___)
(Wilton) 149
Clemence 155
Esther 40
Frances (___) 149
Hannah 135 212
277
Hannah (Bushnell)
149
James 149
Katharine (Hoskins)
(Wilton) 279
Mary 239 271
Mary (___) 149
Sarah 151
Sarah (White) 149
Stephen 149
Thomas 149 279
HOUCHIN
Hester (Pigeon) 149
Jeremiah 149
HOUGH
Abiah 82
Ann 151
Ann (Rainsford)
150
Atherton 150

Elizabeth 137
Elizabeth (Bulkeley)
(Whittingham)
150
Hannah 30
Hannah (Orvis) 150
Mary (Bates) 150
Samuel 137 150
263
Sarah 263
Sarah (Symmes)
150
Susanna
(Hutchinson)
(Storre) 150
Susanna (Wrotham)
150
HOUGHTON
Abigail (Fisher)
150
Experience 55
John 150
Mary 127 276
HOULTON
Ann (___) 150
Robert 150
HOUSE
Elizabeth 45 249
Elizabeth
(Hammond) 150
Hannah 175
Rebecca (Nichols)
150
Samuel 150
HOVEY
Abigail (Andrews)
150
Daniel 150
Nathaniel 150
Sarah (Fuller) 150
HOW/HOWE
Abraham 150
Ann (Hough) 151
Daniel 150
Deborah 17
Dorothy (Martin)
151
Edward 43 150 151
Eleanor 189
Eleazer 151
Elizabeth 36
Elizabeth (Dane)
151
Elizabeth (Jackson)
151
Elizabeth (Kerley)
150
Elizabeth (Ward)
151
Elizabeth (___) 151
Ephraim 151
Frances 151
Frances (Woods)
151
Hannah 151
Hannah (Howe)
151

Hannah (Ward) 150
Isaac 151
James 151
Jeremiah 151
John 151
Joseph 151
Josiah 150 151
Margaret (Wells) 43
151
Martha (Bent) 151
Mary 2 31 150 270
Mary (___) 151
Mary (Cooper)
(Dorman) 151
Mary (Haynes) 151
Mary (Howe) 150
Mary (Needham)
151
Rebecca 16 219
Samuel 151
Sarah 35 248 264
Sarah (Hosmer)
151
Sarah (Leavitt)
(Clapp) 151
Sarah (Peabody)
150
Sarah (Towne) 151
Thomas 151
William 151
HOWARD
Abigail (___)
(Dimon) 79
Edward 79
Frances 82
Hannah 178 185
232
John 150
Martha (Hayward)
150
Mary 43 154
Robert 185
Sarah 109 225
Tabitha (Kinsman)
150
William 150
HOWCHEN
Hester (Pigeon)
150
Jerimy 150
HOWD
Anthony 150
Elizabeth
(Hitchcock) 150
191
HOWE see How
HOWELL
Arthur 151
Elizabeth (Gardiner)
151
HOWES
Jeremiah 151
Mary 124
Mary (___) 214
Peninah 174
Sarah (Prence) 151
Thomas 214

HOWKINS
Anthony 130 265
Hannah 265
Ruth 130
HOWLAND
Abigail 286
Abigail (___) 152
Arthur 151
Bethiah (Thatcher)
152
Desire 116
Elizabeth 5 139
Elizabeth (Prence)
151
Elizabeth
(Southworth) 152
Elizabeth (Tilley)
152
Elizabeth (Vaughn)
152
Hannah 30
Henry 38 71 152
Hope 54
Isaac 152
Jabez 152
John 139 152
Joseph 152
Lydia 38
Margaret (___)
(Walker) 151
Martha 12
Mary 71
Mary (___) 152
Mary (Lee) 152
Mary (Sampson)
152
Mary (Walker) 152
Rebecca (Hussey)
152
Ruth 72
Samuel 152
Sarah 78 152
Zoeth 152
HOWLETT
Abigail (Powell)
152
Alice (French) 152
John 152
Lydia (Peabody)
152
Mary 205
Mary (Perkins) 152
Rebecca (___)
(Smith) 152
Samuel 152
Sarah 71
Sarah (Clark) 152
Susanna (Hudson)
152
Thomas 152
William 152
HOWSON
Ellen (___) 152
Peter 152
HOXIE
Gideon 152
Grace (Gifford) 152

331

HOYLE
Elizabeth (Challis)
153
John 153
HOYT
Benjamin 152
Elizabeth (Challis)
27 153
Elizabeth (___) 153
Hannah (Holly) 153
Hannah (Weed)
152
John 152 153 215
Joshua 153
Mary 177
Mary (Bell) 153
Mary (Brundish)
(Purdy) 152 215
Mehitable
(Rockwood or
Rockwell)
(Keeler) 164
Miriam 97
Moses 153
Nicholas 153
Rhoda (___)
(Taylor) 153
Samuel 153
Sarah 97
Simon 153
Susanna (___)
(Joyce) 153
Susanna (___) 153
Walter 153
Zerubbabel 164
HUBBARD
Alice (___) 153
Alice (Sabeere)
279
Ann 18
Benjamin 153
Elizabeth (Goodwin)
(Emery) 91 153
Elizabeth (Ibrook)
153
Elizabeth (Whiting)
153
Jeremiah 153
Judith (___) 153
Margaret 229
Martha 92 275
Mary (Giddings)
(Pierce) 153 209
Mary (Rogers) 153
Nathaniel 153
Peter 153
Philip 91 153
Richard 153
Sarah 51
Sarah (Bradstreet)
153
William 92 153 209
see also Hobart
HUBBELL
Abigail 104
Ebenezer 153
Mary (Harris) 153

HUCKENS
Rose (___) (Tilley)
255
Thomas 255
HUCKINS
Sarah (Pope)
(Hinckley) 142
Thomas 142
HUDSON
Abigail 27
Abigail (Turner)
153
Ann (___) 154
Elizabeth (Alford)
153
Elizabeth (Watkins)
153
Elizabeth (___) 153
Francis 152 153
Hannah 173 219
John 153
Jonathan 153
Mary (___) 153
Mary (Browne)
(Founell) 102 154
Mary (Watts) 154
Nathaniel 153
Ralph 154
Sarah 86
Susan (___) 154
Susanna 152
William 102 154
HUES
Lewis 135
Martha (___)
(Shreive) (Hazard)
135
HUFF
Ferdinando 154
Mary (Moses) 154
HUGHES
Elizabeth 16
Martha 38
HULBIRD
Ann (___) (Allen)
154
Ann (___) 154
Hannah (Whitaker)
154
John 154
Mary (Baker) 154
Mary (Howard) 154
Ruth (Salmon) 154
William 154
HULET
Helena (Applegate)
(Farrington) 94
Louis 94
HULING
Martha (Palmer)
154
Walton 154
HULINS
Margaret 28
HULL
Abigail (Kelsey)
154

Agnes (___) 154
Andrew 154
Benjamin 154
Blanche (___) 136
155
Dodovah 154
Dorothy 165
Edward 154
Eleanor (Newman)
154
Elizabeth 109 135
139
Elizabeth (Loomis)
155
Elizabeth (___)
(Storer) 155
George 154 210
Griselda 266
Hannah (Ferniside)
155
Hannah (Townsend)
268
Hopewell 154
Jerusha (Hitchcock)
155
Joanna 44 75
John 154
Joseph 75 154
Josias 155
Judith (Pares)
(Quincy) (Paine)
155 216
Judith (Quincy) 154
Katharine (___)
154
Martha 192
Mary 147 210
Mary (Manning)
155
Mary (Martin) 154
Mary (Merwin) 154
Mary (Rishworth)
(White) (Sayward)
155
Mary (Seward) 154
Naomi 44 74
Phineas 155
Rachel (York) 154
Reuben 155
Robert 155 216
Samuel 155
Sarah (___)
(Phippen) 154
Temperance 25
Thomasine
(Mitchell) 154
Tristram 136 155
HULLING
Josiah 155
Jesse 155
HUMFREY
Mary 265
Robert 265
HUMMERY
Deliverance 105
HUMPHREY
— 197

Ann 199
Elizabeth (Pelham)
155
Elizabeth (Seamer)
(Foster) 155
Frances (Coley)
155
Hannah 41
Hannah (Lane) 155
Isabel (Williams)
155
Jane (Clapp)
(Weeks) 155
John 155 197
Jonas 155
Mary 132
Susan (Fiennes)
155
Thomas 155
HUMPHRIES
Sarah 44
HUNDSDEN
Joan 217
HUNKING
Mark 155
Sarah (Sherborn)
155
HUNN
Anne (___) 155
George 155
Nathaniel 155
Sarah (Keene) 155
HUNNEWELL
Elizabeth (Harris)
155
John 155
Lydia (Edwards)
155
HUNT
Abigail (Hustis)
156
Ann 283
Ann (___) 192
Ann (Richards) 155
Clemence (Hosmer)
155
Edmund 155
Elizabeth 18 277
Elizabeth (Redding)
156
Ephraim 155
Jane (___) 156 255
Jonathan 155
Josiah 156
Mary 209
Mary (___) 156
Mercy (___)
(Brigham) (Rice)
36
Peter 277
Richard 156 255
Samuel 156
William 36
HUNTER
Christian 187
Elizabeth 283
Mary (Carter) 156

332

Rebecca (Bessey)
156
Sarah 202 263
Scissilla (Corish)
156
Susan 145
Susanna (___) 145
William 156
HUNTING
Elizabeth 203
Elizabeth (Paine)
156
Esther 84 98
Hannah (Hagburne)
156
Hester (Seaborne)
156
John 84 156
Margaret 265
Mary 160
Samuel 156
HUNTINGTON
Abigail (Lathrop)
14
Christopher 156
Hannah (Crane)
156
Joan (Bayly) 156
Margaret (Barrett)
156 247
Ruth (Rockwell)
156
Simon 156 247
Thomas 156
William 156
HUNTLEY
Abigail (Chappell)
(Comstock) 156
Moses 156
HURD
Adam 156
Anna (Tuttle)
(Judson) 156 164
John 17 156 164
Joseph 156
Sarah (Long) 156
Sarah (Thompson)
17 156
HURRY
Hannah (Hett) 156
William 156
HURST
Gertrude (Bennister)
156
James 156
Joan 255
Patience 57
HUSSEY
Ann (Capon)
(Mingay) 156
Christopher 156
157
Huldah 237
Jane (Canney) 157
John 157
Martha (Bunker)
157

Mary 197
Rebecca 152
Rebecca (Perkins)
157
Richard 157
Stephen 157
Theodate (Bachiler)
157
HUSTIS
Abigail 156
Anne (Moon) 157
Elizabeth 19
Elizabeth (Buston)
157
Elizabeth (Pell) 157
Elizabeth (___) 157
Robert 157
Samuel 157
Sarah 25
HUSTON
Sarah 263
HUTCHINS
Daniel 157
Eleanor (___) 157
Elizabeth (Farr) 157
Joanna (Corliss) 82
157
Joseph 82 157
Love 234
Mary (Edmonds)
157
Nicholas 157
Sarah (Cushman)
(Hawkes) 157
Sarah (Hardy) 157
William 157
HUTCHINSON
Abigail (Firmage)
(Button) 157
Alice (Bosworth)
158
Anna 205
Anne 63 84 85 261
Anne (___) 132
Anne (Marbury)
158
Bethiah (Clarke or
Prince) 158
Bridget 227
Edward 84 157
Elisha 157
Elizabeth 230
Elizabeth (Clark)
(Freak) 157
Faith 228
Francis 157
George 157
Hannah 30 263
Hannah (Hawkins)
157
Joseph 158
Katharine 18
Katharine (Hamby)
157
Margaret (___) 157
Martha (Curwin)
(Case) 50

Mary (___) 157
Mary (Cushman)
157
Nathaniel 158
Richard 9 30 158
Samuel 158
Sarah (___) 157
Sarah (Baker) 158
Susanna 58 61 150
Susanna (___)
(Archer) 9
Thomas 50
William 158 227
HUTSON
Rebecca 15
HUTTON
Richard 84
Susanna (More)
(Dutch) 84
HUXLEY
Sarah (Spencer)
158
Thomas 158
HYDE
Hannah (Stedman)
158
Jane (Lee) 25 158
Joanna (___) (Abell)
2
Mary 39
Samuel 158
William 2
HYLAND
Elizabeth 182
Elizabeth (James)
158
John 158
HYNES
Ann 149
IBROOK/IBROOKE
Christian 58
Elizabeth 143 153
Ellen 143
Rebecca 143
Richard 143
ILSLEY
Barbara (Stevens)
158
John 158
Mary 187
Sarah (Haffield)
158
William 158
INCE
Jonathan 125
Mary (Miles) 125
INDIAN
Hannah 276
Sam 1
INES
Hannah (Browne)
(Oklye) 158
Matthew 158
INGALLS
Annis (Telbe) 158
Edmund 158
Henry 2

Sarah (Farnham)
(Abbott) 2
INGERSOLL
Abigail (Bascomb)
158
Agnes (Langley)
158
Alice 262 282
Bathsheba 168
Elizabeth 121
Elizabeth (___) 158
George 121 158
Hannah (Collins)
158
Joan 206
John 158
Judith (Felton) 158
Nathaniel 158
Richard 158
Sarah 134
INGERSON
Elizabeth (Symonds)
(Newhall) 158
192
John 158 192
INGHAM
Dorothy (Stone)
158
Ebenezer 158
Joseph 158
Mary (___) (Atwell)
158
Rebecca (Williams)
158
Samuel 158
Sarah 50
Sarah (Bushnell)
158
INGLESBY/
INGOLDSBY
Olive 160
Sarah 230
INGRAM
Joan (Rockwell)
(Baker) 13
Richard 13
INGS
Hannah 57
Maudit 57
INION
John 158
Question (Tyler)
158
INMAN
Barbara (___)
(Phillips) 159
Edward 159
Elizabeth (Bennett)
159
Joanna 190
John 159
Mary (Whitman)
159
INNES
Alexander 159
Anne (Browne) 159
Elizabeth 129 217

333

335

337

338

339

340

MANTER
John 222
Mary 222
MANWARING
Elizabeth 128
Hannah 127
Prudence 21
MAPLEHEAD
Mary (Richards) 42
MARABLE
John 275
Mary (Knower)
(Whittemore) 275
Sarah (Bell) 178
Thomas 178
MARBURY
Anne 158
MARCH
Dorcas (Bowman)
(Blackleach) 27
Hugh 27 178
John 73
Martha (___) 73
Sarah (Coker) 178
MARE
Hannah (Howard)
178 232
Robert 178 232
MARION
John 178
Sarah (Eddy) 178
MARKS
Roger 178
Sarah (Holt) 178
MARRIET
Susanna (Shanke)
179
Thomas 179
MARRIOTT
Susanna 18
Thomas 18
MARSH
Elizabeth 24 196
Elizabeth (___) 31
George 31
Grace 115
Hannah 97
Hepzibah (Ford)
(Lyman) 177
John 177 179
Jonathan 179
Mary (Verry) 179
Susanna (Skelton)
179
MARSHALL
Ann (Cross) 95
Anna (Cross) 179
Elizabeth 173 258
Elizabeth (Lyong)
179
Hannah (Rockwell)
179
Hester (Lugg) (Bell)
22 179
John 179 225
Mary (Chantrell)
179

Mary (Wiltor) 179
Rebecca 231
Richard 22 179
Roger 173
Ruth 192
Ruth (Hawkins)
179
Ruth (Kempton)
179
Samuel 179
Sarah 225
Sarah (Webb) 179
Thomas 95 179
MARSHFIELD
Margaret 201
Mercy 83
Thomas 83 179
MARSON
Elizabeth 204
MARSTON
Prudence 68 249
Sarah 208
Sabina (___) 218
William 218
MARTEN
Lydia 236
MARTIN
Abigail (Norton)
179
Alice (___)
(Farnum) 93
Ann (___) 87
Christopher 179
Dorothy 151
Elizabeth (Bordon)
179
George 179
Hannah 111 267
Hannah (___) 179
Joanna (Upham)
179
John 154
Magdalen 42
Mary 154
Mary (___) (Prower)
179
Phebe (Bisby)
(Bracy) 33
Rachel 25
Rebecca (Higgins)
179
Richard 179
Robert 179
Samuel 33 179
Solomon 93
Susanna 160
Susanna (North)
179
Thomas 179
MARTYN
Anne 42
Elizabeth (Salter)
179
Elizabeth (Sherborn)
(Langdon) (Lear)
170
Richard 170 179

MARVIN
Elizabeth 264
Phebe (Lee) 179
Reinold 179
MASKELL
Bethiah (Parsons)
179 278
Thomas 179
MASON
Abigail 35
Abigail (Eaton) 180
Abigail (Fitch) 46
180
Ann 38
Ann (Peck) 180
Arthur 179
Daniel 180
Elizabeth 99
Elizabeth (Peck)
180
Hannah (Hawes) 180
Helena 12
Israel 26
Jane 83
Joanna (Parker) 179
John 46 180
Judith (Smith) 180
Lydia (Tabor)
(Tillinghast) 255
Margaret (Denison)
180
Mary (___) (Heath)
231
Mary (Eaton) 180
Mary (Holman) 180
Mary (Wise) 180
Priscilla 99
Rachel 139
Rebecca (Hobart)
180
Robert 180
Samuel 180 255
Walter 231
MASSEY
Ellen (Fox) 180
Jeffery 180
John 180
Sarah (Wells) 180
MASTERS
Elizabeth 174
Jane (___) 180
John 174 180 250
Lydia 250
Nathaniel 180
Ruth (Pickworth)
180
Sarah 80
MASTERSON
Elizabeth (Cogswell)
180
Mary (Goodall) 180
239
Nathaniel 180
Richard 180 239
Sarah 10 283
MATCHET
Bridget 99

MATHER
Eleazer 180
Esther (Warham)
180
Richard 68
Sarah (___) (Story)
(Cotton) 68
MATHEWS
Benjamin 165
Dorothy (Hull)
(Kent) 165
MATHEWSON
Elizabeth
(Clemence) 180
James 180
MATSON
____ (Thomas) 181
Abigail 271
Amy (Chambers)
181
Elizabeth (Thomas)
180 186
Jane (___) 180
John 180
Joshua 180 186
Mary (___) (Read)
181
Mary (Cotton) 180
Nathaniel 181
Thomas 181
MATTHEWS
____ (Strickland)
(Wood) 283
James 181
Margery (Hoar) 100
Samuel 283
Sarah (Hedges) 181
MATTHEWSON
Ruth 271
MATTOCKS
David 217
Sarah (___) 217
MATTOON
Philip 181
Sarah (Hawkes)
181
MAUDSLEY
Samuel 209
MAVERICK
Abigail 178
Amias (Cole)
(Thomson) 181
253
Anna (Harris) 181
Antipas 181
Elias 181
Eunice (___)
(Roberts) 181
Jane (Andrewes)
181
John 181 199
Mary 10 198 199
Mary (Gye) 181
Moses 133 181
Rebecca 133
Rebecca
(Wheelwright) 33

341

Remember
  (Allerton) 181
  Samuel 33 181 198
    253
MAY
  Abigail (Stansfield)
    162
  Charity 71
  Elizabeth (Franklin)
    113 181
  George 181
  Mary 45
  Samuel 162
MAYHEW
  Bethiah 127 268
  Hannah 80
  Jane (___) 181 268
  Jane (Gallion)
    (Paine) 181 198
  Martha 258
  Thomas 181 198
    268
MAYNARD
  Editha (Stebbins)
    (Day) 76
  Elizabeth 117
  Elizabeth (Carter)
    181
  Elizabeth (Wight)
    (Heaton) (Pell)
    136 181
  John 11 76 136 181
  Mary (___) (Axtell)
    11
  Mary (Starr) 181
  Sarah (___) 207
MAYO
  Elizabeth 257
  Elizabeth (___) 107
  Hannah (Graves)
    181
  Hannah (Prence)
    181 241
  Jane (Browne)
    (Lunt) 177
  John 107 181
  Joseph 177
  Mary 15
  Mary (Brown) 181
  Nathaniel 181 241
MCALLISTER
  Angus 182
  Margaret (___) 182
MCCARTHY
  Elizabeth (Johnson)
    182
  Thaddeus 182
MEAD
  Experience 136
  Gabriel 43
  Hannah (Potter)
    182
  John 182
  Joseph 182
  Lydia 43
  Martha 220 278
  Mary (Brown) 182

Philip (___) 182
William 182
MEADE
  Gabriel 86
  Joanna (___) 86
MEADES
  Mary (Cobbett)
    (Bennett) 24
  Richard 24
MEADS
  David 182
  Hannah (Warren)
    182
MEAKINS
  Elizabeth (Tulston)
    182
  Katharine (Bell)
    182
  Katherine (Greene)
    182
  Sarah (___) 182
  Thomas 182
MEALES
  Judith 273
MEDDOWES
  Mary 75
MEIGS
  Emm (___) 182
  John 182 264
  Thomasine (Fry)
    182
  Trial 264
  Vincent 182
MEINER
  Hannah 134
MEKUSETT
  Mordecai 182 212
  Sarah (Scant) 182
    212
MELLOWS
  Abraham 182
  Anne 237
  Catherine 193
  Edward 141 182
  Elizabeth
    (Hawkredd)
    (Coney) 182
  Hannah 43
  Hannah (Smith)
    141 182
  Martha (Bulkeley)
    182
  Mary 51
  Mary (James) 182
  Oliver 182
MELYEN
  Abigail 284
MENDALL
  ____ (Hewes)
    (Burroughs) 44
    182
  John 44 182
MENDUM
  Jonathan 182
  Judith (___) 182
  Mary (___) 182
  Mary (Raynes) 182

Robert 182
Sarah 190
MERCER
  Elizabeth (Hawkins)
    183
  Thomas 183
MERIMAN
  Abigail 142
MERKS
  Mary 251
MERRIAM
  Elizabeth 87
  Hannah 11
  John 183
  Joseph 183
  Mary (Wheeler)
    183
  Sarah 271
  Sarah (Jenkins) 183
  Sarah (Wheeler)
    183
MERRICK
  Rebecca (Tracy)
    183
  William 183
MERRILL
  Abel 183
  Abigail 196
  Daniel 183
  Elizabeth (Vincent)
    183
  John 183
  Priscilla (Chase)
    183
  Sarah (Clough) 183
MERRIOTT
  Abigail 98
MERRITT
  Deborah (___) 183
  Elizabeth (Pincen)
    183
  Elizabeth (___) 183
  Henry 183
  John 183
  Mary (Ferris)
    (Lockwood) 174
  Thomas 174
MERRY
  Elizabeth (Cunnill)
    183
  Martha (Cottrill)
    183
  Mary (Doling) 183
  Rebecca (___) 183
  Walter 183
MERWIN
  Abigail 229
  Abigail (Clapham)
    183
  Deborah 45
  Elizabeth 47
  Elizabeth (Powell)
    183
  Hannah 144
  Hannah (Wilmot)
    (Miles) 183
  John 183

Martha 214
Mary 154
Mary (Welch)
  (Holbrook) 183
Miles 183
Samuel 183
Sarah (Platt)
  (Beach) 183
Sarah (Wooden) 183
Sarah (Youngs)
  (Scofield) 183
Thomas 183
MESSANT
  Anne 114
MESSENGER
  Abigail 74 185
  Andrew 183 184
  Edward 184
  Elizabeth 120
  Mary 23
  Nathaniel 112
  Rachel (___) 183
  Rachel (Hayes) 184
  Rebecca (Kelsey)
    112
  Rebecca (Pickett)
    (St. John) 184
  Samuel 184
  Sarah 120 198
  Susanna (___) 184
METCALF/
METCALFE
  Martha 247
  Mary (Fairbanks)
    184
  Mary (Sothy)
    (Pidge) 208
  Michael 184 208
  Sarah (Pidge) 184
  Thomas 184
MEW
  Ellis 184
  Sarah 66
MICHELL
  John 184
MIDDLEBROOK
  Esther 275
  Mary 219
MIDDLECOTT
  Richard 243
  Sarah (Winslow)
    (Standish) (Payne)
    243
MIGHILL
  John 184
  Sarah (Batt) 184
MILBURY
  Mary 27 103
MILCOME
  Eleanor 159
MILES
  Abigail (Thompson)
    (Alsop) 6
  Elizabeth 113
  Elizabeth
    (Buckland)
    (Adams) 2

Susanna 84
William 5 187
MORELY
Ralph 187
MOREY
Constance (Bracy)
187
Hannah (Bourne)
187
John 187
Jonathan 187
MORGAN
Abigail (Phelps)
(Parsons) 201
Deborah (Hart)
187
Elizabeth 264
Francis 121 177
Joseph 187
Margaret (Norman)
187
Mary 27
Pelatiah 201
Rebecca (Holdred)
187
Richard 187
Robert 187
Sarah (Tilley)
(Lynn) (Gunnison)
(Mitchell) 121
177
MORGYN
Carle 94
Helena (Applegate)
(Farrington)
(Hulet) 94
MORRELL
Sarah 88
MORRICE
Elizabeth (Fishcock)
(Cornell) 67
John 67
MORRILL
— 33
Catherine 237
Hannah 34
Isaac 187
Sarah 76
Sarah (___) 187
Vashti (___) 33
MORRIS
Hester (___) 187
John 187
Leonora (Pawley)
(Underhill) 188
Mary (___) 188
Philip (___) (Cole)
61
Rice 187
Richard 188
Sarah (Johnson)
187
William 61
MORRISON
Edward 188
Elizabeth 49
Grace (Bett) 188

MORSE
Abigail 92 163
Abigail (Stearns)
188
Bethiah 206
Daniel 188 206
Elizabeth 74
Elizabeth (Rawlins)
188
Elizabeth (Sawtell)
188
Grace (Warren) 188
Hannah 76
Hannah (Phillips)
32
Jeremiah 188
John 76 188
Joseph 32 36 188
Lydia (Fisher) 188
Mary 16 37
Mehitable (Cheney)
188
Obadiah 188
Sarah (Tucker) 188
Susanna (Shattuck)
36
MORTON
Ann (Cooper) 188
Deborah 66
Ephraim 188
George 165 188
Hannah (Faunce)
188
Joanna (Kempton)
188
John 188 221
Juliana (Carpenter)
165 188
Lettice (___) 188
221
Lydia (Cooper) 188
Mary 104
Mary (Burnham)
188
Mehitable (Graves)
188
Nathaniel 188
Patience 94
Richard 188
Rose (___) 188
Ruth (Edwards)
188
Sarah 29
Thomas 188
William 188
MOSELEY
Anne (Addington)
209
Mary 58
Samuel 209
MOSES
— 69
Aaron 189
Alice (___) 189
Anne (___) (Jones)
189
Elizabeth 263

Henry 189
Joanna 76
John 189
Mary 154
Mary (___) 189
Remember (Giles)
189
Ruth (Sherborn)
189
MOSHER
Ann 171
Elizabeth (___) 189
Hugh 189
John 189
MOSLEY
Maria (Eyre) 189
Richard 189
MOSS
Bethiah 84
Elizabeth 142
MOTLEY
Anne 82
MOTT
Dorothy 250
John 250
MOULD
Hugh 273
Martha (Coit) 273
MOULTHROP
Elizabeth 120
Hannah (Thompson)
189
Jane (Nichol) 189
Matthew 189
MOULTON
Abigail (Goad)
189
Alice (___) 189
Alice (Chadbourne)
(Donnell) 81
Dorothy 87 96
Elizabeth 236
Hannah 3 255
Henry 189
Jacob 189
Jane (___) 189
Jeremiah 81
Mary 134 141 186
Mary (___) 91
Robert 189
Ruhamah (Hayden)
189
Sarah 280
Sobriety (Hilton)
189
Thomas 141 189
MOUMFORD
Jane 8
MOUNTFORD
Ann 88
MOUSALL
Alice (___) 189
Eleanor (How) 189
Elizabeth
(Richardson) 189
John 189
Mary (Moore) 189

Mary (Richardson)
189
Mercy (Mirick) 189
Ralph 189
Thomas 189
MOWRY
Appiah 198
Benjamin 189 212
Bethiah 198
Hannah 234
Hannah (Pincen)
(Young)
(Witherell) 190
Joanna (Inman) 190
John 189
Jonathan 190
Joseph 190
Martha (Hazard)
(Potter) 189 212
Mary (___) 189
Mary (Bartlett)
(Foster) 190
Mary (Johnson)
190
Mary (Wilbur) 190
Mehitable 37 167
Nathaniel 190
Roger 15 190 234
Susanna (Newell)
190
Thomas 190
MOYCE
Anna (Folcard) 190
Hannah (___) 190
Joseph 190
MUCHMORE
James 190
Sarah (Mendum)
190
MUDD
Henry 60
Ruth (___) (Cole)
60
MUDGE
Martha 275
MULFORD
Elizabeth (Barns)
190
Jemima (Higgens)
190
John 190
Thomas 190
MULLINEX
Elizabeth (Hustis)
190
Worseman 190
MULLINS
Alice (___) 190
Anne (Essex) (Bell)
23 190
Priscilla 4
Sarah 29 95
William 23 190
MUMFORD
Sarah (Sherman)
190
Thomas 190

MUNGER
Samuel 190
Sarah (Hand) 190
MUNJOY
George 190
Mary (Phillips) 190
MUNKE
Ann 244
MUNN
Abigail (Parsons)
190 220
John 190
MUNNINGS
Abigail 99
MUNROE
John 190
Sarah (___) 190
MUNSELL
Lydia (Way) 190
Thomas 190
MUNSON
Elizabeth 67
Thomas 67
MUNT
Dorothy (___) 190
Eleanor (___) 191
Faith 235
Mary 167
Thomas 190 191
MUNTER
Julian Mrs. 60
Susan 161
MURDOCK
Hannah (Stedman)
191
Robert 191
MUSHIT
Margaret 61
MUSSILLOWAY
Daniel 120 191
Mary (Long)
(Griffin) 120 191
MUSTE
Edward 191
Hester (___) 191
MUSTON
Isabell 282
MUZZEY
Esther (Jackman)
104 191
Joseph 104 191
MYCALL
James 191 193
Mary (Farr) 191
193
MYLAM
Humphrey 191
Mary (Gore) 191
NASH
— 227
Dorothy (Littlefield)
191
Elizabeth 65
Elizabeth
(Hitchcock)
(Howd) 191
Isaac 191

James 191
John 191
Joseph 129
Martha 56
Mary 123
Phebe (___) 191
Rebecca (Stone)
191
Samuel 191
Sarah 251
Sarah (Simorson)
191
Thomas 251
Timothy 191
NASON
Benjamin 50
Sarah (Bolles)
(Chadbourne) 50
NEALE
Edward 191
Francis 191
Hannah 134
Jane (Andrews) 191
John 129
Lydia 129
Martha (Hart) 191
NEAST
Sarah 268
NEATE
Eleanor 122
NEEDHAM
Ann (Potter) 191
Anne 138
Anthony 191
Edmund 151
Mary 151
NEFF
Mary (Corliss) 191
William 191
NEGGRES
Mary 55
negro
Jo 1
Mingo 1
Mott 1
Nimrod 1
Toby 1
NEGUS
Benjamin 191
Elizabeth
(Williamson) 191
Grace 94 162
Hannah (Phillips)
191
Jabez 191
Jane (Deighton)
(Lugg) 177 191
Jonathan 177 191
Sarah (Brown) 191
NELSON
Dorothy (Stapleton)
191
Elizabeth (Cross)
192
Joan (Dummer) 191
Philippa (Andrews)
(Felt) (Platts) 95

Ruth (Foxwell) 191
Thomas 95 191
William 191 192
NETTLETON
Elizabeth 244
John 192
Martha 260
Martha (Hull) 192
Samuel 260
Sarah 127 138
Sarah
(Woodmansee)
192
NEVINSON
Elizabeth 131
John 131
Mary 131
NEWBERRY
Ann 56
Hannah 125
Jane (___) 265
Thomas 265
NEWBITT
Elizabeth (Herris)
(Wheeler) 271
Hugh 271
NEWBOLD
Alice 139
Mary 139
NEWBURY
Sarah 282
Thomas 125 282
NEWCOMB/
NEWCOMBE
Elizabeth 90
Francis 192
John 192
Peter 192
Rachel (Brackett)
192
Ruth (Marshall)
192
Susanna (Cutting)
192
NEWELL
Hannah (Larkin)
192
Jacob 192
James 192
John 192
Martha (Gibson)
192
Mary 19
Mary (___) 192
Ruth 1
Sarah 132
Susanna 190
Thomas 19
NEWGATE
Ann (___) (Hunt)
(Draper) 192
Elizabeth 195
Hannah 173
John 192 195
Lydia (___) 192
Mary 257
Sarah 195

Thomasine (Hayes)
192
NEWHALL
Abigail (Lindsey)
192
Anthony 192
Elizabeth 94
Elizabeth (Laighton)
192
Elizabeth (Potter)
193
Elizabeth (Symonds)
158 192
Esther (Bartram)
192
John 192
Joseph 192
Mary 39
Mary (Hallewell)
192
Mary (White) 192
Mary (Woodland)
192
Nathaniel 192
Rebecca 199
Rebecca (Green)
193
Samuel 192
Sarah (Flanders)
192
Susanna 132
Susanna (Farrar)
192
Thomas 192 193
NEWLAND
Benjamin 50
Catherine (Mellows)
193
Elizabeth (Hall)
(Caswell) 50
Rose (Allen)
(Holway) 147
William 147 193
NEWMAN
Antipas 91
Eleanor 154
Elizabeth (Winthrop)
91
Joanna (Flint) 193
Noah 193
NEWTON
Anna (Loker) 193
Anthony 6 207
Elizabeth (Larkin)
193
Ellen 2 281
Hannah 23 207
Joan 6
Joanna (Larkin) 193
John 193
Mary (Hooker) 193
Moses 23 193
Richard 193
Roger 193
NICHOL
Ellen 176 224
Jane 189

345

346

347

Thankslord 233
Thomas 205
Timothy 205
Tobijah 205
William 205 215
PERLEY
John 205
Martha 59
Mary (Howlett) 205
PERNE
Rachel 217
PERRIN
Elizabeth (Emerson)
(Fuller) 105
Thomas 105
PERRING
Hannah 239
PERRY
Arthur 205
Bethiah (Morse) 206
Deborah 211
Dorothy (Powell)
206
Edward 205
Elizabeth 127 145
Elizabeth (Crow)
205 265
Elizabeth (Lobdell)
206
Elizabeth
(Williamson) 206
Elizabeth (___) 126
206
Esther 130
Francis 205 261
Henry 206
Jane (Cash) (Verin)
205 261
John 126 206
Margaret 103
Mary 136
Mary (___) (Pratt)
206
Mary (Freeman)
205
Mehitable (Eliot)
206
Phebe 78
Phebe (Cramphorne)
206
Ruth (Ripley) 206
Samuel 206
Sarah (Stedman) 206
Seth 206
Susan (Barstow)
206
Susanna (Carver)
206
Susanna (Whiston)
206
Susanna (___) 206
Thomas 206
William 206
PESTER
Dorothy (Stratton)
206
William 206

PETER
Jane 63
PETERS
Elizabeth 228
PETERSON
John 206
Mary (Soule) 206
PETTINGILL
Joan (Ingersoll) 206
Mary 2
Mary (___) 206
Nathaniel 206
Richard 206
Samuel 206
Sarah (Poore) 206
PEVERLY
Jane (Walford) 206
Thomas 206
PHELPS
Abigail 201
Abraham 206
Anne (Dover) 207
Christopher 206
Elizabeth (___)
(Copley) 207
Experience (Sharp)
206
George 129 206
Hannah (Baskel)
(Phelps) 206 207
Hannah (Newton)
207
Henry 206
Isabel (Wilson) 207
John 206
Joseph 207
Mary 15 216
Mary (___)
(Salmon) 207
Mary (___) 207
Mary (Griswold)
207
Mary (Pinney) 206
Nathaniel 207
Nicholas 206 207
Philura (Randall)
206
Samuel 207 210
Sarah 262
Sarah (Buckland)
206
Sarah (Griswold)
207 210
Sarah (Pinney) 178
207
Timothy 207
William 207
PHETTIPLACE
Philip 207
PHILBRICK
Anne (Knopp) 207
Elizabeth (Knapp)
207
James 207
John 207
Sarah (Silver) 207
Thomas 207

PHILLIPS
___ (Sergeant)
207
Abiel 17
Abigail 16
Alice 232
Ann (Cooper)
(White) 272
Barbara (___) 159
Bethiah (Keedell)
208
Bethiah (Wakeman)
(Kelley) 164
Bridget
(Hutchinson)
(Sanford) 227
David 164
Elizabeth 26 92
Elizabeth (___)
(Welden) 207
Ephraim 209
Faith (Clarke)
(Doty) 81
George 17 207
Hannah 32 191 272
Henry 207
Joanna (___) 207
John 32 81 207
Jonathan 207
Martha (Tapping)
(Herrick) 208
Mary 190 264
Mary (___)
(Jefferson) 208
Mary (Bennett) 208
Mary (Dwight) 207
Mary (Hoskins)
(Cobb) 57
Mary (Hunt) 209
Michael 159
Phebe 112
Samuel 57 207
Sarah 258
Sarah (___)
(Maynard) 207
Sarah (___) 207
Sarah (Appleton)
207
Sarah (Holland)
207
Sarah (Stedman)
(Brackett)
(Alcock) (Graves)
32
Theophilus 208
Thomas 208
William 92 227
258
Zorobabel 208 272
PHILPOT
Anne (___) (Hunn)
155
William 155
PHINNEY
Abigail (Bishop)
(Coggan) 58
John 58

PHIPPEN
David 154
Gamaliel 19 208
Judith 134
Mary 27 264
Sarah (___) 154
Sarah (Purchase)
208
PHIPPS/PHIPS
Elizabeth (Wood)
208
Margaret 7
Solomon 208
PICKERAM
Esther (___) 208
John 208
PICKERING
— 208
___ (Chambers)
208
Abigail 68
Elizabeth (___) 77
John 77 208 217
Mary 15
Mary (Gee) 208
Mary (Stanyan) 208
Rebecca 217 223
Thomas 208
PICKETT
Rebecca 184
PICKMAN
Lydia (Palfrey) 208
Martha 20
Samuel 208
PICKWORTH
Anna 166
Anne (___) 208
Benjamin 208
Elizabeth (___) 208
John 208
Rachel 235
Ruth 180
Samuel 208
Sarah (Marston)
208
PIDGE
Elizabeth
(Newcomb) 90
John 90 208
Martha 41
Mary 283
Mary (Farrington)
208
Mary (Sothy) 208
Sarah 184
Thomas 208
PIERCE
Abiah 101
Abigail 223
Abraham 208
Alice 13
Ann (Greenway)
209
Anne (___) (Allen)
5
Anne (Addington)
(Moseley) 209

350

351

352

353

355

357

359

361

TAINTER/TAINTOR
— 122
Elizabeth (Warren)
250
Jonathan 250
Joseph 250
Mary (Eyre) 250
Mary 71
TALBY
Dorothy
(Rawlinson) 250
Hannah (Place) 250
John 250
Priscilla
(Southworth) 250
Samuel 250
Stephen 250
TALCOTT
Dorothy (Mott) 250
Elizabeth 262
Hannah (Holyoke)
251
Helena (Wakeman)
251
John 250 251 262
Mary 225
Mary (Cooke) 251
Rachel 245
Samuel 251
Sarah 262
TALLMAN
Susanna 22
TALMADGE/
TALMAGE
Christian 22 285
Elizabeth (___) 251
Elizabeth (Alsop)
251
Jane 263
Katharine (Hay) 251
Robert 251
Sarah (Nash) 251
Simon 251
Thomas 251 263
William 251
TANKERSLEY
George 251
Tabitha (Abdy) 251
TAPP
Anne 8 110
Anne (___) 251
Edmund 251
Jane 257
Mary 102
TAPPAN
Ann (Ward) 251
Hannah 265
Hannah (Garrett)
251
James 251
TAPPIN
John 11 251
Mary (Woodmansee)
11 251
TAPPING
Martha 208
Thomas 208

TARBELL
Abigail 274
Mary 228
TATARSOLE
Joan 119
TATMAN
Deborah (Turner)
251
Elizabeth (Davis)
251
Jabez 251
Joanna (___) 251
John 251
TAYLOR
Abigail 115
Alice (___)
(Waterbury) 251
Anne 147
Bethiah (Brown) 252
Deliverance 115
Edward 34 251
Elizabeth 204
Elizabeth (Biggs)
252
Elizabeth (___)
(Bancroft)
(Saunders)
(Bridge) 34
Frances 2
Gregory 251
Henry 251
Jacob 251
Joanna 118
John 153 252
Joseph 252
Lydia (Hatch) 251
Margaret 114
Mary 279
Mary (___) 251
252
Mary (Merks) 251
Mary (Robbins) 252
Mercy 271
Rebecca 119
Rebecca (Weeks)
251
Rhoda 202
Rhoda (___) 153
Samuel 252
Sarah 48 280
Sarah (Cole)
(Pearson) 252
Sarah (Hosford)
252
Sarah (Palmer) 251
Sarah (Scone) 252
Sarah (White) 252
Stephen 252
William 252
TEARN
Elizabeth (___)
(Roice) 223
Michael 223
TED
Elizabeth (Field)
252
John 252

TELBE
Annis 158
TEMPLE
Mary (Barker) 252
Richard 252
TENNEY
Elizabeth 136 164
279
Sarah 10
TENNY
Ruth 126
TERRILL
Abigail (Ufford)
252
Roger 252
TERRY
Abigail 165
Elizabeth 225
Elizabeth
(Wadsworth) 252
Elizabeth (___)
252
Jane (Hardy) 252
John 252
Mary 115
Robert 252
Sarah (Farrington)
252
Stephen 252
TEWELL
Alice 103
THACHER
Elizabeth 74
THATCHER
Anthony 152
Bethiah 152
John 252
Judah 252
Mary (Thornton)
252
Rebecca (Winslow)
252
Thomas 84
THAXTER
Elizabeth (Jacob)
252
Elizabeth (___) 84
John 252
Sarah 255
THAYER
Abigail (Hayden)
252
Agnes 35
Ann (___)
(Freebery) 252
Benjamin 160 252
Cicely 75
Cornelius 252
Deborah 95
Deliverance (Priest)
253
Ebenezer 252
Elizabeth (French)
253
Ferdinando 252
Hannah 134
Hannah (___) 253

Hannah (Hayden)
253
Huldah 4
Huldah (Hayward)
252
Isaac 253
Jane (Hellyer)
(Parker) 199
Joan (Hellyer)
(Parker) 199
Jonathan 253
Josiah 253
Marcy (Rockwood)
253
Margery (Wheeler)
253
Martha (Thompson)
252
Mary 45
Mary (Barrett) 253
Mary (Butterworth)
253
Mary (Poole) 253
Naomi 64
Nathaniel 253
Richard 135 199
Samuel 253
Sarah 135 246
Sarah (___) 253
Sarah (Hayward)
252
Shadrack 253
Susanna (Martin)
(James) (Kelley)
160
Thomas 253
THEALE
Elizabeth (___) 260
Nicholas 260
THISTLE
Mary 226
THOMAS
— 181 242 253
Abigail 176 214
Bethiah 174
Deborah (Jacob)
253
Elizabeth 180 186
253
Elizabeth (___)
(Billings) 25
Francis 253
James 253
John 176 253
Martha (Goddard)
253
Nathaniel 174 180
253
Rebecca (Innes)
253
Rice 25
Ruth (Bassett)
(Sprague) 242
253
Susanna (___)
(Rogers) 223 253
William 223 253

365

366

367

VINTON
  Blaise 261
  Hannah (Green)
    261
  John 261
  Lydia (Hayden) 261
VITTREY
  Lewis 256
  Mehitable (Betts)
    (Tippett) 256
VITTUM/VITTOON
  Jane (___) 261
  John 261
VOOREHOTEN
  Elizabeth (Fletcher)
    16
  Michiel 16
VORE
  Abigail 40
  Richard 40
  Sarah 201
WADE
  Deborah (Dudley)
    261
  Dorothy (Buckley)
    261
  Elizabeth 239 265
  Elizabeth (Cogswell)
    262
  Elizabeth (Dunster)
    261
  Elizabeth (Hanford)
    261
  Hannah (Ensign)
    261
  Jonathan 261 265
  Joseph 261
  Mary 235
  Mercy (Bradstreet)
    261
  Nathaniel 261
  Nicholas 261
  Prudence 70
  Robert 261
  Sarah 223
  Sarah (Ensign) 261
  Sarah (Phelps) 262
  Susanna (Birchard)
    261
  Susanna (___) 261
  Thomas 261 262
  William 262
WADLAND
  Agnes 12
WADLIN
  Elizabeth
    (Gattensby) 262
  William 262
WADSWORTH
  Abigail (Andrews)
    262
  Abigail (Lindall)
    262
  Christopher 262
  Elizabeth 252
  Elizabeth (Barnard)
    262

Elizabeth (Stone)
  262
Elizabeth (Talcott)
  262
Grace (Cole) 252
John 262
Joseph 262
Mary 7 247
Mary (___) 262
Samuel 262
Sarah 9 276
Sarah (Stanley)
  262
Sarah (Talcott) 262
Thomas 262
William 252 252
WAIT
  Deborah 197
  Eunice (Roberts)
    262
  Eunice (___) 262
  Gamaliel 262
  Grace 214
  Grace (___) 262
  Hannah (___) 227
  John 262
  Martha (Brownell)
    84
  Mary (___) 262
  Mary (Hills) 262
  Rebecca (Hepburn)
    262
  Richard 262
  Samuel 227
WAITE
  John 199
  Joseph 161
  Mehitable 200
  Mercy (Tufts) 161
  Sarah (___) (Parker)
    199
  Sarah (Cutler) 262
  Thomas 262
WAKEFIELD
  Martha 40
WAKELEY
  Alice (___) (Boosy)
    30
  James 30
WAKEMAN
  Bethiah 164
  Elizabeth 9
  Elizabeth (___) 262
  Esther 265
  Ezbon 262
  Hannah 122 272
  Hannah (Jorden)
    262
  Helena 251
  Samuel 9 262
WALCOTT
  Alice (Ingersoll)
    262
  John 262
  Mary (Wrentmore)
    262
  William 262

WALDEN
  Ann 236
  Hannah 94
WALDO
  Cornelius 262
  Hannah (Cogswell)
    262
WALDREN
  Edward 262
  Tamesin (___) 262
WALES
  Elizabeth 134
  Jonathan 262
  Nathaniel 263
  Sarah (Baker) 262
  Susanna (Greenway)
    263
WALFORD
  Elizabeth 228
  Hannah 163
  Jane 206
  Jane (___) 263
  Jeremiah 263
  Martha 142
  Mary 37
  Mary (___) 263
  Thomas 263
WALKER
  Abigail (Prudden)
    263
  Ann (___) (Houlton)
    150
  Bathsheba (Brooks)
    263
  Elishua 254
  Elizabeth 167
  Elizabeth (Moses)
    263
  Elizabeth (Soule)
    263
  Elizabeth (Wheeler)
    (Blackman) 263
  Francis 263
  Grace 18 50
  Hannah
    (Hutchinson) 263
  Hannah (Leager)
    263
  Jacob 263
  James 263
  Jane (Talmage) 263
  John 263
  Joseph 263
  Katharine (___) 263
  Lydia (Colburn)
    263
  Margaret (___) 151
  Mary 85 152
  Mary (Manning)
    231
  Mary (Prudden)
    263
  Mary (Walford)
    (Brookings) 37
  Obadiah 263
  Patience (Jewett)
    81 263

Peter 263
Richard 85 150 263
Robert 263
Samuel 202 263
Sarah 175 227 266
Sarah (___) 263
Sarah (Goodenow)
  263
Sarah (Hough) 263
Sarah (Hunter) 202
  263
Sarah (Huston) 263
Sarah (Leager) 263
Sarah (Snow) 263
Shubal 263
Susanna (Rossiter)
  263
Tabitha 166
William 37 263
Zachary 263
WALL
  John 263
  Susan (Bell) 263
WALLACE
  Christian 58
WALLEN
  Joyce (___) 175 263
  Mary 92
  Ralph 175 263
WALLER
  Elizabeth (Marvin)
    264
  Hannah
    (Hampstead)
    (Moore) 264
  John 264
  Mary (Daniels) 264
  Mary (Durant) 264
  Samuel 264
  Sarah (Wolterton)
    264
  Thomas 264
  William 264
WALLEY
  John 264
  Sarah (Blossom)
    264
WALLING
  Margaret (White)
    (Colwell) 264
  Mary (Abbott) 264
  Thomas 264
WALLINGTON
  Ann 60
WALLIS
  Benjamin 264
  Dorcas 170
  Elizabeth (Morgan)
    264
  Elizabeth (___) 264
  James 264
  John 27 264
  Josiah 264
  Martha (Standford)
    265
  Mary (Phippen) 27
    264

Mary (Standford)
264
WALTERS
Sarah 218
WALTON
Elizabeth 64
WANNERTON
Ann (___) 264
Thomas 264
WANTON
Edward 264
Mary (Phillips) 264
WARD
___ (Ogden) 265
Andrew 264
Ann 251
Anne 60 193
Deborah
(Lockwood) 265
Elizabeth 126 151
Esther 166
Esther 30
Hannah 150
Hannah (Brigham)
(Eames) 85
Hannah (Howkins)
(Nichols) 265
Hannah (Tappan)
265
Henry 264
Hester 44
Hester (Sherman)
264
Jane (___)
(Hopkins) 148
John 264
Lucy 197
Mary 44
Mary (Dyre) 264
Mary (Harris) 264
Nathaniel 148
Remember (Farrow)
264
Samuel 264 265
Sarah 44
Sarah (Hills) 264
Sarah (Howe) 264
Susan 97
Thomas 265
Trial (Meigs) 264
William 85 265
WARDELL
Alice 113
WARDWELL
Alice (___) 265
Elihu 265
Elizabeth (Crow)
(Perry) (Gillett)
205 265
Elizabeth (Wade)
265
Grace (___) 265
Leah 256
Mary 225
Mary (Kinsman)
(Rindge) 265
Meribah 174

Pyce 265
Samuel 133
Sarah (Hooper)
(Hawkes) 133
Uzall 265
William 205 265
WARE
Anna (Vassall) 265
Anne 82
Joanna (Gay)
(Whiting) 265
274
John 265 274
Margaret (Hunting)
265
Mary 216
Mary (Wheelock)
265
Nathaniel 265
Nicholas 265
Robert 265
WARFIELD
Elizabeth (Shepard)
265
Hannah (Randall)
265
Hester (Harbour)
135 265
John 265
Peregrina
(Wheelock) 265
WARHAM
Abigail 6
Abigail (Searle)
(Branker) 34 265
Esther 180
Jane (___)
(Newberry) 265
John 34 265
Sarah 248
Susanna (Gollop)
265
WARMAN
Abigail (Lay) 265
William 265
WARNER
Andrew 2 141 213
245 265 266
Anna (Norton) 266
Daniel 266
Deliverance (Hawes)
(Rockwell) 222
266
Elizabeth
(Goodman) 266
Elizabeth (Grant)
266
Esther (Wakeman)
(Selden) 265
Hannah 213
Hannah (Boynton)
12
Isaac 266
Jacob 266
John 266
Martha (Boltwood)
266

Mary 141 245
Mary (___) 266
Mary (Humfrey) 265
Nathaniel 12
Priscilla (Symonds)
266
Rebecca (Fletcher)
2 266
Rebecca (___) 266
Robert 222 266
Ruth 164
Sarah (Boltwood)
266
WARR
Sarah 56
WARREN
— 97
Abigail 240
Ann 174
Daniel 266
Deborah (Wilson)
266
Elizabeth 54 167
168 250
Elizabeth (Danson)
231 266
Elizabeth (Whitney)
266
Elizabeth (___) 267
Experience 254
Grace 188
Hannah 182
James 266
Jane 174
Joan 64
Johane/Joan 242
John 168 231 266
Joseph 266
Joshua 266
Margaret (___) 266
Mary 18 25 54 99
Mary (Barron) 266
Mary (Browne) 266
Michal (Jennison)
(Bloise) 266
Nathaniel 266
Phebe (Peckham)
266
Priscilla (Faunce)
266
Rebecca (Church)
266
Richard 174 242
267
Sarah 65
Sarah (Walker) 266
Susan (___) 97
WARRINER
Elizabeth (___)
(Hitchcock) 14
WASHBURN
— 159
Agnes 159
Elizabeth (Irish)
267
Elizabeth (Mitchell)
267

Jane (Nichols) 267
John 9 267
Margery (Moore)
267
Martha 256
Philip 267
Rebecca (Lapham)
267
Sarah (Cornell) 9
William 267
WASSILBE
Bridget (Playfer) 26
195 267
Samuel 195 267
WATERBURY
Alice (___) 251
267
John 267
Rose (___) 267
William 251 267
WATERMAN
— 60
Anne (Olney) 267
Bethiah (___) 267
John 267
Lydia 231
Mercy (Williams)
267
Mehitable 95
Nathaniel 267
Resolved 267
Richard 267
Susanna (___) 60
Susanna (Carder)
267
Wait 37
WATERS
Hannah (Peach)
(Bradstreet) 34
Josiah 267
Mary 75 231 267
Mary (Waters) 267
William 34
WATHEN
Anne (Annis) 267
Deborah 104 164
Ezekiel 267
George 267 285
Hannah 102
Hannah (Annis) 267
Hannah (Martin)
267
Margerite 268
Margery (Hayward)
267 285
Thomas 267
WATKINS
Elizabeth 153
Elizabeth (Baker)
267
Margaret (Ryall)
267
Thomas 267
WATSON
Alice (Bredda)
(Prentice) 214
268

370

Caleb 267
Dorcas 84
Dorothy (Bissell)
247 268
Elizabeth 218 278
Elizabeth (Frost)
117 216 268
Elkanah 267
George 267
John 117 214 216
268
Margery 115
Mary 172 245
Mary (Eccles) 268
Mary (Hide) 267
Mercy (Hedge) 267
Nathaniel 247 268
Phebe 232
Phebe (Hicks) 267
WATSON-CHALLIS
Mary (Sargent) 268
Philip 268
WATTS
Cicely (___)
(Barlow) 268
Eleanor 38 277
Elizabeth (Steele)
268
Henry 268
Mary 154
Thomas 268
WAY
Aaron 268
Alice 52
Anna 276
Bethiah (Mayhew)
(Harlock) 127
268
Elizabeth (___) 268
George 268
Hannah 276
Hannah (Townsend)
(Hull) (Allen)
(Knight) 268
Henry 268 276
Hester (Jones) 268
Joan (Sumner) 268
Katharine (___)
268
Lydia 190
Richard 127 268
Sarah (Neast) 268
Susanna 204
WEARE
Abigail 96
Christian 12
Elizabeth 69
Elizabeth (Swaine)
268
Mary 249
Nathaniel 268
WEAVER
Christopher 270
Clement 268
Elizabeth 270
Mary (Freeborn)
268

Mary (Springer)
268
Thomas 268
WEBB
Bethiah (Adams)
268
Elizabeth 227
Elizabeth (___)
(Grant) 117 268
Hannah 2
Hester 209
John 268
Marah (Fosdick)
268
Richard 117 268
Sarah 179
Tomas 268
WEBSTER
Ann (Batt) 268
Elizabeth (Brown)
268
Israel 268
James 268
John 90 268
Mary (Dawes) 268
Mary (Shatswell)
90
Robert 61
Sarah (Edwards)
(Colefax) 61
WEDGWOOD
John 60
Mary 60
WEED
Bethiah (Holly) 269
Daniel 268
Dorcas 285
Elizabeth 222
Ephraim 267
George 268
Hannah 152
Hannah (Anris)
(Wathen) 257
Joanna (Westcott)
268
John 268 269
Jonas 269
Margerite (Wathen)
268
Mary 1
Mary (___) 269
Ruth (___) 258
Samuel 269
WEEDEN
Edward 22 269
Elizabeth (Cole) 269
James 120
Phebe 65
Rose (French)
(Grinnell) (Paine)
120
Sarah 22
WEEKES/WEEKS
____ (___) 218
____ (Haynes) 269
Abigail (Trescott)
269

Amiel 269
Amiel 269
Daniel 269
Deliverance
(Sumner) 269
Ebenezer 269
Elizabeth 6 222
Elizabeth (___) 269
Elizabeth (Harris)
269
Elizabeth (Packer)
(Stark) 269
George 155
Henry 269
Jane 19
Jane (Clapp) 155
John 269
Joseph 269
Leonard 269
Mary (Alling) 269
Mary (Redman)
269
Mercy (Robinson)
269
Rebecca 251
Sarah (Sumner)
(Turell) 269
Submit 64
Supply 269
Susanna (Alling)
269
Susanna (Barnes)
269
Thankful 199
William 269
WELBY
Olive 94
WELCH
Deborah 47
Mary 183
Thomas 47
WELD
Barbara (Clapp)
246 269
Dorothy (Whiting)
269
Elizabeth 116
Elizabeth (Wise)
269
Hannah 1
John 116
Joseph 1 127 269
Judith (___) 269
Margaret (___)
269
Mary 127
Thomas 269
WELDEN
Elizabeth (___) 207
270
Robert 207 270
WELLER
Richard 125
Sarah 125
WELLES
Frances (Albright)
61 270

Hannah (Buckland)
270
Joshua 270
Margaret 43
Mary (Beardsley)
270
Mary (Blackleach)
195 270
Sarah 53
Thomas 195 270
WELLINGTON
Benjamin 270
Lydia (Browne)
270
Mary 66
Mary (Palgrave)
270
Roger 66 270
WELLMAN
Elizabeth (Spencer)
164 270
Hannah (Adams)
270
Isaac 270
Martha 185
William 164 270
WELLS
Elizabeth (Deming)
(Foote) 100
Elizabeth
(Rowlandson)
128
Grace 194
Isabel 259
Margaret 151
Sarah 180
Thomas 61 100 180
WENTWORTH
Sarah 16
William 16
WEST
Bartholomew 270
Catherine (Almy)
270
Elizabeth 226
Francis 270
Jane 100
Susanna 232
Susanna (Soule)
270
Thomas 226
WESTBROOK
John 142
Martha (Walford)
(Hinkson) 142
WESTCOTT
Abigail 167
Damaris 9
Joanna 268
Richard 268
WESTLY
Elizabeth 205
WESTON
Abigail (Eames) 17
Deborah (Delano)
270
Elizabeth 64

371

374

WOODBERY
Andrew 283
Mary (Cockerill)
283
WOODBRIDGE
John 283
Mary (Jones) 59
Mercy (Dudley)
283
Thomas 59
WOODBURY
Abigail 140
Abigail (Batchelder)
283
Agnes (___) 283
Elizabeth (Hunter)
283
Elizabeth (___) 80
283
Hannah 13
Hannah (Dodge)
(Porter) 212
Humphrey 283
Johanna (Wheeler)
284
John 80 283
Peter 283
Sarah (Dodge) 283
Thomas 212
William 284
WOODCOCK
Sarah (Cooper) 284
William 284
WOODEN
Sarah 183
WOODFORD
Hannah 5
Mary 233
Mary (Blott) 284
Sarah 5
Thomas 284
WOODIN
John 284
Martha 218
Mary (___) 284
Mary (Johnson)
284
WOODLAND
Mary 192
WOODMAN
John 182
Mary 90
Mary (Raynes)
(Mendum) 182
WOODMANSEE/
WOODMANSEY
Abigail (Melyen)
284
Anna 72
Anna (___) 284
Elizabeth 90
Elizabeth (Carr)
284
Elizabeth (Clark)
284
Gabriel 284
Hannah (___) 284

James 284
John 284
Margaret (___) 284
Mary 11 251 256
Robert 284
Sarah 192
Sarah (___) (Rix)
284
Thomas 284
WOODS
Frances 151
Hannah 172
John 151 284
Mary (Parmenter)
284
Sarah 172
WOODWARD
Ann 76
Elizabeth (___) 284
Experience 211
Hannah (Stacy) 284
Israel 284
James 284
Jane (Godfrey) 284
John 284
Katharine (___)
284
Lambert 226
Margaret (___) 284
Mary (Jackson) 284
Nathaniel 284
Rachel (Smith) 130
Rebecca 98
Robert 130
Sarah (Bloomfield)
(Sackett) 226
Sarah (Crossman)
284
WOODWORTH
Benjamin 284
Caleb 190
Deborah (___) 284
Deborah (Daman)
285
Elizabeth 1 245
Hannah (___) 284
Isaac 284
Joseph 284
Lydia (Standlake)
284
Martha 73
Mary 235 236 261
Sarah (Stockbridge)
284
Thomas 285
Walter 236 245 285
WOODY
John 285
Mary (Coggan) 285
WOOLAND
Sarah 202
WOOLFE
Hannah 240
Martha (___) 285
Peter 285
WOOLRIDGE
John 285

Sarah (___) 285
WOOLSTONE
Jane 95
WOOTON
Elizabeth 205
WORCESTER
Ann 103
Sarah (___) 285
Susanna 209
Susanna (___) 7
Timothy 7
William 285
WORDEN
Mercy 281
WORKMAN
Martha (White)
285
Samuel 285
WORMALL
Joseph 285
Miriam (___) 285
WORMLUM
— 285
Christian (Talmage)
285
WORMWOOD
Ann 99
Christian (Talmage)
22
William 22
WORTHEN
Anne (Annis) 285
George 285
Margery (Hayward)
285
WORTHINGTON
Mehitable (Graves)
(Morton) 188
William 188
WRENTMORE
Mary 262
WRIGHT
— 285
Abigail 55 144 231
Ann 44 106
Anna 44
Dorcas (Weed) 285
Dorothy 99
Edward 217
Elinor 55
Elizabeth 55 197
Elizabeth (Peters)
(Sawdy) 228
Elizabeth
(Townsend) 176
Gideon 176
Hester (Cooke) 285
James 285
Lydia 129 169
Lydia (Moore) 72
Lydia (Sylvester)
(Rawlings) 217
Margaret (___) 285
Martha 209
Mary (Davis)
(Dodd) (Austin)
80

Mercy 5
Nicholas 173
Priscilla (Carpenter)
66 285
Rebecca 173
Richard 144 285
Samuel 72 169
Sarah 128 171
Thomas 129
Walter 228
William 66 80 285
WRITE
Rachel 172
WROTHAM
Susanna 150
WYATT
Hepsibah 213
John 221
Mary (___)
(Riddlesdale) 221
WYBORNE
Anne 91
Hannah 91
WYER
Abigail (Lawrence)
170 285
Edward 285
WYLLYS
Amy 215
Esther 126
WYMAN
Elizabeth
(Richardson) 285
Francis 285
WYNPENNIE
Mary 240
WYOT
Margret 6
YALE
Mary (Turner) 285
Thomas 285
YATES
Dianah 202
John 139
Mary (___) 139
YELLINGS
Elizabeth
(Ballentine)
(Greenland) 66
119 285
Elizabeth
(Ballentine) 120
Roger 66 119 285
YORK
Deborah (Bell)
286
James 286
Rachel 154
Richard 154
YORKE
Dorothy 83
YOUNG
Abigail (Howland)
286
George 190

ENGLISH LOCATIONS

377

www.ingramcontent.com/pod-product-compliance
Lightning Source LLC
Chambersburg PA
CBHW072044020426
42334CB00017B/1380